D0987105

POETRY BY AMERICAN WOMEN, 1900-1975:

A Bibliography

by

Joan Reardon

and

Kristine A. Thorsen

The Scarecrow Press, Inc.

Metuchen, N.J. & London

1979

Library of Congress Cataloging in Publication Data

Reardon, Joan, 1930-
Poetry by American women, 1900-1975.

Includes index.
1. American poetry--Women authors--Bibliography.
2. American poetry--20th century--Bibliography. I. Thorsen, Kristine A., joint author. II. Title.
Z1229.W8R4 [PS151] 016.811'008 78-11944
ISBN 0-8108-1173-1

Manufactured in the United States of America

CONTENTS

INTRODUCTION

Poetry by American Women, 1900-1975: A Bibliography enumerates more than 5,500 women poets who have contributed to the development of American poetry in the twentieth century, and provides access to approximately 9,500 volumes never before subjected to rigorous bibliographic control. Because it extends substantially the perimeters of the standard literary bibliographies which have traditionally limited their attention to ten or fifteen major women poets, the comprehensive nature of this volume augments the bibliographic domain of American literature. As such, it functions as an intermediary between the researcher and a corpus of published material frequently inaccessible due to limited readership, promotion, distribution, and availability. Wishing neither to isolate the contribution of American women poets nor to make even indirectly those judgments proper only to the literary critic, the compilers' intention in the preparation and publication of this bibliography is solely to provide accessibility to a body of literature not generally available.

As stated in its title, this bibliography lists separately published volumes of poetry by women who are United States citizens whose major works have appeared during the period 1900-1975. To qualify for inclusion a poet must have published at least one volume. Audio-visual works, collaborative efforts, mixed genre, reprints, foreign language editions, broadsides, and testimonial pieces have been excluded.

Arrangement of this bibliography is alphabetical by author. Following Library of Congress practice, complete names as well as birth and death dates have been supplied whenever possible. Cross references from pseudonyms, maiden names, and names in religion are made to the correct form (e.g., H.D. see Doolittle, Hilda). Specific volumes are listed chronologically for each poet. Complete bibliographic information--author, title, place of publication, and date of publication is indicated for every entry. In certain cases, editions other than the first have been excluded if they do not represent a significant addition to an individual's work. Access by title is supplied by the Title Index following the bibliography.

By electing to place this work within the larger bibliographic framework of American literature, a deliberate effort to be exhaustive in coverage has been made. Notable collections of American poetry have been searched and selective bibliographies, publishers' catalogs, and review literature have also been thoroughly examined to yield entries which might otherwise have escaped notice. Realizing that a work of this magnitude places great demands on the bibliographer and exposes his efforts to scrutiny, the compilers of this present edition of Poetry by American Women, 1900-1975: A Bibliography have exerted every effort to collocate and produce a complete and accurate bibliography. Anticipating a revised edition to include those works published during the latter quarter of the twentieth century, the compilers plan to correct any inadvertent omissions or errors in the present volume, for which they accept full responsibility.

A bibliography of this scope could not be undertaken and completed without reliance upon numerous institutions and individuals. In addition to the resources, facilities, and staff of the Newberry Library, Chicago; Northwestern University Library, Evanston; Lake Forest College Library and Barat College Library, Lake Forest, Illinois, we wish to acknowledge in a special way the outstanding collections of American poetry found at Brown University, Providence, R.I. and at the University of Chicago. Gratitude, also, must be expressed to the research assistants whose untiring efforts made the completion of this bibliography possible. And lastly, we acknowledge with appreciation the support of the professional men and women who encouraged the completion of this project.

Joan Reardon
Kristine A. Thorsen

ABBREVIATIONS

arr.	arranged
b.	born
d.	died
dist.	distributed
Ed.	Edited
ed.	edition
enl.	enlarged
ℓ.	leaf/leaves
n.p.	no place/no publisher
p.	page(s)
p.ℓ.	preliminary leaf (leaves)
pl.	plate(s)
rev.	revised
v.	volume(s)

THE BIBLIOGRAPHY

AAMODT, MARGARET D. (1910-)
Through Country Lanes. 1st ed. Lake Mills, IA.: Graphic, 1963. 71 p.

ABBOTT, ELSIE (TWINING) (1874-)
Sensations of the Seasons. New York: Fleming H. Revell Co., 1935. 73, [1] p.
Reactions. New York: H. Harrison, 1937. 63 p.

ABBOTT, IRENE McMILLAN
Ministry of Love. Topeka, KA.: Crane & Company, Printers, 1903. 190 p.

ABEL, LUCY E.
Open Road, and Other Poems. Boston: The Gorham Press, 1916. 64 p.

ABELSON, ALTER (1881-)
The Death of Isaiah. New York?: n.p., 1909. 4 ℓ.
Sambatyon and Other Poems. New York: The Ariel Publications, 1931.
Sonnets of Motherhood and Other Poems. New York: The Paebar Co., 1940. 185 p.
Songs of Labor. Newburgh, N.Y.: Paebar Co., 1947. 111 p.
Helen and Shulamith. New York: Whittier Books, 1959.

ABER, LOUREINE
We, the Musk-Chasers. Chicago: R. F. Seymour, 1921. 80 p.

ABNEY, LOUISE
Brief Candles. New York: H. Harrison, 1938. 63 p.
From Life to Me: Poems. New York: H. Harrison, 1946. 63 p.
No Time for Doubt: Poems. New York: Exposition Press, 1950. 64 p.

ABRAM, THERESA WILLIAMS (1903-)
Abram's Treasures. New York: Vantage Press, 1967.
Rhythm and Animals. Oklahoma City, OK.: Best Way, 1971.

ABSHIRE, MARTHA
Odes to Man Along Life's Way. Boston: The Stratford Co., 1925. 4 p.ℓ., 62 p.

ACKERMAN, MORA L.
Verses Interpreted. Plainfield, N.J.: Courier News Publishing Co., 1924. 54 p.

ACOSTA, MERCEDES de
Moods: Prose Poems. New York: Moffat, Yard and Co., 1919.
Archways of Life. New York: Moffat, Yard and Co., 1921. 61 p.
Streets and Shadows. New York: Moffat, Yard and Co., 1922. 6 p.ℓ., 51 p.

ADAM, HELEN (1909-)
The Queen o' Crow Castle. San Francisco: White Rabbit Press, 1958. [15] p.
Ballads. San Francisco: White Rabbit Press, 1961.
At the Window. Berkeley, CA.: Four Seasons, 1963.
Ballads. New York: Acadia Press, 1964. 26 ℓ.
Selected Ballads and Poems. New York: Helikon Press, 1974. 57 p.

ADAMS, CARMEN BOITEL (1920-)
Quiet Reflections. Phoenix, AZ.: O'Sullivan Woodside, 1974. 55 p.

ADAMS, CAROLYN BELLE
Poems. Omaha, NB.: Irvan & Medlar Printing Office, 1923. [19] p.

ADAMS, CYNTHIA deFORD
In Miniature. North Carolina: Four Oaks, 1952. 47 p.
Part of Each Day. Durham, N.C.: Seeman Printery, 1957. 36 p.

ADAMS, EUNICE
Souvenir and Other Poems. Boston: B. Humphries, 1944. 9-77 p.
Fragments. Boston: B. Humphries, 1962. 48 p.

ADAMS, FAYE CARR
Sweet Is the Homing Hour. Dallas, TX.: Kaleidograph Press, 1948. 80 p.
More Than a Loaf. San Antonio, TX.: Naylor Co., 1968. x, 50 p.

ADAMS, GEORGIA B.
The Silver Flute and Other Poems. Philadelphia: Dorrance, 1968. 122 p. (Contemporary poets of Dorrance, 691)

ADAMS, GERTRUDE LEONARD
Poems. New York: F. W. Orvis, 1907. 7 p.ℓ., 21-202 p.

ADAMS, GRACE CLARK
Varied Thoughts in Verse. Chicago: Justitia Publishing Co., 1915. 32 p.

ADAMS, KATHARINE
Light and Mist. Boston: The Cornhill Co., 1918. 5 p.ℓ., 49 p.

ADAMS, LEONIE (FULLER) (1899-)
Those Not Elect. New York: R. M. McBride & Co., 1925. viii, 50 p.
High Falcon and Other Poems. New York: The John Day Co., 1929. viii, 48 p.
This Measure. New York: A. A. Knopf, 1933. 2 ℓ. (The Borzoi Chapbooks no. 7)
Poems, A Selection. New York: Funk and Wagnalls, 1954. 128 p.
Poems, A Selection. New York: Noonday Press, 1960. 128 p.

ADAMS, MARGUERITE (JANVRIN) (1899-)
I Give You Words. New York: I. Washburn, Inc., 1934. xii, 87 p.
Insignia Amoris. New York: The Fine Editions Press, 1940. 9-22 p.
Poems. Portland, ME.: Falmouth Pub. House, 1948. 176 p.

ADAMS, MARY JANE (MATHEWS) (1840-1902)
Sonnets and Songs. New York & London: G. P. Putnam's Sons, 1901. xi, 167 p.
The Song at Midnight. Boston: R. G. Badger, 1903. 128 p.

ADAMS, MYRA WINCHESTER
"Polly" and Other Poems. New York: F. W. Orvis, 1901. 6 p. ℓ., 95 p.
Pathways and Other Poems. New York: F. W. Orvis, 1903. 7 p. ℓ., 19-170 p.

ADAMSON, JOAN
Loosened Cargo, and Other Verses. New York: F. H. Hitchcock, 1925. 64 p.

ADCOCK, BETTY (1938-) [Full Name: Elizabeth (Sharp) Adcock]
Walking Out. Baton Rouge, LA.: Louisiana State University Press, 1975. 58 p.

ADDISON, ELEANOR
Nonamessett, and Other Verses. Philadelphia: Westbrook Publishing Co., 1928. 2 p. ℓ., 7-54 p.
Naushon, and Other Poems. New York: Margent Press, 1940. viii, 60 p.

ADDISON, JULIA DULANY
Sketches, Verses, and Attempts. Boston?: n.p., 1914. [22] p.
More Verses...1915. n.p., n.d. [34] p.
The Field of Honor and Other Poems...1918. n.p., 1918.
Verses. n.p., 1924. [35] p.
More Verses. Brookline?, MA.: n.p., 1952? 30 p.

ADDISON, MEDORA C. (1890-)
Dreams and a Sword. New Haven, CT.: Yale University Press, 46 p., 1 ℓ. (The Yale Series of Younger Poets, 12)

ADEE, LUCY AMELIA KINNARD (1885-)
Selected Poems. Glens Falls, N.Y.: Glencraft Print., 1957. 79 p.

ADLER, CAROL
Arioso. Milwaukee, WI.: Pentagram Press, 1975. [41] p.

ADLER, LUCILE
The Traveling Out and Other Poems. New York: Macmillan, 1967. 64 p.
The Society of Anna. Santa Fe, N.M.: Lightning Tree Press, 1974. 71 p.

AGNEW, MARJORIE LOURISE
--And the Moon Be Still as Bright. Emory University, GA.: Banner Press, 1956. 66 p. (Versecraft series)

AI, pseud. [ANTHONY, FLORENCE (1947-)]
Cruelty. Boston: Houghton, Mifflin, 1973. 46 p.

AIKINS, RUTH
The Smiling Princess. New York: Norcross, 1922. [31] p.

AKIN, KATY
Impassioned Cows by Moonlight. Brooklyn, N.Y.: Hanging Loose Books, 1975. 69 p. (A Red Dot book)

AKIN, MARGARETE ROSE (1868-)
Life's Afterglow. Dallas, TX.: W. T. Tardy, 1937. 6 p. ℓ., 111 p.
Fifty Golden Sonnets. Beebe, AK.: Underhill Press, 1939. 34 p.
Easter Pictures. Dallas, TX.: Artcraft Print. Co., 1943. 3 p. ℓ., 16 p.
White Rose Wonder. Dallas, TX.: Avalon Press, 1945. 48 p.

AKINS, ZOË (1886-1958)
Interpretations; a Book of First Poems. London: G. Richards Ltd., 1912. 120 p.
_______. New York: M. Kennerley, 1912. 120 p.
The Hills Grow Smaller. New York & London: Harper & Brothers, 1937. xv p., 1 ℓ., 102 p., 1 ℓ.

ALBANESE, MARGARET LEWIS (1911-)
Heir to Eden and Other Poems. Mexico: Impresora Antequera, 1951. 4 p. ℓ., 51 p.
_______. San Raphael, CA.: Andrews and Schroeder, 1951. 51 p.

ALBAUGH, DOROTHY PRISCILLA (1903-)
Songs Against the Dark. 1st ed. Worthington, OH.: n.p., 1941.

5-54 p.
By Quill and Candlelight. Worthington, OH.: n.p., 1947. 91 p.
The Green Bough. Delaware, OH.: Gateway Pub. Co., 1952. 114 p.

ALDAN, DAISY (1923-)
Poems. Long Island, N.Y.: n.p., 1946. 3 p. ℓ., 24 p.
The Destruction of Cathedrals and Other Poems. Paris, New York: Two Cities Press; dist. U.S.A.: Folder Editions, 1963. 75 p.
The Masks Are Becoming Faces. Lanham, MD.: Goosetree Press, 1964. 1 v.
Seven: Seven; Poems and Photographs (with Stella Snead). New York: Folder Editions, 1965. [40] p.
Journey; A Poem. New York: Folder Editions, 1970? [26] ℓ.
Or Learn to Walk on Water. New York: Folder Editions, 1970. [24] p.
Breakthrough: Poems in a New Idiom. Dornach, Switzerland: W. Keller; dist. in U.S.A. by Folder Editions, New York, 1971. 1 v. unpaged.
Love Poems of Daisy Aldan. New York: Barlenmir House, 1972. 56 p.
Stones. n.p.: Ragnarok Press, 1973. 26 ℓ.
______. New York: Folder Editions, 1974. [32] p.
Verses for the Zodiac. New York: Folder Editions, 1975. [29] p.

ALDEN, LUCY CHAFFEE
To Hampden. Hampden, MA.: n.p., 1907. 81 p.
Songs of Hope. Hampden, MA.: Pub. by her friends, 1909. 60 p.

ALDEN, MARGARET HAMILTON
Bits O' Verse. Port Huron, MI.: Riverdale Printing Co., 1917. [26] p.

ALDERSON, ALETHEA TODD
The Far Call. Dallas, TX.: The Kaleidograph Press, 1934. xi p., 1 ℓ., 15-96 p.
This Thing Called Peace. Dallas, TX.: The Kaleidograph Press, 1941. x p., 2 ℓ., 15-56 p.

ALDINGTON, HILDA DOOLITTLE see DOOLITTLE, HILDA (1886-1961)

ALDIS, DOROTHY (KEELEY) (1896-1966)
Everything and Anything. New York: Minton, Balch & Co., 1927. x, 99 p. (Verses for children.)
Here, There and Everywhere. New York: Minton, Balch & Co., 1928. x, 99 p. (Verses for children.)
Any Spring. New York: Minton, Balch & Co., 1933. 6 p. ℓ., 3-52 p.
Hop, Skip, and Jump. New York: Minton, Balch & Co., 1934.

xi p., 2 ℓ., 3-95 p. (Verses for children.)
Before Things Happen. New York: G. P. Putnam's Sons, 1939. viii, 85 p. (Verses for children.)
All Together, A Child's Treasury of Verse, Including Selections from Everything and Anything, Here, There, and Everywhere, Hop, Skip, and Jump, Before Things Happen, with Poems Previously Unpublished in Book Form. New York: Putnam, 1952. 192 p.
Hello Day. New York: Putnam, 1959. 64 p. (Verses for children.)
Quick as a Wink. New York: Putnam, 1960. 63 p.
Favorite Poems of Dorothy Aldis. New York: Putnam, 1970. 64 p.

ALDIS, MARY (REYNOLDS) (1872-)
Flashlights. New York: Duffield & Co., 1916. 4 p. ℓ., 130 p.

ALDRICH, MABLE GIERE [GIERE, MABLE LOUISE]
Awakening. Minneapolis, MN.: F. T. Phelps, 1933. 6 p. ℓ., 80 p., 1 ℓ.

ALDRICH, MARGARET CHANLER
Sonnets for Choice. New York: Moffat, Yard & Co., 1910. viii, 52 p.
The Horns of Chance, and Other Poems. London: E. Mathews, 1914. 67 p.
Westminster Abbey. By an American Visitor. Boston: The Merrymount Press, 1939. 4 ℓ.

ALDRICH, MYRTLE ANNA (1872-)
Echoes from the Green Hills. Rutland, VT.: The Tuttle Company, 1922. 110 p.

ALDRIDGE, ADELE (1934-)
...Notpoems. 2d ed. Riverside, CT.: Magic Circle Press, 1972. 1 v. unpaged.
The Strange Coherence of Our Dreams: Poems. Riverside, CT.: Magic Circle Press, 1973. 24 p.
Notpoems. 3d ed. Riverside, CT.: Artists & Alchemists, 1975. 50 p.

ALEXANDER, FAY F.
Reconnaissance. New York: Exposition Press, 1952. 12-64 p.

ALEXANDER, FRANCES (LAURA) (1888-)
Seven White Birds. Dallas, TX.: The Kaleidograph Press, 1938. x, 13-82 p.
Time at the Window. Dallas, TX.: The Kaleidograph Press, 1948. 76 p.
Conversation with a Lamb. Austin?, TX.: Stock Co., 1955. 62 p.
The Diamond Tree. Austin, TX.: Printed by Von Boeckmann-Jones Co., 1970. 39 p.

ALEXANDER, SELMA
The Ether Song and Other Poems. New York: The Aster Press, 1927. 3 p. ℓ., 28 p.

ALIESAN, JODY (1943-)
Thunder in the Sun. Seattle, WA.: Young Women's Christian Assn., University of Washington Branch, 1971.
To Set Free. Seattle, WA.: Second Moon, 1972. 37 p.
Soul Claiming: Poems. Northampton, MA.: Mulch Press, 1975. 76 p. (A Haystack book)

ALLEN, ADA (YORK)
Moods and Moments. New York: H. Harrison, 1943. 95 p.
Children of Earth: Poems. New York: Exposition Press, 1947. 96 p.

ALLEN, FLORENCE ELLINWOOD (1884-)
Patris. Cleveland, OH.: H. Carr, 1908. 4 p. ℓ., [7]-49 p.

ALLEN, MINERVA C(RANTZ) (1935-)
Like Spirits of the Past Trying to Break Out and Walk to the West. Albuquerque, N.M.: Wowapi Productions, 1974. 51 p.

ALLEN, PAULA GUNN
The Blind Lion. Berkeley, CA.: Thorp Springs Press, 1974. [44] p.

ALLEN, SARA VAN ALSTYNE
The Season's Name. Francestown, N.H.: Golden Quill Press, 1968. 80 p.

ALLEN, VELTA MYRLE (1898-)
Me and My Shadows. Chicago: Dierkes Press, 1948. 48 p.
Within Adobe Walls. Sunland, CA.: C. L. Anderson, 1948. 45 p.
Random Treasure. Sunland, CA.: C. L. Anderson, 1949. 14 p.
No Narrow Grooves. Dallas, TX.: Story Book Press, 1954. 45 p.
Men... Not Angels! Dexter, MO.: Cander Press, 1960. 28 p.

ALLISON, KIM, pseud. see GARBISCH, RUTH

ALLISON, MARGARET M.
The Sun Looked Upon Me and I Am Black. Madison, WI.: By the Author, 1970.

ALLMAN, REVA WHITE (1913-)
I've Known Love. New York: Vantage Press, 1975.

ALLYN, AIMEE
Thought Flowers. New York: The Knickerbocker Press, 1927. 6 p., 1 ℓ., 7-64 p.
Daydreams and Visions. New York: The Knickerbocker Press, 1929. 64 p.

ALTA (1942-)
Freedom's in Sight. Berkeley?, CA.: Noh Publications Press, 1969. [28] p. (Aldebaran review, no. 5)
________. n.p., 1970. [32] p. "First printed January, 1969... second printing March, 1970."
Letters to Women. San Lorenzo, CA.: Shameless Hussy Press, 1970? [28] p.
Burn This & Memorize Yourself: Poems for Women. New York: Times Change Press, 1971. 16 p.
No Visible Means of Support. San Lorenzo, CA.: Shameless Hussy Press, 1971. 71, [1] p.
Song of the Wife. Song of the Mistress. San Lorenzo, CA.: Shameless Hussy Press, 1971? [32] p.
I Am Not a Practicing Angel. Trumansburg, N.Y.: Crossing Press, 1975. 80 p.
Theme & Variations: Longpoem. San Lorenzo, CA.: Shameless Hussy Press, 1975. [49] p. (Aldebaran review, 18)

ALTROCCHI, JULIA (COOLEY) (1893-1972)
The Poems of a Child. New York: R. H. Russell, 1904. vi, [1], 150 [1] p.
The Dance of Youth, and Other Poems. Boston: Sherman, French & Co., 1917. 5 p. ℓ., 149 p.
Snow Covered Wagons, A Pioneer Epic; The Donner Party Expedition, 1846-7. New York: Macmillan, 1936. xxiii, 202, [1] p.
Girl with Ocelot, and Other Poems. Boston: Bruce Humphries, 1964. 150 p.
Chicago: Narrative of a City. Chicago?: n.p., 1968? 76 p.

ALVES, JULIET
Seven Oaks. New York: L. Raley, 1939. 5-64 p.
Philosopher, What Word? New York: L. Raley, 1941. 11-64 p.

ALYEA, DOROTHY ELIZABETH (COLLINS) (1898-)
All My Argument, A Book of Poems. New York: R. W. Ellis, 1935. 6 p. ℓ., 11-81 p., 1 ℓ.
Beach Fire. New York: Dutton, 1951. 52 p.

AMES, BERNICE (1915-)
Where the Light Bends. Los Angeles: Wagon & Star Press, 1955. 78 p.
In Syllables of Stars. Francestown, N.H.: Golden Quill Press, 1958. 64 p.
Antelope Bread. Denver, CO.: A. Swallow, 1966. 60 p.

AMES, EVELYN (PERKINS) (1908-)
The Hawk from Heaven. New York: Dodd, Mead, 1957. 93 p.

AMINI, JOHARI [LATIMORE, JEWEL C.]
Black Essence. Chicago: Third World, 1968. [9], 17 p.
Images in Black. Chicago: J. C. Press, 1968. 13 p.
________. Chicago: Third World, 1969. 13 p. rev. ed.

Let's Go Somewhere. Chicago: Third World, 1970. 31 p.

ANYX, KATHERINE McCLURE (1901-)
The Changing Hills. Dallas, TX.: Royal Pub. Co., 1959. 64 p.

ANDELSON, PEARL
Fringe. Chicago: W. Ransom, 1923. 5 p. ℓ., 9-59 p.

ANDERS, HALEN
A Pinch of Stardust. Philadelphia: Dorrance, 1967. 90 p. (Contemporary poets of Dorrance, 675).

ANDERSON, BESSIE WAYNE
Without Fear, and Other Poems. Philadelphia: Dorrance, 1939. 91 p. (Contemporary poets of Dorrance, 196)
A Temple Made Without Hands, and Other Verse. Francestown, N.H.: M. Jones Co., 1953. 80 p.

ANDERSON, CAMILLE
Abstractions 101. Chicago: R. F. Seymour, 1958. 111 p.

ANDERSON, EDNA L.
...Through the Ages. Philadelphia: Dorrance, 1946. 58 p. (Contemporary poets of Dorrance, 317)

ANDERSON, FLORENCE BELLE
Heart's Ease. San Diego, CA.: The Harmonial Publishers, 1921. 32 p.

ANDERSON, IDA FRANCES
In Love's Garden and Other Verses. Los Angeles: Arroyo Guild Press, 1909. 95, [1] p.

ANDERSON, ISABEL WELD (PERKINS) (1876-1948)
I Hear a Call. Cambridge, MA.: The Riverside Press, 1938. vi p., 2 ℓ., 3-81, [1] p.
The Whole World Over. Boston: B. Humphries, 1944. 71 p.
Near and Far. Boston: B. Humphries, 1949. 70 p.

ANDERSON, MARGARET STEELE (1867-1921)
The Flame in the Wind. Louisville, KY.: J. P. Morton & Co., 1913. 3 p. ℓ., 5-49.
________. Louisville, KY.: J. P. Morton, 1914. 59 p.
________. 3d printing. Louisville, KY.: J. P. Morton & Co., 1930. 6 p. ℓ., 71 p.

ANDERSON, MARJORIE (1892-1954)
A Web of Thought. Boston: The Four Seas Company, 1921. 57 p.
Maine Legend, and Other Poems. Freeport, ME.: Bond Wheelwright Co., 1960. 45 p.

ANDERSON, MARY LOUISA
The Child and Other Verse. New York: Knickerbocker Press, 1915. vi, 55 p.

ANDERSON, OMA CARLYLE
Bright Is the Tempo. Prairie City, IL.: Decker Press, 1949. 91 p.

ANDERSON, VIRA B.
Whisperin' Winds. New York: Exposition Press, 1974.

ANDREWS, EDITH FARGO
Vagrant Visions. Boston: Sherman, French & Co., 1917. 4 p. ℓ., 80 p.

ANDREWS, JENNE
In Pursuit of the Family. Morris, MN.: Minnesota Writers' Publishing House, 1974. 28 p. (Minnesota Writers' Publishing House Booklet)

ANDREWS, MARIETTA (MINNIGERODE) (1869-1931)
Songs of a Mother. New York: E. P. Dutton & Co., 1917. 79 p.
Out of the Dust. New York: E. P. Dutton & Co., 1920. x p., 1ℓ., 91 p.
The Darker Drink. Boston: R. G. Badger, 1922. 2 p. ℓ., 3-122 p.

ANDREWS, MARY RAYMOND (SHIPMAN) (1860-1936)
Crosses of War. New York: C. Scribner's Sons, 1918. 5 p. ℓ., 3-22 p.

ANDREWS, REBECCA GRAHAM AYARS (1849-)
Vineland: A Narrative Poem. Vineland, N. J.: n. p., 1911. 15 p.

ANDREWS, ROSE (1881-) [Full Name: Rose Ellen Andrews]
The Glory in Common Things. Winnsboro, TX.: Winnsboro Weekly News, 1938. [10] p.
The Glory in Common Things: Selected Poems. North Quincy, MA.: Christopher Pub. House, 1973. 91 p.

ANGELOU, MAYA (1928-)
Just Give Me a Cool Drink of Water: 'Fore I Diiie; the Poetry of Maya Angelou. New York: Random House, 1971. viii, 48 p.
_______. New York: Bantam, 1973. 52 p.
Oh Pray My Wings Are Gonna Fit Me Well. New York: Random House, 1975. x, 67 p.

ANGLUND, JOAN WALSH (1926-)
A Cup of Sun: A Book of Poems. New York: Harcourt, Brace & World, 1967. 63 p.
_______. London: Collins, 1968. 63 p.
Morning Is a Little Child. New York: Harcourt, Brace & World,

1969. [32] p.
A Slice of Snow: A Book of Poems. New York: Harcourt, Brace & World, 1970. 63 p.

ANGNEY, LYDIA FRANCES (WITHAM)
California, and Other Poems. San Jose, CA.: Press of A. C. Eaton, 1900. 5 p. ℓ., 13-96 p.

ANTHONY, FLORENCE (1947-) see AI, pseud.

APPLETON, SARAH (1930-) [Full name: Sarah Appleton Weber]
The Plenitude We Cry For. Garden City, N.Y.: Doubleday, 1972. 67 p.

ARCHER, KATE RENNIE
Now My Eyes Fade: A Narrative Poem. San Francisco?: n.p., 193-? [9] p.
Jock Tamson's Bairns and Other Poems. Glasgow and London: Cowans and Gray, Ltd., 1934. 4 p. ℓ., 56 p.
"Songs of a Little Brother," Souvenir-Vignette Verses. San Francisco: Zenith Press, Inc., 1934. 1 p. ℓ., 41 p.
Tumbleweed Trail. San Francisco: The Canterbury Press, 1936. 3 p. ℓ., 64 p.
Call Frae the Heather. Mills College, Oakland, CA.: The Eucalyptus Press, 1940. 3 p. ℓ., 61, [1] p.
Petals of the Guelder-Rose. Berkeley, CA.: Gillick Press, 1941. 3 p. ℓ., 9-73., 1 ℓ.
Recurrent Vigil. Berkeley, CA.: The Gillick Press, 1943. 3 p. ℓ., 95, [1] p.
Coffee Shop. Berkeley, CA.: The Gillick Press, 1947. 2 p. ℓ., 72 p.
Persimmon Harvest. San Francisco: The Abbey Press, 1955. 68 p.

ARCHER, LEOLA (1901-)
A White Ship Sailing. New York: Henry Harrison, 1940. 31 p.

ARCHER-BURTON, MARY-ELA (DENNE) (1853-)
Silver Wings and Other Gems of Thought and Verse. East Aurora, N.Y.: The Roycrofters, 1920. 4 p. ℓ., [11]-58 p.

ARDAYNE, JULIA COLLINS
Prismatic Window: Poems. New York: Exposition Press, 1950. 60 p.
Bright Morning, Bright Land. Philadelphia: Dorrance, 1969. 63 p.

ARMFIELD, LUCILLE (ARMFIELD) (1873-)
Songs from the Carolina Hills. New York: Doxey's, 1901. 68 p.
________. 1902. 68 p.

ARMSTRONG, PHYLLIS ELEANOR (1910-)
A Witness in Washington. Georgetown, CA.: Dragon's Teeth

Press, 1972. vi, 64 p. (Living poets library. Penultimate series, no. 10)

ARNOLD, CLARA PRATT
Ripple Marks. Newark, N. J.: n. p., 1925. 36 numb. ℓ.

ARNOLD, E. IRENA
Poems of a Salvationist. New York: Fleming H. Revell Co., 1923. 160 p.

ARTHUR, BARBARA
Common Sense Poetry. Berkeley, CA.: Respect International, 1969.

ASH, SARAH LEEDS (1904-)
Just Little Things. Presented by the Folio Club. Philadelphia: Eldon Press, 1941. 16 p.
Changeless Shore. 1st ed. Haverford, PA.: Haverford House, 1962. 39 p.
Moment in Time. Francestown, N. H.: Golden Quill Press, 1972. 79 p.

ASHBY, MAY
Figments. Boston: University Press, 1961. 50 p.

ATHENS, IDA GERDING
Brethren. Cincinnati, OH.: Talaria, 1940. 70 p., 1 ℓ.

AUL, JANE, pseud. see GUMP, LOUISE

AUSTIN, AURELIA (1912-)
Bright Feathers: Poems. Atlanta?: n. p., 1958. 59 p.

AUSTIN, DEBORAH S.
The Paradise of the World. University Park, PA.: Pennsylvania State University Press, 1964. 71 p.

AUSTIN, GRACE JEWETT (1872-1948)
My Father. Bloomington, IN.: Gummerman Printing Office, 1939. [11] p.
Vignettes of Texas. Dallas, TX.: n. p., 1946. [15] p.
Poems of Here and There. Dallas, TX.: Story Book Press, 1947. 40 p.
Poems from the Poetry Corner. Dallas, TX.: Story Book Press, 1947. 40 p.
Poems for Christmas Time. Dallas, TX.: Story Book Press, 1947. 40 p.
Poems for a Child Under a Big Tree. Dallas, TX.: Story Book Press, 1948. 44 p.
Songs and Ballads. Dallas, TX.: Story Book Press, 1948. 40 p.

AUSTIN, MARY (HUNTER) (1868-1934)
The American Rhythm. New York: Harcourt, Brace & Co., 1923.

The Children Sing in the Far West. Boston and New York: Houghton Mifflin Co., 1928. xiii, [1], 187, [1] p.
The American Rhythm. New and enl. ed. Boston & New York: Houghton, Mifflin Co., 1930. x, 174 p.

AUSTIN, MAXINE SANFORD (1910-)
The Spring of the Spirit. San Antonio, TX.: Naylor Co., 1972. xiii, 71 p.

AUSTRIAN, DELIA
Love Songs. Chicago: W. B. Conkey, 1902. 91 p.

AUXIER, SYLVIA (TRENT) (1900-)
Meadow-Rue. Prairie City, IL.: Decker Press, 1948. 51 p.
Love-Vine. Dallas, TX.: Story Book Press, 1953. 51 p.
The Grace of the Bough. Dallas, TX.: Royal Pub. Co., 1957. 50 p.
No Stranger to the Earth. Mill Valley, CA.: Wings Press, 1957. 56 p.

AVERILL, ANNA BOYNTON
Birch Stream, and Other Poems. Dover, ME.: The Cricket Club, 1908. xiii p., 1 ℓ., 297 p.

AVERY, LILLIAN MABEL (HIGGINS) (1861-)
Gems of Thought. Boston: The Roxburgh Publishing Co., 1917. 177 p.

AYERS, VIVIAN
Spice of Dawns. New York: Exposition Press, 1953. 39 p.
Hawk. Houston, TX.: Hawk Press, 1957. viii, 64 p.

BABBITT, EDITH COURTENAY
Chapel by the Sea. Brattleboro, VT.: The Stephen Daye Press, 1933. 70 p., 1 ℓ.
The Shady Road. Portland, ME.: Falmouth Publishing House, 1940. 5 p., 1., 3-37 p.
This Man of Galilee. Portland, ME.: Falmouth Publishing House, 1942. 4 p. ℓ., 3-97, [1] p.

BABCOCK, EDWINA STANTON
Greek Wayfarers and Other Poems. New York: G. P. Putnam's Sons, 1916. viii, 118 p.
The Flying Parliament, and Other Poems. New York: J. T. White & Co., 1918. 128 p.
Nantucket Windows. Nantucket Island, MA.: The Inquirer and Mirror Press, 1924. 124 p.

BABCOCK, MARGARET
Flashlights. Boston: Sherman, French and Co., 1917. 4 p. ℓ., 129 p.

BABER, IRENE ANGELE
Carolanus and Merone. The First Bouquet & Other Poems.

Boston: The Gorham Press, 1917. 224 p.

BABSON, HELEN CORLISS (1881-)
Tide Rhythms. Mill Valley, CA.: Wings Press, 1958. 89 p.

BACON, JOSEPHINE DODGE (DASKAM) (1876-)
Poems. New York: Scribner's & Sons, 1903. viii, [1] 72 [1] p.
The Twilight of the Gods. New York: M. Kennerley, 1915. 43 p.
Truth o' Women: Last Words from Ladies Long Vanished. New York: D. Appleton and Co., 1923. vii, 137 p.

BACON, MARTHA SHERMAN (1917-)
Lament for the Chieftains and Other Poems. New York: Coward-McCann, Inc., 1942. viii, 54 p.
Things Visible and Invisible. New York: Coward-McCann, Inc., 1947. vii, 56 p.

BACON, PEGGY (1895-) [Full Name: Margaret Frances Bacon]
Funerealities. New York: Aldergate Press, 1925. 59 p.
Two Poems & a Drawing. New York: Latterday, 1928. [4] ℓ. (The Latterday Pamphlets, No. 2)
The Ballad of Tangle Street. New York: The Macmillan Company, 1929. 4 p.ℓ., 22 p., 2 ℓ.
Animosities. New York: Harcourt, Brace and Company, 1931. 106 p., 1 ℓ.
Cat-calls. New York: R. M. McBride and Company, 1935. viii p., 1 ℓ., 11-87 p., 1 ℓ.

BAIL, GRACE SHATTUCK (1898-)
Daily Bread. New York: Pageant Press, 1952. 35 p.
Heartstrings. London: Mitre Press, 1968. 64 p.
Golden Days. London: Mitre Press, 1970. 64 p.

BAILEY, GERTRUDE BLACKWELL
If Words Could Set Us Free. Jericho, N.Y.: Exposition Press, 1974. 59 p.

BAILEY, MARGARET EMERSON (1880-1949)
First-Fruits. Boston: The Stratford Co., 1924. 2 p.ℓ., 41 p.
White Christmas. New York & London: G. P. Putnam's Sons, 1931. xii, 73 p.
Collected Writings; Manuscripts. New Canaan, CT.: n.p., 19-?-1949. 3v. Vol. 1-2, Poems; Vol. 3, Prose works.

BAILEY, MINNIE KEITH (1869-)
Life's Undertow. Topeka, KA.: Crane & Company, 1905. 1 p.ℓ., 43 p.

BAILY, HANNAH LAVINIA (1837-)
By the Sea, and Other Verses. Boston: R. G. Badger, 1907. 2 p.ℓ., [7]-75 p.

BAIR, FRIEDA
Feather in the Wind. Philadelphia: Dorrance, 1975. 60 p. (Contemporary poets of Dorrance)

BAIRD, MARTHA JOANNA (1921-)
Nice Deity. New York: Definition Press, 1955. 82 p.

BAKER, ANNA M.
The Voice of the Waters and Other Poems. Philadelphia: Dorrance, 1944. viii p., 1 ℓ., 11-97 p. (Contemporary poets of Dorrance, 267)
The Song of the Mountain Stream, and Other Poems. Philadelphia: Dorrance, 1947. 176 p. (Contemporary poets of Dorrance, 335)

BAKER, CATHERINE (1879-)
...Prayer for Storm. Philadelphia: Dorrance & Co., 1944. 58 p. (Contemporary poets of Dorrance, 283)
Land of Morning Splendor. Chicago: Dierkes Press, 1951. 40 p.
Capriccio. Eureka Springs, AK.: Dierkes Press, 1955. 38 p.
Late Finding, Collected Poems. Philadelphia: Dorrance, 1956. 123 p. (Contemporary poets of Dorrance, 493)

BAKER, HELEN GRANVILLE
Songs in Cities and Gardens. New York: Putnam, 1919. 132 p.

BAKER, JULIA ALDRICH
Gleams of Truth. General ed. Spartanburg, S.C.: Wadell & Band, 1904. 92 p.
______. Family ed. Spartanburg, S.C.: Wadell & Band, 1904. 149 p.
Mispah...A Calendar for 1911. London: E. Nister, 1910? [24] p.
In Mellow Light. Boston: The Christopher Publishing House, 1936. ix, [1], 11-88 p.

BAKER, Mrs. KARLE (WILSON) (1878-)
Blue Smoke. New Haven: Yale University Press, 1919. 116 p.
Burning Bush. New Haven: Yale University Press, 1922. 93, [1] p.
Dreamers on Horseback. Dallas, TX.: The Southwest Press, 1931. xii, 195 p.

BAKER, LIZZIE LEONARD
Yonderland. Cincinnati: Jennings and Graham, 19-?. 110 p.
Yonderland, and Other Verses. Boston: J. H. Earle & Co., 1904. 96 p.

BAKER, MARTHA S.
Songs of Home and Others. Boston: Cornhill, 1921. 5 p. ℓ., 79 p.

BAKER, MARY SHAW
Footprints on the Sands of Time. Boston: R. G. Badger, 1904. 114 p.

BAKER, MERCY E.
White Elephant Sale; A Collection of Previously Used Verse. Cedar Rapids, IA.: Torch Press, 194- . 83 p.
Bird Logic and Other Verse. New Bedford, MA.: Reynolds Printing, Inc., 1955. 36 p.

BALCH, ALLIE SHARP
Sunshine, Rain, and Roses. New York: G. P. Putnam's Sons, 1911. vi, 132 p.

BALDWIN, MARY NEWTON (1903-)
Here in These Hills.... Cleveland, OH.: n.p., 1946. 27 p. (Durham chapbook, no. 3)
Time's Winged Chariot. Francestown, N.H.: Golden Quill, 1975. 80 p.

BALDWIN, MERCY
Gray Songs. New York: H. Vinal, 1927. x p., 1 ℓ., 41 p.

BALDWIN, MYRA
Nancy's Easter Gift (A Poem). New York & London: The Abbey Press, 1902. 2 p. ℓ., 10 p.

BALE, JOY (1912-)
never less than love. Louisville: Kentucky Poetry Press, 1972.
The Storm's Eye: A Narrative in Verse Celebrating Cassius Marcellus Clay, Man of Freedom, 1810-1903. Edited by Wade Hall, Alice Scott, Gregg Swem. Louisville: Kentucky Poetry Press, 1974. 32 p. (Poets of Kentucky series, no. 7)

BALES, MARTHA E.
Souvenir Poems of Willoughby. Plainsville, OH.: n.p., 1923. 80 p.

BALL, ALICE (1906-)
In Old Carmelo. A Love Story of California. Prairie City, IL: Press of J. A. Decker, 1947. 63 p.

BALL, ALICE ELIZA (1867-)
A Year with the Birds. New York: Putnam, 1916. 191 p.
________. New York: Dodd, Mead and Company, 1918. 191 p.

BALLARD, JULIET (LYLE) BROOKE (BOND) (1913-)
Under a Tropic Sun. North Montpelier, VT.: The Driftwind Press, 1944. 60 p.
Winter Has Come. North Montpelier, VT.: The Driftwind Press, 1945. 84 p.

BALLOU, ELECTRA PEARL (1905-)
Jim's Place in the Sun. Chicago: Dierkes Press, 1951. 61 p.
Narcissus Poems. Dallas, TX.: Story Book Press, 1951. 39 p.
Jim's Place in the Sun, and Other Poems. New York: Exposition Press, 1953. 112 p.

BANBURY, CHRISTINE HOPE
Underneath a Bough. New Haven, CT.: Priv. print., 1920. 110 p.

BANCROFT, EMMA PUTMAN
Verses. New Orleans: Tulane University Press, 1921. 2 p. ℓ., 9-110 p., 1 ℓ.
"Mummie" Talks. Wauwatosa, Wis.: Print. by the Kenyon Press Publishing Co., 1932. 2 p. ℓ., [3]-47, [1] p.
When the Wind Blows. West Los Angeles, CA.: Wagon & Star, 1941. 5 p. ℓ., 15-60 p., 1 ℓ.

BANES, LUCIE GILLETT
... Lamps Are Burning. Philadelphia: Dorrance & Co., 1945. 65 p. (Contemporary poets of Dorrance, 300)
The Sun Is Up. Philadelphia: Dorrance, 1949. 157 p. (Contemporary poets of Dorrance, 402)
Transcendent Flight. Houston, TX.: The Anson Jones Press, 1952. 7 p. ℓ., 95 p.

BANFIELD, EDITH COLBY (1870-1903)
Place of My Desire, and Other Poems. Boston: Little, Brown & Company, 1904. 2 p. ℓ., [vii]-xiii p., 1 ℓ., 154 p.

BANGS, JANET (NORRIS) (1885-)
Cornstalk Fiddle. Prairie City, IL.: Press of J. A. Decker, 1948. 141 p.

BANY, AMALIA M.
Dear Richard. Denver, CO.: A. Swallow, 1965. [17] p.

BARBER, BETTY
The Original Face: Poems, 1948-1959, & One Poem from the Seventies. Hicksville, N.Y.: Exposition Press, 1975. 48 p.

BARBER, FRANCES
Realms We Fashion: A Book of Poems. Boston: B. J. Brimmer Company, 1923. xii, 78 p.
________. Special edition, numbered and signed by the author.

BARKER, ELSA (1869-1954)
The Frozen Grail, and Other Poems. New York: Duffield & Co., 1910. 2 p. ℓ., 3-4 p., 1 ℓ., 5-126 p.
The Book of Love. New York: Duffield & Company, 1912. xii, [2], 23 [1] p.
Songs of a Vagrom Angel. New York: M. Kennerley, 1916. 5 p. ℓ., 3-55 p.

BARKER, LAURA COOKE
Mezzotints. Wausau, WS.: The Philosopher Press, 1900. 70 p.
______. 1901. 70 p.
Looking Upward; Being a Collection of Inspirational Verse. New York: The Roycrofters, 1928. 133 p.

BARKER, MARY LUCRETIA
Voices That Sang. Cedar Rapids, IA.: The Torch Press, 1940. 98 p.
In Light and Shade. Golden, CO.: Sage Books, 1949. 48 p. (Poets of the West, 1)

BARKER, SHIRLEY (1911-1965) [Full name: Shirley Frances Barker]
The Dark Hills Under. New Haven, CT.: Yale University Press, 1933. 59 p. (The Yale Series of Younger Poets, 32)
A Land and a People. New York: Crown Publishers, 1952. 78 p.

BARKINS, ELIZABETH
Poems by a Young Girl. New York: Frederick Fell, 1954. 44 p.
Poems by a College Girl. New York: F. Fell, 1958. 46 p.

BARKINS, EVELYN (WERNER) (1918-)
The Magic Pod and Other Poems. New York: Island Workshop Press, 1945. 2 p. ℓ., 7-65 p.
Hospital Happy. New York: F. Fell, 1959. 109 p.
Love Poems of a Marriage. New York: F. Fell, 1970. 48 p.
A Grandparent's Garden of Verses. New York: F. Fell Publishers, 1973. 46 p.

BARNARD, MARY (ETHEL) (1909-)
A Few Poems. Portland, OR.: Graphic Arts Workshop, Reed College, 1952. [15] p.

BARNES, DIANTHA
Poems. Boston: R. G. Badger, 1925. 59 p.

BARNES, LEOLA CHRISTIE
Purple Petals, Poems Mainly of Texas, U. S. A. Devonshire, Eng.: Channing Press, 1934. 48 p. (Channing poets lib., no. 30)
Silver Century. San Antonio, TX.: The Naylor Company, 1936. xiii p., 1 ℓ., 65 p.
Purple Petals. San Antonio, TX.: Naylor Co., 1960. 38 p.
West to Glory, A Poem. New York: Exposition Press, 1961. 59 p.
Silver Century. San Antonio, TX.: Naylor, 1973. xiii, 83 p.

BARNES, MARY EMILIA (CLARK)
Athanasia. Boston: S. D. Towne, 1907. 7 ℓ.
Life Exultant. New York: Schulte Press, 1925. 15 p.

BARNES, PHOEBE (WASHBURN) (1908-)
Through Prisms. Boston: B. Humphries, 1961. 40 p.
Soundings and Bearings. Boston: Branden Press, 1967. 41 p.

BARNEY, NATALIE CLIFFORD
Poems and Poèmes; Autre Alliances. Paris: Emile-Paul Freres, New York: Geo. H. Doran, 1920. 3 p. ℓ., 9-38, 29, [2] p.

BARNHILL, MYRTLE FAIT (1896-)
Afterglow. San Antonio, TX.: Naylor Co., 1964. xi, 92 p.

BARNITZ, MAIDIE EMERSON (d. 1910)
Some Stray Poems. Washington, D. C.: Printed by Judd and Detweiler, 1913. 40 p.

BARNSTONE, ALIKI
The Real Tin Flower: Poems About the World at Nine. New York: Crowell-Collier Press, 1968. 54 p.

BARON, LINDA
Black is Beautiful and.... n. p., 1971.

BARON, MARY (KELLEY) (1944-)
Letters for the New England Dead. Boston: Godine Press, 1974. 32 p. (First Godine poetry chapbook series, no. 4)

BARR, C. H., pseud. see HORD, Mrs. CLARENCE

BARR, ISABEL (HARRIS)
Sword Against the Breast. New York, London: G. P. Putnam's Sons, 1935. 92 p.
The Ship of Glass. Prairie City, IL.: Press of J. A. Decker, 1946. 75 p.
Let Time Relate (Williamsburg Sonnets). Richmond, VA.: Dietz Press, 1947. 39 p.
Dialogue Without End. Richmond, VA.: Dietz Press, 1962. lx, 53 p.

BARRETT, KATHARINE RUTH (ELLIS) (1879-)
Red Shoes. New York: The Womans Press, 1930. viii p., 2 ℓ., 3-77 p. Verses for Children.
The Trenchant Wind: Poems of Patagonia. Cambridge, Eng.: W. Heffer & Sons Ltd., 1932. xii, 73, [1] p.
Katy of the Eighties. Cedar Rapids, IA.: The Torch Press, 1936. 83 p.

BARRETT, MADELEINE
Poems. Boston: American Poetry Association, 1924. 59 p.

BARRETTE, DENISE
Nocturne and Other Poems. Boston: B. Humphries, 1940. 63 p.
Nijinsky Dancing. Boston: B. Humphries, 1955. 32 p.

BARROW, KATE TRADER (1860-1939)
The Joy of Christmas, Mount of Ambition, etc.: Miscellaneous Medley of Modern Verse. Memphis, TN.: Dixon-Paul Printing Co., 1916. 100 p.
A Happy House of Life, and Other Verse. Memphis, TN.: S. C. Toof & Co., 1941. 9 p. ℓ., 171 p., 1 ℓ.

BARROWS, ANITA (1947-)
Emigration: A Collection of Poems, 1970-1972. Boston: The Spindrift Press, 1972. [53] p.

BARTELS, SUSAN LUDVIGSON (1942-)
Step Carefully in Night Grass; A Collection of Poems. Winston-Salem, N.C.: John F. Blair, 1974. 55 p.

BARTLETT, ALICE E[LINOR BOWEN] (1848-1920)
Birch Leaves: Homely Verse for Homely People with Homely Virtues and Sentiments. Detroit: Franklin Press, 1905. 168 p.

BARTLETT, ELIZABETH (WINTERS) (1911-)
Poems of Yes and No. Mexico City: Editorial Jus, 1952. 66 [1] p.
Behold This Dreamer. Mexico City: Editorial Jus, 1959. 30 p.
Poetry Concerto. Flushing, N.Y.: Sparrow Magazine, 1961. 14 p. (Vagrom chapbook no. 7)
It Takes Practice Not to Die. Santa Barbara, CA.: Van Riper & Thompson, 1964. 114 p.
Threads. Santa Barbara, CA.: Unicorn Press in association with Unicorn Bookshop, 1968. [20] p. (Santa Barbara poetry series)
Twelve-Tone Poems. Santa Barbara, CA.: Sun Press, 1968. [8] ℓ.

BARTLETT, HELEN (BIRCH) (1884-1925)
Capricious Winds. Boston & New York: Houghton, Mifflin Co., 1927. xvii, [1] p., 2 ℓ., 3-91 p.

BARTLETT, JENNIFER
Cleopatra I-IV. New York: Adventures in Poetry, 1971. [89] ℓ.

BARTON, Mrs. ARDELIA MARIA (COTTON) (1843-)
Thoughts. San Francisco: The Murdock Press, 1903. 213 p.
Autumn Leaves. San Francisco: Press of B. Brough, 1908. xii, 231 p.
Fragments.... San Francisco: The Philopolis Press, 1915. 243 p.

BARTON, MARIE
South Wind Calling. Dallas, TX.: The Kaleidograph Press, 1935. xi, 13-94 p.
Faith Is the Star. Dallas, TX.: The Kaleidograph Press, 1944. viii p., 1 ℓ., 11-64 p.

BARTON, MARY COURTNEY (1907-)
Another April. Prairie City, IL.: Press of J. A. Decker, 1946. 28 p.
Spirals of Sound. A Book of Sonnets. Boston: B. Humphries, 1954. 48 p.

BASCOT, JOSEPHINE RHETT
Shreds of Rhyme. Charleston, S. C.: n. p., 1924. 84 p.

BASS, CORA C.
Songs for All Seasons and Other Poems. Lowell, MA.: The Lawler Printing Co., 1901. 4 p. ℓ., 103 p.

BASS, ELLEN (1947-)
I'm Not Your Laughing Daughter. Amherst, MA.: University of Massachusetts Press, 1973. 96 p.

BASS, MADELINE TIGER (1934-)
The Chinese Handcuff. Fort Smith, AK.: South and West, 1975.

BASSETT, MARY JEANETTE (1895-)
We Ask No Dreams. Baltimore, MD.: n. p., 1961. 64 p.

BATCHELOR, JEAN MURIEL (1892-1945)
The Poems of Jean Batchelor. Selected and edited by Florence Edsall and Abbie Huston Evans. New York: Rockport Press, 1947. xi, 98 p.

BATEMAN, SYLVIA (1907-1926)
Branches to the Sky. Boston: The Stratford Co., 1927. 6 p. ℓ., 3-99 p.

BATES, CORA
Toll of the Mills and Other Poems. Sacramento, CA.: Anderson Print Shop, 1916. 64 p.

BATES, HARRIET SAWYER
Diversified Verse. New Orleans: Printed by Robert H. True Co., 1917. [22] p.

BATES, KATHERINE LEE (1859-1929)
America the Beautiful and Other Poems. New York: Thomas Y. Crowell Co., 1911. xii, 305 p.
________. 2nd ed.
Fairy Gold. New York: E. P. Dutton Co., 1916. viii, 232 p.
The Retinue and Other Poems. New York: E. P. Dutton Co., 1918. xii p., 1 ℓ., 138 p.
Yellow Clover, A Book of Remembrance. New York: E. P. Dutton, 1922. xv, 111 p. "Poems to Katharine Coman."
The Pilgrim Ship. New York: The Womans Press, 1926. 8 p. ℓ., 13-215 p.
America the Dream. New York: Thomas Y. Crowell Co., 1930. xi, 210 p.

Selected Poems of Katherine Bates. Edited by Marion Pelton Guild. Boston & New York: Houghton, Mifflin Co., 1930. xxv, [1], 230 p.

BATES, Mrs. MARGARET HOLMES (ERNSPERGER) (1844-1927) [HOLMES, MARGARET, pseud.]
Hildegarde, and Other Lyrics. New York: Broadway Publishing Co., 1911. 5 p., 1 ℓ., 7-86 p.

BATTAGLIA, BETTE (1925-)
The Blood of Roses. Philadelphia: Dorrance, 1968. 71 p. (Contemporary poets of Dorrance, 671)

BATTLE, EFFIE T.
Gleanings from Dixieland. Okolona, MS.: Priv. print., 1914. [4], 24 p.

BAXTER, MARION (BABCOCK)
Bits of Verse and Prose. Seattle, WA.: Printed by Lowman & Hanford Co., 1910. 54 ℓ.

BEACH, JESSIE
The Baby Poetess: A Book of New Poems. Lakeport, CA.: Mrs. J. Beach, 1904. 110 p.

BEACH, MARY
The Electric Banana. Cherry Valley, N.Y.: Cherry Valley Editions, 1975. 36 p.

BEACHLEY, ELIZABETH
Coconut Slide, and Others; Poems. Boston, MA.: Stratford, 1925. 3 p. ℓ., 83 p.

BEALL, DOROTHY LANDERS
Poems. New York: M. Kennerly, 1910. 132 p.
The Bridge and Other Poems. New York: M. Kennerley, 1913. 218 p.

BEALL, LAURA F.
The Agate Lamp. Boston: Cornhill, 1922. 4 p. ℓ., 3-86 p.

BEAN, ANNIE SHEPARD (1863-)
Breath of the Rose and Other Verse. San Jose, CA.: Melvin Printing Co., 1916. [48] ℓ.

BEAN, MARGARET PETRIE (1893-)
Magic Apple, and Other Poems. Charleston, IL.: W. S. Tremble, Prairie Press, 1965. 1 v.

BEATTY, MIRIAM
He Never Left Me: A Narrative Poem. New York: Exposition Press, 1975. 24 p.

BEATY, JOSEPHINE (POWELL) (1896-)
Milestones. Dallas, TX.: Kaleidograph Press, 1951. 99 p.
Tapestries. Dallas, TX.: The Story Book Press, 1953. 61 p.
For Us the Living. Dallas, TX.: Triangle Pub. Co., 2d ed., 1960. 40 p.
Reverie. Dallas, TX.: The Bookcraft, 1964. 70 p.
The Road to Jericho. Philadelphia: Dorrance, 1965. 154 p.

BECK, RACHEL WYATT ELIZABETH (TONGATE)
City Beautiful. A Tribute to the Capital of the United States. Boston: Christopher Publishing House, 1917. [16] p.

BECKER, CHARLOTTE
The Glass of Time. Chicago: The Blue Sky Press, 1900. 4 p. ℓ., 13-44 p., 1 ℓ.
________. 1901. 43 p.

BEDELL, CORNELIA FRANCES (1876-)
Sea Secrets. New York: Stewart & Co., 1911. 47 p.

BEECHER, MAY HOWELL
No Trespassing, and Other Verses. New York: F. Tennyson Neely Co., 1901. v, 147 p.

BEEDE, LILLIAN BARKER
Through the Mists. Marshalltown, IA.: Marshalltown Printing Co., 1910. 52 p.

BEELER, EMMA FLORENCE (ASHLEY) (1865-)
Brown Studies: Poems. New York: Cosmopolitan Press, 1911. 61 p.

BEHELER, LAURA FLO (1921-)
A Random Medley. Santa Fe, N.M.: Rydal Press, 1955. 39 p.

BEHENNA, CATHERINE ARTHUR (1860?-) [PRENDREGEIST, JOHN, pseud.]
Love Victorious. London: Kegan Paul, Trench, Trubner & Co., Ltd., 1904. 124 p.
Mystic Songs of Fire and Flame. Boston: Cornhill, 1921. x, 78 p.

BEHNEY, EVELYN
November.... Wilmington, DE.: Wilmington Poetry Press, 1946. 16 p. Limited edition.
Each Pale and Trembling Leaf. Wilmington, DE.: Wilmington Poetry Society & Delaware Writers, Inc., 1954.
________. Provincetown, MA.: Advocate Press, 1954. 27 p.
Fragment from a Letter. Philadelphia: Dorrance, 1962. 52 p. (Contemporary poets of Dorrance, 546)

BEIGHLE, NELLIE (CRAIB) (1851-)
Psychic Poems. San Francisco: Hicks-Judd Co., 1907. 3 p. ℓ., 62 p.

BELL, ELEANORA MAY
Bits of Dreams. Boston: The Stratford Company, 1923. 4 p. ℓ., 36 p.

BELL, MARY BETTIE see BELL, MARY ELIZABETH (STONE) (1848-)

BELL, MARY ELIZABETH (STONE) (1848-)
Old Kentucky Rhymes. Chicago: J. E. Fellers and Co., 1906. 4 p. ℓ., 5-51 p.

BELL, RUBY MARIE
Time Doth Wind. A Poetry Collection. New York: William-Frederick Press, 1951. 32 p. (The William-Frederick poets, 71)
In the Turn of the Wheel. New York: William-Frederick Press, 1953. 15 p. (The William-Frederick poets, 111)

BELLAMANN, KATHERINE (JONES)
Two Sides of a Poem. Denver: A. Swallow, 1955. 48 p. (The New poetry series [11])
A Poet Passed This Way. Mill Valley, CA.: Wings Press, 1958. 134 p.

BENDIT, EMILY TUPPER
Thoughts and Other Verses. Independence, MO.: n.p., 1905. 17 p.

BENEDICT, MADELINE (1895-)
Spring Will Not Fail. Emory University, Atlanta: Banner Press, 1940. 70 p. (Verse craft series)
Sudden Door. Francestown, N.H.: Golden Quill Press, 1960. 64 p.
That Bridge Again. Francestown, N.H.: Golden Quill Press, 1973. 78 p.

BENET, LAURA (1884-)
Fairy Bread. New York: T. Seltzer, 1921. 40 p.
Noah's Dove, A Book of Poems. Garden City, N.Y.: Doubleday, Doran & Co., 1929. 7 p. ℓ, 3-50 p.
Basket for a Fair. Garden City, N.Y.: Doubleday, Doran & Co., 1934. xiii, 93 p.
Is Morning Sure? New York: Odyssey Press, 1947. x, 64 p.
In Love with Time: Poems. Sanbornville, N.H.: Wake-Brook House, 1959. 53 p.
Bridge of a Single Hair: A Book of Poems. Boston: Branden Press, 1974. 45 p.

BENJAMIN, ABBIE CLEVELAND
In the Path of the Gleam. Boston: The Poet Lore Company, 1918. 80 p.

BENNETT, ANNA ELIZABETH (1914-)
Aeolian Airs. n. p., 193-?
Cantibile, Poems. New York: Fine Editions Press, 1954. 71 p.

BENNETT, C. FAYE (1890-)
Saying Sonnets & a Few Mavericks. Homestead, FL.: Olivant Press, 1969. 54 p.

BENNETT, GEORGIA E.
Vagrants. Chicago: R. F. Seymour, 1921. 2 p. ℓ., 64 p.

BENNETT, GERTRUDE RYDER
Etched in Words. New York: G. P. Putnam's Sons, 1938. xi p., 1 ℓ., 15-96 p.
The Harvesters. Francestown, N. H.: Golden Quill Press, 1967. 96 p.
Ballads of Colonial Days: With Historical Background. Francestown, N. H.: Golden Quill, 1972. 160 p.
Fugitive: With Historical Background. Francestown, N. H.: Golden Quill Press, 1975. 118 p.

BENSEL, ANNA B.
A Voice from the Silence. Boston: Sherman, French & Co., 1917. 7 p. ℓ., 91 p.

BENSKINA, PRINCESS ORELIA (1915-)
No Longer Defeated, and Other Poems. New York: Carleton Press, 1972. 64 p. (A Lyceum book)
The Inflammable Desire to Rebel. New York: Vantage, 1973. 44 p.
I Have Loved You Already. Hicksville, N. Y.: Exposition Press, 1975. 47 p.

BENTLEY, BETH RITA (1928-)
Phone Calls from the Dead. Athens, OH.: Ohio University Press, 1970. 78 p.
Country of Resemblances. Athens, OH.: Ohio University Press, 1975. 72 p.

BENTLEY, ELLIDA (PATTISON) (1856-)
Wind's Far Sowing. Emory University, Atlanta, GA.: Banner Press, 1940. 28 p. (Verse craft series)

BENTLEY, LAVINIA TIFFANY
The Gentle People. New York: Vantage Press, 1974. 56 p.

BENTON, DOROTHY GILCHRIST (1919-)
Mountain Harvest. Peterborough, N. H.: Windy Row Press, 1973. 68 p.

BENTON, PATRICIA (1907-) [MEDNIKOFF, PATRICIA BENTON]
Pebbles: A Collection of Poems. Mt. Vernon, N. Y.: The Walpole Printing Office, 1939. 59 [1] p.

Voice in the Willows. Chicago: Dierkes Press, 1947. 96 p.
The Whispering Earth. New York: n. p., 1950. 47 p.
Signature in Sand. New York: Greenberg, 1952. 69 p.
Medallion Southwest. Santa Fe, N. M.: Rydal Press, 1954. 64 p.
Cradle of the Sun. New York: F. Fell, 1956. 55 p.
Arizona, the Turquoise Land. New York: F. Fell, 1958. 41 p.
Love Is. New York: F. Fell, 1963. 45 p.
A Friend Is for Always. New York: Fell, 1964. [35] p.
The Magic of Christmas. New York: F. Fell, 1964. 1 v.
Manhattan Mosaic. New York: F. Fell, 1964. 1 v.
Love Has Many Faces. New York: F. Fell, 1965. 1 v. unpaged.
Of the Heart's Own Telling. New York: F. Fell, 1966. 28 p.

BERGE, CAROL PEPPIS (1928-)
The Vulnerable Island. Cleveland, OH.: Renegade Press, 1964. [10] ℓ.
Lumina. Cleveland, OH.: Flowers Press, 1965. 3 double ℓ.
Poems Made of Skin. Toronto: Weed/Flower Press, 1968. 50 p.
An American Romance; The Alan Poems, a Journal. Los Angeles: Black Sparrow Press, 1969. 88 p.
The Chambers. Capel-y-ffin, Abergavenny: B. Sewell, 1969. 18 p.
______. Aylesford Priory, Kent: Aylesford Review Press, 1969.
Circles, As in the Eve. Santa Fe, N. M.: Desert Review Press, 1969. 22 p.
From a Soft Angle: Poems About Women. Indianapolis, IN.: Bobbs-Merrill, 1971. xiii. 190 p.

BERGHOLZ, MARY MARANCEY (LYON)
Rhymes from Different Climes. Boston: The Cornhill Company, 1918. 5 p. ℓ., 52, [2] p.

BERNHEIM, BEATRICE B.
Impressions. New York: The Vail-Ballou Co., 1917. 3 p. ℓ., 5-62 p.
______. 2nd ed. New York: Jaques and Co., 1917. 82 p.
America's Great Northwest. New York: National Book Publishers, 1919. 93 p.
Life's Vagaries. New York: Jaques and Company, 1920. 109 p.
Norway's Snows to Egypt's Treasure-Trove. New York: Luxor Publishing Co., 1923. 116 p.

BERRY, JEAN
My Child; A Book of Verse. New York: E. P. Dutton, 1919. viii p., 1 ℓ., 69 p.
Psalms. London: G. Routledge and Sons, Ltd., 1923. 72 p.
Midian Meditations: Vignettes From the South of France. New York: Putnam, 1925. viii, 70 p.

BERRY, SYLVIA
Rose Petals. Chicago: New Day Publications, 1973. 32 p.

BERRY, VIOLA RILEY
The Alamo, and Other Poems. Denton, TX.: News Publishing Co., 1906. 153 [6] p.

BERRY, VIOLETTA LANSDALE
The Great Blue Heron and Other Poems. New York, London: G. P. Putnam's Sons, 1933. 112 p.
Tall Oneida Mountains and Other Poems. New York, London: G. P. Putnam's Sons, 1934. ix p., 1 ℓ., 13-86 p.

BERRYHILL, HELEN (1915-)
A Habit of Listening: Poems. San Francisco: Printed by Grabhorn-Hoyem, 1968. 50 p.

BERSSENBRUGGE, MEI
Summits Move with the Tide. Greenfield Center, N.Y.: Greenfield Review Press, 1974. 50 p.

BESS, OLEAN (1936-)
Mixed Feelings. St. Albans, N.Y.: n.p., 1972. 1 v. unpaged.

BEST, SUSIE MONTGOMERY
Arbor Day in the Primary Room. Philadelphia: Penn Publishing Co., 1907. 16 p.
Altar Candles. Boston: R. G. Badger, 1927. 78 p.
Leaves from Life's Tree, a Book of Verse. Philadelphia: Dorrance, 1947. 137 p. (Contemporary poets of Dorrance, 348)

BEVINGTON, HELEN (SMITH) (1906-)
Dr. Johnson's Waterfall and Other Poems. Boston: Houghton, Mifflin, 1946. viii, [1], 164 p.
Nineteen Million Elephants and Other Poems. Boston: Houghton, Mifflin, 1950. xi, 115 p.
A Change of Sky and Other Poems. Boston: Houghton, Mifflin, 1956. 144 p.

BEVIS, KATHERINE
God's Power and Other Poems. Boston: Bruce Humphries, 1955. 40 p.

BEYE, HOLLY (1922-)
Do Keep Thee in Stoney Bowes. San Francisco: Inferno Press, 1951. 49 p.
______. San Francisco: Greenwood Press, 1953. 47 p.
In the City of Sorrowing Clouds. San Francisco: The Print Workshop, 1955. 79 p.
Stairwells and Marriages. San Francisco: Print Workshop, 1955. 79 p.
XVI Poems. San Francisco: The Print Workshop, 1955. 25 p.

BIANCHI, MARTHA GILBERT (DICKINSON) (1866-1943)
The Cathedral, and Other Poems. New York: C. Scribner's Sons, 1901. x, 149 p.
Gabrielle, and Other Poems. New York: Duffield & Company, 1913. 5 p. ℓ., 3-141 p.
The Wandering Eros. Boston & New York: Houghton, Mifflin Co., 1925. xii p., 2 ℓ., [3]-115 p.

BICKLEY, BEULAH VICK
Love's Tapestry. Boston: B. J. Brimmer Co., 1925. 4 p. ℓ., 7-78 p.
The Grail of Spring. Cedar Falls, IA.: Holst Printing Co., 1934. 120 p.
The Flowering Rod. Cedar Rapids, IA.: Parnassian Press, 1937. 119, [1] p., 1 ℓ.
______. Paterson, N. J.: Gayren Press, 1939. 119, [1] p., 1 ℓ.
Discs of Time. Boston: B. Humphries, 1947. 158 p.

BIGELOW, CHARLOTTE BARNES
Life-Voyage Verse. Chicago: n. p., 1916. vii, 85 p.

BIGELOW, L. ADDA (NICHOLS) (1849-)
From Sea to Sea: Complete Poems. Burlington, VT.: Free Press Printing Co., 1914. 471 p., viii p.
Reminiscences. Chula Vista, CA.: Denrich Press, 1917. [36] p.

BILLIPP, BETTY
Please Pass the Salt... Poems. Peterborough, N. H.: Windy Row Press, 1974. 63 p.

BIRCH, ALISON WYRLEY (GREENBIE) (1922-)
Say Ah-h! Penobscot, ME.: Traversity Press, 1959. 54 p.
East of Manhattan. Penobscot, ME.: Traversity Press, 1965. vi, 101 p.
A Little of This and That. London: Mitre Press, 1965. 32 p.

BIRCHALL, SARA HAMILTON
Book of the Singing Winds. Boston: A. Bartlett, 1905. 5 p. ℓ., 17-46 [2] p.
Songs of Saint Bartholomew. Boston: A. Bartlett, 1909. 4 p. ℓ., 17-69 p., 1 ℓ.
The Game of Hearts; A Book for Lovers of Each Other or the Game. Boston & Chicago: W. A. Wilde Company, 1911. [15] ℓ.

BIRD, BESSIE CALHOUN
Airs From the Woodwinds. Philadelphia: Alpress Publishers, 1935. 1 p. ℓ., lx, 23, [1] p.

BISHOP, ELIZABETH (1911-)
North & South. Boston: Houghton, Mifflin Co., 1946. v, 54 p.
Poems: North & South. A Cold Spring. Boston: Houghton

Mifflin, 1955. 95 p.
Poems. London: Chatto and Windus, 1956. 50 p.
Questions of Travel. New York: Farrar, Straus & Giroux, 1965. 95 p.
_______. New York: Noonday Press, 1967. 95 p.
Selected Poems. London: Chatto and Windus, 1967. 117 p.
The Ballad of the Burglar of Babylon. New York: Farrar, Straus & Giroux, 1968. [43] p.
The Complete Poems. New York: Farrar, Straus & Giroux, 1969. 216 p.
_______. London: Chatto and Windus, 1970. [8], 216 p.
Poem. New York: Phoenix Bookshop, 1973. [11] p. (Phoenix Book Shop Oblong Octavo Series, v. 16)

BISHOP, JEAN A.
Just Dogs. New York: Lion Press, 1918. [27] p.
_______. New York: G. H. Watt, 1927. 64 p.

BISHOP, JOAN STAFFORD (1911-)
Truth for Orange Trees. Francestown, N. H.: Golden Quill Press, 1958. 63 p.

BISSELL, BESS G.
Milltown Days & Nights. Philadelphia: Dorrance, 1973.
A Log Cabin Log: Poems. New York: Vantage Press, 1973. 31 p.

BLACK, EDNA VAUGHAN
Meditations. Cleveland, OH.: Pegasus Studios, 1938. 21 p. (Torchbearers' Chapbooks, no. 31)

BLACK, EFFIE S.
Heart-Whispers. Cleveland, OH.: F. M. Barton, 1900. 93 p.

BLACKBURN, MARY CARY
Toward the Highlands. St. Louis, MO.: Pub. for the author by Christian Board of Publication, 1912. 133 p.

BLACKWELL, HARRIET GRAY (1898-)
The Lightning Tree. Richmond, VA.: Dietz Press, 1954. 73 p.
The Trees of Heaven. Richmond, VA.: Dietz Press, 1970. xi, 80 p.

BLAIR, ANNE
... Candlelight Dreams. New York: H. Vinal, 1928. 5 p. ℓ., 30 p. (The friendly books)
A Modern Penelope. Manchester, ME.: Falmouth Pub. House, 1951. 53 p.

BLAKE, ELIZABETH JESSUP
Up and Down. New Haven, CT.: Yale University Press, 1924. 50 p. (Yale Series of Younger Poets, 19)

BLAKE, EVA S.
Rhymes from the Kitchen. Meredith, N.H.: n.p., 1923. 3 p. ℓ., 9-78 p.
Lines from the Garden. Rutland, VT.: The Tuttle Company, 1930. 68 p.

BLANARD, FREDA EFTER (1910-)
Through Cynics Scoff. Philadelphia: Dorrance, 1965. 80 p. (Contemporary poets of Dorrance, 603)

BLAND, CLARA OPHELIA
Songs from the Capital. New York: R. G. Badger, 1906. 4 p. ℓ., 7-90.
Songs from the Southland. Macon?, GA.: n.p., 192-. [8] p.
_______. Macon, GA.: n.p., 1921. 8 p.
Songs from the Heart of Georgia. Macon?, GA.: n.p., 1923?. 2 p. ℓ., [7] p.
Songs of Spring. Macon, GA.: Bibb Printing Co., 1923. [12] p.
Ragged Robins; or, Verses for Juniors. Macon, GA.?: n.p., 1934. 30, [1] p.

BLANKNER, FREDERIKA
All My Youth, a Book of Poems. New York: Brentano's, 1932. 6 p. ℓ., 3-86 p. "First edition."
_______. New York: Brentano's, 1934. 86 p.

BLANTON, NATALIE (McFADEN) (1895-)
In That Day, Poems of the Second World War. Richmond, VA.: n.p., 1950. 72 p.
The Door Opened. Richmond, VA.: n.p., 1959. 55 p.

BLISS, ALICE (WITHERSPOON) (1925-)
Words for Dancing, and Other Poems. Atlanta, GA.: Russell & Wardlaw, 1958. 28 p.
Ellipse of Sonnets and Other Poems. Athens, GA.: McGregor's, 1960. 28 p.

BLISS, ANNIE MARIE
Smile and Sing, and Other Verses. Reading, MA.: A. M. Bliss Publishing Co., 1905. 4 p. ℓ., 11-27 p.

BLISS, SYLVIA HORTENSE (1870-1963)
Quests; Poems in Prose. Montpelier, VT.: Capital City Press, 1920. 101 p.
Sea Level. North Montpelier, VT.: The Driftwind Press, 1933. 90 p.
Quests: Poems in Prose. Montpelier, VT.: Capital City Press, 1965. 5 p. ℓ., 74 p., 1 ℓ. "Contains excerpts from the 1920 first edition."

BLITCH, MARY M. [MIGUELLA, pseud.]
Perfect Silence and Other Poems. Boston: Meador Publishing Co., 1933. 80 p.

BLOMFIELD, ADELAIDE
White Ash. Tacoma, WA.: Charas Press, 1974. 58, [1] p.

BLOOD, MINNIE E.
When Good Men Meet as Foe to Foe. Boston: The Southgate Press, 1916. 1 p. ℓ., 29 p.

BLOUNT, IVA MILAM
Through the Years. San Antonio, TX.: Naylor Co., 1959. x, 40 p.

BLOUNT, NELL RANDOLPH
"Sincerely Yours"; Verses. Phoenix?, AZ.: n.p., 1905. 110 p.

BLUM, ETTA (1908-)
...Poems. New York: Golden Eagle Editions, 1937. 62 p., 1 ℓ.
The Space My Body Fills: Poems. Hicksville, N.Y.: Exposition Press, 1975. 62 p.

BLUMENKRON, CARMEN (1920-)
Spearhead Toward the Dawn. New York: Vantage Press, 1973. 122 p.

BOBIER, CATHERINE
Vice Versa. Philadelphia: Dorrance, 1974. 58 p. (Contemporary poets of Dorrance)

BODENSCHATZ, VIOLA (HEISE)
Fireworks Poems. Louisville, KY.: Brandy & Fowler, 1932. 2 p. ℓ., 7-49 p.

BODINE, EDNA J.
Jewels of Memory. New York: Vantage Press, 1962. 55 p.

BODLEY, LAVINA M.
Wandering and Wondering. Kansas City, MO.: Burton Publ. Co., 1932. 86 p.

BOFF, ANNA McCOY
Inspirational Poems. Albany, N.Y.: n.p., 1933. 33 p.
Poems. Albany, N.Y.: Fort Orange, Press, 1943. 82 p.

BOGAN, LOUISE (1897-1970)
Body of This Death. New York: R. M. McBride & Co., 1923. 5 p. ℓ., 30 p.
Dark Summer. New York: C. Scribner's Sons, 1929. x, 72 p.
Women. Pasadena, CA.: Printed by Ward Ritchie, 1929. [4] p.
The Sleeping Fury. New York: C. Scribner's Sons, 1937. xii, 42 p.
Poems and New Poems. New York: C. Scribner's Sons, 1941. xi, 116 p.
Collected Poems, 1923-1953. New York: Noonday Press, 1954.

126 p.
________. London: P. Owen, 1956. 126, [1] p.
The Blue Estuaries: Poems, 1923-1968. New York: Farrar, Straus & Giroux, 1968. 136 p.
________. New York: Octagon Books, 1975. 136 p.

BOGART, LAURA GERTRUDE
The Way Out. Pasadena?, CA.: n.p., 1949. 100 p.
Prisms. Pasadena?, CA.: n.p., 1951. 110 p.

BOGUE, LUCILE MAXFIELD (1911-) [BOGUE, MAX and MAX, LUCY]
Typhoon! Typhoon! An Illustrated Haiku Sequence. Rutland, VT: C. E. Tuttle Co., 1969. 67 p.

BOGUE, MAX see BOGUE, LUCY MAXFIELD (1911-)

BOHANON, MARY
Earth Bosom and Collected Poems. New York: Carlton Press, 1973. 48 p.

BOHRS, MARY ANN (1934-)
Ironing Board Altars. Nashville, TN.: Broadman Press, 1969. 32 p.

BOLCOURT, DOROTHY
I Wandered Far.... Kansas City, MO.: n.p., 1951. 116 p.

BOLE, MILDRED LOUISE (1907-)
Better Than Laughter. Minneapolis, MN.: University of Minnesota Press; London: G. Cumberlege, Oxford University Press, 1946. 4 p.ℓ., 68 p.

BOLLES, MARY NIMS (1871-)
Paths That Be: Poems. Ann Arbor, Mich.: Lithographed by Edwards Brothers, 1967. xi, 72 p.

BOLLOCK, MARGOT
The Calibrated Woman. Berkeley, CA.: Thorp Springs Press, 1973. 74 p.

BOND, AGNES (DAVENPORT)
The Lure of the Open and Other Rhymes. Cincinnati: Caxton Press, 1930. 96 p.
Rainbow Trails. Dallas, TX.: The Kaleidograph Press, 1934. x p., 1 ℓ., 13-96 p.
Ships That Pass. North Montpelier, VT.: The Driftwind Press, 1938. 89 p.
Happy Landing. Dallas, TX.: The Kaleidograph Press, 1942. xi p., 1 ℓ., 15-80 p.
This Hour Is Mine. Dexter, MO.: Candor Press, 1953. 80 p.

BOND, CARRIE (JACOBS) (1862-1946)
Little Stories in Verse as Unpretentious as the Wild Rose. Chicago: The Author, 1905. 3 p. ℓ., 9-70 p.
The Path o' Life. Chicago: J. G. Cannom, 1909. [14] p.
Tales of Little Cats. Chicago: P. F. Volland Co., 1918. 19 ℓ.
Tales of Little Dogs. Chicago: P. F. Volland Co., 1921. unpaged.

BOND, LUCILE (1898-) [Full Name: Hallie Lucile Bond.]
River Harvest. Caldwell?, ID.: n.p., 1951. 72 p.

BOND, PEARL
The Sensual Image: Poems. Eagle Creek, OR.: New Age, 1952. 4 p. ℓ., 70 p. (New Age, Eagle Creek, OR.: Publications, no. 2)

BONHAM, CECILE
Cecilian Love Songs. Los Angeles, CA.: New Age Publishing Co., 1949. 100 p.
Listen! O World. Los Angeles, CA.: New Age Publishing Co., 1950. 7 p.

BONNETTE, JEANNE De LAMARTER (1907-) [De LAMARTER, JEANNE]
Colored Sails. Chicago: R. Packard Co., 1930. 1 ℓ., 13-79 p.
Seven Stars. Chicago: R. F. Seymour, 1939. 4 p. ℓ., 7-66 p.
Chess Game and Other Poems. Chicago: R. F. Seymour, 1952. 70 p.
In This Place. Fort Smith, AR.: South and West, Inc., 1971. 48 p.

BOOTH, AMANDA M. E.
In a Country Land, and Other Poems. Cincinnati, OH.: Editor Publ. Co., 1900. 90 p.

BOOTH, BARBARA
Storm Dark Trails. n.p.: Apex Publishers, 1972.

BOOTH, EDNA PERRY
The Shadow-Man, and Other Poems. New York: The Grafton Press, 1907. 41 p.
Nursery Rhymes for the Grown-Ups and Some of Another Kind. New York: Grafton Press, 1910. viii, 60 p.

BOOTH-SMITHSON, ALICE ROSE (O'NEILL)
Songs of Gladness. Boston, MA.: n.p., 1924. 96 p.
Heart to Heart with the Kiddies; Original Poems for Boys and Girls. Boston: The Author, 1927. 45 p.

BOSS, LEONORA MILLIKEN
Poems. Los Angeles, CA.: Austin Publishing Co., 1918. 2 p. ℓ., [7]-79 p.

BOST, EMMA (INGOLD)
Songs in Many Keys. Hickory, N. C.: Clay Printing Co., 1920. 80 p.

BOSWELL, MARGIE BELLE (1875-)
The Mocking Bird and Other Poems. Los Angeles: J. C. Farley, 1927. 125 p. "second edition."
The Upward Way. Dallas, TX.: W. T. Tardy, 1937. 6 p. ℓ., 3-89 p.
Wings Against the Dawn. Dallas, TX.: Avalon Press, 1945. 93 p.
The Light Still Burns. Dallas, TX.: Story Book Press, 1952. 68 p.
Starward. Arlington, TX.: Dudley Hodgkins Co., 1956. 107 p.
Sunrise in the Valley. Arlington, TX.: Dudley Hodgkins Co., 1959. 137 p.

BOTTS, IDA (BASSETT) BOTTS (1869-1958)
Across the Years. San Antonio, TX.: Naylor Co., 1959. xvi, 110 p.

BOUGHTON, MARTHA ELIZABETH (ARNOLD) (1857-1928)
The Quest of a Soul, and Other Verse. New York, Chicago: Fleming H. Revell Co., 1911. 127 p.
Mystery and Other Poems. New York: H. Vinal, 1926. 5 p. ℓ., 37, [1] p.

BOUGHTWOOD, ALICE MARIAN (1897-)
Mathematical Music. Quincy, MA.: President Press, 1967. 30 p.

BOULT, ELLA MAUD (1868-)
Romance of Cinderella; being the true history of Eleanor de Bohun, and her lover, Hallam Beaufort, duke of Somerset.... New York: R. H. Russell, 1902. 2 p. ℓ., 146 p.

BOVEE, HELEN HARDY
The Hour Glass. Seattle, WA.: n.p., 1925. 2 p. ℓ., 7-64 p.

BOVELL, CECILE
A Point of View. New York: Vantage Press, 1963. 60 p.

BOWCHER, MAY ALICE
Jingles from the Far West. New York: Whittaker Ray, 1904. 39 p.

BOWDEN, GUSSIE COOPER
Jolly Jingles. San Antonio, TX.: Naylor Co., 1965. v, 30 p.

BOWDOIN, GENEVIEVE B.
Bouquet of Eggs. Boston: Branden Press, 1968. 60 p.

BOWEN, MARGARET (BARBER) (1874-)
Singing Places. Boston: The Cornhill Co., 1919. 5 p. ℓ., 48 p.

BOWERS, CHARLOTTE (1911-)
Poems From My Pen and My Heart. San Antonio, TX.: Naylor Co., 1967. x, 97 p.

BOWERS, HAZEL
Cricket Voices. Francestown, N.H.: Golden Quill Press, 1970. 64 p.

BOWERS, MILDRED
Twist o' Smoke. New Haven, CT.: Yale University Press; London: H. Milford, Oxford University Press, 1928. 35 p. (The Yale Series of Younger Poets, 24)

BOWIE, BEVERLEY (MUMFORD) (1914-)
Know All Men by These Presents. New York: Bookman Associates, 1958. 64 p.

BOYCE, FLORENCE E.
Sunshine and Cheer from Vermont. North Montpelier, VT.: The Driftwind Press, 1931. 86 p.

BOYCE, MONICA (PLAXCO) (1893-) [BOYCE, WILLIE BELL PLAXCO]
Poems of Wisdom and Wit. Dexter, Mo.: Candor Press, 1964. 64 p.
Gurgling Fountains. Charleston, IL.: Prairie Press, 1967. ix, 45, [1] p.
Challenge to Laughter. Dexter, MO.: Candor Press, 1968. 64 p.

BOYCE, WILLIE BELL PLAXCO see BOYCE, MONICA (PLAXCO)

BOYD, MARION MARGARET see HAVIGHURST, MARION M. (BOYD)

BOYD, SUE ABBOTT (1921-)
Decanter; Poems: 1952-1962. Fort Smith, AR.: South and West Publications, 1962. 40 p.
The Sample Stage. Fort Smith, AR.: South and West, 1964. 38, [3] p.
Fort Smith and Other Poems. Fort Smith, AR.: Border Press, 1965. 33 p.
How It Is; Selected Poems, 1952-1968. Homestead, FL.: Olivant Press, 1968. 172 p.

BOYDEN, POLLY CHASE
Toward Equilibrium. New York: Covici, Friede, 1930. viii, 51 p.

BOYER, Mrs. FLOY
The Heart Unbowed. New York: H. Harrison, 1936. 64 p.

BOYER, JILL WITHERSPOON
Dream Farmer. Detroit: Broadside Press, 1975. 24 p.

BOYLAN, JOSEPHINE WINDER
Marble Satyr and Other Poems. New York: The Knickerbocker Press, 1928. vi, 58 p.

BOYLAN, OCTAVIA WINDER
An Arresting Voice. Baltimore, MD.: The Norman Remington Co., 1924. 23 p.

BOYLE, KAY (1903-)
A Statement. New York: The Modern Editions Press, 1932. [8] p., 1 ℓ.
A Glad Day. Norfolk, CT.: New Directions, 1938. 85 p., 1 ℓ.
American Citizen Naturalized in Leadville, Colorado. New York: Simon and Schuster, 1944. 15, [1] p.
Collected Poems. New York: A. A. Knopf, 1962. 105 p.
Testament for My Students and Other Poems. Garden City, N.Y.: Doubleday, 1970. 90 p.

BOYLE, VIRGINIA (FRAZER) (1863-1938)
Robert Edward Lee: The South's Gift to Fame. n.p., 19--.
Love Songs and Bugle Calls. New York: A. S. Barnes, 1906. ix, 236 p.
Abraham Lincoln, A Centennial Poem... written for the Philadelphia Brigade, February 12, 1909. Memphis, TN.: S. C. Toof & Co., 1909. 8 ℓ.
Songs from the South. Memphis, TN.: S. C. Toof & Co., 1939. 5 p. ℓ., 9-81 p.

BOYLES, VERA POWELL
Golden Loaves and Silver Fishes. Chicago: Windfall Press, 1963. 32 p.

BRACKETT, KATE (1902-)
The Lonely Guest; Lyrics 1945 to 1953. Cleveland, OH.: American Weave Press, 1956. 38 p. (Durham Chapbook, 11)

BRADBURY, BIANCA (1908-)
Half the Music. New York: The Fine Editions Press, 1944. 48 p.

BRADBURY, GEORGIEE REED
Rose Leaves and Old Dreams. New York: P. G. Boyle, 1922. 95 p.

BRADFORD, BERNICE MARGARET
Poems. Baltimore, MD.: Saulsbury Publishing Co., 1918. 24 p.

BRADFORD, GEORGIA (MORTENSON) (1874-)
Thoughts in Rhyme. San Francisco: Franklin Linotyping Co., 1911. 1 p. ℓ., 24 p., 1 ℓ.

BRADLEY, LAURA M.
West Woods. New York: Exposition Press, 1967. 80 p.

BRADLEY, MARY LINDA (1886-)
From the Foothills. Portland, ME.: The Mosher Press, 1914. ix, 86, [1] p., 1 ℓ.
Reconnaissances. New York: H. Harrison, 1937. 128 p.

BRADT, EDITH VIRGINIA
Songs by the Way. New York: Neale, 1904. 74 p.

BRADY, ANNE HAZELWOOD
Unfinished Conversations. New York: Pageant Press, 1970. 5 p. ℓ., 61 p.

BRADY, EILEEN M.
Amber Moods. New York: Exposition Press, 1951. 56 p.

BRADY, KATHRYNE HELEN
The Dream Path. Denver, CO.: n.p., 1928. 31 p.

BRAGG, LINDA BROWN
A Love Song to Black Men. Detroit: Broadside Press, 1975. 32 p.

BRAGG, VIRGINIA HAGGENJOS
The Heart Remembers. Easton, PA.: John S. Correll Co., 1943. ix, 67 p.

BRAMBLETT, AGNES EZELL COCHRAN (1886-)
Legend of the Weaver of Paradise. Macon, GA.: The J. W. Burke Co., 1928. 136 p.
Wind-Mad. North Montpelier, VT.: W. J. Coates, 1935. 5 p. ℓ., [9]-74 p.
The Wolves of Trollness; a narrative poem of German-occupied Norway, told by a Norwegian grandmother. Emory University, GA.: Banner Press, 1944. 40 p. (Versecraft series)
Eve and the Fallen Star. Emory University, GA.: Banner Press, 1948. 68 p. (Versecraft series)
With Lifted Heart. Boston: Branden Press, 1965. 64 p.

BRANCH, ANNA HEMPSTEAD (1875-1937)
The Heart of the Road, and Other Poems. Boston: n.p., 1901. 120 p.
______. Boston: and New York: Houghton Mifflin, & Co., 1902. vi, 120 [1] p.
St. Valentine. New York: Privately printed, 1905. 12 p.
The Shoes That Danced, and Other Poems. Boston and New York: Houghton Mifflin Co., 1905. ix, 201 [1] p.

_______. Boston: Houghton, 1906, c1905. 201 p.
Rose of the Wind, and Other Poems. Boston and New York: Houghton Mifflin Co., 1910. 4 p. ℓ., 229 [1] p.
Sonnets from a Lock Box and Other Poems. Boston and New York: Houghton Mifflin Co., 1929. vii, [1], 125 [1] p.
Last Poems of Anna Hempstead Branch. Ed. by Ridgely Torrence. New York, Toronto: Farrar & Rinehart, Inc., 1944. xii, 71 p.

BRANDT, THEODINE E.
Dawn to Dusk. Emory University, GA.: Banner Press, 1944. 84 p. (Versecraft series)
Horizons, Poems. Chicago: Dierkes Press, 1948. 48 p.
Let There Be Gladness. Chicago: Dierkes Press, 1949. 72 p.
When the Dreaming Ends. Denver, CO.: Big Mountain Press, 1953. 48 p.

BRANNAN, EULA M.
Smoke Screens. Sewanee, TN.: The University Press, 1945. 6 p. ℓ., 76 p.

BRASIER, VIRGINIA
The Survival of the Unicorn, and Other Poems. Claremont, CA.: Creative Press, 1961. 48 p. (Poems of Distinction 1)

BRAY, MARY (MATTHEWS) (1837-)
Wayside Blossoms. Boston: R. G. Badger, 1912. 3 p. ℓ., 5-115 p., 1 ℓ.

BRAYTON, TERESA
Songs of the Dawn and Irish Ditties. New York: P. J. Kenedy, 1913. lv, 92 p.

BREED, IDA MARION see ROBINSON, IDA MARIAN (BREED) (1903)

BREEDLOVE, MILDRED MATTHEWS (1904-)
Those Desert Hills and Other Poems. Los Angeles, CA.: Vogue House, 1959. 95 p.

BREGY, KATHERINE MARIE CORNELIA (1888-1967)
Bridges, with Other Verse in Varying Moods. Atlanta, GA.: E. Hartsock, 1930. 47 p. "Limited first edition."
Ladders and Bridges; A Book of Verse. Philadelphia: David McKay, 1936. 79 p.

BREHM, EDYTHE LUCILLE (1904-)
Heart Wrought Filigree. San Antonio, TX.: Carleton Printing Co., 1943. 66 p.
Heritage of Song. San Antonio, TX.: Carleton Printing Co., 1945. 72 p.

BREIG, JEAN HAMILTON
One to Remember; Collected Poems. Philadelphia: Dorrance, 1950. 61 p. (Contemporary poets of Dorrance, 421)

BREITFELD, ROSE (1885-)
... Voices from the Great Beyond. New York: Fortuny's, 1940. 64 p.

BREITHAUPT, THELMA
No Silence Heard. Dallas, TX.: Tardy Publishing Co., 1937. 5 p. ℓ., 3-73 p.

BRELAND, LYDIA FOSTER
My Patchwork Quilt, and Other Poems. New York: Exposition Press, 1959. 32 p.

BREMER, ANNE (d. 1923)
The Unspoken and Other Poems. San Francisco: Printed for A. M. Bender by J. H. Nash, 1927. vii, 31 p.

BRENNAN, BETH A. (1876-)
Meg, the Pioneer, and Other Poems. Lincoln?, Neb.: n.p., 1955. viii, 157 p.

BRENT, HALLY CARRINGTON
Moods and Melodies. Philadelphia: Dorrance and Company, 1928. 64 p. (Contemporary poets of Dorrance, 69)
Music and Meditation. Philadelphia: Dorrance and Co., 1931. 58 p. (Contemporary poets of Dorrance, 105)

BRENT, IMOGEN DeLOACH (1885-)
Not in New Lands. Richmond, VA.: The Dietz Printing Co., 1947. 7 p. ℓ., 11-100 p.

BREWER, AMANDA FRANCES MEADE (1903-)
Romantic West Virginia. Kermit, W. VA.: n.p., 1963. 22 p.

BREWER, EDITH GADDIS
Of Inter-Weaving Significance. Cambridge?, MA.: n.p., 1952. 61 p.

BRIDGES, MADELINE, pseud. see DE VERE, MARY AINGE

BRIDGEWATER, EDITH
Wimble Folk and Rimble Seed. New York: Exposition Press, 1951. 48 p.

BRIDGMAN, AMY SHERMAN
Song-Flame, Poems. Boston: The Stratford Co., 1918. viii, [1] p., 2 ℓ., 145 p.

BRIEL, LOIS WOODWARD
Kiss o' Hollow Hours and Other Poems. Boston: Chapple Publishing Co., 1930. ix, 102 p.

BRIGGS, BESSIE EMMELINE (1885-)
Poems. Marion, IN.: The Marion Tribune Co., 1908. [27] p.

BRIGHAM, BESMILR (1923-)
Agony Dance: Death of the Dancing Dolls. Portland, OR.: Prensa de Lagar, 1969. 1 v. (unpaged)
Heaved from the Earth. New York: Alfred A. Knopf, 1971. xi, 75 p.

BRIGHT, NORMA KATHRYN (1883-)
The Dream Child & Other Verses. New York: The Grafton Press, 1905. 4 p. ℓ., 7-80 p.

BRIGMAN, ANNE
Songs of a Pagan. Caldwell, ID.: Caxton Printers, 1949. 90 p.

BRIN, RUTH FIRESTONE (1921-)
A Time to Search. New York: Jonathan David Co., 1959. 56 p.
A Rag of Love. Minneapolis, MN.: Emmett Publ. Co., 1969. 48 p.

BRINKLEY, MAY
A Handful of Life. Atlanta, GA.: Bozart Press, 1927. 57 p.

BRISBANE, MARGARET HUNT
Poems. Boston: R. G. Badger, 1925. 200 p.

BRITTON, ESTELLE R.
Piari (Beloved) Prints. Philadelphia: Dorrance, 1965. 50 p. (Contemporary poets of Dorrance, 601)
Say to the Wind. Philadelphia: Dorrance, 1966. 61 p. (Contemporary poets of Dorrance, 609)
I Dreamed I Grew a Grape Tree. Philadelphia: Dorrance, 1967. 50 p. (Contemporary poets of Dorrance, 647)

BROADHURST, PATTI (SMITH) [Full Name: Medora Patti (Smith) Broadhurst.]
Worn Shoes. Philadelphia: Dorrance & Co., Inc., 1932. 82 p. (Contemporary poets of Dorrance, 111)
For Florida. New York: Dial Press, Inc., 1937. ix p., 2 ℓ., 15-111 p.
Any Century. New York: The Dial Press, 1940. xii, 93 p.
Lightning Hour. Philadelphia: Dorrance, 1954. 55 p.

BROBECK, FLORENCE RICHARDS (1895-)
Against the Dark. New York: Ram Press, 1962. 41 p., 1ℓ.

BROCKMAN, ZOE KINCAID (1893-)
Heart on My Sleeve. Emory University, GA.: Banner Press, 1951. 73 p. (Verse craft series)

BROMAN, JESSIE GODDARD (1882-)
Design for Words. Minneapolis, MN.: Imperial Print. Co., 1947. 103 p.

BROOKS, ERICA MAY (1894-)
Into Space. New York: House of Field, Inc., 1939. 5 p. ℓ., 3-88 p.

BROOKS, ESTELLA M.
Poems from the Country. Concord, MA: Printed at the Minuteman Press, 1927. 42 p.

BROOKS, FLORENCE (1860-1948)
The Destiny and Other Poems. Boston: Small, Maynard, 1901. viii, 92 p.
______. Boston: Sherman, French and Company, 1907. viii, 92 p.
XXXIII Love Sonnets. New York: J. Marone, 1908. 43 p.
______. Ed. by Gwendolen Brooks Penniman. San Jose?, CA.: n.p., 1950. ix, 54 p.

BROOKS, GWENDOLYN (1917-)
A Street in Bronzeville. "First edition." New York: Harper and Row, 1945. vi, 57, [1] p.
______. 3d ed. New York: Harper and Row, 1945. 57 p.
Annie Allen. 1st ed. New York: Harper, 1949. x, 60 p.
Bronzeville Boys and Girls. New York: Harper, 1956. 40 p.
The Bean Eaters. New York: Harper, 1960. 71 p. (Verse for children)
Selected Poems. 1st ed. New York: Harper and Row, 1963. x, 127 p.
In the Time of Detachment, In the Time of Cold. Springfield, IL.: Civil War Centennial Commission of Illinois, 1965.
For Illinois, 1968; A Sesquicentennial Poem. Chicago: Illinois Sesquicentennial Commission, 1968. [4] p.
In the Mecca: Poems. 1st ed. New York: Harper and Row, 1968. vii, 54 p.
Riot. Detroit: Broadside Press, 1969. 22 p. "A poem in three parts: Riot; The Third Sermon on the Warpland; An Aspect of Love, Alive in the Ice and Fire."
Family Pictures. Detroit: Broadside Press, 1970. 23 p.
Aloneness. 1st ed. Detroit: Broadside Press, 1971. [16] p.
The World of Gwendolyn Brooks. New York: Harper & Row, 1971. xii, 426 p. Contents: A Street in Bronzeville. --Annie Allen. --Maud Martha. --The Bean Eaters. --In the Mecca.
Beckonings. Detroit: Broadside Press, 1975. 16 p.

BROOKS, LELAH HARRISON
World's Fair Poems. St. Louis, MO.: n.p., 1904. 3-7 p.

BROOKS, OLIVE
Panama Quadrant. New York: Bookman Associates, 1960. 95 p.

BROOME, MYRTLE B.
Along My Way. Columbia, S.C.: n.p., 1964. xi, 243 p.

BROSMAN, CATHERINE (HILL) SAVAGE (1934-)
Watering. Athens, GA.: University of Georgia Press, 1972. 89 p.

BROSSEAU, OLIVE
Shadows on the Water. Ashland, WI.: Northland College Press, 1933. 5 p. ℓ., 27 p.
Madeline and Other Poems. Kenosha, WI.: Kenosha News Press, 1935. 57 p.

BROUSSARD, VIVIAN L.
Song of the Shall. Prairie City, IL.: Decker Press, 1948. 54 p.

BROWER, ALICE K.
Mediterranea. New York: H. Vinal, Ltd., 1928. 4 p. ℓ., 39, [1] p.

BROWN, ABBIE FARWELL (1871-1927)
A Pocketful of Posies. Boston & New York: Houghton, Mifflin and Co., 1902. viii p., 1 ℓ., 162, [4]p. (Verses for children)
Fresh Posies; Rhymes to Read and Pieces to Speak. Boston & New York: Houghton, Mifflin Co., 1908. xvi p., 2 ℓ., 3-199, [1]p.
Songs of Sixpence. Boston & New York: Houghton, Mifflin, Co., 1914. xviii, [1] 214, [2]p.
Heart of New England. Boston & New York: Houghton, Mifflin Co., 1920. x, [1], 144 p., 1 ℓ.
The Silver Stair. Boston & New York: Houghton, Mifflin, Co., 1926. ix p., 1 ℓ., 148 p.

BROWN, ADELE HART
Yamparika (Spirit of Wind). Dallas, TX.: The Kaleidograph Press, 1939. xiii p., 1 ℓ., 17-107 p.

BROWN, AGATHA, pseud. see CHURCH, VIRGINIA WOODSON (FRAME)

BROWN, ALISON
The Candle's Beams: A Book of Poems for Children. Duluth, MN.: The Le Tourneau Press, 1919. [27] p., 1 ℓ.
Songs of the Northland, and Other Poems. Duluth, MN.: The LeTourneau Press, 1923. [55] p.
Lake Superior Magic. Duluth, MN.: Press of Mattocks-McDonald Co., 1927. [56] p.

BROWN, ANNE VAN NESS
Open Windows. Prairie City, IL.: Press of James A. Decker, 1947. 72 p.

BROWN, DOROTHY
Calico Rags and Bits of Silk. San Pedro, CA.: Krieger Printing Co., 1932. 42 ℓ.

So Must I Sing. San Pedro, CA.: Marions, 1941? 82 ℓ.

BROWN, EDITH MAE
From Earth Arising, a Collection of Poems.... New York: House of Field, Inc., 1942. 70 p.
Moon Under. New York: Exposition Press, 1946. 62 p.

BROWN, ELINOR EDITH (HENRY) (1911-)
Dream Awake and Remember. Hollywood, CA.: Camas Press, 1945. 27 p.
The Merry-Go-Round Has Wings. North Hollywood, CA.: Camas Press, 1948. 27 p.
Of Little Songs, and Other Poems. North Hollywood, CA.: Camas Press, 1949. 48 p.
Old Days in Camas Valley. North Hollywood, CA.: Camas Press, 1951. 60 p.

BROWN, GRACE ADA
Song and Story: Poems. Pittsfield, MA.: The Eagle Publishing Co., 1902. vii, 188 p.

BROWN, GRACE McCLEAN
Flowers of Hope. Chicago: Dierkes Press, 1951. 64 p.
Jeweled Hours. Eureka Springs, AK.: Dierkes Press, 1954. 64 p.

BROWN, HELEN LOUIS
"Soul Glow." Los Angeles, CA.: The Times-Mirror Press, 1924. 64 p.

BROWN, HELEN WILLISTON
Elan Vital. Boston: The Gorham Press, 1917. 55 p.

BROWN, IDA ELIZABETH (1865-1927)
Visions. Baltimore, MD.: Print. by Meyer & Thalheimer, 1933. 5 p. ℓ., 7-57 numb. ℓ.

BROWN, INA (LADD) (1902-)
...Just for Luck. Bangor, ME.: Furbush-Roberts Printing Co., 1946. 65 p.
More of the Same. Portland, ME.: Falmouth Pub. House, 1949. 54 p.
Homespun. Francestown, N.H.: Golden Quill Press, 1959. 77 p.
Leaves on the Wind. Francestown, N.H.: Golden Quill Press, 1963. 80 p.
Cross Roads. Francestown, N.H.: Golden Quill Press, 1970. 80 p.

BROWN, INEZ MARGUERITE
Will-o'-the-Wisp and Other Poems. New York: Pageant Press, 1955. 5 p. ℓ., 85 p.

BROWN, JUNE
You Are Music. Kansas City, MO.: Burton Pub. Co., 1954. 116 p.

BROWN, LOTTIE PRATT
It Shows in Your Face. Dallas, TX.: M. Van Nort & Co., 1941. 6 p.ℓ., 60 p.

BROWN, MABEL (SMITH) (1890-)
A Bouquet from the Garden of Life. Wichita, KA.: n.p., 1925. 35 p.

BROWN MAREL, pseud. see BROWN, MARGARET ELIZABETH (SNOW) (1899-)

BROWN, MARGARET ELIZABETH (SNOW) (1899-) [BROWN, MAREL, pseud.]
Hearth Fire. Nashville, TN.: Broadman Press, 1943. 104 p.
Fence Corners. Nashville, TN.: Broadman Press, 1952. 103 p.
The Shape of a Song. Grand Rapids, MI.: Baker Book House, 1968. 96 p.

BROWN, MARGARETTA
Reflections. Knoxville, TN.: n.p., 1956. 127 p.

BROWN, MARY THORNTON
Doctor's Dream and Other Poems. Chicago: n.p., 1913. 126 p.

BROWN, PEARL ELIZABETH (1887-)
Freedom's Land. San Antonio, TX.: The Carleton Printing Co., 1943. 69 p.
Heritage. New York: Pageant Press, 1952. 70 p.

BROWN, REBECCA
Mouse Works. New York: Siamese Banana Press, 1971. 10 ℓ.

BROWN, RITA MAE (1944-)
The Hand That Cradles the Rock. New York: New York University Press, 1971. 64 p.
Songs to a Handsome Woman. Baltimore, MD.: Diana Press, Inc., 1973. 39 p.
Sally Forth. Iowa City, IA.: Iowa City Women's Press, 1974.

BROWN, ROSALIE (MOORE) (1910-)
The Grasshopper's Man, and Other Poems. New Haven, CT.: Yale University Press, 1949. 66 p. (Yale Series of Younger Poets, 47)

BROWN, ROSELLEN
Some Deaths in the Delta and Other Poems. Amherst, MA.: University of Massachusetts Press, 1970. 66 p.

BROWN, VIOLA BAILEY WILSON (1881-)
Gathered Beauty. 1st ed. Kansas City, MO.: Moss Pub. Co., 1950. 94 p.

BROWN, WINIFRED LANGWORTHY
...Weeds and Rue. New York: H. Harrison, 1941. 63 p.

BROWNE, ALICE HARRIMAN (1861-1925)
Songs o' the Olympics. Seattle, WA.: The Alice Harriman Co., 1909. 70 p., 1 ℓ.

BROWNE, ELIZABETH
Poems. Uniontown, PA.: n.p., 1938. 40 p.
...Litany of Life. Philadelphia: Dorrance and Co., 1941. 111 p. (Contemporary poets of Dorrance, 214)
Strands of Emotion. Cedar Rapids, IA.: The Torch Press, 1942. ix, 85 p.
Tryst with Life. Cedar Rapids, IA.: The Torch Press, 1944. 135 p.
Life Triumphant. Cedar Rapids, IA.: The Torch Press, 1945. 128 p.
Crucible of Life. Cedar Rapids, IA.: The Torch Press, 1946. 135 p.
Amidst Life's Pageantry. Cedar Rapids, IA.: Torch Press, 1947. 128 p.

BROWNE, EVELYN GAGE
At Mother's Shrine. Pittsfield, MA.: The Arpodene Studio, 1918. 13 p.
Beyond the Shadows. Pittsfield, MA.: The Arpodene Studio, 1918. 13 p.
Cloth of Gold. Pittsfield, MA.: The Arpodene Studio, 1918. 13 p.
Of Such Is the Kingdom. Pittsfield, MA.: The Arpodene Studio, 1918. 13 p.
Smiles of God. Pittsfield, MA.: The Arpodene Studio, 1918. 13 p.
Wings of Silver. Pittsfield, MA.: The Arpodene Studio, 1918. 13 p.

BROWNE, HARRIET AUGUSTA
Dew Drop on Ocean Wave. Wallnakee, WS.: J. M. Williams & Son, 1907. 3 p. ℓ., 3-144 p.

BROWNE, LEDA GANO
Eva's Choice and Other Poems. New York: Cochrane Publishing Co., 1910. 58 p.

BROWNE, LEILA KENDALL
Little Child Looking. 1st ed. New York: Pageant Press, 1955. 87 p.

BROWNE, MAUD M.
Scattered Mists. Boston: The Gorham Press, 1918. 72 p.

BROWNING, EUNICE
Poems. Sacramento, CA.: Wilbur Printing Co., 1921. 72 p.

BRUCE, (IRMA) IRENE (1905-)
Crag and Sand.... Reno, NV.: Silver State Press, 1945. 1 p. ℓ., 5-45 p.
Night Cry. Reno, NV.: Poetry West, 1950. 61 p.

BRUENINGHAUSEN, ELEANORE HERBERT
Out of the Wilderness. New York: n.p., 1921. 32 p.
Paths in the Desert. New York: n.p., 1922. 46 p.

BRUFF, NANCY see GARDNER, NANCY (BRUFF) (1909-)

BRUGNOLA, ORLANDA
King of Thornbushes. Berkeley, CA.: Oyez, 1972. 38 p.

BRUNDAGE, ALICE HOLT
Along the Way. Boston: Christopher Pub. House, 1949. 96 p.

BRUNER, MARGARET ELIZABETH (1886-197?)
The Hill Road. Dallas, TX.: The Kaleidograph Press, 1932. 4 p. ℓ., vii-ix, 11-110 p.
Mysteries of Earth. Dallas, TX.: The Kaleidograph Press, 1934. xi, 13-108 p.
In Thoughtful Mood. Dallas, TX.: The Kaleidograph Press, 1937. xii p., 1 ℓ., 15-122 p.
Midstream. Dallas, TX.: The Kaleidograph Press, 1940. x p., 1ℓ., 13-106 p.
Be Slow to Falter. Dallas, TX.: The Kaleidograph Press, 1941. xi p., 1 ℓ., 15-84 p.
The Constant Heart. Dallas, TX.: The Kaleidograph Press, 1952. 79 p.
Above Earth's Sorrow. Boston: Bruce Humphries, 1955. 64 p.
The Deeper Need. Boston: Christopher Publ. House, 1957. 94 p.
The Road Lies Onward. Boston: Christopher Publ. House, 1960. 85 p.
The Hills Were Friends. Boston: Christopher Publ. House, 1962. 93 p.
The Unwritten Law. Boston: Christopher Publ. House, 1963. 110 p.
Eternal Quest. Boston: Christopher Publ. House, 1968. 94 p.

BRUNT, FANNY GUDMUNDSEN
Sage and Syringa, Collected Poems. Los Angeles, CA.: Wetzel Pub. Co., 1952. 67 p.

BRYANT, NANNA MATTHEWS
Phantasies. Boston: The Gorham Press, 1914. 5 p. ℓ., 9-94 p.

BRYNING, WINIFRED LIVINGSTONE
The Search for Light, and Other Poems. Boston: Bruce Humphries, 1941. 95 p.

BUBOLTZ, ETHEL
Under the Firefly Lamp. New York: Comet Press Books, 1955. 94 p.

BUCHANAN, ALICE
...Blood in the East. Philadelphia: Dorrance & Co., 1945. 117 p. (Contemporary poets of Dorrance, 301, i.e. 310?)

BUCHANAN, BESSIE GLEN
Silver Strand, A Candelabra of Lyric Verse. Prairie City, IL.: Press of J. A. Decker, 1947? 75 p.
For Every Yesterday. Prairie City, IL.: Decker Press, 1949. 45 p., 1 ℓ.
Pattern for Orioles. 1st ed. North Hollywood, CA.: Camas Press, 1952. 31 p.
Poems in the Chinese Manner. Tujunga, CA.: Cecil L. Anderson, 1953? 23 p.

BUCHER, HELEN HALL (MULLIN)
Mountain Echoes. 1st ed. Boiling Springs? PA.: n.p., 1958. 63 p.
______. Harrisburg, PA.: The Telegraph Press, 1958. 68, [1] p.

BUCHMAN, MARION
A Voice in Ramah. New York: Bookman Associates, 1959. 72 p.

BUCHNER, GLADYS (CLOSE)
My Garden. San Antonio, TX.: Naylor Co., 1952. xi, 92 p.

BUCHTENKIRK, ELIZABETH J. (1898-)
Small Answer. Philadelphia: Dorrance, 1949. 42 p. (Contemporary poets of Dorrance, 394)

BUCK, ALICE
Somebody's Brother and Other Poems. Oklahoma City, OK.: n.p., 1935. 18 p.

BUCK, ANNE DODSON (1883-)
This Was April. New York: Exposition Press, 1949. 64 p.
By All Their Wonder. New York: New Voices Pub. Co., 1954. 53 p.

BUCK, MARION STEARNS
Words of Cheer. Boston: The Gorham Press, 1918. 1 p. ℓ., 173 p.

BUCK, NELLIE MANLEY
By Winding Trails. Boston: The Christopher Publishing House, 1928. 64 p.

BUCK, NINA CORDELIA
The Eternal Eulogy. Boston: R. G. Badger, 1920. 52 p.

BUCKINGHAM, GERTRUDE TOOLEY
Poems at Random. Fair Lawn, N. J.: Kimball Press, 1948. xiii, 129 p.

BUCKLE, GRACE WIGHT
A Cluster of Lyrics. Lowell, MA.: n. p., 1926. 4 p. ℓ., 89 p.
Birds, Buds, and Loving Hearts. Warner, N. H.: Warner Press, 1956. 130 p.

BUCKLEY, MARY-ELIZABETH
Sanctuary. Paris: n. p., 1931. [16] p.

BUCKLEY, NANCY
Laughter and Longing. San Francisco: M. Cloyd, 1921. 5 p. ℓ., 3-59 p.
Wings of Youth. San Francisco: The Cloister Press, 1922. 68 p.
Cameos; A Book of Poetry. San Francisco: The Cloister Press, 1926. 4 p. ℓ., 11-103 p., 1 ℓ.

BUCKLEY, SARA VIRGINIA
Ships Spray. Emory University, Atlanta, GA.: Banner Press, 1932. 43 p. (Verse craft series)
Chianti and Other Poems. New York: n. p., 1936. 32 p.

BUFFUM, LILLIE
Lilies from the Valley. Los Angeles, CA.: B. N. Robertson Pub. Co., 1941. 43, [1] p.

BUHLER, MARY EDITH (1864-)
The Grass in the Pavement. New York: J. T. White & Co., 1918. 1 p. ℓ., 112 p.

BUIRGY, MARY HIGGINS (1911-)
... Through a Little Green Gate. New York: H. Harrison, 1937. 95 p.
Strangers in My Heart. Emory University, Atlanta, GA.: Banner Press, 1944. 58 p. (Verse craft series)
Escape from Pink Wall Paper. Philadelphia: Dorrance, 1947. 61 p. (Contemporary poets of Dorrance, 346)

BULLOCK, AMY HOWARD WALES
Moon-Moths and Wing-Flowers. New York: The Avondale Press, Inc., 1927. ix, 154 p.

BUMPUS, CORA HOOD
Rhythm in the Wind. A Collection of Verse. New York: Pageant Press, 1956. 4 p. ℓ., 49 p.

BUNDY, RUTH LaSHORNE
Doors to the Beautiful. New York: E. Harrison, 1948. 64 p.

BUNKER, ANNIE (CROSBY) (1865-)
The World's Desire: A Book of Poems. Boston: The Four Seas Company, 1921. 3 p. ℓ., 9-82 p.

BUNSTON, ANNA see DE BARY, ANNA (BUNSTON)

BUNTING, CHRISTOBELLE (VAN ASMUS)
Reverie; Verses and Rhymes. Stamford? CT.: 1949. 71 p.

BURBANK, BLANCHE MARIE (BUSWELL)
Reed Notes. San Francisco: A. M. Robertson, 1903. 62 p.

BURCH, ADELLE E. (SHOEMAKER) (1858-)
Know Thyself and Other Poems. Buchanan, MI.: Burch Printing Co., 1909. 4 p. ℓ., 182 p.

BURCH, LOIS
Memory Lane. New York: Harbinger House, 1945. 3 p. ℓ., 11-84 p.

BURCH, VIOLA S.
Designs in My Quilt. Boston: B. Humphries, Inc., 1943. 62 p.
While the Mock Orange Waits. Philadelphia: Dorrance, 1968. 145 p.

BURDEN, HAZEL
My Barge of Dreams. Los Angeles, CA.: West Coast Publishing Co., 1931. 4 p. ℓ., 15-156 p.

BURDEN, JEAN (1914-)
Naked as the Glass. New York: Clarke & Way, 1963. 72 p.

BURDICK, ANNIE M.
The Stolen Bride; or, A Tale of Old Watch Hill. New York: Middlemore Press, 1903. 31 p.

BUREN, ANONA ELINOR
Fleeting Hours. Tacoma, WA.: Press of Smith-Kinney Co., 1926. 31 p.

BURGE, MARIE LOUISE
Sylva and Other Poems. Boston: The Gorham Press, 1902. 39 p.

BURGER, MYRTLE (GRIGSBY)
Fallen Leaves. Washington, MO.: Cameo Press, 1936. 1 p. ℓ., 5-48 p.

BURGESS, FLORENCE INA (1892-)
Watch for the Morning: A Group of Inspirational Poems. n. p., 193-? 22 p.
Fallen Petals... A Collection of Verse. Portland, OR.: Printed by Bushong and Co., 1939. 32 p.

BURGESS, STELLA FISHER (1881-)
A Peking Caravan. Shanghai: The Shanghai Times, 1924. 4 p. ℓ., 32 numb. ℓ., 1 ℓ.
Toward the Summit. New York: Woman's Press, 1948. 31 p.

BURGUM, JESSAMINE (SLAUGHTER)
Dakota Ballads, and Other Poems. Hunter, N. D.: The Viking Press, 1939. 5 p. ℓ., 10-61, [2], 62-68, [1], 69-76 p.
Cactus and Magnolia Blossoms, and Other Poems. Valley City, N. D.: E. P. Getchell, Printer, 1944. 78 p.

BURK, ALMA
Echoes from My Native Hills. Denver: Big Mountain Press, 1960. 72 p.

BURKE, CAROL
Close Quarters. Ithaca, N. Y.: Ithaca House. Dist. by Serendipity Books, Berkeley, CA., 1975. 52 p.

BURKE, MARIE LOUISE (1916-)
Verse for Christmas. San Francisco: Printed by Jackson Burke at Pocket Press, 1938. 8 ℓ.
17 Verses and Curses. San Francisco: Press of M. L. and J. Burke, 1940. [13] p.
Verses and Curses. San Francisco: n. p., 1941. 16 ℓ.
Little Music. Belmont? CA.: Aquarius Press, 1948. 4 p. ℓ., 3-88 p.

BURKE, MARY CECELIA (1869-)
School Room Echoes, Book One. Boston: R. G. Badger, 1909. 215 p.
________. 1909-1911. 2 v.
________. 1909-1912. 3 v.
Flowers of Fancy. Boston: R. G. Badger, 1913. 7 p. ℓ., 13-185 p.

BURKE, NORA T.
Chrysanthemums, White. Boston: Meador Publishing Co., 1941. 170 p.

BURKET, GAIL (BROOK) (1905-)
Courage, Beloved! Chicago: Dierkes Press, 1949. 55 p.
Blueprint for Peace. Chicago: Dierkes Press, 1951. 38 p.
Far Meadows. Eureka Springs, AR.: Dierkes Press, 1955. 55 p.

BURLEN, MAY GIBSON

By the Highway. Lynn, MA.: The Nichols Press, 1930. 1 p. ℓ., iii, 3-99 p.

BURLIN, HELEN

In the Midst of Death. New York: Harbinger House, 1944. 47 p.

BURMEISTER, MAGDALENE

At the Sign of the Zodiac, and Other Poems. New York: Liveright, 1950. 200 p.

Against the Shifting Sands. Francestown, N.H.: Golden Quill Press, 1974. 159 p., [1] leaf of plates.

BURNS, MATTIE A.

Rhymes of the Workers. Homestead, PA.: n.p., 1904. 34 p.

BURR, AMELIA JOSEPHINE (1878-)

The Roadside Fire. New York: G. H. Doran Co., 1912. 111 p.

Afterglow, A Poem. Ithaca, N.Y.: Comstock Publishing Co., 1913. 12 p.

In Deep Places: A Book of Verse. New York: G. H. Doran, 1914. xi p., 1 ℓ., 132 p.

Life and Living: A Book of Verse. New York: G. H. Doran Co., 1916. 3 p. ℓ., ix-xi, [2] 15-130 p.

The Silver Trumpet: A Book of Verse. New York: G. H. Doran, 1918. xi p., 1 ℓ., 15-133 p.

Hearts Awake. New York: G. H. Doran Co., 1919. x p., 1 ℓ., 13-155 p.

A Child Garden in India. West Medford, MA.: Central Committee on the United Study of Foreign Missions, 1922. 76 p., 1 ℓ.

Little Houses; A Book of Poems. New York: George H. Doran, 1923. xiii p., 1 ℓ., 17-120 p.

Selected Lyrics. New York: G. H. Doran, 1927. xii p., 1 ℓ., 15-149 p.

Highways and Byways. New York: Ad Press, Ltd., 1933. 3 p. ℓ., 3-42 p.

BURR, JANE pseud. [PUNCH, ROSALIND MAE GUGGENHEIM]

City Dust. New York: F. Shay, 1916. 3 p. ℓ., 9-42 p., 1 ℓ.

_______. New York: The Baker & Taylor Co., 1917. 3 p. ℓ., 9-42 p., 1 ℓ.

I Build My House. New York: J. T. White & Co., 1918. x, [11]-126 p.

BURR, WINIFRED ADAMS

Design for Courage; Collected Poems. New York?: n.p., 1959. 105 p.

BURROUGHS, MARGARET G. (1917-) [STEPHANY, pseud.]

Moving Deep. 1st ed. Detroit: Broadside Press, 1969. 32 p.

BURROW, PEARL (COVINGTON)
Golden Vase. Dallas, TX.: The Kaleidograph Press, 1944. xi p., 1 ℓ., 15-79 p.

BURROWES, ELIZABETH
Poems for Christmas. Philadelphia: Dorrance, 1969. 22 p.

BURT, CLARE LOUISE (1874-)
Bowl of Petunias. Ellerbe, N.C.: Ellerbe School Press, 1936. 2 p. ℓ., 19 numb. ℓ.
Wicks in Earthenware. Raleigh, N.C.: The Author, 1937. 2 p. ℓ., 2-17 (i.e. 18) p.
Ordered Chaos. Boston: The Christopher Publishing House, 1937. 4 p. ℓ., vii-viii p., 1 ℓ., 13-88 p.
Call Me Not Dead. Raleigh, N.C.: Capital Printing Co., 1939. vii numb. ℓ., 55 p.

BURT, KATHARINE (BROWN) (1879-)
New England Dusk. New York City: The Poet's Press, 1938. 6 p. ℓ., 15-81 [1] p.
...This Our Eden, Poems. New York: H. Harrison, 1940. 96 p.
Connecticut Legend. Mount Vernon, N.Y.: Priv. print at the Walpole Printing Office, 1942. 3 p. ℓ., 9-75 p., 1 ℓ.

BURTON, GRACE (OAKES)
Songs of My Heart. Lynchburg, VA.: J. P. Bell Co., 1951. 41 p.
Sonnets and Songs of My Heart. New York: Vantage Press, 1956. 83 p.

BURTON, MARION STURGES
Prelude to Summer. Albuquerque? N.M.: n.p., 1960. 28 p.

BURTON, MARTHA VIRGINIA
Sons of the Sun: Poems. Chicago: Bessette & Sons, 1907. 124 p.

BURTON, RUTH GUTHRIE (THOMSON) HARDING (1882-) [HARDING, RUTH GUTHRIE (THOMSON)]
Lark Went Singing, and Other Poems. Concord, N.H.

BURWELL, CORA GERTRUDE (1883-)
...Neatly Packed. Philadelphia: Dorrance, 1947. 59 p. (Contemporary poets of Dorrance, 342)
Woodwinds. Eureka Springs, AR.: Dierkes Press, 1957. 68 p.

BUSH, GRACE ELIZABETH (PICKELL) (1885-)
Cipriana, and Other Poems. Los Angeles, CA.: David H. Shol Co., 1925. 34 p.
High Heritage. Los Angeles, CA.: De Vorss and Co., 1939. 3 p. ℓ., 9-93 [1] p.

With This Bright Armor. Hollywood, CA.: Boulevard Press, 1950. 114 p.

BUTCHER, GRACE (1934-)
The Bright-Colored Dark. Cleveland, OH.: 7 Flowers Press, 1966. [22] p. on double leaves.
Rumors of Ecstasy... Rumors of Death. Ashland, OH.: Ashland Poetry Press, 1971. 62 p.

BUTLER, JENNIE McBRIDE
My Soul Goeth Winging. San Diego, CA.: J. A. Mallory, 1927. 3 p. ℓ., 9-68 p.

BUTLER, KATE
Harlequin Day. Emory University, Atlanta: Banner Press, 1937. 76 p.
We Walk in Wonder. Emory University, Atlanta: Banner Press, 1940. 74 p.

BUTTERFIELD, CAROLINE M.
Jacob, and Other Poems. Denver, CO.: n.p., 1907. 357 p.

BUTTERFIELD, CORA L.
The Springtime Melody; A Book of Poetry. New York: Exposition Press, 1951. 63 p.

BUTTLES, MARY A.
Bluets, and Other Poems. n.p.: Broadway Publ., 1912. 16 p.

BUTTS, ELEANORA DAYTON
By Candlelight. New York: The Caravan Publishing Co., 1943. 5 p. ℓ., 13-94 p.

BUTTZ, RACHEL QUICK (1847-)
Blades and Blossom. Boston: R. G. Badger, 1911. 9-100 p.

BUXTON, LUCY
Hay Harvest, and Other Poems. London: John Lane; New York: John Lane, 1918. 47 p.

BYARD, DOROTHY (RANDOLPH)
Not Creatures But Creations. London: F. Wright, 1930. 3 p. ℓ., 9-58 p.
Poems. Norwalk, CT.: n.p., 1937. 17 p.
Poems. Norwalk, CT.: Pell Studio Press, 1938. 9 ℓ.
Selfward Journey. Portland, ME.: Falmouth Publishing House, 1939. 43 p.

BYINGTON, CHLOE CASTLE
Sunset Songs. Pasadena, CA.: A. C. Vroman, Inc., 1919. 37 p.

BYNON, MARY A. (d. 1962)
My Boy, and Other Poems. New York: Vantage Press, 1964. 48 p.

BYRD, AMANDA BLOCKER
Reveries of a Homesteader. Denver, CO.: The Smith-Brooks Printing Co., 1916. [16] p.

BYRD, LUCILLE D.
The Singings of My Heart. New York: Exposition Press, 1963. 64 p.

BYRNE, AGNES F.
Fiddlesticks. Concord, N.H.: The Rumford Press, 1941. 47 p.

BYRON, MAY
Wind on the Heath: Ballads and Lyrics. New York: Doran, 1912. 139 p.

CABLE, CATHERINE, pseud. see FOUTS, NELLIE CATHERINE (BORING)

CABOT, ELSIE (PUMPELLY) (1875-)
Arizona, and Other Poems. New York: E. P. Dutton & Co., 1919. x, 110 p.
Balloon Moon. New York: H. Holt and Co., 1927. viii, 99 p. (Verses for children)

CABRAL, OLGA (1909-)
Cities and Deserts. New York: Roving Eye Press, 1959. 69 p.
The Evaporated Man. Homestead, FL.: Olivant Press, 1968. 58 p.
Tape Found in a Bottle. Homestead, FL.: Olivant Press, 1971. 57 p.

CAEN, LILLIAN CRANER
Cheer. Boston: Four Seas Co., 1922. 31 p.

CAESAR, DORIS
Phantom Thoughts. New York: G. P. Putnam's Sons, 1934. 67 p.
Certain Paths. New York: G. P. Putnam's Sons, 1937. 3 p. ℓ., ix-x p., 1 ℓ., 13-55 p.

CAFFREY, DOROTHY CRUIKSHANK
Stars and Candles. Mill Valley, CA.: Wings Press, 1952. 62 p.

CAHILL, MARY
The Desert Speaks. San Antonio, TX.: Naylor, 1968. viii, 52 p.
Vagabond Gold. Tucson? AZ.: n.p., 1972. 42 p.

CAILLEAU, RELDA M.
The Public Square, and Other Short Verse. San Francisco, CA.: n.p., 1924. 63 p.

CAIN, BELLE MAXWELL
Soul Beams. Washington, D.C.: The Crane Printing Press, 1922. 31 p.

CAIN, MAUDE LUDINGTON
Dusty Shoes, and Other Poems. Dallas, TX.: The Kaleidograph Press, 1940. ix p., 1 ℓ., 13-115 p.
Oath to the Sod, A Narrative Poem of the Hills. Philadelphia: Dorrance, 1949. 49 p. (Contemporary poets of Dorrance, 397)
Traveler's Return and Other Poems. New York: Pageant Press, 1960. 64 p.

CAIN, MILDRED PALMER
A Chinese Seal, and Other Poems. Philadelphia: Dorrance, 1923. 47 p. (Contemporary poets, 7)

CALCEDO, DOROTHY
These Are the Lists of My Despairs. New York: Philosophical Library, 1966. viii, 87 p.

CALDWELL, DORIS
Dawn & Other Verses. New York, Santa Barbara: W. Hebberd, 1929. viii, 56 p.

CALDWELL, ELEANOR BAIRD
Poems and Verses.... Firenze: Succ. B. Seeber, Editori Librai, 1927. 66 p.

CALDWELL, INGA GILSON
Still Waters. Boston: B. Humphries, 1950. 80 p.

CALDWELL, LIZZIE
The Courtship Rhymes of Hebec and Lesbia. Lamar, MO.: G. J. & L. C. Hunt, 1900. 2 p.ℓ., 157, [1] p.

CALDWELL, LOUISE WHITMAN
Out from a Little World into a Larger World: Poems and Crumbs. n.p., 1950. 3 p.ℓ., 67 p.

CALDWELL, MABELLE (MOLDER)
Wind-Blown Leaves. Dallas, TX.: The Kaleidograph Press, 1946. xii p., 1 ℓ., 15-72 p.

CALDWELL, ZULA IRENE
The Rolling Stone; Poems. 1st ed. New York: Exposition Press, 1955. 55 p.

CALHOUN, BERTHA ANN
...My Vagabond Dreams. Philadelphia: Dorrance and Co., 1943. 89 p. (Contemporary poets of Dorrance, 255)

CALHOUN, JANET
The Thief, and Others. n.p.: Privately printed, 1930. 27 p.
Reflecting Many Moods. San Francisco, CA.: Grabhorn Press, 1948. 36 p.

CALHOUN, MARY R.
Original Poems. Seattle, WA.: Metropolitan Press Printing Co., 1916. 2 p. ℓ., 7-28 p.

CALKINS, BERTHA BRANDES
Let the Heart Sing. Ed. by M. B. Dickson. Spokane, WA.: Custom Printers, 1956. 1 v.

CALLAGHAN, GERTRUDE
Inheritance. New York: Blue Faun Publications, 1924. 63 p.
Witch Girl. New York: Blue Faun Publications, 1926. 4 p. ℓ., 11-58 p.
Who Goes Lightly. Portland, ME.: Falmouth Pub. House, 1950. 69 p.

CALLAHAN, GRACE (NOTTLESON)
Flowers by the Highway and Other Poems. Los Angeles: n.p., 1930. 30 p.

CALLAND, ANNICE
Voo Doo. New York: H. Vinal, 1926. 6 p. ℓ., 64 p.
Grape with Thorn. Carmel-by-the-Sea, CA.: n.p., 1933. [65] p.

CALLAWAY, DOROTHY ELIZABETH (1897-1939)
Lantern and Lyre. Dallas, TX.: The Kaleidograph Press, 1939. xiv p., 1 ℓ., 17-217 p.

CALLENDER, GEORGETTA (1917-)
Dream Dust. 1st ed. New York: Pageant Press, 1952. 3 p. ℓ., 25 p.

CAMERON, ELLEN GORDON
Rhymes and Lines. Philadelphia: Dorrance and Co., 1926. 48 p. (Contemporary poets of Dorrance, 37)

CAMP, PAULINE FRANCES
Poems. Boston: R. G. Badger, 1904. 60 p.

CAMPBELL, ANNE (1888-)
Companionship, and Other Poems. New York, Newark, N.J.: Barse & Hopkins, 1924. 3 p. ℓ., xi-xv, 17-185 p.
Back Home. New York, Newark, N.J.: Barse & Hopkins, 1926. 6 p. ℓ., 179, [1] p.
The Heart of Home, Poems of Love and Understanding. Phila-

delphia, Chicago: John C. Winston Co., 1931. xiii p., 1 ℓ., 238 p.
Anne Campbell's Poems of Love and Understanding. Chicago: n.p., 1935. unpaged.
The House That Love Built. Detroit: Arnold-Powers, Inc., 1940. 111 p.

CAMPBELL, DELPHINE
A Reach of Touch. New York: Vantage Press, 1975. 96 p.

CAMPBELL, ELIZABETH A.
Ballet of Leaves. Chicago: Dierkes Press, 1951. 56 p.

CAMPBELL, ELSIE JANE (COSLER)
The Book of Thrills. Dayton, OH.: Dayton Publishing Co., 1934. 32 p.

CAMPBELL, EMMA F. R. (1830-)
Hymn "Jesus of Nazareth Passeth By," Its History and Other Verses. New York: M. E. Munson, 1909. xvi p., 1 ℓ., xvii-xx, 130 p.

CAMPBELL, FAY STRAWN (1884-)
...Bamboo Songs. Philadelphia: Dorrance and Co., 1945. 109 p. (Contemporary poets of Dorrance, 309)

CAMPBELL, GRACE TRUMAN
Blue Deep. San Antonio, TX.: Naylor Co., 1955. viii p., 1 ℓ., 46 p.

CAMPBELL, HELEN STEWART
Some Love-Lit Lines and Others: A Cluster of Poems. Boston: B. Humphries, 1935. 268 p.

CAMPBELL, MARY ALDEN
As a Vapor Rising, and Other Poems. Denver, CO.: Big Mountain Press, 1955. 64 p.

CANANT, EDITH RAYZOR
Fringe of Stardust. Rome: Centro Studi e Scambi Internazionali, 1962. 16 p. (Quaderni di Poesia)
And Also I. Chicago: Windfall Press, 1966. 37 p.

CANBY, MARION (1885-) [Full name: Marion Ponsby (Gause) Canby.]
High Mowing. Boston & New York: Houghton, Mifflin Company, 1932. x, 94 p.
...On My Way. Boston: Houghton, Mifflin Company, 1937. xi, [1] p., 3 ℓ., 5-161 p, [1] p.

CANDEE, ELLA BRADY
Human Passions. Syracuse, N.Y.: The Mason Publishing & Printing Co., 1901. 5 p. ℓ., 112 p.

CANDLER, BEATRICE POST
Vision, and Other Poems. New York: The Nation Press, 1917. 30 p.
Life's Garden. Portland, ME.: The Mosher Press, 1930. x, 53, [2] p., 1 ℓ.
Songs and Echoes. Brooklyn, N.Y.: Printed by Foil Printing Co., Inc., 1938. iii-ix, 3-28 p.

CAPEHART, RACHEL FRIEND
Green Lace. Danbury, CT.: T.N.P.C., 1968. 2 p. ℓ., 36 p.
For Hearts Grown Cold. Neosho, MO.: Willis & Associates, 1972. 48 p.

CAPPS, MARY NEELY
When God Made Texas. San Antonio, TX.: Naylor Co., 1955. 53 p.

CARASSO, KATHARINE
The Candle Burns. New York: H. Harrison, 1936. 95 p.
Crystal Arabesques. Brooklyn, N.Y.: Biography Press, 1937. 87 p.
Apostrophes, Sonnets. Brooklyn, N.Y.: Biography Press, 1938. 63 p.
Leaf on the Sill. Brooklyn, N.Y.: Biography Press, 1939. 64 p.

CARAWAY, CONSTANCE CATHERINE (1906-)
The Immortal Bride, and Other Poems. New York: Margent Press, 1946. 116 p.

CARD, DOROTHY EDITH
Prairie Harvest, and Other Poems. New York: Vantage Press, 1954. 3 p. ℓ., 48 p.

CARDOZO, ELIZABETH CLAYTON (1867-)
Salvage. Boston: R. G. Badger, 1912. 48 p.

CAREY, CLAIRE B.
Gems of Thought. New York: Comet Press Books, 1958. 5 p. ℓ., 69 p. (A Lyceum book)

CAREY, NELL SHELDON
...A Book of Verse. Holly Springs, MS.: W. T. Barry, Printer, 1900. 21 numb. ℓ., 1 ℓ.

CARHART, ELLEN SOULE
Overflow... Poems. Pasadena, CA.: Privately printed, 1917. 41 p.
Overflow; Poems. Boston: R. G. Badger, 1924. 80 p.

CARLISLE, HELEN TURNER
The Music from the Carousel. Philadelphia: Dorrance, 1975. 30 p.

CARPENTER, AUDREY F.
<u>One Star.</u> Sybil, W. VA.: Leatherwood Press, 1941. 5 p. ℓ., 39 p.
<u>The Constant Pattern.</u> Chicago: Dierkes Press, 1948. 40 p.

CARPENTER, EDITH FOOTE
<u>Songs of My Years.</u> Philadelphia: Dorrance, 1968. vii, 64 p. (Contemporary poets of Dorrance, 666)

CARPENTER, EVELYN
<u>Remembrance Will Be Lasting.</u> San Antonio, TX.: Printed by the Naylor Co., 1959. 3 p. ℓ., 18 p.

CARPENTER, KATHRYN [McKAY, KAY, <u>pseud.</u>]
<u>Secrets.</u> New York: The Paebar Company, 1946. 5 p. ℓ., 97 p.
<u>Grains of Salt.</u> Philadelphia: Dorrance, 1959. 49 p.

CARR, AGNES
<u>My Mother's Garden, and Other Poems.</u> Boston: Chapple Publishing Co., 1931. 48 p.
<u>Where Happiness Is, and Other Poems.</u> Boston: Waverly House, 1939. xiii, 161 p.

CARR, SADIE
<u>Goldenrod; A Book of Poems.</u> Edgar? NB.: n. p., 1909. 141 p.

CARREL, CORA GAINES (1860-1927)
<u>Buckeye Ballads.</u> Cincinnati, OH.: Editor Publ., Co., 1900 [i. e. 1901]. 151 p.

CARREL, MINNIE E.
<u>Fireside Poems.</u> Madison, WI.: The Quality Printers, 1923. 90 p.

CARRIER, CONSTANCE (VIRGINIA) (1908-)
<u>The Middle Voice.</u> Denver, CO.: A. Swallow, 1955. 53 p.
<u>Peter at Fourteen.</u> San Jose, CA.: Talisman Press, 1956. 4 p. (Talisman poetry folio number 1, pt. 2)
<u>The Angled Road.</u> Chicago: Swallow Press, 1973. viii, 60 p.

CARRIER, DOROTHY CHAPIN
<u>. . . Collected Poems.</u> New York: Harbinger House, 1943. 32 p.

CARRIGAN, DAISEY PATTERSON
<u>Lyrics and Songs of Other Days.</u> Burlington, N. C.: The Author, 1926. 2 p. ℓ., [3]-60 p.

CARRIGAN, NETTIE W.
<u>Rhymes and Jingles for the Children's Hour.</u> Boston: Christopher Publishing House, 1940. 3 p. ℓ., v-vi p., 1 ℓ., 9-57 p.

CARRINGTON, ELIZABETH
The Garden of My Heart. Westerly, R.I.: Utter Company, 1928. 2 p. ℓ., 7-39, [1] p.

CARRINGTON, MARY COLES
Pilgrim Paths. Cedar Rapids, IA.: The Torch Press, 1929. 95 p.
Totin' Home de Wash. Richmond, VA.: Whittel & Shepperson, 1947. 62 p.

CARROLL, ELLEN M.
Lonely Shores.... Atlanta, GA.: Banner Press, Emory University, 1934. 66 p.
Late Evening. Shelbyville, IN.: The Blue River Press, 1938? 12 p.

CARROLL, MARIE NETTLETON (1890-)
Beyond These Walls; Complete Collection of Poems by Marie Nettleton Carroll. Kansas City, MO.: Burton Publishing Company, 1941. 2 p. ℓ., 7-121 p.

CARTER, ALINE BADGER
Halo of Love. Rogers, AR.: Avalon Press, 1946. 78 p.
Doubt Not the Dream. San Antonio, TX.: Naylor Co., 1968. xi, 76 p.

CARTER, ELIZABETH PERRY
Random Seeds. San Antonio, TX.: Naylor Co., 1969. viii, 44 p.

CARTER, EMMA SMULLER
Lays of the Lake, and Other Lyrics. New York, Chicago: Fleming H. Revell, 1910. 232 p.

CARTER, JANE
On a Theban Hill. Gradyville, PA.: n.p., 1965. 62 p.

CARTER, JANE GREENOUGH (AVERY) (1838-)
The Sunset Road. Boston: Sherman, French & Co., 1913. 146 p.
At Eventide. Springfield, MA.: Bassette, 1927. 66 p.

CARTER, JESSIE (ZANE)
The Chrysalid. Muskogee, OK.: The Star Printery, 1918. 72 p.

CARTER, LAURA ARMISTEAD (d. 1935)
Wind and Blue Water. Boston: The Cornhill Company, 1920. 5 p. ℓ., 3-65 p.

CARTER, LAURIE A. (1874-)
In Quiet Hours. West Asheville, N.C.: n.p., 1959? 24 p.
________. Birmingham, AL.: Banner Press, 1926. 63 p. (A Banner book)

CARUS, HELENA
Everyman Argument in Sonnets. La Salle, IL.: The Open Court Publishing Co., 1942. 1 p. ℓ., 15 p.

CARUTHERS, MAZIE V.
The Legend of the Holy Thorn and Other Poems. Baltimore?, MD.: Printed at the Sign of the Raven, 1912. [46] p.
Songs Out of Sadness. Baltimore, MD.: Salt House Press, 1926. 4 p. ℓ., 36 p., 1 ℓ. "Certain typewritten pages laid in."
_______. 1927. 4 p. ℓ., 36 p., 2 ℓ.

CARVELL, ALICE MAUDE
Songs of Deliverance. Chicago: The Bible Institute, 1925. 64 p.

CARVER, ALICE (SHEPARD) (1874-)
Enthusiasms. Nashville, TN.: Broadman Press, 1950. 81 p.

CARVER, GERTRUDE NASON
Jupiter's Moons. Philadelphia: Dorrance & Co., 1924. 64 p. (Contemporary poets, 15)
Outside Eden. Philadelphia: Dorrance & Co., 1927. 46 p. (Contemporary poets of Dorrance, 58)

CARVER, MABEL McDONALD
The Golden Rain Tree, Poems of China. Branson, MO.: New Athenaeum Press, 1950. [20] p.
Out of Asia, and Other Poems. New York: Bookman Associates, 1957. 92 p.

CASBON, ALICE BELLE
So Much of Beauty. 1st ed. New York: Vantage Press, 1956. 66 p.

CASCIANI, EDA (1932-)
Great Blue Heron. Brooklyn, N.Y.: Serv-u-Press, 1965. 12 p.
Omnibus; Poems, 1961-66. Fort Smith, AR.: South and West, 1967. 52 p.

CASE, ELIZABETH YORK
Faith and Reason: A Poem. New York: I. Somerville & Co., 1907. 8 ℓ.
There Is No Unbelief: A Poem. New York: I. Somerville & Co., 1907. 12 ℓ.

CASEBEER, FLORENCE CHURCHILL
Stars. Los Angeles, CA.: n.p., 1918. 45 p.
Amaranths. Chula Vista, CA.: Denrich Press, 1923. [15] p.

CASEY, PEARLE ROSENCRANS
Facing West. Caldwell, ID.: The Caxton Printers, Ltd., 1936. 77 p.
Coronado. Emory University, Atlanta, GA.: Banner Press, 1940. 95 p.

CASH, GRACE (1915-)
Pattern for Living, and Other Poems. Philadelphia: Dorrance, 1950. 123 p. (Contemporary poets of Dorrance, 408)

CASSIN, MAXINE
A Touch of Recognition. Denver, CO.: A. Swallow, 1962. 56 p. (New poetry series 25)

CASTELLO, ALMEDA MERCHANT (1856-)
Wild Animal Verses Made at the New York Zoological Park. New York: Broadway Pub., 1913. 4 p. ℓ., 58 p.

CASTLE, ELIZABETH
A Verse of Bells. Boston: H. Vinal, Ltd., 1931. 5 p. ℓ., 9-71 p.

CASTLE, GWEN
Salt Winds. San Francisco: J. Howell, 1938. 52 p., 1 ℓ.
Song Above the Storm. San Francisco: J. Howell, 1942. 3 p. ℓ., 9-61 p.
The Highest Hill. San Francisco: J. Howell, 1945. 3 p. ℓ., 9-60 p.

CASTLEMAN, VIRGINIA CARTER (1864-)
Pocahontas, A Poem. New York: Broadway Publishing Co., 1907. 4 p. ℓ., ii, 44 p.
Betweenwhiles; A War Tramp's Musings. Washington, D.C.: Press of F. E. Sheiry, 1919. 28 p.

CATHER, WILLA SIBERT (1873-1947)
April Twilights: Poems. Boston: R. G. Badger, 1903. 52 p.
April Twilights, and Other Poems. New York: A. A. Knopf, 1923. 66 p. "The verses in Part I of this volume are reprinted from an early volume, April Twilights, published in 1903."
________. New York: A. Knopf, 1924. 66 p.
________. London: W. Heinemann, 1924. 66 p.
________. New York: A. A. Knopf, 1933. 70 p., 1 ℓ. "Published April, 1923...fourth printing June, 1933."
________. Ed. and with an intro. by Bernice Slote. Lincoln, NB.: University of Nebraska Press, 1962. xxxxviii [sic], 72 p., 1 ℓ.

CAUDLE, WILMA
Words on the Wind. Fort Smith, AR.: South and West, 1970. 44 p.

CAVALIERI, GRACE
Why I Cannot Take a Lover. Washington, D.C.: The Washington Writers' Publishing House, 1975. [28] p.

CAVANAGH, NANCY
Poems of Old New Orleans, and Others. New York: Harbinger

House, 1945. 47 p.
_______. 1949. 3 p. ℓ., 7-47 p.

CAVE, SALLY BULLOCK
Inland Voices. Boston: The Christopher Publishing House, 1943. viii, 9-63 p.

CECIL, EMMA TALBOTT
Songs in the Night and Other Poems, Emphasizing Essential Elements of High Christian Character through Living Examples. New York: Broadway Pub., 1913. 8 p. ℓ., 19-110 numb. ℓ.

CHAAPEL, HENRIETTA HOUGHTON
Poems. Rockford, IL.: W. P. Lamb, Printer, 1900. 179, [1] p.

CHADWELL, PAULINE SOROKA (1910-)
Beyond the Flame. Cambridge, MA.: Hampshire Press, 1948. 94 p.

CHADWICK, BESSIE MAY
Under the Locust Trees. New York: H. Vinal, 1927. 5 p. ℓ., 61 [1] p.
Creation. Washington: n. p., 1943. 52 p.

CHAFFEE, ELEANOR ALLETTA (1899-)
Temporary Truce. Brooklyn, N. Y.: The Lantern, 1934. 16 ℓ. (Lantern poet series, no. 3)

CHAFFIN, LILLIE (DORTON) (1825-)
Lines and Points. Pikeville, KY.: Pikeville College Press, 1966. 51 p.
A Stone for Sisyphus. Fort Smith, AR.: South and West, 1967. 52 p.
Bear Weather. New York: Macmillan, 1968. [32] p.
First Notes. Pikeville, N. Y.: Golden Horseshoe Press, 1969. 48 p.
8th Day 13th Moon. Pikeville, KY.: Hilltop Editions, 1974. [46] p.

CHALFIN, MATTIE MABEL (1878-)
Fine and Fussy Feathers. Los Angeles, CA.: Press of Gem Publishing Co., 1925. 6 p. ℓ., [15]-60 p.

CHALMERS, AGNES
Travel Orders. Grand Rapids, MI.: The Crescent Publishers, 1922. 178 p.

CHALMERS, JANE
Manhattan Serenade. New York: Fortuny's, 1935. 60 p.

CHAMBERS, BETTIE KEYES
Idylls of the South. New York: The Neale Publishing Co., 1912. 168 p.

CHANCELLOR, MABEL MAY
Lights and Shadows. Dallas, TX.: Royal Pub. Co., 1966. 7 p. ℓ., 31 p.

CHANDLER, BESSIE (1856-) [Full Name: Elizabeth Lowber (Chandler) Parker.]
Verses. Chicago: The Blue Sky Press, 1901. 121, [1] p.

CHANDLER, SARAH A.
Homey Poems and Others. Providence, R.I.: The Providence Press, 1923. 6 p. ℓ., 7-127 p.

CHANEY, ELSIE NORTHRUP
Poems of the Far East. New York, London: Fleming H. Revell Company, 1939. 108 p.
The Ivory Carver. 2d ed. Claremont, CA.: Creative Press, 1955. 61 p. "Originally published in Rangoon in 1941."

CHANLER, ALIDA
Songs and Sonnets. Boston: The Cornhill Company, 1919. vii, 58 p.

CHANNING, BLANCHE MARY (1863-1902)
Lullaby Castle, and Other Poems. Boston: Little Brown and Co., 1904. x, 62 p.

CHAPIN, HELEN BURWELL
Echoes. Berkeley, CA.: Printed at the Gillick Press, 1938. [62] p.

CHAPIN, KATHERINE GARRISON (1890-)
Outside of the World. New York: Duffield and Co., 1930. ix, 94 p.
______. 2d ed., 1931.
Bright Mariner. n.p., 1933. [6] p.
Time Has No Shadow. First edition. New York: Dodd, Mead & Co., 1936. xii, 100 p.
Lament for the Stolen: A Poem for a Chorus. Philadelphia: The Centaur Press, 1938. [7] p.
Plain-Chant for America. New York: Harper & Brothers, 1942. xi, 141 [1] p.
______. New York & London: Harper & Brothers, 1942. xi, 141, [1] p. "Second edition."
The Other Journey; Poems New and Selected. Minneapolis, MN.: University of Minnesota Press, 1959. 4 p. ℓ., 98 p.

CHAPIN, MARY R. L.
Little Songs. Washington, D.C.: Printed by B. S. Adams, 1917. 24 ℓ.

CHAPIN, VIRGINIA (1908-)
Beat of Wings. New York: Dodd, Mead & Co., 1935. xi p., 2 ℓ., 3-121 p.

The Final Accolade. 1st ed. New York: Fine Editions Press, 1956. 50 p., 1 ℓ.

CHAPMAN, ELIZABETH
The Merest Chants. Chicago: n.p., 1933. 45 p.

CHAPPELL, JEANNETTE
Destination Uncharted. Francestown, N.H.: Golden Quill Press, 1964. 80 p.

CHAPPELL, PEARL WALLACE
Long Must We Listen. Dallas, TX.: Mathis, Van Nort & Co., 1941. 4 p. ℓ., 88 p.
Blue Heron and Other Poems. Dallas, TX.: Hamrick Pub. Co., 1959. 50 p.

CHARLES, MARY GRANT
Across a Covered Bridge. Manchester, N.H.: Granite State Press, 1958. 90 p.

CHARMLEY, BEULAH JACKSON
Flying Joy. Dallas, TX.: The Kaleidograph Press, 1938. x p., 2 ℓ., 15-79 p.
_______. 1940. xi p., 1 ℓ., 15-71 p.
As a Strong Bird. Dallas, TX.: The Kaleidograph Press, 1940. xi p., 1 ℓ., 15-71 p.
Isle Royale, and Other Poems. Dallas, TX.: The Kaleidograph Press, 1943. xi p., 1 ℓ., 15-87 p.
Sleeping Indian Mound. Dallas, TX.: The Kaleidograph Press, 1950. 68 p.
The Lincoln Legend; A Biography in Verse and Trilogy for Today; A Group of Shorter Poems. Lena, IL.: Stephenson-Carroll, 1961. 180 p.

CHASE, HENRIETTA M.
Poems. Boston: Nathan Sawyer & Son, Inc., 1920. 26 p.

CHASE-RIBAUD, BARBARA
From Memphis and Peking: Poems. New York: Random House, 1974. 112 p.

CHASIN, HELEN
Two Poems. Somerville, MA.: Barn Dream Press, 1970. [4] p.
Coming Close and Other Poems. New Haven, CT.: Yale University Press, 1968. 54 p. (The Yale Series of Younger Poets, v. 63)
Casting Stones. 1st ed. Boston: Little, Brown, 1975. viii, 47 p.

CHATTEN, LILLY WALLER
Out in the Country, and Other Poems from "Pennyroyal Pearls." Chicago: n.p., 1915. [11] p.

CHAUNCEY, FLORENCE ISABEL
Songs. Boston: R. G. Badger, 1911. 80 p.

CHEFFEY, JESSIE ANN
Jewels by the Wayside. New York: Harbinger House, 1942. 55 p.

CHENERY, RUTH BALDWIN
At Vesper Time, Poems. New York & London: G. P. Putnam's Sons, 1917. vii, 89 p.

CHENEY, ANNE CLEVELAND
By the Sea and Other Poems. Boston: Sherman, French & Company, 1911. 5 p. ℓ., 69 p.

CHENEY, ANNIE ELIZABETH
Dreams of Hellas, and Other Poems. New York & Los Angeles: Lloyd Publishing Co., 1917. 2 p. ℓ., v p., 1 ℓ., 11-219 p.

CHENOWETH, FANNIE E.
Montana Pioneers. Kalispell, MT.: Printed by E. C. O'Neill, 1914. [22] p.

CHERRINGTON, EDITH (DE WITT) (1894-)
Phantom Caravan. Dallas, TX.: The Kaleidograph Press, 1940. xi p., 1 ℓ., 15-78 p.

CHERRY, JEANNE (YATES) (1879-) [D'ORGE, JEANNE, pseud.]
Lobos. Carmel, CA.: The Seven Arts, 1928. 29 p.
Voice in the Circle. Santa Barbara, CA.: N. Young, Printer, 1955. 3 p. ℓ., 96 p., 1 ℓ.

CHESHAM, SALLIE
Walking with the Wind. Waco, TX.: Word Books, 1969. 132 p.
Trouble Doesn't Happen Next Tuesday. Waco, TX.: Word Books, 1972. 160 p.

CHESTER, LAURA
Tiny Talk. n.p.: Roundhouse, 1972. 1 v. (unpaged)
Primagravida. Santa Barbara, CA.: Christopher's Books, 1975. 116 p.

CHEUVRONT, LILLIAN B.
'Round Home. Denver, CO.: Printed by the Highland Chief, 1938. 4 p. ℓ., 51, [1] p.
Life in Rhyme. New York: Vantage Press, 1956. 108 p.

CHIESA, CAROL DELLA see DELLA CHIESA, CAROLYN M. (1887-)

CHILD, LESLIE
Dream-Forest, Afternoon of a Faun and a Flower. Portland, ME.: The Mosher Press, 1928. 5 p. ℓ., 3-40 p.

CHILES, ROSA PENDLETON (1866-)
"He Whom Thou Lovest Is Sick"; A Poem. Richmond, VA.: Whittet & Shepperson, 1904. 54 p.
________. 3d ed., 1904. 54 p.

CHIPP, ELINOR (1898-) [MILLER, ELINOR CHIPP]
The City, and Other Poems. Boston: The Four Seas Company, 1923. 83 p.
Day and Night. New York: H. Harrison, 1938. 63 p.
New Poems. Portland, ME.: Falmouth Pub. House, 1949. 70 p.

CHITTENDEN, LULU (BROWER) (1877-) [Full Name: Lulu Wilcox (Brower) Chittenden.]
My Heart Goes Home. New York: G. P. Putnam's Sons, 1939. 86 p.

CHOLMELEY-JONES, HENRIETTA HOWARD BOIT (STURGIS) (1896-)
...Slow Advance (1914-1944). Philadelphia: Dorrance and Co., 1944. xiv p., 1 ℓ., 17-115 p. (Contemporary poets of Dorrance, 281)

CHRISTENSON, CLARA BIRGITTE (1883-)
Passing Thoughts, Poems. New York: Exposition Press, 1952. 96 p.

CHRISTESON, AMELIA V.
When Time Returns, Caddo, and Other Poems. LaJunta, CO.: La Junta Printing Co., 1954. 46 p.
Silence and Stars. Dallas, TX.: American Guild Press, 1957. 48 p.
Vibrations and Visions. Dallas, TX.: Royal Pub. Co., 1962. 40 p.
Voice of Stillness. San Antonio, TX.: Naylor Co., 1965. 50 p.

CHRISTIANSEN, RUTH BUNKER
The Golden Trillium. Chicago: Windfall Press, 1963. 32 p.

CHRISTIE, HELEN [H. C.]
Leaflets of Melody. Chicago: Lipman Supply House, 1900. 44 p.

CHRISTMAN, BERNIECE BUNN
Grey Pools and Reflections. Philadelphia: Dorrance, 1951. 95 p. (Contemporary poets of Dorrance, 427)

CHRISTOFF, MADELINE JOSEPHINE (1920-)
Gate of Freedom. New York: Hobson Book Press, 1947. 187 p.

CHRISTOPHER, ANN
Poems. Chicago: B. P. Branham Company, 1935. [26] p.

CHUNN, LEONA HAYES
Rouse with the Dawn. Birmingham, AL.: Banner Press, 1965. 60 p.

CHURCH, MARY ELIZABETH
Messenger of Thoughts. San Jose, CA.: n. p., 1944. 100 p.

CHURCH, PEGGY POND (1903-)
Foretaste. Santa Fe, N. M.: Writers' Editions, 1933. 5 p. ℓ., 3-73, [1] p.
_______. 2d ed. Santa Fe, N. M.: Writers' Editions, 1933. 5 p. ℓ., 3-73 [1] p.
Familiar Journey. Santa Fe, N. M.: Writers' Editions, 1936. 69 p.
Ultimatum for Man. Stanford, CA.: Stanford University, James Ladd Delkin, 1946. 4 p. ℓ., 32 p., 1 ℓ.
_______. 1947. 4 p. ℓ., 32 p., 1 ℓ. "One of 400 copies printed at the Greenwood Press, San Mateo, CA. Second edition."

CHURCH, VIRGINIA WOODSON (FRAME) (1880-) [BROWN, AGATHA, pseud.]
Teachers Are People. Hollywood, CA.: Authors Publishing Co., 1925. 3 p. ℓ., 60, [1] p.
_______; being the lyrics of Virginia Church sometime teacher of English in the Hilldale High School. Hollywood, CA.: David Graham Fischer Corp., 1926. 60 p.
_______. New York, Santa Barbara: W. Hebberd, 1929. xiii, 63 p.
_______. Rev. ed. Santa Barbara, CA.: W. Hebberd, 1945. xiii, 82 p.
Silhouettes of the Latin Quarter. Atlanta, GA.: The Bozart Press, 1931. 49 p.

CHURCHIELLO, JOSEPHINE M.
Portrait in Thoughts. Brooklyn, N. Y.: Postar Press, 1954. 72 p.

CHURCHWARD, DAISIE BELL
The Turn of the Wheel. New York: Privately printed, Brown Printing Co., 1928. 72 p.
Brown Linnets. New York: The Knickerbocker Press, 1931. vii, 75 p.

CHUTE, MARCHETTE GAYLORD (1909-)
Rhymes About Ourselves. New York: The Macmillan Company, 1932. 5 p. ℓ., 72 p., 1 ℓ.
Rhymes About the Country. New York: The Macmillan Company, 1941. 5 p. ℓ., 74, [1] p.
Rhymes About the City. New York: The Macmillan Company, 1946. 3 p. ℓ., 57, [1] p.
Around and About: Rhymes. New York: Dutton, 1957. 124 p.

CLAFFORD, PATRICIA MARY WISE (1907-)
Even the Wind. Chicago: Dierkes Press, 1949. 55 p.

CLAPP, MARY BRENNAN (1884-)
And Then Re-Mold It. Missoula, MT.: H. G. Merriam, 1929.

55 ℓ.
Gifts. Christmas Poems. Missoula, MT.: n. p., 1932. 22 [1] p.

CLARE, JOSEPHINE
Deutschland, A Sequence. Milwaukee, WI.: Morgan Press, 1970. [28] p. (Hey lady supplement, no. 6)
Deutschland & Other Places. Plainfield, VT.: North Atlantic Books, 1974. [12], 45 p.

CLARK, ANNIE MARIE LAWRENCE (1835-)
Poems. Boston: R. G. Badger, 1904. 83 p.

CLARK, ESTHER M[ARY]
Verses by a Commonplace Person. Topeka, KS.: n. p., 1906. unpaged.
The Call of Kansas, and Other Verses. Lawrence, KS.: C. C. Seewir, 1910. 16 p., 1 ℓ.
_______. 2d ed., 1911. 20 p.
_______. 1916. 36 p.

CLARK, GERTRUDE KELLOG
Verses. Buffalo, N. Y.: Gay Press, 1922. 31 ℓ.
_______. Village of Eden, N. Y.: Aries Press, 1927, i. e., 1928. viii, 37 p., 1 ℓ.

CLARK, LAVINIA RUMSEY
Lines for Lillian. Dallas, TX.: Kaleidograph Press, 1947. viii p., 1 ℓ., 11-68 p.
Pine Needles. New York: Exposition Press, 1950. 64 p.

CLARK, LESLIE SAVAGE
Star for Beacon. Dallas, TX.: The Kaleidograph Press, 1941. xi p., 1 ℓ., 15-77 p.
Still There Is Peace. Claremont, CA.: Creative Press, 1960. 39 p. (Creative poetry series, no. 1)

CLARK, LUELLA
April Days. Boston: R. G. Badger, 1904. 178 p.

CLARK, MARGUERITE DIXON
Wind Free. Portland, ME.: The Mosher Press, 1924. viii p., 2 ℓ., 3-51, [1] p.

CLARK, MARY
Within Each Day. Philadelphia: Dorrance, 1974. 69 p.

CLARK, MARY BAYARD
Poems. New York: Broadway Pub., 1905. 31-193 p.

CLARK, MARY KATHERINE
Verses. Sandusky, OH.: Register Press, 1900. 2 p. ℓ., 70 p.

CLARK, MAY ROBERTS
Eternal Quest. Philadelphia: Dorrance & Co., Inc., 1933. 136 p. (Contemporary poets of Dorrance, 116)

CLARK, MAZIE EARHART
Garden of Memories. Cincinnati: Eaton Publishing Co., 1932. 1 p. ℓ., 7-62 p.
Life's Sunshine and Shadows. Cincinnati: Eaton Publishing Co., 1940. 112 p.

CLARK, OLIVE ADELLA
Lady Pocotopaug: Moods, History and Legend. Moodus, CT.: n.p., 1925. 16 p.

CLARK, ROSE CAVE GOULD
My Old Photograph Album. Duluth, MN.: n.p., 1914. [4] p.
Autumn Afternoon, and Other Poems. Philadelphia: Dorrance, 1923. 55 p. (Contemporary poets, 6)

CLARK, RUTH GREER
Echoes from the Hills. Texarkana, TX.: Printed by Southwest Printers and Publishers, 1952. 76 p.

CLARKE, BETTY JEAN (1929-)
44, Almost 45. Philadelphia: Dorrance, 1974. 69 p.

CLARKE, BIRDIE BAXTER
Little Rimes of the Garrison. Kansas City, MO.: Franklin Hudson Press, 1909. 2 p. ℓ., 11-139 p.

CLARKE, HENRIETTA
Little Towns. Philadelphia: Poetry Publishers, 1934. 40 p.
________. Boston, 1935. 2d printing.
Unseen Blossoms, and Other Poems. New York: Exposition Press, 1951. 62 p.

CLARKE, MARGARET ELECTRA (1904-)
Time Was. New York: H. Harrison, 1941. 63 p.

CLARKE, MARIANNE
Miss America. New York: Leacy N. Green-Leach, 1929. 115 p.
Sunlit Trails. New York: The Poet's Press, 1938. 128 p.

CLARKE, MARION LOUISE
Annie Bell, and Other Poems. Worcester, MA.: The Blanchard Press, 1906. 141 p.

CLARKE, PHEBE ANN
Ye Shall Have a Song; Poems. Philadelphia: Dorrance & Co., 1947. 55 p. (Contemporary poets of Dorrance, 362)

CLAUDEL, ALICE MOSER (1918-)
Southern Season. Pikeville, KY.: Pikeville College Press, 1972. 78 p.

CLAY, SUSAN
Poems. Chicago: R. F. Seymour, 19--? 32 p.

CLAYES, EDITH MARTIN
Some Indian Legends Done into Verse. San Francisco, CA.: Sanborn, Vail & Co., 1924. 4 p. ℓ., 5-90 p.
Undelibet. San Francisco, CA.: n.p., 1927. [57] p.

CLAYTOR, GERTRUDE BOATWRIGHT (1890?-1973)
Sunday in Virginia and Other Poems. New York: Dutton, 1951. 79 p.
Mirage at Midnight and Other Poems. London: Villiers Publications, 1960. 76 p.

CLEAVELAND, ELIZABETH HANNAH (JOCELYN)
No Sects in Heaven. n.p.: Elder, 1902. 24 p.

CLEGHORN, SARAH NORCLIFFE (1876-)
Hillsboro People... With Occasional Vermont Verses. New York: H. Holt, 1915. 1 p. ℓ., iv-v, 1 ℓ., 346 p.
Portraits and Protests. New York: H. Holt, 1917. 2 p. ℓ., vii-viii, 82 p.
Ballad of Gene Debs. North Montpelier, VT.: The Driftwind Press, 1928. 8 p.
The True Ballad of Lionel Licorish. New York: Survey Graphic, 1930. 8 p.
Ballad of Tuzulutlan. Berne: Busag, Ltd., 1932. 1 p. ℓ., 5-28 p.
The True Ballad of Glorious Harriet Tubman. Manchester, VT.: n.p., 1933. 12 p.
The True Ballad of the Extraordinary Fortitude of William Griffin. Manchester, VT.: n.p., 1933. 12 p.
The True Ballad of the Camden Boy. Manchester? VT.: n.p., 1933. 7 p.
The True Ballad of Lionel Licorish. New York: Survey Graphic, 1937. 8 p.
Poems of Peace and Freedom. Fulton? N.Y.: The New York State Branch of the Women's International League for Peace and Freedom, 1945. 93 p.
Poems. n.p., 1956? 18 p. ℓ., [302]. "A collection of 224 poems edited by Anna Pettit Broomell."

CLEMANS, BERTHA JOHANNA (1875-)
California, Nature's Paradise. Los Angeles: Press of Shaw & Riley, 1914. 14 p.

CLEMMONS, GERTRUDE
Pictures of Silver. Birmingham, AL.: Banner Press, 1965. 48 p. (Versecraft series)

CLENDENEN, LAURA HENDERSON
A Beacon of Light. Denver, CO.: Sutton Press, 1938. 120 p.
An Open Door. Denver, CO.: Sutton Press, 1939. 112 p.

CLENDENING, LURA KELSEY
Ropes of Sand; Poems and Sketches. Boston: R. G. Badger, 1908. 141 p.

CLIFFORD, CARRIE WILLIAMS
Race Rhymes. Washington, D. C.: Printed by R. L. Pendleton, 1911. 28 p.
The Widening Light. Boston: Walter Reid Company, 1922. ix, 65 p.

CLIFTON, LUCILLE (1936-)
Good Times; Poems. New York: Random House, 1969. [85] p.
Good News About the Earth; New Poems. New York: Random House, 1972. 1 v. (unpaged)
An Ordinary Woman. New York: Random House, 1974. 94 p.

CLINEDINST, CATHERINE AMES (1915-)
To the Virgin and Other Poems. New York: H. Harrison, 1938. 60 p.

CLINKSCALES, BERTIE H. (LOUISE)
The Far Horizon. Philadelphia: Dorrance, 1958. 56 p. (Contemporary poets of Dorrance, 503)

CLINTON, ELEANOR M.
Fire and the Wheel. New York: Greenwich Book Publishers, 1954. 64 p.

CLOUD, VIRGINIA WOODWARD (1861-1938)
A Reed by the River. Boston: R. G. Badger, 1902. 75, [1] p.
From an Old Garden. Baltimore, MD.: The Norman, Remington Co., 1922. 30 p.
Candlelight. Baltimore, MD.: The Norman, Remington Co., 1924. 34 p.
The Collected Poems of Virginia Woodward Cloud. New York: H. Harrison, 1939. 96 p.

CLOUGH, RUTH (CRARY) see CRARY, RUTH

COATES, FLORENCE VAN LEER (EARLE) NICHOLSON (1850-1927)
Mine and Thine. Boston & New York: Houghton, Mifflin Company, 1904. 7 p. ℓ., 175, [1] p.
________. 1905. (II), 175 p.
Poems. Boston: Houghton, Mifflin & Co., 1905. vii, 136, [1] p.
Mine and Thine. Boston & New York: Houghton, Mifflin Company, 1906.
Lyrics of Life. Boston & New York: Houghton, Mifflin Company, 1909. x p., 11 ℓ., 114, [4] p., 1 ℓ.
________. 1910.
The Unconquered Air, and Other Poems. Boston & New York: Houghton, Mifflin Company, 1912. x, 112 p., 1 ℓ.
Poems. Collected ed. Boston and New York: Houghton, Mifflin Co., 1916. 2 v.

Pro Patria. Philadelphia: n.p., 1917. 8 ℓ.

COATES, GRACE STONE (1881-)
Mead and Mangel-Wurzel. Caldwell, ID.: The Caxton Printers, Ltd., 1931. 151 p.
Portulacas in the Wheat. Caldwell, ID.: The Caxton Printers, Ltd., 1932. 71, [1] p.

COATSWORTH, ELIZABETH JANE (1893-)
Fox Footprints. New York: A. A. Knopf, 1923. 9 p. ℓ., 3-78 p., 1ℓ.
Atlas and Beyond. New York & London: Harper & Brothers, 1924. xvi, 61, [1] p.
Compass Rose. New York: Coward McCann, Inc., 1929. xi, 13-96 p.
The Cat Who Went to Heaven. New York: The Macmillan Co., 1934. 5 p. ℓ., 122 p.
Away Goes Sally. New York: The Macmillan Co., 1934. 5 p. ℓ., 122 p.
Country Poems. New York: The Macmillan Co., 1942. x, 103 p.
Summer Green. New York: Macmillan Co., 1948. x, 86 p.
The Creaking Stair. New York: Coward-McCann, 1949. 110 p.
Night and the Cat. New York: Macmillan, 1950. 4 p. ℓ., 55 p.
Mouse Chorus. New York: Pantheon, 1955. [32] p.
Poems. New York: Macmillan, 1957. 6 p. ℓ., 115 p.
The Peaceable Kingdom, and Other Poems. New York: Pantheon Books, 1958. [41] p.
The Sparrow Bush: Rhymes. New York: Norton, 1966. 63, [1] p.
Down Half the World. New York: Macmillan, 1968. xi, 96 p.

COBB, ANN
Kinfolks, Kentucky Mountain Rhymes. Boston & New York: Houghton, Mifflin Co., 1922. x, 82 p.

COBB, CARRIE CLEMENTS
Fireside Poems, and Other Selections. Jackson, TN.: C. M. E. Publishing House, 1923. 98 p.

COBB, MARGARET MACLEISH (1913-)
The Root and the Leaf, Poems. Limited ed. Cleveland, OH.: American Weave Press, 1950. 22 p. (Durham chapbook, no. 5)

COBB, MARY ESTHER
Chords. Boston: McGrath-Sherrill Press, 1926. 18 p.
Geode. Laconia, N. H.: Laconia Press Association, 1929. 20 p.
Above the Mists. Boston: Peabody Master Printers, 1930. 50 p.
I Reaped a Field. Franklin, N. Y.: Dairyman Press, 1930? 16 p.

COBB, MARY (McKINLEY) (1884-1927) [Full Name: Mary Beattie McKinley Cobb.]
Swallow Flights. Oglethorpe University, GA.: Oglethorpe University Press, 1929. xvi p., 1 ℓ., 187 p.
Swallow Flights, The Posthumous Poems of Mary McKinley Cobb. New York: Exposition Press, 1948. 123 p.

COBB, WINIFRED BRADLEY
The Greening Branch. San Antonio, TX.: Naylor Co., 1964. x, 58 p.
Spin the Golden Thread. San Antonio, TX.: Naylor Co., 1966. viii, 60 p.
Let the Mountains Stand. San Antonio, TX.: Naylor Co., 1971. 41 p.

COBBLE, EDITH SANBORN
Drifting Sands. New York: New Voices Publishing Co., 1952. 5 p.ℓ., 105 p.
Whispering Winds. New York: Vantage Press, 1969. 96 p.

COBLENTZ, FLORA (BACHRACH)
A Selection of Epigrams.... Los Angeles: Overland-Out-West Publications, 1934. 2 p.ℓ., 62 p. On cover: Scattered Kernels.
To Each a Path. Mill Valley, CA.: Wings Press, 1955. 48 p.

COBURN, LOUISE HELEN (1856-)
Kennebec, and Other Poems. Boston: Sherman, French & Co., 1916. 4 p.ℓ., 139 p.

COBURN, MYRNA H.
The Eighth Day, and Other Poems. New York: Exposition Press, 1960. 46 p.

COCHRAN, MARY NORRIS
Desultory Verses. Philadelphia, Chicago, etc.: The John C. Winston Company, 1923. ix, 90 p.

COCHRAN, RITA EAUDENE
A Smaller Bauble, and Other Poems. New York: Exposition Press, 1960. 54, [1] p.

COCKE, ZITELLA (1848?-)
The Grasshopper's Hop and Other Verses. New York: H. M. Caldwell Co., 1901. 113 p.
_______. Boston: D. Estes & Co., 1901. 2 p.ℓ., viii p., 1 ℓ., 11-113 p.
Cherokee Rose, and Other Southern Poems. Boston: R. G. Badger, 1907. 96 p.

CODY, ROSALIE MAY (1853-)
In Flight. New York: Duffield & Co., 1916. 8 p.ℓ., 83 p.

COE, ALICE ROLLIT
A Sprig of Lavendar and Other Poems. Seattle, WA.: n.p., 1902. 12 p.
Lyrics of Fur and Foam. Seattle, WA.: The Alice Harriman Co., 1908. 51 ℓ.
Chimes Rung by the University District Herald. Seattle, WA.: Press of Univ. Publishing Co., 1921. 22 p.

COEUR, KATHRYN ALLEN (1885-)
Thought Crystals. Hollywood, CA.: House-Warven, 1952. 98 p.

COFFEY, MABEL R.
Towns and Towers. New York: H. Vinal, Ltd., 1927. 6 p. ℓ., 67, [1] p.

COFFMAN, JUDIE MICHAEL
A Cup of Honor. Philadelphia: Dorrance, 1965. 40 p. (Contemporary poets of Dorrance, 610)

COIN, LISBETH G. (WHITEHURST) (1878-1948)
Vagabond Leaves. Philadelphia: Dorrance, 1936. 60 p. (Contemporary poets of Dorrance, 144)
Wanderer's Gold. Philadelphia: Dorrance, 1950. 64 p. (Contemporary poets of Dorrance, 412)

COLDIRON, DAISY LEMON (1876-1946)
Songs of Oklahoma. Dallas, TX.: The Kaleidograph Press, 1935. xiii p., 1 ℓ., 17-132 p.
There Was a Garden. Dallas, TX.: The Kaleidograph Press, 1940. x p., 1 ℓ., 13-68 p.
Who Touches This. Dallas, TX.: The Kaleidograph Press, 1940. xi p., 1 ℓ., 15-88 p.
Ballads of the Plains. Dallas, TX.: Kaleidograph Press, 1950. 86 p.

COLE, HELEN EMMA (WIEAND) (1885-)
Spring Moods and Fancies; A Book of Verse. Boston: Sherman, French, & Co., 1914. 5 p. ℓ., 69 p.
Music and Memory, and Other Poems. Boston: R. G. Badger, 1919. 64 p.
Many Voices. New York: H. Harrison, 1938. 64 p.

COLE, MARY ELIZABETH
My Tapestry. La Habra? CA.: n.p., 1951. 54 p.

COLE, MAUDE E. (CRAIGHEAD)
Clay-Bound. Dallas, TX.: Kaleidograph Press, 1935. xi p., 1 ℓ., 15-82 p.

COLE, MAY (1877-)
Lyrics of Love and Laughter. Chicago: R. R. Donnelley & Sons, 1914. x p., 1 ℓ., 130 p.

COLEMAN, ELEANOR MANGAN
The Last Frontier; Poems. Hicksville, N.Y.: Exposition Press, 1975. 63 p.

COLEMAN, LUCILE LEWIS
Strange Altar. Prairie City, IL.: J. A. Decker, 1947. 120 p.
This Laughing Dust. Dallas, TX.: Story Book Press, 1951. 80 p.

COLEMAN, WINIFRED HARPER
Western Window, Poems. New York: Exposition Press, 1951. 64 p.

COLES, CHRISTIE LUND (1906-)
Some Spring Returning; A Collection of Poems. Provo, UT.: Faucette, 1958. vii, 54 p.
Speak to Me; Poems. Provo, UT.: n.p., 1970. 64 p.

COLGROVE, LAURA WALKER
A Romance of the Lake and Other Poems. New York: H. Harrison, 1931. 64 p.

COLIE, ROSALIE LITELL (1924-)
Atlantic Wall, and Other Poems. Princeton, N.J.: Princeton University Press, 1975. viii, 85 p.

COLLETT, SARAH RAINSFORD
Thoughts and Flowers. New York: H. Harrison, 1937. 63 p.
Peace with Christianity and Other Poems. Edgefield, S.C.: n.p., 1951. 3 p.ℓ., 51 p.
Songs of Edgefield. New York: Exposition Press, 1956. 63 p.

COLLINS, ERNESTINE L. R.
"A Garnered Autumn Sheaf." Boston: The Cornhill Publishing Co., 1921. 3 p.ℓ., 149 p.

COLLINS, ETHEL D. W.
Banner of Song; Poems of Things in Heaven and Earth. New York: Exposition Press, 1952. 144 p.

COLLINS, FAITH WADSWORTH
Poems. New York: H. Vinal, 1926. 59 p.

COLLINS, LAURA G. (1826-1912)
Egypt: A Poem. Cincinnati, OH.: The Robert Clarke Co., 1900. 19 ℓ., 3 p.ℓ.

COLLISTER, LEONIE DAVIS
Stowaways. New York: T. Seltzer, 1925. 6 p.ℓ., 5-118 p.

COLWELL, ELIZABETH
Songs of Tristram and Yseult; Quatrains. Chicago: n.p., 1907. 52 p.

Songs and Sonnets. New York: F. F. Sherman, 1909. 85 p.

COMBE, MURIEL
Inflammable Wine. Dallas, TX.: The Kaleidograph Press, 1937. 3 p. ℓ., xi-xii p., 1 ℓ., 15-65 p.

COMBES, GLADYS EWING (1893-)
Homespun. North Montpelier, VT.: Driftwind Press, 1946. 46 p.

COMBS, ESTELLE H.
Poems about This and That. New York: The Paebar Co., 1945. 3 p. ℓ., 34 p.

COMFORT, FLORENCE CROCKER
Time Turns Under. Prairie City, IL.: J. A. Decker, 1945. 132 p.

COMMELIN, ANNA OLCOTT
Atala, An American Idyl: A Poetic Dramatization of the Work of Chateaubri and, with Original Poems. New York: E. P. Dutton & Co., 1902. iv, 76 p.
Song of Christmas. Brooklyn, N.Y.: n.p., 1906. 2 p.

COMPNEY, CARMEN C.
Whispering Echoes. Philadelphia: Dorrance, 1952. 48 p. (Contemporary poets of Dorrance, 432)
Silver Shadows. Philadelphia: Dorrance, 1956. 56 p. (Contemporary poets of Dorrance, 480)

COMSTOCK, JANE see CLARKE, JANE COMSTOCK

COMSTOCK, MARY EDGAR
Flickering Candlelight. Philadelphia: Dorrance & Co., 1926. 72, [1] p. (Contemporary poets of Dorrance, 43)
...A Penny a Dream. New York: H. Harrison, 1930. 63 p.

CONANT, HELEN PARR
Recompense: A Book of Verse. Boston: Sherman, French, & Co., 1916. 51 p., 4 ℓ.

CONANT, ISABELLA (FISKE) (1874-) [Full Name: Isabella Howe (Fiske) Conant.]
Verses. Boston: Printed by F. Wood, 1900. 79 p.
A Field of Folk. Boston: R. G. Badger, 1903. 67 p.
Songs before Birth. Portland, ME.: The Mosher Press, 1912. x, 39 p. 1 ℓ.
Pageant of the Charles River, September 19, 1914 at 3 o'clock Metropolitan Parkland, Quinobequin Road, Newton Lower Falls. Wellesley, MA.: Magus Printing Co., 1914. [8] p. (In verse.)
Sonnets and Lyrics. Boston: Printed at the Industrial School for Crippled Children, 1915? 8 ℓ. Cover title: "Hands across

the sea; sonnets in praise of King Albert and his Belgians."
_______. 1917? 15 p.
Sonnets of Protest...for the Allied Relief.... n.p., 1917. [13] p.
_______. n.p., 19--. 12 p.
Many Wings. Boston: B. J. Brimmer Co., 1923. 79 p.
Frontier. Portland, ME.: The Mosher Press, 1924. ix, [1], 69, [1] p.
Puritan. New York: H. Vinal, 1925. 6 p.ℓ., 60 p.
Dream Again. London: Fowler Wright, 1929. vi, 90 p.
These Coloured Balls. London: Fowler, Wright, 192-? 78 p.
_______. 1931. 78 p.
_______. London: Wright, 1932. 78, [1] p.
Aisle-Seat; Lyrics, Sonnets, Quatrains. Portland, ME.: The Mosher Press, 1937. vi, 53, [2] p.
Campus Sonnets. Winter Park, FL.: The Rollins Press, 1938. 8 ℓ.
Remembered Journey: Lyrics, Quatrains, Sonnets. Dallas, TX.: The Kaleidograph Press, 1938. ix p., 2 ℓ., 15-91 p.
Storrowton Sonnets. Storrowton, West Springfield, MA.: Pond-Ekberg Co. Press, 1938. 15 p.
Wellesley Sonnets. Winter Park, FL.: The Rollins Press, 1938. 8 ℓ.
Orange Feather: Lyrics, Sonnets, Quatrains. Boston: B. Humphries, Inc., 1939. 73 p.
Window-Shopping; Lyrics, Sonnets, Pieces of Eight. Dallas, TX.: The Kaleidograph Press, 1940. ix p., 1 ℓ., 13-85 p., 1 ℓ.
Crystal Cage. Dallas, TX.: The Kaleidograph Press, 1941. vi p., 2 ℓ., 11-85 p., 1 ℓ.
Sky-Color: Lyrics and Sonnets. Dallas, TX.: The Kaleidograph Press, 1943. xi, [1] p., 1 ℓ., 15-75, [2] p.
Short Waves. Hartwick, N.Y.: Reflections Press, 1944. 16 p.

CONANT, LORA M.
Things as We See Them. Dallas, TX.: Story Book Press, 1950. 48 p.
As the Wheel Turns. Dallas, TX.: Story Book Press, 1955. 48 p.
Willie Magee of the Ranch Sandee. Denver, CO.: Big Mountain Press, 1959. 39 p.

CONDE, CECILIA S.
An Empty Shell. Boston: Four Seas, 1918. 14 p.

CONDEE, NANCY
The Rape of Saint Emad. Providence, R.I.: Burning Deck, 1974. [16] p., 1 ℓ.

CONDON, AMASA S. (1849-)
Handful of Flowers with Sprays of Evergreen. Boston: Sherman, French & Co., 1913. 143 p., 5 ℓ.

CONE, HELEN GRAY (1859-1934)
Soldiers of the Light. Boston: R. G. Badger, 1911. 72 p.
A Chant of Love for England and Other Poems. New York: E. P. Dutton & Co., 1915. viii, 103 p.
The Coat Without a Seam, and Other Poems. New York: E. P. Dutton & Co., 1919. viii, 100 p.
Harvest Home, Selected Poems. New York: The Knickerbocker Press. x, 147 p.

CONKLIN, ELMA KENDALL
A Booklet of War Poems. San Francisco, CA.: n.p., 1923. 45 p.

CONKLIN, MYRTLE SAUERBIER (1881-)
Beneath Montana Skies; Poems. New York: Exposition Press, 1962. 32 p.

CONKLING, GRACE WALCOTT (HAZARD) (1878-1958)
Afternoons of April; A Book of Verse. Boston & New York: Houghton, Mifflin Co., 1915. viii, [1], 89, [3] p. (The New poetry series)
Wilderness Songs. New York: H. Holt & Co., 1920. ix, [1], 102 p.
Variations on a Theme. Charleston, S.C.: The Poetry Society of South Carolina, 1922. 15, [1] p.
Ship's Log and Other Poems. New York: A. A. Knopf, 1924. viii p., 2 ℓ., 13-143 p.
Flying Fish; A Book of Songs and Sonnets. New York & London: A. A. Knopf, 1926. 111, [1] p.
Witch and Other Poems. New York: A. A. Knopf, 1929. x, 84 p., 1 ℓ.
Rose Rhymes from a Child's Garden in Mexico. Northampton, MA.?: n.p., 192-? [8] p.

CONKLING, HILDA (1910-)
Poems by a Little Girl. New York: Frederick A. Stokes Company, 1920. xxiv, 120 p.
_______. London and Sidney: G. G. Harrap & Co., Ltd., 1920. xxii, 119, [1] p.
_______. New York: Frederick A. Stokes Company, 1921. xxiv, 120 p. "This edition containing the author's autograph is limited to 365 copies."
_______. New York: Frederick A. Stokes Company, 1924. 120 p.
Shoes of the Wind: A Book of Poems. New York: Frederick A. Stokes Company, 1922. xiii, 170 p.
_______. London: Harrap, 1923. xiii, 170 p.
Silverhorn, The Hilda Conkling Book for Other Children. New York: Frederick A. Stokes Company, 1924. xii p., 1 ℓ., 159 p.

CONNELL, CATHERINE (1908-) [Full Name: Catherine May Connell.]

Vagaries in Verse. Boston: Bruce Humphries, 1952. 61 p.

CONNER, ADELINE MERRIAM
Old Trails and New. Sacramento, CA.: Western Building Review, 1939. 3 p. ℓ., 11-75 p.

CONNER, MARY
Songs of a Smoky City. New York: The Poets Press, 1956. 4 p. ℓ., 7-54 p.

CONNOP, FELIX, pseud. see GEISSE, MARY A.

CONNOR, ELIZABETH H.
Poems of Peace and War. Haverhill, MA.: The Record Press, 1917. [55] p.
Poems. Boston: The Cornhill Publishing Company, 1923. 4 p. ℓ., 3-45 p.

CONNOR, MARY JOSEPH (1874-)
Soul-Voices. New York: Broadway Publishing Co., 1906. 4 p. ℓ., 35 p.

CONTESSA DOROTEA de SAUTEIRON de ST. CLEMENT see de ST. CLEMENT, DOROTHY (BERRY)

CONVERSE, CAROLINE (LANGMAN) (1878-)
Lantern in the Prairie. Dallas, TX.: The Story Book Press, 1954. 71 p.

CONVERSE, FLORENCE (1871-)
The Happy Swan. Wellesley, MA.: The Merrythought Press, 1924. [8] p. (Wellesley poems, no. 2)
Efficiency Expert. A Poem. New York: The John Day Company, 1934. 172 p., 1 ℓ.
...Collected Poems of Florence Converse. New York: E. P. Dutton & Co., Inc., 1937. 223, [1] p.
Prologue to Peace: The Poems of Two Wars. Wellesley, MA.: Hathaway House Bookshop, 1949. 52 p.

CONWAY, KATHERINE ELEANOR (1853-1927)
The Color of Life. Boston: T. J. Flynn & Co., 1927. xii, 109 p.

COOK, ELISABETH
Rose on the Sand. Los Angeles: The Ward Ritchie Press, 1938. 39, [1] p.

COOK, ETHEL CASE
Tread Softly, A Book of Poems. New York: The Paebar Co., 1949. 51 p.

COOK, ETHEL (SUTTON) (1895-)
Fond Memories. Julare, CA.: n.p., 1961? [22] p.

All of These Things. Julare, CA.: n.p., 1965. 25 p.
Jonah. Julare, CA.: n.p., 196-? 8 p.
Memories Carry Me Back. Julare, CA.: n.p., 196-? 10 p.

COOK, JOSEPHINE MERWIN
Bandana Days. New York: Broadway Publishing Co., 1908. 3 p. ℓ., 21 p.

COOK, MYRA B. (1933-)
Chalkdust. Philadelphia: Dorrance, 1969. 46 p.

COOK, RAMONA (GRAHAM) see GRAHAM, RAMONA

COOKE, ELIZABETH THROCKMORTON
A Few Herbs and Apples. New York: Vantage Press, 1975. 72 p.

COOKE, MAGDALEN
Heart Pangs. New York: The Neale Publishing Co., 1917. vi, 7-44 p.

COOLBRITH, INA DONNA (1842-1928)
Songs from the Golden Gate. Boston & New York: Houghton, Mifflin and Company, 1907. vii, [1], 159 p. 3d impression.
Retrospect: in Los Angeles. San Francisco: Printed for E. Dawson by J. H. Nash, 1925. 2 ℓ.
Wings of Sunset. Boston & New York: Houghton Mifflin Co., 1929. xxxvii, [1], 214, [1] p.
Retrospect. "In Los Angeles." Los Angeles: Ampersand Press, 1930. 4 ℓ.

COOLEY, JULIA see ALTROCCHI, JULIA (COOLEY) (1893-)

COOLIDGE, HELEN ELIZABETH
Poems. Boston: R. G. Badger, 1907. 102 p.
Sweetly Solemn Thoughts. Milwaukee, WI.: The Young Churchman Company, 1911. x, 123 p.
With Unclipped Wings. Carmel-by-the-Sea, CA.: The Carmel Pine Cone Press, 1941. 4 p. ℓ., 51 p.

COOMBES, MARGIE BRANYON
Smoke Rings. Dallas, TX.: Mathis, Van Nort, 1947. 123 p.

COOPER, EDNA (POPPE) (1889-1918)
The Song of the Wind and Other Poems. Petaluma, CA.: Northern Crown Publishing Co., 1915. [18] p.
Songs from the Valley of the Moon. San Francisco: n.p., 1926. 61 p.

COOPER, INEZ
Miscellaneous Poems. Philadelphia: Dorrance, 1968. 47 p. (Contemporary poets of Dorrance, 688)

COOPER, JANE (MARVEL) (1924-)
The Weather of Six Mornings; Poems. New York: Macmillan, 1968. 53 p.
Calling Me from Sleep; New and Selected Poems, 1961-1973. Bronxville, N.Y.: Sarah Lawrence College, 1974. [32] p. (Essays from Sarah Lawrence faculty. v. 2, no. 2)
Maps and Windows. New York: Macmillan, 1974. x, 80 p.

COOPER, LENORE
Beside the Open Door. Denver, CO.: Big Mountain Press, 1956. 39 p.

COOPER, LUCY PARHAM
...A Nightingale Singing. Philadelphia: Dorrance, 1949. vii, 71 p. (Contemporary poets of Dorrance, 378)

CORBETT, OPAL HAUSER
From Dawn to Dusk. New York: Vantage Press, 1959. 60 p.

CORBIN, ALICE see HENDERSON, ALICE (CORBIN) (1881-1949)

CORBIN, ROSE
Poems. Sullivan? IL.: n.p., 1907. 83 p.

CORDES, AMANDA
Memory, and Other Poems. Richmond, VA.: Richmond Press, Inc., 1926. 78 p.

CORE, MARY ELIZABETH (1874-)
Poems. Denver, CO.: Big Mountain Press, 1954. 52 p.

CORLIES, MARGARET LONGSTREBLE (1867-)
The Old Schloss. Philadelphia: J. C. Winston, 1906. 22 ℓ.

CORNELIUS, HELEN (1892-1933)
In Tract of Time: Poems. New York: Oxford University Press, 1936. xii, 75 p.

CORNELL, ANNETTE (PATTON)
The Forbidden Woman. Cincinnati, OH.: Talaria Publication, 1939. 55 p.

CORNELL, GLADYS MYERS
Bemused by Mews. Chicago: Windfall Press, 1964. 64 p.

CORRIGAN, HELEN FRANCES
Dream Dresses. Milwaukee, WI.: Marquette University Press, 1931. x p., 1 ℓ., 13-48 p.

CORRY, EUDORA VIRGINIA (SWASEY) (1870-)
Wayfarers. Boston: Sherman, French & Co., 1914. 4 p. ℓ., 92 p.

CORTEZ, JAYNE
Pisstained Stairs and the Monkey Man's Wares. New York?: Phrase Text, 1969. 52 p.
Festivals and Funerals. New York: Bola Press, 1971. [41] p.
Scarifications. New York: Bola Press, 1973. 61 p.

COSGRAVE, CATHERINE (CAFFEY)
Sand in My Shoes. Dallas, TX.: Mathis, Van Nort & Company, 1945. 5 p. ℓ., 47 p.

COTTON, ETHEL
When the Waves Dash High, and Other Poems. San Francisco: Press of Chase & Rae, 1918. [28] p.
Down Lyric Lanes. San Francisco: Harr Wagner Publishing Co., 1922. 43 p.

COUGHLIN, ANNA EMMA
Knots of Straw, and Other Verses. Portland, ME.: The Mosher Press, 1926. vii, [1] 84 p., 2 ℓ.
Shore Neighbors; A Book of Verses. Brooklyn, N.Y.: The Comet Press, 1936. 3 p. ℓ., 9-103, [1] p.
Master Mariner, and Other Poems. Portland, ME.: Printed by the Southworth-Anthoensen Press, 1944. viii, 70 p.

COUGHLIN, ROSE MARGARET
Another Year, and Other Catholic Poems. New York: Vantage Press, 1953. iv, 90 p.

COULSON, LOUISE (NEIGHBOR) (1847-)
Poetic Gems to the World I Love. Rahway, N.J.: Quinn & Boden Co., Press, 1912. xii, 175 p.

COURCIER, HELEN (1918-)
Poems for a Lonely Evening. Philadelphia: Dorrance, 1967. 4 p. ℓ., 79 p. (Contemporary poets of Dorrance, 669)
November Burning. Reseda, CA.: Mojave Books, 1974.

COURTNEY, GRETCHEN LEWIS
My Garden of Verse. Richmond, VA.: G. C. Courtney, 1922. 42 p.
Encore. Richmond, VA.: The Hillcourt Press, 1925. 87 p.

COURTNEY, NELLIE
Whirling Thoughts: A Book of Poems. Havana, Cuba: H. E. Swan, 1918. 168 p.
_______. New Orleans: Hauser Printing Company, 1918. 168 p.

COURTNEY, PAULINE
Under the Green Helm. La Porte, IN.: Dierkes Press, 1947. 27 p.
Twelve Moons, A Book of Poetry. New York: Exposition Press, 1953. 95 p.

COWAN, MARY IDA
The Sea of Lillies, and Other Poems. Philadelphia: Dorrance and Company, 1928. 58 p. (Contemporary poets of Dorrance, 64)

COWAN, SADA
Star-Glint. New York: Published for the author by Brentano's, 1925. viii p., 1 ℓ., 33 p.

COWDERY, MAE V.
We Lift Our Voices and Other Poems. Philadelphia: Alpress, 1936. 68 p.

COX, ELEANOR ROGERS (d. 1931)
A Hosting of Heroes and Other Poems. Dublin: Sealy, Bryers, & Walker, 1911. viii p., 1 ℓ., 60 p.
Singing Fires of Erin. New York: John Lane Company, 1916. 112 p.

COX, ETHEL LOUISE
Poems, Lyric and Dramatic. Boston: R. G. Badger, 1904. vi, 195 p.
Julian and Other Poems, Lyric and Dramatic. Boston: R. G. Badger, 1925. 232 p.

COXON, ROSE (1879-)
The Silver Butterflies and Other Poems. New York: Hobson Book Press, 1947. 92 p.

COZBY, AMY PEARL
Songs of the Plains; A Volume of Short Poems. Long Beach, CA.: Press of F. C. Foote, 190-? 104 p.
The Bell of the Alamo and Other Texas Poems. San Antonio, TX.: San Antonio Print. Co., 1902. 32 p.

COZINE, HELEN GILBERT
Trees and Wayside Flowers. Chicago: N. Halfen, 1920. [38] p.

CRADY, KATE McALPIN
Free Steppin'. Dallas, TX.: Mathis, Van Nort & Co., 1938. 6 p. ℓ., 3-83 p.
Travelin' Shoes. Dallas, TX.: Mathis, Van Nort, 1948. 86 p.

CRAIG, ELLEN FRANCES
The Wonderful Spring and Other Poems. Morgantown, W.V.: Acme Publishing Co., 1903. 47 p.

CRAIG, MARJORIE
The Known Way. Francestown, N.H.: Golden Quill Press, 1955. 80 p.

CRAIGHEAD, DOROTHY
Bits of Driftwood. Philadelphia: The John C. Winston Co., 1928. 45 p.

CRAM, DOROTHY M. (1905-)
Small Gleanings. Portland, ME.: A. Dirigo Edition, 1949. 40 p.

CRAMER, NELLY RUTH (1866-)
Poems for You and You. New York: William-Frederick Press, 1951. 58 p. (The William-Frederick poets, 82)

CRAMER, RUTH
And All My Life. Portland, ME.: The Mosher Press, 1928. 5 p. ℓ., 3-37, [1] p., 1 ℓ.

CRANDALL, ELEANOR
While Enemies Conspire. North Montpelier, VT.: The Driftwind Press, 1946. 37 p.

CRANDALL, ROSA RUTH (NEIL) (1865-)
Poems. Jamestown, N.Y.: Jamestown Publishing Co., 1907. 63, [1] p.

CRANE, ELIZABETH GREEN
Sylva: Poems. New York: A. D. F. Randolph Co., 1900. 2 p. ℓ., viii, 90 p.
Poems. New York: New York Poetry Book Shop, 1920. 38 p.

CRANE, NATHALIA-CLARA RUTH ABARBANEL (1913-)
The Janitor's Boy, and Other Poems. New York: T. Seltzer, 1924. xix p., 1 ℓ., 28-82 p.
Lava Lane, and Other Poems. New York: T. Seltzer, 1925. viii, 7 ℓ., 68 p.
The Singing Crow and Other Poems. New York: A. & C. Boni, 1926. 85 p.
Venus Invisible, and Other Poems. New York: Coward-McCann, Inc., 1928. 7 p. ℓ., 11-90 p.
Pocahontas. New York: E. P. Dutton & Co., Inc., 1930. 103 p.
The Janitor's Boy. New York: T. Seltzer, 1934. 82 p.
Swear by the Night and Other Poems. New York: Random House, 1936. 59 p.

CRAPSEY, ADELAIDE (1878-1914)
Verse. Rochester, N.Y.: The Manas Press, 1915. 1 p. ℓ., 5-95 p.
Verse. New York: A. A. Knopf, 1922. 107 p.
Verse. new ed. New York: A. A. Knopf, 1934. 10 p. ℓ., 19-132 p., 1 ℓ.

CRARY, FRANCES E.
All Without Protest and Other Poems. San Francisco: Double-H Press, 1966. 1 p. ℓ., 21, [1] p.
Revival. San Francisco?: Double-H Press? 1966. 1 p. ℓ., 24 p.
Temples of Sun; Collected Poems. Ukian, CA.: Panpipes Press, 1968. 53, 2 p. "Limited edition."

CRARY, RUTH [CLOUGH, RUTH (CRARY)]
Forty Shillings. Prairie City, IL.: The Press of J. A. Decker, 1945. 94 p.
Legends from Ancient China. Mill Valley, CA.: Wings Press, 1952. 63 p.

CRAWFORD, AMY P.
Flower Secrets in Rhyme. Boston: The Christopher Publishing House, 1941. 62 p.

CRAWFORD, ANNIE C.
Songs from Dixie. Columbus, GA.: Gilbert Printing Co., 1927. 65 p.

CRAWFORD, MAUDE SPARKS
Kentucky Poems and Others. Newport, KY.: n.p., 1942. [32] p.

CRAWFORD, PAULINE MARGUERITE (AVERY)
Sonnets from a Hospital. Boston: Bruce Humphries, Inc., 1936. 79, [1] p.

CREGLOW, MARY ELIZABETH (RODHOUSE)
The Fairy Phlox and Other Verses. Boston: R. G. Badger, 1931. 61 p.

CREVELING, CLARA BRADWAY
Interludes. Philadelphia: The John C. Winston Co., 1913. 89 p.

CREVER, ANNA ROZILLA (1866-)
Variant Voices. San Francisco: Harr Wagner Publishing Co., 1925. x p., 1 ℓ., 80 p.

CREWE, HELEN COALE
Aegean Echoes, and Other Verses. Boston: Poet Lore, 1910. 80 p.
________. Boston: Badger, 1911. 80 p.

CRISP, LUCY CHERRY
Brief Testament. North Montpelier, VT.: Driftwind Press, 1947. 114 p.

CRISS, MILDRED (1890-) [McGUCKIN, MILDRED CRISS]
In the Name of Love. New York: The Knickerbocker Press, 1917. vii, 94 p.
...Wind Flower. Boston: R. G. Badger, 1922. 39 p.

CRISWELL, JULIA
Wind and Waters. Denver, CO.: Smith-Brooks Press, 1936. 92 p.
Home Land. Longmont, CO.: Longmont Ledger Press, 1939. 3 p. ℓ., 98 p.

CROKER, MARIA BRISCOE
Vision and Verity. Baltimore, MD.: The Norman Remington Co., 1926. 6 p. ℓ., 3-61 p.

CROMER, DOROTHY GIRD
Ten O'Clock in Kitchen. Los Angeles, CA.: Wetzel Publishing Co., 1935. 71 p.

CROMWELL, GLADYS (1885-1919)
The Gates of Utterance, and Other Poems. Boston: Sherman, French, & Co., 1915. 4 p. ℓ., 40 p.
Poems. New York: The Macmillan Co., 1919. x, 12 p.

CROSBY, CARESSE (1892-1970)
Crosses of Gold, A Book of Verse. Paris: n. p., 1925. 93 p.
Crosses of Gold. Nouv. ed. Augm. Paris: A. Messein, 1925. 4 p. ℓ., iii, 69, [1] p.
Graven Images. Boston & New York: Houghton Mifflin Co., 1926. ix, 101, [1] p.
Painted Shores. Paris: Editions Narcisse, 1927. [51] p.
The Stranger. Paris: Editions Narcisse, 1927. [21] p.
Impossible Melodies. Paris: Editions Narcisse, 1928. 5 p. ℓ., 38 p., 2 ℓ.
Poems for Harry Crosby. Paris: Black Sun Press, 1931. vii p., 28 ℓ.

CROSBY, ELIZABETH MAE
Along the Bypaths. 2d ed. Boston: R. G. Badger, 1925. 174 p.
Here and There. Lynn, MA.: Printed by Nichols-Ellis Press, 1931. 64 p.
A Thought or Two; in Rhymes and Sonnets. n. p., 1936.

CROSNOE, THELMA (SLAYDEN)
Afterglow; Poems. New York: Exposition Press, 1957. 64 p.

CROSS, KATHRYN
Heights and Depths. Boston: R. G. Badger, 1927. 93 p.

CROSSER, NORA BADGER
Poems. Baltimore, MD.: Day Printing Co., 1929. 5 p. ℓ., 3-144 p.

CROSSMAN, GERTRUDE COUCH
Sharply Remembered. Portland, ME.: Falmouth Book House, 1937. 3 p. ℓ., 31, [1] p.
Change at Jamaica. Portland, ME.: Falmouth Publishing House, 1939. 4 p. ℓ., 3-43 p.

CROTHERS, ELIZABETH (MILLS) (1882-1920)
The Ascent & Other Poems. San Francisco, CA.: Sunset Press, 1921. [51] p.

CROUDACE, LENORE

The Misty Day. San Francisco: J. R. La Fontaine, 1907. 91 p.

The Opening Vista, and Other Poems. San Francisco: The Pacific Goldsmith, 1907. 122 p.

The Burning Gauze, and Other Poems. San Francisco: J. R. La Fontaine, 1910. 233 p.

Poems of Destiny. San Francisco: Norton Printing Co., Inc., 1931. 68 p.

CROWDER, LAURA

And Life Is Sweet. Dallas, TX.: Mathis, Van Nort, 1952. 56 p.

CROWELL, GRACE (NOLL) (1877-)

White Fire. Forth Worth, TX.: n.p., 1925. 3 p. ℓ., 11-93 p.

Silver in the Sun. Dallas, TX.: P. L. Turner Company, 1928. viii, 77 p.

Miss Humpety Comes to Tea and Other Poems. Dallas, TX.: The Southwest Press, 1929. 119 p.

Flame in the Wind. Dallas, TX.: The Southwest Press, 1930. ix, 105 p.

Songs for Courage. Dallas, TX.: The Southwest Press, 1930. viii, 32 p.

Flame in the Wind. Rev. ed. Dallas, TX.: Turner, 1934. 84 p.

Silver in the Sun. Rev. ed. Dallas, TX.: P. L. Turner Co., 1934. 88 p.

White Fire. Rev. ed. Dallas, TX.: P. L. Turner Co., 1934. 88 p.

_______. New York: Harper, 1934. x, 88 p.

Bright Destiny; A Book of Texas Verse. Dallas, TX.: Turner Co., 1936. vi, 41 p.

Light of the Years. New York & London: Harper and Brothers, 1936. xii p., 1 ℓ., 55, [1] p.

This Golden Summit. New York & London: Harper & Brothers, 1937. ix p., 2 ℓ., 79 p., 1 ℓ.

Songs for Courage. New York & London: Harper & Brothers, 1938. 42 p., 1 ℓ.

Songs of Hope. New York & London: Harper & Brothers, 1938. 50 p., 1 ℓ.

White Fire. New York and London: Harper & Brothers, 1938. x, 88 p.

Songs of Faith. New York & London: Harper & Brothers, 1939. 50 p., 1 ℓ.

The Radiant Quest. New York & London: Harper & Brothers, 1940. xiv p., 1 ℓ., 94 p., 1 ℓ.

Splendor Ahead. New York & London: Harper & Brothers, 1940. x p., 52 p.

Facing the Stars. New York & London: Harper & Brothers, 1941. viii p., 1 ℓ., 53, [1] p.

The Lifted Lamp. New York & London: Harper & Brothers, 1942. 3 p. ℓ., ix-x, 55, [1] p.

Some Brighter Dawn. New York & London: Harper & Brothers,

1943. viii, 56 p.
Between Eternities. New York & London: Harper & Brothers, 1944. viii, 56 p.
The Wind-Swept Harp. New York & London: Harper & Brothers, 1946. xiii p., 1 ℓ., 76 p., 1 ℓ.
Songs for Comfort. New York: Harper, 1947. 46 p.
The Crystal Fountain. New York: Harper, 1948. 84 p.
Apples of Gold. New York: Harper, 1950. 90 p.
A Child Kneels to Pray. Minneapolis, MN.: Augsburg Publishing House, 1950. 33 p.
The Wind-Swept Harp. New York & London: Harper & Brothers, 1950. xiii p., 1 ℓ., 76 p., 1 ℓ.
Bright Harvest. New York: Harper, 1952. 87 p.
Journey into Dawn. New York: Harper, 1955. 80 p.
Come See a Man. New York: Abingdon Press, 1956. 125, [2] p.
Songs of Triumph. New York: Harper, 1959. 52 p.
Poems of Inspiration and Courage; The Best Verse of Grace Noll Crowell. New York: Harper & Row, 1965. x, 214 p.
Let the Sun Shine In. Old Tappan, N.J.: F. H. Revell Co., 1970. 128 p.

CROWELL, RHODA M.
The Soul's Evolution. New York: Vantage Press, 1953. 60 p.

CROXTON, IRENE COLE
Book of Golden Thought. Detroit: Myrtle Printing Co., 1925. 83 p., 1 ℓ.

CROY, RUTH JANE
My Song of Life and Other Poems. Hicksville, N.Y.: Exposition Press, 1975. 136 p.

CROZIER, ADA B.
The Hush of Hills. Indianapolis, IN.: Levey Printing Company, 1934. 75 p.

CRUM, ELIZA (TILDEN) (1832-)
Nature, and Other Verse. Oberlin, OH.: E. J. Goodrich, 1909. 2 p.ℓ., iv p., 1 ℓ., 7-115 p.

CRUMPTON, BEATRICE
The Princess Papers, and Poems. Chicago: Scroll Publishing Co., 1901. 60 p., 1 ℓ.

CULBRETH, EDNA V.
Secretarily Yours, Cullie. New York: Exposition Press, 1951. 171 p.

CULLER, JULIA BELLE
Sunlight and Shadows.... New York: The Caravan Publishing Co., 1944. 63 p.

CULP, PAULA (1941-)
A Thousand Portholes. Minneapolis, MN.: Pacul Publications, 1973. 95 p.

CUMMING, MARION
Let's Make the Most of It; A Volume of Verse. San Francisco?: n. p., 1948. 36 p.

CUMMING, PATRICIA
Afterwards. Cambridge, MA.: Alice James Books, 1974. 63 p.

CUMMINGS, CYNTHIA HOLT
Into the World. Philadelphia: Dorrance, 1969. 50 p.

CUMMINS, MARY FRANCESE
Rhymes of a Lifetime. Chicago: Private printing, 1907. 155 p.

CUMMINS, VIRGINIA KENT
On Wind of Chance. New York & London: G. P. Putnam's Sons, 1931. xv, 189 p.
Pierre; or, A Parisian and a Puritan. New York: Brentano, 1949. 175 p.

CUNNINGHAM, ALICE HATHAWAY
Book of Verses. New York: Cochrane Publishing Co., 1910. 16 p.

CUNNINGHAM, MARY MOFFAT
Verses. New York: Bonnell, Silver & Co., 1908. 99 p.

CUNNINGHAM, WANDA G.
In a Spasm of Enthusiasm! Francestown, N. H.: Golden Quill Press, 1964. 80 p.

CURLEY, FRANCES W. (1906-)
Fragments of Fancy. New York: The Poets Press, 1939. 79 p.

CURRIER, ADELLA LOVEJOY
Clover Bloom. Lincoln, NB.: The Woodruff Press, 1914. 74 p.
Candle Light. Lincoln, NB.: The Woodruff Press, 1928. 129 p.

CURRIER, MARY MEHETABEL
A Few Songs. Concord, N. H.: Rumford Printing Co., 1905. vii, 93 p.
Songs to One Silent. Franklin Falls, N. H.: The Journal-Transcript Press, 1905. 2 p. ℓ., 5-24 p.

CURRIN, RUBY WILLIAMS
The Evening and the Morning. Dallas, TX.: Royal Pub. Co., 1960. 100 p.

CURRY, MARY C. (1867-)
Poems. New York: Exposition Press, 1950. 86 p.

CURRY, MARY EARLE LOWRY (1917-)
Looking Up! New York: Paebar Co., 1949. 102 p.
Looking Within. Philadelphia: Dorrance, 1961. viii, 88 p. (Contemporary poets of Dorrance, 531)

CURRY, PEGGY (SIMSON) (1911-)
Red Wind of Wyoming. Denver, CO.: Sage Books, 1955. 64 p.

CURTIS, CAROL (1950-)
Where Do You Keep Your Heart? Philadelphia: Dorrance, 1975. 51 p. (Contemporary poets of Dorrance)

CURTIS, CHRISTINE TURNER
Narrow Keyboard, A Poem. New York: William-Frederick Press, 1951. 39 p.
Fragile Lineage. Mount Vernon, N.Y.: Printed at the Peter Pauper Press, 1955. 62 p.
Passport to Autumn, and Other Poems. New York: Exposition Press, 1961. 55 p.

CURTIS, ELIZABETH
Equinox. New York: H. Vinal, 1925. 3 p.ℓ., 34 p.

CURTISS, JOSIE DAYTON
Rays of Thought. Elgin, IL.: Brethren Publishing House, 1907. ix, 2 ℓ., 15-159 p.

CUTHBERT, MARION VERA (1896-)
April Grasses. New York: The Womans Press, 1936. 3 p.ℓ., 30 p.
Songs of Creation. New York: Woman's Press, 1949. 46 p.

CUTHRELL, FAITH (BALDWIN) (1893-)
Sign Posts. Boston: Small, Maynard & Co., 1924. xii, 119 p.
Widow's Walk: Variations on a Theme. New York: Rinehart, 1954. ix, 84 p.

CUTLER, MAUD EMETT
River Rhymes and Rhymes Betimes. New York: Dean & Co., 1928. 88 p.

DABEY, BETTY PAGE (1911-)
The Ancient Bond. Richmond, VA.: Dietz Press, 1954. 6 p.ℓ., 47 p.

DABNEY, JULIA PARKER (1850-)
The Primal Poet. Boston, MA.: The Vedanta Centre, 192-? 17 p.
________. Brookline, MA.: n.p., 1923. 13 p.
Echoes from India. Cedar Rapids, IA.: The Torch Press, 1925. 90 p.

DAFFAH, KATIE
As Thinketh a Woman. Houston, TX.: Southwest Publishing Company, Printers, 1912. 5 p. ℓ., [15]-95 p.

DAHLEN, BEVERLY
Out of the Third. San Francisco: Momo's Press, 1974. 52 p.

DAKIN, EMMA SAHLER
... Figure and Landscape. New York: The Fine Editions Press, 1946. 6 p. ℓ., 15-32 p.

DALLIBA, GERDA (1885-1913)
Fate and I, and Other Poems. New York: The Grafton Press, 1902. 81 p.
An Earth Poem, and Other Poems. New York & London: G. P. Putnam's Sons, 1908. xiv p., 1 ℓ., 323 p.
Poems. New York: Duffield & Co., 1921. 3 p. ℓ., v-xiii, 119 p.
________. London: Ingpen, 1929. 156 p.
Poems: Second Series. London: Ingpen, 1933. 144 p.
Last Poems. London: Ingpen & Grant, 1935. xiv, 230 p.

DALTON, MINNIE M. (1894-)
The Sidewalks of Life. New York: Vantage Press, 1968. 79 p.
Heaven and Earth; Poems. New York: Exposition Press, 1969. 136 p.
Bread on the Waters; Poems. New York: Exposition Press, 1971. 192 p.
Crumbs of Comfort. New York: Exposition Press, 1973. 137 p.
Homeward Bound. Jericho, N.Y.: Exposition Press, 1974. 255 p.
Pegs of Love. Radford, VA.: Commonwealth Press, 1975. vi, 119 p.

DALY, EDITH
The Angel in the Sun. San Jose, CA.: The Pacific Short Story Club, 1917. 58 p.
The Golden Dome. Dallas, TX.: Turner Co., 1936. ix, 90 p.
Silver-Twilight. San Jose, CA.: Printed by the Smith Printing Co., 1940. 93, [1] p., 2 ℓ.

DALY, EMMA RING (1883-)
Flowering Agates. Caldwell, ID.: The Caxton Printers, Ltd., 1938. 77 p.
Silver Moccasins. Mill Valley, CA.: Wings Press, 1955. 64 p.

D'AMBROSIO, VINNIE-MARIE (1928-)
Life of Touching Mouths. New York: New York University Press, 1971. 64 p. (Contemporaries)

DAME, HAZEL STEVENS
This Too-Brief Moment. Chicago: Dierkes Press, 1950. 48 p.

DAME, RUBY M.
Down the Walks of Life. Plattsburg, N.Y.: The Imperial Press, 1927. 67 p.

DAMON, FANNIE A.
In the Shadow of the Pines. Clinton, MA.: The W. J. Coulter Press, 1907. xii, 13-76 p.

DANA, SHIRLYE
For the Rest of My Life. Francestown, N. H.: Golden Quill Press, 1956. 44 p.

DANFORTH, ELIZABETH (HANLY)
In Rio on the Ouvidor, and Other Poems. Rio de Janeiro: Meier and Blumer, 1938. 3 p. ℓ., 55 p., 1 ℓ.
Firewood, and Other Verse. Portland, ME.: Falmouth Publishing House, 1950. 158 p.

DANIEL, MARY HELEN
My Gift; Poems. New York: Exposition Press, 1965. 102 p.

DANIELEWICZ, ROSA
Rose Petals.... Oakland, CA.: n. p., 1911. 161 p.
Logic and Love, Poems of Peace. Oakland, CA.: Triangle Printing Co., 1924. [42] p., 2 ℓ.

DANIELL, ROSEMARY (1935-)
A Sexual Tour of the Deep South. New York: Holt, Rinehart & Winston, Inc., 1975. 97 p.

DANIELS, HILDA PETERSON
My Kitchen Sings; Poems. New York: Exposition Press, 1963. 56 p.

DANIELSON, EDYTHE IVEY
Along the Way.... Minneapolis, MN.: Argus Co., Inc., 1934. 40 p.

DANIELSON, RUTH WATTERS
Sand in My Shoes. New York: Exposition Press, 1955. 62 p., [1] p.
Rocking Chair Rhymes. Dallas, TX.: Triangle Pub. Co., 1957. 57 p.

DANNER, MARGARET ESSIE (1915-)
Impressions of African Art Forms in the Poetry of Margaret Danner. Detroit: Broadside Press, 1960. [19] p.
To Flower. n. p.: Hemphill Press, 1963. 30 p. (The Counterpoise Series, no. 4)
Iron Lace. New York: Designed by the Poet's Press, and printed at Kriya Press, Millbrook, N. Y., 1968. [32] p.

DANNER, SARA KOLB (1894-)
Gallery Tour. Stanford, CA.: Stanford University Press, 1952. 58 p.

DANYSH, LIBBY
Deny the Day. San Francisco, CA.: n. p., 1940. 3 p. ℓ., 5-24 p., 1 ℓ.

DARE, GLORIA
Out of the Mist. San Francisco, CA.: California Press, 1925. 2 p. ℓ., 146, [2] p.

DARE, VIOLA

Little Poems for Little Folks. Boston: The Stratford Co., 1930. 2 p. ℓ., 33 p.

DARGAN, OLIVE (TILFORD) (1869-1968)

Path, Flower and Other Verses. London: J. J. Dent & Sons; New York: Chas. Scribner's Sons, 1914. vi p., 1 ℓ., 119, [1] p.

The Cycle's Rim. New York: C. Scribner's Sons, 1916. 4 p. ℓ., 3-73 p.

Lute and Furrow. New York: Scribner's and Sons, 1922. viii, 140 p.

The Spotted Hawk. Winston-Salem, N. C.: J. F. Blair, 1958. 128 p.

DARLING, ESTHER (BIRDSALL) (d. 1965)

Up in Alaska. Sacramento, CA.: Jo Anderson Press, 1912. 4 p. ℓ., 11-59 p.

D'ARPAJON, NOEL (1922-)

Tankas. Philadelphia: Dorrance, 1948. 65 p. (Contemporary poets of Dorrance, 374)

DARR, ANN

St. Ann's Gut. New York: William Morrow and Co., 1971. 94 p.

The Myth of a Woman's Fist. New York: William Morrow and Co., 1973. 82 p.

DARROUGH, ROSE

White Thorn. Dallas, TX.: The Kaleidograph Press, 1938. 4 p. ℓ., xi-xii p., 1 ℓ., 15-49 p.

DARROW, ALICE JENNINGS

Threads in the Weave. Brunswick, ME.: Pejepscot Press, 1956. viii, 30 p.

DART, EDITH

Earth and Her Bars; and Other Poems. London: Longmans, Green & Co., 1915. 64 p.

DASHIELL, MARGARET MAY

Spanish Moss and English Myrtle. Boston: The Stratford Co., 1920. 3 p. ℓ., 46 p.

Richmond Reverie. Richmond, VA.: Dudley Printing Co., Inc., 1942. 4 p. ℓ., 39 p.

D'AURIA, GEMMA ABKAZOFF

High Noon. Prairie City, IL.: Decker Press, 1949. 85 p.

DAVENPORT, CHARLOTTE C. (SHEPHERD)

My Christmas Wish, and Other Rhythms. Boston: The Cornhill Publ. Co., 1922. 7-127 p.

DAVID, ELIZABETH (HARBISON)

A Book of Verses. New London, CT.: The Tudor Press, 1926. 74 p.

DAVID, JUNE CLEELAND
Thoughts in Verse and Rhyme. Berkeley? CA.: n.p., 1948. 53 p.

DAVIDMAN, JOY
Letter to a Comrade. New Haven, CT.: Yale University Press, 1938. 94 p., 1 ℓ. (Yale Series of Younger Poets, v. 37)

DAVIDSON, BONNIE J.
Heartbeats of Our Time. New York: Exposition Press, 1961. 47 p.

DAVIDSON, FLORENCE ROSE (1907-1955)
Rose Petals. La Crescenta, CA.: n.p., 1956. 78 p.

DAVIDSON, ROSE
The Year's Holidays in Verse. New York: n.p., 1904. 36 p.
Songs of Living. Dallas, TX.: The Kaleidograph Press, 1938. 85 p.
Breeze over Texas. Dallas, TX.: The Kaleidograph Press, 1940. x p., 1 ℓ., 13-85 p.

DAVIDSON, YVONNE ROBESON (1916-)
Heart Talk. Los Angeles: W. Ritchie Press, 1949. 48 p.

DAVIES, ADA HILTON (1893-)
Signature. Francestown, N.H.: Golden Quill Press, 1964. 64 p.

DAVIES, GENEVA (1905-)
Whence the Wind. Emory University, GA.: Banner Press, 1952. 63 p. (Verse craft series)
Songs of Valor: Civil War Poems, 1863-65. n.p., 1964. 15 p.
Softly on the Christmas Air. Decatur, GA.: n.p., 1965. 31 p.

DAVIES, LAURA VICTORIA (1865-)
Davies Poems. Minneapolis, MN.: Printed by the Syndicate Printing Co., 1912. 99 p.
Victory Edition of Davies Poems. Great Falls, MT.: n.p., 1919.
... Gold Star Edition of Davies Poems. Duluth, MN.: n.p., 1922.
Picturesque Montana. Great Falls, MT.: Equity Print Shop, 1917. [13] p.

DAVIES, MARY CAROLYN
The Drums in Our Street; A Book of War Poems. New York: Macmillan, 1918. xi, 131 p.
... Songs.... Berkeley, CA.: University of California Press, 1913.
A Little Freckled Person; A Book of Child Verse. Boston & New York: Houghton Mifflin Company, 1919. 3 p.ℓ., 104 p., 1 ℓ.
Youth Riding; Lyrics. New York: The Macmillan Company, 1919. 5 p.ℓ., 3-179 p.
Outdoors and Us. Philadelphia: The Penn Publishing Co., 1922. 70 p.
Marriage Songs. Boston: H. Vinal, 1923. 3 p.ℓ., 16 p.
The Skyline Trail; A Book of Western Verse. Indianapolis: The Bobbs-Merrill Company, 1924. 6 p.ℓ., 15-159 p.

Penny Show. New York: H. Harrison, 1927. 95, [1] p.
White Parachutes and Other Poems. New York: Board of Education, W. P. A., New Reading Materials Program, 1937. 31 p.
Pirate, and Other Poems. New York: Board of Education of the City of New York. Published for the New Reading Materials Program. Federal Works Agency. W. P. A. for the City of New York, 1940? 30 p.

DAVIS, CAROL BEERY
Alaska Driftwood. Denver, CO.: Big Mountain Press, 1953. 80 p.
Home Is North. Francestown, N. H.: Golden Quill Press, 1974. 68 p.

DAVIS, CHERYL
Imani. Madison, WI.: By the Author, 1969?

DAVIS, CORINNE EASTMAN
Selected Poems. Vermont?: n. p., 1951. 44 p.

DAVIS, EDITH ELLA
Echoes from the Temple. New York: Bloch Publishing Co., Inc., 1926. viii, 64 p.

DAVIS, ELIZABETH STOUT
Excuse for Singing. Philadelphia: Dorrance, 1951. 40 p.

DAVIS, ERCELLE O'BRIEN
I March to My Own Drum. Francestown, N. H.: M. Jones Co., 1953. 64 p.

DAVIS, ESTHER EUGENIA
Smouldering Dusk. Boston: R. G. Badger, 1928. 72 p.

DAVIS, FANNIE STEARNS see GIFFORD FANNIE STEARNS (DAVIS) (1884-)

DAVIS, FLORENCE
A Little Book of Verse. New York: n. p., 1908. 31 p.

DAVIS, FLORENCE (BOYCE) (1873-1938)
Selected Ballads and Poems. Burlington, VT.: Free Press Printing Co., 1946. 77 p.

DAVIS, HELEN BAYLEY
Moth-Wings. Baltimore, MD.: O'Donovan Callis & Co., 1929. 3 p. ℓ., [1]-56 p.
I Shall Sing a Song. Baltimore, MD.: J. J. O'Donovan, 1936. 58 p.
They That Dwell Therein. Baltimore, MD.: J. H. Furst Co., 1943. xii, 73 p.
Tomorrow Is Here. Chicago: Dierkes Press, 1950. 48 p.

DAVIS, HILDA PAULINE
Love Me, Love My Thoughts. New York: Exposition Press, 1946. 63 p.

DAVIS, JULIA JOHNSON
The Garnet Ring. New York: Fine Editions Press, 1951. 104 p.

DAVIS, MARALEE G. (1924-)
Soliloquy's Virgin, Poems. Francestown, N. H.: Golden Quill Press, 1964. 5 p. ℓ., 68 p.
The Valley of Self. Norfolk, MA.: NBS Co. Pub. Services Division, 1969. vii, 72 p.

DAVIS, MARY ANNE
From My Window. Siloam Springs, AR.: Bar D. Press, 1939. 4 p. ℓ., 11-61 p.

DAVIS, RONDA MARIE
The Elizabeth Series. n. p.: Doron Innerprizes, 1972.

DAVIS, RUTH RUSSELL
The Questing Self. Detroit: Alved of Detroit, 1948. 54 p.
South of Market, and Other Poems. New York: Exposition Press, 1951. 64 p.
Traitor Spring. Birmingham, MI.: Silverado Press, 1951. 1 p. ℓ., 4 f., 1 ℓ.
Auction in Manassas, A Poem. New York: Exposition Press, 1953. 136 p.
Opening Stanzas of Chiarra. Bloomfield Hills, MI.: Silverado Press, 1954. 6 ℓ.
Chiara. Denver: A. Swallow, 1957. 42 p. (Big mountain book)
A Saint in Being. Denver: Big Mountain Press, 1961. 109 p.

DAVIS, UDOLPHIA
Leisure Hours; A Book of Short Poems on Nature. Hornellsville, N. Y.: The Author, 1903. 43, [1] p.

DAVISON, LOIS ANNE
Ask of the Eagle. Lewisburg, PA.: Bucknell University Press, 1954. 46 p.

DAW, BEATRICE [Full Name: Elizabeth Beatrice Daw.]
Songs of Inexperience. Boston: The Gorham Press, 1916. 32 p.

DAWES, LENORE
I Reached for a Star, Poems. New York: Exposition Press, 1951. 63 p.

DAWSON, EMMA FRANCES (d. 1926)
Ballade of Liberty, and Other Patriotic Verses. Palo Alto, CA.: Stanford Univ., CA.: Stanford University Press, 1917. 14 p.

DAWSON, MARIE HUNTER
Candle-Flame. Manchester, ME.: Falmouth Pub. House, 1952. 4 p. ℓ., 96 p.

DAY, EDITH SHINER (1887-)
Silver Linings. Dallas, TX.: Story Book Press, 1954. 49 p.

DAY, GWYNN McLENDON (1908-)
God Lit a Candle; A Volume of Religious Verse. New York: Exposition Press, 1951. 95 p.

DAY, KATHERINE HUNTINGTON
Pictures from the Past. Indianapolis, IN.: Rough Notes Press, 1922. 96 p.

DAY, LENA HALL
...The Clearer View. Philadelphia: Dorrance & Co., 1945. 51 p. (Contemporary poets of Dorrance, 306)
...Signal Light, and Other Poems. Philadelphia: Dorrance & Co., 1947. 4 p. ℓ., 7-57 p. (Contemporary poets of Dorrance, 353)

DAY, LUCIE GAGE
Miscellaneous Poems. Oregon City, OR.: Press of the Oregon City Enterprise, 1923. 64 p.

DAY, SARAH J. (1860-1940)
From Mayflowers to Mistletoe; A Year with the Flower Folk. New York & London: G. P. Putnam's Sons, 1900. vii, 95 p.
Fresh Fields and Legends Old and New. New York: n.p., 1909. ix, 178 p.
Mayflowers to Mistletoe; A Year with the Flower Folk. 2d ed. New York & London: G. P. Putnam's Sons, 1909. viii, 115 p.
Wayfares and Wings. New York & London: G. P. Putnam's Sons, 1924. ix, 103 p.

DAYTON, IRENE (1922-)
The Sixth Sense Quivers. Peterborough, N.H.: Windy Row Press, 1970. 78 p.
The Panther's Eye. Peterborough, N.H.: Windy Row Press, 1974. 80 p.

DEACON, ANGELINE HAWKINS
Childhood Days, and Other Poems. Los Angeles, CA.: n.p., 1918. 28 p.

DEAGON, ANN (1930-)
Carbon 14. Amherst, MA.: University of Massachusetts Press, 1974. 54 p.
Poetics South. Cambridge, MA.: John F. Blair, 1974. x, 54 p.

DEAN, AGNES LOUISE
Let Us Be Merry. New York: A. A. Knopf, 1941. xiii, 169, [1] p., 1 ℓ.
Songs for My Grandmother. Holyoke, MA.: Unity Press, Inc., 1945. 83, [1] p.
Devonshire Cream. Holyoke, MA.: Unity Press, 1950. 49 p.

DEAN, ELOISE EARLE
Christmas of Long Ago, and Other Poems. Atlanta, GA.: Index Printing Co., 1921. 32 p.
Evergreen Leaves. New York: A. M. Shields, 1942. 64 p.

DEAN, EVA
In Peanut Land. New York: I. Somerville & Co., 1907. [137] p.

DEASE, RUTH ROSEMAN
Scan-Spans. New York: Vantage Press, 1967. 79 p.

DE CAMP, HELEN ESTELLE
Apples of Sodom. Emory University, Atlanta, GA.: Banner Press, 1933. 48 p. (Verse craft series)

DE CHERKEZ, FLORENCE EUPHEMIA (1872-)
Driftwood, and Other Poems. Boston: R. G. Badger, 1910. 121 p.

DEERING, IVAH (EVERETT) (1889-)
Stormy Petrel. Philadelphia: Dorrance, 1949. 140 p. (Contemporary poets of Dorrance, 375)

DE FAZIO, MARJORIE
A Quiet Noise. New York: The Poets Press, 1972. 24 p.

de FORD, MIRIAM ALLEN (1888-)
Children of Sun. New York: The League of Support Poetry, 1939. [22] p.
Penultimates. New York: Fine Editions Press, 1962. 69 p.

DE FORD, SARA (WHITCRAFT) (1916-)
The Return to Eden. New York: H. Harrison, 1940. 31 p.
The City of Love: A Poem in Sonata Form. New York: Exposition Press, 1958. 59 p.

DE FOREST, JULIA (MORROW)
Belfry Chimes and Other Rimes. New York: Vantage Press, 1974. 64 p.

DE FREES, MADELINE (1919-) [MARY GILBERT, SISTER]
From the Darkroom. Indianapolis, IN.: Bobbs-Merrill, 1964. 64 p.

DE GOOD, JEANNE (1924-)
The Long Weight. St. Louis, MO.: State Pub. Co., 1955. 128 p.

DE GRAFF, MARIANNE
Lilies of Love. Boston: Meador Publishing Co., 1932. 42 p.
The Poets Log, In Reminiscence. Boston: Meador Publishing Co., 1932. 56 p.

DE GROOT, MARGARET DRAKE
Wanodah, and Other Poems. Boston: The Four Seas Company, 1923. 116 p.

DE HUARTE, HELEN (1907-)
Michaelmas Spring. Philadelphia: Dorrance, 1952. 48 p. (Contemporary poets of Dorrance, 438)

DE LAMARTER, JEANNE see BONNETTE, JEANNE DE LAMARTER (1907-)

DE LAZIER, BERTHA (VREELAND)
"Poems by Bertha De Lazier." Paterson, N.J.: Lont & Overkamp Pub. Co., 1940. 102 p.

DEL CASTILLO, MARY VIRGINIA (1865-)
The Runes of Virginia the Vala. Boston: The Christopher Publishing House, 1916. 44 p.

DE LEEUW, ADELE LOUISE (1899-)
Berries of the Bittersweet. Boston: B. J. Brimmer Company, 1924. 96 p.
...Life Invited Me. New York: H. Harrison, 1936. 63 p.

DELESDERNIER, MARIE LOUISE
These Things I Love. New York: Vantage Press, 1956. 62 p.

de LIESSELINE, ETHEL (McDONALD) (1888-)
My Dear Mother. Emory University, Atlanta, GA.: Banner Press, 1943. 62 p. (Verse craft series)
One Small Candle. Boston: Branden Press, 1969. 96 p.

DE LONGCHAMPS, JOANNE (LAURIE) (CUTTEN) (1923-)
And Ever Venus. West Los Angeles, CA.: Wagon & Star Publishers, 1944. 19 p. (Destiny editions)
Eden Under Glass. Francestown, N.H.: Golden Quill Press, 1957. 70 p.
The Hungry Lions. Bloomington, IN.: Indiana University Press, 1963. 60 p. (Indiana University poetry series, 25)
The Wishing Animal. Nashville, TN.: Vanderbilt University Press, 1970. 88 p.

DELPHINE, FREDA
I Promise You Tomorrow. Houston, TX.: Pacesetter Press,

dist. by Gulf Publishing Co., 1974. [98] p.

DELTWYN, AGNES (PROCTOR) (1854-)
Echoes from Shadow-Land. New York: The Alliance Publishing Co., 1900. 88 p.
Believest Thou This. Chicago: M. A. Donohue & Co., 1913. 117 p.

DE MENEZES, RUTH
Thunder in Spring. Dallas, TX.: The Kaleidograph Press, 1934. viii p., 1 ℓ., 11-62 p.

DEMING, ADELE CHESTER
Lyrics of Life. Boston: The Christopher Publishing House, 1916. 52, 1 p.

DENIS, ALBERTA JOHNSON
Questionings. Los Angeles, CA.: Times-Mirror Printing and Binding House, 1920. 17 p.

DENIS, HELEN B(ISCHOFF)
Gardens of Eden. New York: Fleming H. Revell Company, 1937. 2 p.ℓ., 7-178 p.

DENISON, GLADYS BROWN (1909-)
Smoke Around the Sun. New York: H. Harrison, 1938. 64 p.

DENNETT, MABEL (FREESE)
Some Day. Dallas, TX.: The Kaleidograph Press, 1945. xi p., 1 ℓ., 15-71 p.

DENNING, FRANCES KRAMER
Discovery, & Other Poems. Dallas, TX.: The Kaleidograph Press, 1946. viii p., 1 ℓ., 11-50 p.
Verbs and Seasons. San Antonio, TX.: Naylor Co., 1962. xii, 82 p.

DENNING, MARY MARGARET
Treasure Chest. New York: H. Harrison, 1938. 63 p.

DENNING, RUTH MILLER
...Song of the Okimow and Other Poems. New York: H. Harrison, 1941. 62 p.

DENNIS, ZELMA LAVERNE SWAIN (1921-)
Flamesong. California?: n.p., 1951. [20] p.

DENNY, ELEANOR M.
Earth Music. Kansas City, MO.: The Lowell Press, 1927. 64 p.

DENSMORE, FRANCES
Poems from Sioux and Chippewa Songs. Washington, D.C.: n.p., 1917. 23 p.

DE RAN, EDNA SMITH (1870-)
Verses by the Wayside. Boston: R. G. Badger, 1907. 133 p.
The Grief Shadow Between, and Other Poems. Kalamazoo, MI.: The Author, 1911. 2 p. ℓ., 3-153, [1] p.
The Heritage of Hope. Detroit, MI.: E. S. De Ran, 1918. 108 p.
The Dawn of Day. Detroit, MI.: The Author, 1919. 166 p.
Muted Melodies. Kalamazoo, MI.: Ihling Bros. Everard Co., 1926. 3 p. ℓ., 5-168 p.
Memories and Moods. Cleveland, OH.: Pegasus Studios, 1938. 67 p. (Torchbearers' chapbooks, no. 26)
Love's Legacy. Cleveland, OH.: Pegasus Studios, 1939. 24 p. (Torchbearers' chapbooks, no. 37)
Singing in the Sunset. Los Angeles, CA.: n.p., 1951. 91 p.

DE ST. CLEMENT, DOROTHY (BERRY) [LA CONTESSA DOROTEA de SAUTEIRON de ST. CLEMENT]
Prairies and Palaces. Philadelphia: Dorrance, 1963. 72 p. (Contemporary poets of Dorrance, 578)

DESHAIES, EMELDA
"Miscellaneous Moods." Washington, D.C.: Washington Journal Press, 1930. 71 p.

DE SHANDS, LOTTIE BELLE (WILLS)
Golden Gems of a New Civilization. New York: Exposition Press, 1955. 95 p.

DESHON, DOROTHY
All Things Great and Small. Boston: J. W. Luce Co., 1949. 1 ℓ., 9-64 p.

DEUTSCH, BABETTE (1895-)
Banners. New York: George H. Doran Co., 1919. x p., 1 ℓ., 13-104 p.
Honey Out of the Rock. New York, London: D. Appleton & Co., 1925. ix p., 2 ℓ., 3-129 p.
Fire for the Night. New York: J. Cape and H. Smith, 1930. vi p., 3 ℓ., 3-77 p.
Epistle to Prometheus. New York: J. Cape and H. Smith, 1931. 95 p.
One Part Love. New York: Oxford University Press, 1939. 4 p. ℓ., 11-86 p.
Take Them Stranger. New York: H. Holt and Co., 1944. 5 p. ℓ., 3-72 p.
Animal, Vegetable, Mineral. New York: Dutton, 1954. 59 p.
Coming of Age, New & Selected Poems. Bloomington, IN.: Indiana University Press, 1959. 160 p. (Indiana University poetry series, 17)
Collected Poems, 1919-1962. Bloomington, IN.: Indiana University Press, 1962. 182 p. (Indiana University poetry series, 26)
I Often Wish: Poems. New York: Funk & Wagnalls, 1966.

1 v. unpaged.
Collected Poems of Babette Deutsch. Garden City, N. Y.: Doubleday, 1969. xxii, 230 p.

DEUTSCH, HELEN
The White Magnolia Tree. New York: Frank Music Corp., 1957. [4] p.

DEVAMATA, SISTER
The Open Portal. La Crescenta, CA.: Ananda-Asrama, 1929. 120 p.
My Song-Garden; Child-Poems. La Crescenta, CA.: Ananda-Ashrana, 1930. 71 p.

DE VERE, MARY AINGE [BRIDGES, MADELINE, pseud.]
Wind-Swept Wheat: Poems. Boston: R. G. Badger, 1904. 95 p.
The Open Book, Humorous Verse. New York: Knickerbocker Press, 1915. viii, 120 p.

DEVLIN, JANE
Gypsy Lyrics. Chicago, IL.: Mueller Press, 1935. 1 p. ℓ., 61 p.

DEWEY, MILDRED NYE
Breakers Calling. Dexter, MO.: Candor Press, 1965. 73 p.

DICKASON, CAROLINE
...Outside Time. Los Angeles, CA.: The Green Horn Press, 1940. 3 p. ℓ., 20 numb. 1., 1 ℓ.

DICKERSON, MARILYN
Silver Ladder. San Antonio, TX.: Naylor Co., 1961. 58 p.

DICKEY, BESS
Steps of Youth. Philadelphia: Dorrance and Co., 1943. 89 p.

DICKINS, EDITH PRATT
The Port O'Dreams, and Other Poems. New York & London: G. P. Putnam's Sons, 1909. vii, 128 p.

DICKINSON, HELEN TRENHOLM
St. Michael's Chime, and Other Verses. Chicago: R. F. Seymour, 1906. 55, [1] p.

DICKINSON, HESTER
Songs En Route. Boston: Sherman, French & Co., 1911. 4 p. ℓ., 78 p.

DICKINSON, KATE LETITIA (1886-)
Flesh and Spirit. New York: H. Vinal, 1926. viii, 68 p.

DICKINSON, LAURA AUSTIN
Optimism and Other Poems.... Amherst, MA.: The Elms, 1929. 51 p.
Pen Pictures. Amherst, MA.: n.p., 1937. xiii, 83 p.

DICKINSON, MARY
Truths That Shine. New York: Fleming H. Revell, 1940. 63 p.

DICKSON, MARGARETTE BALL (1884-)
Tumbleweeds, Thirty-Four Poems. New York: H. Vinal, 1926. 6 p. ℓ., 3-49 p.
One Man and a Dream. Minneapolis, MN.: Argus Pub. Co., 1938? 72 p. (Minnesota poetry series)
A Son Enlists. Minneapolis, MN.: Argus Pub. Co., 1941. 27 p.
Fuel of One Flame. Rapid City, S.D.: Troyer Print. Co., 1956? 67 p.

DIEHL, LUCILLE MEYER
To Paint with Words. Philadelphia: Dorrance, 1964. 96 p. (Contemporary poets of Dorrance, 579)

DIEHNEL, ELLIE (TATUM)
Joy-Rhymes. Kingston-in-the-Ozarks, KS.: O. E. Rayburn, 1928. 32 p.
The Soul's Window-Box. Kingston, AR.: O. E. Rayburn, The Kingscraft Press, 1928. 31, [1] p.
Beyond the Blue Hills, and Other Poems. Kansas City, MO.: Burton Publ. Co., 1952. 130 p.

DIER, CAROLINE (LAWRENCE)
Out of the West. New York: H. Vinal, 1927. 7 p. ℓ., 129 p.
...The Luring Flute. Philadelphia: Dorrance and Company, 1937. 119 p. (Contemporary poets of Dorrance, 159)

DIETZ, FLORENCE (ANDERSON)
Brocade and Burlap: A Varied Collection of Verse. Los Angeles, CA.: New Age Publishing Co., 1956. 59 p.
Stitches in Time. Francestown, N.H.: Golden Quill Press, 1965. 87 p.

DIFFIN, LESLYE T.
April's Songs about Maine. Manchester, ME.: Falmouth Pub. House, 1951. 56 p.

DI GIULIO, ELEANOR
Beloved of My Heart: Poems. New York: Vantage Press, 1960. 112 p.
Love Pursues. Madras: Printed at St. Joseph's Technical School, 1967. 67 p.
The Seventh Flute. Madras: Printed at St. Joseph's Technical School, 1968. 91 p.
Lotus Buds: American Haiku. Madras: Salesian Institute of

Graphic Arts, 1969. 85 p.
Miramichi. Madras: Salesian Institute of Graphic Arts, 1970. 111 p.
Happiness Is.... Madras: Salesian Institute of Graphic Arts, 1975. 93 p.

DILL, BETTY CAROTHERS
...Fragments. Philadelphia: Dorrance & Co., 1943. 73 p. (Contemporary poets of Dorrance, 262)

DILLARD, ANNIE
Tickets for a Prayer Wheel. Columbia, MO.: University of Missouri Press, 1974. 128 p. (Breakthrough books)
_______. New York: Bantam Books, 1975. 113 p.

DILLEY, OPAL (LAWRENCE)
Fragrance of the Hours. New York: Pageant Press, 1952. 4 p. ℓ., 26 p.
Pearls of Yesteryear. New York: Pageant Press, 1952. 4 p. ℓ., 31 p.

DIMMETTE, CELIA PUHR
Toward the Metal Sun. Boston: B. Humphries, 1950. 62 p.
Horizon Far as Ocean. Cleveland, OH.: American Weave Press, 1965. 30 p.
The Winds Blow Promise. Francestown, N.H.: Golden Quill Press, 1969. 80 p.

DIMMICK, RUTH CROSBY
Poems of Emotional Love, and Other Poems. Chicago: W. B. Conkey, 1907. 127 p.

DINES, CORA PRITCHARD
White Moonlight. Dallas, TX.: Printed by C. C. Cockrell, 1930. 7 p. ℓ., 93 p.
Someone Must Dream. San Antonio, TX.: Naylor Co., 1950. 55 p.

DINSMORE, JULIA STOCKTON
Verses and Sonnets. New York: Doubleday, Page & Co., 1910. viii p., 2 ℓ., 151, [1] p.

DIORIO, MARGARET (TOARELLO)
Morning Fugues, A Collection of Poems. New York: William-Frederick Press, 1953. 44 p., 1 ℓ. (The William-Frederick poets, 109)
Listening. Baltimore, MD.: Falcon Books, 1970. 52 p.

di PRIMA, DIANE (1934-)
This Kind of Bird Flies Backward. New York: Totem Press, 1959. 43 p.
The Monster. New Haven, CT.: Penny Press, 1961. 1 ℓ.
The New Handbook of Heaven. San Francisco: Auerhahn Press,

1963. [13] p.

Unless You Clock In. Palo Alto, CA.: Patchen Cards, 1963. 2 ℓ.

Poets Vaudeville. New York: Feed Folly Press, 1964. 8 p.

Combination Theatre Poem and Birthday Poem for Ten People. New York: Brownstone Press, 1965. 4 ℓ.

Poems for Freddie. New York: Poets Press, 1966.

Haiku. Topanga, CA.: Love Press, 1967. 1 ℓ., 36 ℓ.

Earthsongs: Poems, 1957-59. New York: Poets Press, 1968. [58] p.

Hotel Albert: Poems. Millbrook, N.Y.: Printed by Kriya Press for Poets Press, New York, 1968. [12] p.

New Mexico Poem, June-July, 1967. New York: I. Roodendo, 1968. [8] p. on double leaves.

The Star, The Child, The Light. n.p., 1968. folder [2] ℓ.

Revolutionary Letters. New York: Communications Co., 1968. 15 p.

______. London: Long Hair Books, 1969. [28] p. (Long hair books, ser. 1)

L. A. Odyssey. New York: Poets Press, 1969. [16] p.

New As.... New York: Privately printed, 1969.

Notes on a Summer Solstice. n.p., 1969. [3] p.

The Book of Hours: Poems. San Francisco: Brownstone Press, 1970. 27 ℓ. In wood box.

For Blake. Santa Barbara, CA.: Unicorn Press, 1971. folder [4] p.

Kerhonkson Journal, 1966. Berkeley, CA.: Oyez, 1971. 1 v. unpaged.

Prayer to the Mothers. New York: Privately printed, 1971.

Revolutionary Letters, etc. 2d ed. San Francisco: City Lights Books, 1971. 80 p. (The Pocket poets series, no. 27)

The Calculus of Letters. San Francisco: Priv. Printed, 1972.

The Calculus of Variation. San Francisco: n.p., 1972. 1 v. unpaged.

Loba, Part I. Santa Barbara, CA.: Capra Press, 1973. 31 p. (Yes! Capra chapbook ser., no. 10)

Freddie Poems. Point Reyes, CA.: Eidolon Editions, 1974. [72] p.

Revolutionary Letters, etc. 3d ed. San Francisco: City Lights Books, 1974. 104 p.

Brass Furnace Going Out: Song, After an Abortion. Syracuse, N.Y.: Pulpartform Unltd., 1975. [13] p. (The Beau Fleuve series, 9)

Loba as Eve. New York: Phoenix Bookshop, 1975. [20] p. (Phoenix Bookshop oblong octavo series, no. 18)

Selected Poems, 1956-1975. Plainfield, VT.: North Atlantic Books, 1975. 345 p.

DIRADOUR, VIRGINIA

A Pocketful of Verses. Philadelphia: Dorrance, 1968. 27 p. (Contemporary poets of Dorrance, 696)

DITHRIDGE, ETHELWYN
As Thou Wilt, and Other Poems. Boston: The Stratford Co., 1918. vii, [1], 89 p.

DITHRIDGE, RACHEL LEWIS (1873-)
At Twilight, A Book of Verse. New York: House of Field, Inc., 1939. 4 p. ℓ., 11-77 p.

DIXON, CLAIRE (AUSTIN) (1876-)
The Crown of Life, and Other Poems. New York: Exposition Press, 1959. 159 p.

DIXON, RILLA MACKIE
Meditations of a Dreamer. Dallas, TX.: The Kaleidograph Press, 1942. ix, 11-95 p.

DODGE, JULIA ELIZABETH
Sant' Alessio and Other Poems. New York: The Knickerbocker Press, 1905. vii, 129 p.

DODGE, MARY (MAPES) (1831-1905) [Full Name: Mary Elizabeth (Mapes) Dodge.]
Rhymes and Jingles. New York: C. Scribner's Sons, 1903. xii, 255 p.
Poems and Verses. New York: Century Co., 1904. xiii, 216 p.

DOE, BLANCHE S.
Quest. Philadelphia: Dorrance and Co., 1927. 46 p.

DOERNER, CELIA
Little Ripples of Song. Boston: The Gorham Press, 1914. 80 p.

DOERR, ETTA
Song Poems. Kansas City, MO.: Chittenden Printing Co., 1922. 23 p.

DONALDSON, JEAN CHALMERS
Cup of Stars. Emory University, Atlanta, GA.: Banner Press, 1939. 62 p.
Bridge Against Time.... Dallas, TX.: Avalon Press, 1945. 2 p. ℓ., 7-44 p.
Velvet Foil. Mill Valley, CA.: Wings Press, 1958. 89 p.

DON LEAVY, KATHLEEN
Bunch of Flowers. Boston: Angel Guardian Press, 1904. 9 p. ℓ., 90 p.

DONNAN, MAY (WINTERS) (1859-1913)
Various Verses. Cambridge, MA.: Riverside Press, 1914. ix, [1], 102, [1] p.

DONNELLY, DOROTHY (BOILLOTAT) (1903-)
Trio in a Mirror. Tucson, AZ.: University of Arizona Press, 1960. 4 p. ℓ., 47 p.
Houses. Providence, R. I.: Burning Deck, 1970. [12] ℓ.

DONNELLY, ELEANOR CECILIA
Secret of the Statue, and Other Verse. Boston: R. G. Badger, 1907. 80 p.

DOOLITTLE, HILDA (1886-1961) [H. D. and ALDINGTON, HILDA (DOOLITTLE)]
Sea Garden. Boston: Houghton, Mifflin Co.; London: Constable and Co., 1916. 3 p. ℓ., v-[vi], 1-47, [1] p.
The Tribute and Circe--Two Poems. Cleveland, OH.: Printed at the Clerk's Private Press, 1917. 3 p. ℓ., 3-39 p.
Hymen. London: Egoist Press, 1921. 46, [1] p.
______. New York: H. Holt & Company, 1921. 46, [1] p.
Heliodora and Other Poems. London: J. Cape; Boston & New York: Houghton Mifflin & Co., 1924. 127 p.
Collected Poems. New York: Boni and Liveright, 1925. viii, 306 p.
Palimpsest. Boston: Houghton Mifflin Co., 1926. 338 p.
______. Paris: Contact Editions, 1926. 4 p. ℓ., 3-338 p.
Selected Poems. Selected and edited by Hugh Mearns. New York: Simon & Schuster, 1926. 31 p.
Hedylus. Stratford-upon-Avon: Printed by the Shakespeare Head Press for B. Blackwell, Oxford and Houghton Mifflin, Boston and New York, 1928. 3 p. ℓ., 185 p.
The Usual Star. London: Printed by Imprimérie Darantière at Dijon, France, 1928. 3 p. ℓ., 9-116 p.
Red Roses for Bronze. New York: Random House, 1929. 4 ℓ. (The poetry quartos)
Kora and Ka. Vaud, Switzerland: Privately printed, 1930. 101 p.
______. Dijon, France: Privately printed, 1934. 101 p.
Nights. Dijon, France: n. p., 1935. 124 p.
Red Roses for Bronze. Boston & New York: Houghton Mifflin Co., London: Chatto & Windus, 1931. viii, 147, [1] p.
The Hedgehog. London: Brendin Pub. Co., 1936. 78 p.
The Walls Do Not Fall. London & New York: Oxford University Press, 1944. 48 p.
What Do I Love? London: Privately published by Brendin Publishing Co., 1944? 24 p.
Tribute to the Angels. London & New York: Oxford University Press, 1945. 3 p. ℓ., 9-42 p.
The Flowering of the Rod. London, New York: Oxford University Press, 1946. 2 p. ℓ., 7-50 p.
Selected Poems. New York: Grove Press, 1957. 128 p.
Helen in Egypt. New York: Grove Press, 1961. [i-xii], 1-315, [1] p.
Evening. Stoke Ferry, Norfolk, VA.: Daedalus Press, 1969? [2] p.
2 Poems by H. D. Berkeley, CA.: Arif, 1971. [12] p.
"These poems appeared in Life and Letters Today in Winter

of 1937."

Hermetic Definition. New York: New Directions Pub. Corp., 1972. 117 p. (A New Directions book)

Trilogy. Chaedle: Carcanet Press, 1973. xiii, 172 p. Contains--The Walls Do Not Fall--Tribute to the Angels--The Flowering of the Rod.

Helen in Egypt. New York: New Directions Pub. Corp., 1974. xi, 304 p. (A New Directions book)

The Poet and The Dancer. San Francisco: Five Trees Press, 1975. 30 p. Appeared originally in Life and Letters Today, Dec., 1935.

DOOSE, UNA V.

Gypsey Flame. Dallas, TX.: Mathis Van Nort, 1941. 6 p. ℓ., 92 p.

DORAN, BEVERLEY

Breath of the Mountains. Boston: The Poet Lore Company, 1907. 79 p.

DORAN, CAROLYN RUTH

Reflective Twilights. Boston: The Cornhill Publishing Co., 1926. 6 p. ℓ., 3-72 p.

DORAN, LOUISE A.

From a Rose Jar. San Francisco: The Cloister Press, 1923. 5 p. ℓ., 17-61 p.

D'ORGE, JEANNE see CHERRY, JEANNE (YATES)

DORLAND, ALICE B. (1890-)

Roaming the Wind, and Other Selections. New York: Spiral Press, 1955. 5 p. ℓ., 123 p.

DORMAN, LOUISE JESSIE (1887-)

Thoughts; Poems of Cheer. Washington, D.C.: Sheiry Printing Co., 1920. 19 p.

DORMAN, MILDRED

...If Night Falls. Philadelphia: Dorrance & Company, 1941. 2 p. ℓ., 3-47 p.

DORMAN, SONYA

Poems. Columbus, OH.: Ohio State University Press, 1970. x, 74 p.

Stretching Fence. Athens, OH.: Ohio University Press, 1975. 61 p.

Vanishing Points. Columbus, OH.: Cider Press, 1975.

DOROTHY ANNE, Sister

The Whale We Cherish. Milwaukee, WI.: Bruce Press, 1963. viii, 120 p.

DORR, JULIA CAROLINE RIPLEY (1825-1913)
Afterglow: Later Poems. New York: Scribner, 1900. x, 84 p.
Beyond the Sunset: Latest Poems. New York: Scribner, 1909. ix, 94 p.
Poems. Complete ed. New York: C. Scribner, 1912. xiii, 471 p.
Last Poems. New York: C. Scribner, 1913. xiii, 206 p.

DORRIS, ANNA VERONA
When My Heart Sings; Poems. New York: Exposition Press, 1959. 64 p.

DORSEY, BERTHA ANNABELLE (GAY) (1893-) [GERRO, CARON, pseud.]
Hark to the Bells, A Collection of Poems. New York: Greenwich Book Publishers, 1963. 66 p.

DOSS, VIRGINIA
Man Upon Earth. Nashville, TN.: Parthenon Press, 1938. 104 p.
Lights and Shadows. Nashville, TN.: Broadman Press, 1943. 51 p.
Man Upon Earth. Nashville, TN.: Broadman Press, 1945. 111 p.

DOTY, NAOMI
Along the Way. Cambridge, MA.: Dresser, Chapman & Grimes, 1964. 79 p.

DOW, DOROTHY MINERVA (1903-) [Full Name: Dorothy Minerva Dow Fitzgerald.]
Black Babylon. New York: Boni & Liveright, 1924. vii p., 1 ℓ., 11-90 p.
Will-o'-the-Wisp. New York: Boni & Liveright, 1925. ix p., 1 ℓ., 13-93 p.
Time and Love. New York: Liveright Publishing Corporation, 1942. ix p., 1 ℓ., 13-107 p.

DOW, LILLA PAGE
...Sunbeams, and Other Poems. Boston: The Stratford Company, 1928. 3 p. ℓ., 5-28 p.

DOWNEY, JUNE ETTA (1875-1932)
The Heavenly Dykes. Boston: R. G. Badger, 1904. 63 p.

DOWNING, EVA COTTLE (1895-)
Stars over My Shoulder. Kanona, N.Y.: J. & C. Transcripts, 1966. 5 p. ℓ., 63 p.

DOWNING, LAURA CASE
Poem-Pictures. Boston: R. G. Badger, 1904. 5 p. ℓ., 137 p.

DOWNS, EDITH
Underneath the Bough. Chicago: Dierkes Press, 1951. 32 p.

DOWS, ALICE
Idle Hours. Philadelphia: Dorrance & Company, 1927. 119 p. (Contemporary poets of Dorrance, 63)
Illusions. Philadelphia: Dorrance & Company, 1931. 145 p. (Contemporary poets of Dorrance, 100)

DOYLE, BARBARA (1933-)
Pen on Fire; A Collection of Poems. New York: Greenwich Book Publishers, 1958. 48 p.

DOYLE, MARION STAUFFER
Strange Exodus. Brooklyn, N. Y.: A Lantern Publication, 1934. [32] p. (Lantern poet series, no. 2)

DRACHLER, ROSE (1911-)
Burrowing In, Digging Out. Berkeley, CA.: Tree Books, 1974. 45, [2] p. (A Tree book)

DRAGONETTI, MARY
Lure Elusive. Dallas, TX.: Story Book Press, 1950. 39 p.
Wind Prints. Kanona, N. Y.: J. & C. Transcripts, 1967. 14 p.

DRAKE, BARBARA (ANN) (1939-)
Narcissa Notebook. Okemos, MI.: Stone Press, 1973. [16] p.
Field Poems. Okemos, MI.: Stone Press, 1975. [12] p.

DRAKE, EDNA DUMMER
The Mad Lover and Other Poems. Boston: The Christopher Publishing House, 1937. 64 p.

DRAKE, IRIS M.
Iris Gems, A Collection of Verse. New York: Pageant Press, 1955. 3 p. ℓ., 49 p.

DRAKE, LEAH BODINE (1904-)
A Hornbook for Witches; Poems of Fantasy. Sauk City, WI.: Arkham House, 1950. viii, 70 p.
This Tilting Dust. Francestown, N. H.: Golden Quill Press, 1955. 61 p.

DRANSFIELD, JANE [Full Name: Mrs. Jane (Dransfield) Stone.]
Marks upon a Stone, Selected Lyrics and Sonnets, 1920-1940. Prairie City, IL.: Press of J. A. Decker, 1940. 60, [1] p.

DRAPER, ELIZABETH FOWLER (1904-)
Girl about Town. Dallas, TX.: Mathis, Van Nort & Co., 1938. 3 p. ℓ., 54 p.
A Co-ed Sings. Dallas, TX.: Mathis, Van Nort & Co., 1939. 62 p.

Come Stag. Dallas, TX.: Mathis, Van Nort & Co., 1940. 76 p.
Mouse to Mouse. Dallas, TX.: Mathis, Van Nort & Co., 1946. 90 p.
Curb Service. San Antonio, TX.: The Bibb Publishing Co., 1947. 192 p.

DRAPER, JESSAMINE KIMBALL
The Shadow Babe and Others. Boston: Sherman, French & Co., 1914. 5 p. ℓ., 61 p.

DRAWBRIDGE, DORIS
Poems. Boston: R. G. Badger, 1925. 32 p.

DREESEN, MINNIE ROBERTS (1888-)
Green Dusk. Dallas, TX.: Tardy Pub. Co., 1937. 4 p. ℓ., 61 p.
When Spring Comes On. Dallas, TX.: The Book Craft Publisher, 1938. 6 p. ℓ., 100 p.

DRENNAN, MARIE (1890-1950)
The World I Live In. Cedar Rapids, IA.: Torch Press, 1952. 153 p.

DREW, IVA H.
Some Signs and Other Simple Rhymes. Colebrook, N. H.: News-Sentinel Press, 1908. 57 p.
Antiques; A Book of Verse. Boston: The Four Seas Company, 1926. 76 p.
Dust and Cobwebs. Boston: The Ball Publishing Co., 1929. 4 p. ℓ., 81 p.

DREW, MARGARET A.
Let's Go A-Fishing. Devils Lake, N. D.: n. p., 1931. 94 p.

DREYER, CORA WILCOX
Green Journey, and Other Poems. Mill Valley, CA.: Wings Press, 1956. 97 p.

DREYFUS, LILIAN GERTRUDE (SHUMAN)
In Praise of Leaves and Other Verse. Boston: Lothrop, Lee & Shepherd Co., 1906. 124 p.

DRISCOLL, LOUISE (1875-1957)
The Garden of the West. New York: Macmillan, 1922. 98 p.
Garden Grace. New York: Macmillan, 1924. 4 p. ℓ., [7]-132 p.

DRIVER, OLIVE ELIZABETH (WAGNER) (1905-)
The Christmas Story. New York: Exposition Press, 1951. unpaged.
New England Sketches. Manchester, MA.: Falmouth Pub. House, 1952. 3 p. ℓ., 75 p.
New England Moods. Northampton, MA.: Metcalf Print. & Pub. Co., 1967. 61 p.

DUANE, MARY MORRIS (1872-)
Hidden Wings. Philadelphia: Dorrance & Company, 1928. 6 p. ℓ., 105, [1] p.
Barn Yard Ditties. Boston: Chapman and Grimes, 1937. 3 p. ℓ., 38 p.
Star-Drift. Boston: Chapman and Grimes, 1938. 4 p. ℓ., 91 p.

DU BARRY, CAMILLE (1914-)
Challenge. St. Paul, MN.: Caravan Pub. Co., 1934. 56 p.

DUBERSTEIN, HELEN LAURA (1926-)
The Human Dimension. Brooklyn, N.Y.: Gnosis, 1970. 10 p. (A Gnosis Supplement)

DU BOIS, JANE
Sonnets, 1932-1934.... New Haven, CT.: Yale University Press, 1935. 19 ℓ.

DU BOSE, NINA HOUSTON
It's Spring Again. San Antonio, TX.: Naylor Co., 1963. x, 44 p.
Black Panther Story, and Other Poems. San Antonio, TX.: Naylor Co., 1966. xi, 55 p.

DUCKWORTH, SOPHIA HAGEMANN
Love of Quintell; A Modern Romance in Verse. Boston: B. J. Brimmer, 1922. 3 p. ℓ., 151 p.

DUFF, MARIE
Whispering Leaves. New York: Paulus-Ullmann Printing Corporation, 1934. 3 p. ℓ., 9-108 p.
Songs after Dawn. New York: Paulus-Ullmann Printing Corporation, 1936. 94 p.

DUFFEE, MAY M.
Patriotic Poems. Washington Court House, OH.: The Murphy Print Shop, 1917. 12 p.
Poems That Are Real, That Appeal, That You Feel. Washington Court House, OH.: Murphy Print Shop, 1917. 2 p. ℓ., 3-103, [1] p.
Memorium. Washington Court House, OH.: Reeder Printing Co., 1926? [31] p.
Greetings... A Trek Through Florida and Other Poems. Washington Court House, OH.: Fayette Times Print., 1939. [20] p.
God's Gift to Me. Washington Court House, OH.: The Old Reliable Book Co., 1940. [92] p.
Patriotic Poems. Washington Court House, OH.: The Old Reliable Book Co., 1942. [22] p.

DUFFIELD, ELLA W.
...The Moonbeam's Lace, and Other Poems. Philadelphia: Dorrance and Co., 1938. 48 p. (Contemporary poets of Dorrance, 182)

DUKES, HARRIET ELIZABETH GROSE
Sunlit Heights. Boston: R. G. Badger, 1928. 241 p.
Music of the Soul. Berne, IN.: Berne Witness Company, 1939. 3 v.
Sweets of Redeeming Grace. Berne, IN.: Berne Witness Co., 1939. 3 v.

DULANEY, EMMA CAROLINE (1857-1904)
Sky Panorama. Boston: R. G. Badger, 1904. 28 p.

DUMONT, LOUISA SEILER
...Awake.... Philadelphia: Dorrance & Co., 1949. 58 p. (Contemporary poets of Dorrance, 398)

DUNCAN, HAZEL
Poemettes of the Hour. Chicago: The General Printing Co., 1944. 7 p. ℓ., 82 p.

DUNCAN, KUNIGUNDE (1886-) [Full Name: Flora Kunigunde Duncan.]
Kentish Fire. Boston: Humphries, 1951. 36 p.
Dream for Tomorrow. Boston: B. Humphries, 1964. 12 p.
Bird People. Boston: Bruce Humphries, 1965. 79 p.
When I Consider Thy Heavens. Boston: Branden Press, 1966. 117 p.
In the Laboratory. Boston: Branden Press, 1968. 126, [2] p.
Prairie Song. Boston: Branden Press, 1968. 218 p.

DUNLOP, FLORENCE A.
Concerto for the Heart. New York: Vantage Press, 1967. 46 p.

DUNN, EMILY MYRTLE
Silver Lining and Other Poems. New York: n.p., 1925. 150 p.

DUNSHEE, CHARLOTTE FITCH (1901-)
Through the Ages. Los Angeles, New York, etc.: Suttonhouse, 1936. 2 p. ℓ., xi-xvi, 115 p.

DUNWELL, LOUISE WILSON
Mountain Symphony, and Other Poems. Dallas, TX.: The Kaleidograph Press, 1939. ix p., 2 ℓ., 15-90 p.
Shadows of Beauty. Dallas, TX.: The Kaleidograph Press, 1941. xiv, 15-168 p.
Song of the Silence. Berkeley, CA.: Howell-North Press, 1949. 103 p.

DU PONT, MARCELLA MILLER
Sonnets and Lyrics. New York: Spiral Press, 1950. 56 p.
Poems: Folio Two. New York: Spiral Press, 1956. 60 p.

DU PRE, LUCILLE
Poems. Boston: B. J. Brimmer, 1923. 114 p.

DU PUY, ELIZABETH (1868-1932)
The River of Dreams. New York: J. T. White, 1919. 96 p.

DURAN, SUSANA E.
Florilegia of Light/Florilegios de Luz: Poems. Hicksville, N.Y.: Exposition Press, 1974. 88 p.

DURANT, NANCY MILES
A Book of Verses. Charleston, S.C.: Press of Walker, Evans & Cogswell Co., 1906. 5 p.ℓ., 6-87 ℓ.

DURHAM, ELIZABETH MALCOLME
Price of Wisdom. Wilmington, DE.: Pandora Press, 1927. 3 p.ℓ., 49 p.

DURHAM, FRANCES (RUFFIN)
Sea Woman. Portland, ME.: House of Falmouth, 1964. 6 p.ℓ., 51 p.
Swallows in the Air, Certain Haiki. Charleston, IL.: Prairie Press Books, 1969. vii, 19 p.

DURHAM, KATHLEEN MacNEAL
Thoughts from Oregon to Greet a Friend. Portland, OR.: F. W. Baltes and Co., Printers, 1916. 4 p.ℓ., 13-59 p.

DUROSKA, EMILIA O.
The Carousel. New York: New Orlando Publications, 1970. 66 p.
Charisma. New York: New Orlando Publications, 1971.

DURST, SOFIE PATTON
Mosaics. Berkeley, CA.: Professional Press, 1948? 64 p.

DURYEE, MARJORIE
The Image Collector. Portland, ME.: House of Falmouth, 1963. 3 p.ℓ., 58 p.

DURYEE, MARY BALLARD (1896-)
Avenues of Song. New York: E. B. Hackett, The Brick Row Book Shop, Inc., 1926. 80 p.
No Special Pleading. New York: G. P. Putnam's Sons, 1940. x, 70 p.
Free Enterprise; A Book of War Poems. New York: The Fine Editions Press, 1943. 41 p.
______. Second edition. New York: G. P. Putnam's Sons, 1940. x, 70 p.
Ring Around a Family. New York: n.p., 1949. 45 p.
This Instant Joy. New York: Pageant Press, 1958. 58 p.

DUSENBERY, GAIL (CHIARELLO)
The Mark. Berkeley, CA.: Oyez, 1967. 68 p.
The Sea-Gull. Berkeley, CA.: Oyez, 1968. [4] p.
The Bhangra Dance, Poems, 1967-1970. Berkeley, CA.: Oyez, 1970. 34 p.

DUSTIN, EDNA S.
Sage Brush and Wagon Wheels. Salt Lake City, UT.: Bookcraft, 1946. 60 p.

DU VAL, JEANNE
The Perfect Gift. Baltimore, MD.: The Norman Remington Co., 1922. 16 p.

DYAR, BLANCHE HEUSTIS
Musings in Verse. New York: The Exposition Press, 1944. 47 p.

DYE, ELIZABETH OSBORNE
Violets. Ballston Spa? N.Y.: n.p., 1900. 26 p.

DYER, ADA MAY (1876-)
Echoes from Forestside. Columbus, OH.: C. C. Hartley, 1949. 137, [5] p.

DYER, ROBERTA COLDREN
Message from Gabriel. Dallas, TX.: Royal Pub. Co., 1961. 70 p.

DYRENFORTH, MARJORIE
Verses. Chicago: n.p., 1910. 66 p.

DYSART, MARY
Poems. New York: The Paebar Company, 1947. 2 p. ℓ., 66 p.

EAGAN, ALICE LIVINGSTON
Released: A Poem. New York: Broadway Pub., 1907. 3-21 p.
________. 1908. 3 p. ℓ., 3-21 p.

EAKES, MILDRED
Women Are That Way. New York: Exposition Press, 1950. 53 p.

EARLEY, CARRIE L. (1880-1907)
Poems. Newton? IA.: n.p., 1909. 1 p. ℓ., [7]-81 p., 1 ℓ.

EARNSHAW, EDITH
Verses. Raleigh, N.C.: Edwards & Broughton, 1961. 6 p. ℓ., 69 p.

EASTMAN, MAE McCOMAS
Wind-Blown. Dallas, TX.: The Kaleidograph Press, 1941. 55 p.

EASTON, IDA LOIS
Songs of the Southland. Boston: R. G. Badger, 1912. 36 p.

EATON, CHARLOTTE
Desire. New York: G. W. Dillingham Co., 1904. 159 p.

_______. New and enl. ed. New York: Duffield & Co., 1918. 3 p. ℓ., 5-199 p.

EATON, ESTELLE ATLEY
Out of My Dreams, and Other Verses. Boston: Christopher Pub. House, 1959. 105 p.

EBERHART, NELLE RICHMOND (McCURDY) (1871-1944)
From the Land of Sky Blue Water. New York: H. Vinal, 1926. 6 p. ℓ., 71 p.

EBERLING, GEORGIA EDITH (MOORE) (1887-1975) [MOORE, FAITH, pseud.]
Songs of Solitude. Boston: The Christopher Publishing House, 1936. vi p., 1 ℓ., 9-32 p.

EBLE, Mrs. JESSIE G.
The Red Trail. New York: H. Harrison, 1931. 5 p. ℓ., 9-57 p.

ECKRICH, CATHERINE (LE MASTER)
Never Tell the Vision, and Other Poems. Boston: Bruce Humphries, 1951. 86 p.

EDDY, LEFA MORSE
Where the Hours Go. New York: H. Vinal, Ltd., 1927. 6 p. ℓ., 48 p.
Eve, and Other Poems. Brooklyn, N.Y.: Lantern Publication, 1933. 15 ℓ.
Sarah.... Brooklyn, N.Y.: Lantern Publication, 1935. 2 p. ℓ., 26 p.
Mary. Brooklyn, N.Y.: Lantern, 1936. 2 p. ℓ., 25, [1] p.
Eve. Brooklyn, N.Y.: Lantern Publication, 1940. 26 p.

EDDY, MARY MORSE (BAKER) GLOVER (1821-1910)
Christ and Christmas, A Poem. 5th ed. rev. Concord, N.H.: Rumford Press, 1900.
_______. Boston: Allison V. Stewart, 1910. 25 p.
Poems. Boston: A. V. Stewart, 1910. 3 p. ℓ., v-x p., 1 ℓ., 79 p.
Christ and Christmas, A Poem. Boston: A. V. Stewart, 1915. 25 p.
Early Verse. n.p.: Privately printed, 1933. 52 p.

EDDY, RUTH BASSETT
Altar Fires. Boston: The Cornhill Company, 1919. x p., 1 ℓ., 97 p.

EDDY, RUTH MURIEL
Poems for Christian Youth. Providence, R.I.: Oxford Press, 1941. [15] p.
Stardust, Silver, and Gold. Providence, R.I.: Oxford Press, 1949. 16 p.
Impressions of the Terminal. Providence, R.I.: Reynolds Press, 1959. 25, [2] p.

EDELMAN, KATHERINE (GUILFOYLE) (1885-)
Shamrock and Prairie Grass. Kansas City, MO.: F. Glenn Pub. Co., 1954. 6 p. ℓ., 121 p.

EDELSON, MARIE CHERRY (1887-)
Sparkling Embers. Chicago: Capitol Publishers, 1941. 79 p.

EDGELL, MAUD SCOTT
Key to Heaven. Dallas, TX.: Story Book Press, 1948. 44 p.

EDGERTON, ANGIE ROSE
Mosaics of the Mind. Dexter, MO.: Candor Press, 1962. 112 p.

EDGERTON, GLADYS
Walled Garden. Berkeley Heights, N.J.: Pub. priv. by the Oriole Press, 1934. 76 p., 1 ℓ.

EDGERTON, MARY WHEELER
The Heart Must Listen. Hallowell, ME.: L. Tebbetts, 1958. 6 p. ℓ., 57 p.

EDWARDS, CECILE PEPIN (1916-)
Days of Radiance. Francestown, N.H.: Golden Quill Press, 1964. 92 p.

EDWARDS, FRANCES JANE MERRILL (1832-)
Leaves from the Almond Tree. Milwaukee, WI.: n.p., 1901. 219 p.
Reminiscences, and Other Poems. Milwaukee? WI.: n.p., 1906. viii, 194 p.

EDWARDS, JEANETTE SLOCOMB (1890-)
Songs Against the Dark. North Montpelier, VT.: The Driftwind Press, 1936. 124 p.
Salt Blown Wood. Wilmington, DE.: n.p., 1944. 7 ℓ. (Wilmington poetry society publications)
Inward from the Sea. Philadelphia: Dorrance, 1948. 83 p. (Contemporary poets of Dorrance, 369)
Once Upon a Time. Branson, MO.: Hand set and printed by the New Athenaeum Press, 1952? [6] p.

EDWARDS, LETA MARGUERITE
Nebraska Nocturne. New York: Exposition Press, 1950. 64 p.
The Poem Is Carved. Kanona, N.Y.: J. & C. Transcripts, 1965. 4 p. ℓ., 43 p.

EDWARDS, MARGARET MARIE (MAHONEY) (1902-) [PORTER, ALICE, pseud.]
Casuals. Atlanta, GA.: E. Hartsock, The Bozart Press, 1929. 83 p.

EDWARDS, MARGARET (ROYALTY)
New Leaves. Waco, TX.: Baylor University Press, 1947. [12] p.
Quatrains. Waco, TX.: Baylor University Press, 1947. [12] p.
Reflections on the Twenty-Third Psalm. Waco, TX.: Baylor University Press, 1947. 14 ℓ.
The Lure of the Road, and Other Poems. San Antonio, TX.: Naylor Co., 1959. x, 35 p.

EDWARDS, RHODA WALKER
The Rhythm of Life. New York & London: G. P. Putnam's Sons, 1927. ix p., 1 ℓ., 58 p.

EDWARDS, ZAIDA PACKARD
Coin of Life. New York: The Poets Press, 1938. 46 p.
Kottabos, a Medley of Verse. Boston: B. Humphries, 1943. 128 p.

EGGLESTON, AMY (WHITTINGTON) (1874-)
Like a Shining Cloak and Other Poems. San Diego, CA.: Priv. printed, 1931. 111, [1] p.

EHRMAN, LILLIAN M.
Time Stood Still. La Porte, IN.: Dierkes Press, 1947. 42 p.

EHRMAN, MARY (BARTHOLOMEW) (1862-)
Melodies in Verse. Cincinnati, OH.: Stewart & Kidd, 1918. 32 p.
The Lure of Miami. Cincinnati, OH.: The Author, 1933. 6 ℓ.

EISENDRATH, BLANCHE GOODMAN
Poems. New York: Bloch Publishing Co., 1914. 5 p.ℓ., 9-78 p.

ELDER, SUSAN BLANCHARD (1835-1923)
Elder Flowers. New Orleans, LA.: The L. Graham Co., Ltd., 1912? 101 p.

ELDERT, ISABELLA KATE (CAMERON) (1852-)
Threads for the Soul's Garment. Boston: R. G. Badger, 1912. 55 p.

ELDREDGE, DOROTHY PUTNAM
Heartstrings in Poetry. Orleans, MA.: Harry's Print Shop, 1942? 66 p., 2 ℓ.

ELDREDGE, ELIZABETH FLORENCE
Heart Songs. Cincinnati, OH.: Pica Press, 1902. 28 p.

ELDRIDGE, ELLEN M.
Invitation, and Other Poems. Philadelphia: Dorrance, 1949. 63 p. (Contemporary poets of Dorrance, 392)

ELEANORE, Sister see MICHEL, ELEANORE (1890-1940)

ELFRETH, EMILY ALLEN
War Echoes. Southern Pines, N. C.: n. p., 1944. 38 p.

ELICK, EVA MARIE
Everyday Saints. New York: Vantage Press, 1954. 493 p.

ELKIN, BONNIE DINKLE
Outside Eden. Wichita Falls, TX.: Railey Pub. Co., 1936. 88 p.
This Harvest. Wichita Falls, TX.: Terry Bros., 1945. 5 p. ℓ., 69 p.

ELLARD, VIRGINIA G.
The Unity of Life and Spirit. New York: The Grafton Press, 1906. 4 p. ℓ., 56 p.

ELLENWOOD, MARION CARRINGTON
Songs of the Outdoors. New York: Exposition Press, 1957. 47 p.

ELLETT, M. DEBORAH (1949-)
From Them I Came. n. p.: A Free Will Publication, 1973.

ELLICOTT, ELVIRA ANN
Poems. St. Mary's City, MD.: Whitmore Publishing Co., 1925. 33 p., 1 ℓ.
________. Reisterstown, MD.: n. p., 1931. 33 p.

ELLIOT, MARIETTA M.
As They Came to Me. Bangor, ME.: O. F. Knowles & Co., 1908. 168 p.

ELLIOT, RUTH
Night Magic, and Other Poems. Boston: The Stratford Co., 1919. iv, 60 p.

ELLIOTT, ELLEN COIT (BROWN)
Rosy Thorn. Stanford University, CA.: Stanford University Press, 1924. 4 p. ℓ., 3-63 p.
Silver Bells and Cockle Shells. Number three. n. p., 193-? 9 p.
Footholds in Chaos. Los Angeles, CA.: The Ward Ritchie Press, 1939. 5 p. ℓ., 59 p.
Unicorns Browsing at Dawn. Stanford University: Stanford University Press, 1942. 3 p. ℓ., 27 p.
The Winds. Los Angeles, CA.: The Ward Ritchie Press, 1952. 33 p.
The Leaves of Vallombrosa. Palo Alto, CA.: Pacific Books, 1954. 25 p., 1 ℓ.

ELLIOTT, MARTHA JULIA (1899-   )
Poems. Ithaca, N.Y.: The Cayuga Press, 1917. [67] p.

ELLIOTT, MARY ADDEMAN
Whimsies. Putnam, CT.: The Chase Printery, 1932. 3 p. ℓ., 3-47 p.

ELLIS, OLYETTE
Autumn Leaves. De Forest, WI.: Time Publishing Co., 1908. 256 p.

ELLISTON, Miss GEORGE
Everyday Poems. Cincinnati, OH.: Stewart & Kidd Company, 1921. 112 p.
Changing Moods. Cincinnati, OH.: Sign of the Pen and Pad, 1922. 52 p.
Through Many Windows. Boston: B. J. Brimmer Company, 1924. 14 p., 1 ℓ., 15-82 p.
Bright World. New York: H. Vinal, Ltd., 1927. 94 p.
Cinderella Cargoes, Poems for Poets and Those Who Love Poetry. New York: G. Sully and Co., 1929. xvii p., 1 ℓ., 146 p.

ELLITHORPE, ADELAIDE
A Wreath of Monkey Flowers. New York: Exposition Press, 1955. 56 p.

ELMENDORF, MARY (JOHNSON)
Two Wives and Other Narrative Poems. Caldwell, ID.: The Caxton Printers, Ltd., 1935. 153 p.

ELTON, MAUDE LAY
Chit-Chat Philosophy. Emory University, GA.: Banner Press, 1932. 48 p. (Verse craft series)
As a Woman Thinks. Emory University: Banner Press, 1942. 79 p. (Verse craft series)
Blended Voices. Emory University, GA.: Banner Press, 1952. 5 p. ℓ., 11-103 p. (Verse craft series)

ELY, EFFIE SMITH (1879-1968)
My Mountains. Nashville, TN.: Parthenon Press, 1959. 79 p.
Devout Poems. Bristol, TN.: King Printing Co., 1969. 104 p.

EMANS, ELAINE V.
Earth's Child. Prairie City, IL.: Decker Press, 1950. 92 p.

EMBRY, ELOISE WILLIAMS (1916-   )
Hands Full of Honey. New York: Exposition Press, 1959. 40 p.

EMERSON, ALICE FERNALD
A Cycle of Song. Indianapolis, IN.: Continental Printing Co., 1928. [19] p.
Marsh Fire, Poems. Indianapolis, IN.: Butler University Press, 1935. 6 p. ℓ., 126 p. "Includes 'A Cycle of Song' published separately in 1928."

EMERSON, FLORENCE BROOKS
The Destiny, and Other Poems. Boston: Small, 1901. 8-92 p.

EMERY, ALICE E.
Sacred Thoughts. Indianapolis, IN.: Hollenbeck Press, 1917. 4 p. ℓ., 71 p.

EMERY, EMMA WILSON
Velvet Shadow. New York: Parnassus Press, 1934. 111, [1] p.
Bleeding Heart and Rue. Chicago: M. A. Donohue & Co., 1937. 79 p.
...Songs of Victory; Verses Old and New. Philadelphia: Dorrance & Co., 1944. 50 p. (Contemporary poets of Dorrance, 284)

EMERY, SARAH M.
Song of My Heart. New York: The Exposition Press, 1944. 3 p. ℓ., 9-61 p. (Poets of America. Series four)

EMMET, ALIDA CHANLER
The Hidden Places, and Other Poems. New York: R. G. Cooke, Inc., 1907. 2 p. ℓ., vii-ix p., 1 ℓ., 108 p.
Psyche Sleeps, and Other Poems. New York: Moffat, Yard and Company, 1910. 2 p. ℓ., vii-xi p., 1 ℓ., 193 p. Pt. 1, The Hidden Places and Other Poems. Pt. 2, Psyche Sleeps....

EMMONS, AMELIA D.
The Creative Spirit. Detroit: Harlo Press, 1966. 127 p.

EMMONS, ELISE
Autumn Songs Among the Leaves. London: J. M. Watkins, 1921.
The Surprise and Other Poems. London: A. H. Stockwell, 1922.
The Parliament of Birds and Other Poems. Boston: The Christopher Publishing House, 1924. 5 p. ℓ., 9-200 p.
The Crystal Sea, and Other Poems. London: A. H. Stockwell, 1925.
The Lone Eagle. Boston: The Christopher Publishing House, 1928. 202 p.
"The Valley of Vision"; and Other Poems. London: A. H. Stockwell, 193-. 6, [3]-80 p.

EMMS, JOSEPHA MURRAY (1894-)
April Music. n.p., 1962. 60 p. (Ozark sunlight series).

ENDRES, CATHERINE ROE-HARRIS
Light and Shadow. St. Paul, MN.: n.p., 194-? 21 numb. ℓ.
With Wind and Sun.... New York: The Exposition Press, 1943. 2 p. ℓ., 7-30 p.

ENGALITCHEFF, EVELYN PARDRIDGE
Poems. New York: n.p., 1917. 31 p.

ENGELHARDT, JANET (WORTHINGTON)
Be Good Sweet Maid. Philadelphia: Dorrance, 1963. 95 p. (Contemporary poets of Dorrance, 555)

ENGLE, ADA MAY
Singing in the Rain. New York: Vantage Press, 1956. 148 p.
Singing in the Shadows. New York: Vantage Press, 1959. 149 p.

ENGLISH, LOIS E.
Of Dreams and Memories. New York: Exposition Press, 1949. 63 p.
Leave Me My Dreams. New York: Exposition Press, 1955. 119 p.
The Most Precious Word; Verse Variations on Several Themes. New York: Exposition Press, 1957. 160 p.
The Poet and the Psalms; An Interpretation in Verse. New York: Exposition Press, 1957. 44 p.
Of Course I've Faith; Verses of Affirmation. New York: Exposition Press, 1958. 119 p.
The Golden Stairway; Religious Poems. New York: Exposition Press, 1959. 95 p.
Sweetness of Memory; Poems on Love, Friendship, Nature, and Children. New York: Exposition Press, 1959. 72 p.
Progress of the Pilgrim, "Farewell Night, Welcome Day." New York: Pageant Press, 1963. 5 p. ℓ., 70 p.
The Miracle of Miracles, A Poem. New York: Exposition Press, 1964. 47 p.

ENLOW, LUCILE CORDELIA (JOHNSON) (1895-)
The Heart of a Girl. Boston: The Stratford Co., 1919. vii p., 2 ℓ., 3-68 p., 1 ℓ.

ENTREKIN, CLARA (PIPER)
After Eden. Cedar Rapids, IA.: The Torch Press, 1942. 64 p.
Earth Is So Round. Cedar Rapids, IA.: The Torch Press, 1942. 3 p. ℓ., 5-61 p.

EPPERSON, ALOISE (BARBOUR)
The Hills of Yesterday and Other Poems. Norfolk, VA.: Printed by J. A. Brown, 1943. 74 p.
Unto My Heart, and Other Poems. Boston: Christopher Pub. House, 1953. 201 p.

EPSTEIN, ALMA THAYER
Pathway in Verse. San Antonio, TX.: Printed by the Naylor Co., 1959. viii, 98 p.

EPSTEIN, JUDY
Keeping Score. Ithaca, N.Y.: Ithaca House, 1975. 33 p.

ERICKSON, RUTH LINNEA
Homespun Verse. Providence, R.I.: Rollinson & Hey, 1956. 82 p.

ERSKINE, BARBARA (PEATTIE) (1885-1915)
The Little Poems of Barbara Erskine. n. p., 1916. 75 p.

ERSKINE, EDITH DEADERICK
The Power Flows. Dallas, TX.: Story Book Press, 1950. 4 p. ℓ., 9-48 p.
Here They Live and Die. Dallas, TX.: Story Book Press, 1953. 64 p.
From Sea to Sky. Emory University, Atlanta, GA.: Banner Press, 1954. 59 p. (Verse craft series)
The Millions Climb. Emory University, Atlanta, GA.: Banner Press, 1958. 72 p.
This Day; This Hour. Emory University, Atlanta, GA.: Banner Press, 1959. 50 p.
Time Roads. London: Mitre Press, 1962. 61 p.

ERWIN, MARGARET
Canyon Garden. San Francisco, CA.: A. M. Robertson, 1922. 4 p. ℓ., 103 p.

ERWIN, RACHEL MELISSA
Her Garden. Chicago: Bert. L. White, Company, 1917. 3 p. ℓ., [9]-99 p.
Reclaimed. Chicago: B. L. White Co., 1921. 4 p. ℓ., 11-46 p.

ESDEN, EFFIE ISABEL (GRAY) (1876-)
Poems. Baltimore, MD.: Saulsbury Publishing Co., 1918. 24 p.

ESHER, MARGARET
New Leaves. New York: Pegasus Publishing Co., 1937. 82 p.

ESPINOSA, MARIA
Love Feelings. Sausalito, CA.: Four Winds, 1967. [16] p.
Night Music. Sausalito, CA.: The Tides, 1969. 42 p.

ESSMAN, CHARLOTTE
There's Music in the Rain. Dallas, TX.: The Kaleidograph Press, 1943. x p., 3 ℓ., 17-79 p.

ESTABROOK, FIDELLA E.
Berkshire Wild Flowers. New York & London: The Abbey Press, 1902. 89 p.

ESTERNAUX, MARIE LOUISE
Outdoor Voices. New York: The Poets Press, 1936. 100, [1] p.

ESTES, DOROTHY
Man Has Forever. Emory University, Atlanta, GA.: Banner Press, 1957. 59 p. (Verse craft series)

ESTLIN, MARIE
...Nature Sketches, and Other Poems. Philadelphia: Dorrance

& Co., 1946. 44 p. (Contemporary poets of Dorrance, 338)

ESTY, JANE
Seven Spiders. New York: Mutiny Press, 1956. 13 p.
Two Poems, as they appeared in Prairie Schooner, The Sewanee Review, 1964-1965. n.p.: Mutiny Press, 1965. [4] p.

ETS, MARIE HALL
Beasts and Nonsense. New York: Viking Press, 1952. 64 p.
_______. 1968. 64 p.

EUDY, MARY CUMMINGS (PAINE) (1874-)
Quarried Crystals and Other Poems. New York & London: G. Putnam's Sons, 1935. xv p., 1 ℓ., 19-189 p.
Crystals.... New York: n.p., 1947. 6 ℓ.
Quicken the Current. New York: Harper, 1949. x, 116 p.

EVANGELISTA, EDITH LOUISE (1921-)
Phases of Life. Philadelphia: Dorrance, 1975. 60 p. (Contemporary poets of Dorrance)

EVANS, ABBIE HUSTON (1881-)
Outcrop. New York & London: Harper and Brothers, 1928. xiii, 86 p., 1 ℓ.
The Bright North. New York: The Macmillan Company, 1938. x, 85 p.
Fact of Crystal. New York: Harcourt, Brace, 1961. 48 p.
Collected Poems. Pittsburgh, PA.: University of Pittsburgh Press, 1970. xvi, 216 p. (Pitt poetry series)

EVANS, ALICE MARY
And Did You Wonder, and Other Verse. New Haven, CT.: The Tuttle, Morehouse & Taylor Company, 1927. 3 p. ℓ., 55 p.

EVANS, ANNE MARIE (1886-)
Little Bits of Living. Boston: R. G. Badger, 1929. 53 p.

EVANS, FLORENCE (WILKINSON) [WILKINSON, FLORENCE]
The Far Country: Poems. New York: McClure, Phillips & Co., 1906. xi, 259 p.
Connecticut. London: The Tamburlane Press, 1932. 67 p.

EVANS, LUCILLE (1872-)
...Bright Meridian. West Los Angeles, CA.: Wagon & Star Publishers, 1944. [20] p. (Destiny editions)
Harp Toward Morning. Los Angeles, CA.: Wagon & Star Press, 1948. v, 12 numb. ℓ., [2] p.

EVANS, MARI (1923-)
Where Is All the Music? London: Paul Breman, 1968. 24 p. (Heritage series, v. 6)
I Am a Black Woman. New York: Morrow, 1970. 95 p.

I Look at Me! Chicago: Third World Press, 1974. [28] p.

EVANS, MARY ANNA (BUCK) (1857-)
The Moonlight Sonata, and Other Verses. New York & London: G. P. Putnam's Sons, 1910. ix, 172 p.
The Caliph's Secret, and Other Verses. New York & London: G. P. Putnam's Sons, 1916. ix, 176 p.
The Cry of Vashti, and Other Verses. New York & London: G. P. Putnam's Sons, 1922. x, 184 p.

EVANS, NELLIE CHALCRAFT (1883-)
Nellie's Scrapbook. New York: Pageant Press, 1961. 3 p. ℓ., 58 p.

EVANS, NELLIE SEELYE
Poems. Englewood, N. J.: Press Printing Establishment, 1906. 2 p. ℓ., vii-xii p., 2 ℓ., 17-176 p.
September Roses; A Collection of Verse. Englewood, N. J.: n. p., 1908. 5 p. ℓ., [13]-46 p.

EVANS, VIRGINIA MORAN (1909-)
When March Sets Free the River.... Cleveland, OH.: n. p., 1946. 36 p.
In Silence and In Thunder. Dallas, TX.: Kaleidograph Press, 1951. 88 p.
Bee in the Wind. Francestown, N. H.: Golden Quill Press, 1965. 96 p.
Eyes of the Tiger. Francestown, N. H.: Golden Quill Press, 1970. 87 p.

EVANS, WILVA SCOTT
Embers of Truth. San Antonio, TX.: Naylor Co., 1965. viii, 52 p.
Forty Winks. San Antonio, TX.: Naylor Co., 1965. viii, 28 p.

EVARTS, LULU EMMA (KUSEE) (1879-)
A Book of Poems. Oklahoma City, OK.: Printed by H. R. Stephens, 1917. [24] p.
______. Oklahoma City, OK.: Phelps Printing Co., 1918. [14] p.

EVERETT, LEOLYN LOUISE (1888-)
The Closed Book, and Other Poems. New York: Wessels & Bissell, 1910. 2 p. ℓ., vii-xvi, 226 p.
The Pipes o' Pan. n. p., 1916. 36 p.
The Hills of Arcetri. London & New York: John Lane Co., 1921. 3 p. ℓ., 9-79, [1] p.
Fauns at Prayer. London: J. Lane, The Bodley Head, 1922. 107 p.
______. New York: Brentano's, 1922. 107 p.
The Hills of Arcetri. New York: Brentano's, 1923. 3 p. ℓ., 9-79 p., [1] p.
Byways to Crossroads. New York: Brentano's, 1927. 127 p.

EVERLEY, DORIS CHRISTINE
Words Be My Steed; Poems. New York: Crown Publications, 1944. 64 p.

EVERTS, LILLIAN (1910-1960)
Poems. Brooklyn, N. Y.: n. p., 1940. 4 ℓ.
While the Past Burns. New York: The Author, 1945. [8] p.
Lost Edition. Limited ed. Brooklyn? N. Y.: n. p., 1948. [10] p.
In Time of Change. Brooklyn, N. Y.: Fairfield Press, 1953. [28] p.
Journey to the Future. New York: Farrar, Straus and Cudahy, 1955. 104 p.

EWING, ANNA (HEBERTON)
Reveries. Washington, D. C.: The Neale Co., 1900. x, 11-110 p.

FABILLI, MARY (1914-)
The Old Ones; Poems. Berkeley, CA.: Oyez, 1966. 1 v. unpaged
Aurora Bligh & Early Poems. Berkeley, CA.: Oyez Press, 1968. 108 p.
The Animal Kingdom: Poems 1964-1974. Berkeley, CA.: Oyez, 1975. 69 p.

FABIO, SARAH WEBSTER (1928-)
A Mirror, A Soul: a Two-Part Volume of Poems. San Francisco: J. Richardson, 1969. 29, 15 p.
Black Talk: Soul, Shield and Sword. New York: Doubleday, 1973.

FAGNANI, FLORA CARLETON
Ink Flings. New York: Dodd, Mead and Co., 1901. 3 p. ℓ., 6-126 [1] p.
Verses. New York?: Privately printed, 1908. 30 p.

FAHNESTOCK, RUTH
Shoulder the Sky. New York: Margent Press, 1941. xii p., 2 ℓ., 17-61 p.

FAINLIGHT, RUTH (ESTHER) (1931-)
A Forecast, A Fable. Dulwich Village: Outposts Publications, 1958. 12 p.
Cages. London: Macmillan; New York: St. Martin's Press, 1966. [6], 42 p.
______. Chester Springs, PA.: Dufour Editions, 1967. 41 p.
18 Poems from 1966. Ed. by Edward Luce-Smith. London: Turret Books, 1967. 22 p. (Turret booklet, no. 13)
To See the Matter Clearly, and Other Poems. London: Macmillan, 1968. vi, 78 p.
______. Chester Springs, PA.: Dufour Editions, 1969. vi, 77 p.

The Region's Violence. London: Hutchinson, 1973. 79 p.
21 Poems. London: Turret Books, 1973. 29 p.

FAIR, OLIVIA
Love's White Flower. Hollywood? CA.: n.p., 1953. 52 p.

FAIRBANK, EULA MAE (STURDIVANT) (1900-) [FAIRBANK, PRISCILLA]
Life in a Nutshell. Richmond, VA.: Dietz Press, 1950. xiv, 77 p.

FAIRBANK, PRISCILLA (STURDIVANT) see FAIRBANK, EULA MAE (STURDIVANT)

FAIRCHILD, MINNIE L.
Just Thoughts. Dillon, MT.: n.p., 1928. [32] p.

FAIRCLOTH, ANNIE B.
Rhyme and Reason. Winston-Salem, N.C.: Clay Printing Co., 1948. 81 p.

FAIRMONT, ETHEL
The Lovely Garden. New York: Algonquin Publishing Co.; London: John Lane, 1937? [40] p.
Rhymes for Kindly Children; Modern Mother Goose Jingles. New York: The Wise-Parslow Company, 1937. [127] p.

FALK, STELLA
Nursery Rhymes for Perilous Times; Poems of Dissent and Lament. New York: Vantage Press, 1967. 64 p.

FALL, NELLIE M.
Your Mother and Mine, Through the Maze of Pride, Lust, Labor, Color, and Creed. Los Angeles, CA.: Grafton Publishing Corp., 1922. 10 ℓ.
Definition of a Dog. Los Angeles, CA.: Fall Publishing Co., 1924. 7 ℓ.
Mrs. Jonése. Los Angeles, CA.: Fall Publishing Company, 1939. [31] p.

FARGASON, INA
Ghostwood. San Antonio, TX.: Naylor Co., 1970. 5 p.ℓ., 37 p.

FARGASON, NELL COOKE
From the Tender Years. New York: Exposition Press, 1953. 64 p.

FARGO, KATE MILLS
Songs Not Set to Music: Poems. New York: Abbey Press, 1902. 201 p.

FARLEY, CORINNE SICKEL
L-I-G-H-T. Emory University, Atlanta: Banner Press, 1937. 100 p. (Verse craft series)

FARLEY, JEAN (1928-)
Figure and Field. Chapel Hill, N.C.: University of North Carolina Press, 1970. 52 p. (Contemporary poetry series)

FARNELL, GENEVIEVE (BROWNE)
The Faun, and Other Poems. Boston: Sherman, French & Company, 1913. 6 p. ℓ., 91 p.
Love Me While You May, and Other Poems. New York: Exposition Press, 1954. 95 p.

FARNSWORTH, ELIZABETH ARNDT
This Live Tree. New York: Vantage Press, 1963. 76 p.

FARNUM, LOUISE KOBBE
For All Her Knowing. New York: Doc Press, 192-? 112 p.
A Song of Sicily, and Other Verses. New York: n.p., 1923. 115 p.

FARNUM, MARY V.
Tall Shadows. Chicago: Dierkes Press, 1952. 55 p.

FARRELL, ANNA E.
Gleanings. Boston: R. G. Badger, 1923. 4 p. ℓ., 7-82 p.

FARRELL, CATHERINE HYLAND
Lavender and Old Rags. New York: H. Harrison, 1940. 63 p.

FASEL, IDA (1909-)
A Prairie View. Dallas, TX.: Story Book Press, 1954. 40 p.

FAUBLE, CLOTA HATCHEL
From Sense to Soul. San Diego, CA.: Frye and Smith, 1920. [64] p.

FAVOR, FLORENCE (KIMBALL)
Songs of the Field. Hillsboro, N.H.: Rumford Press, 1914. 3 p. ℓ., 58 p.

FAY, ALICE (Countess di Castagnola, Alice McIntire Fay) (1894-)
The Realm of Fancy; Poems and Pictures. New York: Broadway Publishing Company, 1912. 3 p. ℓ., 35 p.
My Country. New York: Gotham Press, 1915. 19 p.
Our America; A Symphony of the New World. New York, London: G. P. Putnam's Sons, 1927. 4 p. ℓ., 104 p.
The Soul's Quest. New York, London: G. P. Putnam's Sons, 1936. 95 p.

FAY, GABRIELLE
Poems of the Four Seasons. Brooklyn, N.Y.: The Preston Press, 1935. [40] p.

FAYERWEATHER, MARGARET DOANE (GARDINER) (1883-)
Gathering. Albany, N. Y.: C. F. Williams & Son, Inc., 1929. 78 p.

FAYLOR, ROSALYN [Full name: Mrs. Floy Rosalynn Faylor.]
Sparks o' the Heart. San Jose, CA.: n. p., 1928. 5 p. ℓ., 15-76 p.

FELDER, BEULAH DUKES
When Jonquils Bloom. Chicago: Dierkes Press, 1947. 45 p.

FELPS, JETTIE IRVING (1889-)
Life's Contrasts. Dexter, MO.: Candor Press, 1945. 20 p.
Our Hero and Other Poems. Dallas, TX.: Story Book Press, 1948. 40 p.
Poems for Thought. Corpus Christi, TX.: Christian Triumph Press, 1951. 64 p.
Bible Gems and Other Poems. Corpus Christi? TX.: Christian Triumph Press? 1952. 20 p.
Life's Hectic Olio. Boston: Forum, 1961. 115 p.

FENOLLOSA, MARY McNEILL (d. 1954) [McCALL, SIDNEY]
Blossoms from a Japanese Garden; A Book of Child-Verses. New York: Frederick A. Stokes Company, 1913. vii, 60 p.

FENTON, ELIZABETH
Public Testimony. Cambridge, MA.: Alice James Books, 1975. 72 p.

FERGUSON, DOROTHY FRANK
In His Hand: Poems. New York: Exposition Press, 1960. 56 p.

FERNANDIS, SARAH COLLINS
Poems. Boston: R. G. Badger, 1925. 59 p.

FERRARI, MARY SELBY
The Flying Glove. New York: Adventures in Poetry, 1973. [49] p.

FERRIS, CONSTANCE
Curtain Calls. San Francisco, CA.: Harr Wagner Publishing Co., 1930. 5 p. ℓ., 62 p.
Orchards and Orchids. San Francisco, CA.: Williams Publishing Co., 1933. 70 p.

FEST, MATTIE LOIS
Turn up the Corners of Your Mouth and Smile. San Francisco, CA.: n. p., 1924. 11-77 p.

FEUSNER, RUTHEDA
The Heart Revealed. Chicago: Dierkes Press, 1948. 48 p.

FIEDLER, LOIS (WAGNER) (1928-)
The Sound of Silence. Westwood, N.J.: F. H. Revell Co., 1965. 126 p.

FIEDLER, SALLY ANDERSEN
Skin and Bones. n.p.: Ceres Press, 1972.

FIELD, ALICE GERTRUDE
Sun in My Sky, and Other Verse. North Montpelier, VT.: The Driftwind Press, 1938. 116 p.

FIELD, BEULAH
A Silver Pool. New York: Moffat, Yard and Company, 1922. 50 p.

FIELD, RACHEL LYMAN (1894-1942)
The Pointed People: Verses & Silhouettes. New Haven, CT.: Yale University Press, 1924. xii, 98 p.
Taxis and Toadstools. Garden City, N.Y.: Doubleday, Page, and Co., 1926. xii p., 1 ℓ., 129 p.
A Little Book of Days. Garden City, N.Y.: Doubleday, Page and Co., 1927. [59] p. (Verses for children.)
A Circus Garland. Washington, D.C.: The Winter Wheat Press, 1930. vii, [1] p.
The Pointed People: Verses & Silhouettes. New York: The Macmillan Co., 1930. ix, [1], 110, [1] p.
Points East, Narratives of New England. New York: Brewer and Warren, Inc., 1930. 126 p., 1 ℓ.
________. New York: Macmillan Co., 1933. 126 p., 1 ℓ.
Branches Green. New York: The Macmillan Co., 1934. x p., 2 ℓ., 3-66 p.
Fear Is the Thorn. New York: The Macmillan Co., 1936. viii, 88 p.
Christmas Time. New York: The Macmillan Co., 1941. [32] p.
Poems. New York: Macmillan, 1957. 118 p.

FIELD, SARA BARD (1882-)
The Great White Christ. n.p., 19--. [4] p. "A poem."
The Gift. n.p., 1914. 8 p.
To a Poet Born on the Edge of Spring; A Poem Unfolding a Secret, with a Prologue and an Epilogue. San Francisco, CA.: Press of Johnck, Kibbee & Co., 1925. 14 p., 2 ℓ.
The Pale Woman & Other Poems. New York: W. E. Rudge, 1927. 6 p.ℓ., 3-81 p.
Vineyard Voices. San Francisco, CA.: Press of Johnck and Seeger, 1930. 12 p., 1 ℓ.
Barabbas; A Dramatic Narrative. New York: A. & C. Boni, Inc., 1932. x p., 3 ℓ., 17-200 p.
Darkling Plain. New York: Random House, 1936. 8 p.ℓ., [3]-92 p., 1 ℓ.

FIELDER, MILDRED (CRAIG) (1913-)
Wandering Foot in the West. Boston: Bruce Humphries, 1955. 114 p.

FIELDING, ANNA M.
Collected Poems of Anna M. Fielding. New York: Margent Press, 1940. 5 p. ℓ., 146 p.

FIELDS, JULIA (1938-)
Poems. Millbrook, N.Y.: Kriya Press, 1968. [32] p.
East of Moonlight. New ed. Charlotte, N.C.: Red Clay Books, 1973. 52 p. (Red Clay Reader, v. 8, no. 4)

FIELDSTEEL, MARGARET (NICKERSON)
Not All the Green Hills; Poems. Denver, CO.: Big Mountain Press, 1960. 81 p.

FIGGS, CARRIE LAW MORGAN
Poetic Pearls. Jacksonville, FL.: Edward Waters College Press, 1920. 32 p.
Nuggets of Gold. Chicago: Jaxon Printing Company, 1921. 2 p. ℓ., 7-31 p.

FIKE, BERTHA (READ) (1872-)
Against the Thorn, Poems. New York: Exposition Press, 1956. 80 p.

FIKE, HELEN DUKE (1925-)
Make It a Gentle Farewell, and Other Poems. New York: Vantage Press, 1969. 47 p.

FILLMORE, GRACE ETHEL
The Comfort of Quietude. Boston: Meador Publishing Company, 1942. 63 p.

FINCH, MAY STANLEY see STANLEY, MAE

FINCH, REBECCA L.
Heart Lyrics. Oklahoma City, OK.: Printing by H. R. Stephens, 1918. [31] p.

FINDLEY, EDGARDA L.
Fancies of Childhood. New York: n.p., 1916. 4 p. ℓ., 26 numb. ℓ.

FINLEY, LORRAINE NOEL
John Comes First. Francestown, N.H.: Golden Quill Press, 1968. 117 p.
Forever in Eden. Francestown, N.H.: Golden Quill Press, 1971. 128 p.

FINN, MARY ELIZABETH see FINN, Sister MARY PAULINA (1842-1935)

FINN, Sister MARY PAULINA [PINE, M.S., pseud. and FINN, MARY ELIZABETH]
A Glory of Maryland. Philadelphia: Salesian Press, 1917. 88 p.

<u>Sacred Poems.</u> Washington, D.C.: Pub. for Georgetown Visitation Convent, 1924. 4 p. ℓ., 7-320 p.

FISCALINI, JANET (1931-1967)
<u>Evasions.</u> Santa Fe, N.M.: Sunstone Review and Press, 1972. 64 p.

FISCHER, GRETL KRAUS
<u>The Emigrant, and Other Poems.</u> New York: Vantage Press, 1962. 126 p.

FISH, HENRIETTA A.
<u>Heart to Heart Poems.</u> Oakland, CA.: Harrington-McInnis Co., 1931. 5 p. ℓ., 178 p.

FISH, LISBETH
<u>Wild Iris; Odes and Lyrics.</u> Denver, CO.: E. J. Hurd & Co., 1936. 91 p.
<u>Chinook, A Welcome Wind.</u> Denver, CO.: The World Press, Inc., 1940. ix, 11-100 p.
<u>Late Harvest; Poems.</u> Denver, CO.: Smallwood Press, 1951. 24 p.

FISHBACK, MARGARET (1904-)
<u>I Feel Better Now.</u> New York: E. P. Dutton & Co., 1932. 128 p.
<u>Out of My Head.</u> New York: E. P. Dutton & Co., 1933. 128 p.
<u>I Take It Back.</u> New York: E. P. Dutton & Co., Inc., 1935. 128 p.
<u>One to a Customer; Collected Poems of Margaret Fishback.</u> New York: E. P. Dutton & Co., 1937. 6 p. ℓ., 9-450 p.
<u>Time for a Quick One.</u> New York: Harcourt, Brace and Company, 1940. xv, 172 p.
<u>I Feel Better Now; and Out of My Head. Two volumes of verse.</u> Cleveland, OH.: World Publishing Co., 1942. 250 p. Tower books edition.
<u>Poems Made Up to Take Out.</u> New York: D. McKay Co., 1963. ix, 117 p.

FISHER, AILEEN LUCIA (1906-)
<u>The Coffee-Pot Face.</u> New York: R. M. McBride & Co., 1933. x p., 1 ℓ., 13-95, [1] p. (Verse for children.)
<u>Inside a Little House.</u> New York: R. M. McBride & Co., 1938. 112 p. (Verse for children.)
<u>Guess Again!</u> New York: R. M. McBride and Co., 1941. 111 p.
<u>That's Why.</u> New York, Edinburgh: T. Nelson & Sons, 1946. 96 p.
<u>Runny Days, Sunny Days: Merry Verses with Silhouettes.</u> London, New York: Abelard-Schuman, 1958. 126 p.
<u>Up the Windy Hill: A Book of Merry Verse with Silhouettes.</u> N.Y.: Abelard Press, 1958. 128 p.
<u>Like Nothing at All.</u> New York: Crowell, 1962. Unpaged.
<u>Cricket in a Thicket.</u> New York: Scribner, 1963. 63 p.

(Verse for children.)

<u>In the Middle of the Night.</u> New York: Crowell, 1965. 1 v. unpaged. A narrative poem for children.

<u>In the Woods, In the Meadow, In the Sky.</u> New York: Scribner, 1965. 64 p.

______. Tadworth, Surrey: The World's Work, 1967. 64 p.

<u>In One Door and Out the Other: A Book of Poems.</u> New York: Crowell, 1969. 7 p. ℓ., 65, [1] p.

<u>Feathered Ones and Furry.</u> New York: Crowell, 1971. 37 p.

FISHER, AMY (WOODWARD) (1889-)

<u>Colored Leaves, A Book of Ninety Sonnets.</u> Caldwell, ID.: The Caxton Printers, Ltd., 1933. 102 p.

<u>Gems of the Gem State.</u> Moscow, ID.? n. p., 1940. 14 p.

<u>Two Stars in a Window.</u> Caldwell, ID.: The Caxton Printers, Ltd., 1946. 3 p. ℓ., 5-79 p.

<u>Portrait of Paradise Acre.</u> Spokane? n. p., 1951. 119 p.

FISHER, ANNIE L.

<u>The City of Sweet Content.</u> Cambridge, MA.: n. p., 1903. [8] p.

<u>Wayside Thoughts.</u> Boston: Smith & Porter Press, 1903. 7, [1] p.

<u>Songs of Comfort.</u> Boston: Lincoln & Smith Press, 1910. 3 p. ℓ., 18 numb. ℓ.

<u>Comforted....</u> Boston: n. p., 1913. [81] p.

<u>Little Verses for Little People.</u> Boston: n. p., 1913. [12] p.

<u>A Man from the Hills.</u> Chicago: Arts and Crafts Book Shop, 1917. 20 p.

FISHER, CONSTANCE

<u>Varied Verse, The Dreams of a Decade.</u> Rockford, IL.: Rockford Printing Company, 1923. 2 p. ℓ., 7-30 p.

FISHER, DOROTHY

<u>Another Night for America.</u> New York: H. Harrison, 1942. 61 p.

FISHER, ELLA WARNER

<u>Idylls from Champlain.</u> Boston: L. Phillips, 1918. 4 p. ℓ., 70 p.

<u>Green Mountain Echoes.</u> Rutland, VT.: The Tuttle Company, 1927. 154 p.

<u>Homeland in the North.</u> North Montpelier, VT.: The Driftwind Press, 1936. 100 p.

FISHER, GERTRUDE ARGUERE

<u>Original Poems.</u> Parsons, KA.: Foley Railway Printing Co., 1910.

FITCH, BERTHA E.

<u>Lyrics of L. A. Hinterlands and Lakes.</u> Bear Valley ed. Los Angeles, CA.: The Franklin Press, 1925. 15, [1] p.

FITTS, ADA M. (1869-)
A Little Book of Verse. Buffalo, N.Y.: Henry B. Brown Co., 1906. 4 p.ℓ., 68 p.

FITTS, ANNA SNOW
Poems. Williamsport, PA.: n.p., 1927. 35 p.

FITZGERALD, MARY (SMALL)
An Etching. Cedar Rapids, IA.: The Torch Press, 1927. 19 p.
The Way of Beauty. Dallas, TX.: The Kaleidoscope Publishers, 1931. 7 p.ℓ., 17-86 p.
Aspen Gold. Dallas, TX.: The Kaleidograph Press, 1938. x p., 2 ℓ., 15-68 p.

FITZGIBBONS, MARY ELLEN
The Old Organist, and Other Poems. New York: Vantage Press, 1958. 60 p.

FITZ-PATRICK, NAN (BARTOS) (1883-)
Winding Road. Minneapolis, MN.: The Lund Press, Inc., 1945. 128 p.
Far Horizons. Dexter, MO.: Candor Press, 1957. 138 p.

FLANAGAN, DOROTHY BELLE (1904-) [HUGHES, DOROTHY BELLE FLANAGAN]
Dark Certainty. New Haven, CT.: Yale University Press; London: H. Milford, Oxford University Press, 1931. 68 p. (Yale Series of Younger Poets, [30])

FLANAGAN, JEWEL MACE
Maybe Tomorrow. Claremont, CA.: Saunders Press, 1944. 5 p.ℓ., 3-66 [1] p.

FLANDERS, ISADORE ELIZABETH
The Red upon the Hill. Cedar Rapids, IA.: Bookfellows at the Torch Press, 1930. 61 p.
A Thimble Cup. Cedar Rapids, IA.: The Torch Press, 1939. 61 p.

FLANIGAN, MARY LEEDY
A Summer Idyl. New York: The Cosmopolitan Press, 1911. 105 p.

FLANNER, HILDEGARDE (1899-) [Full name: June Hildegarde Flanner.]
Young Girl, Awarded the Emily Chamberlain Cook Prize at the University of California, 1920, and Other Poems. San Francisco: Printed for private distribution by H. S. Crocker Company, Inc., 1920. x, 11 p., 1 ℓ.
This Morning, Poems. New York: F. Shay, 1921. 14 p.
A Tree in Bloom and Other Verses. San Francisco: The Lantern Press, Gelber, Lilienthal, Inc., 1924. 2 p.ℓ., 15, [1] p.

That Endeth Never; A Gift, Christmas 1921. Pittsburgh, PA.: The Laboratory Press, 1926. xi, 28, [1] p.
Time's Profile. New York: The Macmillan Co., 1929. 156 p.
In Galilee. Los Angeles? Printed by Gregg Anderson and Ward Ritchie, 1932. 2 ℓ.
If There Is Time, Poems. Norfolk, CT.: New Directions, 1942. 29, [2] p. (The Poet of the Month [1942])
Winter Rain. San Francisco: Printed by the Eucalyptus Press, Mills College, 1947. 2 ℓ. (Book Club of California, San Francisco. The California Poetry Folios, Part 10)
In Native Light. Calistoga, CA.: n.p., 1970. x, 61 p.

FLANNER, JUNE HILDEGARDE see FLANNER, HILDEGARDE

FLATT, Mrs. J. M. see FLATT, WILLA MARY

FLATT, WILLA MARY
Home Lyrics. Keene, TX.: The College Press, 1931. 176 p.

FLEBBE, GRACE CHANEY
Songs from the Prairie. Denver, CO.: Big Mountain Press, 1966. 56 p.

FLEMING, GRACE
The Life of Christ, and Other Poems. New York: Crown Publications, 1939. 3 p. ℓ., 9-59 p.

FLEMING, IDA CAPEN
Wind-Swept Strings, Selected Poems. San Francisco: The Author, 1934. 48 p.

FLEMING, MARY
Ireland, Broadway, and Other Loves. New York: G. Bruno, 1921. 47 p.

FLEMING, SARAH LEE BROWN
Hope's Highway. New York: Neale Publishing Co., 1918. 156 p.
Clouds and Sunshine. Boston: The Cornhill Company, 1920. 5 p. ℓ., 53 p.

FLETCHER, FRANCES
The Banquet and Other Poems. Philadelphia: Dorrance & Co., 1925. 44 p. (Contemporary poets)
A Boat of Glass. Philadelphia: Dorrance and Co., 1926. 37 p. (Contemporary poets, 33)

FLETCHER, LOUISA
The Land of Beginning Again. Boston: Small, Maynard and Company, 1921. 6 p. ℓ., 3-92 p.

FLETCHER, MARJORIE
Us: Women. Cambridge, MA.: Alice James Books, 1973. x, 59 p.

FLEWELLING, STELLA ISENHOWER (1902-)
Listen! I Dream. Torrance? CA.: n.p., 1956. 112 p.

FLEXNER, HORTENSE (1885-)
Clouds and Cobblestones. Boston & New York: Houghton, Mifflin Co., 1920. xi, 91, [1] p.
This Stubborn Root and Other Poems. New York: Macmillan Co., 1930. xii p., 1 ℓ., 78 p.
North Window and Other Poems. New York: Coward-McCann, 1943. ix, 78 p.
Selected Poems. London: Hutchinson, 1963. 40 p.

FLING, JESSIE SARISSA (PETTIT) (1853-)
Wonder-land of Nature. Boston: The Christopher Publishing House, 1918. 34, [1] p.

FLOHR, NATALIE
The White Unicorn. New York: Exposition Press, 1950. 63 p.

FLORENCE, STELLA GRENFELL
Dawn on the Distant Hills. New York: William Edwin Rudge, Inc., 1920. 3 p.ℓ., 16 p., 1 ℓ.

FLORENCE, YVONNE (1909-)
Flesh Against the Earth, Poems. New York: Exposition Press, 1952. 96 p.

FLORINE, MARGARET HELEN
Songs of a Nurse. San Francisco: Philopolis Press, 1917. 71, [1] p.
________. 2d ed. rev. and enl., 1918. 79 p.

FLOYD, EDNA L.
A Time to Mourn. Boston: Chapman & Grimes, 1958. 20 p.

FLUGSTAD, PATTY
A Little Fresh Air. Philadelphia: Dorrance, 1975. (Contemporary poets of Dorrance)

FOCHT, MILDRED (1881-)
Four Trees and Other Poems. New York: G. P. Putnam's Sons, 1937. 77 p.

FOGEL, RUBY
Of Apes and Angels, and Other Poems. Denver, CO.: A. Swallow, 1966. 48 p. (New poetry series, 33)

FOLEY, BARBARA ELIZABETH
The Cloister and Other Poems. Boston: Bruce Humphries, 1938. 36 p.

FOLEY, BETTY SMITH
...Wood Pile Poems. Philadelphia: Dorrance and Company, 1936.

86, [1] p. (Contemporary poets of Dorrance, 142)
...Bible Chillun. Philadelphia: Dorrance and Company, 1939. 52 p. (Contemporary poets of Dorrance, 197)

FOLGER, ALICE ADELE
Songs from the Heart. New York: The Grafton Press, 1905. 2 p. ℓ., 7-59 p.

FOOSHEE, CLARE MURRAY
Sea Pieces. New York: Harbinger House, 1945. 42 p.

FOOTE, DORREN H.
Ports of Call. New York: Poets' Press, 1941. 48 p.

FOOTE, ELVIRA
Aspen Leaves. San Francisco: Printed by Helen Gentry, 1929. [40] p.

FORBUSH, HARRIET W.
Lancaster, and Other Poems. Boston: R. G. Badger, 1930. 8 p., 1 ℓ., 9-104 p.
By Nashua's Banks, Legends and Lyrics. Boston: R. G. Badger, The Gorham Press, 1933. 3 p. ℓ., 9-64 p.
Intervale & Upland. Boston: Chapman & Grimes, 1935. 3 p. ℓ., 5-54 p.

FORD, ANNA FOSTER
Souvenir of Thoughts and Things, A Poetic Medley. New York: William-Frederick Press, 1951. 31 p. (The William-Frederick poets, 72)

FORD, CHARLOTTE IRENE
Rhymes of a Postman. New York: The Exposition Press, 1940. 40 p.

FORD, GENA
Tall Tales from Far Corners, and Other Poems. New Rochelle, N. Y.: Elizabeth Press, 1962. 29 p.
A Planting of Chives; Poems. New Rochelle, N. Y.: Elizabeth Press, 1964. 20 p.
This Time, That Space, Poems, 1964-1967. New Rochelle, N. Y.: Elizabeth Press, 1968. [49] p.
Homesickness for Big Men. New Rochelle, N. Y.: Elizabeth Press, 1972. 51 p.

FORD, JULIA ELLSWORTH (SHAW) (1859-1950)
King Solomon and the Fair Shulamite: A Poetic Idyl Arranged in Sequence. New York: n. p., 1908.

FORD, LUCY MILDRED
Maestro Harmonies. Boston: B. Humphries, Inc., 1943. 40 p.

FORKIN, KATHERINE M.
Prelude; Poems. Dallas, TX.: The Kaleidograph Press, 1934. x p., 1 ℓ., 13-52 p.
...Open Letter. Menasha, WS.: Printed by the Collegiate Press, G. Banta Publishing Co., 1941. xi, 51 p.

FORMAN, ELIZABETH (CHANDLEE)
King of the Air, and Other Poems. Boston: R. G. Badger, 1919. 119 p.
The Singing Day, and Other Poems. Ed. by Henry Chandlee Forman. New York: Exposition Press, 1951. 99 p.

FORSTER, MINNIE JANE (WYATT) (1875-)
The Carrier Pigeon. New York: Comet Press Books, 1959. 4 p. ℓ., 54 p.

FORSYTHE, HELEN (NIXON)
Thoughts from the Thicket. Philadelphia: Dorrance, 1952. 66 p. (Contemporary poets of Dorrance, 436)

FORTUNATO, MARY SHEA
Meditation; Poems. Denver, CO.: Big Mountain Press, 1961. 64 p.

FORTUNE, JAN ISBELLE (1892-)
Black Poppies. Dallas, TX.: The Southwest Press, 1921. xiii, 110 p.
Tower to the East, A Sonnet Sequence. Dallas, TX.: Southwest Press, 1934. [82] p.

FOSTER, AGNESS (GREENE) (1863-1933)
You, & Some Others, Being Poems for Occasions. San Francisco & N.Y.: P. Elder & Company, 1909. vii, 63 p., 1 ℓ.
Love Is Best, and Other Verses. Boston: n.p., 1915. 11 p.
Your Happy Way, and Other Verse for Occasions. Boston: The Stratford Company, 1924. 6 p. ℓ., 88 p.

FOSTER, CAROLINE HOLCOMBE (WRIGHT) (1864-1929)
Winds of the World. Boston: B. Humphries, Inc., 1932. xiii p., 1 ℓ., 17-156 p.

FOSTER, CYNTHIA (1919-)
Swords into Plowshares. Boston: Meador Pub. Co., 1950. 56 p.

FOSTER, EDITH
...Beside the Wishing Well. New York: H. Harrison, 1937. 64 p.
To Wind a Chain; Poems of Love and Nature. New York: Exposition Press, 1952. 64 p.

FOSTER, ELIZABETH MAY
Poems. New York: Broadway Publishing Co., 1905. viii, 175 p.

FOSTER, ELMA WILKINS
The Sound of Shadows, Poems. Denver, CO.: A. Swallow, 1960. 48 p. (The New poetry series)

FOSTER, JEANNE ROBERT (OLIVER) (1884-)
Neighbors of Yesterday. Boston: Sherman, French & Co., 1916. 8 p. ℓ., 125 p.
Wild Apples. Boston: Sherman, French & Company, 1916. 6 p. ℓ., 193 p.
Rock-Flower. New York: Boni & Liveright, 1923. ix, 118 p.

FOSTER, LAURA CHASE
Thread of the Loom. Columbus, OH.: n.p., 1943. 75 p.

FOSTER, LOUISE NELLIE
Songs of the Alps. Syracuse, N.Y.: W. Y. Foote Co., 1908. 4 p. ℓ., 3-51 p.

FOSTER, MARGUERITE STEVENS (1890-)
The Young Fliers, and Other Poems. Cambridge, MA.: Priv. print., 1944. vi, 42 p.
Homeward Flight, and Other Poems. Cambridge, MA.: Priv. Print. Harvard University Printing Office, 1946. vii, 56, [1] p.

FOSTER, MARTHA J.
Fireside Chimes in New Thought Rhymes. New York: Alliance Pub. Co., 1901. 4 p. ℓ., 13-65 p.

FOSTER, MARY EVA
The Dream of Life, and Other Poems. Pittsburgh, PA.: J. E. Banks, 1913. 70 p.

FOSTER, NANCY KIER
Sonnets and Lyrics. San Francisco, CA.: P. Elder and Company, 1917. viii, 40 p., 1 ℓ.

FOUTS, NELLIE CATHERINE (BORING) (1877-) [CABLE, CATHERINE, pseud.]
Light and Shadows. Central City, NB.: Fitch Brothers, Printers, 1930. 126 p.

FOWLER, ELOISE COOPER
Verses of Love, Faith, and Appreciation. Boston: The Roxburgh Publishing Company, 1919. 133 p.

FOWLER, ELSIE MELCHERT
For His Return; Poems. Chicago: R. F. Seymour, 1943. 77 p.
Merry-Go-Round of Verse. Chicago: Creative Enterprises, 1956. 80 p. (Happy hour books)

FOWLER, TRUTH MARY
Haiku for All Day. Francestown, N. H.: Golden Quill Press, 1968. [71] p.

FOX, CLARA MASON
In Pleasant Places; Poems. Los Angeles, CA.: Grafton Publishing Corporation, 1924. 6 p. ℓ., 17-124 p., [1] p.

FOX, IDA
In the Wind; An American Poet in Wales. St. Davids, Wales: Antiphon Press, 1970. 99 ℓ.

FOX, IONE SELMAN
Dust on Shafts of Gold. Dallas, TX.: Manfred, Van Nort & Co., 1939. 6 p. ℓ., 77 p.

FOX, LOIS
Carnation Petals. New York: The Schilling Press, Inc., 1915. 5 p. ℓ., 15-111 p.

FOX, RUTH BERRIEN (1910-1969)
A Catch or Key: Selected Poems. Peterborough, N. H.: Noone House, 1969. 77 p.
________. Dublin, N. H.: Wm. L. Bauhan, Inc., 1969.

FOX, SIV CEDERING
Cup of Cold Water; Poems and Photographs. New York: New Rivers Press, 1973. 92 p.
Letters from the Island; Poems. Fredericton, N. B.: Fiddlehead Poetry Books, 1973. 24 p.
Mother Is. New York: Stein and Day, 1975. 63 p.

FOXWORTH, NILENE ELIZABETH (1936-)
If I Were a Miracle Hen. New York: Amuru, 1973.

FRAGASSE, MARGARET
Seeds in the Wind. New York: Vantage Press, 1965. 48 p.

FRANCE, ALICE
Sung in the Shadow; Poems. Little Rock? AR.: Sketch Book Pub. Co., 1908. [94] p.

FRANCIS, MARILYN (1920-)
Tangents at Noon. San Antonio, TX.: Naylor Co., 1961. vii, 40 p.
Space for Sound. San Antonio, TX.: Naylor, 1962. v, 42 p.
Mirror Without Glass: Oak Creek Canyon. Flagstaff, AZ.: Northland Press, 1964. 61, [1] p.
Symbols for Instants. San Antonio, TX.: Naylor Co., 1965. [40] p.

FRANCK, INEZ E.
First Candleflame; Poems. St. Matthews, S. C.: Calhoun Times,

1938. [52] p.
Forget-Me-Nots of Glory. Cleveland, OH.: Pegasus Studios, 1943. 20 p. (Torchbearers' Chapbooks, no. 79)
Sunward, Poems. Prairie City, IL.: Decker Press, 1948. 74 p.

FRANK, ESTELLE R.
Pulse Beats, A Group of Freudian Poems. New York: Greenberg, 1948. 61 p.

FRANK, FLORENCE (KIPER)
The Jew to Jesus, and Other Poems. New York: M. Kennerley, 1915. 4 p. ℓ., 3-90 p.
The Silver Grain; Poems. New York: Bookman Associates, 1956. 64 p.

FRANK, RACHEL (BEREZOW) (1917-)
Selected Poems. Brooklyn, N.Y.: R. Frank Pub. Co., 1958. 35 p.
The Hero and His Voices; Eclogue. Brooklyn, N.Y.: n.p., 1960. [10] p.

FRANKLIN, ETHEL MARY
A Wild Bird's Scarlet Feather. Dallas, TX.: The Kaleidograph Press, 1941. ix p., 1 ℓ., 18-71 p.

FRANTZ, MABEL (GOODE)
The Divine Adventure; Poems. New York: H. Harrison, 1938. 95 p.

FRASER, EDITH L.
Bay Blossoms; Poems. New York: H. Harrison, 1936. 64 p.

FRASER, KATHLEEN (1937-)
Change of Address, & Other Poems. San Francisco, CA.: Kayak, 1966. 47 p.
Stilts, Somersaults, and Headstands; Game Poems Based on a Painting by Peter Brueghel. New York: Atheneum, 1968. 37 p.
In Defiance of the Rains; Poems. San Francisco, CA.: Kayak Books, 1969. 50 p.
Little Notes to You from Lucas Street; Poems by Kathleen Fraser, 1970-71. Urbana, IL.: Penumbra Press, 1972. 16 p.
What I Want. New York: Harper & Row, 1974. xii, 129 p.

FRASER, MARJORIE FROST
Franconia. New York: The Spiral Press, 1936. 37 p.

FRAZEE-BOWER, HELEN (1896-)
Garment of Praise; Poems. Boston: Bruce Humphries, 1956. 95 p.
He Came with Music; Poems. Chicago: Moody Press, 1963. 96 p.

FRAZIER, RUBY PRIMUS
Ruby's Black Emeralds. New York: Amuru, 1973.

FREAR, MARY EMMA (DILLINGHAM) (1870-)
My Islands; Verses. New York: F. D. Beattys & Co., 1911. ix, 70 p.
Hawaiian Days and Holidays and Days of Long Ago. Boston: The Stratford Co., 1927. 6 p. ℓ., 50 p.

FREDERICK, FRANCE
Just Echoes. New York: F. H. Hitchcock, 1925. iv p., 1 ℓ., 60 p.
Query. New York: H. Vinal, Ltd., 1927. 6 p. ℓ., 88 p.

FREELAND, ISABELLE McMURRAY
Thoughts in Verse. Columbus, OH.: n.p., 1909. 3-45 p.

FREEMAN, BLANCHE K. (1865-)
Winds of Tomorrow; Poems. New York: Pageant Press, 1958. 5 p. ℓ., 83 p.

FREEMAN, ELIZABETH ANDERSON
A Pilgrimage to Rubidoux. Riverside, CA.: Printed by W. D. Clark, 1911. 14 ℓ.

FREEMAN, ELLEN RICKER
Pine Grove Poems. Cincinnati, OH.: n.p., 1901. 54 p., 1 ℓ.

FREEMAN, MABEL (MILLER)
April Fantasy; The Poems of Mabel Miller Freeman. Santa Ana, CA.: The Fine Arts Press, 1938. 5 p. ℓ., 63 p.

FREEMAN-ISHILL, ROSE (FLORENCE) (1895-)
Rain Among the Bamboos. Stelton, N. J.: J. Ishill, 1917. 57 p., 1 ℓ.
Petals Blown Adrift. New York: J. Ishill, 1918. 89, [4] p.
Dream and Advent. Berkeley Heights, N. J.: Published privately by The Oriole Press, 1929. 8 p., 1 ℓ.
Poems. Berkeley Heights, N. J.: Priv. pub. by The Oriole Press, 1930. 35, [1] p.
Dedications, a Group of Poems. Berkeley Heights, N. J.: Pub. and printed privately by The Oriole Press, 1948. 79 p., 2 ℓ.
O-Jin-San; from "Rain Among the Bamboos." Berkeley Heights, N. J.: Oriole Press, 1958. [3] ℓ.
To the Unknown Martyrs. Berkeley Heights, N. J.: Oriole Press, 1959. [4] p.
Petals Blown Adrift. Berkeley, N. J.: Oriole Press, 1962. 49, [1] p. (Her Collected Works, v. 1)
Poems. Berkeley, N. J.: Oriole Press, 1962. 32 p., 1 ℓ. (Her Collected Works, v. 3)
Rain Among the Bamboos. Berkeley, N. J.: Oriole Press, 1962. 23, [1] p. (Her Collected Works, v. 2)

Seer in Darkness; A Group of Three Poems. Berkeley Heights, N. J.: The Oriole Press, 1964. [12] p.

Wellspring & Later Poems. Berkeley Heights, N. J.: Oriole Press, 1965. [22] p.

FRENCH, ELSIE JANET

May Festival and Other Poems. Berlin Heights, OH.: Press of the Berlin Call, 1925. 1 p. ℓ., 5-97 p.

Evensongs from Blossoming Sanctuaries. New York: House of Field, Inc., 1941. 81 p.

FRENCH, MARION LEONE (1899-)

Buds Not Yet in Blossom. Chicago: Printed by Kenfield-Leach Co., 1916. 35 p.

FRENCH, NORA MAY (1881-1907)

Poems. San Francisco, CA.: The Strange Company, 1910. 5 p. ℓ., 91 p.

...Poems. With a foreword by Sara Bard Field. San Francisco, CA.: Published by the Book Club of Calif., 1936. 4 p. ℓ., 23, [1] p.

FRESTON, ELIZABETH HELENE

Italia's Fornarina: Poem. New York: Broadway Pub., 1904. 40 p.

Poems. New York: Broadway Publishing Company, 1908. 2 p. ℓ., iii, 143 p.

Scattered Leaves and Other Poems. Dobbs Ferry, N. Y.: The Clermont Press, 1937. 134 p.

FREYMAN, ANNE ROBINSON

Suddenly the Earth Is Singing. Baltimore, MD.: n. p., 1951. 102 p.

FRIEND, BYRD (Mrs.)

Yucca Lilies. Dallas, TX.: The Kaleidograph Press, 1941. xiii p., 1 ℓ., 17-92 p.

FRITZ, MARTHA

If the River's This High All Summer. Cambridge, MA.: Pym-Randall Press, 1974. 42 p.

FRIZELL, MARTHA G. (SINKS) (1893-)

...A Stranger and Afraid.... New York: Crown Publications, 1941. 4 p. ℓ., [11]-92 p.

FROST, ALICE A.

Poems. Seattle, WA.: Printed by Frank McCaffrey at his Dogwood Press, 1945. [48] p.

FROST, ELIZABETH (HOLLISTER)

The Lost Lyrist. New York & London: Harper & Bros., 1928. xiii, [1] p., 2 ℓ., 3-96 p.

Hovering Shadow. New York & London: Harper & Bros., 1929. xii, 29 p., 1 ℓ.
The Closed Gentian. New York & London: Harper & Brothers, 1931. ix, [1] 52 p.

FROST, FRANCES MARY (1905-1959)
Hemlock Wall. New Haven, CT.: Yale University Press; London: H. Milford, Oxford University Press, 1929. 36 p. (Yale Series of Younger Poets, 27)
Blue Harvest; Poems. Boston & New York: Houghton Mifflin Company, 1931. xi, [1], 112, [1] p.
_______. Peterborough, N. H.: Transcript Printing Co., 1932. xi, [1], 112, [1] p. Ed. limited to 250 copies.
These Acres. Boston & New York: Houghton Mifflin Co., 1932. 5 p. ℓ., 3-72 p.
Pool in the Meadow, Poems for Young and Old. Boston & New York: Houghton, Mifflin Co., 1933. vii, [1], 73, [2] p.
Woman of This Earth. Boston & New York: Houghton Mifflin Company, 1934. 4 p. ℓ., 3-95, [1] p.
Road to America. New York: Farrar & Rinehart, Inc., 1937. 5 p. ℓ., [3]-59 p.
Mid-Century; Poems. New York: Creative Age Press, 1946. x, 99 p.
Christmas Is Shaped Like Stars. New York: Thomas Y. Crowell Co., 1948. 86 p.
The Little Whistler. New York: Whittlesey House, 1949. 48 p. (Children's poetry.)
This Rowdy Heart. Francestown, N. H.: Golden Quill Press, 1954. 71 p.
The Little Naturalist. New York: Whittlesey House, 1959. 47 p.
The Little Whistler. New York: McGraw-Hill, 1966. 48 p. (Children's poetry.)

FROST, MARGARET
Chin Up, Poems. Franklin, IN.: The Service Shop Printers, 1937. 5 p. ℓ., 26 p.

FROST, MARGUERITE (SCRIBNER) (1876-)
Love of Earth. New York: The Poets Press, 1937. 110, [1] p.

FROSTIC, GWEN (1906-)
My Michigan. Frankfort, MI.: n.p., 1957. unpaged
A Walk With Me. Benzonia, MI.: Presscraft Papers, 1958. [56] p.
These Things Are Ours. Benzonia, MI.: Presscraft Papers, 1960. [62] p.
A Place on Earth. Frankfort, MI.: n.p., 1962. 1 v.
_______. Benzonia, MI.: Presscraft Papers, 1965. [72] p.
To Those Who See. Benzonia, MI.: Presscraft Papers, 1965. [64] p.
Wing-Borne. Benzonia, MI.: Presscraft Papers, 1967. [62] p.
Wisps of Mist. Benzonia, MI.: Presscraft Papers, 1969. 1 v. unpaged

Beyond Time. Benzonia, MI.: Presscraft Papers, 1970. [62] p.

FROTHINGHAM, ELIZABETH WHITE

Broken Silences; Poems. New York & London: G. P. Putnam's Sons, 1925. vi, 51 p.

Broken Silences; Poems. 2d ed., rev. and enl. New York & London: G. P. Putnam's Sons, 1929. vii, 68 p.

FRY, DOROTHY (WHIPPLE) (1897-)

Verses. Cambridge, MA.: Priv. Print. at the Riverside Press, 1912. vii, 89 p.

Lyrics and Sonnets. Cambridge, MA.: Priv. Print. at the Riverside Press, 1914. ix, [1] p., 1 ℓ., 115, [1] p.

Driftwood. Cambridge, MA.: Priv. Print., The Riverside Press, 1916. xiii, [1], 265 p., 2 ℓ.

Rainbows and Echoes from Fairyland. Boston: The Four Seas Company, 1927. 119 p.

FRY, MAGGIE CULVER (1900-)

The Witch Deer. Dallas, TX.: Story Book Press, 1954. 40 p.

The Witch Deer; Poems of the Oklahoma Indians. 2d enl. ed. New York: Exposition Press, 1955. 40 p.

FUCHS, WILMA

So Bright the Light; Poems. New York: Pageant Press, 1955. 79 p.

FULLER, ETHEL ROMIG

White Peaks and Green. Chicago, New York: Willett, Clark and Colby, 1928. 7 p. ℓ., 91 p., 2 ℓ.

Kitchen Sonnets (and Lyrics of Domesticity). Portland, OR.: Metropolitan Press, 1931. 8 p. ℓ., 3-108 p., 1 ℓ.

White Peaks and Green. Portland, OR.: Metropolitan Press, 1933. 7 p. ℓ., 91 p., 2 ℓ.

Skylines. Portland, OR.: Binfords & Mort, 1952. 91 p.

Kitchen Sonnets (and Lyrics of Domesticity). 2d ed. Portland, OR.: Binford & Mort, 1956. 7 p. ℓ., 110 p., 1 ℓ.

________. 3d ed., 1956.

FULLER, MARGARET WITTER (1872-1959)

The Complete History of the Deluge, in Verse and Pictures. Windham, CT.: Hawthorn House, 1936. 55 p., 2 ℓ.

It Is All So Simple, Poems. Chicago: Dierkes Press, 1947. 30 p.

Sonnets and Songs; A Collection of Poems. Mill Valley, CA.: Wings Press, 1956. 100 p.

FULLWOOD, ANNE HUNT

Itinerary of Thoughts. New York, Los Angeles: The Caruthers Company, 1935. 1 p. ℓ., 5-28 p.

Tidal Waves: Book of Unpublished Verse. Boston: The Christopher Publishing House, 1941. ix, 11-64 p.

FULTON, DOLORES CASSEL
My Favorite Things. New York: Vantage Press, 1966. 63 p.

FULTON, ELLEN (1887-)
Acadian Summers. Penobscot, ME.: Tampa University Press, 1954. 48 p.

FUNK, SARAH MAE (FLOYD) (1878-)
The River and Other Poems. Warsaw, IN.: The Warsaw Union Printers, 1917. [12] p.

FUQUA, CLARA MAI HOWE
Two Dozen. Boston: R. G. Badger, 1912. 32 p.

GABLE, MARIELLA, Sister (1899-) [GABLE, MARY MARGARET and MARIELLA, Sister]
Blind Man's Stick. Boston: B. Humphries, Inc., 1938. 64 p.

GABLE, MARY MARGARET see GABLE, MARIELLA, Sister (1899-)

GADDY, LULU NETTLETON
Twilight Melodies. Boston: Manthorne & Burack, Inc., 1942. 87 p.

GAGE, JEANNE E.
This Then Is Life. Los Angeles, CA.: Ward Ritchie Press, 1957. vii, 42 p.

GAGE, THALIA
Prelude to Pentecost. New York: B. Wheelwright Co., 1952. 71 p.

GAHM, ANNA HIGBEE
Pepper Tree Lane and Other Verse. Pasadena, CA.: The Mission Press, 1936. 84 p.

GAILY, ISABEL TRACY
...Harp Strings. New York: H. Vinal Limited, 1928. 4 p. ℓ., 56 p. (The Friendly Books)

GAINER, INA
Silver Bells and Cockle Shells. Oklahoma City, OK.: n.p., 1923. [27] p., 1 ℓ.

GAINES, ALICE AUGUSTA
What Counts; Poems. San Antonio, TX.: n.p., 1923. [41] p.

GALBREATH, LORA
Various Poems. Pulaski, VA.: B. D. Smith & Bros., Printers, 1925. 145 p.

GALE, ANNA (MORLEY)
Pearls and Pebbles From the Sea of Thought. Kalamazoo, MI.: Press of Ihling Bros. Everard Co., 1916. 89 p.

GALE, MARION PERHAM
Vignettes in Violet. New York: H. Vinal, Ltd., 1928. 7 p. ℓ., 85 p.

GALE, VI
Several Houses. Denver, CO.: Alan Swallow, 1959. 47 p. (The New Poetry Series, 20)
Love Always. Denver, CO.: Alan Swallow, 1965. 60 p.
Nineteen ing Poems. Portland, OR.: Press 22, 1970. 1 v. unpaged.
Clouded Sea. Portland, OR.: Press 22, 1971. 10 ℓ. in portfolio.
Clearwater. Chicago: Swallow Press, 1974. 64 p.

GALE, ZONA (1874-1938)
The Secret Way. New York: Macmillan, 1921. x, 118 p.

GALL, GRETCHEN
Touch Earth. Vermillion, S.D.: University of South Dakota Press, 1973. 68 p.

GALLOWAY, JULIA REBECCA (1873-)
When the Lilacs Bloom, and Other Poems. Boston: R. G. Badger, 1905. 64 p.

GALLOWAY, LOUANNIE STRATTON
Transient Spring. Boston: Chapman & Grimes, 1936. 64 p.

GALT, LISA
Radar. Sacramento, CA.: Runcible Spoon, 1966.

GAMBLE, LAURA HITCHCOCK
Songs from the Hills. Los Angeles, CA.: The Ward Ritchie Press, 1941. vii, 34 p., 1 ℓ.

GAMBLE, MARY ROLOFSON
Hearts of Gold and Other Poems. Peoria, IL.: Manual Arts Press, 1923. 80 p.
Legend of the Four-Leaved Clover, and Other Rhymes. Chicago: H. G. Adair Printing Co., 1930. 3 p. ℓ., 77 p.

GANO, LOUISE HEINKE (1885-)
From My Muse to You. Portland, ME.: Falmouth Pub. House, 1948. 123 p.

GANT, SOPHIA
Smattering of Time and Sense. Philadelphia: Dorrance, 1964. 40 p. (Contemporary poets of Dorrance, 576)

GARBER, VIRGINIA (ARMISTEAD)
Pocahontas. New York: Broadway Pub., 1906. 4 p. ℓ., iii, 39 p.

GARBISCH, RUTH
The Wine Press; A Collection of Poems and Epigrams. Los Angeles, CA.: Wetzel Pub. Co., 1936. 48 p.
This Dog-Gone World. Philadelphia: Dorrance, 1965. 58 p.

GARDE, EDNA
Harp of One String. New York: Pageant Press, 1963. 5 p. ℓ., 48 p.

GARDNER, ISABELLA (McCORMICK) (1915-)
Birthdays from the Ocean. Boston: Houghton Mifflin Co., 1955. xii p., 1 ℓ., 43 p.
The Looking Glass: New Poems. Chicago: University of Chicago Press, 1961. 45 p.
West of Childhood: Poems 1950-1965. Boston: Houghton Mifflin Co., 1965. ix, 93 p.

GARDNER, JULIA MATTHEWS (1879-)
Poetry Panorama. Dallas, TX.: Story Book Publishers, 1952. 60 p.

GARDNER, LILLIAN (THOMPSON) (1870-)
Cupid's Capers. New York: E. P. Dutton & Co., 1915. 33 ℓ.

GARDNER, NANCY (BRUFF) (1915-)
My Talon in Your Heart. New York: Dutton, 1946. 60 p.

GARDNER, ORPHA MAY (1912-)
Chosen of Beauty. Spokane, WA.: n.p., 1933. 112, [4] p.

GARDNER, PATTI VANDENBARK
Some Exciting Times in Rhythm and Rhymes, and Other Poems. Harrisburg, PA.: The Evangelical Press, 1941. 56, [5] p.

GARDNER, VIOLA
Song and Laughter. Los Angeles, CA.: n.p., 1963. 11 p.
The Immortal Cast. Kanona, N.Y.: J. & C. Transcripts, 1965. 83 p.
Penny a Piece Poems. Kanona, N.Y.: J. & C. Transcripts, 1965. 4 p. ℓ., 20 p.
Bittersweet. Danbury, CT.: Published by T.N.P.C., 1967. 1 p. ℓ., 34 p.
When Violets Blue the Meadow. Kanona, N.Y.: J. & C. Transcripts, 1972. v, 33 p.
Mistletoe of Oklahoma. Kanona, N.Y.: J. & C. Transcripts, 1974. 28 p.
Love Vine Knot. Kanona, N.Y.: J. & C. Transcripts, 1975. 22 p.

GARDYNE, MARY ELKINS
Oup in Ole Vermont and Other French Dialect Poems. Boston: R. G. Badger, 1920. 64 p.
Encore Oup in Ole Vermont, French Dialect and Other Poems. Burlington, VT.: Free Printing Co., 1927. viii, 51 p.

GARLAND, MARGARET WOLFF
The Good Wine; Poems Written During a Lifetime. Waverly, IA.: Waverly Pub. Co., 1972. 48 p.

GARLAND, MARIE (TUDOR) (1870-) [TUDOR, MARIE]
The Potter's Clay; Poems. New York & London: G. P. Putnam's Sons, 1918. v, 80 p.
The Winged Spirit, and Other Poems. New York & London: G. P. Putnam's Sons, 1918.
The Marriage Feast. New York & London: G. P. Putnam's Sons, 1920. x, 147 p.

GARLICK, ETHA REBECCA (1874-1913)
Verses. San Francisco, CA.: R. J. Orozco, 1912. 34 p.

GARNETT, JUDITH LIVINGSTON COX (1862-)
Sermons in Rhyme. New York: The Neale Publishing Company, 1916. 59 p.
Twenty-Two Messages for You. New York: The Neale Publishing Company, 1918. 2 p. ℓ., 7-42 p.
Temple Torches. New York: Authors & Publishers Corporation, 1921. 43 p.
The Celestial Garment. New York: Authors & Publishers Corporation, 1927. v, 7-22 p.

GARNETT, LOUISE AYRES
Eve Walks in Her Garden. New York: Macmillan, 1926. 133 p.

GARNETT, PEGGY WINDSOR (1895-)
Audubon Trail. San Antonio, TX.: Printed by Carleton Print Co., 1951. 76 p.

GARNSEY, MARY VESTA
Gods in Modeling Clay. New York: Pageant Press, 1962. vii p., 1 ℓ., 131 p.

GARRABRANT, VERA RUTH (1888-) [GARRY, RUTH, pseud.]
My Way of Life. New York: Vantage Press, 1952. 64 p.

GARRETSON, RADELLA
Tulu Menika; An Art Poem. Chicago: W. B. Conkey Co., 1917. 3 p. ℓ., 9-59, [1] p.

GARRETT, FLORENCE ROME
Edge of Day. Sanbornville, N. H.: Wake-Brook House, 1954. 60 p., 2 ℓ.
More Than the Quiet Pond. Francestown, N. H.: Golden Quill Press, 1969. 63 p.

GARRETT, HARRIET
An Old Refrain, and Other Poems. New York: Paebar Co., 1936. 5 p. ℓ., 28 p.
Nostalgia. New York: H. Harrison, 1941. 63 p.
Tears and Glory. Cedar Rapids, IA.: Torch Press, 1947. 95 p.
Far Horizons. Cedar Rapids, IA.: Torch Press, 1957. 45 p.
Into the Morning Sun. Cedar Rapids, IA.: Torch Press, 1960. 32 p.

GARRETT, RETTA SCOTT
My Children. Dallas, TX.: C. C. Cockrell Company, 1935. 77 p.
Dream Smoke; Poems. New York: The Phaebar Co., 1937. 68 p.

GARRETT, SADIE DOWNING
Sunland Seams. New York: The Exposition Press, 1940. 3 p., 9-63 p.

GARRIGUE, JEAN (1912-1972)
The Ego and the Centaur; Poems. New York: New Directions, 1947. 126 p.
The Monument Rose; Poems. New York: Noonday Press, 1953. 58 p.
A Water Walk by Villa d'Este. New York: St. Martin's Press, 1959. 96 p.
_______. London: Macmillan, 1960. 96 p.
Country Without Maps, Poems. New York: Macmillan, 1964. xi, 82 p.
New and Selected Poems. New York: The Macmillan Company, 1967. vii, 168 p.
Studies for an Actress and Other Poems. New York: Macmillan, 1973. x, 85 p.

GARRIGUS, AILENE MARIE (FOWLER)
The Awakening, and Other Poems. New York: Exposition Press, 1952. 48 p.

GARRISON, ALETHEIA
Impressions of Mexico. New York: Robert W. Kelly Publishing Corporation, 1937. 63, [1] p.
Harp in the Midnight. New York: Robert W. Kelly Publishing Corporation, 1938. 70 p.
Words--the Weapon of Dictators. New York: R. W. Kelly Pub. Corp., 1939. 22 p.
Surf Against the Rocks. New York: R. W. Kelly Publishing Corporation, 1941. 4 p. ℓ., [11]-63 p.

GARRISON, THEODOSIA (PICKERING) (1874-)
The Joy o' Life, and Other Poems. New York: M. Kennerley, 1909. 5 p. ℓ., 9-148 p.
The Earth Cry and Other Poems. New York: M. Kennerley, 1910. 159 p.

The Dreamers and Other Poems. New York: G. H. Doran Co., 1917. x p., 1 ℓ., 13-133 p.
Et in Arcadia Ego. Chicago: Brothers of the Book, 1917. [5] p.
As the Larks Rise. New York & London: G. P. Putnam's Sons, 1921. xii, 119 p.

GARRY, RUTH, pseud. see GARRABRANT, VERA RUTH (1888-)

GARVIN, ALICE ESTHER
...Autumn Journey, and Other Poems. New Haven, CT.: The John J. Corbett Press, 194-? [16] p.

GARVIN, MARGARET ROOT
A Walled Garden and Other Poems. Portland, ME.: The Mosher Press, 1913. viii, 57, [1] p., 1 ℓ.
Peacocks in the Sun. New York: H. Vinal, 1925. 4 p. ℓ., 5-54 p.

GARVIN, MARY
Golden Rose.... New York: The Exposition Press, 1946. 32 p.

GARVIN, VIOLA GERARD (1898-)
Dedication. New York: Alfred A. Knopf, 1928. 66 p.

GATES, BERTHA LAVINA
By the Potomac, A Collection of Verse. San Leandro, CA.: The Greater West Publishing Company, 1941. 60 p.
Plum Blossoms. San Leandro, CA.: The Greater West Publishing Company, 1941. 95 p.

GATES, ELLEN MARIA (HUNTINGTON) (1835-1920)
The Dark. New York: The De Vinne Press, 1904. 10 ℓ.
To the Unborn Peoples, and Other Poems. New York: n. p., 1906. [17] p.
_______. New York: The Baker & Taylor Co., 1910. ix p., 2 ℓ., 3-65, [1] p.
The Marble House and Other Poems. New York & London: G. P. Putnam's Sons, 1921. xv, 190 p.

GATES, ESTHER BOONE (1922-)
Softness in the Wind. Hicksville, N. Y.: Exposition Press, 1975. 64 p.

GATES, MARY C. (BISHOP) (d. 1905)
Hymns of Nature and Songs of the Spirit; Poems. New York: F. H. Revell Company, 1908. xv p., 1 ℓ., 11-224 p.

GAUSS, MARGARET PAYNE
Unpublished Lyrics and Other Verse. Rochester, N. Y.: Printed by Swinburn and Co., 1914. 18 p.

GAVIN, RUTH
No More Springs, and Other Poems. Chicago: Paul Edward Pross, The Penny Post Press, 1955. 16 p.

GAW, ETHELEAN (TYSON)
Drums of El Dorado, and Other Poems. New York: Exposition Press, 1951. 96 p.
Misty Sundown. North Hollywood, CA.: Camas Press, 1959. 18 p.

GAZZAM, ANNA READING
Gleams and Echoes. Philadelphia: J. B. Lippincott, 1903. 32 ℓ.

GAZZAM, CLARE GRIFFITH
Port o' Dreams, and Other Poems. Utica, N.Y.: The Evande Company, 1911. [27] p.

GEAR, LUELLA (GLASSER) (1875-)
Winged Victory. New York: H. Vinal, 1925. 4 p. ℓ., 57 p.

GEE, PATTIE WILLIAMS (1867-)
Ode to North Carolina. 2d and rev. ed. Hasbrouck Heights, N.J.: n.p., June 1st, 1906. 8 p.
The Palace of the Heart, and Other Poems of Love. Boston: R. G. Badger, 1904. 63 p.
________. 2d ed.

GEISSE, MARY A. [CONNOP, FELIX, pseud.]
Poems by Felix Connop. Philadelphia: Campion & Co., 1904. 1 p. ℓ., 80 p.

GELFOND, RHODA (1946-)
The First Trail. Providence, R.I.: Hellcoal Press, 1972. 32 p.

GENEE, EDYTHE HOPE
Brief Aprils. New York: Dodd, Mead & Co., 1947. 142, [1] p.
Sequins for Calico. Hollywood, CA.: House-Warven, 1951. 143 p.

GENEREAUX, ELIZABETH
Just Little Things. Sacramento, CA.: Anderson Printing Co., 1919. 4 p. ℓ., 7-40 ℓ.

GENTRY, PEARL (OWEN)
Memories. Dallas, TX.: Tardy Pub. Co., 1936. 4 p. ℓ., 90 p.
Hilltops and Hollows. Dallas, TX.: Mathis, Van Nort & Co., 1946. 5 p. ℓ., 85 p.

GEORGE, HELLYN
Only New England. Springfield, MA.: The Valley Press, 1911. [53] p.

New England Days. Boston: The Four Seas Co., 1921. 60 p.

GEORGE, MARGUERITE
Wings on the Hilltop. Dallas, TX.: The Kaleidograph Press, 1933. 4 p. ℓ., xi-xii p., 1 ℓ., 15-76 p.

GEORGNS, ESTHER VALCK
Snow at Night, and Other Poems. Boston: B. Humphries, Inc., 1939. 79 p.

GERBAULET, NINA JOY
Contours. New York: Columbia University Press, 1931. 4 p. ℓ., 32 p.

GERBERDING, ELIZABETH (SEARS)
Verse. San Francisco, CA.: W. N. Brunt Press, 1915. [15] p.

GERMAINE, FLORIDA DRAKE
Some Verses and Songs. Philadelphia, PA.: n. p., 1917. [24] p.

GERRO, CARON, pseud. see DORSEY, BERTHA ANNABELLE (GAY) (1893-)

GERRY, HELEN
Sonnets of Simonetta. New York: The Georgian Press, 1927. 23 p.
Songs of Simonetta. Mexico: Elizondo Publishers, 1938. 30 ℓ.
Mexican Summer; A Book of Poems. New York: The Fine Editions Press, 1941. 50 p., 1 ℓ.

GETMAN, GRACE M. (1886-)
Lake Shore Reflections. Greenfield, IN.: Printed by Gobles, 1947. 93 p.

GETMAN, SALLIE GREGORY
The Watcher, The Pathway, and Other Poems. Frankfort, N. Y.: The Hardell Printing Co., 1924. [123] p.

GHENT, KATE DOWNING
A String of Pearls, and Other Poems. Boston: The Christopher Publishing House, 1925. 42 p.

GIANCRECO, MARIANNE RANSON
Canoe Country Poems. New York: Vantage Press, 1974. 44 p.

GIBBONS, HELEN K.
Verses.... Philadelphia: Barandon Press, 1917. 3 p. ℓ., 128 p.

GIBBS, AGNES K.
Songs of Colorado and Other Places. Boston: The Gorham Press, 1916. 182 p.

GIBBS, BARBARA (1912-)
...The Well; Poems. Albuquerque: A. Swallow, 1941. 31, [1] p.
The Green Chapel. New York: Noonday Press, 1958. viii, 110 p.
Poems Written in Berlin. Pawlett, VT.: Claude Fredericks, 1959. xiv, [2] p.
Poems by Barbara Gibbs: The Meeting Place of the Colors. West Branch, IA.: Cummington Press, 1972. 63 p.

GIBBS, BEATRICE RUTH (1894-)
Vision. Philadelphia: University of Pennsylvania Press, 1950. 20 p.
The Voices and Other Poems. London; New York: Hutchinson, 1951. 72 p.

GIBBS, JEANNE OSBORNE
The Other Side of the Water. Decatur, GA.: Georgia Magazine, 1970. 63 p.

GIBBS, SALLY
Beauty for Ashes. Philadelphia: Dorrance and Co., 1931. 100 p. (Contemporary poets of Dorrance, 98)

GIBSON, FLORENCE (BURDICK)
Mountain Laurel. New York: Avon House, 1937. 64 p.

GIBSON, FRANCES REED
The Moon-Maiden, and Other Poems. Boston: Sherman, French and Company, 1913. 3 p. ℓ., 39 p.

GIBSON, IVA THOMAS
God's Steadfast Power. San Antonio, TX.: Naylor Co., 1959. vii, 34 p.

GIBSON, KATHLEEN C.
A Bard's-Eye View. Philadelphia: Dorrance, 1970. 49 p. (Contemporary poets of Dorrance)

GIBSON, LOUISE M.
Poems Straight from the Heart. Boston: Christopher Pub. House, 1962. 71 p.

GIBSON, MARGARET
Lunes: Poems. Washington, D.C.: Some of Us Press, 1973. 31 p.

GIDLOW, ELSA (1898-)
On a Grey Thread. Chicago: W. Ransom, 1923. 5 p. ℓ., 9-77 p. (Series of First Volumes, no. 6)
California Valley with Girls, and Other Poems. San Francisco, CA.: Privately published, 1932. 9 p.
From Alba Hill (A Mountain Interlude). San Francisco, CA.:

n. p., 1933. [8] p.
Wild Swan Singing. n. p.: Priv. Print., 1954? [12] p.
Letters from Limbo. n. p., 1956. [12] p.
Mood of Eros. Mill Valley, CA.: Druid Heights Books, 1972? 24 ℓ.
Makings for Meditation. Mill Valley, CA.: Druid Heights Books, 1973. [39] p.

GIERE, MABLE LOUISE see ALDRICH, MABLE GIERE

GIERASCH, GEORGIA BOIT
Out of the Night and Other Poems. Akeley, MN.: Printed by the Cabin in the Pines, 1934. 64 p.
Skyline Mirages. Emory University, GA.: Banner Press, 1941. 65 p. (Verse craft series)

GIFFORD, FANNIE STEARNS (DAVIS) (1884-) [DAVIS, FANNIE STEARNS]
Myself and I. New York: Macmillan and Co., 1913. viii p., 1 ℓ., 129 p.
Crack o' Dawn. New York: Macmillan Co., 1915. vi p., 2 ℓ., 3-109 p.
The Ancient Beautiful Things. New York: Macmillan Co., 1923. 82 p.

GILBERT, ANNA (KELLEDY)
The Angle of the Battlefield & Other Poems. New York: H. Vinal Ltd., 1928. 8 p. ℓ., 109 p., 1 ℓ.

GILBERT, HAZEL A.
All for Jesus, Poems. New York: Exposition Press, 1948. 63 p.

GILCHRIST, MARIE EMILIE
Wide Pastures. New York: The Macmillan Company, 1926. 4 p. ℓ., 7-103 p.

GILDEA, FLORENCE
Lest You Forget. Philadelphia: Dorrance & Company, 1946. 4 p. ℓ., 7-56 p. (Contemporary poets of Dorrance, 326)

GILE, BLANCHE FINKLE
Song of the Onion River.... n. p., 1918? 4 p.
Echoes of the Great. Boston: R. G. Badger, 1919. 29 p.
Songs of the Glad Years. Rutland, VT.: The Tuttle Company, 1922. 34 p.
Second Youth. Rutland, VT.: The Tuttle Company, 1929. 31 p.

GILL, BETTY HOLLIDAY
Flights of Fancy and Fun; Simple Poems about Home and Children. New York: Exposition Press, 1952. 80 p.

GILL, DAISY SANIAL
Poems. New York: H. Vinal, 1927. 6 p. ℓ., 77 p., 1 ℓ.
Out of the Lips of Life. North Montpelier, VT.: The Driftwind Press, W. J. Coates, 1936. 70 p. (Driftwind chapbook, no. 5)

GILL, FRANCES
The Little Days. Boston & New York: Houghton Mifflin Co., 1917. 5 p. ℓ., [3]-50, [2] p.
Windy Leaf. New York: The Macmillan Company, 1924. 58 p.

GILLESPIE, MARIETTA
Life's Lyre. New York: The Hobson Book Press, 1947. xi, [1] p., 2 ℓ., 159 p.

GILLESPIE, YETZA
The Bird in the Willow. Dallas, TX.: The Kaleidograph Press, 1946. ix p., 1 ℓ., 13-72 p.

GILLESPY, JEANNETTE BLISS
The Eastward Road. New York: J. Pott & Co., 1903. 73 p.

GILLETT, ISABELLA
Gleanings and Weavings. San Francisco, CA.: M. Cloyd, 1922. 3 p. ℓ., 3-89 p.

GILLETT, LUCIE KARME
First Children. Philadelphia: Dorrance & Co., 1933. 63 p. (Contemporary poets of Dorrance, 114)
...Out with the Tide. Philadelphia: Dorrance & Co., 1937. 71 p. (Contemporary poets of Dorrance, 166)

GILLILAND, LEONIA DODDS
A Thimbleful of Living; Poems. New York: Vantage Press, 1960. 59 p.

GILMORE, ELSIE L.
Our Flag and Other Verse. Toledo, OH.: McManus Troup Co., 1918. 32 p.

GILMORE, JESSIE MAY (1872-)
The River's Bride. New York: The William-Frederick Press, 1945. 30 p., 1 ℓ. (The William-Frederick poets, no. 16)

GILPIN, RUTH F. (1895-)
The Other Side of the Cloud. San Antonio, TX.: Naylor, 1952. xiii, 69 p.

GILTINAN, CAROLINE (1884-)
The Divine Image; A Book of Lyrics. Boston: The Cornhill Company, 1917. x p., 1 ℓ., 60 p.
The Veiled Door. New York: The Macmillan Company, 1929. 101 p.

GIOVANNI, NIKKI (1943-)
Black Feeling, Black Talk. 1st ed. n.p.: Priv. print., 1968. 19 p.
______. 2d ed. New York: Afro-Arts, 1968. 26 p.
Black Judgement. 1st ed. Detroit: Broadside Press, 1968. 36 p.
Black Feeling, Black Talk. 3d ed. Detroit: Broadside Press, 1970. 26 p.
Black Feeling, Black Talk, Black Judgment. New York: W. Morrow, 1970. vii, 98 p. (Morrow paperback editions)
Poem of Angela Yvonne Davis. New York: Printed by Afro-Arts, 1970. [4] p.
Re: Creation. 1st ed. Detroit: Broadside Press, 1970. 48 p.
Spin a Soft Black Song; Poems for Children. New York: Hill and Wang, 1971. [64] p.
My House: Poems. New York: William Morrow, 1972. xviii, 69 p.
Ego Tripping & Other Poems for Young Readers. New York: L. Hill, dist. by Independent Pub. Group, 1974. 37 p.
The Women and the Men. New York: William Morrow, 1975. [64] p.

GITHENS, BEVERLEY (1903-)
Novitiate. n.p., 1938. [15] p.
No Splendor Perishes. La Porte, IN.: The Dierkes Press, 1946. 50 p.

GITIN, MARIA
Little Movies. Ithaca, N.Y.: Ithaca House, 1974. 59 p.

GLADDING, MARY HIGH
Pomegranate Seeds. Boston: n.p., 1926. 101 p.

GLASCOCK, KATHRYN IRENE (1909-1923)
Poems. South Hadley, MA.: A. L. F. Snell, 1923. 2 p. ℓ., iii-xi, 25 p.

GLASGOW, ELLEN ANDERSON GHOLSON (1873-1945)
The Freeman, and Other Poems. New York: Doubleday, Page and Co., 1902. 3 p. ℓ., 9-56 p.

GLASS, NANCY REBECCA (CAMPBELL) (1842-)
The Mountain Spring, and Other Poems. Boston: Sherman, French & Co., 1913. 4 p. ℓ., 59 p.

GLASSIE, ADA BOYD
The Cause; A Bit of War Verse. Washington, D.C.: Printed by W. B. Dawson, 1917. [13] p.

GLAZER, ETTA (1913-) [MARKS, LILA, pseud.]
Flutings. Boston: Meador Publishing Co., 1945. 24 p.

GLEASON, MADELINE
Poems by Madeline Gleason. San Francisco, CA.: The Grabhorn Press, 1944. 4 p. ℓ., 3-59 p., 1 ℓ.
The Metaphysical Needle; Poems. San Francisco, CA.: Centaur Press, 1949. 53, [1] p.
Concerto for Bell and Telephone. San Francisco, CA.: Unicorn Press in association with Unicorn Book Shop, 1967. 52 p.
The Interior Castle. Santa Barbara, CA.: Unicorn Press, 1967. 1 ℓ.
Selected Poems. Ltd. 1st ed. Georgetown, CA.: Dragon's Teeth Press, 1972. viii, 61 p. (Living poets' library. Penultimate series, no. 1)
Here Comes Everybody: New and Selected Poems. San Francisco, CA.: Panjandrum Press, 1975. [52] p.

GLEASON, MARIAN (GILES)
Light Version. Francestown, N.H.: Golden Quill Press, 1958. 64 p.
All Our Yesterdays. Francestown, N.H.: Golden Quill Press, 1960. 64 p.

GLEN, EMILIE CAROLYN (1924-)
Laughing Lute, and Other Poems. Chicago: Chat Noir Press, 1963. 35 p.
At Random from the Dragon's Den. New York: n.p., 1966. 11 ℓ.
Coffee House Poems. New York: n.p., 1966. 10 ℓ.
Painted Door, and Other Poems. n.p.: 1967. [8] ℓ.
Mad Hatter and Other Poems. n.p., 1968. [9] ℓ.
Paint and Turpentine. n.p.: R. Ignalls, 1969. [12] ℓ.
Just Because; Poems. n.p.: R. Ignalls, 1970. [8] ℓ.
Twat Shot. New York?: R. Ignalls, 1970. 11 ℓ.
Up to Us Chickens. New York: The Poet's Press, 1972. [24] p.

GLEN, EMMA LEE (PATTERSON)
Like a Meteor. Dallas, TX.: The Kaleidograph Press, 1938. xi p., 2 ℓ., 17-101 p.
Graven Beauty. Dallas, TX.: The Kaleidograph Press, 1941. x p., 1 ℓ., 13-96 p.

GLENN, SIBYL (1891-)
Candles Three; Poems. New York: H. Harrison, 1939. 62 p.

GLINES, ELLEN
Garden Untended. Portland, ME.: The Mosher Press, 1933. xi, [1], 115, [2] p.

GLUECK, ANITRA JOYCE
...Light and Shadow, and Other Poems. Philadelphia: Dorrance & Co., 1943. 47 p. (Contemporary poets of Dorrance, 259)
...Moods and Madrigals. Philadelphia: Dorrance & Co., 1944. 65 p. (Contemporary poets of Dorrance, 235)

Three Worlds. Philadelphia: Dorrance & Co., 1946. 59 p.
The Gothic Look; Poems. Cambridge, MA.: Riverside Press, Priv. print., 1957. xii p., 1 ℓ., 74 p.

GLÜCK, LOUISE (1943-)
Firstborn. New York: New American Library, 1968. 53 p.
Firstborn. Northwood (Middx): Anvil Press Poetry, 1969. [8], 53 p.
The House on Marshland. New York: Ecco Press/Viking, 1975. 42 p. (The American poetry series; v. 5)

GODDARD, GLORIA (1897-)
A Breadline for Souls. New York: L. Copeland, 1930. x p., 2 ℓ., 8-122 p.

GODFREY, CAROLINE (HARDEE)
The Christmas Fireplace. New York: Paebar Co., 1948. 45 p.
The Woman of Promise. Atlanta, GA.: Banner Press, Emory University, 1949. 48 p.
Home in the Orange Grove. Nashville, TN.: Benson Printing Co., 1956. 76 p.
God's Christmas Trees. Atlanta, GA.: Printed by Harper Printing Co., 1957. 25 p.

GOEDICKE, PATRICIA (McKENNA) (1921-)
Between Oceans; Poems. New York: Harcourt, Brace & World, 1968. 69 p.

GOLDBERG, FRIEDA
A Sweet Duet. New York: Vantage Press, 1955. 68 p.

GOLDBERG, MIMI
The Lover, and Other Poems. Philadelphia: Kraft Pub. Co., 1961. [i]-vi p., 1 ℓ., 1-54 p., 1 ℓ.

GOLDMARK, SUSAN
High Adventure, and Other Poems. Los Angeles, CA.: The Auk Press, 1935. vii, 73 p., 1 ℓ.

GOLDSMITH, BEATRICE (1915-1950)
The World Grows Smaller; Poems & Songs. New York: Grenich Printing Corp., 1953. 96 p.; 48 p. Yiddish part: 48 p.

GOLDSMITH, BELLE M.
Happiness Is: Sez Belgee, the Spiritual Clown Philosopher. Philadelphia: Dorrance, 1974. 39 p.

GOLDSMITH, ELIZABETH FITTEN
Patches from the Sky. Atlanta, GA.: H. M. Long Printing Company, 1937. 64 ℓ.
Gleanings. Boston: The Christopher Publishing House, 1938. 2 p. ℓ., vii-ix, 11-50 p.
Patches from the Sky. Atlanta, GA.: W. W. Brown Pub. Co., 1957. 5 p. ℓ., 62 p.

GOLDSTEIN, ROBERTA BUTTERFIELD (1917-)
The Searching Season; Poems of Faith, Hope, and Love by a Modern Mother. Burlington, VT?: n. p., 1961. 62 p.
Fling Jeweled Pebbles. Francestown, N. H.: Golden Quill Press, 1963. 82 p.
The Wood Burns Red. Francestown, N. H.: Golden Quill Press, 1966. 94 p.
Cry Before Dawn. Francestown, N. H.: Golden Quill Press, 1974. 80 p.

GOLDSTONE, ALINE LEWIS see LEWIS, MAY

GOLOMB, MOLLIE R.
How Fair My Faith and Other Poems. Philadelphia: Dorrance, 1968. 56 p. (Contemporary poets of Dorrance)

GOLTRA, MABEL HALL (1874-)
Impressions. Cedar Rapids, IA.: The Torch Press, 1946. 128 p.

GONZALES, ALBERTA JETT (1913-)
Shadow of His Wings. Philadelphia: Dorrance, 1968. 60 p. (Contemporary poets of Dorrance series)

GOODALE, DORA READ (1866-)
The Test of the Sky. Philadelphia: Dorrance and Company, 1926. 79 p. (Contemporary poets of Dorrance, 45)
Mountain Dooryards. Cedar Rapids, IA.: The Torch Press, 1946. 63 p.
_______. Ed. by Chad Drake and Katherine Ayer. 2d ed. Berea, KY.: Council of the Southern Mountains, 1961. 63, [1] p.

GOODE, KATE TUCKER
The First Fruits, and Other Poems. New York: Fleming H. Revell Company, 1914. 221 p.

GOODE, MAUD L.
Poems. East Liverpool, OH.: n. p., 1926. 8 p.

GOODE, NELLIE
Face to the Sun. Dallas, TX.: The Kaleidograph Press, 1945. xi, 13-80 p.

GOODENOUGH, CAROLINE LOUISA (LEONARD) (1856-)
Long, Long Ago on the Farm, and Other Poems. Oberlin, OH.: Obtainable from A. G. Comings & Son, 1912. 4 p. ℓ., [11]-124 p., 1 ℓ.

GOODING, LORIE (CONLEY)
Let There Be Music; A Book of Worship in Verse. Scottdale, PA.: Herald Press, 1962. 112 p.

GOODMAN, CHLEO DESHLER (1913-)
The Hourglass. Denver, CO.: Big Mountain Press, 1954. 48 p.

GOODMAN, LINDA
Venus Trines at Midnight: Astrological Verses about Lions, Rams, Bulls, Twins, Archers, and Other Sun Signs and You. New York: Taplinger Pub. Co., 1970. 127 p.

GOODMAN, MAE WINKLER (1911-)
Foam Against the Sky.... Cleveland, OH.: American Weave Press, 1945. 32 p.
The Single Flame. Cleveland, OH.: American Weave Press, 1948. 61 p.
In Time of Swallows: 52 American Birds, Poems. New York: Devin-Adair, 1951. 54 p.
Verge of Eden, New and Selected Poems. New York: Devin-Adair, 1962. 81 p.

GOODMAN, RYAH TUMARKIN
Toward the Sun. Boston: B. Humphries, 1952. 128 p.

GOODWIN, EMMA EUGENIE (QUIGLEY) (1866-)
Poems for Those Who Work and Hope and Love. New York: The De Vinne Press, 1915. 1 p. ℓ., 13 numb. ℓ., 1 ℓ.
Intimate Words of Life and Love. New York? n.p., 1926. 12 ℓ.
Poems for Those Who Work and Hope and Love. New York: H. Vinal, Ltd., 1928. 6 p. ℓ., 3-140 p.

GOODWIN, GRACE DUFFIELD (1899-)
Horizon Songs. Boston: Sherman, French & Co., 1912. 6 p. ℓ., 3-153 p.

GOODWIN, JULIA EMMONS (1867-)
Singing Pictures. Burlington, VT.: Free Press Interstate Printing Corporation, Inc., 1937. viii, 86 p.

GOODWIN, RUBY (BERKLEY)
From My Kitchen Window; The Poems of Ruby Berkley Goodwin. New York: W. Malliet and Company, 1942. 5 p. ℓ., 13-66 p.
_______. 2d ed., 1946. 5 p. ℓ., 11-67 p.

GOOLD, CLARA ADELIA
To Portland on Casco Bay. Portland, ME.: Smith & Sale Printers, 1916. 16 ℓ.

GORDON, BERTHA FRANCES (1879-)
Overtones; A Little Book of Verse. n.p., 1909. [30] p.
Songs of Courage and Others. Herrin, IL.: Privately printed, The Herrin News, 1910. 12 ℓ.
Songs of Courage, and Other Poems. New York: The Baker and Taylor Co., 1911. 70 p.
...The Orange Lantern, Poems. Philadelphia: Dorrance & Com-

pany, 1941. 88 p. (Contemporary poets of Dorrance, 221)
Beyond the Horizon. Cedar Rapids, IA.: The Torch Press, 1943. vii, 86 p.
Wings of the Dawn, A Trilogy of Aspiration. Cedar Rapids, IA.: The Torch Press, 1943. 47 p.

GORDON, ELIZABETH (1866-1922)
Flower Children; The Little Cousins of the Field and Garden. Chicago: P. F. Volland & Co., 1910. [92] p.
Lyrical Liltings of Lonesome Liz. n.p.: Parker, 1911.
Some Smiles; A Little Book of Limericks. Boston: W. A. Wilde Co., 1911. [29] p.
Bird Children, The Little Playmates of the Flower Children. Chicago: P. F. Volland & Co., 1912. 11-95 p., [1] p.
Just You. Minneapolis, MN.: Geo. W. Parker Art Co., 1912. 10 ℓ.
The Book of Bow-Wows; A Book of Pets. Chicago: M. A. Donohue & Co., 1913. 20 ℓ.
A Sheaf of Roses. Chicago: Rand, McNally & Company, 1915. 36 ℓ.
Just You. Chicago: P. F. Volland Company, 1920. 11 ℓ.
Happy Home Children. Joliet, IL.: The P. F. Volland Co., 1924. 20 ℓ.
Bird Children, The Little Playmates of the Flower Children. Rev. ed., Chicago: P. F. Volland & Co., 1930. 4 p. ℓ., 11-95 p., [1] p.
Flower Children; The Little Cousins of the Field and Garden. Rev. ed., New York: The Wise-Parslow Company, 1939. [92] p.

GORDON, EVE MADELINE
In Caverns of Today. New York: T. Gaus' Son, Inc., 1941. 31 p.

GORDON, GUANETTA STEWART (1905-)
Songs of the Wind. Washington?: n.p., 1953. 92 p.
Under the Rainbow Arch. Chicago: Windfall Press, 1963. 106 p.
Petals from the Moon. Francestown, N.H.: Golden Quill Press, 1971. 96 p.
Shadow Within the Flame. Francestown, N.H.: Golden Quill Press, 1973. 96 p.

GORDON, HELEN (VAN METRE) VAN-ANDERSON (1859-)
Radiant Star: A Poem. San Francisco, CA.: The Little Brother Publishing Co., 1911. 5 p. ℓ., 19 p.

GORDON, SUSAN JOAN (1942-)
The Road I Travel; Collected Poems. Ventnor, N.J.: Ventnor Publishers, 1964. 56 p.

GOREN, JUDITH (1933-)
Coming Alive. Okemos, MI.: Stone Press, 1975. 71, [1] p.

GORGES, GRACE
My Little Songs. Florence: n.p., 1926. 3 p.ℓ., 3-76 p.
The Bells of Italy, and Other Poems. New York: H. Vinal, Ltd., 1927. 6 p.ℓ., 93 p., 1 ℓ.

GORMAN, KATHERINE
This Alien Earth. Boston: B. Humphries, 1951. 60 p.
Flesh the Only Coin. Fort Smith, AR.: South and West, 1968? 44 p.
Album. Homestead, FL.: Olivant Press, 1969. 29 p.

GOSNELL, BETTY see GOSNELL, ELIZABETH DUKE TUCKER

GOSNELL, ELIZABETH DUKE TUCKER [GOSNELL, BETTY]
The Poet Who Was a Painter of Souls: Poems. Fort Smith, AR.: South and West, 1969. 28 p.
Silk and Silence. Fort Smith, AR.: South and West, 1971. 44 p.

GOSTIN, ROSA JESSUP
Leaves of Amber. Macon, GA.: Press of the J. W. Burke Co., 1925. 64 p.

GOTTHARDT, NAOMI
Thoughts That Linger. San Antonio, TX.: Naylor Co., 1966. xiii, 62 p.

GOULD, ALICE LAWRY
Flotilla. Boston: R. G. Badger, 1925. 39 p.

GOULD, CORA (SMITH) [Full Name: Cora Anna (Smith) Gould.]
The Caribbean Sea. New York: National Americana Society, 1927. 87 p.
The Town at the Top o' the World and Other Poems. New York: Street & Smith Corporation, 1928. 94 p.
Winged Journeys. Jersey City, N.J.: Priv. Print., The Author, 1935. 9 p.ℓ., 136 p.
Flash Lights on Florida. New York: Fredrick Photo-Gelatine Press, Inc., 1937. [37] p., 1 ℓ.
Dream Land on the Isle of Nassau in the Bahamas. New York: Fredrick Photo-Gelatine Press, Inc., 1938. [40] p.
Winter in Florida. New York: Printed by Fredrick Photo-Gelatine Press, 1939. [38] p.
Fugitive Poems Make a Happy Landing. Milledgeville, GA.: Ogelthorpe University Press, 1942. 1 v. unpaged.

GOULD, EDITH KINGDON
The Poems of Edith Kingdon Gould. New York & Chicago: W. H. Sadlier, Inc., 1934. 56 p.

GOULD, ELIZABETH PORTER (1848-1906)
One's Self I Sing, and Other Poems. Boston: R. G. Badger, 1904. 3 p.ℓ., 155 p.

GOULD, JEANE L.
Path of Life, a Book of Modern Verse. Boston: B. Humphries, 1931. 85 p.

GOVE, MARY ELIZABETH (DENISON)
Poems of Faith. Wichita, KA.: M'Cormick-Armstrong Press, 1912? 16 ℓ.

GOVERN, RENA GREENLEE
Democracy's Task. New York: By the Author, 1945. 36 p.

GOWAN, IDA CLARICE
Santa Claus at Waikiki; Including Songs: The Waves Kept on Dancing, On My Surfboard. Los Angeles, CA.: Wetzel Publishing Co., 1941. 1 p. ℓ., 5-119 p.
______. New York: The William-Frederick Press, 1944. [73] p.
The Striker. New York: The William-Frederick Press, 1944. 16 p.
Wreaths of Glory, Poems on Historical Events. New York: Exposition Press, 1951. 93 p.

GRADICK, LAURA EMERSON
Burning Bush. Prairie City, IL.: Decker Press, 1948. 30 p.
Silver Buckles. Dallas, TX.: Royal Pub. Co., 1958. 64 p.
Golden Apples. Dallas, TX.: Royal Pub. Co., 1964. 68 p.
Far Horizons. Jacksonville, FL.: n.p., 1970. 117 p.

GRAHAM, BERTHA WHITLEY (1892-)
Garden in the Sky. Moscow, ID.: n.p., 1954. 62 p.

GRAHAM, EDITH MacDONALD
Harp That Sings. Philadelphia: Dorrance, 1947. 52 p. (Contemporary poets of Dorrance, 351)

GRAHAM, ELFREDA
From Dust to Stars. Charleston, IL.: Prairie Press, 1967. x, 22 p.

GRAHAM, GLADYS WILMOT
The Inn of Bells. Sioux Falls, SD.: S.D.M.D. Scott, 1919. 7 ℓ.
Auras of Earth. Crescent City, FL.: New Athenaeum Press, 1962. 56 p.

GRAHAM, JOYCE MAXTONE see TAYLOR, JOYCE (GRAHAM) (1901-)

GRAHAM, LUCILLE (1887-)
...Hills and Valleys. New York: H. Harrison, 1936. 63 p.
No One Ever Told Me. Portsmouth, OH.: n.p., 1947. 63 p.

GRAHAM, MARGARET CABEL
Flight of the Spirit and the Children of Crooked Lake. St. Meinrad, IN.: The Abbey Press, 1942. 69 p.

GRAHAM, MARTHA K.
Words for the Music. Prairie City, IL.: Press of J. A. Decker, 1942. 48 p.

GRAHAM, RACHEL
Headlands. Francestown, N.H.: Golden Quill Press, 1960. 80 p.

GRAHAM, RAMONA [COOK, RAMONA GRAHAM]
Hills of New England. Wellesley Hills, MA.: Wills-Rae Pub. Co., 1946. 36 p.
Aeolus Drives. Francestown, N.H.: Golden Quill Press, 1969. 83 p.

GRAHAME, ROBERTA MARGARET
Last Bell at Midcentury. Wellesley, MA.: Hathaway House Bookshop, 1951. 44 p.
In Dark Radiance. New York: Vantage Press, 1964. 80 p.

GRAHN, JUDY (1941-)
Edward the Dyke, and Other Poems. Oakland, CA.: The Women's Press Collective, 1971. [66] p.
The Common Woman. Oakland, CA.: Women's Press Collective, 1972. 8 p.
A Woman Is Talking to Death. Oakland, CA.: The Women's Press Collective, 1974. [12] p.

GRAINGER, ELLA (STROM) [Full Name: Ella Viola Strom Grainger.]
The Pavement Artist, and Other Poems. London: Hutchinson & Co., Ltd., 1940. 122 p.
A Wayward Girl; Poems. Springfield, MO.: Procurable from Crossways Book Shop, 1941. iv, 40 p.

GRAMLICH, BERNICE FREE
Star Gazing. Hennessey, OK.: The Hennessey Clipper, 1941. 3 p.ℓ., 57 p.

GRANDE, RUTH
White Narcissus; Poems. New York: Carlton Press, 1962. 25 p. (A Lyceum Book)
Haiku Gathering. Philadelphia: Dorrance, 1974. 42 p.

GRANDY, JULIA SELDEN
Witness the Weather. Philadelphia: Dorrance, 1956. 51 p. (Contemporary poets of Dorrance, 492)
Singing Shadows. Philadelphia: Dorrance, 1959. 98 p. (Contemporary poets of Dorrance, 510)

GRANNISS, ANNA JANE (1856-)
Speedwell; or, The Flower of Saint Veronica... Verses. Keene, N.H.: Press of Darling & Co., 1900. 1 p.ℓ., 64 p.

A Christmas Snowflake; A Rhyme for Children. Hartford, CT.: C. M. Gaines, 1903. 3 p. ℓ., 22 p.
Prayer Beautiful, and Other Verse. East Northfield, MA.: The Bookstore, 1916. 4 p. ℓ., [3]-70 p.

GRANT, NEELY
Mississippi from a Picture Window. Philadelphia: Dorrance, 1956. 54 p. (Contemporary poets of Dorrance, 485)

GRANTHAM, ALEXANDRA ETHELDRED (von HERDER) (1867-)
[Full Name: Alexandra Etheldred Emily Maria Sylvia (von Herder) Grantham.]
Per Aspera Ad Astra; A Collection of Poems. New York: R. G. Cooke, Inc., 1907. 6 p. ℓ., 17-64 p.

GRATON, Mrs. HENRY C. (1838-1910)
Heavenly Jewels; Poems. Worcester, MA.: The Blanchard Press, 1911. 100 p.

GRAVELLE, BARBARA
The Keepsake. Berkeley, CA.: Two Windows Press, 1974. [12] p. (Effie's books, no. 1)

GRAVES, ETTA MERRICK
Take Your Choice; A Friendship Brochure. Jackson, MO.: Bard Press, 1936. 30 p.

GRAVES, FRANCES (MINER) (1863-1932)
The Roses of Grandmother's Time, and Other Poems. New London, CT.: The Bingham Press, 1933. 48 p.

GRAVES, KATHERYNE ELIZABETH
The Kaw Valley Deluge, with Poems. Topeka, KA.: Corning Prtg. Co., 1903. 10 ℓ.

GRAVES, LILLIE S.
This Passing Moment. Wichita Falls, TX.: Terry Bros., 1943. 5 p. ℓ., 60 p.
Windows to Catch the Sun.... Wichita Falls, TX.: Terry Bros., 1945. 5 p. ℓ., 76 p.
With Breeze and Bloom. Wichita Falls, TX.: Terry Bros., 1947. 80 p.

GRAY, AGNES KENDRICK
River Dusk, and Other Poems. New York: Evans-Brown, 1923. 72 p.

GRAY, FRANCES ANGEVINE
Fragile Armor. Cedar Rapids, IA.: The Torch Press, 1942. 73 p.
Winged Passage, A Collection of Poetry. New York: William-Frederick Press, 1951. 58 p. (The William-Frederick poets, 77)

Signature of Time. Portland, ME.: House of Falmouth, 1968. 46 p.
End of the Rainbow. Philadelphia: Dorrance, 1970. 29 p.

GRAY, MARY BELKNAP
The New Environment, and Other Poems. Frankfort, KY.: Roberts Print. Co., 1953. 57 p.

GRAY, MARY (TUDOR) (1886-1952)
Selected Poems. Hartford, CT.: Priv. print., 1936. 2 p. ℓ., 67 p.
Spring Tide. Hartford, CT.: Press of Meyer & Noll, 1941. 2 p. ℓ., 56 p.

GRAY, RUBY ARCHER (1873-)
Hail, Friend! New York: H. Harrison, 1930. 128 p.

GREATHEAD, SARAH ESTELLE (HAMMOND) (1855-)
David Remembers, The Epic of the Colorado and Other Poems. San Jose, CA.: Smith Printing Co., 1935. 92, [2] p.
...Stepping Stones to America's Greatness. Philadelphia: Dorrance, 1945. 95 p. (Contemporary poets of Dorrance, 288)

GRECO, EILEEN M.
Reverberations & Other Poems. New York: Vantage Press, 1975. 51 p.

GREEFF, ADELE (1911-)
Love's Argument. New York: Macmillan, 1952. 43 p.

GREEN, ELVIRA J. LORING-SCALES
Green Leaves; Poems. Oakland, CA.: Pacific Press Publishing Co., 1903. 130 p.

GREEN, JULIA BOYNTON
This Enchanting Coast, Verse on California Themes. Los Angeles, CA.: The Times-Mirror Press, 1928. 63 p.
Noonmark. Redlands, CA.: n.p., 1936. 78 p.

GREEN, ROSE BASILE (1914-)
To Reason Why. South Brunswick, N.J.: A. S. Barnes, 1972. 111 p.
Primo Vino. South Brunswick, N.J.: A. S. Barnes, 1974. 83 p.
76 for Philadelphia. N.Y.: A. S. Barnes, 1975. 106 p.

GREENBERG, BARBARA L(EVENSON) (1932-)
The Spoils of August. Middletown, CT.: Wesleyan University Press, 1974. 72 p. (Wesleyan Poetry Program Ser.)

GREENBERG, JUDITH ANNE
Fire in August; A Poem in 31 Parts. East Lansing, MI.: Zeitgeist, 1969. [44] p. (Zeitgeist publications, no. 13)

Wishing Stone. East Lansing, MI.: Zeitgeist, 1973.
Fields of Light: Poems. Gig Harbor, WA.: Cassiopeia Press, 1974. [27] p.

GREENBIE, MARJORIE LATTA (BARSTOW) (1891-)
...Memories. New Haven, CT.: Yale University Press, 1914. 19 p. (Yale University prize poem, 1914)

GREENE, LORNA (1903-1927)
Morning Moods and Other Poems. New York, London: The Century Co., 1928. lxxx, 109 p.

GREENE, LOUELLA DORSEY
...No Greater Love. Philadelphia: Dorrance and Co., 1942. 91 p. (Contemporary poets of Dorrance, 233)

GREENE, LOUISE PRESTON (1893-)
The Listening Heart. Dexter, MO.: Candor Press, 1954. 103 p.

GREENE, LYN
Harvest of Thoughts; Poems. New York: Exposition Press, 1954. 64 p.

GREENE, MARY
Poems! Copyrighted. Dunellen, N.J.: n.p., 1926. 32 ℓ.

GREENE, ROSALIND HUIDEKOPER (1885-)
A Mother's Garden of Verse. Boston: The Stratford Co., 1922. 7 p.ℓ., 3-105 p.

GREENWOOD, GERTRUDE SHISLER
Each Spring Returning. Mill Valley, CA.: Wings Press, 1941. 64 p.
At April's Altars. Mill Valley, CA.: Wings Press, 1951. 64 p.
Poet, Know Now! Sanbornville, N.H.: Wake-Brook House, 1955. 62 p.

GREENWOOD, JULIA WICKHAM
From Dawn to Eve. Boston: R. G. Badger, 1916. 141 p.
Can No One Understand? New York: G. P. Putnam's Sons, 1937. 91 p.

GREENWOOD, MAE S.
Six Songs from Russian River. Petaluma, CA.: Petaluma Argus Print Shop, 1918. [8] p.

GREENWOOD, THERESA (1936-)
Psalms of a Black Mother. Anderson, IN.: Warner Press, 1970. 96 p.

GREER, EDITH BORDEN
The Stubborn Heart. New York: Pageant Press, 1953. 6 p.ℓ., 73 p.

GREER, HAZEL McELHANY
Ebb and Flow. Angwin, CA.: Priv. Print. [Pacific Union College Press] 1935. 40 p.
As the Stars Forever. Mountain View, CA.: Pacific Press Pub. Association, 1965. 88 p.

GREET, ANNE HYDE
Spring Ecologue; Poems. Francestown, N.H.: Golden Quill Press, 1961. 50 p.

GREGG, CECILIA R.
Autumn, Wait for Me; Poems. New York: Exposition Press, 1968. 96 p.

GREGG, INA LORENE
Whiff of Life. Hereford, TX.: Foster-Merrill Company, 1923. 27 p.

GREGORY, CAROLINE AUGUSTA (1859-)
Poems. Roanoke, VA.: The Stone Printing and Mfg. Co., 1913. 41 p.

GREGORY, VIOLET L.
The Silver Link. Philadelphia: Dorrance, 1969. 63 p.
Full Circle. Boston: Branden Press, 1974. 80 p.

GREIF, AMY (1893-)
Rhyme Without Reason; Contemporary Poems. Baltimore, MD.: Remington, 1955. 6 p. ℓ., 100 p.

GREINER, GLADYS HOUSTON
...Blessed Are the Peace-Makers. New York: H. Harrison, 1941. 63 p.

GREINER, JOYCE
½ Cup; Poems. New York: Vantage Press, 1964. 70 p.

GRELLE, LEONE (RICE)
Country Road. New York: The Macmillan Company, 1945. x p., i ℓ., 83 p.
Remembered Weather. New York: Macmillan Co., 1948. x, 84 p.

GRENELLE, LISA, pseud. see MUNROE, ELIZABETH LEE (1910-)

GREY, ANITA
Weathered Wine. Los Angeles, CA.: The Faun Press, 1933. 32 p.
Tongue of Love. New York: Exposition Press, 1953. 64 p.

GRIFFIN, ESTELLE GERALDINE G.
God's and Goddesse's in Embryo. Philadelphia: Printed by Robert

Edmund, 194-? 48 p.
The Lamp. New York: The Exposition Press, 1944. 5 p. ℓ., 13-126 p. (Poets of America. Series four)

GRIFFIN, MARY ELIZABETH (1897-)
Garland of Song. Chicago: The Blakely Printing Company, 1905. 2 p. ℓ., [9]-215 p.
Shafts from Travel's Quiver, and Random Rhymes. Chicago?: n. p., 191-? 3 p. ℓ., 144 p.

GRIFFIN, SUSAN (1943-)
Dear Sky. San Lorenzo, CA.: Shameless Hussy Press, 1973. [32] p.
Let Them Be Said. Berkeley, CA.: Ariel Books, 1973. 57 p.
Letter: 1973. Berkeley, CA.: Twowindows Press, 1974. [33] p. (Effie's books: II)

GRIMES, NIKKI (1950-)
Poems. New York: Celebrated Blackness, 1970. [19] p.

GRINNELL, ALICE (BOWERSOX)
Land of the Lakes. New York: Exposition Press, 1941. 5 p. ℓ., 13-92, [1] p.

GRISH, DORA S. [SCHIELD, DORAJEAN, pseud.]
Willows and Weeds. New York: Vantage Press, 1965. 46 p.

GRISSOM, IRENE (WELCH) (1873-)
The Passing of the Sagebrush, and Other Verse. Idaho Falls, ID.: Scott's "Quality" Print, 1916. 42 p.
The Passing of the Desert. Garden City, N. Y.: Printed at the Country Life Press, 1924. xi p., 1 ℓ., 69 p.
Verses of the New West. Caldwell, ID.: The Caxton Printers, Ltd., 1931. viii p., 3 ℓ., 3-102 p.
Under Desert Skies. Caldwell, ID.: The Caxton Printers, Ltd., 1935. 54 p.
We Harness a River. Caldwell, ID.: The Caxton Printers, Ltd., 1946. 155 p.
Under Rocky Mountain Skies. New York: Pageant Press, 1952. 5 p. ℓ., 118 p.
Under Desert Skies, and Other Verse. Caldwell, ID.: Caxton Printers, 1956. 5 p. ℓ., 118 p.
The Winds of Chance; A Story in Verse. New York: Exposition Press, 1959. 64 p.

GRISWOLD, FLORENCE YOUNG
Trees and Heart Strings. Dallas, TX.: C. C. Cockrell Co., 1932. 3 p. ℓ., 9-103 p.

GRISWOLD, KATHERINE ELIZABETH (1851-)
Gentlemen's Night; recited by the author at a meeting of the Mary Baker Allen Chapter D. A. R., December 8, 1909. Brandon, VT.: n. p., 1909. [4] p.

Retrospection; a poem recited by the author at a celebration commemorating the one hundred and fiftieth anniversary of the settlement of Cornwall, Nov. 3, 1911. Burlington, VT.: Free Press Printing Co., 1911. [6] p., 1 ℓ.

GROBMANN, EDITH

Time Suspended. Spoon River ed. Prairie City, IL.: Decker Press, 1949. 58 p.

GROESBECK, AMY (JOHNSON)

Tales Gay and Ghastly; Verses. Portland, ME.: House of Falmouth, 1958. 3 p. ℓ., 47 p.

Gull Geometrics. Portland, ME.: House of Falmouth, 1959. 5 p. ℓ., 57 p.

GROOM, CHARLOTTE LOUISE

The Street of Women, a Ballad, and Other Poems. Philadelphia: Dorrance and Company, 1936. 69 p.

...Writing on the Wall. Philadelphia: Dorrance and Company, 1939. 67 p. (Contemporary poets of Dorrance, 194)

Sun Up, Sun Down. Philadelphia: Dorrance & Company, 1947. 78 p. (Contemporary poets of Dorrance, 336)

A Reed's Slight Span; Poems. New York: Exposition Press, 1953. 63 p.

Esau. Philadelphia: Dorrance, 1964. 96 p. (Contemporary poets of Dorrance, 593)

GROSE, SARAH LOUISE

The Flutes of Spring. Boston: R. G. Badger, 1933. 60 p.

GROSS, HILDA LEONTAINE

Word Paintings. Los Angeles, CA.: De Vorss & Co., 1933. 3 p. ℓ., 11-93 p.

GROSS, SUZANNE (1933-)

Sand Verbena. Notre Dame, IN.: University of Notre Dame Press, 1962. 5 p. ℓ., 94 p.

Tern's Bones and Other Poems. Beloit, WI.: n. p., 1965. 37 p. (Beloit poetry journal, v. 15, no. 3, Spring, 1965.)

GROSSMAN, ADRIENNE MOSS

Listen, Swallows; Poems, 1941-1960. Pomona, CA.: Pomona Writers' Workshop, 1960. 117 p.

GROSSMAN, ETHEL B.

Poems.... New York: Priv. Print., 1917. 41 p.

GROSVENOR, VERTA MAE see VERTA MAE

GROTE, HENRIETTE

The Sound of Pink. San Antonio, TX.: Naylor Co., 1971. vii, 32 p.

West of Summer. San Antonio, TX.: Naylor Co., 1974. 34 p.

GROVE, ERMA STULL
The Footprint of God. Philadelphia: Dorrance, 1969. 74 p.

GUE, BELLE WILLEY
Some Human Hearts. Philadelphia: Dorrance, 1925. 61 p. (Contemporary poets of Dorrance, 19)
Songs and Sonnets of the Sea. Philadelphia: Dorrance & Co., 1927. 64 p. (Contemporary poets of Dorrance, 66)

GUEST, BARBARA (1920-)
The Location of Things. New York: Tibor de Nagy Editions, 1960. 67 p.
Poems: The Location of Things, Archaics, The Open Skies. Garden City, N.Y.: Doubleday, 1962. 95 p.
The Blue Stairs; Poems. New York: Corinth Books, 1968. 48 p.
I Ching: Poems and Lithographs. New York: Mourlot, 1969.
Moscow Mansions. New York: Viking Press, 1973. 81 p.

GUETTEL, SUZANNE E.
Of Anger and of Glee.... Boston: B. Humphries, 1947. 52 p.

GUIDEN, SARAH LAKER
The Verses of Sarah L. Guiden. New York: Morehouse-Gorham Co., 1950. 96 p.

GUILD, MARILLA MERRIMAN (1873-)
The Old House Speaks, and Other Poems. New York: The Paebar Co., 1944. 4 p. ℓ., 52 p.

GUILLAUME, RUTH
Stepping on Stars. Boston: Branden Press, 1968. 63 p.

GUINEY, LOUISE IMOGEN (1861-1920)
A Roadside Harp; A Book of Verses. Boston: Houghton, Mifflin & Co., 1906. 62 p.
Happy Ending; The Collected Lyrics of Louise Imogen Guiney. Boston: & New York: Houghton, Mifflin Co., 1909. xiii, [1], 176, [2] p.
________. New ed. with newly collected poems. Boston & New York: Houghton, Mifflin Co., 1927. xiv p., 2 ℓ., 3-194, [1] p.

GUIO, CARRIE ABBOTT
First Bud, Last Leaf; A Chorus of the Seasons. New York: Exposition Press, 1957. 63 p.

GUION, KATHERINE ST. JOHN (NOYES) (1849-) [ST. JOHN, KEITH, pseud.]
Three Gifts, and Other Poems. New Haven, CT.: The Tuttle, Morehouse & Taylor Company, 1904. 50 p., 1 ℓ.

GULI, FRANCESCA
I Sing of Summer. Francestown, N.H.: Golden Quill Press, 1964.

72 p.
The Boy and the Stars; A Lyrical Tale of Dante Alighieri. Francestown, N. H.: Golden Quill Press, 1965. 64 p.
Be Gentle, April; Songs & Sonnets of a Young Girl in Love. Francestown, N. H.: Golden Quill Press, 1969. 80 p.
Land of My Loving. Francestown, N. H.: Golden Quill Press, 1971. 64 p.
Bitter Lime. Francestown, N. H.: Golden Quill Press, 1973. 89 p.

GUMP, LOUISE (1911-) [AUL, JANE, pseud.]
Poems. Los Angeles, CA.: Printed by Columbia Art Studios, 1931. 32 p.

GUNDERSON, LORNA FRANK
Clover and Calico; Poems. New York: Exposition Press, 1951. 64 p.
Spice Auction; Poems. New York: Exposition Press, 1952. 96 p.

GUTHRIE, FRANCES ELIZABETH
Reveries. Dallas, TX.: n. p., 1926. 62 p.

H. C. see CHRISTIE, HELEN

H. D. see DOOLITTLE, HILDA (1886-1961)

HAAS, ROSAMOND (1908-)
Delay Is the Song. New York: E. P. Dutton and Company, Inc., 1944. 4 p. ℓ., 56 p.
This Time, This Tide. New York: Dutton, 1950. 62 p.
North Portal. New York: Dutton, 1957. 61 p.

HACKER, MARILYN
The Terrible Children. New York? n. p., 1967. 26 p.
Presentation Piece. New York: Viking, 1974. 115 p.

HADAS, RACHEL
Starting from Troy. Boston: David R. Godine, 1975. 47 p. (A Godine poetry chapbook; second series)

HADDEN, MAUDE (MINER) (1880-)
...Garnet Rock. New York: The Comet Press, 1944. 64 p.
High Horizons, A Collection of Poems. New York: Whittier Books, 1957. 64 p.

HADDOX, ELLA MAXWELL
Poems of Sentiment. Cincinnati, OH.: Printed for the author by Jennings and Graham, 1912. 31 p.

HADEN, ALICE E.
Love and Linger Poems. Asheville? N. C.: n. p., 1927. 31 p.

HADGOPOULOS, SARALYN P.
Poems of Africa. Peterborough, N. H.: Windy Row Press, 1973. 102 p.
Poems of Greece. Peterborough, N. H.: Windy Row Press, 1975. 72 p.

HADLEY, CAROL
The Song of the Singer, and Other Poems. Los Angeles, CA.: Academy Publishers, 1952. 59 p.

HAEFNER, JESSIE BUSBY
... Bright Intervals. Philadelphia: Dorrance & Co., 1945. 59 p. (Contemporary poets of Dorrance, 298)

HAEMER, PEARL GENTRY
Pull Down the Clouds. Sanbornville, N. H.: Wake-Brook House, 1961. 64 p.

HAGAR, LILLIAN M.
A Garden of Thoughts; A Book of Poems. Mexico, MO.: The Missouri Printing and Publishing Company, 1924. 64 p.

HAGEDORN, JESSICA TARAHATA (1949-)
Heart Attack. San Francisco, CA.: Momo's Press, 1974.
Dangerous Music. San Francisco, CA.: Momo's Press, 1975. [56] p.

HAGEMEYER, DORA (1891-)
Swords of the Grass. Carmel, CA.: The Seven Arts, 1927. [27] p.
Songs of the Green Flame. Oceano, CA.: Halcyon Press, 1930. [26] p.
The Periwinkle Patch. New York: n. p., 1931. 26 p.
Leaf and Stone. n. p., 1932. [21] p.
Sonnets of the Green Star. Carmel-by-the-Sea, CA. ? n. p., 1934? [20] p.
Spring in October. Carmel-by-the-Sea, CA.: The Carmel Pine Cone, 1939. 4 p. ℓ., 53 p., 1 ℓ.
Sonnets and Other Songs. Wellington, N. Z.: H. H. Tombs Ltd., 1940. 52 p., 1 ℓ.
Leaf and Shadow. Carmel-by-the-Sea, CA.: The Carmel Pine Cone Press, 1941. 4 p. ℓ., 53 p., 1 ℓ.
The Periwinkle Patch; Rhymes for Little Children. Carmel-by-the-Sea, CA.: The Carmel Pine Cone Press, 1942. 5 p. ℓ., 49 p., 1 ℓ.
Instead of a Gift. Carmel-by-the-Sea, CA.: The Carmel Pine Cone Press, 1943. 5 p. ℓ., 21 p., 1 ℓ.
The Shining Wind.... Carmel-by-the-Sea, CA.: The Carmel Pine Cone Press, 1944. 4 p. ℓ., 48 p., 1 ℓ.
Anne in the Periwinkle Patch. Carmel-by-the-Sea, CA.: The Carmel Pine Cone Press, 1945. 4 p. ℓ., 39 p., 1 ℓ.
Overtones. London: Mitre Press, 1947. 59 p.
The White Sands of Carmel.... Philadelphia: Dorrance & Com-

pany, 1947. 72 p. (Contemporary poets of Dorrance, 349)

The Quicken Tree. Carmel-by-the-Sea, CA.: The Carmel Pine Cone Press, 1953. 4 p. ℓ., 56 p., 1 ℓ.

The Secret Parables; Poems, 1952-54. Christchurch, N. Z.: Pegasus Press, 1955. 63, [1] p.

HAGER, EUNICE (1908-)

A Constant Song, Poems. Peterborough, N. H.: Sim's Press, 1949. 55, [1] p.

HAGER, GERTRUDE J.

...The Violin Speaks.... New York: The Exposition Press, 1941. 96 p.

HAHN, HANNELORE

Taking a Giant Step. Boston: Little, Brown, 1960.

HAHN, LEONA PAULINE

Appassionata. Dallas, TX.: Mathis, Van Nort & Co., 1940. 8 p. ℓ., 3-79 p.

HAIEN, JEANNETTE MICHAEL

Rip Van Winkle's Dream. Garden City, N. Y.: Doubleday & Co., 1947. 95 p.

HAIRS, NAN MACKINTOSH

...Purple Vintage and Other Poems. Carmel-by-the-Sea, CA.: n. p., 1934. [39] p.

HALD, MARIE M.

Love in My Heart. New York: Vantage Press, 1965. 63 p.

HALDERMAN, BELA RHEA (1889-)

Just Poems. Boston: Meador Publishing Co., 1935. 6, 9-97 p.

HALE, ANNE GARDNER (1823-1914)

Seedlings from My Wild Garden: Poems. New York, London: The Abbey Press, 1902. 239 p.

HALE, ARLENE (1924-)

Nightfall. Prairie City, IL.: Decker Press, 1948. 72 p.

HALE, EMMA THARPE

Songs of Hope, and Other Poems. New York: The Cosmopolitan Press, 1913. 3 p. ℓ., [9]-178 p.

HALE, KATHERINE M.

The Music of the Rest, and Other Verse. Appleton, WI.: Printed by Moyle & Moyle, 1913. [46] p.

HALE, SUSAN (1833-1910)
Inklings for Thinklings. Boston: Marshall Jones Company, 1919. 69 ℓ.

HALEY, MARGARET
The Gardener Mind. New Haven, CT.: Yale University Press, 1937. 76 p., 1 ℓ. (Yale Series of Younger Poets, 36)

HALEY, MARY CARMEL
Blown Petals. New York: Knickerbocker Press, 1923. 70 p.

HALEY, MOLLY WHITFORD (ANDERSON) (1888-)
Gardens and You. New York: Wise-Parslow Co., 1925. 12 ℓ. (The Greeting Books)
Heritage, and Other Poems. Philadelphia: Dorrance & Company, 1925. 52 p. (Contemporary poets of Dorrance, 28)
The Window Cleaner, and Other Poems. Boston: B. Humphries, 1930. 60 p.

HALKETT, SARAH PHELPS STOKES
Aunt Sadie's Rhymes and Rhyme-Stories. New York: E. P. Dutton & Co., 1916.
Beyond the Mountain. New York: E. P. Dutton & Co., 1917. ix, 90 p.
Elf King's Flowers. New York: E. P. Dutton & Co., 1924. ix p., 1 ℓ., 79 p.

HALL, AILEEN S.
My Sunrise. Dallas, TX.: Royal Pub. Co., 1957. 71 p.

HALL, ALEDA
Aleda. Coral Gables, FL.: Priv. printed, 1956. 148 p.

HALL, ALICE CLAY
April-Hunger. Alpine, TX.: Different Press, 1958. 40 p.

HALL, ALICE R.
Songs of a Sourdough. New York: Pageant Press, 1953. 6 p. ℓ., 44 p.

HALL, AMANDA BENJAMIN (1890-)
The Dancer in the Shrine and Other Poems. New York: George H. Doran Co., 1923. 4 p. ℓ., xi-xiii p., 1 ℓ., 17-106 p.
Afternoons in Eden. Boston: B. Humphries, Inc.; London: C. W. Daniel Co., 1932. 120 p.
Cinnamon Saint, A Narrative Poem. Boston: B. Humphries, Inc., 1937. 153 p.
Honey out of Heaven. Dallas, TX.: The Kaleidograph Press, 1938. 89 p.
Unweave a Rainbow. Prairie City, IL.: The Press of James A. Decker, 1942. 51 p.
Frosty Harp. Francestown, N.H.: Golden Quill Press, 1954.

80 p.

The View from the Heart. Francestown, N.H.: Golden Quill Press, 1964. 71 p.

The Blue Pigeon & Other Poems. Boston: Branden Press, 1973. 80 p.

HALL, CAROL

Poems. Portland, OR.: Portland Art Museum, 1959. 7 p.

Portrait of Your Niece, and Other Poems. Minneapolis, MN.: University of Minnesota Press, 1959. 55 p.

HALL, CLARISSA

Improvising in the Evening. Cedar Rapids, IA.: The Torch Press, 1933. 64 p. (A Bookfellow Book)

HALL, EILEEN

The Fountain and the Bough. New York: C. Scribner's Sons, 1938. 6 p.ℓ., 3-53 p.

HALL, GRACE E.

Homespun. New York: Dodd, Mead and Company, 1922. 6 p.ℓ., 130 p.

Patchwork. New York: Dodd, Mead and Company, 1924. 6 p.ℓ., 107, [1] p.

HALL, HATTIE VOSE

Songs of the Coast of Maine. Augusta, ME.: n.p., 1931. 56 p.

HALL, HAZEL (1886-1924)

Curtains. New York: John Lane Co.; London: John Lane, 1921. 118 p., 1 ℓ.

Walkers. New York: Dodd, Mead & Co., 1923. xi p., 1 ℓ., 94 p.

Cry of Time. New York: E. P. Dutton & Co., 1928. 99 p.

HALL, KATIE VICTORIA (1867-)

Gems of Comfort, Praise and Victory. Chicago: The Olive Branch, 1937. 240 p.

HALL, KAY DEBARD

Poems of the Sea. New York: Harbinger House, 1948. 44 p.

HALL, LENA

Late Adventure: Poems. New York: H. Vinal, 1926. 8 p.ℓ., 3-59 p., 1 ℓ.

HALL, MABEL (WILSON) (1893-)

The Years Rolled By. Denver, CO.: Big Mountain Press, 1964. 72 p.

HALL, MARY (LANDIS) (1911-)

A Book of Verse. 2d ed. London: Brookside Press, 195-? 56 p.

Excerpts from Spring and Other Poems. London: Brookside Press, 195-? 64 p.

HALL, ROBA (CHRISTIAN) (1888-)
Leisure-Time Lyrics. San Antonio, TX.: Naylor Co., 1950. xiii, 128 p.

HALL, SHARLOT MABRIDTH (1870-1943)
Cactus and Pine: Songs of the Southwest. Boston: Sherman, French & Company, 1911. 5 p. ℓ., 204 p.
_______. 2d ed. rev. and enl. Phoenix, AZ.: Arizona Republican Print Shop, 1924. 4 p. ℓ., 250 p., 1 ℓ.

HALL, ZULA
Blossom Town Ad-Visor. New York: Exposition Press, 1950. 61 p.

HALLET, MARY (THOMAS) (1892-) [Full Name: Mary Keller (Thomas) Hallet.]
Poems. New York: Profile Press, 1951. 50 p.

HALLETT, BARBARA (1907-1936)
Dream's Shadow. North Montpelier, VT.: The Driftwind Press, 1937. vi, 7-103 p.

HALLEY, ANNE (1928-)
Between Wars, and Other Poems. Northampton, MA.: Gehenna Press, 1965. 69 p.
_______. Amherst, MA.: University of Massachusetts Press, 1965. 70 p., 1 ℓ.

HALLIN, RUTH (MARSHALL)
Bitter Honey; Poems. Los Angeles, n.p., 1963. 104 p.

HALLMARK, ERMA ELDER
Along Simple Lines. San Antonio, TX.: The Naylor Company, 1946. 5 p. ℓ., 74 p.
Spoken Songs. San Antonio, TX.: The Naylor Company, 1947. viii, 44 p.
Time Is a Caravan. San Antonio, TX.: Printed by the Naylor Co., 1960. xvii, 75 p.

HALLSTEAD, ANNA WORTHINGTON
"Pastoral Beauty" or, "The Meadows," and Other Poems. Anderson, IN.: n.p., 1924. 20 p.

HALSEY, LEDA M.
Come Home to the Mountains, a Collection of Idaho Poems. New York: The William-Frederick Press, 1947. 3 p. ℓ., 22 p., 1 ℓ. (The William-Frederick Poets, no. 36)

HALSTEAD, ORELLA D.
Rambling Thoughts. Dallas, TX.: Story Book Press, 1952.

40 p.
Stardust and Mist, Poems. New York: New Orlando Publications, 1962. 30 p.

HALSTED, LILLIE BAKER
Overtones. New York: The Trow Press, 1903. vi p., 1 ℓ., 49 p.

HAMIL, LURA CODLEY (1878-1933)
Little Book of Garden Songs. Boston: Four Seas Co., 1921. 42 p.

HAMILTON, ANNE (1902-)
Broken Crescendo and Other Poems. Los Angeles, CA.: Ward Ritchie Press, 1939. x, 11-55 p.

HAMILTON, EDNA
Spend Your Heart. Cincinnati, OH.: n.p., 1950. 86 p., 1 ℓ.

HAMILTON, ELOISE
Earth My Village. Mill Valley, CA.: Wings Press, 1950. 72 p.

HAMILTON, FANNIE EDWARDS
Southern Melodies. Boston: The Christopher Publishing House, 1931. 111 p.

HAMILTON, FLORA (BRENT) (d. 1933)
When Lilacs Bloom; Reflections in a Garden. Chicago: P. Covici, 1927. xxii, [2] p., 1 ℓ., 123 p., 2 ℓ.
...Sonnets. Boston: B. Humphries, 1934. 26 p., 1 ℓ.

HAMILTON, FLORENCE
A Moment's Monument. New York: Klein-Heimbinder, 1939. [6] ℓ., 3-46 p.
Mirrors and Human Voices. Prairie City, IL.: The Press of J. A. Decker, 1942. 47 p.

HAMILTON, KATHARINE PARR (1881-)
The Purple Tree, A Group of Poems. El Paso, TX.: C. Hertzog, 1953. 79 p.
Eternal Verities; Poems. n.p., 1963. 263 p.

HAMILTON, LEONA
Duel Before Dawn, and Other Poems. Crescent City, FL.: New Athenaeum Press, 1960. 39 p., 1 ℓ.

HAMILTON, MARION ETHEL
...Wild Ginger. New York: H. Vinal, 1926. 28 p.
The Ultimate Lover & Other Poems. Chicago: P. Covici, 1927. 72 p.
Bird at Night, Poems. New York: Fine Editions Press, 1949. 63 p.

HAMILTON, MARY GERTRUDE
Lights and Shadows. Boston: Stratford Publishers, 1920. 5 p. ℓ., 50 p., 1 ℓ.

HAMILTON, MONA
Allspice. San Francisco, CA.: Alex Nicoll Printing Co., 1925. 1 p. ℓ., [5]-57 p.

HAMILTON, SARAH B. (EDMONDS)
Out of My Heart; Poems. New York: Exposition Press, 1961. 96 p.

HAMLETT, MAYME LUCILLE
This Scepter'd Isle. New York: Pageant Press, 1960. 52 p.

HAMMANN, VERA B.
Sky Writing. Washington, D.C.: Leeward Publications, 1968. vi, 167 p.

HAMMERSLEY, EVADNA BREDEHOEFT
A Rhapsody of the Rockies. Denver, CO.: The World Press, Inc., 1944. x, [2], 13-118 p.

HAMMOND, HALA JEAN
Sun-Dial. New York: J. T. White & Co., 1929. xiii, 103 p.
I Pray You, Lapidary. Caldwell, ID.: The Caxton Printers, Ltd., 1934. 86 p.

HAMMOND, MARY E.
Peace from the Battle; Poems of War, Peace, Love, and Faith Collected after the Battle of Life and Work. Philadelphia: Dorrance, 1970. 24 p.
Thirty Years after Pearl Harbor. Philadelphia: Dorrance, 1972. 18 p.

HAMNER, LAURA VERNON
Prairie Vagabonds. San Antonio, TX.: Naylor Co., 1955. xi, 62, [2] p.

HAMPTON, ELIZABETH MARGARET
Songs in the Night. Xenia, OH.: The Aldine Publishing House, 1915. 30 p.

HANAFORD, Mrs. JESSIE FORBUSH
Treasured Thoughts. Brooklyn, N.Y.: The Cast Publishing Co., 1904. 95 p.

HANCOCK, NANNIE PRICE (EMERSON) (1857-)
A Book of Poems. Roanoke, VA.: Press of Stone Ptg. & Mfg. Co., 1900. 74 p.

HANCOCK, NATALIE MORRIS
Misty Memories. Philadelphia: Dorrance & Co., 1929. 87 p. (Contemporary poets of Dorrance, 84)

HAND, LEILA H.
Interlude, Summer Ending, and Other Poems. New York: The Hobson Book Press, 1946. 4 p. ℓ., 52 p.

HAND, MARIE
Ashes and Rainbows; Poems. New York: Exposition Press, 1954. 80 p.

HAND, NINNA STANFORD (1862-)
Eternity; a Poem with Inferential Prologue. San Francisco, CA.: Nin S. Hand & Co., 1918. 23 p.

HANDY, SARA
The Imperishable Dust; Poems. Boston: B. Humphries, 1945. 64 p.

HANNA, ELIZABETH HEMING
High Mountain: An Idyl of the Old South. New York, London: The Abbey Press, 1902. 7-124 p.

HANNAH, EULAH E.
Gleanings of the Seasons. Boston: The Stratford Co., 1927. 5 p. ℓ., 3-50 p.

HANNAS, RUTH
...Thorns Are a Style. New York: H. Harrison, 1930. 78 p.

HANNING, ROSANNA EVELYN (SIMMONS) (1931-)
Poems for Every Mood. New York: Greenwich Book Publishers, 1958. 37 p.
Poems in Fact and Fantasy. New York: Exposition Press, 1962. 64 p.

HANRAHAN, AGNES ITA (1871-)
Aroun' the Boreens: A Little Book of Celtic Verse. Boston: R. G. Badger, 1913. 32 p.
________. London: Duckworth & Co., 1914. [4], 32 p.

HANRAHAN, JANNE
Light from New Steel. Springfield, IL.: Sangamon Poets, 1974. 24 p.

HANS, MARCIE
Serve Me a Slice of Moon. New York: Harcourt, Brace & World, 1965. 58 p.

HANSARD, MARY JEWELL
Western Signature. Philadelphia: Dorrance, 1963. 79 p. (Contemporary poets of Dorrance, 561)

HANSBROUGH, MARY BERRI (CHAPMAN)
Poems. New York: The Knickerbocker Press, 1906. 1 p. ℓ., vi, 153 p.

HANSEN, JEAN CROSSE
Cherry Lane. Hartwick, N. Y.: Reflections Press, 194-? 16 p.
Beggar in the Attic. Emory University, Atlanta, GA.: Banner Press, 1942. 60 p. (Verse Craft series)
A Lady Wears a Rose. Emory University, Atlanta, GA.: Banner Press, 1949. 63 p. (Verse Craft series)

HANSEN, JULIANE GRACE (1878-) [PAULSEN, JULIANE, pseud.]
And Then Came Spring. Boston: The Gorham Press, 1914. 72 p.

HANSON, GERTRUDE (1888-1962)
Come Walk with Me. Minneapolis, MN.: Lund Press, 1962. 80 p.

HANSON, KAREN
Spine; A Book of Poems. Ithaca, N. Y.: Ithaca House, 1971. 69 p.

HANSON, MARIDEL DUKE (1930-)
Spun from the Center. New York: Vantage Press, 1969. 72 p.

HANSON, PAULINE
The Forever Young. Denver, CO.: A. Swallow, 1948. [29] p.
The Forever Young and Other Poems. Denver, CO.: Swallow, 1957. 42 p., 1 ℓ.
Across Countries of Anywhere. New York: Alfred A. Knopf, 1971. 67 p.

HANSON, PHYLLIS SUTHERLAND
True by the Sun. Dallas, TX.: The Kaleidograph Press, 1943. xi p., 1 ℓ., 15-75 p.

HARDEN, MAE BALDWIN
Songs of the Soul. San Jose, CA.: Citizen Publishing Company, 1918. 5 p. ℓ., 44 p.

HARDESTY, LETITIA P.
Sprays of Goldenrod. Boston: The Stratford Company, 1937. 2 p. ℓ., iii, 87 p.

HARDIN, CHARLOTTE
From a Flat Housetop. Boston: The Four Seas Co., 1920. 63 p.
Coins and Medals. Boston: The Four Seas Company, 1921. 40 p., 1 ℓ.
Dream Fugue. Boston: The Four Seas Company, 1923. 104 p.
________. Boston: Branden, 1966.
From a Flat Housetop. Boston: Branden, 1966.

HARDING, MAUDE BURBANK
Water from a Wooden Bowl. Sanbornville, N. H.: Wake-Brook House, 1955. 64 p.

Lilies for Eros. Sanbornville, N.H.: Wake-Brook House, 1957. 81 p., 1 ℓ.
Mother Songs. Sanbornville, N.H.: Wake-Brook House, 1961. 65 p.

HARDING, RUTH GUTHRIE (THOMSON) see BURTON, RUTH GUTHRIE (THOMSON) HARDING

HARDY, ELIZABETH STANTON
Time in the Turning. Portland, ME.: Falmouth Publishing House, 1940. 4 p. ℓ., 3-70 p.

HARDY, IRENE (1841-)
Poems. San Francisco, CA.: D. P. & M. Shepard Elder, 1902. 3 p. ℓ., 3-147 p.

HARDY, LULU DANIEL
The Love Cycle. Boston: R. G. Badger, 1924. 67 p.

HARE, MARY AMORY (1885-) see HUTCHINSON, AMORY (HARE) (1885-)

HARGROVE, LOTTIE H.
Texas History in Rhyme. New York: Broadway Publishing Company, 1910. 2 p. ℓ., 7-133 p.

HARKNESS, DONNA J.
Weather Vane. Cincinnati, OH.: Talaria Publication, 1940. 54 p., 1 ℓ.

HARLAN, MARY EDGE (1889-)
Tell Me a Story. New York: Exposition Press, 1939. 58 p.

HARMAN, DOLLY STEARNS
Sea-Wind and Mountain Trail, Olympic Peninsula Verse. Dallas, TX.: The Kaleidoscope Publishers, 1931. 4 p. ℓ., 38 p.

HARMON, BEATRICE E.
Mosaics. New Haven, CT.: Yale University Press, 1923. 63, [1] p. (The Yale Series of Younger Poets, 18)

HARMON, FLORENCE
Prime; Poems. Elsinore, CA.: Sun Publishing Company, 1969. 50 p.

HARMON, LILLIAN ELIZABETH MARSH
Bits of Life. New York: Vantage Press, 1968. 64 p.

HARNEY, HAZEL (DILLON)
Drifting Petals.... New York: H. Harrison, 1937. 61 p.

HARPER, ALICE
Via Lucis, and Other Poems. Nashville, TN.: n.p., 1911. 63 p.

HARPER, CAROL (ELY) (1909-)
To a Faulty Lover. Denver, CO.: A. Swallow, 1946. 39 p.
Distichs for a Dancer. Denver, CO.: A. Swallow, 1950. [20] p. (The Swallow Pamphlets, no. 8)

HARPER, EMMA (PARVIS) (1867-)
Poems of Auld Lang Syne. New York: F. H. Hitchcock, 1927. viii, 51 p.

HARPER, JEAN
Green Was in the Air, Poems. New York: Hobson Book Press, 1946. 5 p. ℓ., 73 p.
Evocation, & Other Poems. Boston: Plowshare Press, 1966. 64 p.
Mouse in the Wall; Poetry. Boston: Plowshare Press, 1972. 87 p.

HARPER, VELMA (REYNOLDS) (1902-)
The Tide Was Out. Dallas, TX.: Story Book Press, 1950. 60 p.
______. Pauls Valley, OK.: McCarty Printing Co., 1950. 83 p. 2d printing.

HARR, BARBARA
The Mortgaged Wife. Chicago: Swallow Press, 1970. viii, 85 p. (New poetry series, no. 41)

HARRELD, CLAUDIA WHITE
Remembered Encounters. Atlanta, GA.: B. F. Logan Press, 1951. 44 p.

HARRELL, RUTH PEAL
Of Much, of Little. Fort Smith, AR.: South and West, 1970. 40 p.

HARRINGTON, KATHARINE SALISBURY
Ballads of the Hard Hills, and Other Poems. Philadelphia: Dorrance, 1969. 109 p.

HARRIS, ELIZABETH HOWE
Give Me a Hill, and Other Poems. San Francisco, CA.: Congregational Press, 1935. 60 p., 1 ℓ.
...Long Dawn, a Collection of Verse. San Leandro, CA.: The Greater West Publishing Co., 1946. 63 p. (Poets of the Greater West)

HARRIS, ELLA STEVENS
Brown Leaves, and Other Verses. Montclair, N.Y.: Oswald Press, 1912. 5 p. ℓ., 3-56 p.

HARRIS, HAZEL HARPER
Wings of the Morning. Dallas, TX.: C. C. Cockrell Co., 1930. 99 p.
Winds [i.e. Wings] of the Morning. Dallas, TX.: C. C. Cock-

rell Co., 1932. 99 p. 2d printing.
Stars of the Morning. New York: Exposition Press, 1957. 77 p.

HARRIS, JOSEPHINE ALDRICH
As Wild Doves Fly. Emory University, GA.: Banner Press, 1949. 76 p. (Verse craft series)
Leaf in a Seaward Wind. Atlanta, GA.: Banner Press, Emory University, 1960. 65 p. (Verse craft series)

HARRIS, MARGUERITE
A Reconciling of Rivers. Mexico: El Corno Emplumado, 1964. 26 p.
Moon. Cleveland, OH.: 7 Flowers Press, 1965. [6] p. on double leaves.
The Risk of the Vine. Newnham, Tasmania: Wattle Grove Press, 1965. [33] p.
A Reconciling of Rivers. Mexico: El Corno Emplumado; dist. by Cymric Press, New York, 1972. 43 p.

HARRIS, MARIE
Herbal. Bowling Green, OH.: Tribal Press, 1973.
Raw Honey. Cambridge, MA.: Alice James Books, 1975. 65 p.

HARRIS, MARY COLLINS (1910-1927)
Rain Magic, and Other Poems. San Francisco, CA.: Vernon Gregory, 1950. 47 p.

HARRIS, MILDRED WOOD
Cherry Stones. New York: The Pyramid Press, 1941. 67 p.
South Wind Blowing. New York: William-Frederick Press, 1949. 40 p. (The William-Frederick poets, 56)

HARRIS, WILLIE VIOLA
Poetry Commemorating the Bicentennial Year. Philadelphia: Dorrance, 1975. ix, 125 p.

HARRISON, EUNICE B.
Here Is My Heart. New York: Carlton Press, 1962. 4 p. ℓ., 55 p.

HARRISON, JENNIE, pseud. see TOMPKINS, JANE HARRISON (1841-1912)

HARRISON, NANNIE HILLARY
Thine and Mine. Dallas, TX.: Gammel-Statesman Pub. Co., 1907? 40 p.
Texas Emblems for You. Waco, TX.: N. H. Church Printing Co., 1914. 2 p. ℓ., 7-47 p.
______. San Antonio, TX.: Standard Printing Co., 1925. 2 p. ℓ., 7-47 p.

HARRISON, ROSALIE
Stories in Rhyme. Oakland, CA.: East Bay Printing Co., 1923. 4 p. ℓ., 11-95 p.

HARRISON, VIRGINIA BIOREN
A Whisper of Destiny, and Other Poems. New York: E. P. Dutton & Co., 1909. 7 p. ℓ., 3-144 p.

HARROD, ELIZABETH
Seascape with Snow; Poem. Denver, CO.: A. Swallow, 1960. 48 p. (The New Poetry Series)

HARROWER, MARY RACHEL (1906-)
Spiral, and Other Poems. n.p., 1933. 38 p.

HARSEN, UNA W.
Behind This Door, and Other Poems. Boston: B. Humphries, 1947. 80 p.

HART, ESTELLE PUGSLEY
Thoughts in Poetry. New York: Tobias Press, 1911. 5 p. ℓ., 9-143 p.

HART, LOUISE (1911-) [Full Name: Ann Louise Blackmar Hart.]
Little Poems. Columbus, GA.: n.p., 1916. [17] p.
Song-Drops. Columbus, GA.: Gilbert Printing Co., 1917. [20] p.
Poems. Boston: The Cornhill Company, 1921. 2 p. ℓ., viii, 45 p.
Chattahoochee Rolling. New York: The Pyramid Press, 1939. 5 p. ℓ., 15-59 p.

HART, MARY ALICE (1911-)
The Chrysalis. Dallas, TX.: Story Book Press, 1954. 40 p.
The Time for Singing. Dallas, TX.: Story Book Press, 196-? 40 p.

HART, NINA
Blazed Trails. Boston: The Four Seas Co., 1924. 58 p.

HARTE, LILLIAN BRET
A Handful of Stars. Hollywood, CA.: J. Lamothe, 1929. 5 p. ℓ.,. 101 p.

HARTGE, LAURA ESTELLE
Tides of Life. Boston: Meador Publishing Co., 1933. 80 p.

HARTICH, ALICE (1888-)
The Gift of Light. New York: Fine Editions Press, 1949. 64 p.
The Pure White Flame. Francestown, N.H.: Golden Quill Press, 1964. 76, [1] p.

HARTLEY, REBECCA (1941-)
For the Glory of Jesus. Philadelphia: Dorrance, 1964. 63 p. (Contemporary poets of Dorrance, 584)

HARTMAN, LETA BECKER
The Grain and the Chaff. San Gabriel, CA.: Willing Pub. Co., 1955. 47 p.

HARTNEY, MARY PATRICE
Blue Lady. Boston: Meador Publishing Company, 1931. 57 p.

HARTSHORNE, ESTELLE
Some Thoughts in Verse. New York: The Friebele Press, 1932. 30 p.

HARTSHORNE, ESTHER KIMBALL
Dog-gerel. Red Bank, N.J.: Stone's Throw Press, 1933. [55] p.

HARTWELL, KATHLEEN
Poems of the Sea. Worcester, MA.: The Woman's Guild, St. John's Episcopal Church, 1955. [13] p.

HARTWICK, ROSE J.
Miscellaneous Poems. Saginaw, MI.: Saginaw Printing and Publishing Company, 1906. 1 p.ℓ., [5]-56 p.

HARTZ, MINA FRASA
A Book for Us. New York: Pageant Press, 1955. 55 p.

HARTZLER, CHRISTINE M.
Poems on This and That Written Now and Then. New York: Vantage Press, 1963. 60 p.

HARVEY, ELEANOR T. M. (1904-)
Sonnets from Captivity, and Other Poems. Philadelphia: Dorrance, 1949. 70 p. (Contemporary poets of Dorrance, 381)
Sonnets from Captivity. Philadelphia: Dorrance, 1973. 64 p.

HARVEY, EMMELINE DAGGETT
Moods and Tenses. Chicago: Priv. Print., 1923. 3 p.ℓ., 3-53 p.

HARVEY, FANNY CUTLER (JOHNSON)
Brave Pioneers. New York: William-Frederick Press, 1948. 31 p. (William-Frederick poets, no. 45)
Light-Bearers Are Birds; Tributes in Verse. New York: William-Frederick Press, 1949. 3 p.ℓ., 24, [1] p. (The William-Frederick poets, no. 53)

HARVEY, JULIA M.
Little Lines of Thought. Boonville, N.Y.: Printed by the Willard Press, 1932. 1 pℓ., 5-31 p.

HARVEY, PEGGY PENN (1887-)
A Whimsical Vancouverite. Vancouver, British Columbia: n. p., 1936. 16 ℓ.
Crumbs from the Kitchen. Boston: The Christopher Publishing House, 1942. 32 p.

HARVEY, SHIRLEY
The Christmas Trail, and Other Poems. Concord, N. H.: n. p., 1916. xiii, 44 p.

HARVEY, VERA ANDREW
Touching the Stars. Emory University, GA.: Banner Press, 1954. 60 p. (Verse craft series)

HARVEY, VICTORIA UNRUH
50 Poems. Liberty, MO.: Quality Press, 1969. 47 p.

HARWOOD, GRACE
½ a Loaf. San Francisco, CA.: Peace & Pieces Press, 1973. 72 p.

HARWOOD, RUTH (1896-)
Emily Chamberlain Cook Prize Poems, 1921. Berkeley, CA.: n. p., 1922. 15 p.
Songs from the Lyric Road. n. p., 193-. [29] p.
The Lyric Road. Berkeley, CA.: The Guilders Publishing Center, 1937. [53] p.
Paris Cycle. Berkeley, CA.: The Guilders Publishing Center, 1938. 2 p. ℓ., 45 p.
Golden Benediction. Santa Barbara, CA.: Pacific Coast Publishing Company, 1946. 56 p.

HASE, ROXANA (FARNSWORTH)
Delicious Lumps. New York: Vantage Press, 1953. 5 p. ℓ., 77 p.

HASELTINE, BLANCHE (SAGE) (1889-1935)
The Poems of Blanche Sage Haseltine. Kansas City, MO.: Midwest Poetry Publishers, 1936. 60 p.

HASKELL, LUCY A.
Poems of Faith and Nature. Boston: n. p., 1900. 60 p.

HASTE, GWENDOLEN
Young Land. New York: Coward-McCann, Inc., 1930. x p., 1 ℓ., 13-75 p. (Songs of Today Series, 1930)

HASTINGS, CRISTEL
Here and There in the Yosemite. San Francisco, CA.: The Cloister Press, 1923. 4 p. ℓ., 17-64 p., 1 ℓ.

HASTINGS, FANNY de GROOT (1893-)
The Victory of Defeat, and Other Poems. New York: Alice Har-

riman Co., 1912. 6 p. ℓ., 32 f.
Wrappings. n. p., 1915. 3 p.
Ten Minutes. New York: W. E. Rudge, 1917. [22] p.
Christmas 1918. n. p., 1918. 2 p.
Lesser Stars. New York: W. E. Rudge, 1919. 3 p. ℓ., 9-44 p.
Through a Glass. New York: W. E. Rudge, 1921. 54 p.
Christmas Poems. New Canaan, CT.: Dormer House, 1934. [18] p.
One Stone Unturned; Poems. New Canaan, CT.: Dormer House, 1949. 93 p.

HASWIN, FRANCES ROSINA
Some Songs and Verses. Wausau, WI.: Van Vechten & Ellis, 1902. 3 p. ℓ., 15-103, [1] p.

HATCH, MARY PRESCOTT
To a Butterfly and Other Pictures and Memories. Boston: Marshall Jones Company, 1937. 96 p.

HATCHER, LUCY LOUISE
Compassionate Pines, and Other Poems. San Antonio, TX.: Naylor Co., 1956. xii, 56 p.

HATFIELD, MYRTLE MARGUERITE
Crescendo. Chicago: Windfall Press, 1965. 50 p.

HATHAWAY, ANNE
Anne Hathaway; Her Poems. Swampscott, MA.: Printed by H. T. Hadley, 1911. 22, [1] ℓ.

HATHAWAY, MAURINE
Embers. Minneapolis, MN.: Geo. W. Parker Art Company, 1910. 50 p.
Passion Lyrics. Minneapolis, MN.: Geo. W. Parker Art Co., 1911. 1 p. ℓ., 7-61 p.
Affinity. New York: Barse & Hopkins, 1914. 2 p. ℓ., 11-94 p.
Little Steps in Child Training. Indianapolis, IN.: Pub. by the Elsie Lincoln Benedict Lecture courses, 1921. 2 p. ℓ., 7-43 p.
Fire Castles. Cincinnati, OH.: Sign of the Pen and Pad, 1922. 111 p.

HAUENSTEIN, MINNIE FERRIS
Songs from the Silence. Buffalo, N. Y.: The Matthews-Northrup Works, 1909. 6 p. ℓ., 11-111 p.
Oliver Hazard Perry, Born 1785-Died 1919; Ode for Perry Centennial. Buffalo? N. Y., 1918? 8 ℓ.
Sonnets from the Silence. New York & London: G. P. Putnam's Sons, 1922. x, 94 p.

HAUG, HANNAH MARIE
Dimensions. New York: Carlton Press, 1969. 63 p.

HAUSMANN, JOY
Full Circle; Poems. Baltimore, MD.: Contemporary Poetry, 1957. 32 p.

HAVINGHURST, MARION M. [BOYD, MARION M.]
Silver Wands. New Haven, CT.: Yale University Press, 1923. 52 p., 1 ℓ., (Yale Series of Younger Poets, 15)

HAWKINS, ALICE TENNESON
A Child's Guide to the Pacific Coast. Los Angeles, CA.: Wetzel Publishing Co., Inc., 1930. [46] p.
The Mountain, the Desert, the Sea, and Other Poems. Boston: R. G. Badger, 1930. 92 p.

HAWKINS, BOBBIE LOUISE
Own Your Own Body. Los Angeles, CA.: Black Sparrow Press, 1973. [15] p.
Fifteen Poems. Berkeley, CA.: Arif Press, 1974. [32] p.

HAWKINS, EDNA B.
Vagabond Dreams, A Book of Poems. New York: Exposition Press, 1953. 96 p.

HAWKS, SARA E. WILSON
Paths to Beautiful Living. Thornton, AR.: Cayce Pub. Co., 1950. 125 p.

HAWTHORNE, GLADYS
An Angel Touched My Hand. Denver, CO.: Big Mountain Press, 1954. 64 p.

HAWTHORNE, HILDEGARDE [Full Name: Hildegarde (Hawthorne) Oskison.]
Poems. Boston: R. G. Badger, 1905. 37 p.

HAY, SARA HENDERSON (1906-)
Field of Honor. Dallas, TX.: The Kaleidograph Press, 1933. xi p., 1 ℓ., 15-87 p.
This, My Letter. New York: Alfred A. Knopf, 1939. xv, [1], 110 p., 1 ℓ.
Field of Honor. 4th ed. Dallas, TX.: The Kaleidograph Press, 1942. xi p., 1 ℓ., 15-87 p.
The Delicate Balance. New York: Scribner, 1951. x, 52 p.
The Stone and the Shell. Pittsburgh, PA.: University of Pittsburgh Press, 1959. 81 p.
Story Hour. Garden City, N.Y.: Doubleday, 1963. 71 p.
A Footing on This Earth. Garden City, N.Y.: Doubleday, 1966. xv, 220 p.

HAYDEN, ALMA PEXDEXTER
Poems. n.p., 19--? 1 v. unpaged.
Soldier Songs. Rochester, N.Y.: Priv. print., 1917. 10 ℓ.

HAYDEN, DOROTHEA (HOAGLIN)
Deodars, and Other Verse. Pasadena, CA.: n.p., 1923. 79 p.
...The Road to Romany. Boston: The Stratford Company, 1927. 32 p. (The Stratford Poets)
Gifts to the Giver. Los Angeles, CA.: I. Deach, Jr., 1931. 77 p.

HAYDEN, KATHERINE SHEPARD see SALTER, KATHERINE SHEPARD (HAYDEN)

HAYES, ANN LOUISE (1924-)
The Dancer's Step. Pittsburgh, PA.: Three Rivers Press, 1973. [20] p.
The Living and the Dead. Pittsburgh, PA.: Carnegie-Mellon Univ., dist. by University of Pittsburgh, 1975. 71 p.

HAYES, HELEN
Lilacs and Pampa Grass. Buenos Aires, Argentina: Imprenta Roetzler, 1939. 3 p. ℓ., 32 p.
Seven Waves. Buenos Aires: n.p., 1939. 42 p.

HAYES, HILDA ROBERTS
Nature's Medley. San Antonio, TX.: Naylor Co., 1966. iv, 22 p.

HAYMAN, CAROL BESSENT (1927-)
Keepsake; A Book of Poems. Greensboro, N.C.: Piedmont Press, 1962. [40] p.

HAYMOND, NORAH LEE
Verse and Worse. New York: The Author, 1918. 2 p. ℓ., 42 p.

HAYN, ANNETTE
Rapunzel. Fredericton, N.B.: Fiddlehead Poetry Books, 1971. 31 p.

HAYNES, CAROLYN ELIZABETH
Flood Tide, and Other Poems. Boston: The Gorham Press, 1914. 85 p.

HAYNES, LAURA BAKER
Faith, Love and Laughter. San Antonio, TX.: Naylor Co., 1965. xiii, 95 p.

HAYNES, LOUISE MARSHALL
Through the Church Door. Boston: Wright & Potter Printing Co., 1924. 53, [1] p.

HAYNES, MARGARET
Love and After. New York: H. Vinal, Ltd., 1928. 4 p. ℓ., 3-69 p., 1 ℓ.

HAYS, HELEN IRELAND

The Strawberry Stone; Poems. Francestown, N. H.: Golden Quill Press, 1966. 80 p.

Roots. Francestown, N. H.: Golden Quill Press, 1972. 80 p.

HAYS, IRENE ELIZABETH ROSSWIG (1900-)

The Understanding Heart. Baltimore, MD.: The Sun Printing Co., 1948. 114 p.

Around the Bend. Baltimore, MD.: The Sun Printing Company, 1955. 40 p.

HAYS, MARGARET PARKER (GEBBIE) (1874-)

Kiddie Rhymes. Philadelphia: G. W. Jacobs & Co., 1911. [52] p.

Vegetable Verselets for Humorous Vegetarians. Philadelphia & London: J. B. Lippincott Company, 1911. 60 p.

HAYWARD, GRACE GLENWAY (1881-)

Gathering Waters. Philadelphia: Dorrance, 1948. 54 p. (Contemporary poets of Dorrance, 368)

HAYWARD, MILDRED (1889-)

Light Breaking Through. New York?: n. p., 193-? 136 p.

Miracle at Sea, & Other Poems. New York: The Fine Editions Press, 1943. 6 p. ℓ., 15-85, [1] p.

The Forgotten Message; Poems. New York: Designed and printed at the Peter Pauper Press, 1953. 61 p.

While Jesus Walked on Earth. Wakefield, MA.: Montrose Press, 1955.

HAZARD, CAROLINE (1856-1945)

A Scallop Shell of Quiet. Boston & New York: Houghton, Mifflin and Company, 1908. 75 ℓ.

The Yosemite, and Other Verse. Boston & New York: Houghton, Mifflin Company, 1917. ix, 178 p., 1 ℓ.

Three Valleys. n. p., 192-? [16] p.

Songs in the Sun. Boston & New York: Houghton Mifflin Company, 1927. viii p., 3 ℓ., 3-89 p.

The Homing to "This Precious Stone Set in a Silver Sea." New York: The Harbor Press, 1929. 4 p. ℓ., 50 p., 1 ℓ.

_______. London: Fowler Wright, 1930. 4 p. ℓ., 11-60 p.

Shards and Scarabs from Egypt. New York: The Harbor Press, 1931. 4 p. ℓ., 50 p., 1 ℓ.

The Golden State; A Semi-Centennial Collection of California Verse Written from 1889 to 1939. Santa Barbara, CA.: The Schauer Printing Studio, Inc., 1939. 5 p. ℓ., 3-39 p., 1 ℓ.

HAZLEWOOD, CHARLOTTE WILLIAMS

The Garden of Gray Ledge, and Other Poems. Boston: Sherman, French & Co., 1910. 5 p. ℓ., 100 p.

HEAD, GWEN (1940-)
Special Effects. Pittsburgh, PA.: University of Pittsburgh Press, 1975. 53 p. (Pitt poetry series)

HEADEN, SUSAN (1938-)
Caravan. New York: Poets of America Pub. Co., 1963. 4 p. ℓ., 69 p.

HEALY, CATHARINE R.
My Silent Songs. Pottstown, PA.: The Feroe Press, 1925. [39] p.

HEARD, LOU ELLA (1881-)
Lines of Living; Poems. San Antonio, TX.: Naylor Co., 1962. ix, 102 p.
More Lines of Living; Poems. San Antonio, TX.: Naylor Co., 1966. ix, 124 p.

HEARN, MADELINE B.
Road, Turn Home. Chicago: Windfall Press, 1964. 48 p.

HEATH, LUCY HANNAH (1847-)
Heart Songs. Boston: The Cornhill Publishing Co., 1926. 5 p. ℓ., 3-57 p.

HEATON, ABIGAIL
The Lambent Glow. Los Angeles, CA.: Anderson & Ritchie, 1947. 40 p.

HECHLER, BEATRICE (MOZIER)
Rhapsody in Rhyme. New York: Vantage Press, 1953. 4 p. ℓ., 35 p.

HECHT, EDITH
Life's Bazaar and Other Poems. San Francisco, CA.: Printed by Ben Franklin Press, 1931. 3 p. ℓ., 5-163 p.
______. Los Angeles, CA.: Sutton House, 1933. 3 p. ℓ., 5-163 p.

HECHT, MARIE (ARMSTRONG)
Morte. Chicago: P. Covici Press, 1925. 81 p.

HECK, FANNIE EXILE SCUDDER (1862-1915)
Sunrise, and Other Poems. New York: Fleming H. Revell Company, 1916. 47 p.

HECKARD, AIMEE POTTIER
Life's Tapestries, a Volume of Lyric Verse. New York: Bouregy & Curl, 1951. 58 p.

HECKEL, PEARL BASH
If I Could Sing. Portland, ME.: Falmouth Publishing House, 1940. 5 p. ℓ., 3-55 p.

Candles in the Sun. Portland, ME.: Falmouth Publishing House, 1947. 55 p.
From Ark to Zoo. New York: Comet Press Books, 1953. unpaged.

HEDGER, KATHRYN (COLLINS)
Shadows of Vanity, A Collection of Verse. New York: Exposition Press, 1958. 61 p.

HEDGES, ADA HASTINGS
Desert Poems. Portland, OR.: Metropolitan Press, 1930. 7 p. ℓ., 3-65 p.

HEDLEY, ANNE
Tom Non-Stop. Berkeley, CA.: Thorp Springs Press, 1972.

HEFLEBOWER, CLARA KECK
Winged Arrows. New York: H. Vinal, Ltd., 1928. 4 p. ℓ., 60 p.

HEFLIN, JEANNETTE (SHELLEY)
A Lantern in the Heart. Dallas, TX.: The Kaleidograph Press, 1937. xi p., 1 ℓ., 15-106 p.

HEGEMAN, KATHARINE REID
In Maytime, and Other Poems. North Montpelier, VT.: The Driftwind Press, 1943. 59 p.

HEILMAN, EDITH
... Forty Poems. Philadelphia: Dorrance and Company, 1940. 48 p. (Contemporary poets of Dorrance, 205)

HEINER, JESSIE MARGARETHE
Beckoning Paths. New York & Mill Valley, CA.: The Wings Press, 1944. 64 p.
This Flowering Branch. Mill Valley, CA.: Wings Press, 1950. 71 p.

HELLMANN, ANNE McCLURE
Star Holiday. Stratford, CT.: Brew Pub. Co., 1942. 28 p.

HELM, BELLE DOROTHY
Discords and Other Chords, Ventures in Rhyme. Chicago: Henson Brothers, 1906. 2 p. ℓ., 3-91 p.

HELM, MARY (SHIRLEY)
Me and Mine. New York: The Hobson Book Press, 1946. 4 p. ℓ., 58 p.

HELMERSHAUSEN, ADELLA (1867-) [HELMERSHAUSEN, MAUDE MINNIE ADELLA]
Dixon Chimes. n.p., 1915? [20] p.

The Poems of Adella Helmershausen to 1891. Chicago: n.p., 1915. unpaged.
College Chimes, A Decade of the Lyrical Poetry of Adella Helmershausen... 1891-1901. Autobiographical ed. Chicago: B. F. Stevens, 1917. [246] p.
The Voice of the Flag, Patriotic Poems. Chicago: Manz Engraving Corp., 1941. [26] p.

HELMERSHAUSEN, MAUDE MINNIE ADELLA see HELMERSHAUSEN, ADELLA

HEMBLING, NINA (CLARK) (1875-)
Silver Overtones. Mill Valley, CA. & New York: Wings Press, 1941. x p., 1 ℓ., 46 p., 1 ℓ. (Redwood Trail Series of American Poetry)

HEMLER, OPAL FRANCES (1890-)
Vista Through, Selected Poems. Dallas, TX.: Southwest Press, 1940. vii, 88 p.

HEMPSTEAD, FAY (1847-)
Poems by Fay Hempstead, Poet Laureate of Freemasonry. Little Rock, AR.: Democrat Printing and Lithographing Company, 1908. [18] p.

HEMSCHEMEYER, JUDITH (1935-)
I Remember the Room Was Filled with Light. Middletown, CT.: Wesleyan University Press, 1973. 72 p. (The Wesleyan poetry program, v. 66)
Very Close and Very Slow. Middletown, CT.: Wesleyan University Press, 1975. 69 p. (The Wesleyan poetry program, v. 76)

HENDERSON, ALICE (CORBIN) (1881-1949) [CORBIN, ALICE]
The Spinning Woman of the Sky. Chicago: R. F. Seymour, 1912. 61 p.
Red Earth: Poems of New Mexico. Chicago: R. F. Seymour, 1920. 58 p.
The Sun Turns West. Santa Fe, N.M.: n.p., 1933. 5 p. ℓ., 3-75, [1] p.

HENDERSON, ANNA R.
Life and Song; Poems. Buffalo, N.Y.: C. W. Moulton, 1900. 2 p. ℓ., [vii]-viii, 9-113 p.

HENDERSON, ELIZABETH PERRY (FAULKNER) (1876-)
Fire and Flesh, A Woman's Testament. New York: H. Vinal, Ltd., 1928. 5 p. ℓ., 74 p., 1 ℓ.

HENDERSON, HARRIET OLDS (1868?-1936)
Morning Glories and Moonflowers; Selected Published Verse, 1888-1933. Dallas, TX.: The Kaleidograph Press, 1934. 5 p. ℓ., xiii-xv p., 1 ℓ., 19-93 p.

HENDERSON, HELENA
Leo and Virgo; Poems. Cambridge: n. p., 1962. 48 p.

HENDERSON, JANE
The Bird Within; Poems. Chicago: Dierkes Press, 1948. 48 p.

HENDERSON, RUTH EVELYN (1892-)
Whistle of Day. Atlanta, GA.: E. Hartsock, 1930. 36 p.
8:20 A. M. Boston: B. Humphries, Inc., 1937. 120 p.
Summer Dusk. Boulder, CO.: Johnson Pub. Co., 1956. 74 p.

HENDERSON, RUTH GORDON
Poems from the Middle West. Lincoln, NB.: Midwest Pub. Co., 1950. 91 p.

HENDRICKS, FLORA BISHOP
Bowls of Phantasy. Chicago: R. Packard & Co., 1928. 76 p.

HENDRICKSON, GWEN
I Seek the Dawn. Dallas, TX.: The Kaleidograph Press, 1942. xi p., 1 ℓ., 15-87 p.

HENDRIE, PEARL DEMING
The Edge of Gold. North Hollywood, CA.: Camas Press, 1953. 34 p.

HENDRIX, LILY ELIZABETH GRAVES (1868-)
Gleanings; A Book of Poems. St. Louis, MO.: Press of Buschart Bros. Printing Co., 1908. 163 p.

HENNEY, MARTHA
'Tis of Me. New York: Vantage Press, 1957. 198 p.

HENRICH, EDITH (DODD) (1907-)
Uncertain Planet. New York: League to Support Poetry, 1939. 12 ℓ.
The Quiet Center. New York: William Sloane Associates, 1946. 73 p.
Person in the World; Poems. Dallas, TX.: Southern Methodist University Press, 1955. 54 p.

HENRY, MARGARET ELLIMAN
The Doves of Old Saint Paul's and Other Brief Verses. New York: J. G. Scharf & Son, 1939. 75 p.

HENRY, MILDRED PUTNAM
Plumes from a Wild Bird's Wing. Mill Valley, CA. & New York: The Wings Press, 1940. 64 p.

HENSHALL, JEANNETTE (FRASER)
Star Dust. Detroit, MI.: n. p., 1919. 52 p.
Rain and Roses. Boston: The Stratford Co., 1923. 4 p. ℓ., 84 p.

HENSLEY, JULIA BEAUMONT
Golden Tapestry. Dallas, TX.: W. T. Tardy, 1937. 49 p.

HENSLEY, SOPHIA MARGARETTA (ALMON) (1866-)
The Heart of a Woman. New York & London: G. P. Putnam's Sons, 1906. vi, 175 p.
The Way of a Woman, and Other Poems. San Diego, CA.: The Canterbury Company, 1928. 112 p.

HENZE, HELEN (ROWE) (1899-)
Song to Life. Boston: B. Humphries, 1948. 85 p.
Each Man's World. Kansas City, MO.: Frank Glenn Publ. Co., 1950. 1 p. ℓ., 103 p.
Strange Is the Heart. Kansas City, MO.: F. Glenn Publ. Co., 1951. unpaged.
Arise, My Love. Garden City, N.Y.: Doubleday, 1953. 8 p. ℓ., 52 ℓ.

HENZE, KATHERINE (CARR) (1915-)
Unto the Hills. Mill Valley, CA.: Wings Press, 1953. 62 p.
Passing By. Mill Valley, CA.: Wings Press, 1955. 61, [1] p.

HERBERT, NELLIE CANDEE (TUCKER) (1858-)
Lyrics and Idyls. Boston: R. G. Badger, 1907. 119 p.

HERGT, RUTH
Impressions. New York: Vantage Press, 1964. 78 p.

HERMAN, LEONORA (OWSLEY)
Rather Personal.... Brattleboro, VT.: The Stephen Daye Press, 1934. 126 p.

HEROLD, BRENDA (1948-)
The St. Charles Gig. New Haven, CT.: Corinth Books, 1971. 42 p.

HERR, DOROTHY M.
Portraiture. Philadelphia: Dorrance, 1963. 31 p. (Contemporary poets of Dorrance, 558)

HERRICK, ELEANOR
Julie's Such a Pretty Lady! New York: H. Harrison, 1938. 62 p.

HERRING, GLADYS FIELD (1909-)
The Offspring. New York: Vantage Press, 1969. 50 p.

HERRON, EMILY K.
A Florida Cypress and Other Poems. New York: H. Harrison, 1938. 64 p.

HERRON, MARY EULALIA, Sister [Secular Name: Mary Herron.]
Vintage, and Other Poems. Paterson, N. J.: St. Anthony Guild Press, 1938. ix, 61 p.

HERRON, STELLA WYNNE
Bowery Parade and Other Poems of Protest. New York: Delphic Studios, 1936. [40] p.

HERSCHBERGER, RUTH (1917-)
A Way of Happening. New York: Pellegrini & Cudahy, 1948. 56 p.
Poetry by G. B. (pseud.) Buckfastleigh, South Devon: n. p., 1963.
Nature and Love Poems. New York: Eakins Press, 1969. 54, [2] p.

HERSEY, CLARA SHERMAN
A New England Romance and Other Poems. Boston: Press of Geo. H. Ellis Co., 1917. 83 p.

HERSHAW, FAY McKENNE
Verse Along the Way. New York: Exposition Press, 1954. 48 p.
Skip Along With Verse. New York: Carlton Press, 1966. 30 p.
Verse Here and There. New York: Heath Cote Pub. Corp., 1971. 63 p.

HERTWECK, IONE REHM
Forevermore. Boston: Christopher Pub. House, 1956. 190 p.
_______. Enl. ed., 1970. 219 p.

HERVEY, ETHEL JESSIE
A Weaver of Dreams. Boston: R. G. Badger, 1919. 192 p.

HERZIG, PAULINE
Poems and Love Lyrics. Boston: Printed by the Terminal Press, 1934. [11] p.

HESS, LUVA M. (d. 1925)
The Sea Is Singing to God Tonight, and Other Poems. Chicago: Whitlock Publishing Co., 1925. 3 p. ℓ., [4]-89 p.

HESSE, ROSANNE A.
Verses in Rhyme. St. Louis, MO.: Con P. Curran Printing Co., 1939. 2 p. ℓ., 3-107, [2] p.

HESTON, FLORENCE
Just to Point It Out. New York: Vantage Press, 1965. 132 p.

HEYER, MARY B.
Under the Southern Sun: Poems. New York, London: The Abbey Press, 1901. 4 p. ℓ., 3-7, 15-258 p.

HEYMAN, KATE SELMA

Portraits. New York: The Horn Publishing Co., 1927. 3-120 p.

The Stone City. New York: Renaissance Book Company, 1936. 125, [1] p.

Songs out of the Soviet. n. p., 1943. 15, [1] p.

Megilla. New York: Academy Photo Offset, Inc., 1953. 4 p. ℓ., 55 p.

"He, Watching over Israel...." Jerusalem: n. p., 1957. 170 p.

HEYWARD, JANIE SCREVEN (DuBOSE) (1864-1939)

Wild Roses. New York: The Neale Publishing Company, 1905. 56 p.

Songs of the Charleston Darkey. n. p., 1912. 29 p.

Daffodils and Other Lyrics. Charleston, S. C.: Southern Printing & Publishing Co., 1921. 3 p. ℓ., 52 p.

HIBBARD, GRACE (PORTER) [Full Name: Helen Grace (Porter) Hibbard.]

California Violets: A Book of Verse. San Francisco, CA.: A. M. Robertson, 1902. 113 p.

Wild Roses of California, A Book of Verse. San Francisco, CA.: A. M. Robertson, 1902. 1 p. ℓ., 129 p.

Forget-me-nots From California: A Book of Verse. San Francisco, CA.: A. M. Robertson, 1907. 3 p. ℓ., 5-113 p.

California Sunshine, and Other Verses. San Francisco, CA.: A. M. Robertson, 1911. 6 p. ℓ., 3-49, [1] p.

HICKEY, AGNES MacCARTHY

Out of Every Day. Cedar Rapids, IA.: The Torch Press, 1929. 59 p.

Little Stories in Verse. Cedar Rapids, IA.: The Torch Press, 1940. 59 p. (A Bookfellow Book)

HICKLER, ROSALIE (DUNLAP) (1903-) [Full Name: Rosalie Baldwin (Dunlap) Hickler]

Lower Than the Angels. Chicago & New York: Willett, Clark & Co., 1934. vi p., 1 ℓ., 75 p.

HICKS, BETTY BROWN (1914-)

I Sing My Amazement. Philadelphia: Dorrance, 1968. 100 p. (Contemporary poets of Dorrance, 68)

Lyrics from Cor Meum. Philadelphia: Dorrance, 1969. 33 p.

HICKS, DORIS ENFIELD

Rambling Thoughts. New York: The Exposition Press, 1941. 63 p.

Bright Through the Flames. New York: The Exposition Press, 1944. 62 p.

HICKS, EMMA ENDICOTT

Poems. Cambridge, MA.: The Riverside Press, 1922. xi, 167 p.

HICKS, GRACE MADELINE
Pot of Gold Verse. New York: Vantage Press, 1957. 63 p.

HIELSCHER, HELEN HUGHES (1863-)
Miscellaneous Poems. Complete ed. St. Meinrad, IN.: Abbey Press, 1936. xii p., 1 ℓ., 203 p.

HIERS, LOIS SMITH
My House and My Country. New York: Fine Editions Press, 1958. 52 p.

HIGBEE, ALMA ROBISON
Songs for Mountain Men. Dallas, TX.: The Kaleidograph Press, 1943. viii p., 1 ℓ., 11-59 p.
Sunmark on the Sill. Dallas, TX.: Kaleidograph Press, 1947. viii p., 1 ℓ., 11-64 p.

HIGBIE, JANE CAMPBELL
Stray Leaves. San Jose, CA.: Rosicrucian Press, 1931. 32 p.

HIGGINS, CLAIRE M.
Scattered Feathers. Ridgewood, N.J.: Gayren Press, 1935. 3 p. ℓ., 38 p.

HIGGINS, LILLIAN AINSLEY (1870-1961)
Heart Praises, and Other Poems. Ed. and with an introd. by Anna M. Schell. New York: Exposition Press, 1961. 1 v.

HIGGINS, LUCY TERRY
Poems. New Britain, CT.: Lincoln Printing Company, 1947. 67, [4] p.

HIGGINSON, ELLA (RHOADS) (d. 1862)
Four-Leaf Clover. Whatcom, WA.: Edson & Irish, 1901. 27 p.
The Voice of April-Land and Other Poems. New York: Macmillan; London: Macmillan & Co., Ltd., 1903. x p., 1 ℓ., 121 p.
The Vanishing Race and Other Poems. Bellingham, WA.: C. M. Sherman, 1911. 28 p.
A Tribute. Ed. by the Washington State Federation of Women's Clubs. Bellingham, WA.: Union Printing Co., 1941. 88 p.

HIGGINSON, MARY POTTER (THACHER) (1844-1941)
The Drum-Beat. Cambridge, MA.: Privately printed for Small, Maynard by the University Press, 1904. 11 p.
The Playmate Hours. Boston & New York: Houghton, Mifflin and Company, 1904. 3 p. ℓ., 50 p., 1 ℓ.
Fugitives. Portland, ME.: The Mosher Press, 1929. vii, 73, [1] p., 1 ℓ.

HILBORN, MARGARETA
Close by the Bud, in Crude Expectant Time. New York: Exposition Press, 1966. 48 p.

HILDRETH, MATTIE OLIVE
Sunshine; A Book of Poems. Camden, N. J.: n. p., 1925. 3 p. ℓ., 3-100 p.

HILL, AGNES (LEONARD) SCANLAND (1842-1917) [LEONARD, AGNES]
"Said Confidentially." Denver, CO.: The Smith-Brooks Printing Co., 1902. 67 p.

HILL, ALICE TAYLOR
The Service Flag and Other Poems. Brooklyn, N. Y.: Connell Press, 1919. [63] p.

HILL, ANNE KAMARRARRA
Aurora; Poems. New York: Anne K. Hill, 1948. 53 p.

HILL, BERYL LEWIS
Philomela's Song, and Other Poems. New York: Exposition Press, 1953. 56 p.

HILL, DOROTHY BLADIN
Poems from My Heart. Sunland, CA.: C. L. Anderson, 1950. 76 p.

HILL, EILEEN SHEILA
Legend of La Pollera, and Other Poems. Philadelphia: Dorrance & Co., 1947. 80 p. (Contemporary poets of Dorrance, 353)
Like Water Willy-Nilly Flowing. Appalachia, VA.: Young Publications, 1967. ii, 72 p.

HILL, ELIZABETH SEWELL
Western Waters and Other Poems. Chicago: The Roadside Press, 1917.
Bethlehem. Cincinnati, OH.: The Methodist Book Concern, 1921. 40 p.

HILL, JENNIE EARNGEY
Poems. Boston: The Gorham Press, 1918. 40 p.

HILL, LAEL (WOOLSEY)
A Legacy of Years. Salt Lake City, UT.: Utah State Poetry Society, 1966. 76 p.

HILL, MAUDE WYNN GILBERT
The Singing Stars. Denver, CO.: Big Mountain Press, 1963. 72 p.

HILL, MAUDIE BROOKS
Flashes. Newark, N. J.: The Essex Press, Inc., 1929. 83 p.

HILL, MILDRED MARTIN
A Traipsin' Heart. New York: W. Malliet and Co., 1941. 4 p. ℓ., 7-61 p.

HILL, PATI see HILL, PATRICIA (1921-)

HILL, PATRICIA (1921-) [HILL, PATI]
The Snow Rabbit; Poems. Boston: Houghton Mifflin, 1962. vi, 51 p.
Slave Days; 29 Poems, 31 Photocopied. New York: Kornblee, 1975. [62] p.

HILLS, AGNES CONNER
Pioneer Trails and Romances of Oregon. New York: H. Harrison, 1948. 64 p.

HILTON, MINA MYRTHINE
Wild Echoes Flying; Poems. New York: Exposition Press, 1962. 86 p.

HIMES, RUTH (SCHULTZ) (1908-)
Life's Poems. San Antonio, TX.: Naylor Co., 1953. vii, 32 p.

HIMMELL, SOPHIE
A Little Madness. Garden City, N.Y.: The Country Life Press, 1935. vi p., 1 ℓ., 63 p.
Within the Crucible. New York: Wings Press, 1938. 68 p.
...Spontaneous Now. New York: Fine Editions Press, 1948. 61 p., 1 ℓ.
Checkerboard of Talk; New and Selected Poems. New York: Bookman Associates, 1955. 81 p.
In the Month of Green Fire; New and Collected Poems. New York: Arco Publ. Co., 1964. 72 p.

HINCHMAN, ANNE
Poems. Cambridge, MA.: Printed at the Riverside Press, 1910. 2 p.ℓ., [v]-vii, 51, [1] p.

HINCKLEY, MABEL (GOULD) DEMERS (1887-)
Today Is Mine; Poems from the Heart of Maine. Brunswick, ME.: Pejepscot Press, 1955. 54 p.

HINCKLEY, MERCY ADELINE (1871-)
The Home Spirit; A Collection of Poems. New York: Cochrane Publishing Co., 1910. 80 p.
Life-Colors. New York: The Neale Publishing Co., 1914. 95 p.

HINES, EDNA GREENE
Underneath the Bough; Poems. Kingston? Ont.: Crusader Press, 1939. [38] p.
The Valley of Blue Moon; Poems. Prairie City, IL.: The Press of J. A. Decker, 1939. [38] p.
Candle in the Night. Watertown, N.Y.: n.p., 1942. 39 p.
The White Dawn; Poems. Watertown, N.Y.: A. M. Phillips, 1943. 38 p.
The Endless Trail. Watertown, N.Y.: A. M. Phillips, 1946. 40 p.

White Butterflies; Poems. Watertown, N. Y.: A. M. Phillips, 1949. 40 p.
Harp of the Pines; Poems. Watertown, N. Y.: A. M. Phillips, 1952. 39 p.
Forgotten Rapture; Poems. Watertown, N. Y.: Weston Printing Co., 1955. 40 p.
Captured Dreams; Poems. Watertown, N. Y.: Weston Printing Co., 1957. 40 p.

HINES, MARCELLA M[ELVILLE] (1828-) [WILDWOOD, FLORA, pseud.]
Songs of the Wildwood. Boston: C. W. Calkins & Co., 1903. 1 p. ℓ., 5-126 p.

HINSON, ESTELLE ELIZABETH
A Few Rhymes and Rhythms. Boston: The Stratford Company, 1925. 3 p. ℓ., 25 p.

HINTON, CAROLINE (CLARK)
The Pinnacle; A Book of Verse. Atlanta, GA.: A. B. Caldwell, 1917. 52 p.
Mothers o' Men. New York: R. J. Shores Corporation, 1919. 72 p.

HINTON, MARY BOOLE
Other Notes: Poems. Washington, D. C.: The Neale Pub. Co., 1901. 47 p.

HINZ, PATRICIA BOYLE
Gypsy Footprints. Dexter, MO.: Candor Press, 1953. 20 p.

HIQUILY, ARIENE COLUMBUS
The Smile on the Face of the Dragon. New York: Libra Publishers, 1961. 4 p. ℓ., 72 p.

HIRD, MARTHA (1877-)
The Gulls, and Other Poems. n. p., 1948. vii, 83, [1] p.

HIRSH, ALICE
Within My Heart. Philadelphia: Dorrance & Co., 1932. 83 p. (Contemporary poets of Dorrance, 106)
A Book for Me. New York: Paebar Co., 1937. 6 p. ℓ., 96, [1] p.
From Pipes Long Cold. Boston: B. Humphries, 1954. 64 p.

HOBBY, JEANNETTE JAMES
Down Memory Lane. Dallas, TX.: Story Book Press, 1950. 68 p.

HOBBY, MINNA ROTH SAMUELS
Dreams of Love. Memphis, TN.: The Sidney S. Friedman Press, 1918. 1 p. ℓ., 39 p.
______. 2d ed. Memphis, TN.: Dreams of Love Co., 1919. [46] p.

HOBSON, DOROTHY (1905-)
Celestial Interim. Brooklyn, N.Y.: Parnassus Press, 1933. 80 p.
Let There Be Light. New York: B. Fitzgerald, 1943. 4 p. ℓ., 51 p., 1 ℓ.

HOCHMAN, SANDRA (1936-)
Voyage Home: Poems. Paris: Two Cities Editions, 1960. 47 p.
Manhattan Pastures. New Haven, CT.: Yale University Press, 1963. 66 p. (Yale Series of Younger Poets, v. 59)
Love Poems. Hong Kong: S. Hochman, 1966. [32] ℓ.
The Vaudeville Marriage; Poems. New York: Viking Press, 1966. viii, 69 p.
Love Letters from Asia; Poems. New York: Viking Press, 1968. viii, 54 p.
Earthworks; Poems 1960-1970. New York: Viking Press, 1970. xi, 210 p.
Walking Papers. New York: Viking Press, 1971.
_______. New York: Ballantine, 1972.
Futures: New Poems. New York: Viking Press, 1974. 52 p.

HOCKEY, ALIDA FEDERSPIEL
Jumbled Poems. Boston: Meador Publishing Company, 1936. 116 p.

HODGINS, MARY E.
Indian Summer and Other Poems. New York: Fortuny's, 1941. 39 p.

HOEFLING, SUSAN JOAN (1909-)
For You, "Melody of Life Poems".... New Brighton, PA.: n.p., 1962. [16] p.

HOERNECKE, ALMA ELLIS
A Wintry Mind. Mill Valley, CA.: Wings Press, 1949. 111, [1] p.

HOFF, DONNAFRED BAKER
Daughter of Eve. Chicago: Dierkes Press, 1952. 60 p.

HOFFMAN, CALLIE ELIZABETH
Rural Poems. Boston: The Christopher Publishing House, 1923. 31 p.

HOFFMAN, HELEN E.
...Some Humbler Poet. New York: Exposition Press, 1948. 64 p.

HOFFMAN, JILL
Mink Coat. New York: Holt, Rinehart & Winston, 1973. xi, 99 p.

HOFFMAN, OLIVIA WATSON
The Four Seasons; Poems. New York: Exposition Press, 1954. 48 p.

HOGE, MARY RINEHART
Calm Now the Heart; Poems. New York: Exposition Press, 1955. 48 p.

HOGREFE, PEARL
Renewal; Poems. Muscatine, IA.: The Prairie Press, 1940. 5 p. ℓ., 15-71, [1] p.

HOGUE, MAUDE BEATRICE
The Cabin Book. San Francisco, CA.: Harr Wagner Publishing Co., 1924. 2 p. ℓ., v, 59 p.
Every-Other-Woman. Asheville, N. C.: n. p., 1927. 95 p.

HOHSTADT, EMMA LEE
...Life Has Scarlet Threads. Philadelphia: Dorrance & Co., 1945. 46 p. (Contemporary poets of Dorrance, 296)

HOLDEN, ADELE V.
Figurine, and Other Poems. Philadelphia: Dorrance, 1961. viii, 88 p. (Contemporary poets of Dorrance, 542)

HOLDEN, HARRIET WOODS
...The Peg Book.... Philadelphia: Dorrance & Co., 1949. 85 p. (Contemporary poets of Dorrance, 388)

HOLDING, CYNTHIA DAVRIL
...Poems, 1936-1945. Los Angeles, CA.: The Ward Ritchie Press, 1946. ix, 112 p.

HOLDING, VERA
Prairie Nautilus. Tipton, OK.: The Tipton Tribune, Printers-Publishers, 1936. 85 p.
Prairie Moods. Dallas, TX.: American Poetry Association, 1938. 7 p. ℓ., 62 p.
Prairie Brand. Boston: B. Humphries, 1946. 64 p.
Take Time. Abilene, TX.: Quality Printing, 1966.
Listen! The Prairies Speak. Abilene, TX.: Quality Printing, 1968. 110 p.
All God's Children. Abilene, TX.: Quality Printing, 1975.

HOLKENBRINK, IONA (MADISON)
The Garden of Memories. Nashville, TN.: Parthenon Press, 1956. 98 p.

HOLLAND, BARBARA ADAMS (1925-)
Medusa. New York: n. p., 196-? 20 p.
Return in Sagittarius. New York: Eventorium Press, 1965. 27 p.
A Game of Scraps; Poems of the MacDougal Street Midway.

Charleston, IL.: Prairie Press, 1967. viii, 34 p.
Crises of Rejuvenation. New York: Grim Reaper Books, 1974-75. 2 v.

HOLLAND, JEAN FOX
The Frogs and I.... New York: The William-Frederick Press, 1947. 46 p. (The William-Frederick poets, no. 35)

HOLLIS, BARBARA COONLEY
Texture; Poems. Philadelphia: Dorrance, 1966. 3 p. ℓ., 82 p. (Contemporary poets of Dorrance, 622)

HOLLISTER, ELEANOR EUNICE
Color Bearer. New York: Fortuny's, 193-? 48 p.

HOLLOWAY, ARIEL (WILLIAMS) (1905-)
Shape Them into Dreams; Poems. New York: Exposition Press, 1955. 48 p.

HOLLY, ALICE
A Legacy of Poetry. New York: Vantage Press, 1966. 63 p.

HOLMAN, ANNE B.
Lazy Shadows. 2d ed. San Diego, CA.: R. O. Akers, 1955. 57 p.
Demitasse. Coraville, IA.: Olympic Press, 1964. 105, [1] p.

HOLME, Mrs. JAMIE SEXTON
Star Gatherer. New York: H. Vinal, 1926. 58 p.
Floodmark. New York: H. Harrison, 1930. 79 p.
I Have Been a Pilgrim, Poems. New York: H. Harrison, 1935. 96 p.

HOLMES, CLARA H.
Scattered Autumn Leaves. Colorado Springs, CO.: n.p., 1926. 122 p.

HOLMES, JEAN WILLA
Lines Lyrique. Montgomery, AL.: Wilson Printing Company, 1924. 67 p.

HOLMES, MARGARET, pseud. see BATES, MARGARET HOLMES (ERNSPERGER)

HOLMES, MARGARET COOPER
Green Gold. Richmond, VA.: William Byrd Press, Inc., 1941. vi p., 1 ℓ., 62 p.
God's Sigh. Boston: The Christopher Publishing House, 1945. 80 p.
Sun and Shade. Lanford? S.C.: n.p., 1949. 182 p.
Christmas Glints. Boston: Christopher Publishing House, 1956. 144 p.

HOLMES, MARGARET ELIZABETH
Moods of Earth. Cleveland, OH.: The Pegasus Press, 1936? 24 p.

HOLMES-TIDY, VIOLET
White Magic and Other Poems. Detroit, MI.: Laughing Dragon Press, 1935. 45 p.

HOLMSTROM, FRANCES
Western Windows. Portland, OR.: Metropolitan Press, 1937. 6 p. ℓ., 17-92 p.
Rich Lady. Portland, OR.: Binfords & Mort, 1941. 93 p.
Oregon Mist. Portland, OR.: Binfords & Mort, 1951. 87 p.

HOLT, GRACE BUCKINGHAM (1902-)
Confessions; Love Ballads and Other Poems. Los Angeles, CA.: Wetzel Publishing Co., 1937. 3 p. ℓ., [5]-37 p.

HOLT, HELEN
Winged Glory. New York: The Poets Press, 1935. 11 ℓ.

HOLT, MARJORIE FAIRBANKS (1900-)
Shape of a Leaf. New York: The League to Support Poetry, 1939. 12 ℓ.

HOLTER, ELIZABETH SAGE [HOLTER, SAGE]
This, My Earth. New York: Gotham Bookmart Press, 1942. 96 p.

HOLTER, SAGE see HOLTER, ELIZABETH SAGE

HOLTON, HELEN AGNES
Where Are the Yesterdays? and Other Poems. Milwaukee, WI.: Kulk & Pauli, Printers, 1922. 3 p. ℓ., 9-110 p.

HONIG, ANNA ELIZABETH (1864-)
Story Poems. Author's ed. Dallas, TX.: Southwest Press, 1940. viii, 143 p.

HOOD, GRACE HUMPHREYS
Soft Soap. Dallas, TX.: Tardy Publishing Co., 1937. 5 p. ℓ., 72 p.

HOOKER, VIOLA LEWIS
Driftwood. New York: Vantage Press, 1965. 121 p.

HOOPER, AMY (RHODES)
Poems; Religion--Travel--Reflections. Boston: Meador Publishing Co., 1943. 96 p.

HOOPER, MARY AMIS
The Mystery of Life, and Other Verses. New York: E. S. Gorham, 1925. 4 p. ℓ., 7-63 p.

HOOPLE, CARRIE MUNSON
Along the Way with Pen and Pencil. New York: The Grafton Press, 1909. 3 p. ℓ., [v]-ix p., 2 ℓ., 3-213 p.

HOPE, ELEANOR MASSIE (1874-)
...Hopeful Thoughts. 2d ed. Kansas City, N.Y.: Franklin Hudson Publishing Co., 1911. 48 p.
...Visions of Hope. Paris: Editions de l'Esperance, 1926. 37, [1] p., 2 ℓ.

HOPEFUL, GRACE, pseud. see KELLER, GRACE ADELLE (1884-1908)

HOPKINS, FRANCES MONROE
Verses. Washington, D.C.: G. E. Howard, Printer, 1911. 83 p., [1] p.

HORD, CLARENCE (Mrs.) [BARR, C. H., pseud.]
Eulogy on the Moon. San Antonio, TX.: Naylor Co., 1937. 20 p.

HORKAN, NELLE IRWIN (1892-)
The Awakening and Other Poems. Philadelphia: Dorrance, 1957. 51 p. (Contemporary poets of Dorrance, 495)

HORLOCKER, MAXINE
Cinquains. New York: House of Field, Inc., 1940. 16 p.

HORNBROOK, ELIZA HOGGAN
Homespun Verses. Montague, MA.: Printed by C. P. Rollins at the Dyke Mill, 1917. 2 p. ℓ., 3-35 p.

HORNE, IDA CAROLINE (HARRELL)
Songs of Sentiment. Ed. by Herman Harrell Horne. New York: The Neale Publishing Company, 1917. 12 p., 1 ℓ., 13-155 p.

HORT, GERTRUDE M.
Tomorrow's Road, and Later Poems. Portland, ME.: T. B. Mosher, 1916. vi, 66, [1] p., 1 ℓ.

HORTON, ELIZA ANN (DUSENBURY) (1822-)
The Poems of Annie Hawthore (Eliza Ann Horton). Arr. & comp. by E. Jay Hanford. New York: The Grafton Press, 1910. 6 p. ℓ., 11-221 p.

HOSKINS, ANN [Full Name: Elizabeth Ann Hoskins.]
Beneath This Bushel. Hastings-on-Hudson, N.Y.: The Mistral Press, 1933. 1 p. ℓ., [7]-28 p., 1 ℓ.

HOSKINS, KATHERINE (de MONTALANT) (1909-)
A Penetential Primer: Poems. Cummington, MA.: The Cummington Press, 1945. [35] p.

Villa Narcisse: The Garden, the Statues and the Pool. New York: Noonday Press, 1956. 94 p.
The Partridge Tree. San Francisco, CA.: n.p., 1957. 1 ℓ.
Out in the Open; Poems. New York: Macmillan, 1959. ix, 99 p. (The Macmillan poets)
Excursions: New & Selected Poems. New York: Atheneum, 1967. ix, 133 p.

HOSKINS, MARTHA MAYE
For Thinking Out Loud... in Meter and Rhyme. Philadelphia: Dorrance, 1967. 32 p. (Contemporary poets of Dorrance, 641)

HOSMER, MARGARET SWIFT
Through Mediaeval Windows. Ontario, CA.: Herals-Silhouettes Press, 1935. 3 p.ℓ., 9-67 p., 1 ℓ.
Poems. Ontario, CA.: Herald-Silhouettes Press, 1937. 1 p.ℓ., 5-68 p.
Flutes Afar. Los Angeles, CA.: Abbey San Encino Press, 1940. v, 6-122 p.
The Wilding Heart. Rev. ed. Hollywood, CA.: Hollycrofters, 1947. 147 p.

HOTALING, ETHELWYN D. (1885-)
Not by Bread Alone, Poems. New York: Exposition Press, 1950. 96 p.

HOUGH, MAUDE CLARK
Occasional Verses. Dallas, TX.: Sheegog Printing Co., 1915. 1 p.ℓ., 46 p.
Youth Dies Not. n.p., 1918. [5] p.
Lines on Life. New York: The Poets Press, 1936. 52 p., 1 ℓ.
In Another Living Room; Poems of Consolation. New York: Call Press, 1938. 39 p.
For Your Inspiration. Brooklyn? N.Y.: n.p., 1940. 36 p.
Out of My Heart. New York: House of Field, Inc., 1940. 64 p.
Life Is a Game, and Other Poems. New York: House of Field, 1941. 73 p.

HOUSE, BEATRICE WADE
Memories. San Antonio, TX.: Naylor Co., 1963. ix, 106 p.

HOUSER, Mrs. TERZAH ADAMS
Into the Sunlight; Poems. New York: H. Harrison, 1936. 63 p.

HOUSTON, MARGARET BELL (d. 1966)
Poems. Boston: R. G. Badger, 1906.
Prairie Flowers. Boston: R. G. Badger, 1907. 71 p.
The Singing Heart, and Other Poems. Nashville & Dallas: Cokesbury Press, 1926. viii, 78 p.
Lanterns in the Dusk. New York: Dodd, Mead & Co., 1930. 6 p.ℓ., 3-86 p.

Collected Poems. San Antonio, TX.: Naylor Co., 1967. xiv, 158 p.

HOUSTON, PEARL BROOKS
Burnt Clay. New York: Dean & Company, 1928. 31 p.

HOVDE, AGNES LOUISE
Song Before Sleep. Chicago: Dierkes Press, 1948. 48 p.
Prelude to a Journey; A Story of the Ukraine. New York: Vantage Press, 1954. xii, 116 p. (Narrative poem)

HOVEY, MARY
Mingled Tints. Boston: R. G. Badger, 1926. 77 p.

HOVNANIAN, LOUISE WHEATLEY COOK
Teach Me to Love, and Other Poems. Kansas City, MO.: Putnam Co., 1948. [21] p.

HOWARD, ALICE HENRIETTA
Onion to Orchid. New York: The William-Frederick Press, 1945. 32 p. (The William-Frederick poets, no. 18)

HOWARD, CATHERINE
Poems. Boston: The Four Seas Co., 1921.

HOWARD, ETTA PEASE
Shadows, and Other Verses. Long Beach, CA.: Worth While Publishing Co., 1925. 3 p. ℓ., 71 p.

HOWARD, FRANCES MINTURN
All Keys Are Glass. New York: Dutton, 1950. 64 p.
Sleep Without Armor. New York: Dutton, 1953. 64 p.

HOWARD, HARRIET M. (1875-)
Through the Years, 1912-1955. Denver, CO.: Big Mountain Press, 1957. 40 p.

HOWARD, HELEN FRANCES
Moods. Boston: H. Vinal, Ltd., 1929. 94 p.

HOWARD, KATHARINE (1858-)
Eve. Boston: Sherman, French & Co., 1913. 4 p. ℓ., 49 p.
Poems. Boston: Sherman, French & Co., 1914. 5 p. ℓ., 78 p.
The Book of the Serpent. Boston: Sherman, French & Co., 1915. 4 p. ℓ., 53 p.
The Little God, Child Verse for Grown-Ups. Boston: Sherman, French & Co., 1916. [76] p.
_______. London: G. Harrap, 1918. 74 p.
The Book of the Serpent. Boston: The Four Seas Co., 1920. 4 p. ℓ., 53 p.
Eve. Boston: The Four Seas Co., 1920. 49 p.

HOWARD, MARTHA WALLING
All Things to Sea, Lyric Poems. New York: H. Harrison, 1942. 62 p.

HOWARD, RENA CARTWRIGHT
The Three Brides, and Other Poems. Los Angeles, CA.: Baumgardt Publishing Co., 1905. 5 p. ℓ., [3]-117 p.

HOWARD, SARAH ELIZABETH (HOWARD) (1846-)
Pen Pictures of the Plains. Denver, CO.: The Reed Publishing Co., 1902. 128 p.

HOWARD, TRUDI
The Poet's Pot. New York: Pageant Press, 1953. 104 p.

HOWARD, VANESSA (1955-)
A Screaming Whisper; Poems. New York: Holt, Rinehart and Winston, 1972. ix, 59 p.

HOWE, EMILINE HARRIET (SIGGINS) (1844-)
Basket of Fragments. Kansas City, MO.: Nazarene Publishing House, 1924. 175 p.

HOWE, FANNY
Forty Whacks. Boston: Houghton Mifflin, 1969. 195 p.
Eggs: Poems. Boston: Houghton Mifflin, 1970. 72 p.
Forty Whacks. London: Gollancz, 1971. [9], 195 p.
The Amerindian Coastline Poem. New York: Telephone Books Press, 1975. [48] p.

HOWELL, DOTTIE
A Clump of Poppies. San Antonio, TX.: Naylor Co., 1967. xi, 56 p.
My Dearest Ann. San Antonio, TX.: Naylor Co., 1969. 4 p. ℓ., 64 p.

HOWELL, EDNA MOORE
The Grapevine Swing. Nacogdoches, TX.: Baker Printing Co., 1931. 46 p.

HOWELL, INEZ BAKER
Life Is Like a Flower. Dallas, TX.: The Kaleidoscope Publishers, 1931. 4 p. ℓ., 52 p.

HOWELL, LOUISE H.
Tomorrow's Vintage, A Book of Poems. Boston: B. Humphries, 1942. 88 p.
In This Hour; Poems. New York: Exposition Press, 1952. 40 p.
The Uncertain Bough. Boston: Bruce Humphries, 1963. 47 p.

HOWELL, MARY JOSEPHINE (McELROY) (1878-)
Potpourri, A Book of Verse. San Antonio, TX.: The Naylor Company, 1941. 6 p. ℓ., 3-120 p.

HOWELL, MILDRED MOON
Star Tipped Wings. Cathlamet, WA.: Howell Pub. Co., 196-? 48 p.
Toward Destiny. n.p., 196-? 60 p.
From Fog and Mist. Faith, S.D.: Faith Independent Printers, 1968? 24 p.

HOWES, BARBARA (1914-)
The Undersea Farmer. Pawlet, VT.: Banyan Press, 1948. vii, 40 p.
In The Cold Country; Poems. New York: Bonacio & Saul in association with Grove Press, 1954. 48 p.
Light and Dark. Middletown, CT.: Wesleyan University Press, 1959. 78 p. (Poetry program series)
Looking Up at Leaves; Poems. New York: Alfred A. Knopf, 1966. 60 p.
The Blue Garden. Middletown, CT.: Wesleyan University Press, 1972. 70 p. (Poetry program series, v. 62)

HOWLAND, JOSEPHINE (1853-)
Think of Me, A Few Inspirational Poems. Boston: The Christopher Publishing House, 1932. 30 p.

HOYER, MILDRED N.
The Master Key; Poems. Francestown, N.H.: Golden Quill Press, 1965. 95 p.

HOYLES, EURETTA A.
In Lotus Land: or, Lovable Life in the Orient: A Volume of Poems. Aurora, IL.?: n.p., 1904. 32 p.

HOYT, HELEN (1887-)
Apples Here in My Basket. New York: Harcourt, Brace & Co., 1924. 4 p.ℓ., vii-viii, 82 p.
Leaves of Wild Grape, Poems. New York: Harcourt, Brace & Co., 1929. xv, 112 p.
The Name of a Rose. San Francisco, CA.: H. Gentry, 1931. [28] p.
Poems of Amis. Los Angeles, CA.: Printed by R. J. Hoffman, 1946. 3 p.ℓ., 5-41, [1] p.

HOYT, HELEN UNDERWOOD (1897-1930)
Bramble-Fruit. Northampton, MA.: Priv. Print. The Hampshire Bookshop, 1931. 156 p.

HUBBELL, PATRICIA (1928-)
The Apple Vendor's Fair. New York: Atheneum, 1963. 4 p.ℓ., 53 p.
8 A.M. Shadows. New York: Atheneum, 1965. viii, 53, [1] p.
Catch Me a Wind. New York: Atheneum, 1968. 52 p.

HUBER, FLORENCE M.
Silver Poems. Columbus, OH.: n.p., 1927. 28 p.

The Golden Stairway, A Book of Verse. London: A. H. Stockwell, 1930. 35, [1] p.

HUDDLESTON, MABEL PARKER
Script of the Sun; Verses. New York: The Knickerbocker Press (G. P. Putnam's Sons), 1915. vii, 82 p.
Transmission, and Other Poems. Langford, East Somerset: Privately Printed at the Latin Press, 1936. 4 p. ℓ., 52 p., 1 ℓ.

HUDSON, CAROL BURDICK
Destination Unknown. Boston: Department of Publications, U. U. A., 1967. 70 p. (The Poetry Shelf, no. 1)

HUDSON, MAXINE
Climbing a Mountain. New York: Vantage Press, 1969. 36 p.

HUDSON, MILDRED E.
Under the Blue and Gold. Portland, OR.: Kilham Stationery & Printing Co., 1917. 35 p.

HUETTL, IRENE ARNDT
The Gathering of the Waters. Mill Valley, CA.: Wings Press, 1959. 46 p.
Esther Morris of Old South Pass & Other Poems of the West. Francestown, N. H.: Golden Quill Press, 1965. 62 p.

HUFF, IMA (KEELING) (1910-)
Shadows of Wings. Dextor, MO.: Candor Press, 1955. 76 p.
Cherry-Ripe. San Antonio, TX.: Naylor Co., 1971. xi, 40 p.

HUFF, LYDA
Black Sheep, and Other Poems. Kansas City, MO.: W. W. Ross, 1938. 4 p. ℓ., 11-45, [1] p.

HUGHES, ADELAIDE MANOLA (MOULD) (1884-1923)
Diantha Goes the Primrose Way, and Other Verses. New York & London: Harper & Brothers, 1920. 4 p. ℓ., 3-77, [1] p.
The Poems of Adelaide Manola, with a memorial by Rupert Hughes. New York & London: Harper & Brothers, 1924. 185, [1] p.

HUGHES, ANN YOUNG
Romancing Widows. Philadelphia: Dorrance, 1961. 53 p. (Contemporary poets of Dorrance, 540)

HUGHES, DOROTHY BELLE (FLANAGAN) (1904-)
Dark Certainty. New Haven, CT.: Yale University Press; London: H. Milford, Oxford University Press, 1931. 68 p. (Yale Series of Younger Poets, v. 30)

HUGHES, DOROTHY BERRY (1910-)
The Green Loving. New York: Scribner, 1953. 41 p.

The Great Victory Mosaic. Columbia, MO.: University of Missouri Press, 1971. 79 p. (A Breakthrough Book)

HUGHES, Mrs. IVOR see HUGHES, RACHEL EMMA

HUGHES, RACHEL EMMA [HUGHES, Mrs. IVOR]
The Picture That I Saw: Poem. Columbus, OH.: n.p., 1904. [18] p.

HULBURD, MARY FLAGG
Bits of Vermont. Shelburne, VT.: The Excelsior Press, 1935. 44 p.

HULL, LUCILE (SHANKLIN) (1902-)
Mountain Festival and Other Poems. New York: The Paebar Company, 1936. 4 p. ℓ., 36 p.
Warm Rain. Dallas, TX.: The Kaleidograph Press, 1938. xii p., 1 ℓ., 15-87 p.

HULST, CORNELIA (STEKETEE) (1865-)
Balder's Death and Loke's Punishment. Chicago: The Open Court Publishing Co., 1913. 4 p. ℓ., 39 p.

HUME, MARTHA HASKINS
Sutras and Shadows. Denver, CO.: Poetry and Prose Editions, 1965. 39 p.

HUMPHREY, FRANCES MARY
Grace Sufficient; Poems. New York: Exposition Press, 1949. 63 p.

HUMPHREY, JANNE
The Moon-Dreamer. San Antonio, TX.: The Naylor Co., 1944. 6 p. ℓ., 150 p.
________. Philadelphia: Dorrance, 1964. xi, 127 p. (Contemporary poets of Dorrance, 659)

HUNN, FLORA LOUISE (SMITH) (1870-)
Unto the Hills, and Other Poems. New Haven, CT.: Priv. Print., 1927. 52 p.
Rainbows, and Other Poems. New Haven, CT.: Priv. Print. [Yale Univ. Press], 1935. 47 p.

HUNT, ELIZABETH (PINNEY)
Tendrils. Philadelphia: Dorrance & Co., 1942. 62 p., 1 ℓ.
Tongues of Fire. Philadelphia: Dorrance & Company, 1942. 64 p.
Cheaters; Poems. Boston: B. Humphries, 1943. 70 p.
Evidence. Boston: B. Humphries, 1944. 47 p.
Maggie. New York: Island Workshop Press Co-op, Inc., 1944. 60 p.
Thin Veils. Boston: B. Humphries, 1945. 32 p.
Marah. Boston: B. Humphries, 1947. 27 p.

Peter's Neighborhood. Plymouth, MA.: Memorial Press, 1950. [39] p.
As Wine Is Red. Paris: Editions de l'Ecole, 1951. 30 p.
Desert Sky Is Gone. London: Priv. print. by Eyre & Spottiswode, 1955. 29 p.
Passed By. London: Priv. print. by Eyre & Spottiswode at the Chiswick Press, 1956. 27 p.
Cautiously Up Hill. Dublin: C. O'Lochlainn, 1957. 47, [1] p.
Mart. Dublin: C. O'Lochlainn, 1958. 47, [1] p.

HUNT, EVELYN TOOLEY
Look Again, Adam. Eden, N.Y.: E. T. Hunt, 1961. 32 p.
Toad-Song; A Collection of Haiku and Other Small Poems. Wolcott, N.Y.: Apple Press, 1966. 48 p., 1 ℓ.

HUNT, INEZ (WHITAKER) (1899-)
Windows Through the Wall. Denver, CO.: Big Mountain Press, 1956. 64 p.
High Country. Denver, CO.: Big Mountain Press, 1962. 50 p.
High Country Ghost Town Poems. Palmer Lake, CO.: Filter Press, 1971.

HUNT, LILLIAN AMBER
Arista, and Other Poems. Los Angeles, CA.: J. F. Rowny Press, 1921. 20 p.

HUNT, MARY LELAND
Moods and Moments. New York: The Knickerbocker Press, 1931. 4 p. ℓ., vii-x, 67 p.

HUNTER, JEANETTE BEGG
Verses. Jamaica, Queensborough, N.Y.: The Marion Press, 1919. 3 p. ℓ., 9-43, [1] p.

HUNTER, MARTHA LAVINIA (1870-)
Far Places. Dallas, TX.: The Kaleidoscope Publishers, 1931. 99 p.
Spirit Flame. Dallas, TX.: Wilkinson Pub. Co., 1949. 75, [1] p.

HUNTER, MARY KATE
Vision. Dallas, TX.: Dealey and Lowe, 1936. 6 p. ℓ., 3-120 p.

HUNTER, MAUD (1867-) [Full Name: Maud Alice Hunter.]
Verses by the Way. Boston: R. G. Badger, 1928. 4 p. ℓ., 9-59 p.

HUNTER, PATRICIA (1918-)
Wisps of Smoke; Poems. New York: Exposition Press, 1957. 71 p.

HUNTER, THERESA MOONE (1877-)
The City Beautiful; A Group of Poems. Austin, TX.: Mimeo-

graph Shop, 1920. [11] ℓ.
Panorama; Poems. Austin, TX.: Printed by Tobins, 1926. 126 p.

HUNTING, CONSTANCE (1925-)
The Heron, A Poem. West Lafayette, IN.: F. Stefanile, 1963. 20 p. (Vagrom Chapbook no. 9)
After the Stravinsky Concert and Other Poems. New York: Scribner, 1969. 73 p.
Cimmerian and Other Poems. Orono, ME.: Puckerbrush Press, 1972. 43 p.

HUNTINGTON, ELIZABETH
The Playground of the Gods, and Other Poems. Boston: The Four Seas Company, 1921. 62 p.

HUNTINGTON, ELIZABETH (BARTLETT)
Poems of Yes and No. Mexico: Editorial Jus, 1952. 66, [1] p.

HUNTINGTON, HELEN
The Solitary Path. New York: Doubleday, Page & Co., 1902. vii, 57 p.
From the Cup of Silence, and Other Poems. New York: G. P. Putnam's Sons, 1909. 3-71 p.

HUNTINGTON, LEA
Lyric Melodies. Boston: The Christopher Publishing House, 1935. 3 p. ℓ., 9-33 p.

HUNTINGTON, VIRGINIA ETHEL (HAIST) (1889-)
Shining Moment. Milwaukee, WI.: Morehouse Publishing Co., 1935. xi, 95 p.
Enough to Hunger. Shanghai: Kelly & Walsh, 1937. 53 p.
The Singing Hour; Poems. New York: Exposition Press, 1951. 96 p.
The Festive Heart; Poems. Wellesley, MA.: Hathaway House Bookshop, 1955. 119 p.
Green Autumn; Poems. Philadelphia: Dorrance, 1959. 71 p. (Contemporary poets of Dorrance, 515)
Sun on the Land; Poems of Mexico. Amherst, MA.: Printed at the Press of Hamilton I. Newell, 1962. 32 p.
The Resonant World. Francestown, N.H.: Golden Quill Press, 1966. 88 p.
Celebrations. Francestown, N.H.: Golden Quill Press, 1971. 88 p.

HUNTOM, RUTH
No Man's Land. n.p.: Roxburgh Pub., 1908. 100 p.

HURD, MARY ABBY (1909-1937)
The Shrine of Beauty, and Other Poems. Boston: R. G. Badger, 1935. 75 p.

HURD, MURIEL (JEFFRIES)
Wild Barley. Dallas, TX.: The Kaleidograph Press, 1941. xiii, 15-78 p.

HURD, PEARL STRACHAN see STRACHAN, PEARL

HUTCHESON, CHRISTINE GORE
Off the High Horse. New York: Pageant Press, 1958. 5 p. ℓ., 113 p.

HUTCHINGS, FLORENCE S.
A Litany of Love. New York: Fine Editions Press, 1956. 66 p., 1 ℓ.

HUTCHINSON, AMORY (HARE) (1885-) [HARE, MARY AMORY]
Tossed Coins. New York: John Lane Co.; London: John Lane, 1921. 2 p. ℓ., xiii p., 1 ℓ., 11-82 p.
The Swept Hearth. New York: John Lane Co.; London: John Lane, 1922. 5 p., 3 ℓ., 15-82 p.
The Olympians, and Other Poems. Philadelphia: Dorrance, 1925. 67 p. (Contemporary poets of Dorrance, 24)
Sonnets. New York: The Macmillan Company, 1927. 41 p.
Between Wars; Sonnets and Road-Songs. Mill Valley, CA.: Wings Press, 1955. 115 p.

HUTCHINSON, RUTH ELMA (1908-)
Underpath, and Other Poems. Boston: Chapman & Grimes, 1941. 4 p. ℓ., 11-48 p.

HUTCHISON, GLADYS
Faith and Fantasy. New York: Vantage Press, 1958. 61 p.

HUTTON, ALTHEA SWINFORD
...To Virginia. Philadelphia: Dorrance & Company, 1935. 63 p. (Contemporary poets of Dorrance, 128)
A Garden of Spices. Philadelphia: Dorrance, 1974. 50 p.

HYDE, GLADYS
...From the Gyral Bit. Philadelphia: Dorrance & Company, 1945. 45 p. (Contemporary poets of Dorrance, 295)

HYER, HELEN VON KOLNITZ
Santee Songs. Columbia, S.C.: The State Company, 1923. 52 p.
Wine Dark Sea. Boston: Marshall Jones Company, 1930. x, 109 p.

HYMERS, MAUDE ESTELLE
Dawn to Dusk. New York: H. Harrison, 1941. 94 p.

IDDINGS, LOLA LA MOTTE (1858-1918)
Poems. New Haven, CT.: Priv. print. at Yale Univ. Press, 1920. 3 p. ℓ., 3-147 p.

INEZ, COLETTE (1931-)
The Woman Who Loved Worms, and Other Poems. New York: Doubleday, 1972. xiv, 102 p.

INGLIMA, CARMELA
My Tapestry. Los Angeles, CA.: Swordsman Pub. Co., 1965. 68 p.

INGLIS, RUTH VICTORIA
Little Pictures. New York: H. Vinal, 1926. viii p., 1 ℓ., 44 p.

INGRAM, MARIA
North Acre. n.p.: Drummer Press, 1974.

IRELAND, THELMA MAY (BROWN) (1900-)
Home Work. Boston: Chapman & Grimes, 1957. 63 p.

IRVING, BLANCHE M.
So Long. New York: Pageant Press, 1959. 63 p.

IRWIN, MERYL
Circular Squares. New York: Arco Pub. Co., 1962. 96 p.

ISAACS, MAY STEVENS
Autumn Leaves. Dallas, TX.: Tardy, 1937. 4 p.ℓ., 57 p.

ISELY, HELEN SUE (1917-)
The Moon Is Red; Poems. Denver, CO.: A. Swallow, 1962. 31 p.

ISHAM, JULIET CALHOUN
Winds and Tides. New York & London: G. P. Putnam's Sons, 1925. x, 46 p.

IVERSON, LUCILLE
Outrage. Pittsburgh, PA.: KNOW, Inc., 1974. 76 p. (Contemporary women poet series)

JACKSON, ANGELA (1951-)
Voo Doo/Love Magic. Chicago: Third World, 1973. 23 p. (First poets series)

JACKSON, AURILDA
Untangled. New York: Vantage Press, 1956. 40 p.

JACKSON, CRUSELLE B. (1901-)
Random Rhymes. Philadelphia: Dorrance, 1955. 135 p. (Contemporary poets of Dorrance, 469)

JACKSON, ELIZABETH W. F.
Daybreak. Atlanta, GA.: The Blosser Co., 1914. 58 p.

JACKSON, GERTRUDE STORMS
Logicals. Mystic, CT.: The Mystic Standard, 1930. 80 p.

JACKSON, HORTENSE CORA
Tanglewild; Miscellaneous Poems. Indianapolis, IN.: The Hollenbeck Press, 1901. 124 p.

JACKSON, KATHERINE H. McDONALD
Summer Songs in Idlenesse. Boston: R. G. Badger; Toronto: W. Briggs, 1903. 71 p.

JACKSON, LAURA F.
Paradise (Cleveland Park) and Other Poems. Washington: R. L. Pendleton, 1920.

JACKSON, LOUISE FRANCES
Messages of Love; Original Poems. Stoughton, MA.: The Pequa Press, Inc., 1919. 4 p. ℓ., 212 p.

JACKSON, LYDIA OCTAVIA (1902-)
Rhymes for Every Season. Cleveland, OH.: Press of Flozari, 1943. 40 p. (Torchbearers' chapbooks, no. 85)

JACKSON, MABEL G. (1872-)
Flights of Fancy. New York: n.p., 1954. 3 p. ℓ., 153 p.

JACKSON, MAE (1946-)
Can I Poet With You. New York: Black Dialogue Publishers, 1969. [4], 16 p.
________. Detroit: Broadside Press, 1973.

JACKSON, MARY ELLEN (1911-)
Pedestrian, A Book of Verse. London: A. H. Stockwell, 1936. 61 p.
Watchman, What of the Night? A Book of Poems. New York: Paebar, 1940. 5 p. ℓ., 45 p.

JACKSON, MAUD FRAZER
Way Side Song. Boston: R. G. Badger, 1922. 72 p.
Starlight and Lamplight. Philadelphia: Aldine Printing Co., 1928. 87 p.

JACKSON, MYRTLE COOK
Sunshine on the Trees. Chicago: Windfall Press, 1962. 32 p.

JACOB, FRANCES see JACOB, SARAH FRANCES

JACOB, SARAH FRANCES [JACOB, FRANCES]
Steel and Stars, Poems. New York: Exposition Press, 1951. 52 p.

JACOBS, FLORENCE BURRILL
Stones and Other Poems. Boston: R. G. Badger, 1932. 128 p.

Neighbors: Poems. New York: Harper, 1949. viii, 53 p.

JACOBSEN, ETHEL
Larks in My Hair. Placentia, CA.: n.p., 1952. 106 p.
Mice in the Ink. Brea, CA.: Progress Press, 1955. 93 p.
Curious Cats. New York: Funk & Wagnalls, 1969. 64 p.

JACOBSEN, JOSEPHINE
Let Each Man Remember. Dallas, TX.: The Kaleidograph Press, 1940. xi p., 1 ℓ., 15-90 p.
...For the Unlost.... Baltimore, MD.: Contemporary Poetry, 1946. 55, [1] p. (Distinguished poets ser. of Contemporary Poetry, v. 4)
The Human Climate, New Poems. Baltimore, MD.: Contemporary Poetry, 1953. 39 p. (Contemporary poetry library series, v. 5)
The Animal Inside; Poems. Athens, OH.: Ohio University Press, 1966. 113 p.
The Shade-Seller: New and Selected Poems. Garden City, N.Y.: Doubleday, 1974. x, 113 p.

JACOBSON, HARRIET PRICE
...Songs in the Night. New York: The Exposition Press, 1947. 63 p.

JACOBY, ROSALIE S.
Kaleidoscope. Hollywood, CA.: Printed by D. G. Fischer Corporation, 1926. 89 p.

JACOBY, ROSE (1891-)
Tom Had a Dreamboat, and Other Poems. Columbus, OH.: Apollo Press, 1948, i.e. 1949. 120 p.

JACQUES, BERTHA EVELYN (CLAUSON) see JAQUES, BERTHA EVELYN (CLAUSON)

JAFFA, AILEEN RABY (1900-)
Three Sonnets. Berkeley, CA.: Churchmouse Press, 1939. 5 ℓ.
Trondheims. Berkeley, CA.: R. Levenson, Tamalpais Press, 1960. 6 p. (Crystal Arrow imprints, 1)
Tiptoe to the Wind. Berkeley, CA.: Professional Press, 1967. xi, 66 p., 1 ℓ.

JAKOWICZ, HEDWIG
Diana, and Other Poems. New York: Exposition Press, 1951. 119 p.

JAMES, ALICE ARCHER (SEWALL) (1870-)
The Ballad of the Prince. New York: R. H. Russell, 1900. 14 ℓ.
The Morning Moon. Philadelphia: Dorrance & Company, 1941. 77 p.

JAMES, BERTHA TEN EYCK
Nine Dragons: Poems. New York: H. Vinal, 1927. 6 p. ℓ., 44 p., 1 ℓ.
Zodiac. Northampton, MA.: Gehenna Press, 1963. [16] ℓ.

JAMES, IDA ELAINE
Gossamered Glory. Philadelphia: Poetry Publishers, 1938. 96 p.
The Deathless Flower. New York: Greenberg, 1939. xvii, 158 p.
Cloak of Wonder. Emory University, GA.: Banner Press, 1941. 131 p. (Verse craft series)
______. 2d ed., 1941. 131 p.
House of Song. Emory University, GA.: Banner Press, 1941. 9 p. ℓ., 17-154 p. (Verse craft series)
Threshold of Light. San Antonio, TX.: Carleton Printing Co., 1945. 206 p.

JAMESON, MARY ADAMS
A Bunch of Poppies. Cincinnati, OH.: Press of Jennings & Graham, 1906. 153 p.

JAMESON, VIRGINIA FARRAR
Poems. Boston: Christopher Publishing House, 1964. 132 p.

JANDA, VICTORIA (MARY)
Star Hunger. Minneapolis-St. Paul, MN.: Polanie, 1942. 5 p. ℓ., 13-103 p.
______. 3d ed., 1943. 103 p.
Walls of Space. Minneapolis-St. Paul, MN.: Polanie, 1945. 96 p.
Singing Furrows. Minneapolis, MN.: Polanie, 1953. 126 p.

JANIK, PHYLLIS (1944-)
The Disaster Expert. Dunkirk, N.Y.: The Basilisk Press, 1971. 60 p., 1 ℓ.
Red Shoes. Milwaukee, WI.: Morgan Press, 1974. 36 p.

JANSSEN, HELEN CARSON (1889-)
Strange Beckoning. New York: Exposition Press, 1951. 78 p.

JANTZEN, GENEVIEVE
Songs Grave and Gay. New York: Fortuny's, 1940. 44 p.

JAQUES, BERTHA EVELYN (CLAUSON) (1863-) [JACQUES, BERTHA EVELYN (CLAUSON)]
Whims. Chicago? Written & Pub. by the Author, 1924? 49 p.
Holiday Greetings. Chicago: Printed by the Libby Company Printers, 1926. 5 p. ℓ., 13-57, [1] p.
Whims. 2d ed. with more whims written and pub. by her. Chicago: The Libby Company, Printers, 1934. [3]-55, [1] p.

JARVIS, A. NELLE (1898-)
The Red Trail, and Other Poems. Grand Rapids, MI.: Powers-Tyson Printing Co., 1916. 30 p.

JARVIS, ANN
Out of the West. New York: Exposition Press, 1940. 5 p. ℓ., 13-92 p.

JEANS, MARYLU TERRAL
Statue in the Stone. Francestown, N.H.: Golden Quill Press, 1966. 87 p.
Moonset. Francestown, N.H.: Golden Quill Press, 1971. 80 p.

JEFFERS, ETTA (HEMPHILL) POND (1882-)
Doves from the Ark. Caldwell? ID.: n.p., 1951. 34 p.

JENKINS, ELIZABETH B.
...Thoughts of Arabel. Boston: The Stratford Company, 1928. 32 p. (The Stratford poets)

JENNINGS, MARTHA W.
...Beyond These Shadows. New York: The Exposition Press, 1947. 127 p.

JENRETTE, CORINE McLEMORE (1903-)
Just for Fun and Pleasure. New York: Carlton, 1970.

JENSEN, CLARA ELLEN
My Album of Verse. New York: Exposition Press, 1961. 30 p.

JEREMIAS, RUTH MATHEW
Realities of Life. Philadelphia: Dorrance, 1961. 48 p. (Contemporary poets of Dorrance, 527)

JERNIGAN, GLADYS (1902-)
We Rose from Rapture. New York: Vantage Press, 1954. 2 p. ℓ., 44 p.

JEROLEMAN, TILLIE C.
Bits of Verse for Christmastide. Nutley, N.J.: Nutley Printing Co., 1917. 22 ℓ.

JESSUP, MARY HALE
Grief Is a Lonely Journey. New York: Comet Press Books, 1952. 4 p. ℓ., 71 p.

JEWELL, MARY CLEVELAND, Sister
The Treasure Garden; or The Lord's Jewel Casket. Los Angeles, CA.: H. E. Gramwell, 1920. 200 p.

JEWETT, ELEANOR
From the Top of My Columns. Chicago: R. F. Seymour, 1927. 7, [1] p., 2 ℓ., 11-49 p.

JEWETT, SARAH ORNE (1849-1909)
Verses.... Boston: D. B. Updike, Merrymount Press, 1916. vi p., [1] ℓ., 33 p.
_______. Centennial ed. Cleveland, OH.: American Weave Press, 1949. 3 p. ℓ., 27 p.

JOBSON, MARJORIE POINSETT
Snare for the Moon. Wilmington, DE.: Wilmington Poetry Press, 1947. [16] p.

JOBSON, MILDRED CARTWRIGHT
Left! Right! Left! Right! Brooklyn, N.Y.: Printed at the Polygon Press, 1938. 31 p.
Topsoil. Boston: Christopher Pub. House, 1950. 46 p.
No Forelock for Time and Other Poems. New York: Pageant Press, 1957. 60 p.

JOCHEN, CAROLYN L.
Calendar Portraits. New York: Vantage Press, 1959. 79 p.

JOHN, GRACE SPAULDING
Memo. Mt. Vernon, N.Y.: Golden Eagle Press, 1949. 52 ℓ.
The Living Line; Drawings and Verse. Houston, TX.: Wall Press, 1962. [92] p.
The Knotless Thread; Drawings and Verses. New York: Pantile Press, 1970. 1 v. unpaged.

JOHNS, ANNE (PAGE)
A Fir Tree Prays, and Other Poems. Richmond, VA.: The Dietz Printing Company, 1943. 8 p. ℓ., 3-140 p.
The King's Lighthouse, and Other Poems. New York: Vantage Press, 1963. 126 p.

JOHNSON, ALICIA (1944-)
Realities vs. Spirits. n.p.: By the Author, 1969.

JOHNSON, ANNA (1892-)
Echoes. Independence, MO.: Print. by Zion's Printing & Publishing Co., 1932. 2 p. ℓ., 3-160 p.
Oriental Rhymes. Salt Lake City, UT.: Printed by the Deseret News Press, 1934. 2 p. ℓ., 9-156 p.
Stardust, Gathered From Day to Day. Salt Lake City, UT.: The Deseret News Press, 1935. 2 p. ℓ., [7]-199 p.
The Trail of the Exile. Salt Lake City, UT.: Printed by the Deseret News Press, 1936. 2 p. ℓ., 7-32 p.
Viking Verse. Salt Lake City, UT.: Printed by the Deseret News Press, 1936. 1 p. ℓ., 5-69 p.
Silver Rain. Boston: Christopher Pub. House, 1940. 4 p. ℓ., 11-106 p.
Rainbow Trails. Caldwell, ID.: Priv. print. The Caxton Printers, Ltd., 1941. 41 p. (Verse for Children.)
Rollicking Rhymes. Salt Lake City, UT.: Giles Press, 1942. 31 p.

For Eyes That See. Kansas City, MO.: Priv. Print., 1945. 97 p.

JOHNSON, CAROL HOLMES (1928-)
Figure for Scamander and Others. Denver, CO.: A. Swallow, 1964. 44 p. (The New poetry series, 28)

JOHNSON, CORA A.
The Art of Living. Dallas, TX.: Story Book Press, 1953. 48 p.

JOHNSON, DAISY VIRGINIA
Poems. Paris, TX.: n.p., 1935. 24 p.

JOHNSON, DORIS (1922-)
A Cloud of Summer, and Other New Haiku. Chicago: Follett Pub. Co., 1967. 48 p.

JOHNSON, DOROTHY COOPER
Dreamdrift. Cedar Rapids, IA.: The Torch Press, 1923. 47 p.

JOHNSON, EDITH WARNER
Hold Lightly, Poems. Philadelphia: Dorrance, 1956. 75 p. (Contemporary poets of Dorrance, 483)

JOHNSON, ELIZABETH MOUNTCASTLE
The Infinite Thought and Other Poems. Los Angeles, CA.: n.p., 1921. [72] p.
A Harp with a Thousand Strings. Los Angeles, CA.: n.p., 1922. 43 p.

JOHNSON, GEORGIA DOUGLAS (CAMP) (1886-1966)
The Heart of a Woman, and Other Poems. Boston: The Cornhill Company, 1918. xii, 62 p.
Bronze: A Book of Verse. Boston: B. J. Brimmer Co., 1922. 101 p.
An Autumn Love Cycle. New York: H. Vinal, Ltd., 1928. xix, 70 p., 1 ℓ.
Share My World; A Book of Poems. n.p., 1962. 32 p.

JOHNSON, HANNAH LYONS
Hello, Small Sparrow. New York: Lothrop, Lee & Shepard Co., 1971. [33] p.

JOHNSON, IDA JUDITH (1882-1928)
Poems. Columbia, MO.: n.p., 1928. 72 p.

JOHNSON, JOSEPHINE (1892-)
The Unwilling Gypsy. Dallas, TX.: The Kaleidograph Press, 1936. ix p., 1 ℓ., 15-78 p.

JOHNSON, JOSEPHINE WINSLOW (1910-)
Year's End. New York: Simon and Schuster, 1937. x, 77 p., 1 ℓ.

JOHNSON, KAY, pseud. see McDONALD, EDWINA LeVIN (DICKERSON)

JOHNSON, MADINE (MADDUX)
Snowflakes and Potter's Clay. San Antonio, TX.: Naylor Co., 1954. x, 63 p.

JOHNSON, MAGGIE (POGUE)
Virginia Dreams, Lyrics for the Idle Hour, Tales of the Time Told in Rhyme. n.p., 1910. 64 p.
Thoughts for Idle Hours. Roanoke, VA.: The Stone Printing & Mfg. Co., 1915. 55, [1] p.
Fallen Blossoms. Parkersburg, W.V.: n.p., 1951. 151 p.

JOHNSON, MARGIE LEE
Timberline, and Other Poems. Philadelphia: Dorrance, 1964. 37 p. (Contemporary poets of Dorrance, 599)
Traceries in Time. San Antonio, TX.: Naylor Co., 1966. x, 90 p.
Homespun Poems. Philadelphia: Dorrance, 1969. 58 p.
The Devastators. Miami Beach, FL.: Florida State Poetry Society, 1971. 92 p.

JOHNSON, MARTHA SHERWOOD (FINCH)
Sauce for the Goose. Siloam Springs, AR.: Bar D Press, 1943. 96 p.
Peddler's Pack. Prairie City, IL.: Decker Press, 1949. 126 p.
Kaleidoscope, A Book of Verse. Muskogee, OK.: Star Printery, 1954. 104 p.
Early Armor. A Book of Verse. Muskogee, OK.: Star Press, 1959. 108 p.
Unshielded Otherwise: A Book of Collected Verse. Oklahoma City, OK.: Harlow Pub. Corp., 1963. viii, 177 p.

JOHNSON, MARY ERNESTINE CLARK
Lacquered Faces; A Book of Poems. New York: Pageant Press, 1954. 70 p.

JOHNSON, ROBERTA ROBERTSON
Blue Flame. Boston: B. Humphries, 1950. 52 p.

JOHNSON, SUSIE (DAWSON)
The Fields Beyond. Columbia, SC.: University of South Carolina Press, 1945. 81 p.

JOHNSON, TERESA
Rest for a While. New York: Vantage Press, 1957. 71 p.

JOHNSON, TRESSA BEATRICE
The Gate in the Wall, Songs and Sonnets. Carmel-by-the-Sea, CA.: Printed for the Author by the Craftsmen of the Press in the Forest, 1932. 37 p.

JOHNSONE, DELPHENE
Glimpses, A Book of Verse. Seattle, WA.: Sherman Printing & Binding Co., 1921. 89 p.
Webs of Harmony. Portland, OR.: Printed by the Metropolitan Press, 1932. 79 p.

JOHNSTON, ANNIE (FELLOWS) (1863-1931)
It Was the Road to Jericho. New York: Britton Publishing Company, 1919. [41] p.

JONAS, SYLVIA LUCILE (REISS) (1895-)
The Inner You. Chicago: Press of A. D. Weinthrop & Company, 1922. 4 p. ℓ., 61 p.
Scarlette's Vagabond Songs. Knox? IN.: n. p., 1945. 113 p.

JONES, BLANCHE E.
Verses 1939-1942. New York: Paebar Co., 1949. 43 p.

JONES, ELIZABETH WARREN
By Way of the Sky. Philadelphia: Dorrance & Co., 1931. 99 p.

JONES, ENID (DANIEL) (1879-)
The Pergola on the Hill and Other Poems. Sierra Madre, CA.: Sierra Madre Press, 1938. 4 p. ℓ., 77 p.
Into the Wind You Rise. Emory University, Atlanta, GA.: Banner Press, 1941. 62 p.
Bells from the Sea. n. p., 1944. [11] p.
Daughters of Zeus, Collected Poems. London: Brookside Press, 1960. 129 p.

JONES, HELEN (HINRICHSEN) (1884-)
A Mother Goes to War; A Sonnet Sequence. New York: William-Frederick Press, 1951. 48 p. (The William-Frederick poets, 74)

JONES, JEANETTA
How to Invoke a Garden, How to Invoke the Same Garden. Berkeley, CA.: Sand Dollar, 1971. [17] p.

JONES, LAURA
Lovecries. Philadelphia: Dorrance, 1963. 79 p. (Contemporary poets of Dorrance, 570)

JONES, LEILA (1885-)
Assent to Autumn. Brattleboro, VT.: The Stephen Daye Press, 1933. 70 p.
Winter Is a Shadow. New York: The Dial Press, 1939. ix, 62 p.

Daughter of Eve. Cleveland, OH.: American Weave Press, 1947. 24 p.
No Season Wits: Poems. New York: Beechhurst Press, 1947. 5 p. ℓ., 3-51 p.

JONES, LUCILLE BLAIR
Songs for a Surgeon. New York: Profile Press, 1944. 53 p.

JONES, MARY HOXIE
Arrows of Desire. New York: The Macmillan Co., 1931. xii, 94 p.
Beyond This Stone. Francestown, N.H.: Golden Quill Press, 1965. 88 p.
Mosaic of the Sun. Francestown, N.H.: Golden Quill Press, 1975. 80 p.

JONES, NINA
Verses. San Francisco, CA.: n.p., 1911. 14 p.
Nina Jones, Her Book. San Francisco, CA.: P. Elder and Company, 1916. 53 p.

JONES, ROSIE LEE LOGAN
Tender Clusters. San Antonio, TX.: Naylor Co., 1969. viii, 108 p.

JONES, RUTH LAMBERT
Symbols, and Other Poems. Bradford, MA.: Bradford Junior College, 1963. 64 p.

JONES, RUTH MURRAY
Hold Fast the Moment. Berkeley, CA.: Wuerth Letter Shop, 1964. 84 p.

JONES, RUTH (NORTON)
Lazing Along on the Bayou, and Other Verses. New York: Exposition Press, 1954. 54 p.

JONG, ERICA
Fruits and Vegetables. New York: Holt, Rinehart & Winston, 1971. viii, 86 p.
Half-Lives. New York: Holt, Rinehart & Winston, 1971. 127 p.
Loveroot. New York: Holt, Rinehart & Winston, 1975. 114 p.

JORDAN, BARBARA LESLIE (1915-)
Web of Days. Portland, ME.: Falmouth Pub. House, 1949. 59 p.
Comfort the Dreamer. Fredonia, N.Y.: Arkwright Press, 1955. 54 p.

JORDAN, JUNE (1936-)
Who Look at Me. New York: Crowell, 1969. 97 p.
Some Changes. New York: Dutton, 1971. x, 86 p. (Black poet series)

New Days; Poems of Exile and Return. New York: Emerson Hall, 1974. vii, 131 p.

JORDAN, KATHERINE
Thoughts to Share. Philadelphia: Dorrance, 1959. 72 p. (Contemporary poets of Dorrance, 514)

JORDAN, REBECCA QUEEN (1861-
Poems. Boston: R. G. Badger, 1913. 128 p.

JORDAN, WINIFRED
The Universe, and Other Poems. Boston: B. Humphries, 1951. 32 p.

JOSEPH, CELTA JOHNSON
A Candle for Your Hand. Abilene, TX.: Chronicle Publ. Co., 1951. 42 p.

JOSLIN, MARY REED (1876-)
Spanish Moss. Emory University, Atlanta, GA.: Banner Press, 1939. 51 p. (Verse craft series)
Winter, Dusk, and Other Poems. New York: Exposition Press, 1954. 77 p.

JUDSON, AGNES
Borderland Poems. New York: Printed by J. J. Little and Ives Company, 1924. 39 p.

KAHLER, SARAH L.
Along My Pathway. New York: The Paebar Co., 1946. 3 p.ℓ., 35 p.

KAHN, HANNAH
Eve's Daughter; Poems. Coconut Grove, FL.: Hurricane House Publishers, 1962. 5 p.ℓ., 69 p.

KAHN, RUTH E.
Accent; Poems. New York: Vantage Press, 1963. 80 p.
My Daddy ABC's. Minneapolis, MN.: T. S. Denison, 1969. 31 p. (Verse for children.)

KAKUGAWA, FRANCES H.
Sand Grains. San Antonio, TX.: Naylor Co., 1970. x, 30 p.
White Ginger Blossom. San Antonio, TX.: Naylor Co., 1971. viii, 35 p.
Golden Spike. New ed. San Antonio, TX.: Naylor Co., 1973. ix, 37 p.

KAMINIS, BOBBIE (1942-)
To Leave the World Too Felt. New York: Vantage Press, 1968. 46 p.

KANDEL, LENORE

An Exquisite Navel. Studio City, CA.: Three Penny Press, 1959. [24] p.

A Passing Dragon. Studio City, CA.: Three Penny Press, 1959. [32] p.

Beat and Beatific. Studio City, CA.: Three Penny Press, 1959. 22 ℓ., [2] p.

San Francisco Art Festival: A Poetry Folio. San Francisco, CA.: East Wind Printers, 1964. 11 ℓ. in portfolio.

The Love Book. San Francisco, CA.: Stolen Paper Review Editions, 1966. 6 numb. ℓ.

Word Alchemy: Poems. New York: Grove Press, 1967. 80 p.

KANE, SHARON

Counting Rhymes. New York: Golden Press, 1960. [24] p. (Verse for children.)

KAPLAN, RUTH

Black Rainbows, Poems. New York: Exposition Press, 1951. 96 p.

KARBAN, POLLY

Just to Take a Peek. New York: Vantage Press, 1968. 82 p.

KARLIN, CELIA C.

The Star of David. Baltimore, MD.: Garamond/Pridemark, 1967. 34 p.

KARLING, EVA HILL LeSUEUR

Leaves from Ancient Oaks. Dallas, TX.: Dealey and Lowe, 1936. 6 p.ℓ., 109 p.

KARN, ESTHER (NELSON)

"Snowflakes." Philadelphia: Press of G. F. Lasher, 1900. 96 p.

Violets. Chicago: n.p., 1904. 100 p.

Wild Roses. Fort Wayne, IN.: Anthony Press, 1915. 3 p.ℓ., 13-143, [1] p.

Lure of the Wilds. Boston: The Four Seas Co., 1925. 107 p.

KARR, MARGARETTA AYRES

The Heavenly Voice; A Life of Christ in Blank Verse; His Work and Word in Sonnets. New York: Printed by Eaton & Mains, 1905. xii, 275 p.

He's No Use Now, and Other Poems: A Symphony of Song. Buffalo, N.Y.: Korydon Book Co., 1915. 6 p.ℓ., 9-284, [4] p.

Heart of the Rose. Buffalo, N.Y.: Press of C. E. Jameson & Son, 1917. 3 p.ℓ., 26 p.

KASER, MARGARET KATHARINE

Silver Strings. New York: H. Harrison, 1940. 31 p.

KASSIMER, ADA MARIE (1877-)
In Dream. Boston: R. G. Badger, 1906. 41 p.
A Garden of Thoughts for You. Kansas City: Crafters Publ. Co., 1911. 20 p.
Beloved: A Driftage of Love Lyrics. Kansas City, MO.: Crafters Publ. Co., 1913. 24 p.

KASTENDIECK, AUGUSTA M.
The Power of Life. Boston: Christopher Pub. House, 1961. 93 p.

KATT, ADELINE SMITH
The Tenth Commandment, a Poem of Renunciation. New York: William-Frederick Press, 1951. 21 p.

KATZ, ELIZABETH
Poems. New York: The Knickerbocker Press, 1909. 2 p. ℓ., 59 p.

KAUFFMAN, DOROTHY BELL (1915-1963)
The Inheritance of My Fathers; Poems of North Carolina and Others. New York: Vantage Press, 1965. 70 p.

KAUFFOLD, MARGARET B.
Rainbows Through the Rain. Hardwick, VT.: Printed by J. E. Appolt, 1931. [40] p.

KAUFMAN, HAZEL SHARRARD
Poems. New York: Bookman Associates, 1958. 60 p., 1 ℓ.

KAUFMAN, SHIRLEY (1923-)
The Floor Keeps Turning; Poems. Pittsburgh, PA.: University of Pittsburgh Press, 1970. 6 p. ℓ., 98 p. (Pitt poetry series)
Gold Country. Pittsburgh, PA.: University of Pittsburgh Press, 1973. 79 p. (Pitt poetry series)

KAUTZ, AUGUSTA
Ink in Bloom. San Diego, CA.: Press of Baker Bros., 1902. 83 p.

KAY, ELLEN
A Local Habitation: Poems. Denver, CO.: A. Swallow, 1958. 51 p. (New poetry series, 18)

KAY, KATHRYN
With Tongue in Cheek. Hollywood, CA.: Circle Publishing Co., 1938. 12 p. ℓ., 85, [1] p.
_______. 2d ed. Hollywood, CA.: Murray & Gee, 1938. 12 p. ℓ., 85 p., [1] p.

KAYER, SOPHIE WILLITS
Rhyme and Rhythm; A Poetic Medley. New York: William-

Frederick Press, 1952. 14 p. (The William-Frederick poets, 81)

KAYLER, MABEL ALMON
As the Prism Swings. San Antonio, TX.: Naylor Co., 1969. viii, 64 p.

KAYLOR, BERNICE CELESTIA (1886-)
Hi Point Poetry. Dallas, TX.: Story Book Press, 1950. 40 p.

KAYSER, EDNA JANES (1903-)
Sunlight and Shadow. Rogers, AR.: Avalon Press, 1946. 47 p.
Leaves of Amber Wine. Boston: Chapman & Grimes, 1949. vi p., 1 ℓ., 9-51 p.
The Bridegroom Cometh. Boston: Christopher Pub. House, 1956. 96 p.

KEASTER, EFFIE LOU
Who Goes with the Road. New York: Vantage Press, 1967. 61 p.

KEATING, NORMA (CONNOLLY)
Giants and Dwarfs. Spring Lake, N.J.: n.p., 1946. 111 p.
Songs of a Salamander. Spring Lake, N.J.: n.p., 1949. 64 p.

KEATS, ELEANOR B.
Songs for Jeremy and Other Poems. n.p.: Sagitta Press, 1974.

KECK, LILLIAN FRANCES (WENNSTROM)
Word Pictures; Verses. Dallas, TX.: The Kaleidograph Press, 1943. xiii p., 1 ℓ., 17-112 p.

KEECH, IONA
Trees of Love. San Antonio, TX.: Naylor Co., 1967. vii, 36 p.

KEECH, LILLIAN SUE
Rosemary. Philadelphia: Dorrance & Co., 1926. 59 p.
Shadows on Water and Other Poems. New York: The Paebar Co., 1937. 4 p.ℓ., 65 p.

KEEFE, MILDRED JONES
White Beauty; Poems. Magnolia, MA.: Expression Co., 1956. 63 p.

KEELER, EDITH FLINT
Vermont. Westborough, MA.: n.p., 1928? [10] p.

KEENER, SUZANNE
Silent Singing. Atlanta, GA.: Mildred Seydell Pub. Co., 1945. 6 p.ℓ., 90 p.

KEENEY, CONLY, pseud. see KEENEY, LOUELLA (1882-)

KEENEY, LOUELLA (1882-)
Sky Lanterns. Vignettes of China. Los Angeles, CA.: Academy Publishers, 1954. 72 p.

KEENEY, SUSAN DOROTHEA
The Circle of the Sun. Portland, ME.: Falmouth Pub. House, 1950. 72 p.
_______. Philadelphia: Allen, Lane & Scott, 1951. 72 p.
The Four Winds Blowing. Wayne? PA.: n. p., 1956. 4 p. ℓ., 66 p.
The Far Horizon Line. Philadelphia: Allen, Lane & Scott, 1961. 4 p. ℓ., 72 p.

KEITH, HENRIETTA JEWETT
Four-o'-Clocks. Minneapolis, MN.: Augsberg Publishing House, 1919. 63 p.
Pipes o' Pan in a City Park. Minneapolis, MN.: Colwell Press, 1922. 6 p. ℓ., 11-121 p.

KEITH, MARCIA
The Wheel of Life. Philadelphia: Dorrance & Company, 1935. 75 p. (Contemporary poets of Dorrance, 139)

KELLAM, LILLIE HOLLIDAY
Old Love. Philadelphia: Dorrance & Company, 1929. 85 p. (Contemporary poets of Dorrance, 83)

KELLAR, DOROTHY AVIS
Kaleidoscope. Philadelphia: Dorrance & Co., 1927. 51, [1] p. (Contemporary poets of Dorrance, 50)

KELLER, ELLA FLATT (1878-)
Thoughts for the Twilight Hour. Toledo, OH.: The B. F. Wade Printing Co., 1903. 48 p.
The Road of Life. Toledo, OH.: B. F. Wade & Sons Co., 1920. 4 p. ℓ., [13]-126 p.
The Friendship Trail. Hudson, MI.: Ella F. Keller, 1926. 3 p. ℓ., 9-62 p.
Mothers--Yours and Mine. Hudson, MI.: Ella F. Keller, 1926. 3 p. ℓ., 3-49 p.
The After-While. Hudson, MI.: Ella F. Keller, 1927. 2 p. ℓ., 9-57 p.
Watching the Stars. Hudson, MI.: n. p., 1927. 60 p.
The Bigger Things. Hudson, MI.: Ella F. Keller, 1928. 3 p. ℓ., 5-60 p.
Worn Paths. Hudson, MI.: Ella F. Keller, 1929. 56 p.
The Call of the Open Road. Hudson, MI.: Ella F. Keller, 1930. 58 p.
Where Memory Leads. Hudson, MI.: Ella F. Keller, 1930. 58 p.
On the Heights; Inspirational Poems of Warm-Hearted Interest

and Sympathetic Understanding. Philadelphia: The John C. Winston Co., 1937. 3 p. ℓ., 166 p.

KELLER, GRACE ADELLE (1884-1908) [HOPEFUL, GRACE, pseud.]
Poems. Chicago: R. R. Donnelley & Sons, 1910. 61 p., 1 ℓ.

KELLER, MARTHA (1902-)
Mirror to Morality. New York: E. F. Dutton & Co., Inc., 1937. 5 p. ℓ., 3-119 p.
Brady's Bend and Other Ballads. New Brunswick, N. J.: Rutgers University Press, 1946. 8 p. ℓ., 3-142 p., 1 ℓ.
War Whoop of the Wily Iroquois. New York: Coward-McCann, 1954. unpaged.

KELLER, MARY CONRAD
A Wreath of Immortelles. Rev. & ed. by Alice Fernald Emerson. Indianapolis, IN.: Priv. Print., 1935. 3 p. ℓ., 3-84, iv p.

KELLER, MILDRED
A Study in Solitude; Poems. New York: Vantage Press, 1960. 41 p.

KELLETT, FLORENCE
Oh Erin My Home, and Other Poems. San Francisco, CA.: P. Elder & Company, 1916. 4 p. ℓ., 3-14 p., 1 ℓ.

KELLEY, ETHEL
As Dreams Are Made of... Sonnets and Other Poems. Granville, N. Y.: Printed by Grastorf Press, 195-? 39 p.

KELLEY, ETHEL MAY (1878-)
When I Was Little. Chicago: Rand, McNally and Company, 1945. 96 p.

KELLEY, SANDY
Instant Tears for Lovers. Millbrae, CA.: Celestial Arts, 1974. [96] p.

KELLOGG, CHARLOTTE (HOFFMAN)
Pacific Light. Washington, D. C.: Anderson House, 1939. x, 67 p.
Prelude. Los Angeles, CA.: Ward Ritchie Press, 1960. 51 p., 1 ℓ.

KELLOGG, FLORENCE (SCRIPPS)
Rhyming 'Round the World. Pasadena, CA.: Post Printing and Binding Company, 1927. [15] p.
My Spirit Sings. Boston: B. Humphries, 1946. 87 p.
My Joyous Spirit Sings. Culver City, CA.: Murray and Gee, 1950. 80 p.

KELLOGG, LOIS
Opposites. Portland, ME.: The Mosher Press, 1933. 29 p., 1 ℓ.

KELLOGG, ROSE STANDISH
What Years of Time. Chicago: P. E. Press, 1966. 32 p.

KELLY, BLANCHE MARY (1881-)
The Valley of Vision. New York: The Encyclopedia Press, Inc., 1916. vi, 56 p.

KELLY, HATTIE BRICKETT
Miscellaneous Poems. Warren, N.H.: n.p., 1919. 1 p. ℓ., 5-36 p.

KELSEY, KATE
Wayside Poems. Menomonie, WI.: Printed by J. Boothby, 1914. 24 p.

KEMP, LEILA RUSH
Ventures in Verse. San Antonio, TX.: Southern Literary Institute, 1934. 36 p.

KEMPHER, RUTH MOON (1934-)
The White Guitar. Homestead, FL.: Olivant Press, 1967. 52 p.
Carnival at Seaside. Fort Smith, AR.: South and West, 1968. 48 p.
Porpoise in the Beer. Homestead, FL.: Olivant Press, 1970. 24 p.

KENDALL, JO M.
Medusa; A Moonshine Melody. Frankfort, KY.: Roberts Printing Co., 1920. 56 p.

KENDALL, KATE, pseud. see GREENE, CLARA MARCELLE (FARRAR)

KENDIG, ELEANOR
Today Is Mine, and Other Poems. New York: R. Speller, 1936. 91 p.

KENNARD, MARIETTA CONWAY
The Poet and the River. Published under the auspices of the Washington State Poetry Foundation: Seattle University Printing Co., 1957. 86 p., 1 ℓ.

KENNEDY, ANNIE (de LARTIQUE) (1875-)
Poems. San Francisco, CA.: Printed by Lanson & Gorfinkel, 1925. 30 p.

KENNEDY, CELIA MARY
Pinafore Poems. Ann Arbor, MI.: G. Wahr, 1924. 4 p. ℓ., 60 p.

KENNEDY, DOROTHEA
Patchwork Dreams. Prairie City, IL.: Decker Press, 1948. 92 p.

KENNEDY, GERTRUDE
Native Island. Boston: Houghton Mifflin, 1956. 41 p.

KENNEDY, KATHARINE (1903-)
Music of Morning. Emory University, Atlanta, GA.: Banner Press, 1937. 79 p.

KENNEDY, MARY
Ride into Morning: Poems. New York: Gotham Book Mart, 1969. 92 p.
Behind the Day. New York: Gotham, 1972. 111 p.

KENNEDY, MILDRED
Etched in Verse. Concord, N.H.: Bridge & Byron, 1959. 56 p.

KENNEDY, SARA BEAUMONT (CANNON) (d. 1921)
One Wish, and Other Poems of Love and Life. Indianapolis, IN.: The Bobbs-Merrill Company, 1915. 5 p. ℓ., 15-90 p.
Poems. New York: The Cameo Press and Publishing Company, 1919. viii p., 1 ℓ., 159 p.

KENNELLY, ALICE E.
Bluegrass. New York: Exposition Press, 1949. 46 p.
Bluegrass, Junior; A Volume of Verse. New York: Exposition Press, 1952. 62 p.
Bluegrass Seasons, Poems. New York: Vantage Press, 1959. 82 p.

KENNEY, EUDORUS CATLIN
Some More Thusettes. Cortland, N.Y.: The Democrat Printery, 1905. 4 p. ℓ., 122 p.
Lafayette and the Rustic Rambler. Cortland, N.Y.: The Democratic Printery, 1907. 1 p. ℓ., 122 p.

KENT, GERTRUDE (HALL) (1874-1956)
Poems. Chicago: Privately printed at the University of Chicago Press, 1957. xii, 69 p.

KENT, LAURA
Two Figures in a Landscape. Berkeley? CA.: n.p., 1952. [4] p. (California University, Emily Chamberlain Cook Prize in Poetry, 36)

KENT, LAURA TILDEN
A Collection of Verses. Boston: The Sparrel Print, 1908. 42 p.

KENT, LENA A.
The Hills of St. Andrew, and Other Poems. Newport? R.I.: Gleaner Co., 1931. xii, 94 p.

KENWORTHY, ELSIE BRAMMALL (1898-)
"Thoughtful Moments"; Poetry. Worchester, MA.: Nemo Press, Printers, 1937.
Weaver of Dreams. New York: H. Harrison, 1941. 62 p.
The Magic Pen, A Book of Poetry. Boston: McIver Johnson Co., 1946. 78 p.

KENWORTHY, MARY BOWLING
Memories That Never Die. Chicago: Tucker-Kenworthy Company, Printers, 1925. 70 p.

KENYON, BERNICE LESBIA (1897-1935)
Songs of Unrest, 1920-1922. New York: C. Scribner's Sons, 1923. ix, 95, [1] p.
Meridian; Poems, 1923-1932. New York & London: C. Scribner's Sons, 1933. x, 67 p.
Night Sky, Poems. New York: Scribner, 1951. 75 p.

KENYON, DORA JOSEPHINE (PRYDE) CARPENTER (1846-)
Gems of Poetry. Washington, D. C.: B. S. Adams, Printer, 1912. 42 p.

KENYON, THEDA
...Certain Ladies. New York: I. Washburn, 1930. 7 p. ℓ., 3-91 p.
Scarlet Anne. New York: Doubleday, Doran & Co., 1939. 4 p. ℓ., 312 p.

KERFOOT, NELL
Eyes of the Soul. Houston, TX.: E. Kerfoot, 1921. 4 p. ℓ., 15-75 p.
Psalms of Servitude. Houston, TX.: E. Kerfoot, 1926. 16 p.

KERIN, SUSIE
Poems of Sunny Colorado. Denver, CO.: The Welch-Haffner Printing Co., 1922. [43] p.

KERNS, DORIS (1921-)
Clear Shining After Rain. Philadelphia: Dorrance, 1948. 57 p. (Contemporary poets of Dorrance, 385)

KERR, DOROTHY FISH
Verses. San Mateo, CA.: Service Press, 1935. 45 ℓ.
My Heart Sings; Verses and Poems. Korbel, CA.: n.p., 1961. 8 p. ℓ., 137, [2] p.

KERR, MINNIE MARKHAM
...This Unquenched Thirst, and Other Poems. Philadelphia: Dorrance, 1938. 87 p. (Contemporary poets of Dorrance,

189)

The American Highway, and Other Poems. Philadelphia: Dorrance, 1949. 76 p. (Contemporary poets of Dorrance, 406)

KEVAN, ELEANOR RANDOLPH

My Best to You; Poems 1959-1966. Petersburg, VA.: n.p., 1966. 48 p.

KEYES, EDITH THRUSTON (1873-)

The Feathered Flute; Indian Legends in Rhyme. Oceanside, CA.: The Langford Press, 1941. [61] p.

The Twilight Trail; Indian Legends in Verse. San Diego? CA.: n.p., 1948. 176 p.

KEYES, FRANCES PARKINSON (WHEELER) (1885-1970)

The Happy Wanderer. New York: J. Messner, Inc., 1935. 96 p.

The Happy Wanderer; The Collected Verse of Frances Parkinson Keyes. 2d ed. New York: J. Messner, 1954. 120 p.

Christmas Gift. New York: Hawthorn Books, 1959. 95 p.

KEYSNER, BLANCHE WHITING (1887-)

Far Hills Are Blue, Poems. Mill Valley, CA.: Wings Press, 1947. 62 p.

KEYTON, CLARA Z.

Poems Enshrined in Memories. Banning, CA.: Deeble Press, 1963. 48 p.

Destiny Beckons. Banning, CA.: Deeble Press, 1964. 136 p.

KICKNOSWAY, FAYE (1936-)

Orange Sailor. Detroit: Alternative Press, 1970. [2] ℓ.

O, You Can Walk on the Sky? Good. New York: Capra Press, 1972. 33 p. (Yes! Capra chapbook series, no. 4)

Poem Tree. Highland Park, MI.: Red Hanrahan Press, 1973. 1 v. (unpaged)

A Man Is a Hook, Trouble! Poems, 1964-1973. Santa Barbara, CA.: Capra Press, 1974. 87 p.

KIDDER, LOUISE WINSLOW

Lyrics. Boston: Priv. Print., 1904. 3 p.ℓ., 5-34 p.

KIDDER, MARTHA ANN (1871-)

Aeonian Echoes, and Other Poems. Boston: Sherman, French & Company, 8 p.ℓ., 219 p.

KIEFER, JENNIE

Fugitive Poems. Los Angeles, CA.: The Author, 1923. 47 p.

KILBURN, HARRIET MASON

The Sign of the Tree. Boston: Sherman, French & Company, 1913. 4 p.ℓ., 64 p.

KILLIAN, BERTHA
Prairie Stakes. Oklahoma City, OK.: National Printing Company, 1943. 56 p.

KILLINGSWORTH, MAE PACE
Dust of Gold; Poems. New York: Exposition Press, 1962. 72 p.

KILMER, ALINE (MURRAY) (1888-1941)
Candles That Burn. New York: G. H. Doran Co., 1919. x p., 1 ℓ., 13-68 p.
Vigils. New York: George H. Doran Co., 1921. x p., 1 ℓ., 13-51 p.
The Poor King's Daughter, and Other Poems. New York: G. H. Doran Co., 1925. x p., 1 ℓ., 13-46 p.
Selected Poems. Garden City, N.Y.: Doubleday, Doran & Co., Inc., 1929. viii, 66 p.

KIMBALL, ALICE MARY (1888-)
The Devil Is a Woman. New York, London: A. A. Knopf, 1929. 5 p.ℓ., 3-128 p., 1 ℓ.

KIMBALL, EMMA ADELINE (1847-)
Pebbles From the Shore: Poems. Boston: R. G. Badger, 1904. 58 p.

KIMBALL, HARRIET McEWEN (1834-1917)
Poems. Boston: Little, Brown and Company, 1911. x, 208 p.
_______. n.p.: Young Churchman, 1916. 220 p.

KIMBALL, HELENJOY
Wandering Cries. New York: H. Vinal, Ltd., 1927. 7 p.ℓ., 48, [2] p.

KIMBALL, MABEL CASSIDY
My House of Dreams, A Collection of Original Verse. Alhambra, CA.: n.p., 1936. 40 p., 2 ℓ.

KIMREY, GRACE SAUNDERS (1910-)
Songs of Sunny Valley. Emory University, GA.: Banner Press, 1954. 60 p. (Verse craft series)
_______. 2d ed., 1954. 3 p.ℓ., [11]-60 p.
Glimpses of Beauty. Emory University, GA.: Banner Press, 1955. 60 p.
The Star of Hope. Emory University, GA.: Banner Press, 1957. 58 p.

KINCHER, ETHELYN M.
Bower of Quiet. Denver, CO.: Big Mountain Press, 1950. 47 p.

KING, ANNIE GRAHAM
Veiled Victory. Boston: B. Humphries, 1950. 64 p.

KING, DAISY CLARK
The Elephant's Trunk and Other Poems. Los Angeles, CA.: Ward Ritchie Press, 1939. 4 p. ℓ., 7-64 p.

KING, DOROTHY
Verses. Boston: n. p., 1901. 3-42 p.

KING, ETHEL M.
Lift Your Hand Skywards. Emory University, GA.: Banner Press, 1931. 31 p. (Verse craft series)
The Calendar in Rime. Portland, ME.: Falmouth Pub. House, 1947. 51 p.
The Four Seasons. Brooklyn, N. Y.: G. J. Rickard, 1960. 5 p. ℓ., 30 p.

KING, FRANCES NASH
The Book of "The White Comrade." New Haven, CT.: The Tuttle, Morehouse, and Taylor Company, 1918. 37 p.

KING, GEORGIANA GODDARD (1871-1939)
The Way of Perfect Love. New York: The Macmillan Company, 1908. viii, 108 p.

KING, GEORGIANNA BOLE
Footsteps, Poems. New York: H. Harrison, 1931. 63 p.
Gibraltar. New York: H. Harrison, 1933. 62 p.

KING, JUNE JAMISON
Soul: Verse Without Punctuation. New York: Printed by the Knickerbocker Press for June J. King, 1920. viii p., 1 ℓ., 99 p.

KING, MARIE HALBERT (1893-)
Call to Remembrance. Asheville? N. C.: n. p., 1951. 74 p.
_______. San Antonio, TX.: Carleton Printing Co., 1951. 74 p.
Forgotten Valleys. Asheville, N. C.: Stephens Press, 1958. 24 p.
Against the Curse of Time. Asheville, N. C.: Biltmore Press, 1966. 50 p.

KING, MARY WENTWORTH
These Things I Love. Boston: The Stratford Company, 1927. 5 p. ℓ., iv, 85 p.

KING-BENHAM, EMMA (1857-)
Wayside Flowers. Indianapolis, IN.: Sentinel Printing Company, 1902. 3 p. ℓ., 5-196 p.

KINGSLEY, ADELAIDE DELIA (NICHOLS) (1844-)
Sky Lines. Boston: The Christopher Publishing House, 1924. 108 p.

KINGSLEY, WINOLA (BEVIER)
The Kindergarten Way. Philadelphia: Dorrance, 1963. 81 p.

KINGSTON, MARION SHERWOOD
The Breath of Birds. Philadelphia: Dorrance, 1963. 72 p. (Contemporary poets of Dorrance, 564)

KINNEAR, HORTENSE McCLELLAN
Tuck in Time, Verses for Children. New York: Exposition Press, 1949. 39 p.

KINNEY, ALMA (HAYES)
Historical Poems. New York: Greenwich Book Publishers, 1963. 96 p.
The Seasons Are Upon Us. New York: Vantage Press, 1966. 104 p.

KINNEY, MARIAN
Summer City. Chicago: Coach House Print Shop, 1969. [16] p.

KINNEY, MURIEL (1865-)
Rainbow Gold, and Other Poems. Boston: R. G. Badger, 1915. 63 p.

KINSER, JESSE GRANVELL
Sparkling Sunbeams. Oklahoma City, OK.: Trave-Trammel Co., 1920. 2 p. ℓ., 48, [1] p.

KINSEY, EVA MAY
Partly for Pleasure; Poems. New York: Exposition Press, 1963. 64 p.

KINSLEY, INEZ MARSHALL
Selected Poems. Burlington, VT.: Studio of Advertising Design, 1958. 84 p. On cover: "Fern Hill Echoes"

KINSOLVING, SALLY (BRUCE) (1876-1962)
Depths and Shallows. Baltimore, MD.: The Norman Remington Co., 1921. 5 p. ℓ., 67 p.
David and Bath-Sheba and Other Poems. Baltimore, MD.: The Norman Remington, Co., 1922. 7 p. ℓ., 3-104 p.
Grey Heather. Portland, ME.: The Mosher Press, 1930. viii p., 2 ℓ., 3-89, [2] p.
Many Waters: Poems. New York: G. P. Putnam's Sons, 1942. xvi, 203 p.

KIRBY, INEZ BARCLAY
River Lights. Mill Valley, CA.; New York: The Wings Press, 1940. 96 p.

KIRCH, PATTI (d. 1963)
The Collected Poems of Patti Kirch. Philadelphia: Dorrance, 1968. [226] p.

KIRK, JOSEPHINE KITTRELL
Crowded Moments. Dallas, TX.: Story Book Press, 1953. 66 p.

KIRK, MURRAY (KETCHAM) (1886-) [Full Name: Edna Murray (Ketcham) Kirk]
The Beacon Light, and Other Poems. New York: H. Vinal, Ltd., 1927. 6 p. ℓ., 3-66 p., 1 ℓ.

KIRKBRIDE, MARTHA SIMS
Love Whispering in My Garden. San Francisco, CA.: Parker Printing Company, 1930. 5 p. ℓ., 7-63 p.

KIRKHAM, KATE
Sun and Shadow. Emory University, Atlanta, GA.: Banner Press, 1936. 72 p. (Verse craft series)
Sunset Hour. Emory University, Atlanta, GA.: Banner Press, 1940. 8 p. (Golden Westward Ho! Poetry Book-Shelf)

KIRKLAND, GRACE
Candle Lights. Atlanta, GA.: The A. B. Caldwell Publishing Company, 1920. 2 p. ℓ., 9-64 p.

KIRKLAND, KAY
Afterthoughts: Poems. Chicago: Adams Press, 1968. 60 p.

KIRKLAND, MARGIE
Profiles of East Texas. New York: Poets of America Pub. Co., 1964. 4 p. ℓ., 44 p.
New-Kindled Fires. San Antonio, TX.: Naylor Co., 1968. xiv, 46 p.

KIRKUP, MARY A.
In the Land of Theocritus and Other Poems. Larchmont, N.Y.?: n.p., 1933? 26 p.

KIRKWOOD, ADELYN
Scratches on Paper. New York: Vantage Press, 1963. 64 p.

KISSLING, DOROTHY HIGHT (RICHARDSON) (1904-) [LANGLEY, DOROTHY]
Fool's Mate, A Sonnet Sequence. Chicago: Traumwald Press, 1970. 116 p.

KISTLER, HELEN RANDEL (1895-)
Silvery Path to God. East Stroudsburg? PA.: n.p., 1951.

159 p.
For This Very Day; Poems. New York: Exposition Press, 1962. 64 p.

KITTELLE, SARAH E.
Fugitive Poems. Phenix, R.I.: J. H. Campbell, 1903. 3 p.

KITTREDGE, ELIZABETH
The Moon Shines at Sundown. Boston: B. Humphries, 1950. 51 p.
________. New York: Vantage Press, 1963. 96 p.

KIZER, CAROLYN (1925-)
Poems. Portland, OR.: Portland Art Museum, 1959. [4] p.
The Ungrateful Garden. Bloomington, IN.: Indiana University Press, 1961. 84 p. (Indiana University poetry series, no. 20)
Knock Upon Silence. Garden City, N.Y.: Doubleday, 1965. viii, 84, [1] p.
Midnight Was My Cry: New and Selected Poems. Garden City, N.Y.: Doubleday, 1971. ix, 132 p.

KLAUBER, ALICE
Poems.... Chula Vista, CA.: Denrich Press, 1928. 48 p.

KLAUMAN, ALICE DAWSON
Pebbles from the Byways of Life. New York: The Exposition Press, 1944. 4 p. ℓ., 11-63 p.
Random Pen Pictures; Poems. New York: Exposition Press, 1946. 127 p.

KLEIN, ROSE (BROCKMAN)
Song from Within. Philadelphia: Dorrance, 1966. 58 p. (Contemporary poets of Dorrance, 623)

KLEINMAN, BERTHA (ANDERSON) (1877-)
Through the Years; A Collection of Poetical Sentiment for All Occasions. Tempe? AZ.: n.p., 1957. 340 p.

KLEINSCHMIDT, ELEANOR STEVENS
Norwegian Year and Other Poems. Boston: Bruce Humphries, 1956. 71 p.

KLEITMAN, ESTHER
Poems. San Francisco, CA.: The Porpoise Bookshop, 1958. 14 ℓ. (Poems and pictures, no. 2)

KLEUSER, LOUISE C. (1890-)
To Heights Beyond. Washington, D.C.: Review and Herald Pub. Association, 1967. 64 p.

KLINCK, JULIA M.
Spindrift.... Lincoln, NB.: n.p., 1933. 32 p.

KLINE, IDAE MAY CLARENDON
A Key for the Game of Life. Boston: The Christopher Publishing House, 1929. 30 p.

KNAAK, NANCY KATHERINE (1928-)
Clouds of Time, Poems. New York: Exposition Press, 1953. 64 p.

KNAPP, ESTELLE MILDRED
Here and There. New York: The Wagner Press, 1906. 3 p. ℓ., 41 p.

KNAPP, HARRIET LORETTA
Echoes from the Prairie and the Hills. Wichita, KA.: The Wichita Publishing Company, 1908. 75, [1] p.
Rhymes for the Children. Wichita, KA.: n.p., 1909. 83 p.

KNEELAND, ISOBEL
Room of Shadows; Poems. Cleveland, OH.: American Weave Press, 1960. viii, 28 p. (Durham chapbook, 15)

KNEELAND, LOUISE WENZEL (1859-)
Sunlight and Shadow. Boston: Sherman, French & Company, 1914. 4 p. ℓ., 93 p.

KNELSON, NELDA RIFE
Out of the Inkwell. Boston: Christopher Publishing House, 1959. 123 p.
Out of the Fire. Boston: Christopher Publishing House, 1960. 104 p.
Out of the Mist. Boston: Christopher Publishing House, 1968. 98 p.

KNIFFIN, EVELYN GAGE
Guide-Posts on the Foot-Path to Peace; A Book of Religious Verse. Brooklyn, N.Y.: The Author, 1910. x, 96 p.
Rose Leaves. Brooklyn, N.Y.: The Author, 1910. vi, 97 p.

KNIGHT, GRETA BUEDINGEN
The Staying Hand. Philadelphia: Dorrance, 1955. 52 p. (Contemporary poets of Dorrance, 478)

KNIGHT, JUDITH B.
Songs in the Night. Philadelphia: Franklin Printing Company, 1902. 82 p.

KNOTT, LUELLA (PUGH) (1871-)
Life-lore Poems. Boston: Sherman, French & Company, 1912. 6 p. ℓ., 3-161 p.
Mary Magdalene. Boston: White-Smith Pub. Co., 1933. [32] p.

The Garden I Love Best. Boston: White-Smith Music Publishing Co., 1937. 2 p.ℓ., 3-42 p.
Uncle Abe Says.... Macon, GA.: The J. W. Burke Company, 1938. 5 p.ℓ., 78 p.
Where We Call Each Other Honey. Macon, GA.: J. W. Burke, 1940. 5 p.ℓ., 66 p.

KNOWLES, RUTH [Full Name: Ruth Loretta Rosecrans Knowles.]
A Boon Book of Poems. Indiana, PA.: Printing House of Park, 1931. 80 p.

KNOWLTON, HELEN GINGRICH
Hearthstones. Philadelphia: Dorrance, 1955. 55 p. (Contemporary poets of Dorrance, 466)

KNOX, JACQUELINE LLOYD
Bittersweets; A Book of Verse. Philadelphia: Dorrance & Co., 1938. 50 p. (Contemporary poets of Dorrance)

KNOX, JEAN LINDSAY
A Key to Brotherhood; Poems. New York: The Paebar Publishing Company, 1934. [24] p.

KNOX, MAUDE LEE (1932-)
A Time for Song; Poems. New York: Exposition Press, 1961. 63 p.

KNUDSEN, DINA
Thoughts from Texas. Boston: Christopher Publishing House, 1953. 82 p.

KOBRIN, KAREN
Marshmallow Seeds, and Other Poems. San Antonio, TX.: Naylor Co., 1967. viii, 48 p.

KOEHLER, MARTHA PETERSON
Ralph Waldo Emerson, and Other Poems. Philadelphia: Dorrance, 1967. 27 p. (Contemporary poets of Dorrance, 646)

KOENIG, ELEANOR CONSTANCE (SHEEHAN) [KOENIG, ELEANOR O'ROURKE]
Herb Woman and Other Poems. New York: H. Vinal, 1926. viii p., 1 ℓ.
Two on an Old Pathway: Poems. Hartford, CT.: E. V. Mitchell, 1929. xii p., 1 ℓ., 74 p.
The Legend of Hartford. Windham, CT.: Hawthorn House, 1935. 18 p., 1 ℓ.

KOENIG, ELEANOR DWYER [MEL, EVELYN, pseud.]
My Gift of Love. New York: Exposition Press, 1960. 53 p.

KOEPKE, ABLONDA PFRIMMER McBETH (1891-)
Of These I Sing. Dexter, MO.: Candor Press, 1960. 84 p.

Song of the Big Hill. Dexter, MO.: Candor Press, 1962. 93 p.

KÖRTE, MARY NORBERT (1934-)
The Beginning Is the Life, Is the Word. Berkeley, CA.: Oyez, 1967. 1 ℓ.
Hymn to the Gentle Sun: Poems. San Francisco: Oyez, 1967. 45 p., 1 ℓ.
Beginning of Lines, Response to "Albion Moonlight." Berkeley, CA.: Oyez, 1968. [31] p.
The Generation of Love. New York: Bruce Publishing Co., 1969. [91] p.
A Breviary in Time of War. San Francisco: Cranium Press, 1970. 32 p.
The Midnight Bridge. Berkeley, CA.: Oyez, 1970. [53] p.

KOFFINKE, ANNE JULIA (1897-)
Sonnets and Autumn Pieces. North Montpelier, VT.: The Driftwind Press, 1945. 46 p.

KOHLS, OLIVE N. ALLEN [ALLEN, DIXIE, pseud.]
Idle Thoughts in Poems. New York: Pageant Press, 1957. 5 p. ℓ., 78 p.

KONLEY, JEANNETTE VAUGHN
Cradled in the Dunelands. Parkville, MO.: Printed by the Park College Press, 1956. 70 p.

KONOPAK, FARONA (1895-)
Adobe in Sunlight; Poems. New York: The Galleon Press, 1935. 4 p. ℓ., 11-64 p.

KONRICK, DUVERNE (1923-)
Flames of Freedom. Shelbyville, IN.: Blue River Press, 1952. 64 p.

KONRICK, VERA BISHOP (1900-)
Moon Flame. Shelbyville, IN.: Blue River Press, 1953. 62 p.

KOOLISH, LYNDA
Journeys on the Living. Berkeley, CA.: Ariel Press, 1973. 68 p.

KOONCE, MAE ELMORE
Poems of the West. New York: Comet Press Books, 1958. 4 p. ℓ., 56 p. (A Lyceum book)

KORALEWSKY, ROSE (1897-)
New England Heritage and Other Poems. Boston: B. Humphries, 1949. 89 p.

KORY, FRANCES P.
Headlines: World War II. Boston: Bruce Humphries, 1954. 67 p.

KOURI, EVA VICTORIA
"Gems of the Heart." Oklahoma City, OK.: Boles Printing Co., 1941. [72] p.

KRAFT, JESSIE LOFGREN
Overtone. New York: Exposition Press, 1947. 63 p.
Moods in Melody. Philadelphia: Dorrance, 1961. 69 p. (Contemporary poets of Dorrance, 586)

KRAKE, MAUDE DE VERE
From the Prairies: A Book of Verse. Chicago: Scroll Publishing and Literary Syndicate, 1900. 63 p., [1] p.

KRARUP, MIRIAM HEIDEMAN
Melodies from a Michigan Marsh: A Collection of Poems. Inkster, MI.: P. Krarup, 1960. 48 p.

KRAUSS, RUTH
Bears. New York: Harper, 1948. [23] p.
The Cantilever Rainbow. New York: Pantheon Books, 1965. [47] p.
There's a Little Ambiguity Over There Among the Bluebells, and Other Theater Poems. New York: Something Else Press, 1968. [94] p.
If Only. Eugene, OR.: Toad Press, 1969. [12] p.
This Beast Gothic. Lenox, MA.: Bookstore Press, 1973. [39] p.

KREIDER, NADA (HART)
Florida Cracker Verse. New York: Exposition Press, 1950. 61 p.

KRIEMLER, MARIE HAYDEN
The Bittersweet; or Smiles and Tears, A Book of Poems. Stanford, CA.: Ed. and published by Forrest Rene Morphew, 1951. 5 p.ℓ., 29 p., 1 ℓ.

KROLL, JUDITH
In the Temperate Zone. New York: Scribner, 1973. 84 p.

KROLL, MILLIE C.
Dream World. New York: Pageant Press, 1951. 56 p.

KRON, ANNETTE
"In the Garden of Self"; Character Studies and Other Poems. Chicago: R. B. Horwich & Co., 1923. 2 p.ℓ., 9-59 p.

KRUCHKOW, DIANE
Odd Jobs. East Lansing, MI.: Ghostdance, 197-? 30 p.

KRUGER, FANIA
The Tenth Jew. Dallas, TX.: Kaleidograph Press, 1919. 93 p.
Cossack Laughter. Dallas, TX.: The Kaleidograph Press, 1937.

xii p., 2 ℓ., 17-83 p., 1 ℓ.
_______. 2d ed., 1938. 83 p.
Selected Poems. Austin, TX.: American University Artforms, 1973. xi, 71 p. (A Benchmark book)

KRUGER, KARIL
Keprikorn Poems. Milwaukee, WI.: Gunrunner Press, 1968? [12] p.

KRUGER, NELL
Miles West of Here; Thoughts in Metres and Miles. New York: Pageant Press, 1958. 42 p.

KRUMM, HAZEL SHINN
The Years Like Foxes. Columbus, OH.: The F. J. Heer Printing Company, 1942. 70 p.

KRUPP, NAHAMI
Tides to the Moon. Chicago: P. Covici, 1927. 8 p., 1 ℓ., 9-66 p.

KUDER, BLANCHE (BANE) (1882-)
April Weather. Boston: The Cornhill Publishing Co., 1922. x, 62 p.

KUEBLER, MILDRED
Soliloquy at Midnight. New York: The Exposition Press, 1946. 93 p.

KUEFFNER, LOUISE MALLINCKRODT
Moods of Manhattan. New York: The Modernist Press, 1920. 59, [2] p.
The Wanderlure. Mount Vernon, N.Y.: The Golden Eagle Press, 1940. [82] p.

KUMIN, MAXINE (WINOKUR) (1925-)
Halfway. New York: Holt, Rinehart and Winston, 1961. 106 p.
No One Writes a Letter to the Snail, Poems. New York: Putnam, 1962. [63] p. (Verse for children.)
The Privilege. New York: Harper and Row, 1965. x, 82 p.
The Nightmare Factory. New York: Harper & Row, 1970. ix, 94 p., 2 ℓ.
Up Country: Poems of New England. New York: Harper & Row, 1972. 83 p.
House, Bridge, Fountain, Gate: Poems. New York: The Viking Press, 1975. 112 p.

KURLAND, PATRICIA BOCKSER (1908-)
Yearning and Yield. New York: Beechhurst Press, 1949. ix, 86 p.

KURTZ, GERTRUDE GRAHAM
The Vine Covered House; Poems and Thoughts, 1924-1958. Providence, R.I.: n.p., 1962. [13] p.

KURZEN, ESTELLE
Eructations of the Damned, and Other Poems. Los Angeles?: Hardy Hanson, 1964. [54] p.

KUSKULIS, ELISABETH
Not Unto Caesar; A Collection of Poems. Long Beach, CA.: Seaside Printing Company, 1943. 106 p.

KUTZIN, ALICE
The Blind Date That Made It. New York: McKay, 1971.

KYGER, JOANNE (1934-)
The Tapestry and the Web. San Francisco: Four Seasons Foundation, 1965. 61 p. (Four Seasons Foundation, San Francisco Writing, 5)
The Fool in April: A Poem. San Francisco: Coyote Books, 1966.
Joanne. New York: Angel Hair Books, 1970.
Places to Go. Los Angeles: Black Sparrow Press, 1970. 93 p., 2 ℓ.
Desecheo Notebook. Berkeley, CA.: Arif Press, 1971. unpaged.
Trip Out, Fall Back. Berkeley, CA.: Arif Press, 1974. unpaged.
All This Every Day. Bolinas, CA.: Big Sky Books, 1975. 96 p.

KYLE, LUCIE (MILES) (1912-) [Full Name: Lucie Clair (Miles) Kyle.]
The Treasure Chest. Columbus, IN.: Weed Printing Company, Inc., 1932. 178 p.
Timber. Philadelphia: Dorrance, 1949. 67 p. (Contemporary poets of Dorrance, 384)

KYLE, PATRICIA MURRAY
Poems from Earth's Fair Corners. Boston: The Stratford Co., 1925. 4 p. ℓ., 37 p.

LaBELLE, CHRISTINE
The Difference Between. Portland, OR.: Wine Press, 1967. [38] p.
Alfalfa Wild; Poems. Cabot, VT.: Vermont Stoveside Press, 1968. 20 p.
The Possibility of an Early Fall. New Rochelle, N.Y.: Elizabeth Press, 1971. 66 p.
Our Own Green Confusion. New Rochelle, N.Y.: Elizabeth Press, 1974. 59 p.

LACEY, GLADYS MARGARET
On Reeds from Niso's Stream. Boston: B. Humphries, 1947. 88 p.

LACEY, RUTH CARMACK (1899-1970)
Sapphire Foundations; A Book of Selected Poems. San Diego? n.p., 1970. 45 p.

LA CLAUSTRA, VERA BERNECIA (1903-)
By the Cool Waters. Dallas: Story Book Press, 1953. 48 p.
The Purple Wheel. Berkeley, CA. ? Berkeley Mimeographing Company, 1954. 4 p. ℓ., 215 p.
Gongs of Light. Los Angeles, CA.: Swordsman Pub. Co., 1971. 187 p.

LACY, MATTIE (HALLAM) (1872-)
Store-City. Dallas, TX.: The Kaleidoscope Press, 1941. xiii, 17-108 p.

LADD, GABRIELLE
The Dark Island; Twenty Poems. Lunenburg, VT.: n.p., 1960. 32 p.

LADEN, GOLDIE
Dreams of Youth. Salt Lake City, UT.: Paragon Printing Company, 1929. 100 p.

LA FAVER, EMMA
Toward the Stars; Poems. New York: Exposition Press, 1951. 63 p.

LA FLEUR, FLOSSIE ADELIA STUDLEY
A Princess in Her Garden of Flowers, Lady Peggy. New York: Printed by Little and Ives Company, 1934. xi, 115 p.

LAFLIN, ELLEN P.
Poems. New York: The Grafton Press, 1909. 33 p.

LAHR, GEORGIANA LIEDER
The Heart Sings! New York: Vantage Press, 1971. 74 p.
Wings of Song. New York: Vantage Press, 1973. 112 p.
Singing Glory! New York: Vantage Press, 1974. 97 p.

LAIDLAW, LOUISE BURTON (1906-)
Wishing on a Comet, and Collected Poems. New York: Dodd, Mead & Company, 1930. 7 p. ℓ., 3-133 p.
Traveler of Earth. New York: Dodd, Mead & Company, 1936. 8 p. ℓ., 5-93 p.

LAING, DILYS (BENNETT) (1906-1960)
Another England; Poems. New York: Duell, Sloan and Pearce, 1941. xi, 67 p.
Birth Is Farewell. New York: Duell, Sloan and Pearce, 1944. x, 53 p.
Not One Atoll. Hanover, N.H.: Dartmouth College Library, 1946. 15 p.
Walk Through Two Landscapes, Poems. New York: Twayne,

1949. 64 p. (The Twayne Library of Modern Poetry, 3)
Poems from a Cage: New, Selected and Translated Poems. New York: Macmillan, 1961. 87 p.
The Collected Poems of Dilys Laing. Cleveland, OH.: Press of Case Western Reserve University, 1967. 464 p.

LAING, Mrs. MARION MacARTHUR
...The Quest and the Temples.... New York: H. Harrison, 1929. 4 p. ℓ., 11-65 p.

LAIRD, ANTONIA BISSELL
A Quiet Voice. Philadelphia: Dorrance, 1970. vi, 62 p.
A Parasol of Leaves. Haddonfield, N.J.: Haddonfield House, 1973. 74 p.

LAKE, LAURA SPOFFORD WILTSIE
Poetry Lane. Paterson, N.J.: Gayren Press, 1938. 6 p. ℓ., 14-72 p.

LAKIN, MATTIE T. (1917-)
Portico of the Temple. Gastonia, N.C.: Minges Printers, 1970.

LALLY, LEE
These Days. Washington, D.C.: Printed by Diana Press for Some of Us Press, 1972. 36 p.

LALLY, MARGE (1904-)
Aloha Poems. New York: Exposition Press, 1940. 5 p. ℓ., 13-64 p.

LA MARRE, HAZEL L. (WASHINGTON) (1917-1973)
Breath in the Whirlwind. Hollywood, CA.: Victory Pub. Co., 1955. 47 p.
Il Silenzio. Hollywood, CA.: Swordsman, 1972.
Half-Past Tomorrow; Poems. Los Angeles, CA.: Swordsman, 1973. 88 p.

LAMB, ESTHER HILL
Verses. Pittsburgh, PA.: Orminston-Dick Co., 1919. 2 p. ℓ., 7-37, [1] p.

LAMBERG, GLENNA
Patchwork Quilts. New York: Pegasus Pub. Co., 1939. 32 p.

LAMBERT, DOROTHY L.
Silhouettes of Life. New York: Vantage Press, 1957. 50 p.

LAMONT, RUBY
The Soul's Language. Jamaica, N.Y.: Beach Printing Company, 1925. 1 p. ℓ., 35 p.

LA MOTTE, Sister MARY WILFRID
Flowers of the Cloister. New York: Benzinger Brothers, 1913. 3 p. ℓ., 5-211 p.

LAMPREY, MARY JOSEPHINE FOLSOM
Rhymes of a Rustic. Boston: The Gorham Press, 1912. 143 p.

LANDIS, MARGARET TUCKER (1871-)
...Stars and Flowers and Other Poems. Philadelphia: Dorrance and Company, 1937. 68 p. (Contemporary poets of Dorrance, 168)

LANDRY, MARGARET MARY
A Garden Enclosed. San Antonio, TX.: Naylor Co., 1974. vii, 15 p.

LANDWER, IDA (KORITZ)
Heart to Heart Poems. New York: Pageant Press, 1959. 154 p.

LANE, FRONA (1903-)
Apples of Gold. Los Angeles, CA.: Welty Printing Co., 1945. 31 p.
The Third Eyelid, Poems. Denver, CO.: A. Swallow, 1951. 44 p.
Make Believe. Alpine, TX.: n.p., 1955. 23 p.
Worm, Feed Gently, and Other Poems. Cabot, VT.: Greenleaf Press, 1957. 43 p.
Eve Made Wise. New York: Carlton Press, 1974. 47 p.

LANE, PINKIE GORDON (1923-)
Wind Thoughts. Fort Smith, AR.: South and West, 1972. 59 p.

LANE, SALLY
Bonaventure. New York: The Exposition Press, 1944. 4 p. ℓ., 11-94 p. (Poets of America. Series four)
My Son Came Home, and Other Poems. New York: The Exposition Press, 1946. 92 p.

LANG, HAZEL N.
Only Human; Poems of Everyday Life. New York: Exposition Press, 1955. 72 p.

LANG, MARGARET R.
Anagrams in Rhyme, To Shorten Long Hours. n.p., 1944. 22, [1] p.

LANGDON, BESSIE E.
Falling Petals. Dallas, TX.: The Kaleidograph Press, 1940. xi p., 1 ℓ., 15-120 p.
Candles at Midnight. Dallas, TX.: The Kaleidograph Press, 1943. xi, 15-120 p.

LANGE, MARIE LOUISE
Petals-of-Music. Emory University, Atlanta, GA.: Banner Press, 1936. 36 p. (Verse craft series)

LANGFORD, RUTH WELLES
Moods and Memories. Boston: The Christopher Publishing House, 1941. viii p., 1 ℓ., 11-77 p.

LANGHEINE, BOBBIE
The Golden Hour. New York: Pageant Press, 1953. 3 p. ℓ., 53 p.

LANGSTON, LUCILE E.
The Peddler. Crescent, OK.: Crescent Publishing Company, 1932. 3 p. ℓ., 6-78 p.

LANTZ, VIRGINIA L.
So Bends the Bamboo. Rutland, VT.: C. E. Tuttle Co., 1959. 54 p.

LAPIDUS, JACQUELINE
Ready to Survive. Brooklyn, N.Y.: Hanging Loose Press, 1975. 30 p.

LA PRADE, RUTH
Woman Free, and Other Poems. n.p.: Rowney, 1918. 72 p.

LARABEE, MARY FLEMING
Persian Pictures. New York: Fleming H. Revell, 1920.

LARAMORE, VIVIAN (YEISER) (1891-) [RADER, VIVIAN LARAMORE]
A Collection of Published Poems. Atlanta, GA.: Ruralist Press, Inc., 1922? 63 p.
Green Acres. New York: H. Vinal, 1926. 5 p. ℓ., 53 p.
Flamingo. New York: H. Harrison, 1932. 63 p.
Miami Muse. n.p.: Beach House, 1932. 61 p.
Had Sappho Written Sonnets. Dallas, TX.: The Kaleidograph Press, 1939. xi p., 1 ℓ., 15-77 p.
The Beggar and the Star. Nashville, TN.: Broadman Press, 1949. 221 p.
Poinciana Poems. Miami, FL.: Pandanus Press, 1953. 26 p.
Ode to Life & Selected Poems. Miami, FL.: Hurricane House, 1967. 90 p.

LARDNER, LENA BOGARDUS (PHILLIPS) (1843-1918)
"This Spray of Western Pine." New York: Broadway Publishing Company, 1903. 4 p. ℓ., 46 p.

LARGENT, THELMA
A Prairie Woman Sings. San Antonio, TX.: Naylor Co., 1967. viii, 64 p.

LARIMER, MABEL (GILBERT) (1893-)
Blending All Colors. San Antonio, TX.: The Carleton Printing Co., 1943. 54 p.

LARKIN, JOAN
Housework; Poems. Brooklyn, N. Y.: Out & Out Books, 1975. 79 p.

LARNED, ANNE MURRAY
"There Was a Time." Boston: R. G. Badger, 1916. 30 p.

LAROCQUE, ELIZABETH
Satan's Shadow. New York: C. Scribner, 1930. x p., 2 ℓ., 3-57 p.

LASATER, ANNE
Golden Nuggets. Dallas, TX.: The Story Book Press, 1948. 40 p.

LA SELLE, EUNICE POND
Chameleons in Livery; A Half-Century of Poems. Chicago: Windfall Press, 1965. 61 p.

LASH, VIRGINIA
Portraits. Boston: B. Humphries, 1950. 48 p.

LASKY, BESSIE MONA (GAINESS) (1890-)
And I Shall Make Music. New York: H. Liveright, 1930. viii p., 2 ℓ., 13-186 p.

LASSEN, MAY C.
Poems. Red Bluff, CA.: W. M. Allen, Printer, 1912. 31 p.
More Poems.... Red Bluff, CA.: n. p., 1914. 6 p. ℓ., 39 p.

LASTER, CLARA (1914-)
The Patter of Poems. Dallas, TX.: Story Book Press, 1948. 40 p.
House on Halfway Hill. Fort Smith, AR.: South and West, 1968. 39 p.

LATCHAW, GLADYS
Neophytes. Boston: R. G. Badger, 1923. 57 p.
Altars to Javeh. Boston: R. G. Badger, 1924. 4 p. ℓ., 11-38 p.

LATHAM, AZUBA JULIA (1866-)
Tales and Tags; Rhymes. New York: A. A. Knopf, 1918. 4 p. ℓ., 13-115 p.

LATHBURY, MARY ARTEMISIA (1841-1913)
Poems of Mary Artemisia Lathbury, Chautauqua Laureate. Minneapolis, MN.: The Nunc Licet Press, 1915. 292 p.

LATHROP, LOUISE
Verses. Jefferson City, MO.: Printed by Hugh Stephens Printing Co., 1912. 1 p. ℓ., 47 p.

LATIMORE, JEWEL C. see AMINI, JOHARI

LATTA, IRENE (KANE) (1910-)
For Seasons of Surprise; Poems. Chicago: Windfall Press, 1965. 36 p.
A Higher Alp. Charleston, IL.: Prairie Press, 1967. x, 34 p.
No Amulet. Newark, N.Y.: n.p., 1970. 60 p.

LAUBACH, CANDACE SAWYER
"A Sheaf of Poems." Topeka, KA.: Crane & Company, 1923. 2 p.ℓ., 7-37 p.

LAUCK, BLANCHE MORRIS
The Picnic, and Other Verses. New York: Cochrane Publishing Company, 1909. 40 p.
_______. Boston: R. G. Badger, 1924. 62 p.

LAUDER, Mrs. JAMES STEWART
Poems and Rhymes. Jeffersonville, IN.: Jeffersonville Printing Company, 1916. 31 ℓ.

LAUFENBURG, MAY MORTENSEN
Grist of the Years. San Antonio, TX.: Artes Graficas, 1952. 93 p.

LAUFMAN, MARILYN JOSELIT (1923-1964)
The Poetry of Marilyn Joselit Laufman, 1923-1964. Chicago: Harbren Pub. Co., 1965. 5 p.ℓ., 83 p.

LAUGHLIN, MARY QUINLAN
Abbeyfeale, and Other Poems. Boston: R. G. Badger, 1928. viii, 9-133 p.

LAVIN, MARGARET MASLAND
To Kate. Francestown, N.H.: Golden Quill Press, 1959. 63 p.
Landscape with Figures. Francestown, N.H.: Golden Quill Press, 1961. 93 p.
Charlie. Francestown, N.H.: Golden Quill Press, 1967. 112 p.

LAW, MARGARET LATHROP (1890-)
Horizon Smoke. Philadelphia: Poetry Publishers, 1932. 68 p.
Horizon Smoke. 2d ed. Philadelphia: Poetry Publishers, 1932. 72 p.
From Gold to Green. Philadelphia: Poetry Publishers, 1933. 96 p.
Where Wings Are Healed; Songs of Nova Scotia. Philadelphia: Poetry Publishers, 1936. 48 p.
White Camellias and Black Laughter. Philadelphia: Poetry Publishers, 1939. 22 p.
Yield from Flame. New York: Exposition Press, 1952. 96 p.
Highroads and Byways. Windsor, N.S.: Lancelot Press, 1970. 35 p.
Songs of Nova Scotia. Windsor, N.S.: Lancelot Press, 1972. 48 p.

LAWNER, LYNNE
Wedding Night of a Nun: Poems. Boston: Little, Brown, 1964. vi, 44 p.
Triangle Dream and Other Poems. New York: Harper and Row, 1969. 95 p.

LAWRANCE, MARGARET (DIX) (1885-) [Full Name: Emily Margaret Gordon (Dix) Lawrance.]
Rosemary for Remembrance. Brookville, L.I.: The Brookville Press, 1941. [182] p.

LAWRENCE, CLARA LOUISE
Some Poems. Crafton, PA.: Cramer Printing & Publishing Co., 1914. 9 ℓ.
Poems Along the Way. San Jose, CA.: Tucker Printing Company, 1927. [54] p.

LAWRENCE, EDA HAHNE
The Truth About Fiction, and Collected Verse. Cleveland, OH.: Printed for the author by H. Carr, 1923. 2 p. ℓ., 9-112 p.

LAWRENCE, EDITH McILVAINE
Winged Thoughts. Pasadena, CA.: Shaw Press, 1945. [63] p.

LAWRENCE, GERTRUDE
The Beggar's Garden. New York: Brentano's, 1903. 106 p.

LAWRENCE, GRACE F.
Of Such Stuff, O Teacher! Poems. New York: Exposition Press, 1952. 64 p.

LAWRENCE, JEAN MITCHELL
Verse Fancies. New York: H. Vinal, Ltd., 1927. 5 p. ℓ., 53, [1] p.

LAWRENCE, MARION (1908-)
Three Shades of Green. Stamford, VT.: n.p., 1967. 80 p.

LAWRENCE, MARJORIE KAHL
The Singing Wind. New York: Vantage Press, 1954. 86 p.
Shining Wings. New York: Exposition Press, 1959. 94 p.
Forest Paths; Poems. New York: Exposition Press, 1962. 64 p.
Song to the Morning. New York: Exposition Press, 1966. 69 p.
High on a Hilltop; Poems. New York: Exposition Press, 1973. 64 p.

LAWRENCE, VARUNA HARTMANN
The Brimming Cup. Dallas, TX.: Tardy Pub. Co., 1937. 5 p. ℓ., 73 p.
Lights and Shadows. Dallas, TX.: The Story Book Press, 1941. 8 p. ℓ., 200 p.
The Last Quarter! Dallas, TX.: Story Book Press, 1951. 117 p.

LAWSHE, ALLISON R.
The City and the Forest by the Sea; a Poem. Trenton, N. J.: The Raindrop Press, 1900. 14 p.

LAWSON, PATRICIA
The Covenants of the Pentateuch; The Promise and the Fulfillment. New York: De Tanko Publishers, 1965. ix, 186 p.

LAY, NORMA
Interval to Sun. Prairie City, IL.: Decker Press, 1949. 86 p.

LAYTON, WINIFRED HEISKELL
This Enchanting Earth. Salem? OR.: Printed by RapCo Litho Service, 1965. 45 p.

LAZARD, NAOMI
Cry of the Peacocks. New York: Harcourt, Brace & World, 1967. vi, 82 p.

LAZIER, DELLA (FELL)
Home Poems for Homefolks. Boston: Christopher Pub. House, 1958. 132 p.

LEA, ESTHER MOOREFIELD
The Heart Whispers. New York: Vantage Press, 1964. 96 p.

LEA, FANNIE HEASLIP (1884-1955)
Take Back the Heart. New York: Dodd, Mead and Company, 1931. 75 p.
Verses for Lovers, and Some Others. New York: Dodd, Mead and Company, 1955. 96 p.

LEACH, MARCIA LEWIS
Dust of Dreams, and Other Poems. New York: The American Guild, 1930. 63 p.

LEACH, RUTH PARK
March Brigade; Poems. New York: Exposition Press, 1971. 79 p.

LEASK, ESTELLE
Pekie Poems by Wu Hoo Git, Taken Down in English Verse. Camden, N. J.: Haddon Press, Inc., 1924. 49 p.

LEATH, MARCELLE CHANCELLOR
Awake in the Night. San Antonio, TX.: Carleton Publisher, 1948. 63 p.

LEATHERBURY, BEATRICE ANNE (1887-)
Poems of Inspiration. Los Angeles, CA.: Wetzel Pub. Co., 1947. 102 p.

LEATHERWOOD, LILLIAN (1898-)
Flowers in the Rain. Dallas, TX.: The Kaleidograph Press, 1944. vii p., 1 ℓ., 11-61 p.
My Heart Has Wings. Dallas, TX.: The Kaleidograph Press, 1947. ix p., 1 ℓ., 13-80 p.
Sing a Bright Song. Dallas, TX.: Kaleidograph Press, 1950. 60 p.
Remember Only Tomorrow. Fort Worth, TX.: D. Cowan Co., Printers, 1956. 48 p.

LEAVENWORTH, ANNIE (CRIM)
Wild Geese and Other Poems. New York: J. T. White & Co., 1921. 98 p.

LECHLITNER, RUTH (1901-)
Tomorrow's Phoenix. New York: The Alcestis Press, 1937. 4 p. ℓ., 3-64 p., 1 ℓ.
Only the Years: Selected Poems: 1938-1944. Prairie City, IL.: Press of J. A. Decker, 1944. 64 p.
The Shadow on the Hour. Iowa City, IA.: Prairie Press, 1956. 44 p., 1 ℓ.
A Changing Season; Selected and New Poems, 1962-1972. Boston: Brandeis Press, 1973. 91 p.

LECKENBY, JOSEPHINE
Bright Thicket of the Stars. Boston: B. Humphries, Inc., 1946. 111, [1] p.

LECKLITER, GRACE D.
Spring Is Tomorrow. Los Angeles, CA.: The Ward Ritchie Press, 1944. xii, 47 p.

LE CLERCQ, LUCILLE
Boy Lore, and Other Poems. Seattle, WA.: Read Printing Co., 1925. 36 numb. ℓ.
Boy Lore, and Nature Poems. Seattle, WA.: Press of Lowman & Hanford Co., 1929. 40 p.

LEDBETTER, ELAINE WALKER
Candles at Noon. San Antonio, TX.: Naylor Co., 1956. ix, [1], 82 p.
Triumphant Moment. San Antonio, TX.: Naylor Co., 1961. viii, 81 p.
Enfold the Splendor. San Antonio, TX.: Naylor Co., 1973. vii, 72 p.

LEDBETTER, ELIZABETH O'CONNOR
Out of the South. Boston: Humphries, 1950. 84 p.

LEDESMAN, NELLY
Collected Poems. New York: Comet Press Books, 1954. 88 p.

LEE, AGNES (RAND) (1868-1939) [Full Name: Mrs. Agnes (Rand) Lee Freer.]
The Round Rabbit, and Other Child Verse. Boston: Small, Maynard & Co., 1901. 2 p. ℓ., ix-xii p., 2 ℓ., 102 p.
The Border of the Lake. Boston: Sherman, French & Co., 1910. 4 p. ℓ., 89 p.
Faces and Open Doors. Chicago: R. F. Seymour, 1922. 120 p.
New Lyrics and a Few Old Ones. Chicago: R. F. Seymour, 1930.
Under One Roof. Chicago: R. F. Seymour, 1940. xii, 184 p.

LEE, AMY (FREEMAN) (1914-)
Remember Pearl Harbor. New York: The Fine Editions Press, 1943. 34 p.

LEE, BEATRICE
Hearts and Flowers, and Other Poems. Muncie, IN.: Press of Central Printing Company, 1906. 3 p. ℓ., 9-134 p.

LEE, BLANCHE
...Singing Gardens; Poems. Boston: The Stratford Company, 1928. 32 p. (The Stratford Poets)
Candle Flowers. New York: J. T. White & Co., 1931. viii p., 1 ℓ., 55 p.

LEE, ELISABETH WARREN
Family Portraits. Narberth, PA.: Livingston Pub. Co., 1961. v, 66 p.

LEE, EVELYN LEWIS
The Call of the West. Boston: B. Humphries, 1949. 56 p.

LEE, FRANCES COLE
Faith of Our Fathers. Alpine, CA.: Handset by Sand Dune Sage, 1938. [12] p.
Opal Dust. New York: The Paebar Company, 1944. 3 p. ℓ., 57 p.

LEE, GERTRUDE
Moods. Boston: The Stratford Company, 1928. 3 p. ℓ., 45 p.
Inside My Garden Wall. Boston: The Stratford Company, 1929. 1 p. ℓ., v p., 2 ℓ., 3-62 p.
Scattered Gems. Boston: The Stratford Company, 1930. 4 p. ℓ., 76 p.

LEE, IDA F.
Life's Impressions. Denver: Kistler's, 1951. 102 p.

LEE, ISABEL
Verses (Just for You). n. p.: Stewart and Kidd, 1912. 16 p.

LEE, JANE DESMOND
Legacy of Dreams. Dexter, MO.: Candor Press, 1949. 60 p.

LEE, LILLIAN
Moods at Midpoint. New York: Greenwich Book Publisher, 1968. 54 p.

LEE, MARIE NELSON
By Special Request. Santa Barbara, CA.: The Youthland Press, 1921. 2 p. ℓ., iii-vi, 7-59 p.

LEE, MARION
Flame and Song, and Other Poems. Greenwood, MA.: Priv. print., 1935. [9] fold. ℓ.
Stones for My Pocket. Dallas, TX.: The Kaleidograph Press, 1940. vi p., 2 ℓ., 11-74 p., 1 ℓ.
Tarry Delight. Portland, ME.: Falmouth Pub. House, 1950. 5 p. ℓ., 3-54 p.

LEE, MARJORIE
What Have You Done All Day? New York: Crown Publishers, 1973. 85 p.

LEE, MARY
Tender Bough; Poems. New York: Crown Publishers, 1969. [95] p.
Hand in Hand. New York: Crown Publishers, 1971. [95] p.

LEE, MARY HINES
Autumn Leaves. Manning, SC.: Printed by the Manning Times, 1962. 85 p.

LEE, MUNA see LEE de MUÑOZ MARIN, MUNA (1895-)

LEE de MUÑOZ MARIN, MUNA (1895-) [LEE, MUNA]
Sea Change. New York: Macmillan, 1923. 76 p.

LEECH, CHARLOTTE
Verses. New York: The Knickerbocker Press, 1917. xv, 293 p.

LEECH, LUCILE PITTMAN
April Will Come. Emory University, GA.: Banner Press, 1944. 70 p.

LEEMING, DOROTHY
Green Wings. Chicago: Peterson Linotyping Co., 1921. 6 p. ℓ., 15-96 p.

LEFFORGE, LOUISE CHEEK
Scintillae of the Soul. Dallas, TX.: The Kaleidograph Press, 1946. viii p., 1 ℓ., 11-51 p.
Tapestry of Thought and Feeling. Dallas, TX.: Kaleidograph Press, 1950. 95 p.

LEFTON, BLANCHE DE GOOD
Mazama & Wecoma. Portland, OR.: Binfords & Mort, 1952. 92 p.

LEGG, BULA E.
I Chose a Way. Dallas, TX.: Kaleidograph Press, 1951. 87 p.

LEGLER, MARY FERGUSON
Until the Day Break. Los Angeles, CA.: The Ward Ritchie Press, 1939. 6 p. ℓ., 51, [1] p.
________. New York & London: Harper & Brothers, 1940. viii p., [2], 54 p.
________. 1949. viii p., 1 ℓ., 54 p.

LE GRAS, BERYL STAR
In My California Garden. Los Angeles, CA.: Wetzel Publishing Co., 1943. [3]-93 p.

LE GUIN, URSULA
Wild Angels. Santa Barbara, CA.: Capra Press, 1975. 50 p. (Capra chapbook ser., no. 27)

LEHMAN, BARBARA SHAW
Ten Poems. Bainbridge, PA.: Katydid Press, 1957. 26 p.
Rex; Homage to a Rooster. Bainbridge, PA.: Katydid Press, 1958. [4] p.
Poems with Titles. Bainbridge, PA.: Katydid Press, 1962. 73 p.

LEHMAN, EMMA A. (1841-)
Poems. New York: Grafton Press, 1904. 47 p.

LEHMAN, VALERIE (ROBERTSON) (1895-)
A Quick Wind Rising. Lake Como, FL.: New Athenaeum Press, 1958. 69 p.
Bare Trees Windward. Mill Valley, CA.: Wings Press, 1959. 46 p.
The Cliff Dweller. Mill Valley, CA.: Wings Press, 1962. 48 p.

LEHNER, LOIS
A Poem or Two for Everyone. Delaware, OH.: Independent Print Shop, 1965. 40 p.
The Song of the Farmer and Other Poems. Delaware, OH.: Independent Print Shop Co., 1966. 33 p.
A Third Book of Poems. Delaware, OH.: Independent Print Shop Co., 1970. 30 p.

LEIGH, JEWELL (1936-)
Lights and Shadows; Poems. New York: Greenwich Book Publishers, 1960. 48 p.

LEIGH, VIOLET
A Little Book of Verse. Eau Claire, WI.: Fremad Publishing Co., 1915. 31 p.

LEIGHTON, ALMEDA MARIE
Spiritual Gems for Thought. New York: Pageant Press, 1952. 3 p. ℓ., 54 p.

LEIGHTON, AMY CROCKER
Candles in the Night. Boston: May and Company, 1931. 3 p. ℓ., 9-74 p.

LEIGHTON, LOUISE (1890-)
The Great Carrying Place. New York: Harbinger House, 1944. 4 p. ℓ., 11-66 p.
Journey to Light. Baraboo, WI.: Printed by Osborne Print. Co., 1953. 102 p.

LEITCH, MARY SINTON (LEWIS) (1876-1954)
The Waggon and the Star. Boston: B. J. Brimmer, 1922. xi, 103 p.
The Unrisen Morrow. Philadelphia: Dorrance, 1926. 93, [1] p.
Spider Architect. New York: G. P. Putnam's Sons, 1937. 108 p.
From Invisible Mountains; War Sonnets & Other Poems. New York: The Fine Editions Press, 1943. 94, [2] p.
Nightingales on the Moon. Richmond, VA.: Dietz Press, 1952. 107 p.

LEITER, SHARON
The Lady and the Bailiff of Time. Ann Arbor, MI.: Ardis, 1974. 58 p. (New poets in America series)

LEITER, WILMA
Bursted Bubbles. Caldwell, ID.: The Caxton Printers, Ltd., 1935. 80 p.

LEITNER, DELLA ADAMS (1881-)
To Share with You.... Dexter, MO.: Candor Press, 1948. 80 p.
Minute Musings. Weiser, ID.: n.p., 1957. 11 p.
White Gold: Idaho Poems. Boise, ID?: Boise Printing Co., 1960. 22 p.

LELAND, EVELYN
I Like to Be a Grandma, and Other Poems. New York: Exposition Press, 1953. 55 p.
This Is For You. Boston: Christopher Pub. House, 1956. 60 p.

LEMMON, TALULAH
First Flight. Columbia, SC.: Gittman's Book Shop, 1942. 84 p.
On the Wing. Columbia, SC.: Gittman's Book Shop, 1943. 5 p. ℓ., 13-91 p.
Here Is Born. Charleston, SC.: Pink House Press, 1946. 39 p.

LEMONT, JESSIE
White Nights. Portland, ME.: The Mosher Press, 1930. viii, [1], 74, [1] p., 1 ℓ.
Where Stillness Lies the Deepest. New York: The Fine Editions Press, 1944. 40 p.

L'ENGLE, MADELEINE
Lines Scribbled on an Envelope, and Other Poems. New York: Farrar, Straus & Giroux, 1969. 7 p. ℓ., 81 p.

LENNON, FLORENCE BECKER (1895-)
Farewell to Walden, Sonnet Sequence. New York: Exile Press, 1939. 4 p. ℓ., 48 numb. ℓ.
Forty Years in the Wilderness. London: Linden Press; New York: Schulte Pub. Co., 1961. 127 p.

LENNON, LILA
Of Time and the Tide, Poems. Chicago: Dierkes Press, 1949. 55 p.

LENSKI, LOIS (1893-)
Alphabet People. New York: Harper & Brothers, 1928. 4 p. ℓ., 104 p.
Animals for Me. New York, London: Oxford University Press, 1941. [48] p.
Spring Is Here. New York, London: Oxford University Press, 1945. [48] p.
_______. New York: H. Z. Walck, 1945. 1 v. unpaged.
Now It's Fall. New York: Oxford University Press, 1948. [48] p.
I Like Winter. New York: Oxford University Press, 1950. 48 p.
On a Summer Day. New York: Oxford University Press, 1953. unpaged.
_______. New York: H. Z. Walck, 1953. unpaged.
The Life I Live; Collected Poems. New York: H. Z. Walck, 1965. 5 p. ℓ., 238 p.
City Poems. New York: H. Z. Walck, 1971. x, 118 p.
Florida, My Florida; Poems. Tallahassee, FL.: Friends of the Library, Florida State University, 1971. 64 p.

LENZ, ANGIE L.
Little Gems for Everybody. New York: The Knickerbocker Press, 1930. ix, 136 p.

LEONARD, AGNES see HILL, AGNES (LEONARD) SCANLAND (1842-1917)

LEONARD, DOROTHY
Buttressed from Moonlight, Poems. New York: Exposition Press, 1951. 63 p.

LEONARD, ELIZABETH S.
Pansies; Poems of Thought and Feeling. New York: M. B. Brown Company, 1902. 1 p. ℓ., 112 p.

LEONARD, FERN SELL (1894-)
Golden Threads for the Loom of Life. Los Angeles, CA.: Wetzel Pub. Co., 1953. 103 p.

LEONARD, FRANCES SWEET
When Evening Shadows Fall; Poems. Caldwell, ID.: The Caxton Printers, Ltd., 1930. 287 p.

LEONARD, HARRIET LYON
White Birds. New York: Little Book House, 1932. 51 p.
Songs of Many Moods.... Cedar Rapids, IA.: Torch Press, 1947. 80 p.

LEONARD, MARY HALL (1847-1921)
My Lady of the Search-Light. New York: The Grafton Press, 1905. v, 58 p.
When Youth Met Life. Boston: The Palmer Company, 1911. 80 p.
My Lady of the Search-Light. Boston: The Four Seas Co., 1920. v, 58 p.
Rest and Unrest. Santee, NB.: Santee N. T. S. Press, 1926. 85 p.

LEONARD, RUTH
Windows.... New York: H. Harrison, 1948. 63 p.

LE PAGE, RITA
Fairy Lore, and Other Poems. n. p.: Stratford, 1925. 68 p.

LE PLA, FANNIE M.
Little Nature Verses. Boston: The Christopher Publishing House, 1930. 88 p.

LE PRADE, RUTH
A Woman Free, and Other Poems. Los Angeles, CA.: J. F. Rowny Press, 1917. 72 p.
Sonnets to Edwin Markham. Los Angeles, n. p., 1937. 2 ℓ.
Songtree. Santa Barbara, CA.: J. F. Rowny Press, 1943. viii p., 1 ℓ., 11-79 p.
Gypsy Love Songs. Los Angeles, CA.: Printed by B. N. Robertson, 1947. 48 p.

LERMAN, ELEANOR (1952-)
Armed Love. Middletown, CT.: Wesleyan University Press, 1973. 64 p. (The Wesleyan Poetry Program, v. 68)
Come the Sweet By and By. Amherst, MA.: University of Massachusetts Press, 1975. 73 p.

LESHER, PHYLLIS
99801, Juneau. Homestead, FL.: Olivant Press, 1968. 3 p. ℓ., A-Z, Aa, [4] p.
The "Ah-ness" of Things! Haiku and Senryu. Homestead, FL.: Olivant Press, 1970. 1 v. unpaged.

LESLIE, SARABETH see LESLIE, SARAH ELIZABETH (SATTERTHWAITE) (1864-)

LESLIE, SARAH ELIZABETH (SATTERTHWAITE) (1864-) [LESLIE, SARABETH]
...Morningshore Children. New York: H. Harrison, 1936. 127 p. (Verse for children.)
Songs from Morningshore. New York: Crown Publications, 1941. 63 p.
Morningshore Calling. New York: Exposition Press, 1944. 30 p.

LESSIN, LOUISE
Cats and Their People, In Haiku. New York: P. S. Eriksson, 1968. [96] p.

LESTER, ALICE MARTIN
Prelude to Midnight. Chicago: Dierkes Press, 1950. 56 p.

LESTER, EMMA SERVICE
Poems to Wu. Shanghai China: The Commercial Press, Limited, 1925. 6 p. ℓ., 3-79 p.

LE SUEUR, MERIDEL
Rites of Ancient Ripening. Minneapolis, MN.: Vanilla Press, 1975. xi, 57 p.

LETTS, ALBINA MARILLA (BROCKWAY)
By Grandsire's Well, and Other Poems. Kansas City, MO.: Kellog-Baxter Pub. Co., 1909. [5]-123 p.

LEVERTOV, DENISE (1923-)
The Double Image. London: Cresset Press, 1946. 45 p.
Here and Now. San Francisco, CA.: City Lights Pocket Bookshop, 1957. 32 p.
5 Poems. San Francisco, CA.: White Rabbit Press, 1958. [8] p.
Overland to the Islands. Highlands, N. C.: J. Williams Jargon, 1958. [47] p.
With Eyes at the Back of Our Head. New York: New Directions Pub. Co., 1959. 3 p. ℓ., 74 p.
The Jacob's Ladder. New York: New Directions, 1961. 4 p. ℓ., 87 p.
City Psalm. Berkeley, CA.: Oyez, 1964. 1 ℓ. broadside.
O Taste and See. New York: New Directions, 1964. 4 p. ℓ., 83 p.
The Jacob's Ladder. London: Cape, 1965. 5 p. ℓ., 83 p.

Psalm Concerning the Castle. Madison, WI.: Perishable Press, 1966.
The Sorrow Dance; Poems. New York: New Directions, 1967. 94 p.
The Cold Spring and Other Poems. New York: New Directions, 1968. [20] p.
A Marigold from North Vietnam. New York: Albondocani Press-Ampersand Books, 1968. 4 ℓ.
The Sorrow Dance. London: Cape, 1968. 94 p.
Three Poems. Mount Horeb, WI.: Perishable Press, 1968. 6 ℓ.
A Tree Telling of Orpheus. Los Angeles, CA.: Black Sparrow Press, 1968. 9 p., 1 ℓ.
Embroideries. Los Angeles, CA.: Black Sparrow Press, 1969. 9 p., 1 ℓ.
A New Year's Garland for My Students, MIT 1969-70. Mount Horeb, WI.: Perishable Press, 1970. [17] p., 1 ℓ.
Relearning the Alphabet. New York: New Directions, 1970. 121 p.
_______. London: Cape, 1970. 3 p. ℓ., 121 p.
Summer Poems 1969. Berkeley, CA.: Oyez, 1970. [16] p.
To Stay Alive. New York: New Directions, 1971. 86 p.
Footprints. New York: New Directions, 1972.
Conversation in Moscow. New York: Pub. & produced by the Hovey St. Press, 1973. [10] p.
The Freeing of the Dust. New York: New Directions, 1975. 114 p.

LEVI, ADELE FRANCES (1912-)
...Dwellers in the Hills. Berkeley, CA.: University of California Press, 1929.

LEVIN, BARBARA
Fingerings. Santa Fe, NM.: American Poet Press, 1966. 18 p.

LEVINE, MIRIAM
Friends Dreaming. Tucson, AZ.: Ironwood Press, 1974. [24] p.

LEVY, LYN
Singing Sadness Happy. Detroit: Broadside, 1972. 32 p.

LEVY, ROSALIE MARIE (1889-)
Happy Moments. New York: Pageant Press, 1963. 6 p. ℓ., 116 p.

LEWINSON, RUTH
...Happy Days. New York: H. Vinal Limited, 1928. 6 p. ℓ., 32 p. (The Friendly books)

LEWIS, AGNES I.
Poetry Time. Boston: Christopher Pub. House, 1955. 232 p.

LEWIS, BESSIE M. (1902-)
Mesa Trails. New York: Paebar Co., 1951. 51 p.

LEWIS, CAROLYN CLAY (McCREERY) (1893-)
...Carols of Carolyn. Detroit, MI.: F. K. Stearns, 1923. iii-xiii, 78 p. (Beverly booklet, number I)

LEWIS, CARRIE LOUISE
Polished Pebbles, Poems. New York: Exposition Press, 1960. 48 p.

LEWIS, CATHERINE de MILLE
A Wilderness of Song; Poems. New York: Pageant Press, 1954. 42 p.

LEWIS, CECILLE ZENIA
Facing East. Boston: B. Humphries, Inc., 1934. viii p., 1 ℓ., 11-70 p.
Tenets, Truths, and Lyrics. Boston: B. Humphries, 1938. 80 p.
Seeds of Growth. Boston: B. Humphries, 1940. 93 p.

LEWIS, CONSTANCE DEMING
More Than Water Broken.... New York: Paebar Co., 1936. 3 p. ℓ., 9-44 p.
The Old House Remembers and Small Town Portraits. Dallas, TX.: The Kaleidograph Press, 1938. 7 p. ℓ., 17-67 p.

LEWIS, DEDE
Just Plain Thoughts. New York: Carlton Press, 1960. 3 p. ℓ., 47 p.

LEWIS, EDITH FLEURINE (LYON) (1869-)
Thoughts in Verse. New York: Springfield Press, 1923. 4 p. ℓ., 49 p.

LEWIS, ELIZABETH
You Take the Glory. Portland, ME.: The Mosher Press, 1932. ix, [1], 37, [1] p.

LEWIS, EMILY SARGENT
The Little Singer, and Other Verses. Philadelphia & London: J. B. Lippincott Company, 1910. 72 p.

LEWIS, EMILY WESTWOOD
Poems. St. Louis: n.p., 1928. unpaged.

LEWIS, ESTEL EVERS
Glimpses Beyond; Being a Number of Poems. East Aurora, N.Y.: The Roycrofters, 1927. 3 p. ℓ., ix p., 3 ℓ., 109 p.

LEWIS, FRANCES OVIATT
Dreams. Cleveland, OH.: Evangelical Press, 193-? [42] p., 1 ℓ.

LEWIS, HARRIET ROSSITER
Glimmering Fireflies. Cambridge, MA.: Priv. print. at the Riverside Press, 1929. viii, 55 p.

LEWIS, JANET (1899-) [WINTERS, JANET LEWIS]
The Indians in the Woods. Bonn: M. Wheeler, 192-? [21] p.
The Wheel in Midsummer. Lynn: The Lone Gull, 1927. 3 p. ℓ., 5-25 p.
The Earth-Bound, 1924-1944. Aurora, N.Y.: Wells College Press, 1946. 47, [1] p.
The Hangar at Sunnyvale. San Francisco: n.p., 1947. 4 ℓ. (Book Club of California, San Francisco. The California Poetry Folios. Part 7)
Poems: 1924-1944. Denver: A. Swallow, 1950. 62 p.
_______. Chicago: Swallow Press, 1970. 62 p.

LEWIS, JESSICA (1892-)
Tiger Moon. Manchester, ME.: Falmouth Pub. House, 1953. 56 p.

LEWIS, JOY
Poetry, of Sorts. Portland? OR.: n.p., 1961. ii, [2], 28 ℓ.

LEWIS, LILLIAN F.
Fagots. Boston: The Gorham Press, 1918. 64 p.

LEWIS, LILLIAN SHEPHERD (1868-)
Verse Versatile. Los Angeles, CA.: Wetzel Publishing Co., Inc., 1944. 104 p.

LEWIS, MARY OWEN (1886-)
The Phantom Bow. Philadelphia: David McKay Company, 1931. 95 p.
Tower Window. Philadelphia: David McKay Company, 1932. 80 p.
_______. 2d ed., 1932. 80 p.
Peddler's Pack. Philadelphia: David McKay Company, 1933. 64 p.
Flight of the Rokh. Philadelphia: David McKay Company, 1936. 5 p. ℓ., [13]-125 p.
The Four Seasons. Pen Argyl, PA.: Printed by V. W. Parsons Print., 1954. 1 v.
At Home and Abroad. Pen Argyl, PA.: Printed by V. W. Parsons Print., 1955. 90, 42, 82 p. Book 1--My city of brotherly love. Book 2--Bits of America. Book 3--Glances around the world.
Music of Water, Air and Fire: Companion to the Four Seasons. Pen Argyl, PA.: Printed by V. W. Parsons Print., 1955. 45, 44, 32, 31, 29 p. Book 1--Music in words. Book 2--Thanks for water. Book 3--On the wing. Book 4--Look at the sky! Book 5--The Inner world.
The Crystal Stair. Pen Argyl, PA.: Printed by V. W. Parsons Print., 1956. 74, 49, 72 p.

Love's Litany. Pen Argyl, PA.: Printed by V. W. Parsons Print., 1956. 2 v.
An Abacus of Memories. Pen Argyl, PA.: V. W. Parsons Printing, 196-? 102 p.

LEWIS, MAY [GOLDSTONE, ALINE LEWIS]
Red Drumming in the Sun. New York: A. Knopf, 1931. xiii p., 2 ℓ., 3-73, [1] p.
Prospect Four Several Ways; Poems. New York: n.p., 1961. x, 103 p.

LEWIS, ROSELL
Memories of XIT. San Antonio, TX.: Printed by the Naylor Co., 1960. vii, 27 p.

LEWIS, WINIFRED
The Greener View. Pittsburg, KA.: Pittcraft, Inc., 1958. 77 p.

LEWISOHN, THELMA BOWMAN (SPEAR)
First Fruits. Paris: E. W. Titus, 1927. 2 p.ℓ., 34 p., 1 ℓ.
Grace Notes. North Montpelier, VT.: The Driftwind Press, 1936. 3 p.ℓ., 85 p.
Many Mansions, and Other Poems. North Montpelier, VT.: The Driftwind Press, 1941. 2 p.ℓ., 7-70 p.

LIBBY, VERA LOUISE
Poetic Trails. Portland, OR.: n.p., 193-? 47 p.

LIEBHARDT, LOUISE (DODGE) (1897-)
Love Is a Thistle. Mill Valley, CA.; New York: The Wings Press, 1941. 57, [1] p.

LIESEE, EDITH (1891-1937)
The Small White Bird. New York: The Harbor Press, 1937. [158] p.

LIFSHIN, LYN (DIANE) (1942-)
Why Is the House Dissolving? San Francisco: Open Skull Press, 1968. [32] p.
Femina 2. Oshkosh, WI.: Abraxas Press, 1970.
Leaves and Night Things. West Lafayette, IN.: Baby John Press, 1970. [24] p.
Black Apples. Trumansburg, N.Y.: New Books, 1971. 44 p.
40 Days, Apple Nights. Milwaukee, WI.: Morgan Press, 1972. [39] p. (Hey Lady supplement no. 17)
I'd Be Jeanne Moreau. Milwaukee, WI.: Morgan Press, 1972.
Lady Lyn. Milwaukee, WI.: Morgan Press, 1972.
Love Poems. Durham, N.H.: Zahir Press, 1972.
The Mercurochrome Sun: Poems. Tacoma, WA.: Charas Press, 1972. 43 p.
Moving by Touch. Traverse City, MI.: Cotyledon Press, 1972? 31 p.
Tentacles, Leaves. Belmont, MA.: Helleric Publications, 1972.

[15] p.
All the Women Poets I Ever Liked Didn't Hate Their Fathers. St. Petersburg, FL.: Konglomerati Press, 1973.
Black Apples. 2d enl. ed. Trumansburg, N. Y.: Crossing Press, 1973. 63 p.
Museum; Poems. Albany, N. Y.: Conspiracy Press, 1973. [22] p.
The Old House on the Croton. San Lorenzo, CA.: Shameless Hussy Press, 1973. 26 p.
Audley End. Long Beach, CA.: MAG Press, 1974. 12 p.
Blue Fingers. Milwaukee, WI.: Shelter Press, 1974.
Plymouth Women. Milwaukee, WI.: Morgan Press, 1974.
Poems. Gulfport, FL.: Konglomerati Press, 1974. 11 p.
Selected Poems. Trumansburg, N. Y.: Crossing Press, 1974.
Shaker Poems. Chatham, N. Y.: Omphalos Press, 1974. 36 p.
Thru Blue Post, New Mexico. Fredonia, N. Y.: Basilisk Press, 1974.
Paper Apples. Stockton, CA.: Wormwood Review Press, 1975. 32 p.
Old House Poems. Santa Barbara, CA.: Capra Press, 1975. 52 p. (Capra chapbook, no. 28)
Shaker House Poems. Tannersville, N. Y.: Tideline Press, 1975. 26 ℓ.
Upstate Madonna: Poems, 1970-1974. Trumansburg, N. Y.: Crossing Press, 1975. 127 p.

LIGHTFOOT, FLORRIE JEAN
Bits of Arden. Fayetteville, N. C.: The Cumberland Printing Co., 1923. [22] p.

LIGHTNER, ALICE M.
The Pillar and the Flame. New York: H. Vinal, Ltd., 1928. 4 p. ℓ., 68, [1] p., 1 ℓ.

LILLIEFORS, MABEL CAROL (RICKENBACHER)
Messages of Spring. Great Kills, Staten Island, N. Y.: The Author, 1941. vi, 128 p.

LILLY, OCTAVE (1908-)
Cathedral in the Ghetto, and Other Poems. New York: Vantage Press, 1970. 96 p.

LILLY, OTHELIA (1908-)
Beyond the Other Poems. n. p., 195-? [7] p.
Wing Your Joy! Berkeley, CA.: Ledereer, Street & Zeus Co., 1953. 95 p.
Galloping Peace. Francestown, N. H.: Golden Quill Press, 1962. 69 p.

LINCOLN, DORIS BRANDT
Greening Twig: Poems. Milwaukee, WI.: Membrane Press, 1975. [45] p.

LIND, MIRIAM SIEBER
Such Thoughts of Thee, and Other Poems. Scottdale, PA.: Herald Press, 1952. xi, 81 p.

LINDBERGH, ANNE (MORROW) (1906-)
The Unicorn and Other Poems, 1935-1955. New York: Pantheon, 1956. 86 p.
_______. London: Chatto, 1958. 86 p.

LINDELL, DOE (1937-)
The Heart's Dark Street. New York? Bosworth Books, 1963. 10 p.

LINDER, JOSEPHINE
Down Friendship Road. New York: House of Field, Inc., 1914. 63 p.

LINDESAY, MARIE (BATTERHAM) (1862-)
The First Shearing. Richmond, VA.: Whittet & Shepperson, 1904. 1 p. ℓ., 11 p., 1 ℓ., [13]-299 p.

LINDGREN, ELSIE M.
Sand and Salt; Poems of Inspiration. New York: Vantage Press, 1967. 63 p.

LINDHOLM, ANNA CHANDLER (1870-)
Wind and Trees and Other Poems. San Francisco: V. F. Pollak Printing Co., 1930. viii, 237 p.

LINDLEY, MAYBON
Carillons and Cow Bells. San Antonio, TX.: Press of the Naylor Co., 1949. 55 p.

LINDSAY, CLARA A. (1844-1909)
In Life's Sweet Afternoon; Rhymes of the Quiet Hour. Philadelphia: Printed for the author by G. W. Jacobs & Co., 1909. 2 p. ℓ., 203 p.

LINDSAY, IRENE
Sun Gold. New York: Vantage Press, 1966. 44 p.

LINDSEY, ALICE (d. 1940)
With These. Dallas, TX.: The Kaleidograph Press, 1941. xi, 13-62 p.

LINDSEY, ALLIENE LIZZIE (HARRIS)
Light Upon a Pilgrim's Way; Poems. Chicago: Printed by Matthews Typesetting Co., 1914. vii p., 1 ℓ., 140, [10] p.

LINDSEY, KAREN
Falling Off the Roof. Cambridge, MA.: Alice James Poetry Cooperative, 1975. 59 p.

LINDSEY, THERESE (KAYSER) (1870-)
Blue Norther: Texas Poems. New York: H. Vinal, 1925. 5 p. ℓ., 54 p.
The Cardinal Flower. Dallas, TX.: The Kaleidograph Press, 1934. xiii p., 1 ℓ., 17-76 p.
A Tale of the Galveston Storm. Dallas, TX.: The Kaleidograph Press, 1936. 40, [1] p.
Collected Poems. San Antonio, TX.: n.p., 1947. viii, 88 p.

LINDSLEY, IVY
What Matter Time or Tide. Dallas, TX.: The Kaleidograph Press, 1936. 92 p.
This Is a Promise. Dallas, TX.: The Kaleidograph Press, 1944. xi p., 1 ℓ., 15-96 p.

LINDSLEY, MARY FLORA
The Uncensored Letter, and Other Poems. New York: Island Press Cooperative, 1949. 6 p. ℓ., 84 p.
Grand Tour and Other Poems. New York: Philosophical Library, 1952. 128 p.
Selected Poems. Brooklyn, N.Y.: T. Gaus' Sons, 1967. 54 p.

LINDSTROM, LILLA (1900-)
Poems on the Bible. Kansas City, MO.: Brown-White-Lowell Press, 1952. xvi, 198 p.

LINEAWEAVER, MARION McLENNAN
The Season Within. Peterborough, N.H.: R. R. Smith, 1967. 77 p., 1 ℓ.

LINHAM, HELEN LOOMIS
I Hear Earth Sing. Dallas, TX.: The Kaleidograph Press, 1936. 82 p.
Lovingly, Helen. Dallas, TX.: The Story Book Press, 1954. 68 p.

LININGTON, ANN
Other Doors. Poughkeepsie, N.Y.: Vassar Co-operative Bookshop, 1927. 30 p.

LINK, CAROLYN CROSBY (WILSON)
Fir Trees and Fireflies. New York & London: G. P. Putnam's Sons, 1920. ix p., 1 ℓ., 69 p.
There Is Still Time. New York: The League to Support Poetry, 1944. 6 p. ℓ., 15-60 p.
Waters Under the Earth. Francestown, N.H.: Golden Quill Press, 1968. 93 p.

LINN, EDITH (WILLIS) (1865-)
A Cycle of Sonnets. New York: J. T. White & Co., 1918. 125 p.
From Dream to Dream. New York: J. T. White & Co., 1918. 126 p.

LINTON, MARY E.
On Wings of the Soul, A Collection of Poems. Kansas City, MO.: Burton Pub. Co., 1947. 3 p. ℓ., 9-119 p.

LIPPI, ANDREA (1918-)
Sea of Faith, Modern Poetry. Faith's Story: A Promise, The Dahlia, and a Sick Boy. Commentary: Lament of a Danish Prince. Private ed. Philadelphia: Printed by Clark Print. House, 1953. 94 p.

LIPPINCOTT, GRACE (ELIZABETH) MINER (1879-)
Skylines of New England. Emory University, Atlanta, GA. & New York: Banner Press, 1938. 63 p. (Verse craft series)
Dancing Shadows. Emory University, Atlanta, GA.: Banner Press, 1940. 64 p. (Verse craft series)
Spun from the Sea. Emory University, Atlanta, GA.: Banner Press, 1943. 62 p., 1 ℓ. (Verse craft series)
Spindrift with Overtones from Madison, Connecticut. Birmingham, AL.: Banner Press, 1965. 72 p.

LIPPINCOTT, JANET (1918-)
Rhapsody. Paterson, N.J.: Gayren Press, 193-? 67 p.

LIPPINCOTT, MARGARET MEREDITH
Poems. Oakland, CA.: Eucalyptus Press, 1951. 68 p.

LIPPINCOTT, MARTHA SHEPHERD
Visions of Life. New York & London: The Abbey Press, 1901. 1 p. ℓ., 398 p.

LIPSCHULTZ, JUDITH E.
Streams of Life. New York: Carlton Press, 1960. 4 p. ℓ., 36 p.

LITCHFIELD, ESTHER
Sands of Scituate. Boston: The Stratford Company, 1933. 2 p. ℓ., iii, 63 p.

LITCHFIELD, GRACE DENIO (1849-1944)
Narcissus, and Other Poems. New York and London: G. P. Putnam's Sons, 1908. 2 p. ℓ., iii-v, 60 p.
Collected Poems. New York and London: G. P. Putnam's Sons, 1913. ix, 341 p.
The Song of the Sirens. New York and London: G. P. Putnam's Sons, 1917. 2 p. ℓ., 99 p.
Collected Poems. New York and London: G. P. Putnam's Sons, 1922. x, 413 p.

LITSEY, SARAH
For the Lonely. London: Favil Press, 1937. 56 p.
The Oldest April. Francestown, N.H.: Golden Quill Press, 1957. 56 p.

LITTLE, MARY BETH see LITTLE, MARYBETH (1927-)

LITTLE, MARY WALLACE (BUNDY)
The Rubaiyat of a Huffy Husband. Boston: R. G. Badger, 1908. 31 ℓ.

LITTLE, MARYBETH (1927-) [LITTLE, MARY BETH]
Silk from a Spool. Dallas, TX.: The Kaleidograph Press, 1944. ix p., 2 ℓ., 15-95 p.
Underside of Leaves. Dallas, TX.: Kaleidograph Press, 1948. 76 p.

LITTLEFIELD, HAZEL see SMITH, HAZEL LITTLEFIELD

LIVERMORE, BERTA S.
Indian Legends of the Te-one-sta. Tionesta, PA.: n.p., 1943. 2 p. ℓ., 3-121 p.
________. 2d ed., 1946. 2 p. ℓ., 3-121 p.

LIVERMORE, EDITH PENNOYER
She Who Has Believed. Staten Island, N.Y.: Alba House, 1968. 111 p.

LIVERMORE, MARAIN (SORLIE) (1827-)
Prairie Flowers & Heather Bells; Poems. St. Joseph, MO.: American Printing Company, 1910. viii, [3]-101 p.

LIVINGSTON, LOUISE (1883-)
A Promise; Songs and Sonnets. San Antonio, TX.: Naylor Co., 1952. xii, 36 p.

LIVINGSTON, MIRIAM DRAKE
Meditations for All Minds. Columbus, OH.: The F. J. Heer Printing Co., 1936. 69 p.
Beacon Lights. New York: The Pyramid Press, 1938. 4 p. ℓ., 84 p.

LIVINGSTON, MYRA COHN
Whispers, and Other Poems. New York: Harcourt, Brace, 1958. 48 p.
Wide Awake, and Other Poems. New York: Harcourt, Brace, 1959. 48 p.
I'm Hiding. New York: Harcourt, Brace, 1961. unpaged.
See What I Found. New York: Harcourt, Brace, 1962. unpaged.
The Moon and a Star and Other Poems. New York: Harcourt, Brace & World, 1965. 48 p.
I'm Waiting. New York: Harcourt, Brace & World, 1966. [32] p.
Old Mrs. Twindlytart. New York: Harcourt, Brace & World, 1967. 48 p.
A Time Beyond Us: A Collection of Poetry. New York: Harcourt, Brace and World, 1968. 280 p.
A Crazy Flight, and Other Poems. New York: Harcourt, Brace

& World, 1969. 47, [1] p.
The Malibu, and Other Poems. New York: Atheneum, 1972. 44 p.
The Way Things Are, and Other Poems. New York: Atheneum, 1974. 40 p.

LLOYD, ANNE PORTER (LYNNES) (1874-)
Banked Fires. New York: E. P. Dutton, 1915. [4] p.
Antiques and Amber. New York: The Derrydale Press, 1928. 7 p. ℓ., 103 p., 1 ℓ.
Brief Procession. New York & London: G. P. Putnam's Sons, 1934. xii, 13-106 p.
Antique Shop. Plainfield, N. J.: Printed by the Recorder Press, 1941. 30 p.
Sight and Sound. New York: The Fine Editions Press, 1944. 56 p.

LLOYD, EILEEN WANDIN
Songs of Southern Land. Boston: The Four Seas Company, 1928. 156 p.

LLOYD, MARJORIE LEWIS
Tangled Threads. Portland, OR.: n. p., 1942. [16] p.

LLOYD, SARAH ELIZABETH
Brain Children. Los Angeles, CA.: Commercial Printing House, 1910. [40] p.

LOCHER, LULA LEE
The Rhymed Record. San Antonio, TX.: Naylor Co., 1961. vii, 39 p.

LOCK, MARY LAND
Shadows of the Swamp. Dallas, TX.: The Kaleidograph Press, 1940. x, 1 ℓ., 13-60 p.

LOCKE, LUCIE H. (1904-)
Naturally Yours, Texas; Nature in Texas. San Antonio, TX.: Naylor Co., 1949. 4 p. ℓ., 60 p.

LOCKE, WENDE
Split Hairs. New York: New York University Press, 1970. 64 p.

LODGE, EDITH
Song of the Hill; Selected Poems. Norfolk? VA.: n. p., 1964. 25 p.
Journey Through Noon. Peterborough, N. H.: Windy Row Press, 1974. 64 p.

LOEWENBERG, FLORENCE ELON
The First Adam and Other Poems. Berkeley, CA.: n. p., 1964. [3] ℓ.

Bread Alone. Berkeley, CA.: n.p., 1967. 2 ℓ.
Flushing Meadows. Berkeley, CA.: n.p., 1967. 2 ℓ.
Marching on May Day. Berkeley, CA.: n.p., 1967. 2 ℓ.
Through the Looking Glass and Back. Berkeley, CA.: n.p., 1967. 2 ℓ.

LOFGREN, MAY (NIXON)
Poems. Revere, MA.: A. R. Von Balsan, 1930. 100 p.

LOFTIN, ELOISE
Jumbish. New York: Emerson Hall Publishers, 1972. 40 p.
Barefoot Necklace: Pome(s). Brooklyn, N.Y.: Jamima House, 1975. 40 p.

LOGAN, FRANCES (DEE)
The Heart of a Woman. Dallas, TX.: Wilkinson Pub. Co., 1953. 79 p.

LOGAN, GERTRUDE MOORE
The Rambler. Cedar Rapids, IA.: Torch Press, 1947. 71 p.

LOGAN, JOSEPHINE (HANCOCK)
Lights and Shadows. Chicago: A. Kroch, 1932. 101 p.
Heights and Depths. Chicago: A. Kroch, 1935. 93 p.
The Collected Poems of Josephine Hancock Logan. Chicago: A. Kroch and Son, 1942. 9 p. ℓ., 226 p., 1 ℓ.

LOGAN, MILDRED DOWNARD (1892-)
Smouldering Fires, and Other Poems. New York: Exposition Press, 1959. 58 p.

LOGAN, MYRTLE FULLER
The Vase of Bronze. Boston: The Christopher Publishing House, 1927. 45 p.

LOGAN, ROSIE LEE (1924-)
Tender Clusters. San Antonio, TX.: Naylor, 1969.

LOGUE, EMILY ROSE (1876-)
Shadows of an Ideal: Poems. Philadelphia: P. Reilly, 1902. 30 ℓ.
"The Quiet Hour" and Other Verses. Philadelphia: D. Reilly, 1907. 7 p. ℓ., 3-69 p.

LOMAX, PEARL CLEAGE (1948-)
We Don't Need No Music. Detroit: Broadside, 1972. 16 p.

LOMBARDI, HELEN PISARELLI
From the Deep. Brooklyn, N.Y.: T. Gaus' Sons, 1966. 5 p. ℓ., 57 p.

LONG, BEE BEACHERIG
Reflections. Dexter, MO.: Candor Press, 1964. 60 p.

Where Treasures Lie. San Antonio, TX.: Naylor Co., 1967. x, 62 p.

LONG, C. THERESSA
Night Thoughts and Day Dreams. Chicago: Press of the Blakely-Oswald Dreams, 1916. 224 p.

LONG, CARLOTTA ESPIE
Muse Upon These. New York: Vantage Press, 1950. 63 p.

LONG, EVELYN
The Hand of God, and Other Poems. New York: Vantage Press, 1963. 41 p.
Worth Remembering; Poems. New York: Exposition Press, 1965. 46 p.

LONG, LILY AUGUSTA (d. 1927)
The Singing Place and Other Poems. Chicago: The Bookfellows(!), 1922. 63 p. (The Little Bookfellow series)

LONG, MABEL SPAUN (1904-)
Country Grandma. Lebo, KA.: Lebo Enterprise, 1957. 26 p.
Doc's Ology II. Danbury, CT.: Published by T. N. P. C., 1965. 28 p.
Pieces of Eight. Danbury, CT.: Published by T. N. P. C., 1966. 32, [2] p.
The Glory of My Scaffold. Los Angeles, CA.: Jackson's Mimeo Service, 1967. 19, [1] p.
Play House of Verse. Danbury, CT.: Published by T. N. P. C., 1967. 52, [2] p.
A Blossom Fell. Valley Center, KA.: Robbins Print. Co., 1968. 24 p.
Roses Bloom for People. n. p., 1971. 48 p.

LONG, MILDRED (1893-)
Hidden Springs. Emory University, Atlanta, GA. & New York: Banner Press, 1938. 36 p. (Golden westward ho! Poetry Bookshelf)
Triumph of Faith. Durham, N. C.: Religion and Health Press, 1954. 29 p.
Listen to the Silence; Meditations. Los Angeles, CA.: De Vorss, 1970. 95 p.

LONG, NAOMI CORNELIA see MADGETT, NAOMI CORNELIA (LONG) (1923-)

LONG, SARA LOUISE
Sundial. Dallas, TX.: The Story Book Press, 1946. 48 p.

LONG, WENDY
Wild Birds and Others; Poems. Millbrae, CA.: Celestial Arts, 1973. 96 p.

LONGFELLOW, MARIAN see O'DONOGHUE, MARIAN ADELE

LONGLEY, SNOW
Sonnets of Spinsterhood; The Spinster's Book of Dreams, Delicate Traceries of Dim Desires. San Francisco, CA.: Paul Elder & Company, 1915. [28] p.

LOONEY, LILLIE LITTRELL
Out of the Mist. San Antonio, TX.: Naylor Co., 1967. vii, 33 p.

LOOS, MADGE
Puppet Without Worlds. Francestown, N. H.: Golden Quill Press, 1969. 80 p.

LOPEZ, BLANCHE
Rubaiyat of a Chronic Golfer. New York: n. p., 1923.

LORD, ALICE EMMA (SAUERWEIN) (1848-1930)
Moods and Tenses. Richmond, VA.: The William Byrd Press, Inc., 1929. 53, [2] p.

LORD, GIGI
Toppling After Itself; Selected Poems. Fort Smith, AR.: South and West, 1969. 48 p.

LORD, MAY CARLETON (1883-)
On the Mown Grass. Denver, CO.: A. Swallow, 1961. 48 p.
On a High Hill. Winston-Salem, N. C.: John F. Blair, 1973. 54 p.

LORDE, AUDRÉ (1934-)
The First Cities. New York: The Poets Press, Inc., 1968. [32] p.
Cables to Rage. London: Paul Breman, 1970. 28 p. (Heritage series, v. 9)
_______. 2d ed., 1973.
From a Land Where Other People Live. Detroit: Broadside Press, 1973. 46 p.
New York Head Shop and Museum. Detroit: Broadside Press, 1975. 56 p.

LORENZINI, MARIA (1885-)
Seeding Democracy. Berkeley, CA.: The Gillick Press, 1943. 2 p. ℓ., 7-64 p.
Singing Stones. San Francisco, CA.: Priv. print., 1945. 87 p.

LORING, MATTIE BALCH
The Stranger. New York: The Abbey Press, 1900. 1 p. ℓ., 80 p.

LORRAINE, BARBARA
Ravellings. Boston: The Stratford Company, 1926. 2 p. ℓ., 81 p.

LOSSY, RELLA
Dryad. No Paint Nor Page. Berkeley? n.p., 1956. [4] p.
Audible Dawn. Alamo, CA.: Holmgangers Press, 1975. [36] p.

LOTHERINGTON, ALICE (1870-) [Full Name: Mary Alice Lotherington.]
Flower Songs, and Others. Boston: Sherman, French & Company, 1914. 3 p. ℓ., 45 p.

LOTT, CLARINDA HARRISS
The Bone Tree: Poems. Baltimore, MD.: New Poets Series, 1971. [20] p.

LOTT, ELSIE (MOORE)
Wagons Rolled West, and Other Poems. Salt Lake City, UT.: Printed by Stevens & Wallis, 1955. ix, 62 p.

LOTT, JULIA
Morning Canticle. New York: Vantage Press, 1950. 87 p.

LOTT, MELVINA ADELE
Facts and Fancies. Los Angeles, CA.: The Author, 1921. [47] ℓ.
Sense and Nonsense. Los Angeles, CA.: n.p., 1924. 105 p.
Facts and Fancies. Los Angeles, CA.: The Author, 1929. 85 p.
Truth and Fiction. Los Angeles? CA.: n.p., 1937. 77 p., 1 ℓ.

LOUCHHEIM, KATIE SCOFIELD (1903-)
With or Without Roses. Garden City, N.Y.: Doubleday and Co., 1966. vii, 64 p.

LOUCKS, VERA M.
Essence of Living. Fort St. John, B.C.: Printed by Alaska Highway News, 1956. 22 p.

LOUD, ETHEL GODFREY (1878-)
Pot Pourri. Portland, ME.: The Dirigo Editions, 1940. 6 p. ℓ., 3-53 p.
Facets. Portland, ME.: Falmouth Publishing House, 1946. vii, [1], 36 p.

LOUGHBOROUGH, CAROLINE
Fragments. Baltimore, MD.: Margie H. Luckett, 1931. 56 p.

LOUGHRAN, HELEN G.
"Hello Teacher." Boston: Chapman & Grimes, 1955. 44 p.

LOUIS, LOUISE
...This Is for You. New York: The William-Frederick Poets, 1947. 4 p. ℓ., 55 p. (William-Frederick poets, no. 37)
The Dervish Dance; Poems of Purpose. N.J.: Westwood Pub. Co., 1958. 40 p.

The Scarlet Net; Collected Poems. Westwood, N. J.: Pen-Art Publishers, 1972. 68 p.

LOUNSBERY, GRACE CONSTANT
An Iseult Idyll, and Other Poems. London & New York: J. Lane, 1901. viii, 79 p.
Love's Testament: A Sonnet Sequence. London & New York: John Lane, 1906. 3 p. ℓ., 135 p.
Poems of Revolt, and Satan Unbound. New York: Moffat, Yard and Company, 1911. 4 p. ℓ., 3-125 p.

LOUTHAN, HATTIE (HORNER) (1865-)
Thoughts Adrift. Boston: R. G. Badger, 1902. 4 p. ℓ., [13]-56 p., 1 ℓ.
Alone in the Afterglow. Denver, CO.: Pub. for the University of Denver by the Baltes Co., 1939. 2 p. ℓ., 7-65, [3] p.

LOVE, ADELAIDE WARREN (PETERSON)
The Slender Singing Tree. New York: Dodd, Mead & Company, 1933. xiv, 102 p.
The Crystal Flute. New York: Dodd, Mead & Company, 1935. xii p., 2 ℓ., 3-75 p.
_______. 2d ed., 1935.
The Star and the Leaf. New York: Dodd, Mead & Company, 1946. xii, 94 p.
Enchanted Drum. Chicago: Dierkes Press, 1950. 32 p.
The Delicate Harp. Chicago: Dierkes Press, 1951. 39 p.

LOVE, BETH
...Ad Lib; A Rambling Book of Verse. Philadelphia: Dorrance and Company, 1937. 50 p. (Contemporary poets of Dorrance, 157)

LOVE, JANE GROOME
Earth-Child. Dallas, TX.: The Kaleidoscope Publishers, 1931. 4 p. ℓ., 41 p.

LOVE, JEANETTE F.
The Fall and Rise of Cushan, and Other Poems. Columbus, OH.: The Stoneman Press Co., 1911. 63 p.

LOVE, KATHERINE NEAL
Passing By. Boston: Christopher Pub. House, 1932. 4 p. ℓ., 11-34 p.

LOVE, MARTHA CORRINE
Thoughts in the Garden of Prayer; Religious Poems. New York: Greenwich Book Publishers, 1958. 48 p.

LOVERIDGE, ROSABEL NOWRY
One Golden Day; Poems. East Poultney, VT.: n. p., 1964. 5 p. ℓ., 64 p.

LOW, MARY
Tres Voces, Three Voices. Habana: Editorial Sanchez, 1957. 94 p.

LOW, MARY CROMWELL
The Lode Star. New York: J. T. White & Co., 1920. 127 p.

LOW, MAY AUSTIN (1863-)
Confession, and Other Verses. Boston: Sherman, French & Company, 1909. 4 p. ℓ., 11-47 p.

LOWATER, NINETTE (MAINE) (1844-)
Songs from the Wayside. Spring Valley, WI.: The Sun Press, 1906. 121, [5] p.
_______. 1908.

LOWELL, AMY (1874-1925)
A Dome of Many Colored Glass. Boston and New York: Houghton Mifflin Co., 1912. xi, 139, [1] p.
Sword Blades and Poppy Seed. New York: Macmillan Co., 1914. xviii, 246 p.
Men, Women and Ghosts. New York: The Macmillan Co., 1916. xv, 363 p.
Can Grande's Castle. New York: The Macmillan Co., 1918. xvii, 232 p.
_______. Boston: Houghton Mifflin Co., 1921. xvii, 232 p.
Pictures of the Floating World. New York: The Macmillan Co., 1919. xx, 237 p.
Can Grande's Castle. Oxford: Basil Blackwell, Broad Street, 1920. xvii, 196 p.
Legends. Boston and New York: Houghton Mifflin and The Riverside Press, Cambridge, 1921. xiv p., 2 ℓ., [3]-289 p.
Pictures of the Floating World. Boston and New York: Houghton Mifflin Co., 1921. xx, 257 p.
The House in Main Street. n. p.: Privately printed? 1922? [14] p.
Can Grande's Castle. Oxford: Basil Blackwell, Broad Street, 1924. xvii, 232 p.
_______. Boston & New York: Houghton Mifflin Co., 1925. xvii p., 1 ℓ., 232 p.
What's O'Clock. Boston and New York: Houghton Mifflin Co., 1925. x, 240 p.
_______. London: J. Cape, 1925.
East Wind. Boston and New York: Houghton Mifflin Co., 1926. 4 p. ℓ., [3]-240 p.
Ballads for Sale. Boston and New York: Houghton Mifflin Co., 1927. xii, 311 p.
Fool o' the Moon. Austin, TX.: Priv. print. by J. S. Mayfield, 1927. [4] p.
The Madonna of Carthagena. n. p.: Privately printed, 1927. [20] p.
Selected Poems of Amy Lowell. Ed. by John Livingston Lowes. Boston and New York: Houghton, Mifflin Co., 1927. ix,

244 p.
Complete Poetical Works. Boston: Houghton Mifflin Co., 1955. xxix, 607 p.
Complete Poetical Works of Amy Lowell. Cambridge ed. Boston: Houghton Mifflin Co., 1955. xxix, 607 p.
The Touch of You; Amy Lowell's Poems of Love and Beauty. Selected by Peter Seymour. Kansas City, MO.: Hallmark Cards Inc., 1972. (Hallmark editions)

LOWERY, CAROL LYNN ROWE
Carol Lynn, A Self-Portrait in Verse. New York: Exposition Press, 1958. 54 p.

LOWES, KATHRYN HOWARD
The Lark's on the Wing. Prairie City, IL.: The Decker Press, 1948. 80 p.

LOWNSBURY, JEANETTE (1901-)
Tenacity in Winter. Prairie City, IL.: Decker Press, 1948. 76 p.

LOWREY, CATHERINE PEARL (FAWCETT)
Nuggets of Thought. Philadelphia: Dorrance, 1963. 40 p.

LOWTHER, WINIFRED E. (1882-)
Winds and Tides. San Antonio, TX.: Naylor Co., 1964. viii, 24 p.
The Old Beach Road. San Antonio, TX.: Naylor, 1973. vi, 91 p.

LOYLES, LENA MYRTLE
...A Religious Garden of Verses. New York: Fortuny's, 1940. 7 p. ℓ., 17-142 p.

LUCAS, ALLIE ISABEL (1858-)
The Raven's Leaf, Poems.... A Message of Spiritual Light, Power, Guidance, Rapture, Harmony and Revelation. Los Angeles, CA.: Fowler Brothers, 1907. 168 p.

LUCAS, ELIZA SYMMES
Toast and Tea. Columbus, OH.: Champlin Press, 1919. 75 p.

LUCAS, GEORGIA B.
Prelude. Austin, TX.: Printed by the Steck Company, 1946. [80] p.

LUCAS, VIRGINIA (1871-)
...June; A Year Book of Sonnets. Strasburg, VA.: Shenandoah Publishing House, 1927. 90 p.

LUCEY, MARY A.
Lavender and Laurel; Poems. New York: The Exposition Press, 1947. 63 p.

LUCK, LAURA
Poems of Love and Wit. Boston: Bruce Humphries, 1956. 175 p.

LUKE, ISOBEL
Mother, Love, and Garden Poems. Boston: Fisher Co., 1921. 15 p.

LUKEI, VESTA NICKERSON (1913-)
Mild Silver and Furious Gold. Redlands, CA.: Citrograph Press, 1952. 63 p.

LUKES, MILLIE
Thoughts and Musings. Chicago, IL.: n.p., 1931. 30 p.

LUND, DORIS HEROLD
Did You Ever? New York: Parents' Magazine Press, 1965. [34] p.
Attic of the Wind. New York: Parents' Magazine Press, 1966. [36] p.
Hello, Baby. Norwalk, CT.: C. R. Gibson, 1968. 89 p.

LUOMALA, KATHARINE
Voices on the Wind; Polynesian Myths and Chants. Honolulu: Bishop Museum Press, 1955. 101 p.

LUPTAK, EMILIA
Melody. Norwood, MA.: The Tower Publishing Company, 1942. [31] p.

LURIE, HANNAH ROSS
The Edge of an Era, and Other Poems. Philadelphia: Philadelphia Chapter of the National Organization for Women, 1973. 82 p.
Journeys Beyond the Edge of an Era, and Other Poems. 2d ed. Port Washington, N.Y.: Ashley Books, 1975. 116 p.

LUSCHEI, GLENNA
Letter to the North. Carta al Norte. Medellin: Talleres de Carpel-Antorcha, 1967. 71 p. (Ediciones papel sobrante, v. 6)
Back into My Body. Berkeley, CA.: Thorp Springs Press, 1974. 75 p.
Spring Break-up. Albuquerque, N.M.: Grasshopper, 1975.

LUSK, ANGELA
Plumes of Song. New York: H. Harrison, 1934. 63 p.

LUSTER, HELEN
A Watcher from That Moment, & Circle Built in: Poems. Los Angeles, CA.: Graphic Eye Press, 1968. 100 p.
The House of Di. San Rafael, CA.: Fur Line Press; dist. by Band H. Books, 1974. [91] p. (HerI(EE), book 4)

LUTTRELL, GEORGIA BELLE
Beyond Doubt's Shadow. New York: Vantage Press, 1963. 72 p.

LUTZ, GERTRUDE MAY (1899-)
Point the Sun Tomorrow. Francestown, N. H.: Golden Quill Press, 1956. 60 p.
More Than Image. Francestown, N. H.: Golden Quill Press, 1966. 87 p.
Song for a New Generation. Francestown, N. H.: Golden Quill Press, 1971. 92 p.
Time Is the Traveler. Francestown, N. H.: Golden Quill Press, 1975. 80 p.

LUTZ, HELEN GERTRUDE
Out Where the West Begins; A Collection of Poetry. New York: William-Frederick Press, 1969. 32 p.

LU VAILE, LYRA (1887-)
This Magic Hour. Batavia, N. Y.: Verservice, 1944. 63 p.

LYMAN, CAROLYN BELLE (PALMER) (1865-)
Fallen Leaves. New York: E. C. Hill, 1913. 63 p.

LYNCH, SOPHRONIA BRINKLEY
Allegheny and Aurora, and Other Poems. Washington ? D. C.: n. p., 1911. 75 p.

LYNN, CLARA A.
Poems of Ye Olden Times; Souvenir, Three Hundredth Anniversary, Portsmouth, New Hampshire, 1623-1923. Amesbury, MA.: n. p., 1923. 68 p.
Poems about Portsmouth. Amesbury, MA.: The Whittier Press, 1929. 3 p. ℓ., 9-68 p.

LYON, LINDA GALE
June's Verses. Rochester, N. Y.: n. p., 1924. 6 p. ℓ., 11-100 p.

LYONS, AMY V.
Christmas Eve's Gift. Chula Vista, CA.: Denrich Press, 1932. [20] p.

LYONS, JENNIE T., pseud.
To My Love; Poems. New York: Exposition Press, 1951. 62 p.

LYTLE, RUBY
What Is the Moon? (Japanese Haiku Sequence). Rutland, VT.: C. E. Tuttle, 1965. 32 p.

LYTTLE, KATHARINE WILLIAMS
Words. Boston: Christopher Pub. House, 1947. 77 p.

LYTTLETON, LUCY BLANCHE see MASTERMAN, LUCY BLANCHE (LYTTLETON) (1884-)

MAAK, EMME
Songs and Poems. Binghamton & New York: Priv. pub. by Vail-Ballou Company, 1914. 52 p.

MABEE, ESTHER (SWART) (1836-)
The Complete Poems of Mrs. G. S. Mabee. Elroy, WI.: The Ericson Co., 1904. 2 p. ℓ., 80 p.

MABEY, NELL
Clover Blooms. Emory University, Atlanta, GA.: Banner Press, 1938. 56 p. (Golden westward ho! Poetry bookshelf)
Whimpie of Bramble Haw. Rockport, ME.: Falmouth Pub. House, 1955. 86 p.

McALLASTER, ELVA ARLINE (1922-)
My Heart Hears Heaven's Reveille. Winona Lake, IN.: Light and Life Press, 1954. 94 p.
Echoes from Intercession. Chicago: Moody Press, 1966. 61 p.
Here and Now. Chicago: Moody Press, 1968. 61 p.

McALLISTER, CLAIRE
Arms of Light, Selected First Poems. New York: A. Knopf, 1964. viii, 71 p.

McALLISTER, ELVA SINCLAIR
Poems. Atlanta, Ga.: Parks Print. Co., 1952. 148 p.

McASSEY, MABEL MOREFIELD
Reflections in Verse. Chicago: n.p., 1934. 2 p. ℓ., 39 p.

McAULAY, MARGARET CRAIG
Christmas Light in San Francisco. San Francisco, CA.: Greenwood Press, 1954. 8 p.

McBAIN, BARBARA MAHONE
Sugarfields. Detroit: Broadside Press, 1970.

McBRIDE, ELLA GRAFF
The Silver Loom; A First Book of Poems. Muscatine, IA.: Weis-Lupton Printing Company, 1928. 33 p., 1 ℓ.

McBROWN, GERTRUDE PARTHENIA
The Picture-Poetry-Book. Washington: Associated, 1935.

McBURNEY, HELEN MITCHELL
Fangs to the Wind; Poems. New York: Exposition Press, 1951. 56 p.

McCAHAN, BELLE TRAVERS
Blowing Bubbles. Kirksville, MO.: The Journal Printing Company, 1941. 240 p.

McCAHAN, LILLIAN
The Year 'Round (in a Little Town); A Record in Verse of a Year in the Life of a Pennsylvania Village. New York: Harbinger House, 1940. 60 p.

McCALL, SIDNEY, pseud. see FENOLLOSA, MARY McNEILL

McCANDLESS, ESTELLA STOKES
Echoes Through the Purple Twilight. New York: Vantage Press, 1962. 60 p.

McCANN, FANNIE G.
Songs in the Night. Minneapolis, MN.: Holiness Methodist Publishing Co., 1932. 52 p.

McCANN, REBECCA (1897-1927)
The Annabel Books. Garden City, N.Y.: Doubleday, Page & Company, 1918. 2 v.
About Annabel; Her Strange and Wonderful Adventures. New York: J. Martin's Book House, 1922. 1 v. (unpaged)
The Cheerful Cherub. Chicago: Covici-McGee, 1923. 8 p.ℓ., 5-208 p.
_______. Chicago: P. Covici, 1927. 8 p.ℓ., 287 p.
Bitter Sweet. New York: Covici, Friede, 1929. xviii p., 2 ℓ., 3-84 p.
The Cheerful Cherub. New ed. New York: Covici, Friede, 1929. 8 p.ℓ., 287 p.
The Cheerful Cherub. First Series. New York: Covici-Friede, 1930. 8 p.ℓ., 287 p.
The Cheerful Cherub, Second Series. New York: Covici, Friede, 1930. 5 p.ℓ., 310 p.
Children's Cheerful Cherub. New York: Covici, Friede, 1932. [63] p.
Complete Cheerful Cherub; 1001 Verses. New York: Covici, Friede, 1932. 512 p.

McCARTHY, FRANCES BOYLE
A Peek Through My Window. New York: Vantage Press, 1963. 122 p.

McCARTNEY, DOROTHY
Lemmus, Lemmus and Other Poems. Boston: Branden Press, 1973. 60 p.

McCARTNEY, HAZEL (SEVERSON)
Poems about Jackie. New York: Vantage Press, 1954. 5 p.ℓ., 90 p.

McCARTY, FLORA L.
My Words Are the Swords; A Collection of Poetry. New York: Vantage Press, 1968. 64 p.

McCASLIN, ELIZABETH
First Came the Night. Philadelphia: Dorrance, 1961. 3 p. ℓ., 26 p.

McCAULEY, EVA
Ring, Ring, A Rhapsody; Poems. New York: Carlton Press, 1968. 65 p.

McCLAIN, NAOMI STEVENS
Thoughts Along the Trail. Bellefontaine, OH.: n. p., 1944. 47 p.

McCLAURIN, IRMA
Black Chicago: Poems. New York: Rannick Playwrights, 1971. [32] p.
Poem I. New York: Rannick Playwrights, 1971. 32 p.
Songs in the Night. n. p.: Pearl Press, 1974.

McCLEARY, CORNELIA WALTER
The Celestial Circus. Boston: The Cornhill Company, 1920. xii p., 1 ℓ., 89 p.

McCLELLAN, EFFIE
Worm on a Leaf. Dallas, TX.: Mathis, Van Nort Company, 1940. 5 p. ℓ., 52 p.

McCLINTOCK, SARA H.
Hasty Puddin'; New England Folk Poems. New York: The Poets Press, 1935. 6 p. ℓ., 15-78 p.

McCLOSKEY, EUNICE MILDRED (LON COSKE) (1906-)
Coal Dust and Crystals. New York: H. Harrison, 1939. 64 p.
Strange Alchemy. North Montpelier, VT.: The Driftwind Press, 1940. 70 p.
The Heart Knows This. North Montpelier, VT.: The Driftwind Press, 1944. 82 p.
This Is the Hour. Prairie City, IL.: Decker Press, 1948. 71 p.
These Rugged Hills. Ridgeway? PA.: The Author, 1954. 64 p.
Symbols of My Life. Philadelphia, PA.: Dorrance, 1970. 88 p.
The Last Furrow: or, The End of the Road for Me. Ridgway, PA?: McCloskey? 1975? 85 p.

McCLUNG, BARBARA ADAIR
The Hidden Self; Poems. New York: Exposition Press, 1954. 64 p.

McCONKEY, SUE
The View from Douglas Hill; A Collection of Poems. Sanbornville, N. H.: Wake-Brook House, 1958. 65 p., 1 ℓ.
Hold Bright the Star; A Book of Poems. Sanbornville, N. H.: Wake-Brook House, 1963. 86 p.

McCONNEL, MARION TRUMBULL
The Jaundiced I. New York: Pageant Press, 1962. 6 p. ℓ., 93 p.

MacCORMACK, VERONICA E.
Doodle of Dee. New York: Vantage Press, 1959. 43 p.

McCORMIC, DACITA (1910-)
What Else Is There! New York: Beechhurst Press, 1949. 64 p.

McCORMICK, VIRGINIA TAYLOR (1873-)
The Hermit, and Other Poems. New York: The New York Poetry Book Shop, 1920. 32? p.
Star-Dust and Gardens. Norwood, MA.: The Plimpton Press, 1920. 3 p. ℓ., 77 p.
Voices of the Wind. New York: J. T. White & Co., 1924. 5 p. ℓ., 3-88 p.
... Radio to Daedalus. Norfolk, VA.: Atlantic Coast Printing Company, 1931. v-xiv, 107, [1] p.
Winter Apples. New York: G. P. Putnam's Sons, 1942. xii p., 1 ℓ., 15-95 p.

McCOUN, ALICE TROXWELL
And Now I Share With You.... New York: The Poets Press, 1941. 63 p.
Limitless Supply; Poems. Denver, CO.: Big Mountain Press, 1961. 54 p.

McCOY, ANNIE WILSON
Youthful Fancies: A Collection of Verses. Baltimore, MD.: J. Murphy Co., 1901. 4 p. ℓ., 58 p.

McCOY, TRUDA (1902-)
"Till the Frost." Pikeville, KY.: n.p., 1952. 15 p.
The Tempter's Harvest. Findlay, OH.: Ellisonian Manse of the Muses, 1954. 79 p.
Winds Will Quote. Chicago: Windfall Press, 1962. 3 p. ℓ., 28 p.

McCROSSAN, MALINDA BELL
The Plainsmen of the Plains, A Narrative of Realism. Amarillo, TX.: Printed by Russel Stationery Co., 1937. [116] p.

McCULLOCH, ELIZABETH ASHFIELD (WALKER)
Far Horizons. Philadelphia: Dorrance & Co., 1933. 48 p. (Contemporary poets of Dorrance, 113)

McCULLOCH, ELIZABETH (McCORMICK) (1865-)
Life's Yesterdays. Eugene, OR.: Shelton-Turnbull-Fuller Co., 1939. 4 p. ℓ., 5-80, [3] p.
A Supplement to Life's Yesterdays. Eugene, OR? n.p., 1944. 20 p.

McCULLOUGH, MABEL L.
From the Heart of a Nurse. San Antonio, TX.: The Naylor Company, 1941. 64 p.

McCURDY, ADA EMERY
Dreams at Twilight. New Albany, IN.: n.p., 1921.

McCURDY, FLORENCE CALDWELL
Greek Heritage and Other Poems. Mill Valley, CA.: Wings Press, 1961. 76 p.

McCURTAIN, LUCILE V.
The After Image.... New York: The William-Frederick Press, 1946. 3 p. ℓ., 7-46 p. (The William-Frederick poets, no. 24)
High Moment. 2d ed. London: Brookside Press, 1957. 71 p.
Thresholds of Awareness. Seattle, WA.: Ballard Printing and Publishing Co., 1966. 81 p.

McDANIEL, HELEN PLEASANTS
War Poems, 1861-1865. New York, London: The Abbey Press, 1901. 1 p. ℓ., 5-110 p.

McDANIEL, LAURA WINANS
The Singer in the Night. Boston: B. Humphries, 1938. xiv, 15-60 p.

McDAVITT, ALICE PYNE
The Homesteader, and Other Poems. New York: The Cosmopolitan Press, 1913. 80 p.

McDERMOTH, CORA A.
...Almost Sleepy Time. Boston: The Stratford Company, 1929. 32 p. (The Stratford poets)

MacDERMOTT, CLARE
There Shall Be Twilights and Other Poems. Dallas, TX.: Turner Company, 1935. 4 p. ℓ., 65 p.

McDERMOTT, MAUD REED
Pen Pictures from a Trail Through the Years. Los Angeles, CA.: Skelton Publishing Company, 1928. 165 p.

McDEVITT, MARIE MARGARITA, Sister
Pocket Poems. New York: Vantage Press, 1969. 61 p.

MacDONALD, ALICE FRASER
...Skimmings. Philadelphia: Dorrance and Company, 1936. 63 p. (Contemporary poets of Dorrance, 149)

McDONALD, ANNA SINGLETON
Columbia, The Land of the Free. New York & Washington: The Neale Publishing Company, 1907. 42 p.

McDONALD, ANNIE CLYDE
Starfield After Twilight. Emory University, Atlanta, GA.: Banner Press, 1957. 71 p.

McDONALD, BEATRICE
Treasured Thoughts. Birmingham, MI.: The Author, 1927. v-xii, 102 p.

McDONALD, CLARA SEEBER
Simple Poems. Boelus, NB.: n.p., 1932. 52 p.

MacDONALD, CYNTHIA
Amputations; Poems. New York: G. Braziller, 1972. 80 p.

MacDONALD, JANET
Tales in Rhyme, by a World War Nurse. Detroit, MI.: n.p., 1935. 26 p.

MacDONALD, JESSICA NELSON (NORTH) (1894-)
A Prayer Rug. Chicago: W. Ransom, 1923. 4 p.ℓ., 7-44 p. (Series of first volumes: no. 5)
The Long Leash. Boston & New York: Houghton Mifflin Company, 1928. vi p., 1 ℓ., 75, [1] p.
Dinner Party; Poems. Muscatine, IA.: Prairie Press, 1942. 82 p.

MacDONALD, SUSANNE RIKE
The Silver Cord. Beverly Hills, CA.: Print. by the Citizen Press, 1933. 59 p.
________. 2d enl. ed. New York: Exposition Press, 1958. 64 p.

MacDONALD, VIRGINIA
Lines and Lyrics. New York: L. Rovere, 1925. [59] p.

McDOUGALL, JO
A Lemon Yeast and Other Mornings. Fort Smith, AR.: South & West, 1965. 43 p.

McDOWELL, LAURA M. (BANKS)
Down Ways of Wonder. San Antonio, TX.: Carleton Printing Co., 1944. 55 p.

McDOWELL, LILLIE GILLILAND
Grandma; A Collection of Poems for Children and Grown-Ups. Topeka, KA.: n.p., 1913. 48 p.
________. 2d ed., rev. and enl. Topeka, KA.: Printed by Capper Printing Company, 1922. 2 p.ℓ., [7]-67 p.

McDOWELL, MARTHA AUSTIN
Christmas Hymn, and Other Poems. New York: L. F. White Company, 1938. 36 p.

McDOWELL, NANCY JOYCE
The First Snow. Cambridge, MA.: Larry Stark Press, 1967. [32] p.

McELEVEY, EVA LITTLE
Dad and I. New York: E. P. Dutton & Co., Inc., 1930. 4 p. ℓ., 11-110 p.

McELROY, COLLEEN
The Mules Done Long Since Gone. n. p.: Harrison-Madronna Press, 1973.

McELWAIN, ETHYL
Sunset Gold. Washington Court House, OH.: The Author, 1938. vi, 56 p.

McFADEN, MILDRED SUSAN (GARRETT) (1860-)
Blossoms by the Wayside; Verses. Kansas City, MO.: Hudson-Kimberly Publishing Co., 1904. 105 p.

McFALLS, CORNELIA A. (PIERCE) (1831-1909?)
Forget-Me-Nots, and Other Poems. Boston: R. G. Badger, 1910. 139 p.

McFARLAND, JEANNETTE
The Guernsey Hills and Other Sketches. Cambridge, OH.: The Callihan & Stottlemire Company, 1930. 86 p.
Roses and Rainbows. Cambridge, OH.: Southeastern Print. Co., 1952. 8 p. ℓ., 106 p.

MacFARLANE, DAISY (MARSH)
Waves in Wind-Bent Grass, and Other Poems. New York: Vantage Press, 1957. 53 p.

MacFARLANE, KATHRYN JEAN (1904-)
I Live Upon an Island; Poems of Hawaii. Honolulu, HA.: Tongg Publishing Company, 1940. 2 p. ℓ., 5-62 p.

McFARLANE, MYRA
The Fat Executioner. n. p.: Very Stone House in Transit, 1971. 12 p.

McGAFFIN, AUDREY ROMOSER (1913-)
The Imagined Country. Baltimore, MD.: Editions Image, 1957. 32 p.

McGAHEY, JEANNE
Oregon Winter. Andes, N. Y.: Woolmer/Brotherson Ltd., 1973. 58 p.

McGAUGHEY, HELEN (1904-)
Wind Across the Night. Emory University, Atlanta, GA.: Banner Press, 1938. 48 p.

Music in the Wind. Emory University, Atlanta, GA.: Banner Press, 1941. 48 p.
Spring Is a Blue Kite. Emory University, Atlanta, GA.: Banner Press, 1946. 64 p.
Reaching for the Spring; Poems. New York: Exposition Press, 1958. 48 p.
Selected Poems. Roma: Centro Studi e Scambi Internazionali, 1961. 16 p.

MacGAVIN, ELIZABETH CUSHING
Sweet & Bitter. Philadelphia: Dorrance, 1971. vii, 45 p. (Contemporary poets of Dorrance)

McGEE, EDITH E.
Poems of Faith. Boston: The Stratford Company, 1937. 4 p. ℓ., 7-80 p.

McGEE, MARGARET B.
No Other Lantern. Portland, ME.: House of Falmouth, 1964. 90 p.

McGEE, MAUD
To Get My Name in the Kingdom Book. Atlanta, GA.: The Author, 1963.

McGEHEE, ELISE
Small Voice. New Orleans, LA.: R. L. Crager, 1960. 76 p.

McGEORGE, ALICE SUTTON
Autumn Leaves; A Collection of Poems. Kansas City, MO.: Burton Publishing Company, 1938. 2 p. ℓ., 9-191 p.

McGETTIGAN, FRANCISCA CARRILLO (VALLEJO)
Along the Highway of the King. San Francisco, CA.: The Howell-North Press, 1943. 1 p. ℓ., 5-104 p., 1 ℓ.
San Francisco Souvenir. San Francisco, CA.: n.p., 1956. 32 p.

McGIFFERT, GERTRUDE HUNTINGTON (BOYCE)
A Florentine Cycle, and Other Poems. New York & London: G. P. Putnam's Sons, 1915. xii, 217 p.
Cast in Bronze. Portland, ME.: The Mosher Press, 1929. ix, 96, [1] p., 1 ℓ.
The Tree of Time. New York: G. P. Putnam's Sons, 1936. xii p., 1 ℓ., 15-251 p.
Radio Concert from Palestrina to Gershwin. New York: G. P. Putnam's Sons, 1942. xv, 191, [1] p.
Gargoyles and Flying Buttresses. New York: G. P. Putnam's Sons, 1943. xi, 13-86 p.

McGINLEY, PHYLLIS (1905-) [Full Name: Phyllis Louise McGinley.]
...On the Contrary. Garden City, N.Y.: Doubleday, Doran & Company, Inc., 1934. vii, [1], 119 p.

One More Manhattan. New York: Harcourt, Brace and Company, 1937. ix, 133 p.
A Pocketful of Wry. New York: Duell, Sloan, and Pearce, 1940. vii, 152 p.
Husbands Are Difficult; or, The Book of Oliver Ames. New York: Duell, Sloan and Pearce, 1941. x, 85, [1] p.
Stones from a Glass House; New Poems. New York: The Viking Press, 1946. 169 p.
All Around the Town. Philadelphia: Lippincott, 1948. [63] p.
The Love Letters of Phyllis McGinley. New York: Viking Press, 1954. 116 p.
_______. London: J. M. Dent & Sons, 1955. ix, 109 p.
_______. New York: Viking Press, 1956. 116 p. "Compass Books ed."
A Pocketful of Wry. Newly rev. ed. New York: Grosset & Dunlap, 1959. vii, 152 p.
Sugar and Spice; The ABC of Being a Girl. New York: F. Watts, 1960. unpaged.
Times Three; Selected Verse From Three Decades, With Seventy New Poems. New York: Viking Press, 1960. xvi, 304 p.
Mince Pie and Mistletoe. Philadelphia: J. B. Lippincott, 1961. 1 v. unpaged.
Times Three; Selected Verse From Three Decades, With Seventy New Poems. London: Secker & Warburg, 1961. xvi, 304 p.
Boys Are Awful. New York: F. Watts, 1962. unpaged.
A Girl and Her Room. New York: F. Watts, 1963. [31] p.
The Love Letters of Phyllis McGinley. New York: Viking Press, 1963. 116 p.
How Mrs. Santa Claus Saved Christmas. Philadelphia: Lippincott, 1963. 32 p.
Wonderful Time. Philadelphia: Lippincott, 1966. 47 p.
A Wreath of Christmas Legends. New York: Macmillan, 1967. 62 p.
Times Three; Selected Verse From Three Decades, With Seventy New Poems. New York: Viking Press, 1968. 304 p. "Compass Book"
A Wreath of Christmas Legends. Toronto: Macmillan, 1969. 62 p.
Confessions of a Reluctant Optimist; Poems. Kansas City, MO.: Hallmark Cards, 1973. 59 p.
A Wreath of Christmas Legends. New York: Collier Books, 1974. 32 p.
Times Three; Selected Verse from Three Decades, with Seventy New Poems. Garden City, N.Y.: Doubleday, 1975. 319 p.

McGOVERN, ANN
Black Is Beautiful. New York: Four Winds Press, 1969. [40] p.

McGOVERN, MARGARET
The Lost Year. New York: Coward-McCann, Inc., 1929. xiii, 95 p.

McGOVERN, ROSE
Chirping from the Nest. Dubuque, IA.: M. S. Hardie, 1906. 84 p.

McGOWAN, CLELIA P.
Plantation Memories, and Other Poems. Philadelphia: The John C. Winston Company, 1923. viii, 52 p.

McGREW, JESSICA JONES
Twilight Embers. Kansas City, MO.: Franklin Hudson Publishing Co., 1912. 47, [1] p.

McGRIFF, JENNEYE
Bits of Stardust. New York: Vantage Press, 1959. 65 p.

McGRIFF, LUCY MOURING
Patchwork. Charlotte, N.C.: n.p., 1957. 54 p.

McGUCKIN, MILDRED CRISS see CRISS, MILDRED (1890-)

McGUIGAN, ALICE
Without a Figleaf; Poems. New York: H. Vinal, Ltd., 1927. 6 p.ℓ., 41 p., 1 ℓ.

McGUIRE, OPAL EVELYN (1906-)
Rhymes of a Hoosier. New York: Paebar Co., 1946. 2 p.ℓ., 44 p.
You and Me. Dallas, TX.: Story Book Press, 1951. 56 p.

McGUIRK, EMMA
In the World's Realm (and Other Poems). Fitchburg, MA.: Sentinal Printing Company, 1902. 1 p.ℓ., 112 p.

McHUGH, JEANNE BAPTISTE
...This and That. Philadelphia: Dorrance and Company, 1938. 50 p. (Contemporary poets of Dorrance, 178)

McHUGH, MARY A.
Echoes of the Great War. Boston: The Christopher Publishing House, 1931. 29 p.

McILWAINE, LUCY ATKINSON (1886-1940)
Nor Fire, Nor Ice; Poems. New York: G. P. Putnam's Sons, 1940. xi p., 1 ℓ., 17-98 p.

McINTIRE, JOSEPHINE
Boot Hill. Boston: Chapman & Grimes, Inc., 1945. 48 p.

McINTIRE, RUBY CLARKE
Poems. New York: Fleming H. Revell Company, 1918. 53 p.

McINTOSH, ADA NATE
Where the Lilacs Bloom and Other Verses. Evanston, IL.:

Modern Printing Service Co., 1931. 23 ℓ.
Where the Roses Bloom and Other Verses. Evanston, IL.: Modern Printing Service Co., 1932. 22 ℓ.

McINTOSH, ANNE T.
Homeward Through the Night. San Antonio, TX.: Naylor Co., 1968. viii, 24 p.

McINTOSH, FLORENCE M.
Time and Tide, and Other Poems. Boston: B. Humphries, 1944. 62 p.

McINTYRE, EASTER WILLDRIDGE
War Is Hell, and Other Poems. New York: n. p., 1927. 5 p. ℓ., 5-33 numb. ℓ.

McINTYRE, FLORENCE
A Book of Verse. Chicago: Eidson Publishing Company, 1909. 93 p.

McINTYRE, MARIE
Unify, Unify; Reflections of a Religion Teacher. Milwaukee, WI.: Bruce Pub. Co., 1969. viii, 141 p.

McJAN, ALICE JANE
Tryst. New York: Hispanic Society of America, 1953. vi p., 1 ℓ., 93 p. (Hispanic Notes and Monographs. Poetry Series)

McKAY, ELIZABETH WHITFIELD
Cobwebs in the Sky. New York: New Haven Press, 1949. 52 p.
Fruits in Season. New York: New Voices Pub. Co., 1952. 3 p. ℓ., 57 p.

McKAY, ELSIE M.
Loveland Stories in Verse. Washington, D. C.: The Washington Book and Art Shop, 1907. 39 p.

McKAY, KAY, pseud. see CARPENTER, KATHRYN

MacKAYE, CHRISTY
Out of Chrysalis.... Winter Park, FL.: The Angel Alley Press, 1930? [17] p.
Wind in the Grass. New York & London: Harper & Brothers, 1931. ix, 89, [1] p.

McKEE, ELLA F.
Plum'ed Depths. Lynchburg, VA.: Coleman & Bradley, 1956. 121 p.

McKEE, MAY
Casual Coins. New York: H. Harrison, 1940. 68 p.

McKEEHAN, IRENE PETTIT (1882-)
Selected Poems. Boulder, CO.: University of Colorado, 1950. 63 p.

McKEEHAN, LITA
Roses in December. Detroit, MI.: Sinclair House Press, 1965. 78 p.

McKENNEY, LILLIAN JERNA
Dawn Daughter and Other Poems. San Diego, CA.: n.p., 1924. 75 p.
Nalini. San Diego, CA.: San Diego Printing Co., 1926. 114 p.

MacKENZIE, CLARA
A Minute or Two to Spare. Boston: B. Humphries, 1943. 31, [1] p.

McKENZIE, ETHEL
Secret Snow. Philadelphia: Roland Swain Company, 1932. xiv p., 1 ℓ., 17-178 p.

MacKENZIE, JEAN KENYON (1874-1936)
The Venture; Poems. Boston & New York: Houghton Mifflin Company, 1925. viii, 44 p.

McKINLEY, IDA SAXTON
Picture That I Saw: A Poem. Columbus, OH.: The Author, 1904.

McKINNEY, KATE (SLAUGHTER) (1857-)
Palace of Silver. New York: H. Vinal, Ltd., 1927. 6 p. ℓ., 128 p., 1 ℓ.

McKINNEY, SARAH
Kate, and Other Poems. Boston: The Stratford Company, 1924. 4 p. ℓ., 84 p.

McKINNON, CECILIA
Fountains of Ordunna. Boston: B. J. Brimmer Co., 1923. 72 p.

McKINNON, KAREN
Stereoscopic. San Luis Obispo, CA.: Solo Press, 1975. 50 p.

MacKINSTRY, ELIZABETH
Puck in Pasture. Garden City, N.Y.: Doubleday, Page & Co., 1925. viii, [2], 79, [3] p.
________. London: W. Heinemann, Ltd., 1926. viii, [2], 79 p.

MACKLIN, EVELYN
Stray Thoughts. 2d ed. Danbury, CT.: Published by T.N.P.C., 1965. 28 p., 1 ℓ.
Memories in Rhyme. Danbury, CT.: Published by T.N.P.C.,

1967. 36, [1] p.
Petals of Thought. Danbury, CT.: Published by T. N. P. C., 1968. 38 p.

McLANE, LUCY NEELY
In Tune with Beauty. Palo Alto, CA.: Pacific Books, 1959. xiii, 81 p.

McLAUGHLIN, EMMA S.
Shining Fearless, Flying Proud. Charleston, IL.: Prairie Press, 1967. x, 36 p., 1 ℓ.

McLAUGHLIN, HONORA
Poems of Life & Love. Boston: R. G. Badger, 1927. 109 p.

McLEAN, EVELYN
Candle in the Wind. New York: Comet Press Books, 1955. 37 p.

MACLEAN, FLORENCE STONE
Poems of Spirit. Bethlehem, PA.: n.p., 1928. 32 p.

McLEAN, TESS
Silver Crickets. Ojai, CA.: Edward Barry Company, 1938. 64 p.

McLEOD, Mrs. E. M.
Love's Offering, and Other Poems. Lansing, MI.: n.p., 1900. 140 p.

MacLEOD, EUPHEMIA
My Rose, and Other Poems. Boston: The Four Seas Company, 1919. 100 p.

MacLEOD, NELLIE G. (OWENS) see OWENS, NELLIE G.

McLUCKIE, HARRIET
Passionate Journey. New York: Pageant Press, 1965. 5 p. ℓ., 45 p.

McMAKIN, CARRIE McNEICE
Heart Blossoms; or The Road to My Heart's Garden. Columbus, GA.: Gilbert Printing Co., 1928. 3 p. ℓ., iv, [5]-85 p.

McMANUS, STASIA
This Shape of Heart. Cleveland, OH.: American Weave Press, 1958. vi, 26 p. (Durham chapbooks, 14)

MacMARTIN, FAYE BRICE
The Effigy Mound National Monument in Iowa, in Poetry and Verse. Des Moines, IA.: Duffy Print. Co., 1950. 44 p.

McMEEKIN, ISABELLA (McLENNAN) (1895-)
Melodies and Mountaineers. Boston, MA.: The Stratford Co., 1921. 5 p. ℓ., 58 p.
...The Bronze Hunter and Other Poems. Philadelphia: Dorrance & Company, 1935. 78 p. (Contemporary poets of Dorrance, 131)

McMICHEAL, MARY AINSLE
Familiar Thought. Stockton, CA.: Print Shop, 1922. 3 p. ℓ., 61 p.

McMILLAN, ELIZABETH
There Are No Words, and Other Verse. New York: Vantage Press, 1966. 43 p.

McMILLAN, LELA F.
Bits of Driftwood. Kanona, N.Y.: J. & C. Transcripts, 1970. 31 p.

McMILLAN, LOUISE WARREN
Poems. Macon, GA.: Printed by the J. W. Burke Co., 1951. iii, 40 p.
Easter Lilies and Other Poems. Louisville, GA.: The News and Farmer, 1961. 67 p.
"The Earth Is the Lord's..." and Other Poems. New York: Vantage Press, 1967. 95 p.

MacMILLAN, MARY LOUISE (1870-)
The Little Golden Fountain, and Other Verses. Cincinnati, OH.: Stewart & Kidd Company, 1916. 2 p. ℓ., 102 p.

McMILLAN, RUTH
Faith in the Space Age. Buffalo, MO.: n.p., 1965. 64 p.

MACMILLIAN, JEAN CAMPBELL
Candle Light to Dawn. San Francisco, CA.: n.p., 1923. 77 p.
Bridge to Dreamland. Los Angeles, CA.: Suttonhouse, 1938. xii p., 2 ℓ., 3-134 p.

McMINDS, FRANCES
All the Year 'Round. Dallas, TX.: For the author by Smith & Lamar, 1913. 136 p.

McMURDO, IDA ANNA (1901-1945)
Poet's Horizon, and Other Poems. San Francisco? CA.: Hooper Printing Co., 19--? [95] p.

McNAIR, LURA THOMAS
Humming Birds in the Mimosas. Lowell, MA.: Alentour House, 1938. [18] p.
Midnight Fire. Francestown, N.H.: Golden Quill Press, 1959. 64 p.

McNALLY, GEORGIA MAUD (1889-)
...May Morning & Apple Blossoms. Boston: H. Vinal Limited, 1930. 5 p. ℓ., 9-50 p. (The friendly books)
Bluebells and Mystic Isles. New York: The Poets Press, 1937. 7 p. ℓ., 11-82 p.

McNAMAR, MYRTLE
Just Muse, Deep Down in the Woods, and Other Poems. Cottonwood, CA.: n.p., 1918. 67, [1] p.
Just Muse, and Other Poems. Cottonwood, CA.: McNamars, 1919. 1 p. ℓ., 78 p.
The Vail of Mist. Cottonwood, CA.: McNamars, 1919. 2 p. ℓ., 31 p.

McNAMARA, FRANCES
Smoke Upon the Hills. New York: Manual Training High School, 1938. 30 p.

McNEILL, LOUISE
Mountain White. Dallas, TX.: The Kaleidoscope Publishers, 1931. 5 p. ℓ., 30 ℓ.
Gauley Mountain. New York: Harcourt, Brace & Co., 1939. xviii, 98 p.
Time Is Our House. Breadloaf, VT.: The Breadloaf Printers, Middlebury College Press, 1942. xii, 30 p., 1 ℓ.
Paradox Hill from Appalachia to Lunar Shore. Morgantown, W.V.: University Library, 1972. 131 p.
Hill-Daughter. Charleston, W.V.: MHC Publications, 1971.
From a Dark Mountain. Charleston, W.V.: Morris Harvey College Publications, 1975?

McNEW, LUELLA HEDRICK
Lilting Lines. New York: Carlton Press, 1966. 1 p. ℓ., 62 p.

McNINCH, MARGARET EMMA
Heartsease and Lilies. Columbia, S.C.: Press of the R. L. Bryan, 1927. 140 p.
My House of Dreams and Other Poems. New York: Exposition Press, 1927. 140 p.

McOMBER, GRETTA M.
Dream Caps and Other Poems. Boston: n.p., 1927. 45 p.

MACOMBER, SUSAN GLOVER (1868-) [Full Name: Mary Susan Glover Macomber.]
A Prison Posie. New York: n.p., 1917. [36] p.

McPHAIL, LAURA
A Child's Treasure of Poems. New York: Exposition Press, 1951. 112 p.

McPHERSON, SANDRA (1943-)
Elegies for the Hot Season. Bloomington, IN.: Indiana University

Press, 1970. 71 p.
Radiation. New York: The Ecco Press; dist. by Viking Press, 1973. 68 p.

McROBERTS, HARRIET PEARL (SKINNER)
Every Christian; Poems.... New York: The Knickerbocker Press, 1921. vi, 37 p.

MADDRY, VERA ELIZABETH
Whisperings. Arlington? TX.: n.p., 1951. 71 p.

MADELEVA, Sister (1887-1964) [Secular Name: Mary Evaline Wolff.]
Knights Errant, and Other Poems. New York, London: D. Appleton & Co., 1923. 8 p. ℓ., 3-76, [1] p.
Penelope and Other Poems. New York, London: D. Appleton & Co., 1927. viii p., 2 ℓ., 59 p.
A Question of Lovers, and Other Poems. Paterson, N. J.: St. Anthony Guild Press, 1935. 6 p. ℓ., 57 p.
The Happy Christmas Wind and Other Poems. Paterson, N. J.: St. Anthony Guild Press, 1936. 4 p. ℓ., 19, [1] p.
Christmas Eve, and Other Poems. Paterson, N. J.: St. Anthony Guild Press, 1938. 4 p. ℓ., 11 p.
Gates and Other Poems. New York: The Macmillan Co., 1938. x, 34 p.
Selected Poems. New York: The Macmillan Co., 1939. xii, 119 p.
Four Girls, and Other Poems. Paterson, N. J.: St. Anthony Guild Press, 1941. 4 p. ℓ., 13 p.
A Song of Bedlam Inn, and Other Poems. Paterson, N. J.: St. Anthony Guild Press, 1946. 4 p. ℓ., 11, [1] p.
Collected Poems. New York: Macmillan Co., 1947. xvii, 166 p.
American Twelfth Night, and Other Poems. New York: Macmillan Co., 1955. xlvii p.
The Four Last Things, Collected Poems. New York: Macmillan Co., 1959. 175 p.
A Child Asks for a Star. Wilkes-Barre, PA.: Dimension Books, 1964. 31 p.

MADELEY, ELILLIAN KELLY
Thoughts Gathered Along the Path of Life. Conroe, TX.: n.p., 1936. 3 p. ℓ., 9-55 p.
Full Moon. Boston: The Christopher Publishing House, 1947. 76 p.

MADGETT, NAOMI CORNELIA LONG (1923-)
Songs to a Phantom Nightingale. New York: Fortuny's, 1941. 30 p.
One and the Many. New York: Exposition Press, 1956. 64 p.
Star by Star. 1st ed. Detroit, MI.: Harlo Press, 1965. 64 p.
________. 2d ed., 1965. 63 p.
________. 3d rev. ed. Detroit, MI.: Evenill, 1970. 64 p.

Pink Ladies in the Afternoon; New Poems, 1965-1971. Detroit, MI.: Lotus Press, 1972. 63 p.

MAGARET, HELENE (1906-)
The Trumpeting Crane. New York: Farrar and Rinehart, 1934. 4 p. ℓ., 8-159 p.
The Great Horse; A Narrative Poem. New York, Toronto: Farrar & Rinehart, Inc., 1937. 5 p. ℓ., 182 p.

MAGENHEIMER, KAY
Love's Stigmata. New York: Pageant Press, 1963. 5 p. ℓ., 54 p.

MAGNA, EDITH (SCOTT) (1885-) [Full Name: Sarah Edith (Scott) Magna.]
Collected Verse. Northampton, MA.: The Hampshire Bookshop, 1934. 5 p. ℓ., 62 p.

MAGUIRE, ANNE
Love Will Never Die. Francestown, N.H.: Golden Quill Press, 1973. 80 p.

MAHLER, EVA ELLIOT
Embers, A Book of Verse. Seattle, WA.: Printed by F. McCaffrey at his Dogwood Press, 1931. 71 p.

MAIN, NORA ELIZABETH (1885-)
The Signing Road, Sonnets. San Antonio, TX.: Naylor Co., 1948. viii, 144 p.

MAIN, VIRGINIA
The Origin of the Pointsetta and Other Poems. Salina, KA.: n.p., 1915. [24] p.

MAITLAND, CARRIE VIRGINIA
A Book of Verse. Chicago: R. R. Donnelley and Sons Company, 1917. [80] p., 1 ℓ.

MAJOR, MARIE AUSTIN (1903-)
Roses with the Throng.... Manchester, N.H.: Granite State Press, 1937. 99 p.

MAJORS, EDNA COE
Winds of the West, and Other Poems. Dallas, TX.: Triangle Pub. Co., 1957. 50 p.

MAKARIUS, CORDELIA B.
Beyond the Moon. Dayton, OH.: Otterbein Press Co., 1922. 32 p.

MALASCHAK, DOLORES
Run in the Morning. Francestown, N.H.: Golden Quill Press, 1969. 72 p.

MALCOM, BARBARA
I Want Me a Home. New Orleans, LA.: Nkombo Publications, 1969.

MALCOSKEY, EDNA WALKER
The Eternal Variant; Love Songs and Lyrics. New York: Dial Press, 1953. 117 p.
The Virgin and the Priestess. New York: F. Fell, 1961. 127 p.
Songs of Greener Pastures. New York: F. Fell, 1962. 104 p.

MALESKY, GAYNELLE S.
Green Autumn. Francestown, N.H.: Golden Quill Press, 1967. 72 p.

MALLORY, SARAH (TROUSDALE) [Full Name: Sarah Ellen (Trousdale) Mallory.]
...Mnemonic and Other Verses. Caldwell, ID.: The Caxton Printers, Ltd., 1935. 64 p.

MALLY, EMMA LOUISE (1908-)
Dedications. New York: Coward-McCann, Inc., 1937. 73 p.

MALMQUIST, MARIE (1866-)
A Message Verse. Boston: The Roxburgh Publishing Company, Inc., 1919. 117 p.
"Forrest Echoes." Brockton, MA.: Franklin Print., 1920. 2 p. ℓ., 7-206 p.

MALONE, ELINORE
Thoughts in Rhyme. San Francisco: Sunset Press, 1941. 47, [1] p.

MANCHESTER, LESLIE CLARE
Blessedness and Other Poems. Cassadaga, FL.: n.p., 1927. 24 p.
Pasture Poems. Cassadaga, FL.: n.p., 1928. [24] p.

MANDEL, URSULA GREENSHAW (1898-)
Random Rhymes. 1st ed. New York: Exposition Press, 1967. vi, 313 p.
______. 2d enl. ed. Hicksville, N.Y.: Exposition Press, 1975. 219 p.

MANDOLA, CAROL M.
Scattered Seeds. New York: House of Field, Inc., 1940. 23 p.
Folly Street, and Selected Poems. Dallas, TX.: The Story Book Press, 1944. 64 p.

MANFRED, FREYA (1944-)
A Goldenrod Will Grow. Minneapolis, MN.: James D. Thueson, 1971. 63 p.

MANGAN, JOAN HELEN (1901-)
Silver Wings. Boston: R. Humphries, 1947. 48 p.

MANLOVE, MARGARET ISABEL
Spiritual Ship. Los Angeles, CA.: n.p., 1922. 108 p.

MANN, DOROTHEA LAWRENCE
An Acreage of Lyric. Boston: The Cornhill Company, 1919. 5 p. ℓ., 57 p.

MANN, ETHEL EDITH (1900-)
Nature Fantasies; Poems. New York: Exposition Press, 1961. 63 p.

MANNING, ELIZABETH
Willie Lamberton. New York: The Macmillan Co., 1927. 64 p.
________. London: W. Heinemann, Ltd., 1927. 3 p. ℓ., 64 p.

MANSFIELD, MADGE ACTON
Flickerings. Boston: Bruce Humphries, 1951. 96 p.
I Heard a Bird-Singing, and Other Poems Redolent of the Joy of Living. Philadelphia: Dorrance, 1956. 47 p.

MANSFIELD, MARGERY
Berkshire Settler. Monterey, MA.: K. Janes, 1961. v, 26 p.

MARCUS, ADRIANNE
The Moon Is a Marrying Eye. Charlotte, NC.: Red Clay Books, 1971. 42 p. (Red Clay Reader, v. 8, no. 1)

MARCY, Mrs. EDMUND D. (1865-)
Buds and Blossoms; A Selection of Songs and Poems. Chicago: Sholty Printing Co., 1920. 2 p. ℓ., 114 p.

MARCY, MARY EDNA (TOBIAS) (1877-)
Rhymes of Early Jungle Folk. Chicago: C. H. Kerr & Co., 1922. 3 p. ℓ., 11-124 p.

MAREAN, EMMA (ENDICOTT) (1854-1936)
Now and Then. Cambridge, MA.: The Riverside Press, 1928. ix, [1] p., 1 ℓ., 120 p.

MARGOLIS, SILVIA (1897-)
Letters to Jesus, by a Jewess. Dayton, OH.: The Lincoln Press Company, 1925. 40 p.
The Argent Flame. Mill Valley, CA.: Wings Press, 1958. 80 p.
The Singing Elm. Mill Valley, CA.: Wings Press, 1959. 80 p.
From the Lips of a River. Mill Valley, CA.: Wings Press, 1962. 85 p.
As the Dial to the Sun. Boston: Bruce Humphries, 1966. 94 p.

MARGOT-PARLE, DELINA
Symphony. Boston: Bruce Humphries, 1955. 119 p.
Ballet Poetique; Poems. Boston: Christopher Pub. House, 1960. 106 p.

MARGRAT, MAE E.
Voices of Yesterday. Mt. Vernon, OH.: The College Press, 1941. 92 p.
Dreams at Sunset. Mt. Vernon, OH.: The College Press, 1944. 96 p.

MARIE MICHAEL, Sister (1923-)
You Have Filled the Days. Boston: Humphries, 1949. 68 p.

MARINONI, ROSA (ZAGNONI) (1891-)
Behind the Mask. New York: H. Harrison, 1927. 64 p.
Red Kites and Wooden Crosses. Chicago: R. Packard & Co., 1929. 128 p.
North of Laughter. Oglethorpe University, GA.: n.p., 1931. 82 p.
Side Show. Philadelphia: David McKay Co., 1938. 160 p.
Timberline, Selected Verse. Cedar Rapids, IA.: Torch Press, 1954. 260 p.
The Ozarks and Some of Its People. Fayetteville, AR.: n.p., 1956. 74 p.
______. 1961. 80 p.
The Green Sea Horse. Francestown, N.H.: Golden Quill Press, 1963. 94 p.
The Ozarks and Some of Its People. 4th ed. Fayetteville, AR.: Villa Rosa, 1965. 84 p.
"Lend Me Your Ears! A Beakful of Humorous Verse. 2d ed. Fayetteville, AR.: n.p., 1966. 60 p.
Whoo-Whoo, the "Howl" of the Ozarks Says: Think and Wink! Fayetteville, AR.: n.p., 1967? 68 p.

MARIOTTI, NANCI
Verses, Mostly by Nanci. Ann Arbor, MI.: n.p., 1953. 63 p.

MARIS, STELLA, Sister (1899-)
Here Only a Dove, A Book of Poems. Paterson, N.J.: St. Anthony Guild Press, 1939. 43 p.
Frost for Saint Brigid, and Other Poems. New York: Sheed & Ward, 1949. 94 p.

MARKEY, VERA P.
Bread and Butter. Dallas, TX.: Story Book Press, 1953. 53 p.

MARKHAM, LUCIA (CLARK) (1870-)
Sonnets to Eve. n.p., 1930. 16 p.
Sonnets. Lexington, KY.: Bur Press, 1944. 5 p. ℓ., 3-66 p., 1 ℓ.
Coolshanagh; "The Meeting Place of Friends." A Sonnet Story of the New Age. Los Angeles, CA.: New Age Pub. Co.,

1958. 154 p.
Sonnets to the Beloved. Maspeth, N. Y.: Poetry Press, 1960. 127 p.

MARKLUND, ELIN
Golden Hours. New York: The Caravan Publishing Co., 1945. 144 p.

MARKS, JEANETTE AUGUSTUS (1875-1964)
Willow Pollen. Boston: The Four Seas Co., 1921. 89 p.

MARKS, LILA, pseud. see GLAZER, ETTA (1913-)

MARKS, MABEL (HATTON) (1887-)
In the Sun or Rain. Los Angeles?: n. p., 193-? 79 p.
Though Men May Pipe. Claremont, CA.: Saunders Press, 1939. 72 p.
Let Song Take Form. Claremont, CA.: Saunders Press, 1941. 79 p.
What Are These Dreams? Culver City, CA.: Highland Press, 1947. 79 p.

MARKS, MARCIA BLISS
Swing Me, Swing Tree. Boston: Little, Brown, 1959. 29 p. (Verse for children.)

MARLATT, JEAN (STEELE)
Westward to Eden; A Collection of Poems. New York: House of Field, Inc., 1940. 111 p.

MARLEY, ANNE B.
Wings, and Other Poems. Charleston, IL.: Prairie Press Books, 1971. viii, 26 p.

MARQUARDT, ANNETTE
Poems of Life and the Seasons. Boston: Branden Press, 1968. 46 p.

MARQUEZ, EMMA SUTTON (CARTER)
Music of the Spheres. New York: Valiant House, 1944. 64 p.

MARR, MABEL EMERY (1877-)
Comrades, and Other Poems. Springfield: The Snow Press, Inc., 1929.

MARR, MARTHA ROBINSON
Colored Leaves. Pasadena, CA.: n. p., 1954. 59 p.

MARSH, ALICE McBRYDE
... Patchwork. Boston: The Stratford Company, 1928. 4 p. ℓ., 7-29 p. (The Stratford Poets)

MARSH, EDITH S.
Thoughts for Busy Days; A Collection of Poems. New York: William-Frederick Press, 1960. 16 p.

MARSH, WENDY
Restless Anchor. New York: The Greystone Press, 1936. 45 ℓ.

MARSHALL, EVA GRANT
Heart Fragments. Cynthiana, KY.: The Hobson Book Press, 1944. viii p., 2 ℓ., 60 p.

MARSHALL, FLORENCE E.
Are You Awake? Lansing, MI.: Shaw Pub. Co., 1936. 96 p.

MARSHALL, HELEN LOWRIE (1904-)
Bright Horizons. Denver, CO.: Halvern Press, 1954. 54 p.
Close to the Heart. Denver, CO.: Halvern Press, 1958. 64 p.
Dare to Be Happy. Denver, CO.: Halvern Press, 1962. 64 p.
Aim for a Star. New York: Distributed by Dodd, Mead, 1964. 64 p.
Hold to Your Dream. Denver, CO.: Halvern Press, 1965. 64 p.
The Gift of Wonder. Garden City, N.Y.: Doubleday, 1967. 64 p.
A Gift So Rare; More Inspirational Verses. Kansas City, MO.: Hallmark Editions, 1969. 61 p.
Hold to Your Dream. London: Muller, 1969. 64 p.
Walk the World Proudly. Garden City, N.Y.: Doubleday, 1969. 64 p.
Quiet Power. Garden City, N.Y.: Doubleday, 1970. 64 p.
Starlight and Candleglow. Garden City, N.Y.: Doubleday, 1970. 64 p.
Let Me Love the Little Things. Kansas City, MO.: Hallmark, 1971. [48] p.
A World That Sings! Favorite Verses of Helen Lowrie Marshall. Selected by James Morgan. Kansas City, MO.: Hallmark Cards, 1971. 69 p. (Hallmark Crown Editions)
Aren't You Glad! Garden City, N.Y.: Doubleday, 1973. 63 p.

MARSHALL, INEZ (MILDRED)
Dream Patterns. Dextor, MO.: Candor Press, 1949. 36 p.

MARSHALL, JANE HULLIHEN
...Moonlight in My Lap. Philadelphia: Dorrance & Co., Inc., 1935. 88 p. (Contemporary poets of Dorrance, 130)

MARSHALL, LENORE (GUINZBURG) (1897-)
No Boundary. New York: H. Holt & Co., 1943. ix, 59 p.
Other Knowledge, Poems New & Selected. New York: Noonday Press, 1956. 92 p.
Latest Will; New and Selected Poems. New York: Norton, 1969. 109 p.

MARSHALL, MARGARET CECILIA (PARKER)
The Message of the Spirit Nun, and Other Poems, Given by Cecile Le Blanc, Transcribed by Cecelia Parker. San Francisco: Miss Cecilia P. Marshall, 1925. 5 p. ℓ., 13-95 p., [1] p.

MARSHALL, NAN
Tell Me More; A Collection of Light Verse. New York: William-Frederick Press, 1954. 48 p. (The William-Frederick Poets, no. 118)
Circle in the Sand; A Collection of Verse. New York: William-Frederick Press, 1968. 64 p. (The William-Frederick Poets, no. 146)

MARSHALL, RENA B.
Young Rivers, A Book of Poems. New York: Carlton Press, 1963. 100 p.

MARSTALLER, LEILA S.
Ebb and Flow. Richmond, IN.: Nicholson Printing Co., 1935. 77 p.

MARTIN, ELLEN
Faith Walks with Me. Dexter, MO.: Candor Press, 1967. 32 p.

MARTIN, MARGARET NICKERSON
The Open Door. Jackson, MI.: Allen Printing Co., 1931. 24 ℓ.
Still Waters. Boston: The Christopher Publishing House, 1933. 64 p.
Ceiling Unlimited. Jackson, MI.: La Rue Print. Co., 1943. [24] p.

MARTIN, MARJORIE
A Friend Asked Me, and Other Poems. Chicago: Windfall Press, 1964. 26 p.

MARTIN, MARTHA
Nature Lyrics, and Other Poems. Boston: R. G. Badger, 1907. 89 p.
The Weed's Philosophy, and Other Poems. Montreal: n.p., 1913. 43 p.
Caught in Flight. New York: Vechten Waring Company, 1931. 103 p.
Poem-Anecdotes of Child-Musicians. New York: The Beekman Hill Press, 1934. 50 p.
Come Into My Garden; A Collection of Flower and Tree Poems. New York: Beekman Hill Press, 1935. 60 p., 1 ℓ.
Out of the Shadows and Other Poems. New York: The Beekman Hill Press, 1937. vii p., 1 ℓ., 11-78 p.
Poet's Pilgrimage. New York: Beekman Hill Press, 1938. 60 p.
Chautauqua Greets You! New York: Gotham Press, 1940. 38 p.

Poems, with the Birth of a Poem. New York: Gotham Press, 1941. 4 p. ℓ., 11-46 p.

MARTIN, MARY CROWNOVER (1907-)
Invisible Vistas. Dallas, TX.: Story Book Press, 1948. 91 p.

MARTIN, MAUD de LORME
Stray Leaves. San Francisco: The Grabhorn Press, 1929. 2 p. ℓ., 103 p.

MARTIN, MAUDE EMORY
We of the Plains. Rockford, IL.: Bellevue Books, 1954. 56 p.

MARTIN, NETTIE PARRISH
Indian Legends of Other Days. Boston: Mayhew Publishing Co., 1904. 3 p. ℓ., 86 p.

MARTIN, NEVA DUNCAN
Twilight Shadows, A Volume of Verse. New York: Greenwich Book Publishers, 1956. 39 p.

MARTIN, ROSE HINTON
Endearing Endeavors. New York: Pageant Press, 1960. 56 p.

MARTINEK, MARIE
The Selected Poems of Marie Martinek. New York: The Exposition Press, 1943. 30 p.

MARTYN, EVA E.
Silent Hill and Other Poems. Ilfracombe: A. H. Stockwell, Ltd., Ltd., 1946? 22, [1] p.
For You! and Other Poems. Ilfracombe: A. H. Stockwell, 1947. 31 p.
...Always, Songs from My Heart. Philadelphia: Dorrance and Company, 1935. 51 p. (Contemporary poets of Dorrance, 134)

MARVIN, BURDETTE K.
Sea Shells. New York: H. Vinal, Ltd., 1928. 6 p. ℓ., 3-148 p., 1 ℓ.

MARX, ANNE
Into the Wind of Waking. Cleveland, OH.: American Weave Press, 1960. 28 p.
The Second Voice. New York: Fine Editions Press, 1963. 72 p.
By Grace of Pain. Fort Smith, AR.: South and West, 1966. 46 p.
By Way of People. Francestown, N. H.: Golden Quill Press, 1970. 96 p.

MARY ANGELINE, Sister [Secular Name: Ellen Hughes.]
Peddler of Dreams. Paterson, N. J.: St. Anthony Guild Press, 1941. x, 69, [1] p.
________. 2d ed., 1948. viii, 71 p.

MARY ANGELITA, Sister (1878-) [Secular Name: Mary Agnes Stackhouse.]
Starshine and Candlelight. New York: D. Appleton and Co., 1925. xi, 99, [1] p.

MARY ANTHONY, Mother see WEINIG, MARY ANTHONY

MARY BLANCHE, Sister [Secular Name: Elizabeth King.]
Poems. New York: The Devin-Adair Co., 1913. 58 p.

MARY DELPHINE, Sister
Aspects and Attitudes; Poems. New York: Pageant Press, 1965. 69 p.

MARY EDWARDINE, Sister see O'CONNOR, MARY EDWARDINE

MARY ELEANOR, Mother (1903-) [Secular Name: Eleanor Chapin Slater.]
Quest. New Haven, CT.: Yale University Press, 1926. 51 p. (Yale Series of Younger Poets, v. 21)
Why Hold the Hound? New York: H. Harrison, 1941. 63 p.

MARY ELEANORE, Sister see ELEANORE, MARY, Sister

MARY EUGENE, Sister [Secular Name: Josephine Early Coleman.]
King of the Hill, and Other Poems. Paterson, N.J.: St. Anthony Guild Press, 1943. x, 186 p.

MARY GILBERT, Sister see DE FREES, MADELINE (1919-)

MARY JEREMY, Sister [Secular Name: Alice Winifred Finnegan.]
Dialogue With an Angel, Poems. New York: Devin-Adair, 1949. xi, 47 p.

MASKEL, ANNA R.
Wild Stubble. Boston: B. Humphries, 1935. 63 p.
From Fallow. Boston: B. Humphries, 1937. 59 p.

MASON, LUCILE MYERS
Moorings and Sails. San Antonio, TX.: Naylor Co., 1972. xiii, 106 p.

MASON, LYLA (1909-)
Forever Now. Dallas, TX.: Story Book Press, 1954. 48 p.

MASON-MANNHEIM, MADELINE (1908-)
Hill Fragments. New York: Brentano's, 1925. xv, 59, [1] p.
The Cage of Years. New York: Bond Wheelwright Co., 1949. 54 p.
The Cage of Years: Poems Out of Print Since 1949. Washington, D.C.: University Press of Washington, D.C., 1962. 54 p.
At the Ninth Hour; A Sonnet Sequence in a New Form. Washington, D.C.: University of Washington, D.C., 1963. 54 p.

MASTEN, MARY
To My Loves. Boston: The Christopher Publishing House, 1928. 50 p.

MASTERS, MARCIA LEE
Intent on Earth. New York: Candlelight Press, 1965. 77 p.

MASTIN, FLORENCE RIPLEY (1896-)
Green Leaves. New York: J. T. White & Co., 1918. 118 p.
Cables of Cobweb. New York: H. Harrison, 1935. 64 p.
Freedom's Dream. Albany, N.Y.: State Commission on Historic Observances, 1960. 10 p.
Over the Tappan Zee, and Other Poems. New York: Fine Editions Press, 1962. 70 p.

MATHEWS, HATTIE SPURLIN (1856-1953)
Thoughts by the Way. San Antonio, TX.: Naylor Co., 1963. 124 p.

MATHEWS, STELLA TYLER
The Life of Abraham Lincoln, In Verse. Seattle, WA.: Press of Lowman & Hanford Co., 1923. 4 p. ℓ., [13]-97 p.

MATHEWSON, GRACE HENDERSON
Silent Forces. Los Angeles, CA.: n.p., 1915. [30] p.

MATHIS, LOUISE OZELLE (1904-)
Open Doors. Philadelphia: Dorrance & Company, 1925. 71 p. (Contemporary poets, 13)

MATHIS, RUTH
Poems. Chicago: Dierkes Press, 1948. 48 p.

MATTESON, ESTELLE LAMBERT
Phryne and Cleopatra: Poem. New York: Stiletto Pub. Co., 1900. 24 p.

MATTHEWS, ALVIA BARTHOLOMEW
Remember Me? Cedar Rapids, IA.: The Torch Press, 1941. 64 p.

MATTHEWS, ELEANOR H.
Ever the Sunrise. Mill Valley, CA.: Wings Press, 1954. 70 p.

MATTHEWS, HELEN E.
God Is Within, and Other Poems. New York: Vantage Press, 1964. 96 p.

MATTHEWS, MARGAREETE
Hope Is Nectar. Philadelphia: Dorrance, 1955. 74 p. (Contemporary poets of Dorrance, 475)

MATTHEWS, MIRIAM CASSEL
Spring Interlude: Poems. New York: H. Vinal, 1927. 6 p. ℓ., 9-45, [1] p.
New Wood. Dallas, TX.: The Kaleidograph Press, 1938. 63 p.

MATTISON, JUDITH N.
From a Woman's Heart. Minneapolis, MN.: Augsburg Pub. House, 1969. 96 p.
Prayers from a Woman's Heart. Minneapolis, MN.: Augsburg Pub. House, 1972. 96 p.

MAUERMANN, BERTHA MERENA
Mosaic. Boston: Meador Publishing Company, 1935. 112 p.

MAULDIN, ETHEL JEANNETTE
The Gipsy Rover. San Antonio, TX.: Naylor Co., 1944. 97 p.

MAUPIN, ELAINE KOHLMETZ
Pen Portraits. New York: Philosophical Library, 1963. 97 p.

MAURA, Sister (1916-)
Where Once the Wild Arbutus Grew. Baltimore, MD.: School Sisters of Notre Dame, College of Notre Dame of Maryland, 1945. 3 p. ℓ., 9-26 p.
Initiate the Heart. New York: Macmillan, 1946. 6 p. ℓ., 3-46 p.
Come Christmas. Baltimore, MD.: Notre Dame College Press, 1951. 1 v. unpaged.
The Word Is Love. New York: Macmillan, 1958. 52 p.
Bell Sound and Vintage. Baltimore, MD.: Contemporary Poetry, 1966. 36 p.

MAVITY, NANCY BARR
A Dinner of Herbs. New York: T. Seltzer, 1923. 6 p. ℓ., 3-54 p.

MAXFIELD, ISOBEL
Twilight Whisperings. New York: Comet Press Books, 1955. 53 p.
Threads of Light. New York: Comet Press Books, 1959. 54 p.

MAXFIELD, JANE (CROWE)
Blue Chicory, and Other Poems. Ann Arbor, MI.: Cushing-Malloy, Inc., 1961. 50 p.

MAXON, GLORIA STROMSETH
Kennings. Boston: Branden Press, 1974. 64 p.

MAXSON, LILLIE ELLEN
On Wings of Whimsey. New York: Vantage Press, 1964. 48 p.

MAXWELL, ELINOR
Little Beggar, and Other Poems. Boston: The Four Seas Company, 1924. 53 p.

MAXWELL, RUTH FORTNEY
As the Seasons Roll. New York: H. Harrison, 1940. 64 p.

MAY, BEULAH (1883-)
Buccaneer's Gold. Santa Ana, CA.: The Fine Arts Press, 1935. 6 p. ℓ., 60 p., 1 ℓ.

MAY, FLORENCE LAND
Lyrics from Lotus Lands. Boston: R. G. Badger, 1911. 5 p. ℓ., 13-178 p.

MAYER, BERNADETTE
Ceremony Latin. New York: Angel Hair Press, 1964? [23] ℓ.
Moving. New York: Angel Hair Press, 1971. 39 p.
Studying Hunger. New York: Adventures in Poetry; Bolinas, CA.: Big Sky, 1975. 71 p.

MAYES, ROBERTA WARREN
Wings of Thought. San Antonio, TX.: The Naylor Company, 1939. ix, [1], 11-56 p.

MAYFIELD, JEAN
Spindrift, Poems from Padre Island. San Antonio, TX.: Naylor Co., 1952. 89 p.

MAYHALL, JANE
Discourse Before Dawn. New York: Qohéleth Press, 1960. 28 p.
Givers and Takers; Poems. New York: Eakins Press, 1968. 47 p.
Givers and Takers 2; Poems. New York: Eakins Press, 1973. 78 p.

MAYNARD, EMMA A.
Stray Forget-Me-Nots. New York: The Arcade Press, 1927. 38 p.

MAYNARD, MARION
Just Remembering.... New York: The Poets Press, 1941. 48 p.

MAYNARD, WINIFRED, pseud.
The Book of Winifred Maynard. New York & London: G. P. Putnam's Sons, 1916. 82 p.

MAYO, CASANDRA
'Twas Ever Thus, Poems. New York: By-Way Press, 1949. 60 p.

MEAD, LUELLE REYNOLDS
And the Stone Is Cold. Claremont, CA.: Saunders Studio Press, 1937. [65] p.

MEADE, BESSIE
The Hand-Wrought Lamp. Cedar Rapids, IA.: The Bookfellows, 1922. 117 p.

MEADOWCROFT, CLARA PLATT
A Wind Blowing Over. New York: H. Vinal, 1925. 4 p. ℓ., 29 p.

MEADOWS, ETHEL BABB
Embers of Memory. Paris, MO.: Printed by the Monroe County Appeal, 1924. viii, 9-50 p., 1 ℓ.

MEANS, LILLIAN BELL
Five Hundred and Twenty-Five Verse Portrations on the History of the United States. Sterling, OK.: n. p., 1903. 115 p.

MEARKLE, ANNIE L.
Faust in Spring; Poems. New York: H. Vinal, 1926. 4 p. ℓ., 59 p., 1 ℓ.
Moon in the City. Brattleboro, VT.: S. Daye Press, 1935. 6 p. ℓ., 15-118 p.
Fair Captive: A Colonial Story. Brattleboro, VT.: Stephen Daye Press, 1937. 134 p.
The Duel With Oblivion. New York: G. P. Putnam's Sons, 1939. vii, 11-81 p.

MEARS, ALICE MONKS
...Brief Enterprise. New York: E. P. Dutton & Co., 1945. 61 p.
Sea and the Nearer Rocks. Rye, N.Y.: Gray Moose Press, 1959. 31 p.

MECHTA, NATALIA MICHAELOVNA (1914-)
...Fragments of Dreams. Philadelphia: Dorrance and Company, 1938. 46 p. (Contemporary poets of Dorrance, 171)
...Out of the Mists. Philadelphia: Dorrance & Co., 1943. 63 p. (Contemporary poets of Dorrance, 263)

MEDLEY, MARY LOUISE
Dogwood Winter, Poems. Raleigh, N.C.: Wolf's Head Press, 1952. 64 p.

MEDNIKOFF, PATRICIA BENTON see BENTON, PATRICIA

MEEHAN, MARGARET (McLAUGHLIN) (1857-)
Souvenir of California Poems. San Francisco: Printed by John Monohan & Co., 1913. 14 p.

MEEKER, MARJORIE
Color of Water. New York: Brentano's, 1928. xiii, 62 p.

MEHLEK, FRANCES BOAL
Moon Silver. New York: W. A. Broder, 1929. 44 p.

A Sinner Contemplates. Cincinnati, OH.: Talaria, 1946. 79, [1] p.

MEHLINGER, EVA ARONSON
Poems of Love and Beauty. Boston: Print. by Shore Brothers, 1933. 105 p., 1 ℓ.

MEIER, JUDITH (1947-)
Hickory and a Smooth Dime. Santa Fe, N.M.: Sunstone Press, 1975. 23 p. (Sunstone poetry series)

MEISEL, MARION
As the Pendulum Swings. North Montpelier, VT.: The Driftwood Press, 1946. 59 p.

MELEHES, CLARA
The Poet Tree; Poems. New York: Exposition Press, 1960. 31 p.

MELLICHAMP, AMELIA ELIZA
Poems of Life and Nature. Columbia, S.C.: The State Company, 1926. 27 p.

MELLICHAMP, INA L.
Scarlet Cap and Bells. Caddo Gap, AR.: Arcadian Life Press, 1940. 24 p.

MELODY, ELLA SHAW
Songs of Grace, A Book of Poems. Los Angeles, CA.: Peniel Herald Publishing Company, 1941. 3 p. ℓ., xv-xvi p., 1 ℓ., 19-126 p.

MELSZINGER, MEDEAH RAWLINGS
Come Walk with Me. Philadelphia: Dorrance, 1964. 95 p.

MELTON, ELVIA GRAHAM
Spectrum, A Volume of Collected Verse. Boston: Chapman & Grimes, 1938. 78 p.

MELTON, INEZ (1916-)
Poems, Both Simple and Serious. New York: Vantage Press, 1968. 45 p.

MELVIN, MAY McINTYRE
Rhymes from Reasons. New York: Vantage Press, 1962. 80 p.

MEMEBROKER, ANN
Three Drums for the Lady. San Francisco?: Second Coming Press, 1972. [20] p.
If You Are Creative, I Will Vanish. River Pines, CA.: Zetitec Press, 1973.

MERCER, LOUISE
My Heart Soars; Poems. New York: Exposition Press, 1952. 64 p.

MERCER, MILDRED MARALYN
Singing Towers. Philadelphia: Dorrance, 1969. 90 p. (Contemporary poets of Dorrance)

MERCHANT, JANE (1919-)
Think About These Things. New York: Abingdon Press, 1956. 96 p.
Halfway up the Sky. New York: Abingdon Press, 1957. 128 p.
Petals of Light. New York: Abingdon Press, 1965. 128 p.
All Daffodils Are Daffy. Nashville, TN.: Abingdon Press, 1967. 64 p.
Because It's Here. Nashville, TN.: Abingdon Press, 1968. 96 p.
_______. 1970. 126 p.

MEREDITH, LOTTIE HAY
Today and Yesterday, A Book of Poems. Chicago: Brock & Rankin, 1912. 63 p.

MEREDITH, LOUISE (MAYERS)
Poems That Make Sense. New York: Vantage Press, 1969. 80 p.

MERNIT, SUSAN
The Angelic Alphabet. Berkeley, CA.: Tree, 1975. [56] p. (A Tree Book)

MERRELL, MABEL
Old Wine in New Bottles. Boston: R. G. Badger, 1927. 42 p.

MERRELL, WILMA
...Winds That Sing. Philadelphia: Dorrance & Company, 1944. 44 p. (Contemporary poets of Dorrance, 278)

MERRIAM, EVE (1916-)
Family Circle. New Haven, CT.: Yale University Press, 1946. 3 p. ℓ., 5-74 p. (Yale Series of Younger Poets, 44)
Tomorrow Morning. New York: Twayne Publishers, 1953. 69 p.
Montgomery, Alabama, Money, Mississippi, and Other Places. New York: Cameron Associates, 1956. [36] p.
The Double Bed, from the Feminine Side. New York: Cameron Associates, 1958. 160 p.
The Words and Music of My Mother. New York: n.p., 1958.
The Double Bed, from the Feminine Side. 2d ed. New York: Marzani & Munsell, 1960. 160 p.
_______. 1st Prometheus ed., 1960.
The Trouble with Love; Poems. New York: Macmillan, 1960. 70 p.

<u>There Is No Rhyme for Silver.</u> New York: Atheneum, 1962. 70 p.
<u>It Doesn't Always Have to Rhyme.</u> New York: Atheneum, 1964. 83 p. (Verse for children.)
<u>Catch a Little Rhyme.</u> New York: Atheneum, 1966. 51 p. (Verse for children.)
<u>Independent Voices.</u> New York: Atheneum, 1968. xi, 79 p.
<u>The Inner City Mother Goose.</u> New York: Simon & Schuster, 1969. 90 p.
<u>Finding a Poem.</u> New York: Atheneum, 1970. 68 p.
<u>The Nixon Poems.</u> New York: Atheneum Publishers, 1970. 97 p.
<u>I Am a Man: Ode to Martin Luther King, Jr.</u> Garden City, N.Y.: Doubleday, 1971. [41] p.
<u>The Double Bed.</u> New York: M. Evans; distributed in assoc. with Lippincott, 1972. 142 p.

MERRIFIELD, ANNABELLE (1883-)
<u>The Grace Notes.</u> Boston: Bruce Humphries, 1951. 96 p.

MERRILL, CLARA A.
<u>Poems.</u> Auburn, ME.: Merrill & Webber Co., Prs., 1915. 3 p. ℓ., [5]-155 p.

MERRILL, DAPHNE WINSLOW
<u>Cones from the Pines of Maine.</u> Manchester, ME.: Falmouth Pub. House, 1953. 24 p.
<u>More Cones from the Pines of Maine.</u> Philadelphia: Dorrance, 1965. 57 p. (Contemporary poets of Dorrance, 600)

MERRILL, ELIZABETH POWERS
<u>Where Bugles Call, and Other Verses.</u> Boston: Sherman, French & Company, 1914. 4 p. ℓ., 106 p.

MERRILL, NELLE
<u>Hillsyde Dew; Poems.</u> Bloomington, IN.: n.p., 1929. 5 p. ℓ., 9-10, 13-62 p.
<u>Gold Filings.</u> Nashville, IN.: n.p., 1933. 61 p.
<u>Happy Jingles.</u> Nashville, IN.: n.p., 1934. [35] p.

MERRITT, ALICE HADEN (1905-)
<u>...Dream Themes, and Other Poems.</u> Philadelphia: Dorrance and Company, 1940. 57 p.
<u>Psalms and Proverbs: A Poetical Version.</u> Philadelphia: Dorrance, 1941.
<u>Whence Waters Flow; Poems for All Ages from Old Virginia.</u> Richmond, VA.: Dietz Press, 1948. 69 p.
<u>A Special Day Program Book.</u> Danville, VA.: A. H. Merritt, 1961. 52 p.

MERSEREAU, EVELYN B.
<u>Suds: Romance, Reality, and Reminiscence.</u> Piermont? N.Y.: n.p., 1952. 74 p.

MESIROW, MILDRED H.
So Proudly We Ail! Philadelphia: Dorrance, 1963. 83 p. (Contemporary poets of Dorrance, 569)
When I Walk in the Sun. Philadelphia: Dorrance, 1965. 32 p. (Contemporary poets of Dorrance)

MESSENGER, HAZEL MOORE
Foam from Grey Deeps; A Collection of Poetry. New York: William-Frederick Press, 1958. 44 p.
Poems. Burton, OH.: n.p., 1961. 22 p.

MESSER, JULIA
Garnered Reveries. Dallas, TX.: Story Book Press, 1954. 40 p.

MESTON, LETA
Alien Votary. Dallas, TX.: The Kaleidograph Press, 1941. xi p., 1 ℓ., 15-104 p.
Lines Written Yesterday. Denver, CO.: Big Mountain Press, 1955. 64 p.
Soliloquy. Denver, CO.: Big Mountain Press, 1958. 36 p.

METZ, DOROTHY
Autumn Leaves. San Antonio, TX.: Naylor Co., 1962. 36 p.

METZGER, HATTIE CAIN (1894-)
I Would Step Lightly Today; Poems. New York: H. Harrison, 1938. 63 p.

METZLER, MAY SOWLES
Awakening of Desert Flowers. Coachella, CA.: n.p., 1930. [16] p.
Desert Memories, and Other Verse. Pasadena, CA.: Login Print. and Binding Co., 1951. 82 p.

MEUDT, EDNA
Round River Canticle. Sanbornville, N.H.: Wake-Brook House, 1960. 104 p.
In No Strange Land. Coral Gables, FL.: Wake-Brook House, 1964. 90 p.
No One Sings Face Down. Madison, WI.: Wisconsin House, 1970. 88 p.
The Ineluctable Sea: Poems. Ft. Lauderdale, FL.: Wake-Brook House, 1975. 128 p.

MEYER, AMY LEAH (HOWLETT) (1879-)
Leaves from the Backwoods. Philadelphia: Dorrance and Company, 1925. 5 p. ℓ., 13-66 p. (Contemporary poets of Dorrance, 20)

MEYER, EMMA (VOORHEES)
First and Last Defense, Selected Poems. New York: Avon House, 1941. 64 p.

MEYERS, BIRDIE (BECKWITH) (1892-)
The Heart Speaks. Denver, CO.: Big Mountain Press, 1961. 71 p.

MEYERS, JOAN SIMPSON
Poetry and a Libretto. Denver, CO.: A. Swallow, 1965. 52 p. (The New poetry series)

MEZQUIDA, ANNA BLAKE
A-Gypsying. San Francisco: M. Cloyd, 1922. 5 p. ℓ., 3-71 p.

MICHAEL, BERTHA INWOOD
Home Poems and Summer Memories. Boston: The Roxburgh Publishing Company, Inc., 1923. 135 p.

MICHAEL, PHYLLIS C.
Poems for Mothers. Grand Rapids, MI.: Zondervan Pub. House, 1963. 61 p.
Poems from My Heart. Grand Rapids, MI.: Zondervan Pub. House, 1964. 160 p.
Beside Still Waters; Poems to Comfort and Encourage. Grand Rapids, MI.: Zondervan Pub. House, 1969. 62 p.

MICHAELIS, ALINE
Courage, and Other Poems. Austin, TX.: Morgan Printing Company, 1931. 105 p.

MICK, PEARL E. (1886-)
"Messengers of Love"; Poems. Kenton, OH.: The Roby Bros. Printing Company, 1912. 6 p. ℓ., 19-91 p.

MIDDENDORF, BARBARA
Thin Mask. New York: Crown Publications, 1939. 4 p. ℓ., 11-59 p.

MIEHM, CLARA
Flotsam and Other Poems. Philadelphia: Dorrance and Company, 1926. 48 p. (Contemporary poets of Dorrance, 36)

MIGUELLA see BLITCH, MARY M.

MILES, EMILY WINTHROP
Coventry and Other Poems. New York: W. E. Rudge's Sons, 1941. 4 p. ℓ., 3-45 p.
Four Wishes, and Other Poems. New York: n. p., 1954. 142 p.
Recompense, and Other Poems. New York: n. p., 1955. 188 p.
Scribes and Other Poems. New York: n. p., 1956. 4 p. ℓ., 172 p.
Appeal, and Other Poems. New York: Helenson Press, 1957. 97 p.
Suggestion, and Other Poems. New York: Helenson Press, 1958. 103 p.
Disclosure, and Other Poems. New York: Helenson Press, 1959. 91 p.

MILES, JOSEPHINE (1911-) [Full Name: Josephine Louise Miles.]
...Lines at Intersection. New York: The Macmillan Company, 1939. viii p., 1 ℓ., 58 p.
Poems on Several Occasions. Norfolk, CT.: New Directions, 1941. [32] p.
...Local Measures. New York: Reynal and Hitchcock, 1946. 5 p. ℓ., 62 p.
After This Sea. San Francisco: The Book Club of California, Hart Press, 1947. [8] p. (Keepsake series)
Prefabrications. Bloomington, IN.: Indiana University Press, 1955. 90 p. (Poetry series)
Poems, 1930-1960. Bloomington, IN.: Indiana University Press, 1960. 160 p.
Civil Poems. Berkeley, CA.: Oyez, 1966. [19] p.
Bent. Santa Barbara, CA.: Unicorn Press, 1967. [4] p.
Kinds of Affection. Middletown, CT.: Wesleyan University Press, 1967. 78 p.
Saving the Bay. San Francisco: Open Space, 1967. unpaged.
Fields of Learning. Berkeley, CA.: Oyez, 1968. 25 p.
American Poems. Berkeley, CA.: Cloud Marauder Press, 1970. [28] p.
To All Appearances: New and Selected Poems. Urbana, IL.: University of Illinois Press, 1974. 163 p.

MILES, SUSAN, pseud. see ROBERTS, URSULA (WYLLIE) (1887-)

MILHOLLAND, MARI HASKINS
One. Mount Vernon, N.Y.: Printed at Peter Pauper Press, 1954. 53 p.

MILLARD, VIVIAN TURNER
The Beckoning Heights. New York: Pageant Press, 1957. 346 p.

MILLAY, CORA (BUZELLE)
Little Otis. New York: W. W. Norton & Co., 1928. 4 p. ℓ., 3-103 p. (Verse for children.)

MILLAY, EDNA ST. VINCENT (1892-1950)
Renascence, and Other Poems. New York: M. Kennerly, 1917. 3 p. ℓ., 73 p.
A Few Figs from Thistles; Poems and Four Sonnets. New York: F. Shay, 1920. 20 p.
A Few Figs from Thistles; Poems and Sonnets. 2d ed. New York: F. Shay, 1921. 16 p.
______. New and enl. ed. New York: F. Shay, 1921. 2 p. ℓ., [7]-28 p.
Second April. New York: M. Kennerly, 1921. 5 p. ℓ., 3-112 p.
The Ballad of the Harp Weaver. 1st ed. New York: F. Shay, 1922. [16] p.
______. 2d ed., 1922.
A Few Figs from Thistles; Poems and Sonnets. New and enl. ed.

New York: F. Shay, 1922. 39 p.
The Harp Weaver, and Other Poems. 1st ed. New York and London: Harper & Brothers, 1923. x, 93 p.
A Few Figs from Thistles; Poems and Sonnets. New York and London: Harper & Brothers, 1923. 3 p. ℓ., 9-39 p.
Poems. London: M. Secker, 1923. 2 p. ℓ., 7-145, [1] p.
Distressing Dialogues. 1st ed. New York and London: Harper & Brothers, 1924. vi p., 2 ℓ., 3-290 p.
The Harp-Weaver. London: M. Secker, 1924. 2 p. ℓ., 7-99 p.
Renascence, A Poem... Printed for the first time in separate form by Frederic & Bertha Goudy on the handpress on which William Morris printed the Kelmscott Chaucer. New York: Anderson Galleries, 1924. 10, [2] p.
Edna St. Vincent Millay. Ed. by Hughes Mearns. New York: Simon & Schuster, 1927. 31 p. (The pamphlet poets)
The Buck in the Snow, & Other Poems. 1st ed. New York and London: Harper & Brothers, 1928. 5 p. ℓ., 69, [1] p.
Edna St. Vincent Millay's Poems Selected for Young People. 1st ed. New York and London: Harper & Brothers, 1929. ix, 113 p.
Fatal Interview, Sonnets. 1st ed. New York and London: Harper & Brothers, 1931. x p., 52 p., 1 ℓ.
Wine from These Grapes. 1st ed. New York and London: Harper & Brothers, 1934. viii p., 2 ℓ., 3-91 p.
________. 2 v. v. 1--Wine from these grapes. v. 2--Epitaph for the race of man.
Conversation at Midnight. 1st ed. New York and London: Harper & Brothers, 1937. xv p., 126 p.
________. xx p., 1 ℓ., 177, [1] p. Ltd. ed. signed by the author.
Huntsman, What Quarry? 1st ed. New York: Harper & Brothers, 1939. ix, 94 p.
________. xii, 108, [1] p. Ltd. ed. signed by the author.
Make Bright the Arrows; 1940 Notebook. 1st ed. New York & London: Harper & Brothers, 1940. viii, 65, [1] p.
There Are No Islands Anymore; Lines Written in Passion and Deep Concern for England, France, and My Own Country. 1st ed. New York: Harper & Brothers, 1940. 10 p., [1] ℓ.
Collected Sonnets of Edna St. Vincent Millay. New York: Harper & Brothers, 1941. xv p., 1 ℓ., 161 p., 1 ℓ.
Invocation to the Muses. New York and London: Harper & Brothers, 1941. 7 p.
Lyrics and Sonnets. Selected, with an introduction by Louis Untermeyer. New York: Editions for the Armed Services, Inc., 1941? 127, [1] p.
The Murder of Lydice. 1st ed. New York and London: Harper & Brothers, 1942. vi p., 1 ℓ., 32 p., 1 ℓ.
Collected Lyrics of Edna St. Vincent Millay. 1st ed. New York and London: Harper & Brothers, 1943. xii, 383, [1] p.
Poem and Prayer for an Invading Army. New York: National Broadcasting Company, 1944. [12] p.
Second April; and, The Buck in the Snow. New York: Harper,

1950. xii, [4], 89, [4], 69 p. (Harper's modern classics)
Mine the Harvest. A Collection of New Poems. 1st ed. New York: Harper and Brothers, 1954. xii, 140 p.
Collected Poems. Edited by Norma Millay. New York: Harper, 1956. xxi, 738 p.
Collected Lyrics. New ed. New York: Washington Square Press, 1959. xxiii, 279 p.
Collected Sonnets. New ed. New York: Washington Square Press, 1959. xxiii, [1], 166 p.

MILLAY, KATHLEEN (1897?-1943) [Full Name: Kathleen Kalloch (Millay) Young.]
The Evergreen Tree; Poems. New York: Boni & Liveright, 1927. ix p., 1 ℓ., 13-110 p.
The Hermit Thrush. New York: H. Liveright, 1929. ix, 11-129 p.
The Beggar at the Gate; Poems. New York: H. Liveright, 1931. 99 p.

MILLER, AGNES
Triptych: Free-Born. North Montpelier, VT.: The Driftwind Press, 1937. x, 13-62 p.
Mural: Journey. Emory University, Atlanta, GA.: Banner Press, 1939. 54 p. (Verse craft series)
Glass: Arborvitae. Emory University, Atlanta, GA.: Banner Press, 1942. 48 p. (Verse craft series)

MILLER, ALICE DAVIS
Flowers from the Garden of My Heart. Oakland, CA.: Printed by Harrington-McInnis, 1942. 79 p.

MILLER, ALICE (DUER) (1874-1942)
Are Women People? A Book of Rhymes for Suffrage Times. New York: George H. Doran Company, 1915. 6 p. ℓ., 11-94 p.
Women Are People! New York: George H. Doran, 1917. vi, 9-98 p.
Wings in the Night. New York: The Century Company, 1918. 5 p. ℓ., 3-17 p.
Forsaking All Others. New York: Simon & Schuster, 1931. 95, [1] p.
The White Cliffs. New York? n.p., 1940? 58 numb. ℓ.
________. New York: Coward-McCann, 1940. 3 p. ℓ., 3-70 p.
________. 1 v. unpaged. Special edition of 5000 copies.
________. 2d ed. London: Methuen & Co., 1941. 3 p. ℓ., 59, [1] p.
Forsaking All Others. London: Methuen & Co., 1941. 2 p. ℓ., 95, [1] p.
Cinderella. New York: Coward-McCann, 1943. [64] p.
The White Cliffs. Toronto: Longmans, Green, 1946. 70 p.

MILLER, CECILIA PARSONS
Not Less Content. Harrisburg, PA.: P. S. Letter Shop, 1960.

32 p.

Peculiar Honors. Harrisburg, PA.: Keystone Press, 1962. 35 p.

Stand on the Edge. Fort Smith, AR.: South and West, 1970. 41 p.

Space, Where Once a Husband Stood; A Small Collection of Poems. Lemoyne, PA.: n.p., 1972. 15 ℓ.

MILLER, DELLA CROWDER (1874-)

Window to the Sun. Kansas City, MO.: Kansas City Pub. House, 1949. 64 p.

And So Through the Year. Kansas City, MO.: Kansas City Pub. Co., 1950. 64 p.

Footprints. Dallas, TX.: Story Book Press, 1953. 64 p.

This Day Is Ours. Kansas City, MO.: Kansas City Pub. Co., 1953. 64 p.

Abraham Lincoln; A Biographic Trilogy in Sonnet Sequence. Ed. by Orville Crowder Miller. Boston: Christopher Pub. House, 1965. 200 p.

MILLER, DORIS C.

Who Burnishes the Lamp. Chicago: Folio Press, 1952. 56 p.

MILLER, DOROTHY JANE

My Rambling Thoughts; Poems. New York: The William-Frederick Press, 1944. 64 p. (The William-Frederick poets, 10)

MILLER, EDITH ABERCROMBIE

Rosemary; A Book of Verse. New York: R. G. Cooke, Inc., 1908. 43 p.

________. New York: F. F. Sherman, 1909. 43 p.

MILLER, FLORENCE MARIA (1872-)

Twilight and Firelight. Leominster, MA.: Leominster Enterprise Co., 1921. [27] p.

MILLER, FLORETTE TRUESDELL

Hadassah, The Star of the Persian Court. Boston: The Stratford Co., 1919. 4 p. ℓ., 83 p., 1 ℓ.

MILLER, FRANCESCA (FALK) (1888-)

Reveries and Rhymes. Chicago: Falk & Co., 1915. 39 p.

The Prodigal and Other Poems. Chicago: Hyman-McGee Co., 1924. 6 p. ℓ., 96 p.

Pink Lightning; A Collection of Verse. Chicago: R. F. Seymour, 1926. 4 p. ℓ., 7-69 p.

Lake of Stars. Philadelphia: Dorrance & Company, 1930. 71 p. (Contemporary poets of Dorrance, 85)

Immortality, and Other Poems. Chicago: R. F. Seymour, 1939. 199 p.

Never Winter & Other Poems. Chicago: Americana House, 1950. 64 p.

Collected Poetry. Chicago: n.p., 1956. 295 p.

MILLER, GERTRUDE (THOMPSON)

Aeolian Harps. Kansas City, MO.: Burton Pub. Co., 1954. 198 p.

For Listening Ears, Poems of Faith, Hope and Love. Huntington, W.VA.: n.p., 1960. 259 p.

Memories in Rhyme; A Sequel to Aeolian Harps. Huntington, W.VA.: Scaggs Printing Co., 1962. 108, [18] p.

MILLER, HEATHER ROSS (1939-)

Tenants of the House. New York: Harcourt, Brace, 1966.

The Wind Southerly; Poems. New York: Harcourt, Brace & World, 1967. 52 p.

Horse, Horse, Tyger, Tyger. Charlotte, N.C.: Red Clay Press, 1973. 52 p.

MILLER, HELEN JANET

Song after War, and Other Poems. New York: Exposition Press, 1947. 64 p.

MILLER, JEWELL

Mountain Water. The Collected Poems of Jewell Miller.... North Montpelier, VT.: W. J. Coates, The Driftwind Press, 1933. 4 p.ℓ., 7-151, [1] p.

MILLER, MABEL (ENDRESEN) (1890-)

Low Clouds at Sundown. Yakima, WA.: Franklin Press, 1966. ix, 54 p.

MILLER, MADELEINE SWEENEY (1890-)

Songs from the Smoke. Cincinnati; New York: The Methodist Book Concern, 1914. 62 p.

MILLER, MARCIA MUTH

Post Card Views and Other Souvenirs. Santa Fe, N.M.: Sunstone Press, 1973. 64 p.

MILLER, MARIE CLARK

Christmas Blooms. Boston: Christopher Pub. House, 1948. 40 p.

Holidays in Verse: Poems for Children. Boston: Christopher Pub. House, 1948. 38 p.

Panorama and Other Poems. Pasadena, CA.: Typecraft, 1957. 90 p.

MILLER, MARY (BRITTON) (1893-)

Menagerie. New York: The Macmillan Company, 1928. xi, 124 p.

Songs of Infancy, and Other Poems. New York: The Macmillan Company, 1928. 5 p.ℓ., 3-144 p.

Without Sanctuary. New York: The Macmillan Company, 1932. ix, 93 p.

Intrepid Bird. New York: The Macmillan Company, 1934. xi, 72 p.

The Crucifixion, A Poem. New York: C. Scribner's Sons, 1944. 4 p. ℓ., 27 p.
Give a Guess; Poems. New York: Pantheon, 1957. unpaged.
All Aboard; Poems. New York: Pantheon, 1958. 47 p.
A Handful of Flowers; Poems. New York: Pantheon, 1959. 46 p.
Listen--The Birds; Poems. New York: Pantheon, 1961. 46 p. (Verse for children.)

MILLER, MARY OWINGS
Sand Dunes, and Other Poems. New York: The Paebar Co., 1935. 3 p. ℓ., 9-48 p.
Only Brown Stubble. New York: Avon House, 1937. 64 p.
Wheel of Paper. Baltimore, MD.: Contemporary Poetry, 1948. 5 p. ℓ., 13-70 p.
High Sun Over Yram; New and Selected Poems. Baltimore, MD.: Contemporary Poetry, 1961. 75 p. (Contemporary poetry library series, 14)

MILLER, MAY
Into the Clearing. Washington, D.C.: Charioteer Press, 1959. 24 p.
Poems. Thetford, VT.: Cricket Press, 1962. [13] p.
The Clearing and Beyond. Washington, D.C.: Charioteer Press, 1974. vii, 49 p.

MILLER, MAY (MERRILL)
Mother Lode, 1849-1949. Culver City, CA.: Murray & Gee, 1949. 32 p.

MILLER, MAYME GARNER
Chandeliers; A Volume of Religious Verse. Nashville, TN.: Parthenon Press, 1952. 160 p.

MILLER, NELL THOMPSON
Live Coals. Emory University, Atlanta, GA.: Banner Press, 1939. 4 p. ℓ., [7]-36 p. (Verse craft series)
Remembered Loves; A Second Book of Verse. Emory University, Atlanta, GA.: Banner Press, 1943. 4 p. ℓ., 7-69 p. (Verse craft series)
This, Too, Has Been My Dream. n.p., 1946. 50 p.

MILLER, NELLIE BURGET (1875-)
In Earthen Bowles. New York; London: D. Appleton & Company, 1924. 126 p.
Pictures from the Plains and Other Poems, Collected Verse. New York: The Poets Press, 1936. 6 p. ℓ., 15-113, [1] p.
The Sun Drops Red, Collected Poems. Denver, CO.: Sage Books, 1947. x, 102 p.

MILLER, RUTH HATHAWAY
Just Everyday Poems; A Poetry Sequence. New York: William-Frederick Press, 1952. 41 p. (The William-Frederick poets, 83)

MILLER, SADIE LOUISE (1870-)
Poems. Upland? IN.: n. p., 1925? [70] p.
A Dip of the Quill. Upland, IN.: Taylor University Press, 193-? 51, [2] p.
Moonlight and Memories. Tucson, AZ.: Acme Printing Co., 1930. 48 p.
Dreams of a Decade. Upland, IN.: n. p., 1940. 64 p.

MILLER, VASSAR (1924-)
Adam's Footprint. New Orleans, LA.: New Orleans Poetry Journal, 1956. 48 p.
Wage War on Silence; Poems. Middletown, CT.: Wesleyan University Press, 1960. 4 p. ℓ., 69 p.
My Bones Being Wiser; Poems. Middletown, CT.: Wesleyan University Press, 1963. 84 p.
Onions and Roses. Middletown, CT.: Wesleyan University Press, 1968. 70 p.
If I Could Sleep Deeply Enough: Poems. New York: Liveright, dist. by Norton, 1974. ix, 48 p.

MILLER-FREEMAN, CALLIE
Garland of Verse. New York: The Writer's Press, 1915. 32 p.

MILLET, MARTHA
Thine Alabaster Cities; A Poem for Our Times. Brooklyn, N.Y.: n. p., 1952. [21] p.
Dangerous Jack, A Fantasy in Verse. New York: Sierra Press, 1953. 78 p.

MILLS, CONSTANCE QUIMBY
My Jewel Box. Santa Barbara, CA.: Schauer Printing Studio, 1952. [18] p.
My Christmas Box. Santa Barbara, CA.: Schauer Printing Studio, 1953. [16] p.
A String of Pearls. Santa Barbara, CA.: Schauer Printing Studio, 1963. [20] p.

MILLS, DOROTHY B.
Cobwebs Half Spun. New York: Exposition Press, 1948. 5 p. ℓ., 140 p.

MILLS, GENEVA
No Lasting Splendor. Dallas, TX.: The Kaleidograph Press, 1945. ix, 11-80 p.

MILLWARD, PAMELA
The Route of the Phoebe Snow. San Francisco: Coyote, 1966. 26 p.
Once and for All. San Francisco: Four Seasons, 1969.

MILNE, FRANCES MARGARET (TENER) (1846-)
Our Little Roman. Verses of Childhood. n. p., 1902. 29, [1] p.

<u>For Today, Poems.</u> San Francisco, CA.: The J. H. Barry Company, 1905. 5 p. ℓ., 9-231 p.

MILTON, ABBY CRAWFORD

<u>The Magic Switch.</u> Boston: The Cornhill Publishing Company, 1925. 5 p. ℓ., 3-46 p.

<u>Caesar's Wife and Other Poems.</u> Atlanta, GA.: E. Hartsock, 1930. 148 p.

<u>Lookout Mountain.</u> Ogelthorpe University, GA.: Ogelthorpe University Press, 1934. 83 p.

<u>Flower Lore.</u> Philadelphia: Dorrance, 1956. 192 p.

MINER, GENEVIEVE FITCH (1906-)

<u>Libations.</u> Boston: The Christopher Publishing House, 1933. viii, 9-48 p.

MINKLER, CARRIE RUTH (STILLWELL) (1845-)

<u>Day Dreams.</u> San Francisco: n.p., 1909. 3 p. ℓ., 11-95 p.

MINTON, ORLENA MARIAN

<u>Ragweed Rhymes of Rural Folks.</u> New York: Aberdeen Publishing Company, 1910. vi, 7-92 p.

MINTY, JUDITH (1937-)

<u>Lake Songs and Other Fears.</u> Pittsburgh, PA.: University of Pittsburgh Press, 1974. 56 p. (Pitt poetry series)

MINTZ, RUTH FINER (1919-)

<u>The Darkening Green.</u> Denver, CO.: Big Mountain Press, 1965. 116 p.

<u>Traveling Through Time.</u> New York: J. David, 1970. 90 p.

MINTZER, YVETTE

<u>Dreamline Express.</u> New York: Inwood Press, dist. by Horizon Press, 1975. 64 p.

MIRIAM, <u>Sister</u> (1886-) [Secular Name: Margaret Miriam Gallagher.]

<u>Woven of the Sky.</u> New York: The Macmillan Company, 1940. xvi, 71 p.

<u>Love Is Enough, New and Selected Poems.</u> New York: Exposition Press, 1962. 103 p.

MIRICK, EDITH (BROWN)

<u>Flower and Weed.</u> New York: J. T. White, 1930. xi, 73 p.

<u>These Twinkling Acres.</u> Dallas, TX.: The Kaleidograph Press, 1935. xii p., 4 ℓ., 21-95 p., 1 ℓ.

MISHLER, MILDRED M.

<u>A Hundred Years Ago, A Miscellany.</u> New York: Vantage Press, 1963. 48 p.

MISHNUN, VIRGINIA
The Inheritors. New York: International Publications, 1962. 79 p.
_______. London: Favril, 1962. 79 p.

MITCHELL, ANNA VIRGINIA
Garden of Dreams; A Book of Poems. Louisville, KY.: J. P. Morton & Company, 1924. 4 p. ℓ., 42 p.

MITCHELL, ANNE COE
Seed of the Wind. Northampton, MA.: Priv. Print., The Hampshire Bookshop, 1929. 2 p. ℓ., 46 p.
Mark of the Tide. Montclair, N. J.: Mountain Press, 1954. 111 p.

MITCHELL, Mrs. E. A. B.
The Lake of Peace, and Other Poems. New York: Press of Eaton & Mains, 1911. 115 p.

MITCHELL, GEORGIA
Last Year and Tomorrow. Camden, N. J.: Printed by the Haddon Craftsmen, Inc., 1941. x p., 1 ℓ., 84 p.
All Is Fair. New Orleans, LA.: Bormon House, 1944. 1 p. ℓ., vii-xiv p., 1 ℓ., [2], 2-116 p.

MITCHELL, IRENE MUSILLO
Portraits; Dramatic Monologs. Boston: Branden Press, 1972. 51 p.
I Don't Own You So I Can't Give You Away. Evanston, IL.: Abstract Pub., 1975. 80 p.

MITCHELL, LULU WHEDON
This Way I Came. Dallas, TX.: The Kaleidograph Press, 1940. ix, 11-92 p.

MITCHELL, RUTH COMFORT (1882-)
The Night Court & Other Verse. New York: Century Co., 1916. 6 p. ℓ., 3-97 p.
Narratives in Verse. New York & London: D. Appleton & Co., 1923. xiv, 181 p., 1 ℓ.

MITCHELL, RUTH HILL (1904-)
Harness Music to Winds. Portland, ME.: Falmouth Pub. House, 1948. 58 p.

MITCHELL, SUSANNA VALENTINE
Journey Taken by a Woman. New York: Farrar & Rinehart, Inc., 1935. xi, 97 p.
Make New Banners. New York: Farrar, Straus & Young, 1954? 4 p. ℓ., 291 p.
Collected Poems. Camden, N. J.: n. p., 1966. ix, 155 p.

MIXTER, FLORENCE KILPATRICK
Out of Mist. New York: Boni and Liveright, 1921. 76 p.

MOCKEL, MYRTLE SIMPSON
...Wild Cherry; Poems. Philadelphia: Dorrance & Company, 1947. 101 p. (Contemporary poets of Dorrance, 334)
Montana's Song, and Poems of the West. Philadelphia: Dorrance, 1964. 32 p.

MODES, ALICE E.
If This Be Wisdom. New York: H. Harrison, 1931. 63 p.

MOFFITT, HELEN REED
Fantasy and Dreams, Poems. Dallas, TX.: Story Book Press, 1951. 40 p.
Green Foam. Denver, CO.: Big Mountain Press, 1954. 32 p.
"Forever Yours." n.p.: Gateway Printers, 1962. 36 p.

MOHLER, IONE
Phantasma. Washington, D.C.: National Capital Press, 1946. 68 p.

MOLINA, JULIA WOLFF
Mingled Sweets and Bitters: or My Legacy. New York; London: The Abbey Press, 1902. 1 p.ℓ., vi, 265 p.

MOLINARO, URSULE
Rimes et Raisons. Monte Carlo: Regain, 1954. 62 p. (Poètes de notre temps, no. 95)
Mirrors for Small Beasts. New York: Noonday Press, 1960. 46 p.

MOLINE, HILMA K.
Echoes; Poems. New York: Exposition Press, 1950. 63 p.

MOLK, SOPHIA (1898-)
A Flame Still Burning. New York: Empire Books, 1935. 96 p.
Prairie Trails. Boston: The Christopher Publishing House, 1937. 3 p.ℓ., v-vii, 9-126 p.
Haunting Shadows. New York: The Exposition Press, 1944. 6 p.ℓ., 17-160 p. (Poets of America. Series four)
On the Wings of the Wind. Avon, IL.: Hamlet Press, 1950. 105 p.
Isle of Tears. Middle Village, N.Y.: J. David, 1971. 54 p.

MOLLICA, HELYN (1926-)
Umbria. Philadelphia: Dorrance, 1953. 57 p.

MONAHAN, MARY ANN
...Stars in a Puddle. Philadelphia: Dorrance and Company, 1938. 54 p. (Contemporary poets of Dorrance, 186)

MONROE, HARRIET (1860-1936)
The Dance of the Seasons. Chicago: Ralph Fletcher Seymour Co., 1911. 20 p.
You and I. New York: Macmillan Co., 1914. x p., 2 ℓ., 3-236 p.
The Difference and Other Poems, Including the Columbian Ode. Chicago: Covici-McGee Company, 1924. 5 p. ℓ., 123 p.
______. 1925. [8], 123 p.
______. New York: Macmillan Co., 1925. 123 p.
Chosen Poems; A Selection from My Books of Verse. New York: Macmillan Co., 1935. xvi, 299 p.

MONROE, ISA W.
... Rhymes o' the Heart. Boston: The Stratford Company, 1929. 31 p. (The Stratford poets)

MONROE, MARY CAMPBELL
The Rainbow Road, and Other Verse. New York: Colonial Printing Co., 1914. [55] p.

MONROE, MARY COLLISTER (1869-)
Legends and Lyrics; Poems. New York: William-Frederick Press, 1951. 14 p. (The William-Frederick poets, 66)

MONTAGUE, ELIZABETH MAY
Southern Songs, Rhymes, and Jingles. New York: The Cameo Press, 1916. 96 p.

MONTGOMERY, BETTY J.
The Elusive Pattern. New York: Pageant Press, 1953. 61 p.

MONTGOMERY, CARRIE JUDD (1850-)
Heart Melody. Oakland, CA.: Office of Triumphs of Faith, 1922. 4 p. ℓ., 13-102 p.

MONTGOMERY, ELIZABETH SHAW (1878?-1968)
Scarlet Runner. New York: T. Crowell Co., 1923. 96 p.
Scarabaeus. New York: H. Vinal, 1926. 40 p.

MONTGOMERY, LOUISE MOSS
Village Vignettes. New York: McBride, 1949. iv, 54 p.
Trail of Years: Lighted by Smiles--Watered by Tears. Clarksdale, MS.: n.p., 1975. 1 v. unpaged.

MONTGOMERY, MARION (HOYT) (1925-)
Dry Lightning. Lincoln, NB.: University of Nebraska Press, 1960. 80 p.
Stones from the Rubble; Poems. Campobello, S.C.: Argus Books, 1965. 62 p.
The Gull, and Other Georgia Scenes. Athens, GA.: University of Georgia Press, 1970. 60 p.

MONTGOMERY, RENA WINTER
Windblown. Columbus, OH.: C. C. Hartley, 1942. 96 p.

MONTGOMERY, ROSELLE MERCIER (d. 1933)
Ulysses Returns, and Other Poems. New York: Brentano's, 1925. 132 p.
Many Devices, Poems. New York & London: D. Appleton, 1929. x p., 1 ℓ., 150 p.

MONTGOMERY, VAIDA (STEWART) (1898-)
Locoed and Other Poems. Dallas, TX.: The Kaleidoscope Publishers, 1930. 5 p. ℓ., 59 p.
Hail for Rain. Dallas, TX.: Kaleidograph Press, 1948. 79 p.

MONTROSE, SANDRA
Poems. Excelsior, MN?: n. p., 1944. 24, [1] p.

MONTROSS, LOIS (SEYSTER) (1897-) [Full Name: Lois Ferne (Seyster) Montross]
The Crimson Cloak. New York: Boni & Liveright, 1924. vii, 71 p.

MOODY, CHRISTINA
A Tiny Spark. Washington: Murray Brothers Press, 1910. 43 p.

MOODY, MARGARET W.
Smoky Hill Trail, and Other Poems. New York: Vantage Press, 1955. 79 p.

MOODY, MARY VIRGINIA (1914-)
The First Hill. York, PA.: The Maple Press Company, 1929. 34 p.

MOON, LUCINA
Autumn Leaves from an Eastern Maple: A Collection of Songs and Verses for the Home Folks. St. Helena, CA.: Pacific Union College Press, 1916. 60 p.
________. 1922. 1 p. ℓ., 5-88, [3] p.

MOORE, ADA J.
Bindweed.... Prairie City, IL.: The Decker Press, 1948. 68 p.

MOORE, ANNE (1872-)
Children of God and Winged Things. Boston: The Four Seas Company, 1921. 126 p.
A Misty Sea. Portland, ME.: The Southworth-Anthoensen Press, 1937. ix, 154 p.

MOORE, CHARLOTTE (McKENNEY) (1908-)
Sword in Eden. New York: Fine Editions Press, 1952. 48 p.

MOORE, CLAIRE
Family. New York: Children's Underground Press, 1971? 38 p. (Verse for children.)
The Edge. New York: The Children's Underground Press, 1972. [46] p.

MOORE, CORDELIA ELIZABETH
Voices of the Heart; A Book of Poems. Louisville, KY.: Pentecostal Publishing Company, 1914. 229 p.

MOORE, EDNA AUGUSTA
Along the Trail. New York: L. N. Green-Leach, 1930. 52 p.

MOORE, ELEANOR AGNES
Poems of Endowment on Realities of Life. Boston: R. G. Badger, 1907. 3-140 p.

MOORE, FAITH see EBERLING, GEORGIA EDITH (MOORE)

MOORE, FRANCES E.
Poems. Kansas City, MO.: Smith-Grieves Company, 1915. [19] p.
The Victorious Life Lyrics. Kansas City, MO.: Franklin Hudson Publishing Co., 1918. 32 p.

MOORE, GEORGIANA T.
White Moth. Malden, MA.: Butler Press, 1930. 3 p. ℓ., 45 p.

MOORE, HELEN TRAFFORD
My Thoughts and I. Boston: R. G. Badger, 1929. 3 p. ℓ., 9-44 p.

MOORE, ISABEL (KELLOGG) (1872-)
The Garden of the Idle Mind. New York: Printed by R. C. Penfield, 1916. 35 p.

MOORE, JOSEPHINE MECHLING
Flame on a Thousand Hills, Lyrics and Sonnets. Boston: B. Humphries, 1949. 136 p.

MOORE, JULIA A. (DAVIS) (1847-1920)
The Sweet Singer of Michigan. Chicago: P. Covici, 1928. 4 p. ℓ., vii-xxvii, 158 p.

MOORE, LA NESE B.
Can I Be Right? New York: Vantage Press, 1971. 48 p.

MOORE, MARIANNE (1887-1972)
Poems. London: The Egoist Press, 1921. 23, [1] p.
Marriage. New York: Monroe Wheeler, 1923. [20] p. (Manikin, no. 3)
Observations. New York: The Dial Press, 1924. 120 p.
________. 2d ed., 1925. 120 p.

Selected Poems. New York: The Macmillan Co., 1935. xvi p., 1 ℓ., 126 p.
_______. London: Faber and Faber Limited, 1935. 142 p. First English ed.
The Pangolin and Other Verse. London: The Brendin Pub. Co., 1936. 4 p. ℓ., 3-24 p., 1 ℓ.
What Are Years. New York: The Macmillan Co., 1941. 5 p. ℓ., 54 p.
Nevertheless. New York: The Macmillan Co., 1944. 5 p. ℓ., 14 p.
A Face a Poem. Cummington, MA.: Printed at the Cummington Press for the New Colophon, 1949. [4] p. on double ℓ.
Collected Poems. New York: The Macmillan Co., 1951. [1]-180 p.
_______. London: Faber and Faber, 1951. 180 p.
Like a Bulwark. New York: Viking Press, 1956. 32 p.
Like a Bulwark. New York: Viking Press, 1957. [1]-32 p.
_______. London: Faber and Faber, 1957. 41 p.
Collected Poems. New York: Macmillan, 1957. 180 p.
O to Be a Dragon. New York: Viking Press, 1959. 37 p.
Marianne Moore Reader. New York: Viking Press, 1961. 301 p.
Eight Poems. New York: Museum of Modern Art, 1962. [32] p.
Occasionem Cognosce. A Poem. Lunenberg, VT.: Stinehour Press, 1963. 2 ℓ.
The Arctic Ox. London: Faber and Faber, 1964. 52 p.
Dress and Kindred Subjects. New York: The Ibex Press, 1965. 11 p.
Marianne Moore Reader. Compass Books ed. New York: Viking Press, 1965. xviii, 301 p.
Silence. Cambridge, MA.: Printed by L. H. Scott, 1965. [1] p.
A Talisman. Cambridge, MA.: Adams House & Lowell House Press, 1965. [2] p.
The Complete Poems of Marianne Moore. New York: Macmillan Co., 1967. xiv, 305 p.
Tipoo's Tiger. New York: Phoenix Book Shop, 1967. [10] p.
The Complete Poems of Marianne Moore. London: Faber and Faber, 1968. xiv, 305, [1] p.
Marianne Moore's First Poem. Philadelphia: Rosenbach Foundation, 1972.
Unfinished Poems. Philadelphia: P. H. and A. S. W. Rosenbach Foundation, 1972. 76 ℓ.

MOORE, MARTHA BAILEY (1884-)
...This I Tell Thee. Philadelphia: Dorrance and Company, 1937. 70 p. (Contemporary poets of Dorrance, 156)

MOORE, ROBERTA ALICE (TAYLOR) (1875-)
Dreams and Fancies. Weatherford, TX.: The Herald Publishing Company, 1910. 48 p.

MOORE, RUTH
Cold as a Dog and the Wind Northeast; Ballads. New York:

Morrow, 1958. 61 p.
The Gold and Silver Hooks. New York: Morrow, 1969. 330 p.
Time's Web; Poems. New York: Morrow, 1972. 81 p.

MOORE, STELLA KILGORE
...Home Logic in Verse. Philadelphia: Dorrance & Company, 1935. 47 p. (Contemporary poets of Dorrance, 141)
Thoughts of an Ordinary Woman. Boston: The Christopher Publishing House, 1944. 60 p.

MOORE, VIRGINIA (1903-)
Not Poppy. New York: Harcourt, Brace & Co., 1926. x, 109 p.
Sweet Water and Bitter.... New York: Harcourt, Brace & Co., 1928. 96 p.
Homer's Golden Chain. New York: E. P. Dutton & Co., 1936. 80 p.

MOORER, LIZELIA AUGUSTA JENKINS
Prejudice Unveiled, and Other Poems. Boston: Roxburgh, 1907. 170 p.

MORE, ANNE
Scotch Thistles. Chicago: Kable Bros. Company, Printed for the Author, 1924. 5 p. ℓ., 13-143 p.
Irish Shamrock, Rhymes. Chicago: Kable Bros. Company, Printed for the Author, 1925. 142 p.

MORGAN, ANGELA
The Hour Has Struck; A War Poem and Other Poems. New York: The Aster Press, 1914. 90 p.
_______. 2d ed., New York: E. C. Lewis Co., 1915. 98 p.
_______. 3d ed., 1915. 98 p.
Battle Cry of the Mothers. n.p., 1915? 7 ℓ.
Utterance, and Other Poems. New York: Baker and Taylor, 1916. 106 p.
God Prays. Answer, World! New York: The Baker and Taylor Company, 1917. 4-24, [1] p.
The Hour Has Struck; A War Poem and Other Poems. 4th ed. New York: The Baker and Taylor Company, 1917. 98 p.
_______. 5th ed., 1917. 98 p.
Forward, March! New York: John Lane Company; London: John Lane, 1918. x, 102 p.
Hail, Man! New York & London: John Lane, 1919. vii p., 1 ℓ., 11-107 p.
The Hour Has Struck; A War Poem and Other Poems. New York: John Lane; London: John Lane, The Bodley Head, 1921. 98 p.
Because of Beauty. New York: Dodd, Mead and Company, 1922. 129 p.
Silver Clothes. New York: Dodd, Mead and Company, 1926. xii, 160 p.
Selected Poems. New York: Dodd, Mead and Company, 1927. xiv, 323 p.
_______. 1928.

Art Triumphant. Philadelphia: Kay Printing Company, 1929. 6 ℓ.
Come You Who Call for Conquerors. Philadelphia: Kay Printing Company, 1929. 6 ℓ.
Creator Man. New York: Dodd, Mead and Company, 1929. xi, 233 p.
______. Philadelphia: Kay Printing Company, 1929. 6 ℓ.
Lordly Spaces. Philadelphia: Kay Printing Company, 1929. 6 ℓ.
Selected Poems. New York: Dodd, Mead and Company, 1929. xiv, 323 p.
______. 1930.
Angela Morgan's Recitals. Philadelphia: The Penn Publishing Company, 1930. xvi, 308 p.
Heaven Is Happening. Philadelphia: Priv. print. Harper Printing Co., 1931. 2 p. ℓ., vii-x p., 1 ℓ., 13-103, [1] p.
Crucify Me! Philadelphia: Poetry Publishers, 1933. 86 p.
Afterwhere. 1st ed. New York: The Poets Press, 1936. 15-63 p.
Gold on Your Pillow. Philadelphia: The Eddington Press, 1936. xv, 143 p.
Drum Beats out of Heaven. Pasadena, CA.: Shaw Press, 1941. 97 p.
The Time for Love Has Come! God Prays. Boston: Beckler Press, 1942. [15] p.
Whirlwind Vision. Boston: Beckler Press, 1943. 34 p.
Let Loose the Splendor. New York: Great-Concord Publishers, 1951. 56 p.

MORGAN, BEATRICE (PAYNE) (1900-)
Amaranth and Myrtle. Philadelphia: Dorrance and Company, 1927. 39 p. (Contemporary poets of Dorrance, 61)
Amryl. Atlanta, GA.: The Bozart Press, 1929. 4 p. ℓ., 7-29 p.
Ophar's Child. Richmond, VA.: Dietz Press, 1951. 34 p.
Seven Jewel Candlesticks. Dallas, TX.: Story Book Press, 1951. 35 p.

MORGAN, CARRIE BLAKE
The Path of Gold; Poems. New Whatcom, WA.: Edson & Irish, 1900. 28 p.

MORGAN, CORAL
To Any Yet Faithful. Dallas, TX.: The Kaleidograph Press, 1941. xi p., 1 ℓ., 15-107 p.

MORGAN, DOLLY ANN
Held by the Heights, Poems. New York: Exposition Press, 1949. 63 p.

MORGAN, JANET BARTON
The Mullein and the Myrtle. Northampton, MA.: Hampshire Bookshop, 1951. 41 p.

The Trumpet Vine. Amherst, MA.: n.p., 1957. 47 p.
Take with You Words. Francestown, N.H.: Golden Quill Press, 1975. 95 p.

MORGAN, JOAN ELIZABETH
The Isles of Thought. Birmingham, AL.: Banner Press, 1966. 64 p.

MORGAN, ROBIN
Monster. New York: Random House, 1972. 86 p.

MORISON, CLARA JEANETTE (NICHOL) (1874-)
My Soldier Boy, and Other Poems. Boston: The Gorham Press, 1916. 46 p.

MORREL, JANE
Wordings Like Love. Springfield, IL.: Sangamon Poets, 1975? 24 p.

MORRILL, BELLE CHAPMAN
Blue Platter. Rochester, N.Y.: Interstate Printing Company, Inc., 1945. 4 p. ℓ., 11-62 p.
Second Helping; Poems. Chicago: Dierkes Press, 1950. 48 p.

MORRIN, MARIANNE
Thirty for Today. Dallas, TX.: Story Book Press, 1954. 39 p.

MORRIS, LAURA (HULL) (1852-)
Apostrophe to Hope, and Other Poems. New York: The Knickerbocker Press, 1915. ix, 161 p.

MORRIS, MARY WRENN
Odd Poems. Cambridge: Priv. print., 1931. 6 p. ℓ., 3-78 p., 1 ℓ.

MORRIS, MARY YOUNGS
Florida, and Other Poems. Philadelphia: Dorrance & Company, 1925. 54 p.

MORRISON, FRANCES
Poems: Frannie's First Book. Indianapolis, IN.: Hampton Printing Company, 1914. 66 p.

MORRISON, LILLIAN
Remember Me When This You See. New York: Crowell, 1961. 182 p. (Verse for children.)
The Ghosts of Jersey City and Other Poems. New York: Crowell, 1967. 55 p.

MORRISON, SARAH PARKE (1833-)
Sicily: A Poem Dedicated to the Memory of Dante Aligheiri. Richmond, IN.: The Ballinger Press, 1910. 32 p.

MORROW, ANNETTE SCHAEFER
Poems for People Who Are Either Emotional Now, or Would Like to Become Emotional. San Antonio, TX.: Naylor Co., 1964. 42 p.
Haiku of Hawaii. Rutland, VT.: Tuttle, 1970. 63 p.

MORROW, ELIZABETH (1873-1955) [Full Name: Elizabeth Reeve (Cutter) Morrow.]
Quatrains for My Daughter. New York: A. Knopf, 1931. 41, [1] p.

MORSE, ELEANOR WHITNEY
Journey's End and Other Poems. New York: Fleming H. Revell, Company, 1937. 44 p.

MORSE, GENEVIEVE F.
Through the Years, and Other Poems. New York: The Paebar Company, 1944. 58 p.

MORSE, KATHERINE DUNCAN (1888-)
A Gate of Cedar. New York: Macmillan Co., 1922. xiv p., 1 ℓ., 17-161 p.
Salt Water in Their Veins. New York: Fine Editions Press, 1947. 48 p.
Assyrian Sword and Spanish Chalice. New York: n. p., 1951. 56 p.

MORTENSON, ALICE HANSCHE (1898-)
Poems from the Heart. Kansas City, MO.: Beacon Hill Press, 1945. 96 p.
Knee-Deep in Snow, and Other Poems. Winona Lake, IN.: n. p., 1954. 96 p.

MORTON, ELIZA HAPPY (1855-1916)
Star-Flowers; or, Songs in the Night. Portland, ME.: Smith & Sale, 1912. x, 130 p., [1] p.

MOSELEY, LOU ELLA
Pebbles from a Brook. San Antonio, TX.: Naylor Co., 1961. vi, 94 p.

MOSES, LILIAN
Nature Poems and Others. Denver, CO.: Big Mountain Press, 1959. 48 p.

MOSHER, MARTHA B.
Almost. New York: Lyric Publishing Company, 1919. 5 p. ℓ., 13-44 p.

MOULTON, LOUISE CHANDLER (1835-1908)
At the Wind's Will; Lyrics and Sonnets. Boston: Little, Brown and Company, 1900. xi p., 1 ℓ., 171 p.

Swallow Flights. New ed. of Poems, published in 1877 with 10 additional poems. Boston: Little, Brown, 1900. 168 p.
The Poems and Sonnets of Louise Chandler Moulton. Boston: Little, Brown & Company, 1909. xxxi, 476 p.

MOVIUS, ANNE MURRY
Lights and Shadows. Ridgewood, N. J.: The Gayren Press, 1936. 1 p. ℓ., [1], 82, [3] p.

MOYER, ALICE
Oklahoma Reveries. North Montpelier, VT.: The Driftwind Press, 1940. 82 p.
Prairie Symphonies. New York: H. Harrison, 1942. 63 p.

MUDER-SMITH, ROSAMOND
Sweet and Bitter; Poems. Limited ed. Poland, OH.: Gold Seal Publications, 1950. 63 p.
Songs from a Gypsy Flute. Greenwell Springs, LA.: Poet's Reed Pub. Co., 1952. 38 p.

MUELLER, LISEL (1924-)
Dependencies; Poems. Chapel Hill, N. C.: University of North Carolina Press, 1965. 60 p. (Contemporary poetry series)
Life of a Queen. LaCrosse, WI.: Northeast/Juniper Books, 1970. 22 p.

MUELLER, PATRICIA
Golden Chalice of Song. Topeka, KA.: Shawnee Chief, 1921. 24 ℓ.

MÜNSTERBERG, MARGARETE ANNA ADELHEID (1889-)
Stained Glass Windows. New York: Literary Publications, 1931. 64 p.
The Wanderer; Songs, Sonnets and Quatrains. New York: The Exposition Press, 1941. 63 p.

MULCAHY, ELIZA LORETTA McCABE (1863-)
Wandewana's Prophecy and Fragments in Verse. Baltimore, MD.: J. Murphy Co., 1905. 107 p.

MULFORD, PAULINE
Vagabond Verse. New York: Carlton Press, 1963. 40 p.

MULLER, OLGA (ERBSLOH) (1894-)
Child of the Sun. New York: Brentano's, 1931. 3-83 p.
The Silvery Flute; Verses for Children. Boston: B. Humphries, 1945. 44 p., 1 ℓ.
As They Who Prevail, Poems. Prairie City, IL.: Decker Press, 1949. 59 p.
German Poems. New York: Weltspiegel, 1953. 39 p.

MULLIGAN, MARION MORGAN
Verses. Lexington, KY.: n. p., 1913. [5]-43 p.

MULLIGAN, MOLLY
Some Verses. Rochester, N.Y.: Priv. Print., 1923. [20] p.
More Verses. Rochester, N.Y.: Priv. Print., 1926. 2 p.ℓ., 7-73, [3] p.

MULLIN, CORA PHEBE (SMITH) (1866-)
The Copper Kettle and Other Poems. Omaha, NB.: Citizen Printing Company, 1925. xiii, 116 p.

MULLINER, GABRIELLE (STEWART) (1868-)
Flowers in Verse. New York: Priv. print., 1918. 6 p.ℓ., 37 numb. ℓ.

MULLINS, HELENE (GALLAGHER) (1899-)
Earthbound and Other Poems. New York & London: Harper and Brothers, 1929. xi, 92 p.
Balm in Gilead. New York & London: Harper and Brothers, 1930. xi, 99 p.
Streams from the Source. Caldwell, ID.: The Caxton Printers, Ltd., 1938. 178 p.
The Mirrored Walls; Poems, 1929-1969. New York: Distributed by Twayne Publishers, 1970. 131 p.

MULLINS, ISLA MAY (HAWLEY) (1859-1936)
An Upward Look for Mothers. Philadelphia: The Griffith & Rowland Press, 1900. 32 p.

MUMMA, BEULAH F. (1895-)
The Fruit of Leisure, Poems. New York: Vantage Press, 1959. 90 p.

MUNN, MARGARET (CROSBY)
Homage and Vision. New York: T. Seltzer, 1925. xii, 136 p.

MUNROE, CLARA MARBLE
Songs in the Night. Boston: J. H. Earle, 1900. 3 p.ℓ., 134 p.

MUNROE, ELIZABETH LEE (1900-)
This Day Is Ours. Chicago: Dierkes Press, 1947. 64 p.
No Light Evaded, Poems. Francestown, N.H.: Golden Quill Press, 1957. 80 p.
Self Is the Stranger. Francestown, N.H.: Golden Quill Press, 1963. 64 p.
No Scheduled Flight. Francestown, N.H.: Golden Quill Press, 1973. 64 p.

MUNSON, IDA NORTON (1877-)
The Surgeon's Hands, and Other Poems. Boston: B. Humphries, 1944. 79 p.
Journeys in Poetry. Mill Valley, CA.: Wings Press, 1953. 87 p.
Borrowed Wings. New York: Pageant Press, 1960. 195 p.

MURDOCH, MARION
The Hermit Thrush, and Other Verses. Boston: The Beacon Press, Inc., 1924. 3 p. ℓ., 31 p.

MURFEY, ETTA JOSEPHEAN (1892-)
Petals of Song. Paterson, N. J.: Gayren Press, 1937. 88 p.

MURPHY, BEATRICE M. (1908-)
Love Is a Terrible Thing. New York: Hobson Book Press, 1945. ix, 65 p.

MURPHY, LEONORA LILLY
Calico Cadence (Storiettes in Rhyme). Cincinnati, OH.: Bookcraft Press, 1933. 4 p. ℓ., 11-55 p.

MURPHY, LETITIA WING
A Poet's Alphabet (Cinquains). Chicago: Barwell Press, 1934. 13 p.

MURPHY, MAUREEN
You Shall Have Songs, A Book of Verse. New York: Carlton Press, 1963. 31 p.

MURRAY, ADA FOSTER (1856-1936)
Flower o' the Grass. New York & London: Harper & Brothers, 1910. viii p., 2 ℓ., 164 p., 1 ℓ.

MURRAY, AMY (1865-)
November Hereabout. New York: H. Holt and Company, 1940. 98 p.

MURRAY, ELIZABETH CREIGHTON
Be Afraid of 1-2-3. London: Unwin Brothers, 1963. 40 p.

MURRAY, GRACE MEL
A Cache of Pearls. Boston: The Christopher Publishing House, 1926. 39 p.

MURRAY, JOAN (1917-1942)
Poems. Ed. by Grant Code. New Haven, CT.: Yale University Press, 1947. 145 p. (Yale Series of Younger Poets, 45)

MURRAY, MABEL WESSON (1877-)
Happy Children, and Other Verses. New York: F. F. Lovell, 1920. 94 p.

MURRAY, MICHELE
The Great Mother and Other Poems. New York: Sheed and Ward, 1974. 103 p.

MURRAY, PAULI (1910-)
Dark Testament and Other Poems. Norwalk, CT.: Silvermine, 1970. 106 p.

MURTAUGH, MARY G.
Snatches from a Diary, 1917-1918. Boston: The Four Seas Company, 1918. 64 p.

MURTON, JESSIE WILMORE
Frankincense and Myrrh. Grand Rapids, MI.: Zondervan, 1939. 57 p.
Whatsoever Things Are Lovely. Washington: Review and Herald Pub. Assn., 1948. 128 p.
The Shining Thread, Selected Poems. Mountain View, CA.: Pacific Press Pub. Association, 1950. 80 p.
A Child's Book of Verses. Washington: Review and Herald Pub. Association, 1952. 62 p.
Christopher Cricket. Washington: Review and Herald Pub. Association, 1955. [31] p.
Grace Notes. Washington: Review and Herald Pub. Association, 1960. 127 p.

MUSKE, CAROL
Camouflage. Pittsburgh, PA.: University of Pittsburgh Press, 1975. 56 p. (Pitt poetry series)

MUSSER, DIANE (1931-1955)
Poems. Brooklyn, N.Y.: T. Gaus' Sons, 1958. 52 p.

MUZZY, FLORENCE EMLYN (DOWNS) (1852-)
Remembered Sonnets. Philadelphia: Dorrance & Co., 1930. 66 p. (Contemporary poets of Dorrance, 91)
As in a Dream. New York: H. Harrison, 1936. 63 p.

MYERS, ANNA BALMER
Rain on the Roof. Philadelphia, PA.: Poetry Publishers, 1931. 64 p.

MYERS, LOUISA PALMIER
An Idyl of the Rhine. New York: F. T. Neely, 1901. 2 p. ℓ., 41 p.

MYERS, LYLA
Here 'Tis. New York, London: Fleming H. Revell Co., 1938. 94, [1] p.

MYERS, WINIFRED R.
From a Tuned Harp. West Los Angeles, CA.: Wagon & Star Press, 1951. 44 p.

NACHANT, FRANCES GRANT
Song of Peace. Francestown, N.H.: Golden Quill Press, 1969. 96 p.

NAMEROFF, ROCHELLE (1943-)
Body Prints. Ithaca, N.Y.: Ithaca House, 1972. 54 p.

NANCE, BERTA HART (1883-1958)
The Round-Up. Cedar Rapids, IA.: The Torch Press, 1927. 38 p.
Flute in the Distance. Dallas, TX.: The Kaleidograph Press, 1935. xi p., 1 ℓ., 15-87 p.
Lines from Arizona. Dallas, TX.: The Kaleidograph Press, 1938. xi p., 1 ℓ., 15-87 p.

NARDI, MARCIA
Poems. Denver, CO.: A. Swallow, 1956. 48 p.

NASH, CLARA
Verses. Cambridge, MA.: The University Press, 1909. vii p., 1 ℓ., 98 p.

NASH, FLORENCE
June Dusk, and Other Poems. New York: George H. Doran Company, 1918. x p., 1 ℓ., 13-104 p.

NASH, LETITIA MORSE
Adventuring. Dallas, TX.: American Poetry Association, Inc., 1938. 5 p. ℓ., 68 p.
Singing Words. Dallas, TX.: Story Book Press, 1949. 79 p.

NATIONS, OPAL L.
5 Poems. Milwaukee, WI.: Morgan Press, 1974. 18 p.

NAVIASKY, ISABEL
People, People. Baltimore, MD.: Navaree Press, 1956. 62 p.

NAVIN, CLARA I.
Their Own Way. New York: Fortuny's, 1939. 32 p.

NEAL, EFFIE C.
Winding Roads; Poems. New York: Carlton Press, 1962. 34 p.

NEALE, LOTTIE B.
The World of Tomorrow, and Other Poems. New York: Exposition Press, 1948. 64 p.

NEALEY, BEULAH RHODES
Random Thoughts in Verse. New York: The Exposition Press, 1944. 3 p. ℓ., 9-64 p. (Poets of America. Series four)

NEASE, LILLA STEWART (DUNLAP) (1858-)
At the End of the Road. Boston: R. G. Badger, 1929. 36 p.

NEFF, FLORA TRUEBLOOD BENNETT
Along Life's Pathway; A Poem in Four Cantos with Recreations. Logansport, IN.: Priv. Print. by the Publisher's Press, Chicago, 1911. 3 p. ℓ., 13-144 p., 1 ℓ.

NEFF, SADIE ASHWORTH
Living Gems of Verse. New York: Pegasus Publishing Co., 1940. 92 p.

NEIS, ANNA MARIE
Lincoln. Boston: George H. Ellis Company, Printers, 1915. 1 p. ℓ., 18 p.

NELSON, BLANCHE KENNON (PARKER) (1898-)
Service and Sacrifice. Dallas, TX.: The Kaleidograph Press, 1947. ix p., 1 ℓ., 13-75 p.

NELSON, CLAIRE E. (1896-)
Down a Country Lane. Dallas, TX.: Story Book Press, 1952. 40 p.

NELSON, DORA
A Farm in Picardy. Boston: The Cornhill Company, 1919. 5 p. ℓ., 49 p.

NELSON, ELIZABETH A.
Legends, and Other Poems. Dallas, TX.: Story Book Press, 1953. 64 p.

NELSON, ELIZABETH LUSINDA
Poems: Spring Blossoms. Columbus? S. C.: n. p., 1901. 80 p.

NELSON, GRACE MIX
The Blue of Alaska, and Other Poems. New York: Bookcraft Publishing Co., 1936. 102 p.

NELSON, HELEN GENEVIEVE
Star Paths. Anaheim, CA.: Rymer Press, 1932. 51 p.

NELSON, MARGUERITE ROGINE [Mrs. N. Lawrence Nelson]
Poems, Crying in the Wilderness. San Francisco: The Mercury Press, 1931. 7 p. ℓ., 130 p.

NELSON, OLIVE HERING
Singing Winds. New York: Pageant Press, 1958. 68 p.

NELSON, PAULA (1892-)
Full Heart Remembering. New York: Vantage Press, 1950. 64 p.
Race in the Sun. New York: Vantage Press, 1954. 3 p. ℓ., 73 p.
Always the Search. Mill Valley, CA.: Wings Press, 1958. 79 p.
Carved in Sand. Mill Valley, CA.: Wings Press, 1961. 48 p.

NELSON, VERA JOYCE (NEWKIRK)
Webs from an Old Loom. Mill Valley, CA.: Wings Press, 1952. 60 p.

Moccasin Prints West; A Legend of the Nez Perces at the Time of Lewis and Clark. Portland, OR?: n.p., 1955. [18] p.

NESOM, ANNE REILEY (1875-1951)
Blue Haze. Tigard, OR.: Cabin in the Pines Press, 1936. 64 p.
Sweet Bay; Louisiana Verse. Cleveland, OH.: The Press of Flozari, 1940. 20 p. (Torchbearers' chapbooks, no. 53)
Turns on the Trail, That Lead by Treasures of Darkness toward Peaceful Goals. St. Francisville, LA.: E. Robinson, 1947. 27 p.

NETTLETON, MARY (GLOVER) (1906-)
Beyond Lies Jupiter. Dallas, TX.: Story Book Press, 1948. 60 p.
It Will Wither; Poems. Bangor, ME.: Furbush-Roberts, 1950. 86 p.
A Bluer Sky; A Book of Poems. Boston: Bruce Humphries, 1952. 48 p.

NEVILE, MURIEL
Prose-poem and Psalm. New York: Sheed and Ward, 1953. 72 p.

NEVIN, ALICE
Poems. New York: The Knickerbocker Press, 1922. 24 p.

NEWBEGIN, ANNA B.
Poems of Life from California. San Francisco, CA.: J. J. Newbegin, 1917. 63, [1] p.

NEWBOLD, ANNA HECKSCHER
Bamboo Curtains. Philadelphia: Dorrance, 1923. 6 p.ℓ., 11-54 p. (Contemporary poets of Dorrance, 8)

NEWBURY, DOROTHY JUNE
My Turn Now. San Antonio, TX.: Carleton Printing Co., 1948. 46 p.

NEWCOMB, ADELLA EASTON (1896-)
Lilacs and the Bittersweet Vine. New York: Carlton Press, 1969. 49 p.

NEWELL, CATHERINE PARMENTER
The First to Kneel. Boston: W. A. Wilde Company, 1944. x, 85 p.

NEWELL, ELIZABETH
Through the Years. Chicago: R. F. Seymour, 1935. 107 p.

NEWEY, HESTER BARBOUR (1893-)
Shifting Sails. Lewiston, ME.: n.p., 1926. 54 p.

NEWHALL, MAFRA
Salute to Lindbergh, and Other Poems. Santa Barbara, CA.: J. F. Rowny Press, 1928? 34 p.

NEWLIN, EDITH CAROLYN
...May Rain. Philadelphia: Dorrance, 1947. 78 p. (Contemporary poets of Dorrance, 371)

NEWLIN, MARGARET (1925-)
The Fragile Immigrants. Oxford (Pin Farm, South Hinksey, Oxford): Carcanet Press, 1971. 62 p.
Day of Sirens. Cheadle, Eng.: Carcanet Press, 1973. 56 p.

NEWMAN, FANNY HODGES
Adventures. Chula Vista, CA.: Denrich Press, 1910. 6 p. ℓ., 9-75, [1] p.
Out of Bondage. San Francisco, CA.: P. Elder and Company, 1913. 3 p. ℓ., v-vii, 92 p., 1 ℓ.

NEWMAN, ISIDORA
Shades of Blue. New York: H. Harrison, 1927. 95 p.

NEWSOME, AGNES MARY
Cape Cod. Boston: Hersey-Webber Co., 1925. [28] p.

NEWSOME, EFFIE LEE [Full Name: Mary Effie (Lee) Newsome.]
Gladiola Garden; Poems of Outdoors and Indoors for Second Grade Readers. Washington, D. C.: The Associated Publishers, 1940. xv, [1], 167 p.

NEWTH, REBECCA (1940-)
Xeme. Fremont, MI.: Sumac Press, 1971. 79 p.

NEWTON, COSETTE (FAUST) (1889-) [Full Name: Mary Cosette (Faust) Newton.]
Relatives in Rhyme at Christmas Time. Dallas, TX.: The Kaleidograph Press, 1938. 128 p.
Around the World in Rhyme. Dallas, TX.: The Kaleidograph Press, 1939. 139 p.
Kinship Songs. Dallas, TX.: Story Book Press, 1939. 132, [1] p.
Dark Interval. Dallas, TX.: The Kaleidograph Press, 1941. 4 p. ℓ., xi-xiii p., 1 ℓ., 17-91 p.
War-Blown. Dallas, TX.: The Kaleidograph Press, 1941. 3 p. ℓ., ix-xii p., 1 ℓ., 15-106 p.
Songs for Singers. New York: Avon House, 1942. 64 p.
The Great American "Accident" (Mr. Truman's Mistakes). Dallas, TX.: Story Book Press, 1951. 44 p.

NEWTON, HALLEY (1871-)
Fernseed. Philadelphia: Dorrance, 1948. 51 p. (Contemporary poets of Dorrance, 372)

NEWTON, MARJORY CONIE
The Isle of My Dreams, Selected Poems. Jamestown, N. Y.: Zonta Club, 1930. 77 p.

NEWTON, MARY LESLIE
A Crooked Staff, and Other Poems. Ed. by Mary Ellen Lynde. New York: Exposition Press, 1951. 92 p.

NEWTON, MAUDE DE VERSE
Songs for the Journey. Kansas City, MO.: Martin Print. Co., 1950. 100 p.

NEWTON, RHODA L.
...Mirages, Sonnets. Philadelphia: Dorrance and Company, 1938. 51 p. (Contemporary poets of Dorrance, 176)

NEWTON, VIOLETTE
Moses in Texas. Fort Smith, AR.: South and West, 1967. 36 p.
The Proxy; Poems. Quanah, TX.: Nortex Offset Publications, 1973. v, 66 p.
Just My Size: Poems. Beaumont, TX.: R. C. "Bob" Andren's, 1975. 33 p.

NEWTON, VIRGINIA LOUISE
Red Clay to Mould. Athens, GA.: The MacGregor Company, 1942. 7 p. ℓ., 3-188 p.

NICHOLES, MARION (1944-)
Life Styles. Detroit: Broadside, 1971. 22 p. (Broadside poets)

NICHOLL, LOUISE TOWNSEND
The Blossom Print. New York: E. P. Dutton & Co., Inc., 1938. 156, [1] p.
Water and Light. New York: E. P. Dutton & Company, Inc., 1939. 111, [1] p.
Dawn in Snow. New York: E. P. Dutton & Company, Inc., 1941. 60 p.
Life Is the Flesh. New York: E. P. Dutton, 1947. 52 p.
The Explicit Flower. New York: Dutton, 1952. 49 p.
Collected Poems. New York: E. P. Dutton, 1953. 243 p.
The Curious Quotient; Poems. New York: E. P. Dutton, 1956. 53 p.
The World's One Clock. New York: St. Martin's Press, 1959. 45 p.
The Blood That Is Language. New York: John Day Co., 1967. 128 p.

NICHOLS, ELIZABETH (BERGER)
Aesop's Fables Rehashed. Los Angeles, CA.: Kellaway-Ide Company, Printers, 1930. 9 p. ℓ., 15-300 p.
Life and Heart Throbs. Los Angeles, CA.: Press of Kellaway-Ide Company, 1931. 273 p.
The Vintage. Los Angeles, CA.: n. p., 1931. 200 p.
In the Land of Bah. Los Angeles, CA.: Press of Kellaway-Ide Company, 1932. 259 p.

NICHOLS, JEANETTE
Mostly People: Poems. New Brunswick, N. J.: Rutgers University Press, 1966. 87 p.
Emblems of Passage. New Brunswick, N. J.: Rutgers University Press, 1968. 79 p.

NICHOLS, LUCY ADDA
Delphine and Other Poems. San Francisco: The Whitaker & Ray Co., 1901. 6 p. ℓ., [15]-74 p.
Sonnets. Nashville? MI.: n. p., 1910. 53 p.
From Sea to Sea; Complete Poems. Burlington, VT.: Free Press Print., Co., 1914. 471, viii p.

NICHOLS, MARCIA
A Woman Speaks. New York, London: H. S. Nichols, 1937. 7 p. ℓ., 111, [1] p.

NICHOLS, MARION LOUISE
The Sheltering Tree. Boston: Christopher Pub. House, 1959. 87 p.

NICHOLS, PHEBE (JEWELL)
Talking Waters. Boston: B. Humphries, Inc., 1944. 83 p.

NICHOLSON, FLORENCE EMILY
The Crow's Nest, and Other Poems. Boston: R. G. Badger, 1912. 136 p.

NICHOLSON, HELEN V.
Poems from the Mystical Pen of Helen V. Nicholson. New York: Vantage Press, 1968. 48 p.

NICHOLSON, MARTHA SNELL (1886-1957)
Wings and Sky. Ashland, OH.: Printed by the Brethren Publishing Company, 1938. 125, [3] p.
Threshold of Heaven. Wilmington, CA.: Martha S. Nicholson, 1943. 104, [2] p.
Heart Held High. Chicago: Moody Press, 1950. 104 p.
Her Best for the Master, Selected Poems. Comp. by F. J. Wiens. Chicago: Moody Press, 1964. 96 p.
Her Lamp of Faith, Selected Poems. Comp. by F. J. Wiens. Chicago: Moody Press, 1968. 94 p.

NICHOLSON, RUTHEDA DYSART (1917-)
Waters in the Wilderness. Denver, CO.: Big Mountain Press, 1953. 104 p.

NICKELL, MEDORA D.
Enoch and Other Poems. Los Angeles, CA.: Primavera Press, 1930. 3 p. ℓ., 99, [1] p., 1 ℓ.

NICKELL, ROSE JASPER
Tree of Freedom. Emory University, Atlanta, GA.: Banner Press, 1952. 67 p. (Verse craft series)

NICKERSON, BEATRICE
The Round Clock. Boston: Priv. print., 1920. 2 p. ℓ., 36 p.

NICKERSON, SHEILA B.
Letter from Alaska and Other Poems. Berkeley, CA.: Thorp Springs Press, 1972. [63] p.

NICOLAY, CLARA LEONORA (1864-)
The Year and the Days; A Book of Verses. Denver, CO.: The Author and Journalist Press, 1925. 64 p.
The Story of Noah's Ark; A Fancy and Medley for Children of Unlimited Age. Boston: The Christopher Publishing House, 1927. 3 p. ℓ., [9]-49 p.

NIE, LILLIAN B.
Grits and Gravy. New York: Comet Press Books, 1959. 4 p. ℓ., 39 p.

NIEDECKER, LORINE (1903-1970)
New Goose. Prairie City, IL.: The Press of James A. Decker, 1946. 3 p. ℓ., 9-50 p.
My Friend Tree; Poems. Edinburgh: The Wild Hawthorn Press, 1962. 20 ℓ.
North Central. London: Fulcrum Press, 1968. [40] p.
T & G; The Collected Poems, 1936-66. Penland, N. C.: The Jargon Society, Penland School, 1968. [71] p.
My Life by Water: Collected Poems, 1936-1968. London: Fulcrum Press, 1970. 126 p.

NEIMANN, KAREN
Wind in the Grass. North Hollywood, CA.: Camas Press, 1954. 39 p.

NIEMANN, YVONNE
The Young Earth. North Hollywood, CA.: Camas Press, 1953. 23, [1] p.

NILES, GWENDOLYN (1914-)
A Changing Sky. Emory University, Atlanta, GA.: Banner Press, 1945. 48 p. (Verse craft series)
The Singing of the Days; Poems. Birmingham, AL.: Banner Press, 1962. 39, [1] p.
The Silence of the Rose. Boston: Franden Press, 1970. 62 p.

NILSSON, ESTHER
Isles of Imagery. Hollywood, CA.: California Health News, 1936. 5 p. ℓ., 3-99 p.

NISSEN, BETTY
When Time Looks Back. Wakefield, MA.: Montrose Press, 1955. 44 p.

NIVENS, HELEN
Testimony of Time. Mill Valley, CA.: Wings Press, 1947. 93 p.
The Crags of Commorley. Mill Valley, CA.: Wings Press, 1952. 60 p.

NIXON, SALLIE
Surely, Goodness and Mercy; A Collection of Poems. Stanley, N.C.: n.p., 1965. vii, 45 p.

NOBLE, FAY (LEWIS)
Testimony of the Root. Boston: B. Humphries, 1941. 59 p.

NOBLE, GURRE PLONER (1902-)
In Southern Seas. Honolulu: Tongg Pub. Co., 1943. 62 p., 1 ℓ.
I Call These Islands Mine. Honolulu: Grass Shack, 1950. 81 p.

NOLAN, MARGUERITE L.
America Our Land, Poems. New York: The William-Frederick Press, 1944. 1 p. ℓ., 14 p. (The William-Frederick poets, no. 9)

NOLAND, ANNE
A January Afternoon and Other Poems. Dunwoody, GA.: N. S. Berg, 1973. 76 p.

NOLAND, PATRICIA
Poems. New York: Exposition Press, 1959. 39 p.

NOLT, EVELYN
The Diana Suite. North Montpelier, VT.: The Driftwind Press, 1944. 65 p.

NOLTE, DOROTHY
Beyond the Bridge. Charleston, IL.: W. S. Tremble, The Prairie Press, 1967? [15] p.

NORBURA, HOPE ROBERTSON
Above the Brink, and Other Poems. Philadelphia: Dorrance, 1949. 59 p.

NORDELL, HELEN JOHANA
Toward the Dawn. San Fernando, CA.: n.p., 1950. [24] p.

NORMAN, ANN
...Earth Rune, and Other Verse. Philadelphia: Dorrance and Company, 1942. 53 p. (Contemporary poets of Dorrance, 238)

NORRIS, KATHLEEN (1947-)
Falling Off. Chicago: Big Table Pub. Co., 1971. 64 p.

NORRIS, SADIE C.
Poems. Lisbon, OH.: Printed by the Buckeye Pub. Co., 1922. [40] p.
_______. n. p., 1925. [40] p.
The Road to Happiness, and Other Poems. Boston: The Christopher Publishing House, 1926. 3 p. ℓ., [9]-49 p.

NORTH, ELEANOR B(ERYL) (1898-)
Star Dust. Cedar Rapids, IA.: Torch Press, 1930.
Fall of Dew. Cedar Rapids, IA.: Torch Press, 1936.
Grace Notes. Cedar Rapids, IA.: Torch Press, 1952. 61 p.
My Heart Sings. n. p.: National Poetry Press, 1969.
High Tide. Detroit: Harlo, 1973. 111 p.

NORTHINGTON, CLARISSA BEARD
The Long White Road, Poems. New York: Exposition Press, 1963. 62 p.

NORTON, ALICE (WHITSON) (1897-) see WHITSON, BETH SLATER

NORTON, ALLA REBECCA (SOPER)
The Old House. Boston: B. Humphries, 1936. 47, [1] p.

NORTON, CAROL
Poems and Verses. Boston: D. Estes & Co., 1903. iv numb. ℓ., 1 ℓ., x-xi, 33 numb. ℓ.

NORTON, GRACE FALLOW (1876-)
Little Gray Songs from St. Joseph's. Boston & New York: Houghton Mifflin Co., 1912. xiv p., 1 ℓ., 77, [1] p., 1 ℓ.
The Sister of the Wind, and Other Poems. Boston & New York: Houghton, Mifflin Co., 1914. 6 p. ℓ., 3-195, [1] p.
Roads. Boston & New York: Houghton, Mifflin Co., 1916. ix, [1], 84, [4] p. (The new poetry series)
What Is Your Legion? Boston & New York: Houghton, Mifflin Co., 1916. 3 p. ℓ., 37, [1] p., 1 ℓ.
The Miller's Youngest Daughter. Boston & New York: Houghton, Mifflin Co., 1924. 5 p. ℓ., 3-32, [1] p.

NORTON, PEARL LULA (1888-)
The Isle of Dreams. Omaha, NB.: Douglas Printing Co., 1914. 88 p.
At the Sign of the Muse. Boston: Sherman, French & Company, 1917. 4 p. ℓ., 66 p.

NORVAL, JANE A.
My Minnesota, and Other Poems. St. Paul, MN.: n. p., 1956. 66 p.

NORVELL, HELEN P.
The Search for the Great Kingdom of the Texas. Beaumont, TX.: Lamb Ptg. & Stat. Co., Inc., 1945. [32] p.

NORWOOD, HILDA MUIRHEAD
The Land I Love. Deland, FL.: The E. O. Painter Printing Co., 1907. 3 p. ℓ., 3-45 numb. ℓ.

NOSSER, MARION A.
Minarets. Boston: H. Vinal, Ltd., 1930. 61 p.

NOTLEY, ALICE (1945-)
165 Meeting House Lane. New York?: "C" Press Publications, 1971.
Incidentals in the Day World. New York: Angel Hair Books, 1973. 1 v. unpaged.
Phoebe Light. Bolinas, CA.: Big Sky Books, 1973. [38] p.

NOTTAGE, MAY HASTINGS
My Father's Voice in Prayer, and Other Poems. Boston: Scriptural Tract Repository, 1901. 55 p.

NOURLAND, JEANETTE
Thought Seeds. New York: Skyline Press, 1940. [19] p.

NOVAK, SONIA RUTHELE (1900-)
Winds from the Moon. New York: The Century Co., 1928. xii, 121 p.

NOVAKOFF, JAN
Rascal Cadence. Philadelphia: Dorrance, 1956. 108 p.
Three Looks: Out, Above, and In. Boston: Branden Press, 1969. 75 p.

NYE, JEAN PALMER
Leaves from the Book of Love. New York: H. Vinal, Ltd., 1928. 5 p. ℓ., 58 p., 1 ℓ.
Oriental Poems. Boston: R. G. Badger, 1930. 110 p.

OAKES, BEATRICE HUSSEY (1915-)
Maine Legend, Poems. Brunswick, ME.: Pejepscot Press, 1953. 26 p.

OAKS, GLADYS (1898-)
Chinese White. New York: Melomine Publications, 1922. [23] p.
Nursery Rhymes for Children of Darkness. New York: R. M. McBride & Company, 1928. x, 59 p.

OATES, JOYCE CAROL (1938-)
Women in Love and Other Poems. New York: Albondocani Press, 1968. 14 p.
Anonymous Sins & Other Poems. Baton Rouge, LA.: Louisiana State University Press, 1969. 79 p.
Love and Its Derangements: Poems. Baton Rouge, LA.: Louisiana State University Press, 1970. 60 p.
Angel Fire; Poems. Baton Rouge, LA.: Louisiana State University Press, 1973. 62 p.

Dreaming America, and Other Poems. New York: Aloe Editions, 1973. [10] p.
Love and Its Derangements and Other Poems, Comprising Anonymous Sins and Other Poems, Love and Its Derangements, and Angel Fire. Greenwich, CT.: Fawcett Publications, 1974. 189 p.

OATMAN, JESSIE MARIE (1917-)
Arcs of Thought. San Antonio, TX.: Naylor Co., 1969. vi, 30 p.

OBERG, ESTELLE
My World. New York: New Voices Pub. Co., 1954. 24 p.

OBERG, MAXINE
I Shall Be I; Poems. New York: Exposition Press, 1956. 43 p.

OBERLEY, GERTRUDE F.
Melody of the Heart; (A Book of Poems). New York: Comet Press Books, 1958. 5 p. ℓ., 43 p.

O'BRIEN, KATHARINE (ELIZABETH) (1901-)
Excavation and Other Verse. Portland, ME.: Anthoensen Press, 1967. 67 p.

O'BRIEN, LUCY FULGHUM (1914-)
The Mourners and the Mourned. Philadelphia: The Pickering Press, 1947. 14, [1] p., 1 ℓ.

OCHS, ELLEN
A Salute in Passing. New York: The Paebar Company, 1945. 4 p. ℓ., 52 p.

O'CONKE, ANN MOREEN
Revealing Verse. Philadelphia: Dorrance, 1953. 48 p. (Contemporary poets of Dorrance, 455)
Via Verse. Philadelphia: Dorrance, 1961. 44 p.
Starlight. Philadelphia: Dorrance, 1964. [32] p.

O'CONNOR, JEAN SMITH
The Quiet Hills. Philadelphia: Dorrance, 1963. 46 p.

O'CONNOR, MARIAN A.
A Mother's Thoughts Through the Years. Cortland? N.Y.: n.p., 1956. 64 p.

O'CONNOR, MARY (1899-)
Reservoir of Thought. Cleveland, OH.: Flozari Pegasus Studios, 1942. 16 p. (Torchbearers' chapbooks, no. 72)
Thought Clusters. Cleveland, OH.: Pegasus Studios, 1943. 18 p. (Torchbearers' chapbooks, no. 75)

The Soaring Flame; A Collection of Poems and Sketches. Rogers, AR.: Avalon Press, 1948. 113 p.

O'CONNOR, MAUDE
Tears and Laughter. San Francisco: Abbey Press, 1955. 69, [7] p.

O'CONOR, ANNIE
All Around Brunswick; or, Uncle Alee's Philosophy. Brunswick, GA.: Glover Brothers, 1922. [70] p.

ODAM, JOYCE
The Confetti Within. San Francisco: J. T. Campbell, 1964. 34 p.
My Stranger Hands. Inglewood, CA.: Wagon & Star Publishers, 1967. vii, 80 p.

ODELL, EVA JOSEPHINE (BEEDE)
Winnipesaukee, and Other Poems. Concord, N.H.: The Rumford Printing Co., 1911. 32 p.
Winnipesaukee, and Other Poems. 2nd ed. Meredith, N.H.: The Meredith News Press, 1923. 34 p.

ODEM, GLORIA
The Naked Frame, A Love Poem and Sonnets. New York: Exposition Press, 1952. unpaged.

ODOM, HELEN B.
Cum Along Thru' Texas. Dallas, TX.: Dealey and Lowe, 1936. 6 p. ℓ., 3-142 p.

O'DONNELL, MARCELLA, Sister
Candlelight Musings. New York: Carlton Press, 1966. 56 p.

O'DONOGHUE, MARIAN ADELE (LONGFELLOW) (1849-1924)
Contrasted Songs. Boston: R. G. Badger, 1905. 103 p.

ODUM, MAMIE OZBURN
...Bits of Southern Sunshine. New York: Exposition Press, 1947. 63 p.
Heart Leaves. Emory University, Atlanta, GA.: Banner Press, 1954. 60 p.
Chosen Bits. Conyers, GA.: Conyers Pub. Co., 1967. 32 p.
Blended Thoughts. n.p., 1968? 62 p.

OFFERLE, MILDRED (GLADYS) GOODELL (1912-)
Moods and Thoughts. Charleston, IL.: Prairie Press Books, 1970.

OGDEN, ALTHEA A.
Bugle Notes of Courage and Love. Chicago: Unity Publishing Company, 1912. 60 p.

O'GORMAN, MAY
Poems. Sioux Falls, S.D.: Convent Guild Board, 1930. 64 p.

O'HALLORAN, ELSPETH (MacDUFFIE) (1898-)
Strange Truth. Boston & New York: Houghton Mifflin Company, 1929. xi, [1], 103, [1] p.
Young Man, Beware! Boston & New York: Houghton Mifflin Company, 1932. ix, [1], 100, [1] p.

O'HARA, JULIE CAROLINE
Attic Memories, and Other Poems. Cincinnati, OH.: Talaria Publication, 1941. 85 p.

O'KEEFE, ROBERTA FLEETWOOD (1903-)
Moods and Monologues. San Antonio, TX.: Naylor Co., 1966. x, 90 p.

OLCOTT, LILLIA M.
Winter Weaving, and Other Poems. New York: Vantage Press, 1967. 48 p.

OLDROYD, ALICE WILSON
It Was His Birthday. Chicago: The Bookfellows, 1924. 8 p.
The House of Gold. Kansas City, MO.: Burton Publishing Company, 1926. 5 p.ℓ., 13-75 p.
It Was His Birthday. Kansas City, MO.: Burton Publishing Company, 1927. 19 ℓ.
Mother. Kansas City, MO.: Burton Publishing Company, 1928. [12] ℓ.

OLIVER, JENNIE HARRIS (1864-1942)
Noon Trail. Guthrie? OK.: n.p., 1926. 11 ℓ.
Red Earth; Complete Collection of Poems. Kansas City, MO.: Burton Publishing Company, 1937. 3 p.ℓ., ix-xii, 13-95 p.
Pen Alchemy. Fallis? OK.: n.p., 1938. 8 ℓ.
_______. Oklahoma City, OK.: Dunn Publishing Co., 1940. 62 p.

OLIVER, MARY HEMPSTONE (1884-1973)
In Moorland Lane, and Other Poems. Cambridge, MA.: n.p., 1953. 3 p.ℓ., 55 p.

OLIVER, MARY JANE (1935-)
No Voyage, and Other Poems. London: Dent, 1963. 56 p.
_______. Boston: Houghton Mifflin, 1965. ix, 67 p.
The River Styx, Ohio, and Other Poems. New York: Harcourt Brace Jovanovich, 1972. viii, 55 p.

OLIVER, VIRGINIA KATHERINE
Smile Along the Way. Boston: B. Humphries, 1946. 58 p.
The Children's Magic Corner. New York: Vantage Press, 1957. 40 p.

OLIVIER, LILLIAN M.
Driftwood Fires. New York: The Exposition Press, 1945. 6 p. ℓ., 15-94 p. (Poets of America. Series four)

OLIVIERE, LUCIA (NEWELL)
Old Houses. New York: Press of O. A. Randel, Inc., 1928. 80 p.

OLMSTEAD, GLADYS SIMMONS (1888-)
Lilacs and Swamp-Pinks. Brunswick, ME.: Pejepscot Press, 1953. 47 p.

OLMSTED, ELIZABETH M(ARTHA) (1825-1910)
Poems of the House, and Other Poems. New York: The De Vinne Press, 1903. xvi, 119, [1] p.

OLMSTED, ROSE
Selah. Glendale, CA.: Poetry X/Change, 1968. [20] p.

O'NAN, MARTHA
Instants: Poems. Boston: Christopher Pub. House, 1965. 38 p.

O'NEAL, OPHELIA
Not with Thorns. Dallas, TX.: The Kaleidograph Press, 1945. x p., 1 ℓ., 13-64 p.

O'NEILL, MARY (LE DUC) (1908-)
Anna. Garden City, N.Y.: Doubleday, 1966. 1 v.
Poor Merlo. New York: Atheneum, 1966. 54 p.
Words, Words, Words. Garden City, N.Y.: Doubleday, 1966. 61 p.
Fingers Are Always Bringing Me News. Garden City, N.Y.: Doubleday, 1969. 40 p.
Winds. Garden City, N.Y.: Doubleday, 1970. [64] p.

O'NEILL, ROSE CECIL (1874-1944)
The Master-Mistress; Poems. New York: A. A. Knopf, 1922. 6 p. ℓ., 277 p.

ONGLEY, GERTRUDE
"Her Book of Memories." Grand Valley, PA.: n.p., 1957. 4 p. ℓ., 88 p.

OPIE, MARTHA J.
Poems. Tavvistock, Eng.; Williamstown, PA.: Times Publ. House, 1911. 5 p. ℓ., 2-103 p.
Friendship's Treasury. London: The Mitre Press, 1931. 48 p.

OPPENHEIM, BERTHA (ELSBERG)
Legends of Life, and Other Poems. Boston, MA.: The Stratford Co., 1921. 6 p. ℓ., 71 p.

OPPENHEIMER, CHRISTINE BACKUS (1920-)
Building the Bridge. Chicago: Columbus Press, 1964. 72 p.

OPPENHEIMER, EVELYN (1907-)
Legend, and Other Poems. San Antonio, TX.: Naylor Co., 1951. 62 p.

OPPENHEIMER, JANE
Of Promises, Dreams, and Visions. New York: Carlton Press, 1969. 64 p.

ORCUTT, ALICE (1922-)
The Song of Magdalen. New York: D. Howell, 1946. [13] p.

O'REILLY, ELIZA BOYLE
My Candles and Other Poems. Boston: Lee and Shepard, 1903. 2 p. ℓ., 3-122 p.

ORR, GLADYS MARIETTA
The Raspberry Patch. Dallas, TX.: The Story Book Press, 1953. 46 p.

ORR, MARYE CROCKETT
Poems of Memory. Boston: R. G. Badger, 1925. 57 p.

ORTH, CAROLINE SOPHIE
Eight Poems. Richmond, VA.: Dietz Prtg. Co., 1924. 18 ℓ.

ORTH, ELIZABETH
Ramblings in Verse. New York: Exposition Press, 1966. 124 p.

ORTHWEIN, EDITH HALL
Petals of Love for Thee. New York: Dodge Publishing Company, 1904. 64 p.
Songs of the Beloved.... New York: Dodge Publishing Company, 1909. 88 p.

ORTIZ, ALICE DU PONT
The Witch of Endor. Boston: The Christopher Publishing House, 1937. vii, 9-85 p.
The Scene Shifter. Boston: The Christopher Publishing House, 1939. 111 p.

O'RYAN, JANE
Assorted Snobs. New York: C. L. Tumasel, 1936. 4 p. ℓ., 7-59 p.

OSBORN, STELLA BRUNT (1894-) [OSBORN, STELLANOVA]
Balsam Boughs. Cedar Rapids, IA.: Torch Press, 1949. 62 p.
________. 1950.
Polly Cadotte, A Tale of Duck Island in Verse. New York: Exposition Press, 1955. 48 p.
Beside the Cabin. Sault Ste. Marie, MI.: Northwoods Press,

1957. 41 p.
Iron and Arbutus. Sault Ste. Marie, MI.: Northwoods Press, 1962. 36 p.

OSBORN, STELLANOVA see OSBORN, STELLA BRUNT (1894-)

OSBORNE, LAURA (HIGGINBOTHAM)
Life's Meaning. (A Collection of Poems). San Antonio, TX.: Naylor Co., 1952. ix, 58 p.

OSGOOD, ELIZABETH SMALLWOOD (DAYTON) (1882-)
River Songs. Emory University, Atlanta, GA.: Banner Press, 1941. 52 p. (Verse craft series)
Winged Victory. Rogers, AR.: Avalon Press, 1946. 48 p.

OSGOOD, IDA STEELE
A Little Bit of Me. Chicago: Alyce Mitchell, 1925. [35] p.
Sonnets of the Desert. n.p., 1932. [9] p.
Burning Leaves. Boston: The Christopher Publishing House, 1938. 110 p.

OSLEY, IRIS B.
Fairy Islands, and Other Poems. Boston: Cornhill, 1918.

OSTENSO, MARTHA (1900-1963)
A Far Land. New York: T. Seltzer, 1924. viii p., 1 ℓ., 11-70 p.

OSTRIKER, ALICIA (SUSKIN) (1937-)
Songs. New York: Holt, Rinehart and Winston, 1969. 4 p.ℓ., 49 p., 1 ℓ.
Once More out of Darkness. New York: The Smith with Horizon Press, 1971. [14] p.
Once More out of Darkness--and Other Poems. Berkeley, CA.: Berkeley Poets' Cooperative, 1974. 32 p.

O'SULLIVAN, HERMELINE
April Harvest. Boston: Chapman & Grimes, 1957. 42 p.

OTT, LILLIAN REZNICK
Teardrops and Dew, Poems. New York: Exposition Press, 1949. 176 p.

OTT, MAUD (BROWN) ["Mrs. Christian Ott"]
Leaflets. Independence, MO.: n.p., 1924. 42 p.
The Hermit of Echo Lake. Independence, MO.: Printed by Midwest Publishing Company, 1927. 105 p.

OTT, VERNA MARLYS
Pennies for Thoughts. Philadelphia: Dorrance, 1960. 54 p.

OTTO, ELEANOR (1908-)
Winged Rhapsodies, A Book of Poems. Philadelphia: Dorrance,

1953. 82 p. (Contemporary poets of Dorrance, 477)
To the Stars; Poems. New York: Exposition Press, 1966. 107 p.

OVERHOLT, MARY ERWIN
Year In, Year Out, at Echoes. Boston: Meador Pub. Co., 1934. 144 p.
Sundown at Echoes. Boston: Meador Pub. Co., 1948. 128 p.
The White Heron. Boston: Meador Pub. Co., 1950. 196 p.
Miracles and Moonbeams. Ed. by Anna Helen Overholt. Boston: Meador Pub. Co., 1952. 95 p.

OVERSTREET, BONARO (WILKINSON) (1902-)
Footsteps on the Earth. New York: A. A. Knopf, 1934. xv, 64 p., 1 ℓ.
Hands Laid upon the Wind. New York: Norton, 1955. 132 p.

OWEN, ELIZABETH
Odes of Odd Moments. Denver, CO.: Bradford-Robinson, 1922. 111 p.

OWEN, LOUISE
Virtuosa: A Book of Verse. New Haven, CT.: Yale University Press; London: H. Milford, Oxford University Press, 1930. 35 p. (Yale Series of Younger Poets, 29)

OWENS, NELLIE G. [MacLEOD, NELLIE G. (OWENS)]
Through the Sycamores. Indianapolis, IN.: n.p., 1948. 52 p.

OWENS, ROCHELLE (1936-)
Not Be Essence That Cannot Be. New York: Trobar Press, 1961. [20] p.
Salt and Core. Los Angeles, CA.: Black Sparrow Press, 1968. 54 p.
I Am the Babe of Joseph Stalin's Daughter; Poems, 1961-1971. New York: Kulchur Foundation, 1972. 140 p.
Poems from Joe's Garage. Providence, R.I.: Burning Deck Books, 1973. unpaged.
The Joe 82 Creation Poems. Los Angeles, CA.: Black Sparrow Press, 1974. 136 p.
Selected Poems. New York: Seabury Press, 1974.

OWENS, VILDA (SAUVAGE)
I've Never Been to Winkle. New York: H. Harrison, 1936. 64 p.

OWINGS, EVELYN
The Royal Battle & Other Poems. Baltimore, MD.: Thomsen-Ellis Press, 1932. 2 p. ℓ., 7-17 p.

OWNBEY, JENNA V.
Cloud Trails. Spearman? TX.: n.p., 1965. 76 p.
Cloud-Moods. San Antonio, TX.: Naylor Co., 1969. x, 194 p.

Star-Moods. San Antonio, TX.: Naylor Co., 1969. x, 141 p.

OXTON, BEULAH SYLVESTER
Poems of Beauty and Spirit. Lewiston, ME.: Lewiston Journal Printshop, 1927. 140 p.

PACKARD, CHARLOTTE MELLON (1839-)
From the Foothills of Song. Boston: R. G. Badger, 1908. 4 p. ℓ., 7-62 p.

PACKARD, FAITH EVELYN
Only the Soft Wind. New York: The Poets Press, 1939. 48 p.
If This Be Night. New York: Harbinger House, 1943. 48 p.

PACKARD, HARRIET
Robins and Ravens. North Montpelier, VT.: Driftwind Press, 1933. 1 p. ℓ., 36 p.

PACKARD, RUTH ELIZABETH (1891-1939)
The World Is Full of Color. Denver, CO.: The Smith-Brooks Press, 1940. 125 p.

PADELFORD, IDA LILLIAN
Who Seeks the Stars. Biltmore, N. C.: n. p., 1934. 3 p. ℓ., 5-71 p., 1 ℓ.
Flutes in the Wind. New York: H. Harrison, 1936. 63 p.

PADEN-PARRISH, MARTHA
Poetic Moments with You. New York: The Paebar Company, 1945. 3 p. ℓ., 44 p.

PAGE, GERTRUDE COOK
Illusion, and Other Poems. Richmond, VA.: The Dietz Press, 1940. 7 p. ℓ., 85 p.

PAGE, LOIS
Lasting Beauty. n. p., 1937. 4 p. ℓ., 11-78 p.
Wake Up and Dream. Kansas City, MO.: Burton Pub. Co., 1950. 127 p.

PAGE, LORENA M(AYBELLE)
Legendary Lore of Mackinac: Original Poems of Indian Legends of Mackinac Island. Cleveland, OH.: n. p., 190 p.

PAGEL, GLADYS (RUTH) (1899-)
Day Dreams. Parkersburg, IA.: Parkersburg Eclipse, 1957. 114 p.

PAILLOU, FRANCESCA
A Handful of Songs. Portland, ME.: The Mosher Press, 1930. xvii, 240, [1] p., 1 ℓ.

PAINE, SELMA WARE
Fugitive Poems. Bangor? ME.: n.p., 1907. 2 p. ℓ., 83 p.

PAINE, VIRGINIA (LAW) (1893-) [Full Name: Virginia Marie (Law) Paine.]
So Loved the World. New York: Fleming H. Revell Company, 1933. 161, [1] p.

PAIR, JENNY
Insight. Birmingham, AL.: Banner Press, 1965. 38 p.

PALADINO, LYN
Kingdom for the Windhooker, and Other Poems. New York: Exposition Press, 1963. 64 p.

PALCHES, LOIS (GRANT) (1905-)
Chiaroscuro. Mount Vernon, IA.: English Club of Cornell College, 194-? 43 p.
Makeup. Mount Vernon, IA.: English Club of Cornell College, 194-? 3 p. ℓ., 7-28 p.
Chiaroscuro. Mount Vernon, IA.: English Club of Cornell College, 1944. 44 p.
The Heart's a Pendulum. n.p., 1948. v, 50 p.

PALEN, JENNIE MAY
Moon over Manhattan. Mill Valley, CA.: Wings Press, 1949. 72 p.
Good Morning, Sweet Prince. Cleveland, OH.: American Weave Press, 1957. 22 p.
Stranger, Let Me Speak. Francestown, N.H.: Golden Quill Press, 1964. 96 p.

PALFREY, SARA HAMMOND (1823-1914)
King Arthur in Avalon and Other Poems. Boston: W. B. Clarke Company, 1900. x, 191 p.
Harvest-Home. Boston: W. B. Clarke Company, 1913. xi, 132 p.

PALMER, ALICE ELVIRA (FREEMAN) (1855-1902)
A Marriage Cycle. Boston and New York: Houghton Mifflin Company, 1915. xvii, 71, [1] p.

PALMER, ANNA SHATTUCK
Illinois Verse. Champaign, IL.: Illini Pub. Co., 1926. 3 p. ℓ., 67 p.

PALMER, BESSIE PRYOR (1878-)
From a California Garden. Philadelphia: Dorrance and Company, 1927. 110 p. (Contemporary poets of Dorrance, 48)
Live Oak Leaves. San Leandro, CA.: The Greater West Publishing Company, 1938. 111 p.

PALMER, CANDIDA (1926-)
Sidings. Madison, WI.: FAS Pub., Printer, 1972. 32 p.

PALMER, CHARLENE
Long Stems Colored. Sausalito, CA.: Golden Goose Press, 1953. 33 p.

PALMER, FANNY (PURDY) (1839-1923)
Sonnets. San Francisco: P. Elder & Company, 1909. 6 p. ℓ., 5-38 p., 1 ℓ.
Of the Valley & the Sea & Other Verses. London: K. Paul, Trench, Trübner & Co., 1912. 62 p.
Dates and Days in Europe, by an American Resident in London (1914-1915). London: K. Paul, Trench, Trübner & Co., 1915. 63 p.
Outpost Messages. Boston: The Four Seas Company, 1924. 77 p.
Sonnets of California. New York: The Purdy Press, 1927. 35 p.

PALMER, GERTRUDE
Of Cabbages and Kings; Poems. New York: Exposition Press, 1969. 56 p.

PALMER, JESSIE
Thought-Bird Warblings. Maquoketa, IA.: Grant Publishing House, 1915. 116 p.

PALMER, LUCILE (1892-)
Heart Throbs from Reno. Hollywood, CA.: Sargent House, 1935. 39 ℓ.
Poems. Hollywood, CA.: Sargent House, 1941. 6 ℓ., 405 p.
"Souse" America, Si! Si! Si!. 2d ed. Hollywood, CA.: Sargent House, 1949. 63, [1] p.
Short Shorts in Rhyme. Los Angeles, CA.: Sargent House, 1950. 102 p.
Songs of the City. Los Angeles, CA.: Sargent House, 1950. 85 p.
________. 2d ed., 1950.
Beyond the Horizon. Los Angeles, CA.: Sargent House Publishers, 1952. 88 p.

PALMER, MARY BLANCHE
Of Life and You and Me. Ann Arbor, MI.: Edwards Brothers, 1952. 2 p. ℓ., 59 p.

PALMER, PAMELA LYNN (1951-)
Rain Is for Dreaming. San Antonio, TX.: Naylor Co., 1968. 3 p. ℓ., 26 p.

PANES, PEARL S.
Moments; Collected Poems. New York: Creative Press, 1960. 61 ℓ.

PAPAYANAKOS, M. ANNETTE
Rainbow Hues.... New York: The Paebar Company, 1946. 3 p. ℓ., 58 p.
Waiting for the Stars; Poems and Limericks. New York: Exposition Press, 1952. 94 p.

PARCELL, LILLIAN
Feet of Dawn. Emory University, Atlanta, GA.: Banner Press, 1939. 50, [1] p.
Horn of the Unicorn. Los Angeles, CA.: Wagon and Star Publishers, 1955. 47 p.

PARDEE, ALICE ROSAMOND (1908?-1926?)
Poems. New Rochelle, N.Y.: The Knickerbocker Press, 1926. 47 p.

PARHAM, EUGENIA
Longing, and Other Poems. Cincinnati, OH.: Jennings and Graham, 1906. 107 p.

PARIS, ANNA M.
Songs from Hawaii. New York: Priv. print., 1910. 45 p.

PARIS, ESTELLE WALLACE
A Song o' the West. Portland? OR.: n.p., 1910. 17 ℓ.

PARITZ, HANNA EMELIA
Twenty Poems. Lexington, KY.: The Keystone Printery, 1933. 7 p. ℓ., 17-37 p.

PARK, LEORA CECELIA
Con Amore. New York: Vantage Press, 1962. 64 p.

PARKE, JEAN
Psalms of the Heart Restored. New York: T. Scott, 1919. 87 p.
Psalms of the Heart Restored. Port Murray, N.J.: Folded Scroll Publishers, 1957. 15 ℓ.

PARKER, BONNIE ELIZABETH
Spindrift. Dexter, MO.: Candor Press, 1954. [8] p.
Dark Tigers of My Tongue. Dallas, TX.: Book Craft, 1957. 3 p. ℓ., 42 p.
Season of the Golden Dragon. Dallas, TX.: Book Craft, 1961. 5 p. ℓ., 78 p.
Leopard on a Topaz Leash. Brooklyn, N.Y.: Parthenon Pub. Co., 1962. 80 p.

PARKER, DIANE
Borrowed Words; Poems. Buffalo, N.Y.: Offerman Printing, 1971. 44 p.

PARKER, DOROTHY (ROTHSCHILD) (1893-1967)
Enough Rope; Poems. New York: Boni and Liveright, 1926.

110 p.

Sunset Gun; Poems. New York: Boni and Liveright, 1928. x p., 1 ℓ., 13-75 p.

The Collected Poetry of Dorothy Parker. New York: The Modern Library, 1931. xii, 210 p.

...Death and Taxes. New York: The Viking Press, 1931. 62 p.

Not So Deep as a Well; Collected Verse. New York: Viking Press, 1936. 4 p. ℓ., vii-xii, 210 p.

_______. Toronto: Macmillan, 1937. 210 p.

_______. London: Hamish Hamilton, 1937. 224 p.

Sunset Gun. New York: Pocket Books, Inc., 1940. 89 p.

Enough Rope. New York: Pocket Books, Inc., 1941. ix, [1], 118 p.

PARKER, EDITH STUBBS

Of Earth, Sea, and Sky. Los Angeles, CA.: n.p., 1939. vii, 77 p.

PARKER, ELINOR M. (1890-)

Nocturne. Philadelphia: Dorrance, 1947. 43 p. (Contemporary poets of Dorrance, 367)

...Souvenirs. New York: Exposition Press, 1947. 64 p.

PARKER, ELIZABETH LOWBER (CHANDLER) see CHANDLER, BESSIE (1856-)

PARKER, FLORENCE M.

Contemplation and Other Poems. Salt Lake City, UT.: n.p., 1915. 15 p.

Lupeta, and Other Poems. Salt Lake City, UT.: n.p., 1915. 81 p.

Song of the Pines, and Other Poems. Salt Lake City, UT.: n.p., 1915. 15 p.

PARKER, FRANCES S.

Walk Quietly. Francestown, N.H.: M. Jones Co., 1954. 111 p.

PARKER, MARY SALTONSTALL

Small Things Antique. Salem, MA.: n.p., 1909. 24 p.

PARKER, MAUD MAY

The Missive: A Dramatic Poem. Boston: The Poet Lore Company, 1907. 48 p.

PARKER, MAUDE

Testament. New York: E. W. Pavenstedt, Priv. Print. at Tri-Arts Press, 1960. [8] p.

PARKER, NANCY

Simple Poems of Everyday Life. New York: The Gibson Publishing Co., 1908. 30 p.

Added Poems. New York: Hamilton Press, 1917. 12 p.

PARKER, PAT (1944-)
Some Poems. London: S. E. Parker, 1966. 10 p.
Child of Myself. San Lorenzo? CA.: Shameless Hussy Press, 1971. [28] p.
Pit Stop. Oakland, CA.: Women's Press Collective, 1974. 48 p.

PARKHURST, ELVA REH
Poems from a Gentle Heart. Boston: Meador Pub. Co., 1956. 47 p.

PARKHURST, MARY EVELINE
The Citadel of Thought. Davenport, IA.: V. Blanche Bromley, Linotype Composition Company, 1917. 61 p.

PARKINSON, FRANZISKA RAABE (1889-)
...The Harvest. Philadelphia: Dorrance & Company, 1943. 68 p. (Contemporary poets of Dorrance, 268)
The Mirror. Philadelphia: Dorrance & Company, 1946. 64 p.
When a Poet Speaks. Mill Valley, CA.: Wings Press, 1955.

PARKS, ANNABEL (DARBY)
Big Texas, Centennial Poems. Dallas, TX.: The Kaleidograph Press, 1935. ix p., 1 ℓ., [13]-68 p.

PARKS, MARIE (de WINSTANLEY)
Sunlight and Shadows. San Leandro, CA.: The Greater West Publishing Co., 1940. 62 p.
...Golden Threads. San Leandro, CA.: The Greater West Publishing Co., 1944. 67 p.
Dancing Dreams. Santa Barbara, CA.: Schauer Print. Studio, 1947. 139 p.

PARKS, MATTIE LOUISE
"Buds." Oroville? CA.: n.p., 1905. [32] p.

PARLETT, VIOLA JONES
Bypaths. Baltimore, MD.: Waverly Press, 1940. 64 p.

PARMELEE, HARRIET E.
Rays of the Eastern Star. New York, London: The Abbey Press, 1901. 3 p. ℓ., 9-41 p.

PARMELEE, LENA W.
Poems. Boston: The Stratford Company, 1938. 3 p. ℓ., iv, 104 p.

PARRISH, BESS M.
Open Mine Eyes That I May See. Dallas, TX.: Kaleidograph Press, 1953. 69 p.

PARRISH, EMMA KENYON (1849-)
The Golden Island. New York: J. T. White & Co., 1921. 108 p.

PARRISH, MARY (MOORE)
How the World Wags. Philadelphia: Dorrance, 1959. 142 p.

PARROT, RETTA
Library Windows. San Francisco: Harr Wagner Publishing Co., 1920. 3 p. ℓ., [5]-62 p.

PARSLOW, EVA ASHLEY
The Star of Gold, and Other Poems. Boston: The Stratford Company, 1921. 4 p. ℓ., 62 p.

PARSONS, KITTY
As the Wind Blows. Chicago: Dierkes Press, 1951. 32 p.
Ancestral Timber. Francestown, N. H.: Golden Quill Press, 1957. 99 p.
People and People. Cleveland, OH.: American Weave Press, 1961. 29 p.
Down to Earth. Francestown, N. H.: Golden Quill Press, 1964. 96 p.
Up and Down and Roundabout; Verses for Children. Francestown, N. H.: Golden Quill Press, 1967. 64 p.
Your Husband... Or Mine. Francestown, N. H.: Golden Quill Press, 1970. 64 p.

PARSONS, MABLE HOLMES
Pastels and Silhouettes; A Book of Verse. Boston: The Stratford Company, 1921. 7 p. ℓ., 89 p.
Listener's Room. Portland, OR.: Binfords & Mort, 1940. 72 p.
On Sun-Dial Road. Portland, OR.: Kilham's, 1944. 6 p. ℓ., 17-52 p.

PARTRIDGE, MARGARET RIDGELY
Lyrics. Venice: Printing-Press of the Industrial Home, 1905. 3 p. ℓ., 27 p.
The Plumes of Dreams. New York: Coward-McCann, 1951. xiv, 97 p.

PASCHALL, ALMA
Horizons. Dallas, TX.: Triangle Pub. Co., 1957. 39 p.
Push Buttons. Dallas: Triangle Pub. Co., 1959? 40 p.

PASTAN, LINDA (1932-)
A Perfect Circle of Sun. Chicago: Swallow Press, 1971. 56 p. (New poetry ser., no. 44)
Aspects of Eve: Poems. New York: Liveright, 1975. viii, 56 p.
On the Way to the Zoo. Washington, D. C.: Dryad Press, 1975. 31 p.

PATON, FLOSSIE LOUISE (1878-)
Recipe for Living, and Other Poems. Philadelphia: Dorrance, 1955. 41 p. (Contemporary poets of Dorrance, 471)

PATTEE, ROWENA
Song to Thee, Divine Androgyne; Seven Steps to Heaven. Millbrae, CA.: Celestial Arts, 1973. unpaged.

PATTEN, ANNA BAKER (1870-)
Washington in Wartime; Poems and Verse. Washington, D. C.: n. p., 1919. 23 p.

PATTERSON, ANTOINETTE (DE COURSEY)
Sonnets and Quatrains. Philadelphia: H. W. Fisher & Co., 1913. xi, 45 p.
Undine: A Poem Adapted in Part from the Romance by de La Motte Fouqué. Philadelphia: H. W. Fisher & Co., 1914. 34 p., 1 ℓ.
The Son of Merope and Other Poems. Philadelphia: H. W. Fisher & Co., 1916. 99, [1] p.

PATTERSON, BELLE McKEAN
The Heart's Garden. Kalamazoo, MI.: Dalm Printing Co., 1925. 2 p. ℓ., 5-48, [1] p.

PATTERSON, HELEN WOHL
See America; Poems. Washington: American Literary Accents, 1967. 67 p.

PATTERSON, LILLIAN M.
From Heart to Heart. Boston: Bruce Humphries, 1952. 168 p.

PATTERSON, LORRAINE
...This Living Urge. New York: H. Harrison, 1938. 64 p.

PATTERSON, MYRTLE REJANE
Fate; A Poet's Answer to Dante's Divine Comedy. Washington, D. C.: Fraternity Press, 1935. [12] p.

PATTERSON, NELLIE
Poems. Dayton, OH.: U. S. Publishing Co., 1926. 1 p. ℓ., 5-62 p.

PATTERSON, RUBY PEARL
Songs from the Florida Everglades, and Other Poems. Philadelphia: Dorrance & Company, 1929. 79, [1] p. (Contemporary poets of Dorrance, 82)

PATTON, HENRIETTA ELIZABETH MARY MARTHA ANNE (1883-)
My Memories. Tipton, IA.: The Conservative, 1903. 48 numb. ℓ.

PAU, CHARLOTTE
Sunbeams and Shadows. New York: Cochrane Publishing Company, 1910. 31 p.

PAUL, HARRIET MAE
Just for You. Danbury, CT.: Published by T. N. P. C., 1965. 24, [2] p.
Just for You #2. Danbury, CT.: Published by T. N. P. C., 1968. 44 p.

PAULEY, LULU MAY
Gateside Lyrics. Prairie City, IL.: Decker Press, 1948. 108 p.

PAULSEN, JULIANE, pseud. see HANSEN, JULIANE GRACE

PAULSEN, LOIS (THOMPSON) (1905-)
Sonnets to My Son. Denver, CO.: Big Mountain Press (A. Swallow), 1963. 35 p.

PAUS, HAZELLE R.
Journeys in Thoughtland. New York: Vantage Press, 1955. 71 p.

PAUSCH, EMILY
The Ungathered River. Berkeley, CA.: Explorations Pub. Co., 1965. 40 p.

PAUST, MARIAN
Honey to Be Savored. San Antonio, TX.: Naylor Co., 1968. x, 50 p.
Everybody Beats a Drum. San Antonio, TX.: Naylor Co., 1970. xi, 74 p.

PAVICH, STELLA M.
The True Story of Packer, the Cannibal. Dallas, TX.: Story Book Press, 1954. 41 p.
Packer, the Cannibal, and Other Story Poems. New York: Comet Press Books, 1961. 5 p. ℓ., 54 p.

PAXSON, ETHEL (1885-)
Sonnets and Other Poems. Stonington, CT.: Pequot Press, 1968. ix, 65 p.

PAXTON, JEAN GRIGSBY
Inward Word. New York: The Womans Press, 1935. 3 p. ℓ., 29 p.

PAYNE, ANNE BLACKWELL (1887-1969)
Released: A Book of Verse. Chapel Hill, N. C.: University of North Carolina Press, 1930. 2 p. ℓ., vii-ix p., 1 ℓ., 63 p.

PAYNE, ELIZABETH
The Eternal Masculine. Boston: R. G. Badger, 1913. 3 p. ℓ., 11-52 p.

PAYNE, EMMA HANKINS
A Winter Garden of Verse. Dallas, TX.: The Kaleidograph Press, 1939. xiv p., 2 ℓ., 19-265 p.

PAYSON, CAROLYN NICHOLSON
To Mother, Memory Blossoms. Boston: The Wheelock Publishing Company, 1931. 2 p. ℓ., [9]-18 p.

PEABODY, JOSEPHINE PRESTON (1874-1922)
In the Silence. New York: Privately printed, 1900. 5 ℓ.
The Singing Leaves: A Book of Songs and Spells. Boston & New York: Houghton Mifflin Co., 1903. xi, 123, [1] p., 1 ℓ.
The Book of the Little Past. Boston & New York: Houghton Mifflin Co., 1908. ix, [1] p., 1 ℓ., 49, [1] p.
The Singing Man: A Book of Songs and Shadows. Boston and New York: Houghton Mifflin Co., 1911. x, 86, [2] p.
Harvest Moon. Boston & New York: Houghton Mifflin Co., 1916. viii p., 3 ℓ., 85, [1] p., 1 ℓ.
______. London: Longmans, Green & Co., 1917.
The Collected Poems of Josephine Preston Peabody. Boston & New York: Houghton Mifflin Co., 1927. xx, 535 p.
The House and the Road. Oakland, CA.: The Eucalyptus Press, 1935. 3 ℓ.

PEABODY, LEILA ROSE (1867-)
A Little Book of Verse. Boston: Sherman, French & Company, 1912. 4 p. ℓ., 41 p.

PEABODY, MILDRED
Good People All. Litchfield, CT.: The Prospect Press, 1941. 95 p.

PEARCE, ELLEN
Life in (Very) Minor Works. New York: October House, 1968. 54 p.

PEARCE, HELEN
The Enchanted Barn. New York: The Watch Hill Press, 1929. [8] p.

PEARL, MARY FRANCES
Sketches from County Seat. Cleveland, OH.: Pegasus Studios, 1940. 24 p. (Torchbearers' chapbooks, no. 50)
Lost and Found: Love. Brooklyn, N.Y.: Priv. print. Skylines Press, 1941. 28 p.
Runner in the Sand. Mount Vernon, OH.: The Kokosing Press, 1941. 55 p.

PEARLE, MARY
California, and Other Poems. San Luis Obispo, CA.: Press of the James H. Barry Co., 1915. 2 p. ℓ., [3]-96 p.

PEARMAN, MABEL (CAPELLE)
Look Seaward! Bermuda. New York: H. Harrison, 1938. 62 p.

PEARSON, CAROL LYNN (1944-)
Beginnings. Provo, UT.: Trilogy Arts, 1967. 63 p.
The Search. Provo, UT.: Trilogy Arts, 1970. 63 p.
Beginnings. Garden City, N.Y.: Doubleday, 1975. 63 p.

PEARSON, LUCY HELEN
Songs along the Way. New York: Lucy H. Pearson, 1928. 93 ℓ.

PEASE, EUNICE S.
Gathered Sunbeams. Pittsfield, MA.: Press of the Sun Printing Company, 1902. 84 p.

PECK, ELISABETH (SINCLAIR) (1883-)
American Frontier. Garden City, N.Y.: Doubleday, Doran and Co., 1937. ix p., 1 ℓ., 13-195 p.

PECK, MAMIE (DOWNARD) (1868-)
California, Los Angeles, and Poems. Corsicana, TX.: n.p., 1924.
Poems of the South. Corsicana, TX.: Stokes Printing Company, 1925. 35, [1] p.
Poems of Yuletide, and Others of the New and Old Year. Corsicana, TX.: American Printing Company, 1926. [16] p.

PECKHAM, LIZZIE CROSS
Poems. Los Angeles, CA.: Out West Company, Printers, 1905. 61 p.

PEDRICK, JEAN (1922-)
Wolf Moon; A Book of Hours. Cambridge, MA.: Alice James Books, 1974. 70 p.

PEELLE, LUNA (CARROLL)
The Mixed Bouquet, and Other Poems. Bucyrus, OH.: J. W. Hopley, 1929. 4 p. ℓ., 13-116 p.

PEGRAM, SHERLEY
Sherley; A Book of Poems, Choice and Rare. Richmond, VA.: The Hermitage Press, 1911. xii, 191 p.

PEGUES, ETTA BEARDEN
Launch Out into the Deep. Emory University, Atlanta, GA.: Banner Press, 1945. 48 p. (Verse craft series)
Doors That Stand Ajar. Birmingham, AL.: Banner Press, 1966. 59 p.

PEIRCE, EMMA
Will-o'-the-Wisps; Poems. Boston: The Stratford Company, 1926. 3 p. ℓ., iv, 108 p.
Neighbor Nature, Poems. Bangor, ME.: The Jordan-Frost Printing Co., 1928. 3 p. ℓ., vi p., 143 p.
Summer Melodies; Poems. La Jolla, CA.: n. p., 1931. vii, 52 p.

PEIRCE, KATHERINE MILNER
A Song of Faith. Boston: The Stratford Co., 1921. 5 p. ℓ., 3-91 p.

PEKTOR, IRENE MARI
War--or Peace! Oceano, CA.: Harbison & Harbison, 1939. 4 p. ℓ., 60 p.
Golden Banners. Boston: The Christopher Publishing House, 1941. ix, 11-211 p.

PEMBER, EDNA DOLE
Rag Carpet Verses. New York: Pageant Press, 1952. 30 p.

PEMBER, ELIZA GEORGINA (GIBBARD) (1841-)
Lyrics and Songs, Sacred and Secular. Boston: Angel Guardian Press, 1913. 3 p. ℓ., 79 p.
The Vision of St. Bride, and Other Poems. Boston: Angel Guardian Press, 1914. 2 p. ℓ., 27 p.

PEMBERTON, EANA
An Indian Love Tale (A Narrative Poem). New York: Exposition Press, 1940. 32 p.

PEMBERTON, GRACE FISHER
Poems. Fall River, MA.: The Munroe Press, 1930. 69, [4] p.

PENCE, ANABEL (ELIASON)
This Time Tomorrow. Richmond, VA.: Dietz Press, 1957. xii p., 1 ℓ., 99 p.

PENDLETON, AGNES EZELL
The Harp and the Rose. 2d ed. Wichita Falls, TX.: Wichita Printing Co., 1949. 76 numb. ℓ.

PENDLETON, BARBARA (EYE) (1861-)
Windows of Agates. Mill Valley, CA.; New York: The Wings Press, 1943. 75 p.

PENDLETON, SUSAN (1870-)
They Will Remain; Poems. Ann Arbor, MI.: Basil and Peters, 1966. 38 p.

PENDLEY, EVELYN (HOGE) (1918-)
Mountain Top Moments. Emory University, Atlanta, GA.: Banner Press, 1953. 91 p. (Verse craft series)

Growing Pleasures. n. p., 1956? 32 p.
Angel Wings. Emory University, Atlanta, GA.: Banner Press, 1957. 40 p.
A Golden Chain; Poems. Brooklyn, N. Y.: Parthenon Publishing Co., 1962. 64 p.

PENFOLD, GERDA
Done with Mirrors. Ellenburg, WA.: Vagabond Press, 1975. 41, [1] p.

PENICK, ELIZABETH ARCHER (1888-)
Petals. Nashville, TN.: Benson Printing Co., 1947. 62 p.

PENICK, MARGARET H.
Coins of Memory. New York: Printed by the John B. Watkins Company, 1943. [110] p.
Beauty's Snare. Mill Valley, CA.: Wings Press, 1952. 98 p.

PENISTON, REINZI EVYLIN (1850-)
A Midnight Reverie. Denver, CO.: The W. F. Robinson Ptg. Co., 1919. 53 numb. ℓ., 1 ℓ.

PENN, AILEEN (EDWARDS) (1902-1948)
Selected Poems. New York: North River Press, 1949. 31 p.

PENNER, HELEN (KNELSEN) (1937-)
Poetry Lane. Strathmore, Alta.: Printed by E. M. Groves, 1969. 53 p.

PENNINGTON, MAY AMANDA (WILLIAMS) (1867-)
Penn Poems.... Brenham, TX.: Banner Publishing Company, 1913. 48 p.

PEPPET, HELEN LOUESE
Lyrics. Philadelphia: Dorrance, 1964. 45 p. (Contemporary poets of Dorrance)

PERCIVAL, OLIVE (1869-1945)
Leaf-Shadows and Rose-Drift; Being Little Songs from a Los Angeles Garden. Cambridge, MA.: Printed at the Riverside Press, 1911. xi, [1], 117, [1] p., 1 ℓ.
...Yellowing Ivy. Los Angeles, CA.: The Ward Ritchie Press, 1946. vi, 40 p.

PERCY, FRANCES COAN
An Illuminated Way, and Other Poems. Boston: R. G. Badger, 1907. 5 p. ℓ., 9-123 p.

PEREIRA, IRENE (RICE) (1907-)
Crystal of the Rose. New York: Nordness Gallery, 1959. xviii, 63 p., 1 ℓ.
The Poetics of the Form of Space, Light and the Infinite. 1st special ed. New York: n. p., 1969. 82 p., 1 ℓ.
________. 2d ed., 1969.

PEREL, JANE LUNIN
The Lone Ranger and the New American Church. Cambridge, MA.: Archival Press, 1974. 48 p.

PERIMAN, MARJORIE DENDY
John an' Me. New York: Vantage, 1975. [8], 39 p.

PERKINS, EMILY TAYLOR
Housekeeper to the Lord. New York: H. Harrison, 1940. 64 p.

PERKINS, LAURA G.
Silhouettes and Samplers. Philadelphia: Dorrance, 1959. 50 p.

PERKINS, MARGARET
Love Letters of a Norman Princess. Topeka, KA.: Crane & Company, 1914. [33] p.

PERRIN, MAY
Left on My Doorstep. Philadelphia: Dorrance, 1951. 98 p.
Pilgrimage to God. Philadelphia: Dorrance, 1952. 67 p.

PERRINGS, MYRA
Shadow on the Stream; Selected Poems. Dallas, TX.: Triangle Pub. Co., 1956. 40 p.
The Circle Is Forever, Selected Poems. Dallas, TX.: Triangle Pub. Co., 1957. 40 p.

PERRY, ANN EVELYN (1880-)
Songs of Life. Los Angeles, CA.: n.p., 1929. 60 p.

PERRY, FERN McCREARY
...Thoughts Are Flowers. Philadelphia: Dorrance & Company, 1945. 5 p. ℓ., 9-106 p. (Contemporary poets of Dorrance, 305)

PERRY, LILLA (CABOT) (1848-1933)
The Jar of Dreams; A Book of Poems. Boston and New York: Houghton Mifflin Company, 1923. xi, [1] p., 1 ℓ., [3]-115 p.

PERRY, MARGARET (1933-)
Something Singing. Boston: Sherman & Company, 1916. 4 p. ℓ., 72 p.

PERRY, MARIE PURCELL
Along the Way; Poems. New York: Exposition Press, 1955. 64 p.

PERRY, SALLIE HOFFMAN
Poems. Pontiac, MI.: Printed by the Roycrofters, East Aurora, N.Y., 1910. 3 p. ℓ., 9-49 p.

PERSOV, ANNE
Whatever You Reap. Detroit, MI.: Shuman's, 1933. 3 p. ℓ., 5-80, [1] p.

PETER, LILY
The Green Linen of Summer, and Other Poems. Nashville, TN.: R. M. Allen, 1964. 114 p.

PETERS, LOUISE EDGAR
Pigeons of St. Marks. New York: Fellowship Press Service, 1922. 2 p. ℓ., 3-40 p.

PETERSON, ALICE ONIONS
Siftings. Los Angeles, CA.: Press of Gem Publishing Company, 1926. 59 p.

PETERSON, FANNIE W.
Rays of Rhyme and Reason. New York: Exposition Press, 1966. 64 p.

PETERSON, FLORA CULP
Life and She. Boston: Christopher Pub. House, 1960. 166 p.

PETERSON, MARY HELENE (1865-)
Lure of Iowa, and Other Poems. Clarinda, IA.: Journal Print, 1925. [24] p.

PETERSON, RUTH STREETER
Stretch Out My Golden Wing. Peterborough, N.H.: Windy Row Press, 1975? 72 p.

PETERSON, SADIE WILSON
Inclined to Lift. New York: Carlton Press, 1962. 6 p. ℓ., 36 p.

PETERSON, VIOLET (1908-)
To You. Hollywood, CA.: Academy Press, 1953. 60 p.
I Will Sing. Hollywood, CA.: Academy Press, 1956. 64 p.

PETRI, LORI
Fools or Gods. Atlanta, GA.: E. Hartsock; The Bozart Press, 1929. 95 p.

PETRUCCI, ANITA
Pomegranate. New York: H. Harrison, 1931. 63 p.
When Incense Burns.... Boston: B. Humphries, 1938. 87 p.
As Stardust Falls. Boston: B. Humphries, 1949. 64 p.

PETTENGILL, MARGARET MILLER
Heart in His Hand. West Los Angeles, CA.: Wagon & Star Publishers, 1944. [24] p. (Destiny editions)

PETTEY, KATHERINE FALL
Songs from the Sagebrush. Tucson, AZ.: State Consolidated Publishing Co., 1910. 69 p.

PETTIT, KATHRYNE YEARGIN
Things That Count, A Book of Poems. San Antonio, TX.: The Naylor Company, 1941. 3 p. ℓ., 58 p.
At Eventide, A Book of Verse. San Antonio, TX.: The Naylor Company, 1943. 5 p. ℓ., 65 p.
Through My Window, A Book of Verse. Boston: The Christopher Publishing House, 1945. 78 p.

PETTIT, MILLICENT LEWIS
Indian Summer; Poems. New York: Exposition Press, 1955. 56 p.

PETTUS, MARTHA ELVIRA
The Wayside Shrine, and Other Poems. Boston: Sherman, French & Company, 1914. 5 p. ℓ., 154 p.

PETTY, SALLIE DeMAREE
Tune in, to Rhymes. Friend, NB.: Studio News, 1947. 5-69 p.
Yuletide Greetings... and Other Poems. Friend, NB.: Studio News, 1948. 1 p. ℓ., 45 p.

PEXTON, JENNIE L.
Lights of Cimarron. Guthrie, OK.: The Cooperative Publishing Co., 1931. 135 p.

PHELAN, ANNA AUGUSTA (von HELMHOLTZ)
The Crystal Cup. Minneapolis, MN.: Delta Phi Lambda, University of Minnesota, 1949. 111 p.

PHELPS, ANNA ELIZABETH
Mountain, Valley, Lake and Stream. New York: The Poets Press, 1936. 71 p.

PHELPS, FLORENCE
Yuletide Candle Light.... New York: The Paebar Company, 1915. 3 p. ℓ., 22 p.

PHELPS, JESSIE ADELINE (COLE) (1864-)
City and Country's Joy, Grief and Romance. New York: The International Press, 1929. 185 p.

PHELPS, MARGUERITE
White Hyacinths. New York: The Poets Press, 1941. 48 p.

PHELPS, MARY
A Bed of Strawberries: Poems. New York: Voyages Press, 1958. vi p., 1 ℓ., 23, [1] p.

PHELPS-RIDER, ALICE
...The Enchanted Hour. Philadelphia: Dorrance & Company, 1940. 87 p. (Contemporary poets of Dorrance, 210)

PHILLEY, ANNA M.
Poems. Fort Wayne, IN.: Fort Wayne Printing Company, 1916. 57 p.

PHILLIPS, AMY CARSON
Poems. Coquille, OR.: Printed by C. E. Darling, 1930. 7 p. ℓ., 118, [7] p.

PHILLIPS, BEULAH WYATT
Grain from My Harvest. New York: Exposition Press, 1964. 64 p.

PHILLIPS, EDNA (REYNISH)
A Mother Sings; Poems. New York: Greenwich Book Publishers, 1961. 41 p.

PHILLIPS, ESTA L. (1917-1956)
The Rock and the Candle. San Antonio, TX.: Naylor Co., 1956. x, 34 p.

PHILLIPS, GERTIE STEWART
Blown Leaves and Petals. Dallas, TX.: The Kaleidograph Press, 1934. xi, 1 ℓ., 15-87 p.
Lonely Apples. Dallas, TX.: The Kaleidograph Press, 1942. xi p., 1 ℓ., 15-100 p.

PHILLIPS, GRACE SPENCER
Seven Sonnets en Puerto Rico. New York: Avon House, 1938. [16] p.

PHILLIPS, HELEN CHARLOT
Pink and Blue Laughter. Los Angeles, CA.: Hollywood House, 1944. [166] p.

PHILLIPS, LOUISE SCOTT
Deep End. Paducah, KY.: Printed by H. H. Martin & Co., 1945. 4 p. ℓ., 60 p.

PHILLIPS, MARIE (TELLO) (1874-)
Book of Verses. New York: Clark & Fritts, 1922. 6 p. ℓ., 81 p.
Greetings from Father Pitt. Pittsburgh? PA.: n. p., 1929. 14 p.
Ten Thousand Candles; A Souvenir of Pittsburgh, Pennsylvania. Pittsburgh, PA.: Observer Press, 1931. 5 p. ℓ., 15-63 p.
The Honeysuckle and the Rose; Lyrics...Sonnets, 1922-1933. Pittsburgh: The Observer Press, 1933. 6 p. ℓ., 92 p., 1 ℓ.
Mary of Scotland, Narrative Poem--Lyrics. Pittsburgh, PA.: Observer Press, 1937. 7 p. ℓ., 17-181 p.
Pittsburgh Saga; Braddock's Defeat, Bouquet's Victory, 1748-1764. Sonnets and Lyrics. Manchester, ME.: Falmouth Pub. House, 1951. 74 p.

PHILLIPS, MARION
A Foot in the Door. New York: Vantage Press, 1966. 62 p.

PHILLIPS, MARY (GEISLER) (1881-)
Spider Webs and Sunflowers. Philadelphia: Macrae Smith Company, 1928. 257 p.
What's Behind the Door? Chicago: Rand McNally, 1963. 27 p.

PHILLIPS, ROSE MYRA
Bird Against the Wind. Winona Lake, IN.: Light and Life Press, 1940. 2 p. ℓ., 7-81 p.
Journey by Night. Winona Lake, IN.: Light and Life Press, 1950. 62 p.

PHYTHIAN, ALICE HAYDEN
Poems. Boston: R. G. Badger, 1929. 48 p.

PICK, ETHEL MIRIAM (d. 1949)
Another Dimension; Poems. Chicago: Dierkes Press, 1950. 46 p.

PICKARD, CYNTHIA
Woman in Apartment. Denver, CO.: A. Swallow, 1957. 48 p.

PICKETT, GLADYS MARIE (1914-)
Wind Through the Bell: A Book of Poetry. Boston: B. Humphries, 1945. 63 p.

PIERCE, EDITH LOVEJOY (1904-)
In This Our Day. New York & London: Harper and Brothers, 1944. viii, 71 [1] p.
Therefore Choose Life: Poems. New York: Harper, 1947. 76 p.
Wind Has No Home. Evanston, IL: E. L. Pierce, 1950. 44 p.

PIERCE, FLORA MAY JOHNSON (1900-)
Sonnets of Eve. Durham, N. C.: Moore Publishing Co., 1973. 80 p.

PIERCE, GRACE ADELE (1858-1923)
The Silver Cord and the Golden Bowl. New York: London: The Abbey Press, 1901. 147, [1] p.

PIERCE, KATHERINE MILNER
Song of Faith. Boston: Stratford, 1921. 91 p.

PIERCE, LEWETTE POLLOCK
...So Brief a Span. New York: H. Harrison, 1938. 64 p.

PIERCE, MAUDE WHEELER
Dream Burdens. North Montpelier, VT.: The Driftwind Press, 1929. iii-viii, [3], 5-68, [1] p.

PIERCY, ESTELLE (ZWOLACK)
Bride's Treasures. Dallas, TX.: Story Book Press, 1948. 48 p.

PIERCY, MARGE (1936-)
Breaking Camp. Middletown, CT.: Wesleyan University Press, 1968. 74 p.
Hard Loving: Poems. Middletown, CT.: Wesleyan University Press, 1969. 77 p.
A Work of Artifice. Detroit: Red Hanrahan Press, 1970.
When the Drought Broke. Santa Barbara, CA.: Unicorn Press, 1971. broadside.
To Be of Use. Garden City, N.Y.: Doubleday, 1973. 107 p.

PIERO, ELDA MAE
Between the Hills of Time. Canton, OH.: Boyer-Buchman Co., 1952. 60 p.

PIERSON, NITA
Sonnets of My Life. San Francisco: Philopolis Press, 1916. 5 p. ℓ., 9-48 p.

PIFER, VIDA
...The Only Gate, and Other Poems. Philadelphia: Dorrance and Company, 1939. 101 p. (Contemporary poets of Dorrance, 200)
...His Own Image, and Other Poems. Philadelphia: Dorrance and Company, 1943. 70 p. (Contemporary poets of Dorrance, 253)
Pearls and Pepperseeds. Philadelphia: Dorrance, 1947. 111 p. (Contemporary poets of Dorrance, 365)

PINCKNEY, JOSEPHINE (1895-1957) [Full Name: Josephine Lyons Scott Pinckney.]
Sea-Drinking Cities: Poems. New York & London: Harper & Brothers, 1927. 6 p. ℓ., 3-86 p.

PINDER, FRANCES (DICKENSON) (1879-1956)
Late Harvest; Poems. Richmond, VA.: Dietz Press, 1959. 271 p.

PINE, M. S., pseud. see FINN, MARY PAULINA, Sister (1842-1935)

PINGEL, MARTHA MARY (1923-)
Catalyst; An Interpretation of Life. New York: Exposition Press, 1951. 64 p.

PINKERTON, HELEN
Error Pursued. Iowa City, IA.: Cummington Press, 1959. [22] p.

PINKNEY, DOROTHY COWLES
The Town Not Yet Awake. New York: Fine Editions Press, 1956. 74 p.

PINNEY, MARY RAY
The Right of Way; A Poem. New York & London: G. P. Putnam's Sons, 1922. 19 p.

PIRONE, MADELYN DALES
Ghosts of Christmas Past and Present. Tucson, AZ.: Printed by V. Carter Service, 1958. 2 p. ℓ., 15 p.
A Minor Minstrel. Shelbyville, IN.: Blue River Press, 1958. 47 p.
Seas, Stars and Seasons. Oneonta? N.Y.: n.p., 1958? [42] p.
Sunlight, Bright Snow, Windsong and Rainbow. Tucson, AZ.: Printed by V. Carter Service, 1958. 24 p.
The Final Leaf. n.p., 1959. 24 p.

PITMAN, EMILY COULTEN
Springtime, and Other Verses. Kirkwood, MO.: n.p., 1910. 37 p.

PITTS, MABEL PORTER (1884-)
In the Shadow of the Crag (A Story of the North), and Other Poems. San Francisco: W. N. Brunt, 1906. 6 p. ℓ., 278 p.
_______. Denver: Smith-Brooks Press, 1907. 6 p. ℓ., 293 p.

PITTSINGER, ELIZA A. (1837-)
The Song of the Soul Victorious; A Poem. Hudson, MA.: The E. F. Worchester Press, 1900. 17 ℓ.

PIXLEY, OLIVE ANN
The Weaver and Other Poems. Tujunga, CA.: C. L. Anderson, 1950. 134 p.

PLANK, ISABELLA CARLISLE
A Woman's Voice. Minneapolis, MN.: Raby Plank Publishing Company, 1903. 5 p. ℓ., 199 p.

PLANTZ, MYRA (GOODWIN) (1856-1914)
Songs for Quiet Hours. New York, Cincinnati: The Methodist Book Concern, 1915. 153 p.

PLATH, SYLVIA (1932-1963)
The Colossus; Poems. London: Heineman, 1960. 88 p.
The Colossus & Other Poems. 1st American ed. New York: Knopf, 1962. x, [1], 83 p., [1], 2 ℓ.
Ariel. London: Faber and Faber, 1965. 86 p.
_______. 1965. Second impression.
Uncollected Poems. London: Turret Books, 1965. 19 p. (Turret booklet, no. 2)
Ariel. New York: Harper & Row, 1966. xi p., 1 ℓ., 85 p., 1 ℓ.

________. London: Faber and Faber, 1967. Fourth impression.
The Colossus. London: Faber & Faber, 1967. 88 p.
Early Poems. Cambridge, MA.: Harvard Advocate, 1967. 40 p.
Wreath for a Bridal. Frensham, Surrey: Sceptre Press, 1970. [12] p.
Crossing the Water. London: Faber and Faber, 1971. 64 p.
Crossing the Water; Transitional Poems. 1st U.S. ed. New York: Harper & Row, 1971. vi, 56 p.
Crystal Gazer and Other Poems. London: Rainbow Press, 1971. [9], 31 p.
Fiesta Melons. Exeter: Rougemont Press, 1971. 21 p.
Lyonnesse: Poems. London: Rainbow Press, 1971. [5], 33 p.
Million Dollar Month. Frensham, Surrey: Sceptre Press, 1971. [5] p.
Winter Trees. London: Faber and Faber, 1971. 3-55 p.
The Colossus. London: Faber and Faber, 1972. 88 p. (Faber paper covered editions.)
Winter Trees. 1st U.S. ed. New York: Harper and Row, 1972. 64 p.
Pursuit. London: The Rainbow Press, 1973. 27 p.

PLATOU, MARIQUITA (VILLARD) (1905-)
Tease the Tiger's Nose; Verses. Boston: Plowshare Press, 1965. [56] p.
One Moment; An Easter Meditation, Thirty-six Sonnet Variations on a Paschal Theme. Boston: Plowshare Press, 1971. 55 p.

PLIMPTON, HARRIET
Out of the North. London, New York: Oxford University Press, 1960. 1961. 95 p.

PLOUGHE, MARY WIMBOROUGH
At Anchorage. Philadelphia: Poetry Publishers, 1937. 127 p.

PLUMMER, MARY CATHERINE
Book of Poems. Washington, D.C.: Milan and Son, 1915. [6] p.

PLUMMER, MARY WRIGHT (1856-1916)
Verses. New York: Priv. print., 1916. 32 p.

PLUMMER, SALLY TERRY
Nature and Stars. Philadelphia: Dorrance, 1960. 47 p.

PLUMMER, SARA A. C.
Falling Leaves. Seattle, WA.: I. N. Davidson, Printer, 1917. 32 p.
The Whipporwills. Seattle, WA.: Clint W. Lee Co., Printers, 1928. 25 p.
The Yellow Butterfly. Seattle, WA.: n.p., 1929. 24 p.
Behind the Holly Trees. Detroit: n.p., 1931. 29 p.
Fragments. Seattle, WA.: Clint W. Lee Co., 1932. 28 p.

PLUNKETT, EUGENIA
If You Listen Quietly. Fort Smith, AR.: South and West, 1970. 55 p.

POGUE, ANNA (HOLM) (1889-)
An Oregon Interlude, A Narrative Poem. Boston: B. Humphries, 1946. 58 p.
A Slant of Years. Mill Valley, CA.: Wings Press, 1955. 72 p.

POINGDESTER, BEATRICE U.
O Virgin Land. New York: Vantage Press, 1974. 53 p.

POLK, BRIGID
Scars. Norwood, PA.: Telegraph, 1973. [78] p.

POLK, GRACE PORTERFIELD
Blossoms From My Enchanted Garden. Indianapolis, IN.: n.p., 1928. 1 p. ℓ., 16 p.
Polk-a-Dots for Tiny Tots. Indianapolis, IN.: n.p., 1928. 1 p. ℓ., 16 p.

POLLARD, PATIENCE (FLORENCE) HOWELL (1898-)
Forgetting All Else. Dallas, TX.: The Kaleidograph Press, 1941. ix p., 1 ℓ., 15-83 p.
Memory Is Bold. Santa Barbara, CA.: J. F. Rowney Press, 1949. x p.
Armed with Song. Alhambra, CA.: Cunningham Press, 1960. x, 92 p.

POLLARD, REBECCA (SMITH) (1831-1917)
Althea; or The Morning Glory. Boston: Sherman, French & Co., 1912. 2 p. ℓ., 37 p.

POLLOCK, DOLLIE LOUISE (CUSTER) (1883-)
My Garden. Pasadena, CA.: San Pasqual Press, 1938. 48 ℓ.

POMMER, SIBYL
Garden of Grace. Emory University, Atlanta, GA.: Banner Press, 1936. 44 p. (Verse craft series)
Muted Melody. Emory University, Atlanta, GA.: Banner Press, 1938. 36 p. (Verse craft series)
Star Beyond Shadow. Emory University, Atlanta, GA.: Banner Press, 1940. 36 p. (Verse craft series)
Collected Poems. Emory University, Atlanta, GA.: Banner Press, 1954. 68 p. (Verse craft series)

POMMY-VEGA, JANINE
Poems to Fernando. San Francisco: City Lights Books, 1968. 60 p. (The pocket poets series, no. 22)
Journal of a Hermit. Cherry Valley, NY.: Cherry Valley Editions, 1974. [28] p.

POND, ELIZABETH KEITH
Easter and Other Poems. Berkeley, CA.: Print. by J. J. Gillick & Co., Inc., 1931. 2 p. ℓ., 7-23 p.
Songs of Gladness. Berkeley, CA.: Print. by J. J. Gillick & Co., Inc., 1931. 2 p. ℓ., 7-69 p.

PONSOT, MARIE (BIRMINGHAM)
True Minds. San Francisco: City Lights Pocket Bookshop, 1956. 32 p. (The pocket poets series, no. 5)

POOLE, BETTIE FRESHWATER
America's Battle Cry, and Other New War Songs. Elizabeth City, N.J.: n.p., 1918. 9-20 p.

POOLE, DORALDINE DEMARIS
A Soul Set Sail. New York: Vantage Press, 1965. 64 p.

POOLE, DOROTHY CAMPBELL (1895-)
Windows; Poems. Charlottesville, VA.: n.p., 1956. 77 p., 1 ℓ.

POOLE, FANNY HUNTINGTON (RUNNELLS) (1863-)
Mugen; A Book of Verse. Bridgeport, CT.: Niles Publishing Co.; Clinton, N.Y.: G. W. Browning, 1907. 4 p. ℓ., 7-94, [3] p.

POOLE, MARY EDNA
Being in Night. Dallas, TX.: Kaleidograph Press, 1950. 74 p.

POOR, NATALIE (1910-1923)
Poems of an Angel Child. Chicago: n.p., 1923.

POPE, FRANCES EMILY (1840-1937)
Poems. Cambridge, MA.: University Press, 1901. x, 182 p.

POPE, MURIEL EAMES (1886-)
Singing Sand, California Desert Verse. Placentia? CA.: n.p., 1952. 49 p.

POPEL, ESTHER A. W. (1896-) [Full Name: Esther (Popel) Shaw.]
A Forest Pool. Washington, D.C.: Priv. print. Modernistic Press, 1934. 6 p. ℓ., 42 p.

PORCHER, MARY F. (WICKHAM)
The Tilted Cup. Philadelphia: Dorrance & Co., 1926. 63, [1] p. (Contemporary poets, 31)

PORTER, ADDIEBELL S.
Lone Star, and Other Travelogue Verse. Tulia, TX.: n.p., 1936. [20] p.

PORTER, AGNES
English B. Boston: Sherman, French & Co., 1917. 5 p. ℓ., 61 p.

PORTER, ANN
White Gold. Jackson, MI.: Tucker Print House, 1952. 40 p.

PORTER, CHARLOTTE ENDYMION (1859-)
Lips of Music. New York: T. Y. Crowell & Co., 1910. xiii, 183, [1] p.

PORTER, ELAINE MARJORIE
Heart Echoes. Detroit: Moore Printing Co., 1915. 3 p. ℓ., 9-42, [1] p.

PORTER, ESTHER (CHURCH)
Life Lines. Oakland, CA.: Goodhue Printing Co., 1931. 3 p. ℓ., 9-46 p.

PORTER, GENE (STRATTON) (1863-1924)
The Fire Bird. Garden City, NY. & Toronto: Doubleday, Page & Co., 1922. 4 p. ℓ., 71 p.
Jesus of the Emerald. Garden City, N. Y.: Doubleday, Page, & Co., 1923. [44] p.

PORTER, JENNY LIND (1927-)
The Lantern of Diogenes and Other Poems. San Antonio, TX.: Naylor Co., 1954. 73 p.
Peter Bell the Fourth. Austin, TX.: Steck Co., 1955. 16 p.
Azle and the Attic Room. Los Angeles, CA.: W. Ritchie Press, 1957. 38 p.
In the Still Cave of the Witch Poesy; Selected Poems. Austin, TX.: Printed by Steck Co., 1960. 71 p.

PORTER, LOUISE M.
Pasqua Florida; The Feast of the Flowers. Philadelphia: Dorrance, 1954. 96 p. (Contemporary poets of Dorrance, 464)

PORTER, MAYBELLE MAYNE
Bells of Memory. Emory University, Atlanta, GA.: Banner Press, 1936. 64 p. (Verse craft series)

PORTILLO, ESTELA
Impressions of a Chicana. n. p.: Quinto Sol, 1974.

POSEGATE, MABEL (1885-)
Silver 'Scutcheon. Paris: n. p., 1928. 84 p.
Once When Arcturus Shone. Brattleboro, VT.: Stephen Daye Press, 1935. 95 p.
...White Moment. Philadelphia: Dorrance and Company, 1938. 80 p. (Contemporary poets of Dorrance, 177)
Burning Gold. Portland, ME.: Falmouth Pub. House, 1947. 40 p.

POST, CAROLINE (LATHROP)
Aunt Carrie's Poems. Battle Creek, MI.: C. W. Post, 1909. 157 p.

POSTELLE, EDNA BLALOCK
Drink the Red Morning. San Antonio, TX.: Naylor Co., 1974. viii, 62 p.

POSTEN, ANNA GARRISON
A Woman Singing. Emory University, Atlanta, GA.: Banner Press, 1937. 60 p. (Verse craft series)

POTTER, CORA BROWN see POTTER, CORA (URQUHART) (1859-1936)

POTTER, CORA (URQUHART) (1859-1936) [POTTER, CORA BROWN]
The Love of the Incas. London: The Orient Press Service, 1927. 45 p.
Poems. London: The Orient Press Service, 1927. 42 p.
_______. New York: P. R. Reynolds, 1928. 38 p.
The Love of the Incas. New York: P. R. Reynolds, 1928. 4 p. ℓ., [7]-45 p.

POTTER, MARGUERITE
With Wings Outspread. New York: Print. by Sales Promotion Co., 1933. 63 p.

POTTS, EVA MAE (GREENO)
Colors That Blend. White Plains, N.Y.: n.p., 1949. 86 p.
Fields of Clover. White Plains? N.Y.: n.p., 1951. ix, 88 p.
Oceans of Dreams. White Plains, N.Y.: Genco Press, 1969. xiv, 75 p.

POUSETTE-DART, FLORA LOUISE
Poems. New York: Oquaga Press, 1936? 31 p.
I Saw Time Open. New York: Island Press, 1948. 152 p.

POWELL, MARY A.
Gems of Thought and Verse. New Haven, CT.: Tuttle, Morehouse & Taylor Co., 1925? 87 p.

POWELL, MARY ELIZABETH
The Dying Musician. Boston: R. G. Badger, 1906. 2 p. ℓ., 96 p.

POWELL, SHIRLEY
Parachutes. New York: Mouth of the Dragon Press, 1975. 59 p.

POWER, MARJORIE PALMER
A Slice of Life with Crumbs. Portland, ME.: Forest City Printing Company, 1939. 5 p. ℓ., 30 numb. ℓ., 31-46 numb. ℓ., 1 ℓ., 47-52 numb. ℓ., 1 ℓ.
Twenty-Four High, Edmund and I. Portland, ME.: F. L. Tower Companies, 1942. 56 p.

POWERS, ELIZABETH LATHROP (1898-)
Rhythm Road. Dallas, TX.: Story Book Press, 1951. 56 p.

POWERS, JESSICA
The Lantern Burns. New York: The Monastine Press, 1939. 6 p. ℓ., 3-53, [1] p.
The Place of Splendor. New York: Cosmopolitan Science and Art Service Co., Inc., 1946. 5 p. ℓ., 13-98 p.
Mountain Sparrow; Ten Poems. Reno, NE.: Carmel of Reno, 1972? 26 p.

POWERS, MARY HELEN
... Flying Bats. New York: Harrison, 1945. 96 p.

POWERS, ROSE MILLS
Psyche's Lamp. Winter Park, FL.: The Angel Alley Press, 1927. 3 p. ℓ., 9-119 p.

POWNING, MARY GLEASON
Star Dust, A Book of Poems. Boston: B. Humphries, 1931. 48 p.

PRATT, FLORENCE EVELYN
Songs of Many Days. Boston: R. G. Badger, 1907. 9-80 p.

PRAY, FRANCES HUNT
Listening. Roscoe, CA., Ann Arbor, MI.: Edwards Brothers, Inc., 1941. 3 p. ℓ., 47 p.

PRAY, MARY FRANCES
Miniatures & Other Poems. Cambridge, MA.: n. p., 1941. 5 p. ℓ., 86 p.

PRENDREGEIST, JOHN, pseud. see BEHENNA, CATHERINE ARTHUR (1860?-)

PRENTISS, CAROLINE EDWARDS (1872-)
Love and Laughter. New York & London: G. P. Putnam's Sons, 1917. xviii p., 1 ℓ., 294 p.

PRENTISS, HARRIET DOAN (McREYNOLDS)
Golden Hours. An Optimistic Book of Verse. New York: House of Field, Inc., 1940. 54 p.

PRESCOTT, GEORGIA SHAW
Whispering Winds. San Antonio, TX.: Naylor Co., 1969. viii, 76 p.

PRESCOTT, LYDIA C.
Planet Descending. Philadelphia, PA.: Poetry Publishers, 1938. 71 p.

PRESS, SIMONE JUDA
Thaw. New York: Inwood Press, dist. by Horizon, 1974. 63 p.

PRESSET, ANNE L.
Cherished Thoughts in Original Poems and Sketches. Provo, UT.: The Skelton Publishing Company, 1901. 221 p., [1] p.

PRESTON, EDNA MITCHELL
Monkey in the Jungle. New York: Viking Press, 1968. [32] p.

PRESTON, JANET NEWMAN
Upon Our Pulses. Francestown, N.H.: Golden Quill Press, 1964. 95 p.

PRESTON, MINNIE HAZELLE PIERCE
Little Songs from Life's Book. Chicago: Priv. Print., R. R. Donnelly, 1918. 43 p., 1 ℓ.

PREVITALI, ROSE ROBINSON MORROW
Pinnacles, A Book of Verse. New York: The Fine Editions Press, 1941. 47, [1] p. (Poetry series of the Fine Editions Press)

PREYSZ, LOUISE ROSALIE (1912-)
Dark Stars. Boston: Meador Publishing Company, 1934. 43 p.
Hills. Dallas, TX.: The Kaleidograph Press, 1936. 51 p.
Moon Dreams. Boston: Meador Publishing Company, 1935. 37 p.

PRICE, ANNA L.
The Old Church, and Other Poems. Marlington, W. VA.: Times Book Company, 1921. 138 p.

PRICE, BLANCHE ADELLE
Debat d'Amour: Twenty-Four Poems. Baltimore, MD.: J. H. Furst Co., 1965. 45 p.

PRICE, BLANCHE ELIZABETH
Across the Years. New York: William-Frederick Press, 1954. 62 p. (The William-Frederick poets, no. 113)

PRICE, EDITH BALLINGER (1897-)
The Four Winds. New York: Frederick A. Stokes Company, 1927. xiii p., 2 ℓ., 181 p.

PRICE, ELEANOR (1911-1929)
Poems. New York: n.p., 1930. 94 p.

PRICE, FRANCES BROWN (1895-)
Blue Flame. San Antonio, TX.: Naylor Co., 1967. xiv, 85 p.

PRICE, LILLA POOLE
The Chant of the Seasons, and Other Poems. Boston: The Christopher Publishing House, 1928. 4 p. ℓ., [7]-25 p.

PRICE, MARJORIE (YATES)
Our Lovely Land; Poems and Sketches. New York: Book Craftsmen Associates, 1960. 6 p. ℓ., 122 p., 1 ℓ.

PRICE, MERLE (1910-)
The Heart Has Its Daybreak. Emory University, Atlanta, GA.: Banner Press, 1950. 60 p. (Verse craft series)
Splendid Rumor. Emory University, Atlanta, GA.: Banner Press, 1953. 60 p. (Verse craft series)

PRICE, NATALIE WHITTED
Ravelings in Rhyme. Chicago: n.p., 1910. 3 p. ℓ., 61 p.
Sketches in Lyric Prose and Verse. Chicago: R. F. Seymour, 1920. 80 p.

PRICE, PAULINE
Into the Void of Time. Ilfracombe, Devon: A. H. Stockwell, 1964. 39 p.

PRICE, SUSAN WILLIS (THORNTON) (1858-)
Sunset Vale, and Other Poems. Waco, TX.: Church Printing Co., 1912. [70] p.

PRIESTLEY, ANNA M. (1883-)
Bright Spires. Dallas, TX.: The Kaleidograph Press, 1938. ix p., 1 ℓ., 13-94 p.
Upon a Rock. Dallas, TX.: The Kaleidograph Press, 1940. xi, 1 ℓ., 15-99 p.
New Walls for Old. Mill Valley, CA.: Wings Press, 1955. 120 p.

PRIME, CYNTHIA
The Sour and the Sweet. New York: William-Frederick, 1972.

PRINCE, CLARA CATHERINE
Trailing Arbutus. n.p., 192-. [1], 27, [1] p.
Interim. Wauwatosa, WI.: Kenyon Press, 1949. 3 p. ℓ., 57 p.
Interlude. Wauwatosa, WI.: Kenyon Press, 1953. 4 p. ℓ., 70 p.

PRINDLE, FRANCES WESTON (CARRUTH)
Vibrations; A Book of Verse. New York: H. Vinal, Ltd., 1927. 6 p. ℓ., 75 p.

PRITCHARD, GLORIA CLINTON
Trees Along the Highway. New York: Comet Press Books, 1953. 3 p. ℓ., 26 p.

PROBST, LEETHA JOURNEY
Poems of the California Missions. Los Angeles, CA.: J. F. Rowney Press, 1923. 53 p.
Steeps of Dawn. Los Angeles, CA.: The Primavera Press, 1935. 44 p.

Six Dance Movements in Words. Los Angeles, CA.: Anderson & Ritchie, The Ward Ritchie Press, 1943. [15] p.

PROBSTFIELD, EDRIS MARY (1907-)
Open Windows. Dallas, TX.: The Kaleidograph Press, 1933. 4 p. ℓ., xi-xii p., 1 ℓ., 15-62 p.

PROCTOR, EDNA DEAN
The Mountain Maid, and Other Poems of New Hampshire. "Old Home Week" ed. Boston & New York: Houghton, Mifflin & Co., 1900. 4 p. ℓ., 60 p.
Songs of the Ancient People. Boston & New York: Houghton, Mifflin & Co., 1903. 69 p.
Songs of America, and Other Poems. Boston & New York: Houghton, Mifflin & Co., 1905. viii, 123, [1] p.
The Glory of Toil, and Other Poems. Boston & New York: Houghton, Mifflin & Co., 1916. vii, [1] p., 1 ℓ., 67, [1] p., 1 ℓ.

PROCTOR, LORINE
Shifting Sands. Philadelphia: Dorrance, 1969. 69 p.

PROCTOR, MARTHA BAILEY
Possessions. Seattle, WA.: Press of Platt & Tomlinson, 194-? [55] p.

PROFFITT, MARY HIGGINS
Airborne Friends, and Other Poems. San Antonio, TX.: Naylor Co., 1965. vi, 95 p.

PROUDFOOT, ANDREA (HOFER)
Trolley Lines, Jotted Down Coming and Going. Chicago: R. F. Seymour, 1919. 1 p. ℓ., 72 p.

PROUTY, MARTHA
Songs of the South Shore. Boston: Marshall Jones, 1922. vii p., 1 ℓ., 90 p.

PRYOR, LOIS A.
Garnered Vintage. Boston: R. Humphries, 1946. 77 p.

PULS, HELEN SEARCY
The Sword. New York: The Monastine Press, 1945.

PULSIFER, SUSAN FARLEY (NICHOLS) (1892-)
Fighting French Ballads. New York: Printed by Richards-Starkey Company, 1943. [3]-30, [1] p.
... L'Esprit de la France, Chants de Liberation. The Spirit of France, Songs of Liberation. New York: Editions de la Maison Francaise, Inc., 1944. 2 p. ℓ., [7]-223 p.
Children Are Poets. Cambridge, MA.: Dresser, Chapman & Grimes, 1963. xiii, 114 p.
Out of the Dust. Portland, ME.: Printed by the Anthoesen Press, 1971. 152 p.

PUNCH, ROSALIND MAE GUGGENHEIM *see* BURR, JANE, *pseud.*

PRUINTON, ANNIE E.
Poems. Boston: The Marymount Press, 1908. 34, [1] p.

PURVIS, CLEO
Barabbas, and Other Poems. Louisville, KY.: Pentecostal Pub. Co., 1959. 28 p.

PURVIS, EVELYN M[ARTIN] (1873-)
Poems. Yazoo City, MS.: Press of the Yazoo Sentinel, 1903. 46 p.

PUTCAMP, LUISE, Jr. (1924-)
Sonnets for the Survivors & Other Poems. Dallas, TX.: Kaleidograph Press, 1952. 56 p.
The Night of the Child; A Christmas Story. Waco, TX.: Word Books, 1971. 39 p.

PUTNAM, CAROLINE (WILLIAMS) (1825-)
In Allah's Garden and Other Poems. Grand Rapids, MI. ? n.p., 1905? [71] p.

PUTNAM, ELIZABETH (LOWELL)
XVIII Sonnets. New York: W. E. Rudge, 1925. 2 p.ℓ., 28 numb. ℓ., 1 ℓ.
On Growing Old.... New York: W. E. Rudge, 1929. 3 p.ℓ., 35, [1] p.
Odors of Hyacinths, and Other Poems. New York: W. E. Rudge, 1930. 41, [1] p.

PUTNAM, GRACE BROWN
Lift up My Cups. Dallas, TX.: The Kaleidograph Press, 1942. xii p., 1 ℓ., 15-112 p.

PUTNAM, HARRIET (1862-)
The Little Candle-Bearer Verses. Roselle Park, N.J.: n.p., 1932. 3 p.ℓ., 54 p.

PYLE, DORIS JOE
Crushed Opals. New York: The Poetry Digest, 1951. 4 p.ℓ., 55 p.

PYLE, KATHARINE
Childhood. New York: E. P. Dutton & Co., 1904. 46 p.
Lazy Matilda, and Other Tales. New York: E. P. Dutton & Co., 1921. 173 p.

QUARLES, ELLIE MAY
Sunlight and Shadows of Human Life. Cincinnati, OH.: F. L. Rowe, 1913. 119 p.
Life's Gleanings. Cincinnati, OH.: F. L. Rowe, 1920. 160 p.

QUICK, DOROTHY (1900-1962)
Threads. New York: H. Vinal, 1927. 72 p.
Changing Winds. New York & London: G. P. Putnam's Sons, 1935. xi, 2 ℓ., 17-103 p.
Spears into Life. New York & London: G. P. Putnam's Sons, 1938. xi p., 1 ℓ., 101 p.
Laugh While You Can. New York: L. Raley, 1940. 44 p.
To What Strange Altar. New York: G. P. Putnam's Sons, 1940. 115 p.
Variations on a Theme. New York: Fine Editions Press, 1947. 94 p.
Interludes. New York: Farrar, Straus & Young, 1953. 118 p.
Bold Heart, and Other Poems. Washington: University Press of Washington, D. C., 1960. 76 p.

QUIGLEY, ADA E. (ELTZROTH) (1871-)
Bubbles. Los Angeles, CA.: The Harmony Press, 1934. [46] p.

QUINN, MELICENT ATHLEEN (BROWN) (1889-)
Jonquils. Tampa, FL.: Laurel Publishers, 1945. 13 p.

QUIRK, CATHLEEN
The Only Child. Somerville, MA.: Barn Dream Press, 1970. [6] p.

RABY, MATTIE PEARL
Voice of Acceptance. New York: Vantage Press, 1953. 42 p.

RACH-WOLSKA, OZELIA (1899-)
The Legend of the Enchanted Mesa and Other Southwest Poems. Santa Fe, N.M.: Privately printed by Clarks Studio, 1937. [10], 3-51 p.
...The Desert Whispers. Philadelphia: Dorrance and Company, 1942. 64 p. (Contemporary poets of Dorrance, 227)

RADER, VIVIAN LARAMORE see LARAMORE, VIVIAN (YEISER) (1891-)

RAGAN, KATHRYN
Jubilee. Cedar Rapids, IA.: Torch Press, 1950. 6 p.

RAIBORN, MILDRED LINDSEY (1913-)
Cactus in Bloom.... Dallas, TX.: The Story Book Press, 1948. 3 p. ℓ., 7-40 p.
Panorama on a Star. San Antonio, TX.: Naylor Co., 1953. 84 p.

RAINER, DACHINE
Outside Time. Bearsville, N.Y.: Retort Press, 1948. 26 p.

RAINSFORD, CHRISTINA
Timeless Moment. Francestown, N.H.: Golden Quill Press, 1962. 92 p.

Upland Pastures. Francestown, N. H.: Golden Quill Press, 1969. 96 p.

RAINSFORD, HELEN (MORGAN)
Me and My House; Fifty Poems. New York: Exposition Press, 1955. 56 p.

RAISCH, MARIE LOUISE
Three Cycles. San Francisco: The Cloister Press, 1929. 122 p.

RAMEL, MAY LEONE
Dawn Wind. Dallas, TX.: The Kaleidograph Press, 1941. 71 p.

RAMSDELL, LEILA R.
A Benediction and Other Verses. New York: E. S. Gorham, 1901. 96 p.

RAMSEY, HELEN PRITCHARD (1886-)
Canary Bird Lady, and Other Poems. New York: Exposition Press, 1953. 63 p.

RAMSEY, RUTH LUSK (1878-)
The Old Plum Tree. St. Paul, MN.: n. p., 1953. 99 p.
The Arc of the Star. Saint Paul, MN.: n. p., 1955. 93 p.
How Far the Fragrance. Saint Paul, MN.: Ramaley Printing Co., 1959. 79 p.

RANCHINO, ESTHER V.
Grains of Sand; Poems. New York: Exposition Press, 1955. 64 p.

RAND, ELIZABETH HUNTINGTON (1875-)
Echoes. Boston: R. G. Badger, 1904. 55 p.

RAND, FLORENCE
As Themis Plays, A Collection of Poems. New York: William-Frederick Press, 1953. 45 p. (The William-Frederick poets, 101)
I Call My Love; Three Poems. Brooklyn, N. Y.: G. J. Rickard, 1958. 50 p.
Spirit on the Winds. Philadelphia: Dorrance, 1960. 50 p. (Contemporary poets of Dorrance, 217)
From My Diary; Poems. Ilfracombe: A. H. Stockwell, 1964. 56 p.

RAND, MARY A.
Windfalls of Poesy. Southington, CT.: News & Times Co., 1920. [56] p.

RANDALL, BELLE
San Quentin and Two Kinds of Conscience. Berkeley, CA.: n. p., 1961. 2 p.
101 Different Ways of Playing Solitaire and Other Poems. Pitts-

burgh, PA.: University of Pittsburgh Press, 1973. 73 p. (Pitt poetry series)
A Wind Among the Sighing Trees. Berkeley, CA.: Arif Press, 1973.

RANDALL, JULIA (1923-)
The Solstice Tree, Poems. Baltimore, MD.: Contemporary Poetry, 1952. 31 p. (Distinguished poets series, v. 8)
Mimic August; Poems. Baltimore, MD.: Contemporary Poetry, 1960. 37 p.
The Puritan Carpenter. Chapel Hill, N.C.: University of North Carolina Press, 1965. 74 p. (Contemporary poetry series)
Adam's Dream. Hollins, VA.: The Tinker Press, 1966. 15 p.
Adam's Dream. New York: Knopf, 1969. x, 113 p.

RANDALL, MARGARET (1936-)
Giant of Tears, and Other Poems. New York: Tejon Press, 1959. 39 p.
Ecstasy Is a Number; Poems. New York: n.p., 1961. [50] p.
Poems of the Glass. Cleveland, OH.: Renegade Press, 1964. [15] p.
October. Mexico: Ediciones El Corno Emplumado, 1965. 62 p.
25 Stages of My Spine. New Rochelle, N.Y.: Elizabeth Press, 1967. 25 p.
Water I Slip into at Night. Mexico City: Printed at Talleres Avelar y de la Parra, 1967. 54 p.
Getting Rid of Blue Plastic; Poems Old and New. Calcutta: Dialogue; Dist. by Writers Work Shop, 1968. 16 p.
So Many Rooms Has a House, But One Roof. Nyack, N.Y.: New Rivers Press, 1968. 12, [1] p.
Only Humans with Songs to Sing. New York: Ikon; New York: Smyrna Press, 1969? [72] p.

RANDALL, MART
Rustlings. San Antonio, TX.: The Naylor Company, 1937. 65 p.

RANDALL-MILLS, ELIZABETH (WEST) (1906-)
Country of the Afternoon. Francestown, N.H.: Golden Quill Press, 1964. 94 p.
All Is Salvations. Francestown, N.H.: Golden Quill Press, 1973. 79 p.

RANDLETT, DOROTHY FROST
Songs of Life. Boston: Humphries, 1949. 121 p.

RANDOLPH, ALTHEA, pseud. see RUSCH, ALTHEA RANDOLPH (BEDLE) (1871-)

RANDOLPH, CLAUDIA PEFLEY
The Enchanted Garden, and Other Poems. New York: Exposition Press, 1952. 62 p.

RANKIN, EMMA ELLER
Not By Bread Alone. New York: Pageant Press, 1953. 73 p.
Now Abideth Faith; A Book of Poems. Boston: Bruce Humphries, 1957. 62 p.

RANLETT, SUSAN ALICE (1853-1942)
Sands on the Shore. Milwaukee, WI.: Morehouse Publishing Co., 1924. 84 p.

RANNEY, MINNIE BOND GARNER
Crystal Gazer, and Other Poems. Chicago: Rand, McNally & Co., 1916. 179 p.

RANSON, NANCY (RICHEY)
The Bucking Burro. Dallas, TX.: The Kaleidograph Press, 1932. x p., 1 ℓ., 70, [2] p.
Texas Evening. Dallas, TX.: The Kaleidograph Press, 1936. 108 p.
My Neighbor's Garden--and Mine. Dallas, TX.: Taylor Pub. Co., 1970. 47 p.

RAPHAEL, ALICE PEARL (1887-)
The Things That Are. New York: October House, 1969. 56 p.

RAPPOSELLI, ANTOINETTE
The Opal Ring. Boston: R. G. Badger, 1927. 128 p.

RASKY, MARIAN M. (1925-)
Beyond My Window; Poems. New York: Exposition Press, 1962. 63 p.

RATHBONE, LAURA LUCILLE (HARNEY)
On Wings of Song. New York: H. Vinal, 1927. 5 p. ℓ., 85 p., [1] p.

RATNER, ROCHELLE (1948-)
A Birthday of Waters. New York: New Rivers Press, 1971. 85 p.
False Trees. New York: New Rivers Press, 1973. 95 p.
The Tightrope Walker. Calgary, Alberta: Pennyworth Press, 1975. 32 p.

RAUH, IDA
...And Our Little Life.... New York: Bookman Associates, 1959. 72 p.

RAVENEL, BEATRICE (WITTE) (1870-1956)
The Arrow of Lightning. New York: H. Vinal, 1926. 5 p. ℓ., 69 p., [1] p.
The Yemassee Lands. Chapel Hill, N.C.: University of North Carolina Press, 1969. 101 p.

RAWLINS, WINIFRED (1907-)
Winter Solstice and Other Poems. New York: Island Press Co-operative, 1952. 1 ℓ., 42 p.
Before No High Altars; Poems. New York: Exposition Press, 1955. 55 p.
Fire Within. Francestown, N. H.: Golden Quill Press, 1959. 75 p.
Russian Pictures. Francestown, N. H.: Golden Quill Press, 1961. [19] p.
Dreaming Is Now; Poems. Francestown, N. H.: Golden Quill Press, 1963. 88 p.
The Small Land; Poems. Francestown, N. H.: Golden Quill Press, 1966. 72 p.
Man Is a Tender Plant. Francestown, N. H.: Golden Quill Press, 1969. 78 p.

RAY, HENRIETTA CORDELIA (d. 1916)
Poems. New York: The Grafton Press, 1910. ix, [5]-169 p.

RAY, LOUISE (CRENSHAW) (1890-1956)
Color of Steel. Chapel Hill, N. C.: The University of North Carolina Press, 1932. viii, 77 p.
Secret Shoes. New York: The Dial Press, 1939. viii, 56 p.
Strangers on the Stars. Dallas, TX.: The Kaleidograph Press, 1944. ix p., 1 ℓ., 15-79 p.
Autumn Token. Emory University, Atlanta, GA.: Banner Press, 1957. 64 p. (Verse craft series)

RAY, RACHEL (BEAZLEY)
Smiles and Tears in Verse. Martin, IN.: Cayces & Turner, 1911. 3 p. ℓ., 130 p.

RAY, REBA
...T Square, and Other Poems. Philadelphia: Dorrance & Company, 1946. 43 p. (Contemporary poets of Dorrance, 316)

RAYBURN, KATHLEEN
Poems of Love. New York: The Paebar Co., 1945. 3 p. ℓ., 53 p.

RAYFIELD, FLORENCE (ROBINSON)
We Thank Thee, Lord. Boston: Christopher Publishing House, 1954. 77 p.

RAYMER, CATHERINE
Poems. Elkhart, IN.: James A. Bell Co., 1920. 47, [1] p.

RAYMOND, EDNA DENHAM (1895-)
Sapphire Nights; Love Poems. New York: A. and C. Boni, 1926. 6 p. ℓ., 84 p.
Sparks and Embers; Poems. New York: T. Seltzer, 1926. 89 p.

RAYMOND, MARY, Sister
Little Mothers. Caldwell, N. J.: n. p., 1929. 105 p.

RAYNOR, VERA
Journey. n. p.: Whaleback Press, 1974.

RE MONDINI, LUISA
Fancy's Garden, & Other Poems. Los Angeles, CA.: The Rowny Press, 1924. 8 p. ℓ., 159, [3] p.

REA, BESSIE CUSTER (1892-)
Oh, Bittersweet. Dallas, TX.: Story Book Press, 1952. 42 p.

REBEC, MARY (LOWELL) (1874-1938)
Poems. Eugene, OR.: University of Oregon, Printed by J. H. Nash, 1938. vii, 162 p.

RECOSKIE, ROSE MARY
Petals of Flowers, Poems. New York: Exposition Press, 1952. 56 p.
Orchids to Lady Maria. New York: Pageant Press, 1953. 46 p.

REDD, ELIZABETH
Of Life and Love; Poems. New York: Vantage Press, 1966. 47 p.

REDDIN, GLADYS M.
The World Passes By. New York: Pageant Press, 1967. 5 p. ℓ., 48 p.

REDDY, MARIE E.
The Country Place; Poems. Darien, GA.: Printed by the Ashantilly Press, 1959. 48 p.

REDFIELD, EDITH SANDERSON
Verses. Boston: Publ. for the author by Lothrop, Lee & Shepherd, 1907. 58 p.

REDHEAD, ALICE CRAIG (HOLLIS)
The Last Battalion. Cincinnati, OH.: Talaria Publication, 1944. 73 p., 1 ℓ.

REDMOND, IDA E.
Thoughts. New York: Fortuny's, 1941. 42 p.

REDMOND, JULIE PARSONS (1880-)
Gay, Grave and Otherwise. New York: Brentano's, 1944. 38 p.

REED, DAISY F.
Moulted Feathers. San Francisco: Cloister Press, 1943. 3 p. ℓ., 40 p.

REED, EVELYN TRUE
Inspirations Rhymed. St. Louis, MO.: Home Printing Company, 1905. 1 p. ℓ., 88 p.

REED, GEORGEIEE KRIECHBAUM
Love and Roses: Poems. Grangeville, ID.: Free Press, 1903. 49 p.

REED, LILY BUIE
...Verse from Mississippi. Boston: The Stratford Company, 1928. 24 p. (The Stratford poets)

REED, MARGERY VERNER
Futurist Stories. New York: M. Kennerley, 1918. 3 p. ℓ., 70 p., [1] p.

REED, MARY GERYRUDE (SNOW)
Music, and Other Poems. Boston: Bruce Humphries, Inc., 1936. 36 p.

REED, MYRTLE (1874-1911)
Sonnets to a Lover. New York: G. P. Putnam's Sons, 1910. ix, 89 p.

REED, NAN LOUISE (TERRELL) (1886-)
Verse. New Haven, CT.: Van Dyck & Company, 1926. 3 p. ℓ., 9-55 p.

REED, RUTH BENDURE
The Book of Ruth, Simple Songs and Other Poems. New York: Vantage Press, 1962. 42 p.

REED, RUTH MILLER
Fragments. Philadelphia: Dorrance & Co., Inc., 1930. 68 p. (Contemporary poets of Dorrance, 89)

REEDER, THELMA (ADAMS) (1908-)
Another Spring. San Antonio, TX.: Naylor Co., 1951. xi, 120 p.

REENSTJERNA, CLAIRE [Full Name: Beulah Claire Reenstjerna.]
Reflections in a Lotus Pool; Poems. New York: Exposition Press, 1953. 55 p.
The Garden of My Beloved, an Idyll. New York: Exposition Press, 1955. [39] p.
Weaver of Dreams, A Pensee. Columbia, S.C.: R. L. Bryan Co., 1955. 36 p.
Season and Landscape Moods; Poems. Charleston, S.C.: n.p., 1956. 37 p.
Of Thee I Sing. Columbia, S.C.: R. L. Bryan Co., 1958. 30 p.
Carolina Drum Song. Charleston, S.C.: n.p., 1969. 59 p.

REES, MILDRED BUCHOLZ
Odyssey of a Soul. New York: Vantage Press, 1966. 64 p.

REESE, LIZETTE WOODWORTH (1856-1935)
A Branch of May. Portland, ME.: T. B. Mosher, 1909. vi, 41, [1] p.
A Wayside Lute. Portland, ME.: T. B. Mosher, 1909. viii, 65, [1] p.
A Handful of Lavender. Portland, ME.: T. B. Mosher, 1915. viii, 52, [1] p.
A Quiet Road. Portland, ME.: T. B. Mosher, 1916. x, 63, [2] p.
A Wayside Lute. 2d ed. Portland, ME.: T. B. Mosher, 1916. viii, 65, [1] p.
A Handful of Lavender. Portland, ME.: T. B. Mosher, 1919. viii, 52, [1] p.
Spicewood. Baltimore, MD.: The Norman Remington Co., 1920. 64 p.
A Wayside Lute. 3d ed. Portland, ME.: T. B. Mosher, 1922. viii, 65, [1] p.
Wild Cherry. Baltimore, MD.: The Norman Remington Co., 1923. 4 p. ℓ., 13-68 p.
A Quiet Road. 2d ed. Portland, ME.: T. B. Mosher, 1924. x, 63, [2] p.
Little Henrietta. New York: George H. Doran Company, 1927. 51 p.
Lizette Woodworth Reese. Ed. by Hughes Mearns. New York: Simon & Schuster, 1928. 31 p. (The Pamphlet poets)
A Wayside Lute. 4th ed. Portland, ME.: T. B. Mosher, 1929. viii, 65, [1] p.
White April, and Other Poems. New York: Farrar & Rinehart, Inc., 1930. xi, 67 p.
...Pastures and Other Poems. New York: Farrar & Rinehart, Inc., 1933. xi p., 1 ℓ., 62 p.
The Old House in the Country. New York: Farrar & Rinehart, Inc., 1936. vii, 54 p.

REESE, SARAH SIMONS
The Little Poem Book. Los Angeles, CA.: Bauer-Peterman Company, 1920. 1 p. ℓ., 5-60 p., 1 ℓ.

REEVES, EDITH C.
...My Mind Is My Castle. Philadelphia: Dorrance and Company, 1941. 31 p. (Contemporary poets of Dorrance, 224)

REEVES, UNA GILBERT
Verse for the Young in Heart. Boston: Christopher Pub. House, 1956. 129 p.

REICH, MARGO
Ashes; Poems. New York: Vantage Press, 1966. 64 p.

REID, DOROTHY E.
Coach into Pumpkin. New Haven, CT.: Yale University Press, 1925. 68 p. (Yale Series of Younger Poets, 20)

REID, ETHEL PETERS
Shapes We Knew. New York: Galleon Press, 1933. vi, 9-63 p.

REID, GRACE
Lightning Bright. New York: Exposition Press, 1967. 47 p.

REID, NELLE JUNE
Pause for Meditation, Poems. New York: Exposition Press, 1960. 47 p.

REINHART, EDITH CLIFTON
The Golden Sycamore, and Other Poems. New York: Vantage Press, 1967. 96 p.

REISS, HENRIETTE
Moods and Melodies. New York: Valencia Press, 1933. 140 p.
________. 2d ed. New York: Gemor Press, 1946. 5 p. ℓ., 140 p.

RELLA, ETTORE
Here and Now; A Collection of Poems. n.p., 1942. 20 p.
Spring Song on an Old Theme, and Other Poems. New York: Trident Press, 1966. 127 p.

REMALEY, SALLY
... Poems of the Heart. Philadelphia: Dorrance and Company, 1945. iv p., 1 ℓ., 7-64 p. (Contemporary poets of Dorrance, 293)

REMSEN, ETHEL WHITE
Stars and Scars. New York: E. S. Gorham, 1924. 33 p.

RENFREW, CAROLYN
Songs of Hope. New York: Moffat, Yard and Company, 1923. 84 p.
My Garden; A Collection of Poems. Kansas City, MO.: Burton Publishing Company, 1933. 3 p. ℓ., 9-125 p.

RENN, MADELINE S.
Whispers of Gold, Poems. New York: Carlton Press, 1964. 53 p.

RENWICK, HELEN (GOODWIN) (1845-) [Full Name: Pamela Helen (Goodwin) Renwick.]
Heaven's Own Mosaic, and Other Poems. Los Angeles, CA.: The Times-Mirror Press, 1929. 95 p.

REPLANSKY, NAOMI (1918-)
Ring Song, Poems. New York: Scribner, 1952. vi p., 1 ℓ., 57 p.

RESTARICK, MAY L. (BAKER)
Everyday Thoughts for Everyday People. Honolulu: n. p., 1919. 40, [1] p.
Dear Hawaii. Honolulu: Paradise of the Pacific Printing Co., 1922. 3 p. ℓ., 9-59 p.

REXROTH, MARY
The Coffee Should Be Warm Now. Berkeley, CA.: Twowindows Press, 1970. [11] p.

REYNOLDS, ELIZABETH
On the Lake, and Other Poems. Boston: The Gorham Press, 1915. 142 p.

REYNOLDS, EVELYN CRAWFORD [LYNN, EVE, pseud.]
No Alabaster Box and Other Poems. Philadelphia: Alpress, 1936. 5 p. ℓ., 37, [2] p.
To No Special Land; A Book of Poems. New York: Exposition Press, 1953. 64 p.
Put a Daisy in Your Hair. Philadelphia: Dorrance, 1963. 31 p.

REYNOLDS, HALLIE ALEXANDER
Co-Mates. Nashville, TN.: Printed for the Author, 1905. 63 p.

REYNOLDS, JULIA LOUISE (PARHAM) (1887-)
The Tower and the Star & Other Poems. New York: Davidson Press, 1934. 3 p. ℓ., 46 p.
No Answer? New York: G. Putnam's Sons, 1937. 96 p.
In This Hour, Poems. New York: Fine Editions Press, 1950. 64 p.

REYNOLDS, NAOMI
Tomorrow. Boston: The Stratford Company, 1924. 4 p. ℓ., 35 p.

RHOADES, LEAH
Sunny Sonnets. Oklahoma City, OK.: Oklahoma City Printery, 1920. [3]-64 p.

RICE, CARRIE SHAW
Where the Rhododendrons Grow. Tacoma, WA.: n. p., 1904. [32] p.
Windows That Shine. Tacoma, WA.: Press of Smith Kinney Co., 1922. 5 p. ℓ., 15-158 p.

RICE, HELEN STEINER
For Your Christmas. New York: Gibson Greeting Cards, 1967. 34 p.
Just for You; A Special Collection of Inspirational Verses. Garden City, N. Y.: Doubleday, 1967. 64 p.
Christmas Classics: A Special Collection of Christmas Verses. New York: Gibson Greeting Cards, 1968. 23, [2] p.
A Gift of Love; Poems from the Heart of Helen Steiner Rice.

Old Tappan, N.J.: F. H. Revell, 1968. 57 p.
Heart Gifts from Helen Steiner Rice; A Special Selection of Her Poems. Old Tappan, N.J.: F. H. Revell, 1968. 96 p.
______. London: Hutchinson, 1970. 73 p.
Lovingly; Poems for All Seasons. Old Tappan, N.J.: F. H. Revell, 1970. 96 p.
Prayerfully. Old Tappan, N.J.: F. H. Revell, 1971. 31 p.
Someone Cares. Old Tappan, N.J.: F. H. Revell, 1972. 128 p.
The Story of the Christmas Guest. Old Tappan, N.J.: F. H. Revell Co., 1972. 28 p.
Everyone Needs Someone; Poems of Love & Friendship. New York: Pyramid Communications, 1973. 79 p.
Life Is Forever. Old Tappan, N.J.: F. H. Revell, 1974. 32 p.
Loving Promises; Especially for You. Old Tappan, N.J.: F. H. Revell, 1975. 128 p.

RICE, LABAN LACY (1870-)
Sonnets to B. B. R. Boston: R. G. Badger, 1921. 56 p.
A Woman's Answer, and Other Verse. Mayland, TN.: The Nakanawa Press, 1946. 118 p.

RICE, MURIEL
Poems. New York: The Grafton Press, 1906. 57 p.
Poems. New York: M. Kennerley, 1910. 70 p.

RICE, RUTH LITTLE MASON (1884-1927)
Afterward. New York: H. Vinal, Ltd., 1927. 75 p.

RICH, ADRIENNE CECILE (1929-)
A Change of World. New Haven, CT.: Yale University Press, 1951. 85 p. (Yale Series of Younger Poets, 48)
Poems. Oxford: Oxford University Poetry Society, 1953. [8] p.
The Diamond Cutters, and Other Poems. New York: Harper, 1955. 119 p.
Snapshots of a Daughter-in-Law; Poems, 1954-1962. New York: Harper & Row, 1963. 71 p.
Focus. Cambridge, MA.: The Lowell-Adams House Printers, 1966. 4 ℓ.
Necessities of Life; Poems, 1962-1965. New York: W. W. Norton, 1966. 79 p.
Selected Poems. London: Chatto & Windus, 1967. 72 p. (Phoenix living poets)
Snapshots of a Daughter-in-Law; Poems, 1954-1962. New York: W. W. Norton, 1967. 64 p.
Leaflets; Poems, 1965-1968. New York: W. W. Norton, 1969. 71 p.
Snapshots of a Daughter-in-Law. London: Chatto & Windus, 1970. 64 p.
The Will to Change; Poems 1968-1970. New York: W. W. Norton, 1971. 67 p.
______. London: Chatto & Windus, 1972. 67 p.
Diving into the Wreck. Poems, 1971-1972. New York: W. W. Norton, 1973. 62 p.
Poems: Selected and New, 1950-1974. New York: W. W. Norton, 1974. xiv, 256 p.

RICHARD, MARGARET A(LICE) (1870-)
Darkey Ways in Dixie. New York, London: The Abbey Press, 1901. 4 p. ℓ., 5-112 p.
Virginia Vaughan, A Romance in Verse. Boston: R. G. Badger, 1907. 4 p. ℓ., 7-151 p.

RICHARDS, ELIZABETH DAVIS (1884-1936)
Leaves of Laurel. Cedar Rapids, IA.: The Torch Press, 1925. 40 p.
The Peddler of Dreams and Other Poems. New York: William Albert Broder, 1928. 96 p.
Thistledown. Medford, MA.: C. A. A. Parker, 1929. viii, 26 p.

RICHARDS, JANE BLAKESLEE
For a Leisure Hour. Boston: The Stratford Company, 1925. 5 p. ℓ., 125 p.

RICHARDS, LAURA ELIZABETH (HOUSE) (1850-1943)
Piccolo. Boston: D. Estes and Company, 1906. 3 p. ℓ., xiii-xiv, 15-121, [1] p.
To Arms! Songs of the Great War. Boston: The Page Company, 1918. 4 p. ℓ., 37, [1] p.
Tirra Lirra, Rhymes Old and New. Boston: Little, Brown and Company, 1932. xx p., 1 ℓ., 194 p.

RICHARDS, ROSA (COATES) (1889-)
Roadways. New York: House of Field, Inc., 1939. 101 p.
Skyways. New York: The Fine Editions Press, 1943. 48 p.
By-ways. New York: William-Frederick Press, 1949. 25 p. (William-Frederick poets, 57)

RICHARDSON, DEBORAH
The Wish to Die. n.p.: Kuchi Press, 1974.

RICHARDSON, DOROTHY LEE
Signs at My Finger-Ends. Cleveland, OH.: American Weave Press, 1961. vi, 34 p.

RICHARDSON, ISLA PASCHAL (1886-1971)
My Heart Waketh, Poems. Boston: B. Humphries, 1947. 96 p.
Wind Among the Pines, and Other Poems. Boston: B. Humphries, 1949. 96 p.
In Beauty's Presence, and Other Poems. Boston: B. Humphries, 1952. 61 p.
Against All Time. Boston: B. Humphries, 1958. 103 p.
Along the Way, and Other Poems. Boston: B. Humphries, 1962. 76 p.
When Springtime Comes. Dallas, TX.: Royal Pub. Co., 1964. 40 p.

RICHARDSON, KATHLEEN M.
Hold Off the Sun. Portland, ME.: Falmouth Book House, 1939. 5 p. ℓ., 3-55 p.

RICHARDSON, MABEL KINGSLEY (1874-)
...Killdeer. Philadelphia: Dorrance & Company, 1936. 47 p. (Contemporary poets of Dorrance, 143)

RICHARDSON, MARION (MUIR) (1859-)
Border Memories. Denver, CO.: n.p., 1903. 144 p.
Shadows of the Sunset, and Other Poems. n.p., 1918. 95 p.

RICHARDSON, NELLIE (SIMPSON) (1871-)
Close to the Soil. Springfield, VT.: Springfield Printing Corporation, 1937. 111 p.
In Memory of Jessie; Seven Poems. Springfield, VT.: n.p., 1943. 17 ℓ.
Once Around the Sun. Boston: B. Humphries, 1944. 141 p.
At the Bow of the Ox, A Year's Doings. Boston: B. Humphries, 1950. 145 p.

RICHARDSON, NOLA (1936-)
When One Loves: The Black Experience in America. Millbrae, CA.: Celestial Arts, 1974. 95 p.
Even in a Maze. Los Angeles, CA.: Crescent Publications, 1975. viii, 54 p.

RICHMOND, CORA LINN VICTORIA (SCOTT) (1840-1923)
Dedication of the Palace of Peace; A Vision. Chicago: n.p., 1915. 22 p.

RICHMOND, FRANCES
Winding Roads. Dallas, TX.: Story Book Press, 1952. 52 p.

RICHTER, ANN KIRK
Lilting Echoes. New York: Exposition Press, 1944. 63 p. (Poets of America. Series four)

RICKER, ELIZABETH (KERRISON)
Dreams and Purple Horizons. Columbia, S.C.: The R. L. Bryan Company, 1933. 145 p.

RICKER, JULIA HURD (SHAW) (1873-1951)
Treasure Chest. Houston, TX.: Carleton Printing Co., 1947. 79 p.
Tomorrow's Dawn. Dallas, TX.: Story Book Press, 1953. 64 p.

RIDDELL, MARY ELLEN
Thoughts in the Night. Philadelphia: Dorrance, 1965. 39 p.

RIDER, LAURA
Venturings. Dubuque, IA.: n. p., 1922.

RIDGE, LOLA (1883-1941)
The Ghetto, and Other Poems. New York: B. W. Huebsch, 1913. 101 p.
Sun-Up, and Other Poems. New York: B. W. Huebsch, 1920. 93 p.
Red Flag. New York: Viking Press, 1927. 103 p.
Firehead. New York: Payson and Clarke, Ltd., 1929. 7 p. ℓ., 13-218 p.
...Dance of Fire. New York: H. Smith & R. Haas, 1935. 104 p.

RIDING, LAURA (1901-)
The Close Chaplet. New York: Adelphi Co., 1926. 76, [1] p.
______. London: Hogarth Press, 1926. 76, [1] p.
Voltaire: A Biographical Fantasy. London: L. & Virginia Woolf, 1927. 30 p.
Love as Love, Death as Death. London: Seizin Press, 1928. 64 p.
Poems: A Joking Word. London: J. Cape, 1930. 171 p.
Though Gently. Deyá, Mallorca: Seizin Press, 1930. 29 p.
Twenty Poems Less. Paris: Hours Press, 1930. 33 p.
Laura and Francisca: A Poem. Deyá, Mallorca: Seizin Press, 1931. 3 p. ℓ., 22 p., 2 ℓ.
The First Leaf. Deyá, Mallorca: Seizin Press, 1933. [6] p.
Poet: A Lying Word. London: A. Barker, Ltd., 1933. vii, 149 p.
The Life of the Dead. London: A. Barker, Ltd., 1933. 48 p.
Americans. Los Angeles, CA.: Primavera, 1934. 28 p.
The Second Leaf. Deyá, Mallorca: Seizin Press, 1935. [6] p.
Collected Poems. New York: Random House, 1938. xxvii, 477 p.
______. London: Cassell, 1938. xxvii, 477 p.
Selected Poems: In Five Sets. London: Faber, 1970. 94 p.
______. New York: Norton, 1973. 94 p.

RIDINGS, GRACE (DUPREE)
Shawl of Song. Dallas, TX.: The Kaleidograph Press, 1934. xi, 3-115 p.
By the Light of the Lone Star. Dallas, TX.: The Kaleidograph Press, 1936. xii p., 1 ℓ., 15-140 p.

RIGGS, Mrs. DIONIS COFFIN
Sea Born Island; Poems. Peterborough, N. H.: Noone House, 1969. 77 p.

RILEY, AGNES
The Dim Past, and Other Poems. Boston: Sherman, French & Company, 1917. 4 p. ℓ., 56 p.

RINEER, HARRIET SNYDER
The Hand of a Child and Other Poems. Lancaster, PA.: n. p., 1932. 60 p.

RINEHART, CONSTANCE
Autographed Copy. Chicago: Dierkes Press, 1951. 56 p.

RIPLEY, FANNIE B.
In No Uncertain Words. Boston: B. Humphries, 1948. 116 p.

RIPLEY, LILLIE ROSALIE
Poems. Boston: R. G. Badger, 1910. 48 p.

RITA, AGNES, Sister (1890-) [Secular Name: Marie Wennerberg.]
Stars Are Shining. Boston: The Christopher Publishing House, 1940. 62 p.

RITCHIE, ELISAVIETTA
Timbot; A Novella in Verse. Notre Dame, IN.: Lit Press, 1970. 40 p.
Tightening the Circle over Eel Country. Washington, D. C.: Acropolis Books, 1974. 111 p.

RITTENHOUSE, JESSIE BELLE (1869-1948)
The Door of Dreams. Boston & New York: Houghton Mifflin Co., 1918. x, [1], 62, [2] p.
The Lifted Cup. Boston & New York: Houghton Mifflin Co., 1921. x, [1], 57, [1] p.
The Secret Bird. Boston & New York: Houghton Mifflin Co., 1930. 3 p. ℓ., ix-1, [1], 99 p.
The Moving Tide; New and Selected Lyrics. Boston & New York: Houghton Mifflin Co., 1939. viii p., 2 ℓ., 3-141, [1] p.

RITTER, MARGARET TOD (1893-)
Mirrors. New York: The Macmillan Co., 1925. 97 p.
Wind Out of Betelgeuse. New York: The Macmillan Co., 1928. 95 p.

RIZK, ESTELLE (SMITH)
To a Timberline Tree. Philadelphia: Dorrance, 1961. 52 p. (Contemporary poets of Dorrance)

ROBB, ELIZABETH S.
The Message of the Bells, and Other Poems. Philadelphia: Dorrance and Company, 1929. 87 p. (Contemporary poets of Dorrance, 78)
Thoughts. New York: House of Field, Inc., 1940. 79 p.

ROBBINS, ANNE MARY
Countryside and Town. New York: James T. White & Co., 1930. ix, 93 p.

ROBBINS, BARBARA
The Hard Ride. Grand Rapids, MI.: Pilot Press Books, 1972. [40] p.

ROBBINS, CORINNA
The Asalea Bush.... New York: The William-Frederick Press, 1945. 2 p. ℓ., 5-31 p. (The William-Frederick poets, no. 13)

ROBBINS, DOROTHY B.
Apricot Gold. Dallas, TX.: The Kaleidograph Press, 1932. x, 69 p.
Come in Awhile.... Dallas, TX.: The Kaleidograph Press, 1941. 4 p. ℓ., 11-38 p.

ROBBINS, SARA
Crushed for Better Wine. New York: Philosophical Library, 1945. 72 p.

ROBERSON, LORENA A.
Of Tears and Rain, A Love Poem. New York: Exposition Press, 1950. 64 p.

ROBERT, KATE AYERS
The Porter's Trip. Mobile, AL.: n.p., 1919. 16 p.

ROBERTS, BERTHA GEYDEN
The Land o' Dream; Verse. New Haven, CT.: Press of J. R. Sutherland, 1927. 53, [2] p.

ROBERTS, ELIZABETH ELEANOR MADOX (1886-1941)
In the Great Steep's Garden. Colorado Springs, CO.: The Gowdy-Simmons Printing Co., 1915. [15] p.
Under the Tree. New York: B. W. Huebsch, Inc., 1922. 4 p. ℓ., 87 p.
_______. London: J. Cape, 1928. 64 p.
_______. Enl. ed. New York: Viking Press, 1930. 5 p. ℓ., 3-85 p.
_______. 1964. 85 p.

ROBERTS, ELIZABETH SIM
Book of Verse. Longview, WA.: Press of the Longview Daily News, 1941. [22] p., 1 ℓ.
Harvest of the Greenwood. Chicago: Dierkes Press, 1947. 64 p.

ROBERTS, FLORENCE CECILIA
Gleanings. Boston: The Gorham Press, 1919. 40 p.

ROBERTS, HOPE LEBAR
...My Heart Sings. Philadelphia: Dorrance and Company, 1938. 67 p. (Contemporary poets of Dorrance, 180)

ROBERTS, JOSEPHINE L.
The Rose of Joy. New York: Neely Co., 1900. 44 p.

ROBERTS, MARTHA
These Go in Flight. Francestown, N. H.: Golden Quill Press, 1970. 56 p.

ROBERTS, MARY A.
Grandma Sue's Diary. Denver, CO.: Big Mountain Press, 1965. 56 p.

ROBERTS, MARY ELEANOR (ROBERTS) (1867-)
Cloth of Frieze. Philadelphia & London: J. B. Lippincott Company, 1911. vii, 9-141 p.

ROBERTS, NANCY [SARGENT, E. N.]
The African Boy. New York: Macmillan, 1963. 77 p.
Love Poems of Elizabeth Sargent. New York: New American Library, 1966. unpaged.
_______. New York: Herder and Herder, 1971. 154 p.

ROBERTS, RUBY (ALTIZER) (1907-)
Forever Is Too Long. Mill Valley, CA., New York: The Wings Press, 1946. 91, [1] p.
Command the Stars. Mill Valley, CA.: The Wings Press, 1948. 85 p.

ROBERTS, RUTH NEWNAM
The Heart Speaks. New York: Crown Publications, 1947. 64 p.

ROBERTSON, Mrs. CLYDE
They Rise Accusing. New York: H. Harrison, 1930. 64 p.
Fool's Gold. Atlanta, GA.: Banner Press, 1934. 95 p.
The Yellow Witch; Ballads about Gold. New York: L. Raley, 1940. 80 p.
Pony Nelson, and Other Western Ballads. New York: Exposition Press, 1954. 128 p.

ROBERTSON, ETHEL
Poems Just for You. New York: Carlton Press, 1962. 31 p.

ROBERTSON, GLADYS VONDY
Overtones, Poems. Chicago: Dierkes Press, 1948. 56 p.

ROBERTSON, HELEN (GRAY) (1900-)
Call of the Tuscarora, and Other Poems. Dexter, MO.: Candor Press, 1955. 58 p.

ROBERTSON, LEXIE (DEAN)
Red Heels. Dallas, TX.: P. L. Turner, 1928. xi, 108 p.
I Keep a Rainbow. Dallas, TX.: C. C. Cockrell Publishing Co., 1932. 6 p. ℓ., 15-103 p.
Acorn on the Roof. Dallas, TX.: The Kaleidograph Press, 1939. xi p., 1 ℓ., 15-93 p.
Red Heels. 10th ed. Dallas, TX.: The Kaleidograph Press, 1939. xi p., 1 ℓ., 15-118 p.

Prelude to Peace. n. p., 194-? 12 p.
Answer in the Night. Dallas, TX.: Kaleidograph Press, 1948. 79 p.

ROBERTSON, OLIVE ALLEN
Violet Rays, Poems. New York: The Poets Press, 1935. 53 p.
Violet Rays and Other Poems. New York: G. P. Putnam's Sons, 1938. xii p., 1 ℓ., 15-94 p.

ROBIE, BERTHA GRACE
In Memory's Garden. Richmond, IN.: The Nicholson Press, 1912. 50 ℓ.

ROBINETTE, VIVIEN
Orchestra of Storm. Dallas, TX.: Story Book Press, 1955. 51 p.
Poems. Dallas, TX.: Triangle Pub. Co., 1956. 83 p.

ROBINS, MARY ELLIS
The Forerunners: A Fancy. Woodstock, N. Y.: Maverick Press, 1913.
Songs Through the Night. Woodstock, N. Y.: Maverick Press, 1913. 185 p.
A Symphony of Life. Boston: R. G. Badger, 1926. 91 p.
... Poems of Dream and Reality. Philadelphia: Dorrance and Company, 1936. 84 p. (Contemporary poets of Dorrance, 153)
... Armatheon and Daphne (A Tale of Reincarnation). Philadelphia: Dorrance & Company, 1937. 96 p. (Contemporary poets of Dorrance, 167)
... The Golden Rose. Philadelphia: Dorrance & Co., 1943. 190 p. (Contemporary poets of Dorrance, 256)

ROBINS, NATALIE S.
Wild Lace. Denver, CO.: A. Swallow, 1960. 30 p.
My Father Spoke of His Riches. Denver, CO.: A. Swallow, 1966. 40 p. (Poets in Swallow paperbooks, 75)
The Peas Belong on the Eye Level. Chicago: Swallow Press, 1971. 70 p.

ROBINSON, ANNE LOUISE (JOHNSON) (1889-1925)
The Singing Blue. Brunswick, ME.: F. W. Chandler & Son, 1925. 72 p.
________. 1926. 74 p.

ROBINSON, ANNIE DOUGLAS GREEN
Days We Remember: Poems. Boston: R. G. Badger, 1903. 3 p. ℓ., 11-60 p.

ROBINSON, CATHARINE
Wayside Gleanings. Emory University, Atlanta, GA.: Banner Press, 1950. 116 p. (Verse craft series)

ROBINSON, CORINNE (ROOSEVELT) (1861-1933)
The Call of Brotherhood, and Other Poems. New York: C. Scribner's Sons, 1912. ix, 93 p.
_______. 2d ed., 1913.
One Woman to Another, and Other Poems. New York: C. Scribner's Sons, 1914. ix p., 1 ℓ., 73 p.
Service and Sacrifice, Poems. New York: C. Scribner's Sons, 1919. xi, 111 p.
The Poems of Corinne Roosevelt Robinson. New York: C. Scribner's Sons, 1921. xiv p., 2 ℓ., 3-280 p.
Out of Nymph--Poems. New York: C. Scribner's Sons, 1930. xii, 108 p.

ROBINSON, FRANCINE PYLE
Underneath the Bough. Boston: H. Vinal, Ltd., 1929. 48 p.

ROBINSON, HELEN CATHERINE
Pallid Pursuit. Dallas, TX.: The Kaleidograph Press, 1941. xi p., 1 ℓ., 13-74 p.

ROBINSON, HELEN TEMPLETON DOUGLAS
Candle and Cup. Toronto: The Crucible Press, 1941. vi, 7-20 p.
Sky Ways. Boston: B. Humphries, 1943. 48 p.
The Call of Life. Boston: B. Humphries, 1957. 60 p.

ROBINSON, IDA MARIAN (BREED) (1903-)
Poems for Pierrot. New York: The Poets Press, 1939. 64 p.

ROBINSON, JESSIE MILLER
Queen Anne's Lace. Mill Valley, CA., New York: Wings Press, 1940. 49 p.

ROBINSON, NORA (SMITH)
Singing Along the Way. Emory University, Atlanta, GA.: Banner Press, 1931. 36 p. (Verse craft series)

ROBINSON, SELMA
City Child. New York: Farrar & Rinehart, 1931. 64 p.

ROBINSON, SERENA (TRUMAN)
Tall Trees and Melodies. Springfield, MA.: Press of the Pond-Ekberg Company, 1938. 3 p. ℓ., [ix]-xi p., 1 ℓ., 17-62 p.

ROBISON, ALBERTA
Poems. Mill Valley, CA., New York: The Wings Press, 1944. 47 p.

ROCHESTER, EDITH GRENSTED
Forenoon and Afternoon and Night. n.p., 1916. 12 p.
From Star to Star. Los Angeles, CA.: Grafton Publishing Corporation, 1919. 166 p.

ROCKWELL, LILLIAN A.
Impatient Lover. New York: Dial Press, 1952. 63 p.

RODENBOUGH, JEAN
If I Were a Ghost. Bassett, VA.: Basset Printing Corp., 1972. [17] p.
ice on a hot stove. n. p.: Pross Publishing, 1974.

RODGER, SARAH ELIZABETH
And If I Cry Release. New York: Doubleday, Doran & Co., 1940. 59 p.

RODGERS, CAROLYN M. (194?-)
Paper Soul. Chicago: Third World Press, 1968. 25 p.
Now Ain't That Love. Detroit: Broadside Press, 1969.
Songs of a Black Bird. Chicago: Third World Press, 1969. 39 p.
Two Love Raps. Chicago: Third World Press, 1969. [4] p.
Long Rap/Commonly Known as a Poetic Essay. Detroit: Broadside Press, 1971. 3 p.
How I Got Ovah, New and Selected Poems. Garden City, N. Y.: Anchor Press, 1975. viii, 81 p.

RODGERS, ELLA CLEMENTINE
From Early Morn, and Other Poems. n. p.: Winston, 1907. 300 p.

RODMAN, BERNECE
The Coming of the Chrysanthemum, and Other Poems. New York: The Knickerbocker Press, 1910. viii p., 1 ℓ., 92 p.
Enchantment, and Other Poems. New York: The Knickerbocker Press, 1927. vii, 72 p.

ROE, CAROLYN ARNOLD
The Angel's Trumpet, and Other Poems. New York: Exposition Press, 1947. 126 p.
The Angel's Gift, and Other Poems. Cedar Rapids, IA.: The Torch Press, 1948. 4 p. ℓ., 5-128 p.

ROE, CLARA B.
The Singing Prairie. Philadelphia: Dorrance, 1960. 122 p.

ROEBLING, STELLA LAWMAN
Collected Poems. New York: n. p., 1933? [58] p.
This Too Shall Pass Away. New York: The Poets Press, 1937. 145 p.

ROGERS, GERTRUDE
Cobwebs. Boston: R. G. Badger, 1907. 55 p.

ROGERS, MARGARET DOUGLAS
The Gift: A Poetic Dream. Cincinnati: Stewart & Kidd, 1914. 7-47 p.

ROGERS, MAY D. (1913-)
Spider's Web. Philadelphia: Dorrance, 1948. 136 p. (Contemporary poets of Dorrance, 370)

ROHLF, IDA CATHERINE
Out of the Night. North Montpelier, VT.: The Driftwind Press, 1946. 64 p.
For Each Day Its Pattern. North Montpelier, VT.: The Driftwind Press, 1947. 70 p.
Twilight Is Here. Cedar Falls? IA.: n.p., 1951. 58 p.

ROLLINS, SABRA FRANCES
First Harvest. Philadelphia: Dorrance & Co., 1932. 5 p.ℓ., 13-120 p. (Contemporary poets of Dorrance, 108)

ROMIG, EDNA (DAVIS) (1889-)
Blue Hills. Philadelphia: Dorrance & Co., 1930. 102 p. (Contemporary poets of Dorrance, 90)
Lincoln Remembers. Philadelphia: Dorrance & Co., 1930. 76 p. (Contemporary poets of Dorrance, 87)
Marse Lee. Philadelphia: Dorrance & Co., 1930. 80 p. (Contemporary poets of Dorrance, 94)
The Torch Undimmed. Philadelphia: Dorrance & Co., 1931. 49 p. (Contemporary poets of Dorrance, 104)
...Sketches and Overtones. Philadelphia: Dorrance & Co., 1936. 85 p. (Contemporary poets of Dorrance, 152)
...An Amherst Garden. Philadelphia: Dorrance & Co., 1938. 4 p.ℓ., 11-100 p. (Contemporary poets of Dorrance, 183)
...The Heart Affirming. Philadelphia: Dorrance & Co., 1939. 126 p. (Contemporary poets of Dorrance, 200)
These Are the Fields. Philadelphia: Dorrance & Co., 1955. 108 p.
Flash of Wings. Boulder, CO.: Johnson Pub. Co., 1967. 50 p.

ROOSEVELT, DIANA LOWELL
A Skull of Flowers. Boston: Dark Woods Press, 1960. 180 p.
Swallow Hill. Haverford, PA.: Dark Woods Press, 1967. 12 p.
Collected Poems. West Grove, PA.: The Dark Woods Press, 1970. 184, [7] p.
The Jungfrau and Other Poems. West Grove, PA.: The Dark Woods Press, 1972. 7 p.
Poems from the Blue Planet. West Grove, PA.: Dark Woods Press, 1972. 5 p.
The Wild Swans at Londonderry. West Grove, PA.: The Dark Woods Press, 1973. 4 p.
Martyrdom. West Grove, PA.: Dark Woods Press, 1974. [11] p.

ROOT, JOAN
Pink Jelly, A Book of Poems. Los Angeles, CA.: Tamarind Lithography Workshop, 1966.

ROOT, JUDITH C.
Little Mysteries. Okemos, MI.: Stone Press, 1974. 8 ℓ.

ROPER, FLORENCE WILSON
A Kiss for Judas. Dallas, TX.: The Kaleidograph Press, 1932. viii p., 1 ℓ., 11-83, [1] p.
Flame Against the Wind. New York: The Wings Press, 1937. 80 p.
Home to the Hills. Mill Valley, CA.: Wings Press, 1954. 64 p.

ROSE, BLANCHE WALTRIP
And So My Love; Poems. Philadelphia: Dorrance, 1958. 56 p.

ROSE, HELOISE DURANT
Dante: A Dramatic Poem. New York: M. Kennerley, 1910. 6 p. ℓ., [11]-244 p.
Dante: A Dramatic Poem. 4th ed. rev. New York; London: Oxford University Press, 1921. 8 p. ℓ., [11]-244 p.

ROSE, MAE
Yesterdays and Tomorrows. Washington, D. C.: n. p., 1942. 32 p.

ROSE, MARY ANN (1835-)
Life's Melody, and The Celestial Hymn. San Francisco: Press of R. R. Patterson, 1904. 65 p.

ROSE, WENDY (1948-)
Hopi Roadrunner Dancing. Greenfield Center, N. Y.: Greenfield Review Press, 1972. 37 p.

ROSEBERY, MARGUERITE (TURNER)
Strange, Sweet Madness. New York: H. Harrison, 1938. 63 p.
War Saga. New York: Pageant Press, 1955. 77 p.

ROSS, ELIZABETH
Homeward Bound, and Other Poems. Mountain View, CA.: Pacific Press Publishing Association, 1959. 32 p.

ROSS, ELIZABETH (WILLIAMS) (1852-1926)
Altarsongs. Cincinnati, OH.: Powell & White, 1925. 108 p.

ROSS, EMMA JEWELL
Sweet Moments. Boston: House of Edinboro, 1945. 155 p.

ROSS, GERALDINE
All Kinds of Weather; Poems. New York: Exposition Press, 1951. 96 p.

ROSS, GRACE
Journey Out of Night. Dallas, TX.: The Kaleidograph Press, 1946. x, 1 ℓ., 13-63 p.

ROSS, JESSIE A.
Voice and Vision. New York: H. Vinal, Ltd., 1928. 5 p. ℓ., 64 p., 1 ℓ.

ROSS, JESSIE HARRIETTE (SLOCOMBE) (1876-)
Happy Hours; Verses and Sketches. Berkeley, CA.: Gillick Press, 1945. [30] p.

ROSS, JOSEPHINE ESTHER
Songs of a Modern Disciple. New York: Vantage Press, 1966. 106 p.

ROSS, LORETTA LYONS
Jus' Plain Livin'. Clarion, IA? n. p., 1952. 78 p.

ROSS, MARGARET WHEELER (1867-)
Vanity Bag; Verses. Topeka, KA.: Frazer Press, 1936. 172 p.

ROSS, MARY (1918-)
Bury Me Deep. Dallas, TX.: Story Book Press, 1948. 40 p.
Trying for Purple. Dallas, TX.: Story Book Press, 1953. 40 p.

ROSS, MAUDE (BARNES)
Turning Leaves. Oklahoma City, OK.: American Printing and Publishing Company, 1941. 4 p. ℓ., 73 p.

ROSS, SUE
The Heart Knows No Reason. New York: Vantage Press, 1966. 64 p.

ROSSER, ELIZABETH
Homeward Bound, and Other Poems. Mountain View, CA.: Pacific Press Publishing Association, 1959. 32 p.

ROSSER, FLAVIA
Oriental Lyrics. New York: Vantage Press, 1955. 68 p.

ROST, IDA S.
... A Green Bough, Poems. Boston: The Stratford Company, 1932. 4 p. ℓ., 7-38 p. (The Stratford poets)

ROTHENBURGER, LEILA (AVERY) (1884-1942)
Candlelights at Dusk. Anderson, IN.: Commercial Service Co., 1939. 63 p.

ROTHERMEL, BERTHA M.
Rhymes for Christmas Chimes. New York: Greenwich Book Publishers, 1956. 64 p.

ROTHGEB, VIRGINIA LEONA (1926-)
The Inner Light, Spiritual Sermonettes in Verse. New York: Exposition Press, 1958. 45 p.

ROTHROCK, ALICE VEST
Autumn Garlands. New York: H. Vinal, Ltd., 1928. 6 p. ℓ., 3-118 p.

ROUNDS, ONA MAHITTA (1876-)
A Book Is Like a Ship with Sails. Boston: Christopher Pub. House, 1952. 61 p.
I Will Write You a Song, and Other Poems. Boston: Christopher Pub. House, 1958. 112 p.

ROUNTREE, ORA BELL
White Birds Flying in the Night. Dallas, TX.: Wilkinson Pub. Co., 1950. 72 p.

ROUQUIE, MARGARET BLANCHE
Picture Poems.... New York: The Paebar Co., 1946. 2 p. ℓ., 28 p.

ROUSE, RUTH
Cadenzas. Dallas, TX.: Kaleidograph Press, 1950. x p., 1 ℓ., 13-79 p.

ROUSH, THEDA DAFFAN
If Ever You Need Me. Houston, TX.: A. E. Rousch, 1957. 94 p.

ROUTH, FREDA KARSIN
My Beloved, My Friend. Philadelphia: Dorrance, 1962. 46 p.

ROWAN, LELIA M.
Trailing Arbutus. Lansing, MI.: R. Smith Printing Company, 1902. 5 p. ℓ., 7-183 p.

ROWLAND, HELEN
The Rubaiyat of a Bachelor. New York: Dodge Publishing Co., 1915. 90 p., 1 ℓ.

ROWLAND, IDA
...Lisping Leaves. Philadelphia: Dorrance and Company, 1939. 55 p. (Contemporary poets of Dorrance, 191)

ROWLEY, EVELYN HUDSON (1909-)
There Is No Spring. New York: House of Field, Inc., 1941. 47 p.

ROYCE, ELIZABETH S.
Bloodroot, and Other Poems. New York: n. p., 1930. 2 p. ℓ., vii-viii p., 1 ℓ., 53 p.

ROYCE, NELL H.
Memory Lane. Danbury, CT.: Published by T. N. P. C., 1967. 31 p.

RUBIN, MAUDE (1891-)
Tiger-on-Leash. Denver, CO.: Verb Publications, 1965. 20 p.
Leaves of Laurel. Chicago: Paul Edwards Press, 1967. 38 p.
Fangs of Midnight. Homestead, FL.: Olivant Press, 1968. 20 p.

RUCKER, KATHARINE KENNON
Echoes. Charlottesville, VA.: n.p., 1931. 24 p.

RUDD, MABEL WARD
To the Bluebird. Lynn, MA.: Nichols Press, 1924. 2 p. ℓ., 7-83 p.
Cornelius to Mary Gay. Lynn, MA.: Nichols Press, 1934. 83 p.
Here in This Pasture. Lynn, MA.: The McCarty Press, 1937. 1 p. ℓ., 105 p.
Pine That Dies Standing. Lynn, MA.: The McCarty Press, 1940. 95 p.

RUDE, BESSIE MANDLES
A Soul Set Free. Boston: The Stratford Company, 1925. 4 p. ℓ., 56 p.

RUDOLPH, BARBARA (BRADSHAW)
The Sum of the Parts. Fayetteville, AR.: Rubert Publications, 1965. 48 p.

RUEDI, NORMA PAUL
If Dreams Came True, and Other Poems. New York: The Avondale Press, 1927. ix, 89 p.

RUFF, ELEANOR CAROLINE (1909-)
Golden Willows. Philadelphia: Dorrance, 1952. 54 p. (Contemporary poets of Dorrance, 441)

RUFFIN, MARGARET ELLEN (HENRY) (d. 1941)
John Gildart: An Heroic Poem. New York: W. H. Young and Company; London: R. & T. Washbourne, 1901. 2 p. ℓ., 5-78 numb. ℓ.
________. 2d ed., 1901.

RUGEL, CLARA (HOOD) (1900-)
These Things Shall I Remember. Dallas, TX.: The Kaleidograph Press, 1941. xii p., 1 ℓ., 15-66 p.

RUGGLES, ALICE McGUFFEY (MORRILL)
Verses. Portland, ME.: The Mosher Press, 1940. viii, [1], 76, [1] p., 1 ℓ.

RUGGLESS, EMMA E.
Pleasant Thoughts. Los Angeles, CA.: Wetzel Publishing Company, 1928. 74 p.
Wheels, Wings, and Other Things. Los Angeles, CA.: Wetzel Publishing Company, 1928. 16 p. (Verse for Children.)

RUHL, BARBARA S.
Semi-Precious Stones. New York: Exposition Press, 1964. 63 p.

RUKEYSER, MURIEL (1913-)
Theory of Flight. New Haven, CT.: Yale University Press, 1935. 86 p. (Yale Series of Younger Poets, 34)
Mediterranean. New York: Writers & Artists Comm. Medical Bureau to Aid Spanish Democracy, 1937? [4] p.
...U.S. 1. New York: Covici Friede, 1938. 5 p.ℓ., 9-147 p., 1 ℓ.
A Turning Wind; Poems. New York: The Viking Press, 1939. 120 p.
The Soul and Body of John Brown. New York: Privately printed, 1940.
Wake Island. Garden City, N.Y.: Doubleday, Doran and Co., Inc., 1942. 3 p.ℓ., 16 p.
Beast in View. Garden City, N.Y.: Doubleday, Doran & Co., 1944. x, 98 p.
The Children's Orchard. San Francisco: Book Club of California, 1947. 4 ℓ. (Book Club of California. The California poetry folios, part 9)
The Green Wave. Garden City, N.Y.: Doubleday, 1948. 95 p.
Elegies. New York: New Directions, 1949. 82 p.
Orpheus. San Francisco: Centaur Press, 1949. [33] p.
Selected Poems. New York: New Directions, 1951. vii, 111 p. (The New classics series)
Body of Waking. New York: Harper, 1958. vii p., 1 ℓ., 118 p.
Waterlily Fire: Poems, 1932-1962. New York: Macmillan, 1962. xi, 200 p.
Selected Poems. Bloomington, IN.: Indiana University Press, 1963. 171 p. (Unesco collection of contemporary works)
The Poem as Mask; Orpheus. Santa Barbara, CA.: Unicorn Press, 1967. [2] p.
The Outer Banks. Santa Barbara, CA.: Unicorn Press, 1967. [20] p.
The Speed of Darkness. New York: Random House, 1968. x, 113 p.
Mazes. New York: Simon and Schuster, 1970. [42] p.
The Speed of Darkness. New York: Vintage Books, 1971. 4 p.ℓ., 113 p.
29 Poems. London: Rapp and Whiting, 1972. 46 p.
Breaking Open. New York: Random House, 1973. vii, 135 p.

RULE, ESTELLE JOHNSON
Poems. St. Louis, MO.: Nixon-Jones Printing Company, 1913. 63 p.

RUMELL, LYNN K.
Poems. Logansport, IN.: Chronicle Printing Co., 1922. [43] p.

RUMRY, FLAURANCE LAYTON
Autumn Had Wept. Chicago: Sangamon Press, 1940. [45] p.

RUNYAN, FRIEDA KAMMERER
The Bible Revisited in Poetry. Philadelphia: Dorrance, 1966. 103 p.

RUPEL, LULA HONEYCOMB
Reaching for the Moon; A Book of Poems. Boston: Chapman & Grimes, 1955. 96 p.

RUSCH, ALTHEA RANDOLPH (BEDLE) (1871-) [RANDOLPH, ALTHEA, pseud.]
A Shower of Verses, Containing Mother's Treasure Book, Fancies, Fairies, and Frolics, Twilight Poems. New York: The H. W. Gray Co., 1914. iii, 115 p.

RUSH, EMMY MATT
My Garden of Roses. Boston: The Four Seas Company, 1925. 64 p.

RUSHING, LUCY CALDWELL
Star Dust and Sunshine, Original Poems. San Antonio, TX.: Clegg Printing Co., 1931. [20] p.

RUSHING, MARIE MORRIS (1910-)
Songs of the Parakeet. Fayetteville, AR.: Avalon Press, 1947. 46 p.
Cry "Shibboleth!" Philadelphia: Dorrance, 1953. 87 p. (Contemporary poets of Dorrance, 448)
Five Golden Mice, A Collection of Poetry. Little Rock, AR.: Allard House Publishers, 1960. vi, 105 p.
Migration to Sand. Fort Smith, AR.: South and West, Inc., 1966. 35 p.

RUSSELL, AMY REQUA
This Native Heart, Poems, 1930-1938. Los Angeles, CA.: n.p., 1938. 4 p.ℓ., 7-66 p.
Alternate Beat. Los Angeles, CA.: Printed by the Ward Ritchie Press, 1945. 29 p.

RUSSELL, BAYKA
A Vision at Versailles; A Book of Sonnets. New York: L. Raley, 1940. 48 p.
Mirror of the Heart. New York: H. Harrison, 1942. 63 p.
Beyond Tomorrow. Portland, ME.: Falmouth Pub. House, 1949. 69 p.

RUSSELL, BESSIE LADD (1873-)
The Gold. Boston: Sherman, French & Company, 1912. 6 p.ℓ., 60 p.

RUSSELL, BETH DUVALL
A White Stone Given. Lake Como, FL.: New Athenaeum Press, 1957. 63, [1] p.
On Earth as It Is. Boston: Christopher Pub. House, 1963. 144 p.

RUSSELL, ETHEL GREEN
Deep Bayou. Lowell, MA.: Alentour House, 1941. 4 p. ℓ., 11-63 p.
Lantern in the Wind. Dallas, TX.: The Kaleidograph Press, 1942. xi p., 1 ℓ., 15-99 p.
Land of Evangeline. Cincinnati: Talaria, 1946. 78 p., 1 ℓ.
_______. 3d ed., 1950.

RUSSELL, KATYE LOU
My Wee Muse Sings; Poems. New York: Exposition Press, 1969. 40 p.

RUSSELL, KAY
Songs from an Ivory Tower. Dallas, TX.: Kaleidograph Press, 1951. 71 p.

RUSSELL, LYNN
Hills of Gold. Houghton, N.Y.: Houghton College Press, 1927. 109 p.
The Little Spanish Princess, and Other Florida Poems. Houghton, N.Y.: Printed at the Houghton College Press, 1937. 38 p.

RUSSELL, QUITILLIA B.
The Star of Christmas and Other Poems. Boston: C. C. Birchard & Co., 1935. v, 7-48 p.

RUST, CARRIE NETER
My Silver and My Gold. New York: Comet Press Books, 1958. 44 p.

RUTH see LE PRADE, RUTH

RUTHERFORD, MARGARET HILL
Down Memory Lane. New York: Carlton Press, 1960. 4 p. ℓ., 27 p.

RUTHVEN, MADELEINE
Sondelius Came to the Mountains. Los Angeles, CA.: The Primavera Press, 1934. 36 p.

RUUTZ-REES, CAROLINE (1865-)
Places and Other Poems. New York: Margent Press, 1947. [48] p.

RYAN, AGNES (1878-1954)
A Whisper of Fire. Boston: The Four Seas Co., 1919. 113 p.
We Women Are to Blame. Bath, Eng.: Ralph Allen Press, 192-? [10] p.

RYAN, ANNE
Lost Hills. New York: The New Door, 1925. 46 p.

RYAN, COLETTA (1876-)
Songs in a Sun-Garden. Boston: N. B. Turner & Co., 1905. viii, 101 p.

RYAN, KATHRYN WHITE
Golden Pheasant, Poems. New York & London: G. P. Putnam's Sons, 1925. xii, 82 p.

RYBERG, BARBARA CORNET (1914-)
A Place of Springs. Chicago: M. P., 1946. 75 p.

RYDZYNSKI, MARIE
Young Thoughts. New York: Vantage Press, 1967. 63 p.

RYMAN, SUNSHINE DICKINSON
Moon Conjure, and Other Poems. Dallas, TX.: Tardy Publishing Company, 1937. 5 p. ℓ., 119 p.
Needle and Thread. Dallas, TX.: Kaleidograph Press, 1951. 83 p.
The Lily Bird, A Tale of Old Matagorda, and Other Poems. Dallas, TX.: Story Book Press, 1955. 59 p.

SACKETT, BLANCHE LONG
...Moods. New York: H. Harrison, 1938. 64 p.

SAFFRON, ROSE
The Miracle of Angel Alley, and Other Poems. New York: Vantage Press, 1961. 66 p.

SAGAN, MIRIAM
Dangerous Body. Berkeley, CA.: Samisdat, 1975. 16 p.

SAGE, KAY
The More I Wonder; Poems. New York: Bookman Associates, 1957. 64 p.
Mordicus. Paris?: n.p., 1962. [28] p.

SAHAKIAN, LUCILLE (1894-)
A Heart Speaks. San Antonio: n.p., 1948. 4 p. ℓ., 86 p.
Stars from a Texas Sky. San Antonio, TX.: Naylor Co., 1956. 36 p.

SAINT CATHERINE, Sister (1878-) [Secular Name: Lee Beavers.]
A Thought at Christmastide, & Other Poems. San Francisco: Printed by J. H. Nash, 1931. v, 26 p.

ST. CLAIR, SOPHIE ROOD
The Christmas Sprites, and Other Poems. Boston: Bruce Humphries, 1954. 44 p.

ST. DENIS, RUTH (1880-)
Lotus Light, Poems. Boston and New York: Houghton Mifflin Company, 1932. ix, [1] p., 1 ℓ., 100 p.
Poems. Glendale, CA.: Morgan, 1952. 51 p.
Poems; Selected from Her Series, Poetic Biography. n.p., 1955. 84 p.

ST. JOHN, EMILY PORTER
Cloudy-Clear. Cedar Rapids, IA.: The Torch Press, 1937. 2 p. ℓ., 7-76 p.

ST. JOHN, JESSIE
Fruit of the Tree. Brattleboro, VT.: The Stephen Daye Press, 1931. 61 p., 1 ℓ.

ST. MAWR, ERIN
Lakes of Light. Ripton, VT.: The Author, 1975. 12 p.

SALEM, ARABEL AMANDA
Pondering the Path of Life; Poems. New York: Vantage Press, 1962. 48 p.

SALISBURY, HELEN MOLYNEAUX
To Touch Infinity; Poems. New York: Exposition Press, 1956. 95, [1] p.

SALLS, HELEN HARRIET
Pensive Citadels. Emory University, GA.: Banner Press, 1931. 41 p. (Verse craft series)

SALONEN, MARTHA
The Shimmering Disk. Mill Valley, CA.: Wings Press, 1948. [1], 55 p.

SALTER, KATHERINE SHEPARD (HAYDEN) (1896-) [HAYDEN, KATHERINE SHEPARD]
Sonnets and Lyrics. Boston: B. Humphries, Inc., 1934. 78 p.

SALTER, Mrs. LESLIE
Homespun Poems. Vallejo, CA.: n.p., 1947. 32 p.

SAMPSON, BLANCHE D.
The Crystal Loom. Holyoke, MA.: The Unity Press, 1939. 4 p. ℓ., 11-61 p.

SAMPTER, JESSIE ETHEL (1883-1938)
The Coming of Peace. New York: Publishers Printing Company, 1919. 35 p.
The Emek. New York: Bloch Publishing Company, 1927. 5 p. ℓ., 3-87 p.

SAMS, DIANE (1947-)
With You in Mind. Baton Rouge, LA.: n.p., 1972. unpaged.

SAMSON, ANNE STRINGER (1933-)
Lines, Spines, and Porcupines. Garden City, N.Y.: Doubleday, 1969. [64] p.

SANBLOM, LOLA
Silk Purses. Montrose, CA.: n.p., 1932. 47, [1] p.
Buffalo Sod. Glendale, CA.: Pioneer Printing Co., 1936. 85, [1] p.

SANBURN, ISABELLA
The Touch of the Master's Hand; Religious Poetry. New York: Vantage Press, 1967. 64 p.

SANBURN, MARJORIE
Through the Emerald; A Modern Novel in Traditional Verse. Portland, ME.: The Mosher Press, 1939. 2 p. ℓ., 25, [1] p., 1 ℓ.

SANCHEZ, SONIA (1935-)
Homecoming. Detroit: Broadside Press, 1969. 32 p.
We a BaddDDD People. Detroit: Broadside Press, 1970. 72 p.
It's a New Day: Poems for Young Brothas and Sistuhs. Detroit: Broadside Press, 1971. 29 p.
Love Poems. New York: Third Press, 1973. 101 p.
A Blues Book for Blue Black Magical Women. Detroit: Broadside Press, 1974. 62 p.

SANDBERG, LUCILLE
Six Islands. New York: Vantage Press, 1953. 65 p.
Roundup. Charleston, IL.: Prairie Press, W. S. Tremble, 1966. 43 p.

SANDBURG, HELGA (1918-)
The Unicorns. New York: Dial Press, 1965. 93 p.
To a New Husband. New York: World Pub. Co., 1970. 79 p.

SANDERS, EFFA STARK (1882-)
The Mirror of Tomorrow. San Antonio, TX.: Carleton Print. Co., 1948. 71 p.

SANDERS, EFFIE EMBRY
Beautiful Stairways; Poems. New York: Exposition Press, 1968. 62 p.
Shining Light; Poems. New York: Exposition Press, 1968. 127 p.
A Mansion over the Hill. New York: Exposition Press, 1970. 96 p.
To Walk in the Light. New York: Exposition Press, 1970. 96 p.

SANDERS, PRISCILLA
With You in Mind. Boston: Branden Press, 1967. 1 p. ℓ., 138 p.

SANDERSON, ISABEL S. (1913-)
Clipped Wings. Chicago: R. F. Seymour, 1947. 90 p.
Corridors of Time. Chicago: R. F. Seymour, 1953. 92 p.
Candles in My Heart. Chicago: R. F. Seymour, 1957. 96 p.

SANDFORD, EMILY WHITE
Chiffons and Mektoub (It Is Written!). New York: Vantage Press, 1953. 3 p.ℓ., 95 p.

SANDS, IRENE BLIGHT
The Rose of California, and Other Ballads. Boston: The Four Seas Company, 1927. 47 p.

SANDS, MARY D. (1914-)
Dark Mirror; Poems. New York: Exposition Press, 1957. 64 p.
After Dawn. New York: Exposition Press, 1970. 64 p.

SANGSTER, MARGARET ELIZABETH (1894-)
Cross Roads. New York: The Christian Herald, 1919. 159 p.
Singing on the Road. New York: Carroll Press, 1923. 120 p.
_______. New York: Round Table Press, 1936. 95 p.
All Through the Day. New York: Round Table Press, 1939. xi, 100 p.

SANGSTER, MARGARET ELIZABETH (MUNSON) (1838-1912)
Lyrics of Love, of Hearth and Home, and Field and Garden. New York, Chicago: F. H. Revell, Co., 1901. 4 p.ℓ., 11-200 p.

SANTLEY, MARY McDERMOTT
Love's Garden. Cleveland, OH.: E. C. Long, 1908. 14 p.
Indian Romances, and Other Poems. Cleveland, OH.: H. Carr, 1911. 115 p.
On Wings of Joy, and Other Poems. Cleveland, OH.: H. Carr, 1919. 3 p.ℓ., 5-142 p.

SARGENT, E. N. see ROBERTS, NANCY

SARGENT, ELIZABETH LEE
Silver Filigree. Los Angeles: Wetzel Pub. Co., 1951. 70 p.

SARGENT, LOUISE (PEABODY) (1856-1949)
Collected Poems. Paris: Akademia R. Duncan, 1949? [32] p.

SARGENT, MARIA deACOSTA
Pierrot's Verses. Boston: Priv. Print., 1917. 2 p.ℓ., 3-27 p., 1 ℓ.

SARTON, MAY (1912-) [Full Name: Eleanor May Sarton.]
Encounter in April. Boston: Houghton Mifflin Company, 1937. vii p., 2 ℓ., 3-85 p.
Inner Landscape; Poems. Boston: Houghton Mifflin Company, 1939. viii, 64 p.

The Lion and the Rose, Poems. New York: Rinehart, 1948. viii, 2 ℓ., 3-104 p.
The Leaves of the Tree; Poems. Mount Vernon, IA.: English Club of Cornell College, 1950. 39 p. (Cornell College chapbooks, no. 22)
The Land of Silence, and Other Poems. New York: Rinehart, 1953. xi, 99 p.
In Time Like Air; Poems. New York: Rinehart, 1958. 80 p.
Cloud, Stone, Sun, Vine; Poems, Selected and New. New York: Norton, 1961. 144 p.
A Private Mythology; New Poems. New York: Norton, 1966. 107 p., 1 ℓ.
As Does New Hampshire, and Other Poems. Peterborough, N.H.: R. R. Smith, 1967. 59 p.
Plant Dreaming Deep. New York: Norton, 1968. 189 p.
A Grain of Mustard Seed: New Poems. New York: Norton, 1971. 72 p., 1 ℓ.
Journal of a Solitude. New York: Norton, 1973. 208 p.
Collected Poems. New York: Norton, 1974. 416 p.

SASSER, HELEN JUNE
My Reminiscence. Lake City, FL.: Arnold Printing Company, 1933. 3 p. ℓ., 3-42 p.

SATIR, VIRGINIA M.
Self Esteem. Millbrae, CA.: Celestial Arts, 1975. [64] p.

SAUNDERS, CECELIA
Out of My Heart. San Antonio, TX.: Naylor Co., 1956. viii, 52 p.

SAUNDERS, JANET LEE
Howling Winds Stir; Poems. New York: Carlton Press, 1969. 32 p.

SAURO, JOAN
Things Lost in Need of Finding. Notre Dame, IN.: Ave Maria Press, 1973. 126 p.

SAVAGE, EUDORA V.
Vibrations of My Heartstrings. New York: The Exposition Press, 1944. 4 p. ℓ., 11-94 p. (Poets of America. Series four)

SAVAGE, FRANCES HIGGINSON (FULLER) (1898-)
Bread and Honey. New York: n.p., 1939. 59 p.
A Pinch of Salt. New York: n.p., 1941. 69 p.
Winter Nocturne. Francestown, N.H.: Golden Quill Press, 1963. 136 p.
Postscript to Spring, and Other Poems. Francestown, N.H.: Golden Quill Press, 1967. 110 p.

SAVARESE, JULIA
...Dreaming Spires.... Philadelphia: Dorrance & Company, 1947. 89 p. (Contemporary poets of Dorrance, 339)

SAVILLE, ANNIE ELIZABETH
Truth, My Guide. New York: Exposition Press, 1949. 98 p.

SAWTELL, ESTELLE ELIZABETH
...Hospital Rhymes. Philadelphia: Dorrance & Company, 1944. 62 p. (Contemporary poets of Dorrance, 271)

SAXON, ELIZABETH (LYLE)
Poems of Elizabeth Lyle Saxon. Dallas, TX.: Clyde C. Cockrell Co., 1932. 3 p. ℓ., 9-119 p.

SAXON, CAROLYN NAUGHT
Sonnets on Identity. Los Angeles, CA.: Wagon & Star Publishers, 1944. [20] p. (Destiny editions)
The Pine and the Power. Philadelphia: Dorrance, 1973. 37 p.

SAYER, LEATHA MATILDA
Priceless Treasures of Our Day. Lansing, MI.: Lansing Letter Service, 1950. 50 p.

SAYRE, GRACE (1884-)
Remembered Aprils. Sunland, CA.: C. L. Anderson, 1949. 87 p.

SCARBOROUGH, DOROTHY (1878-1935)
Fugitive Verses. Waco, TX.: Baylor University Press, 1912. 4 p. ℓ., 11-103 p.

SCHAEFFER, SUSAN FROMBERG (1941-)
The Witch and the Weather Report; Poems. New York: Seven Woods Press, 1972. 54 p.
Granite Lady; Poems. New York: Collier Books, 1974. 144 p.
The Rhymes and Runes of the Toad. New York: Macmillan, 1975. 76 p.

SCHAFFLE, EVALYN WILSON (1914-)
Verses. New York: H. Harrison, 1938. 63 p.

SCHAIBLE, DOROTHY HALLADAY
My Garden of Verse. Grand Rapids, MI.: Bardic Echoes, 1970. 24 p.

SCHARMAN, VERA
Maggior Dolore. New York: Exposition Press, 1965. 56 p.

SCHAUDIES, MARY ALICE
These Gifts I Offer. Dallas, TX.: The Kaleidograph Press, 1936. 71 p.

SCHECHTER, RUTH LISA (1928-)
Near the Wall of Lion Shadows. Syracuse, N.Y.: SMP, 1969. 79 p.
Movable Parts. New York: Folder Editions, 1970? [14] ℓ.

Suddenly Thunder. New York: Barlenmir House, 1972. 72 p.
Offshore. New York: Barlenmir House, 1974.

SCHEEL, ELMA
Yucca Blooms. Aberdeen? SD.: n.p., 1938? 39, [1] p.

SCHEEL, MADOLYNN
A Small Part of Me; Poems. New York: Exposition Press, 1968. 63 p.

SCHELIN, HARRIET TRIELOFF
Thoughts from Nature's Heart. Athol, MA.: W. P. Cook Printer, 1922. 4 p. ℓ., 196 p.

SCHERMERHORN, ELIZABETH L.
Dark Voice Within. Los Angeles, CA.: n.p., 1938. 51 p.

SCHERMERHORN, RUTH (FAHNESTOCK) (1908-)
Testament. Locust Valley: Priv. Print., 1933. 68 p., 1 ℓ.

SCHETTY, MADELEINE
Speech Out of the Rooted Tree, A Selection of Poems. New York: Hippogryph Press, 1947. 94 p.

SCHEUMANN, GLADYS FAWLEY
On Memory's Canvas. Kanona, N.Y.: J. & C. Transcripts, 1968. 48 p.

SCHEVILL, MARGARET ERWIN
Desert Sheaf. Tucson, AZ.: Desert Press, 1942. [30] p.
Desert Center. Tucson, AZ.: Balkow Press, 1953. [55] p.

SCHIELD, DORAJEAN, *pseud.* *see* GRISH, DORA S.

SCHILLER, REBECCA JANE
Poems. n.p.: Evangelical Press, 1900. 8-119 p.

SCHLESINGER, SARA R.
Legends of Manitou, and Other Poems. Colorado Springs? CO.: n.p., 1910. 36 p.

SCHLUNEGER, FRANCES ELEONORE
How Many Springs? Philadelphia: Dorrance, 1969. 5 p. ℓ., 81 p.

SCHNEE, CORA B.
Poems of Nature. Arena, WI.: n.p., 1905. 38 p.

SCHNEIDER, FLORA
Collected Poems. Canton, OH.: n.p., 1959. 111 p.

SCHNEIDER, PATRICIA VOUGHT
Counterpoint in Straw. Gleasondale, MA.: n.p., 1963.

The Wake; A Poem of Remembrance. Boston: Baker's Plays, 1968. 38 p.

SCHOFIELD, JOSEPHINE HOLLY
My Heart and I. Kilbourn, WI.: J. E. Jones & Co., Printers, 1913. 3 p. ℓ., 47 p.
To-Day. Long Beach, CA.: Rex Green Printing Co., 1922. [13] p.

SCHONBORG, VIRGINIA
The Salt Marsh. New York: Morrow, 1969. [32] p.
Subway Swinger. New York: Morrow, 1970. [32] p.

SCHOR, RHEA IRENE
A String of Pearls; Prose, Painting, and Sculpture. Maspeth, N.Y.: Poetry Press, 1956. 102 p.

SCHORR, LAURA (HOWELL)
On Upward Flight. New York: Exposition Press, 1951. 47 p.
In Company; Poems for Devotional Use. New York: Exposition Press, 1965. 69 p.

SCHRADER, EMMA
Half a Hundred Thoughts in Rhyme, Sonnets, Poems. Chicago: The Winona Publishing Company, 1906. 144 p.

SCHRAGE, DOROTHEA AUGUSTE GUNHILDE
Petunia Blossoms; Ballads and Poems. Kansas City, MO.: The Gate City Press, 1921. 80 p.

SCHRAMM, IRENE
Who Is Dead; Poems. Cleveland, OH.: Renegade Press, 1964. [14] p.

SCHUBERT, Mrs. LOUIS H.
Random Rhythms. New York: n.p., 1924. 79 p.

SCHUFF, KAREN E.
Come Take My Hand. Lakemont, GA.: CSA Press, 1968. [48] p.
Barefoot Philosopher. Kanona, N.Y.: J. & C. Transcripts, 1968. 4 p. ℓ., 39 p.
Of Rhythm and Cake. Kanona, N.Y.: J. & C. Transcripts, 1970. 52 p.

SCHULER, ANNE (SWANN) (d. 1936)
Poems. New York: Printed by the Eilert Printing Co., Inc., 1936. 53 p.

SCHULTZ, BIRDIE DILGER
The Heart of Narcissus, and Other Poems. New York: Exposition Press, 1951. 63 p.

SCHULTZ, GARNETT ANN

The Little Things. Philadelphia: Dorrance, 1964. 5 p. ℓ., 154 p.

Something Beautiful. Philadelphia: Dorrance, 1966. 4 p. ℓ., 165 p.

And Then the Dawn. Philadelphia: Dorrance, 1969. 171 p.

But Not My Heart. Philadelphia: Dorrance, 1969. 171 p.

To Touch a Star. Philadelphia: Dorrance, 1971. 172 p.

Moments of Sunshine. Philadelphia: Dorrance, 1974. 168 p.

SCHULTZ, LULU MINERVA (1881-)

Wide Country Dusk. Emory University, New York, Atlanta, GA.: Banner Press, 1938. 52 p. (Verse craft series)

But the Stars Come Out; A Collection of Poems. Milldale, CT.: National Press, 1957. 40 p.

SCHULZ, BERTA BURKE

Song of the Leaves, and Other Poems. Temple, TX.: Gresham's, 1950. 67 p.

SCHUTZ, SUSAN POLIS

Come into the Mountains, Dear Friend. Boulder, CO.: Blue Mountain Arts, 1972. 63 p.

I Want to Laugh--I Want to Cry: Poems on Women's Feelings. Boulder, CO.: Blue Mountain Arts, 1973. 63 p.

The Best Is Yet to Be. Boulder, CO.: Blue Mountain Arts, 1974. 63 p.

Music in the Streets: Poems. Boulder, CO.: Blue Mountain Arts, 1974. 63 p.

Peace Flows from the Sky. Boulder, CO.: Blue Mountain Arts, 1974. 63 p.

SCHUTZE, LENORE CONGDON

In the Southland, and Other Poems. New York: Wagner, Harr, 1932. 25 p.

Poems of Love, Life and Death. New York: The Exposition Press, 1942. 4 p. ℓ., 13-61 p.

SCHWAB, ANTONIA YBOR

Silver Shadows. Atlanta, GA.: E. Hartsock, Bozart Press, 1928. 2 p. ℓ., [3]-40 p.

Distant Wonder. Dallas, TX.: The Kaleidograph Press, 1936. 66 p.

Collected Poems. Dallas, TX.: The Kaleidograph Press, 1948. 89 p.

SCHWARTZ, ESTHER L.

Parents Prefer Babies. New York: E. P. Dutton & Co., Inc., 1930. 3 p. ℓ., 5-103 p.

SCOFIELD, DOLORES MAY (BOWERS) (1884-)

Beacon Lights. Pittsburg, KS.: Beacon Light Publishing Co., 1930. [40] p.

SCOLLARD, ELISABETH
Candle and Cross. Portland, ME.: The Mosher Press, 1925. ix, [1], 3-81, [1] p., 1 ℓ.

SCOTT, CORAL FRANCES
Life's Overtones. Boston: The Stratford Company, 1921. 3 p. ℓ., 40 p.

SCOTT, EVELYN (1893-)
Precipitations. New York: N. L. Brown, 1920. 103 p.
The Winter Alone. New York: J. Cape and H. Smith, 1930. xi, 127 p.

SCOTT, FAY BOND
Seared Leaves. Austin, TX.: Capitol Printing Company, 1933. 2 p. ℓ., 7-39 p.

SCOTT, GRACE MARIE (1920-)
Bittersweet Fragments. Abilene, TX.: Abilene Printing & Stationery Co., Inc., 1947. 108 p.
Beyond All Loneliness. Abilene, TX.: n. p., 1952. 79 p.
Lost Years Restored. San Antonio, TX.: Naylor Co., 1956. xiii, 77 p.
Borrowed Melody. Abilene, TX.: Abilene Printing and Stationery, 1966. 78 p.

SCOTT, IDA JOSEPHINE
A Glitter in the Stream. New York: Exposition Press, 1940. 5 p. ℓ., 13-64 p.
...Come Sing My Songs. Philadelphia: Dorrance and Company, 1943. 51 p.
Leaves of Tender Touch. New York: William-Frederick Press, 1949. 3 p. ℓ., 24 p.

SCOTT, LOUISE
Divining Rod; Poems. Iowa City, IA.: Prairie Press, 1968. 69 p., 1 ℓ.

SCOTT, MARIANA
Only a Moment Golden, Poems. New York: Exposition Press, 1949. 47 p.
Sketches in Black and White; Poems. Boston: Branden Press, 1967. [64] p.

SCOTT, MAYBELLE BURR
My Impressions...A Volume of Patriotic Verse. New York: The Exposition Press, 1944. 5 p. ℓ., 13-62 p.

SCOTT, MEADA
Memoirs of Life on the Ranch. Dallas, TX.: Royal Pub. Co., 1958. 88 p.

SCOTT, VERA E.
Birth of Wings. n. p.: Pioneer Printing Co., 1965. 26 p.

SCOTT, VIOLA (ALLMAN)
Wind in the Pines and Other Poems. Philadelphia: Dorrance, 1961. 3 p. ℓ., 71 p.

SCOTT, VIRGINIA
Poems for a Friend in Late Winter. Bronx, N. Y.: Sunbury Press, 1975. 80 p.

SCOVIL, CORA
Champagne for Christmas. New York?: n. p., 1936? 30 p.

SCUDDER, ANTOINETTE (1898-)
Poems. New York: Priv. Print. De Vinne Press, 1921. x p., 1 ℓ., 82, [2] p.
Story of the Roses, and Other Poems. New York: n. p., 1923. 87 p.
Indian Summer. New York: H. Vinal, 1924. 2 p. ℓ., 28 p.
Provincetown Sonnets, and Other Poems. Philadelphia: Dorrance and Company, 1925. 63, [1] p. (Contemporary poets of Dorrance, 25)
The Soul of Ilaria. New York: F. F. Sherman, 1926. [26] p.
Huckleberries. Philadelphia: Dorrance and Company, 1929. 88, [1] p. (Contemporary poets of Dorrance, 80)
Out of Peony and Blade. New York: H. Harrison, 1931. 62 p.
East End, West End. New York: H. Harrison, 1934. 64 p.
Italics for Life; The Collected Poems of Antoinette Scudder. New York: Exposition Press, 1947. 8 p. ℓ., 589 p.
Hail, New Jersey. n. p., 1957. 48 p.

SCUDDER, NELLIE GENEVA
Wayside Voices. Boston: R. G. Badger, 1925. 46 p.

SCULLY, MARGARET TOWNSEND
White Rose of Essex. New York: The Poets Press, 1936. 30 p.

SCURLOCK, RUTH GARRISON
Voice upon the Wind. San Antonio, TX.: Naylor Co., 1960. xiv, 70, [1] p.

SCUTT, WINIFRED
The Mystical Marriage of Christ. Dallas: Story Book Press, 1954. 121 p.
Tomorrow. Boston: Christopher Pub. House, 1955. 256 p.
Is Your Death Inevitable? New York: Pageant Press, 1962. 6 p. ℓ., 40 p.

SEAFORD, EMILY EASON
Pilgrim Paths. Washington: North Washington Press, 1951. 71 p.

SEAGRAVE, SADIE (FULLER) (1882-)
Cross My Palm. Cedar Rapids, IA.: The Torch Press, 1935. 88 p.
Wild Oats. Midlothian, IL.: T. L. U. Du Press, 1941. 56 p.
Angel Child. Oakdale, IA.: n. p., 1942. 55 p.
These Wiser Years. Cedar Rapids, IA.: Done by the Bookfellows at the Torch Press, 1948. 69 p.

SEALEY, DANGULOE (1931-)
To Regions of No Admittance. New York: Manyland Books, 1968. 4 p. ℓ., 86 p.
Recollections of a Childhood. New York: Manyland Books, 1971. 41 p.

SEALY, MARGARET
A Cluster of Marguerites. New York, London, etc.: The Abbey Press, 1901. 57 p.

SEAMAN, MARGARET LAURIE (1869-)
Roots of Understanding. Dallas, TX.: The Kaleidograph Press, 1932. x p., 2 ℓ., 15-84 p.

SEARLS, IDA SEXTON
Ta-Gosh; An Indian Idyl. St. Paul, MN.: Studio Print Shop, 1923. 32 p.

SEARS, CLARA ENDICOTT (1863-)
Wind from the Hills, and Other Poems. New York, London: G. P. Putnam's Sons, 1936. ix p., 1 ℓ., 13-95 p.

SEARS, JULIA SEATON see SETON, JULIA (1862-)

SEARWAY, RUBY GARRISON
Time to Remember. Francestown, N. H.: Golden Quill Press, 1964. 80 p.

SEBASTAIN, FANNIE B.
Poetry for Today; Subjective in Form. Washington, D. C.: Lithographed by the American Pub. Co., 1951. 160 p.

SEBRING, ARAD JOY (1883-1916)
Girdle of Gladness: Poems. Boston: R. G. Badger, 1905. 63 p.

SECRIST, MARGARET
The Trumpet Time. Denver, CO.: Big Mountain Press, 1958. 40 p.
Before Flight; A Book of Poems. Boston: Branden Press, 1965. 64 p.
All These. Boston: Branden Press, 1972. 32 p.

SEDMAN, LENA
Poems of Life Uplifting. New York: The Paebar Company, 1947. 5 p. ℓ., 133 p.

SEDWICK, ANGIE (1925-)
Synergy. Peterborough, N.H.: Windy Row Press, 1972. 64 p.

SEEBACH, MARGARET REBECCA (HIMES) (1875-)
Here We Have Stars, and Other Poems. Philadelphia: Muhlenberg Press, 1949. 5 p. ℓ., 245 p.

SEEGMILLER, WILHEMINA (1866-1913)
Little Rhymes for Little Readers. Chicago: Rand, McNally and Company, 1903. 81 p.
A Hand Clasp. Chicago: F. P. Volland & Company, 1911. 11 ℓ.
Sing a Song of Seasons. Chicago: Rand, McNally & Company, 1914. 84 p.
A New Garden of Verses for Children. Chicago: Rand, McNally & Company, 1925. ix, 154 p.

SEELEY, VELMA (HITCHCOCK) (1900-1938)
Caravan. Boston: R. G. Badger, 1927. 3 p. ℓ., 9-63 p.
The Collected Poems of Velma Hitchcock. New York: G. P. Putnam's Sons, 1939. 2 p. ℓ., 7-269 p.
While One Bird Sings. Sel. and arr. by Lefa Morse Eddy. Brooklyn, N.Y.: Lantern, 1939. 3 p. ℓ., 24 p. (Lantern poet series, no. 10)

SEFF, BERTHA (JOSEPHSON)
Smilin' Pums (A Book of Humorous Verse). Cedar Rapids, IA.: Torch Press, 1954. 94 p.

SEFRIT, SALLIE M.
Poems. New York: H. Harrison, 1931. 64 p.

SEGAL, EDITH (1902-)
Victory Verses for Young Americans. New York: n.p., 1944? 24 p.
Be My Friend, and Other Poems for Young People. New York: Sylvan Press, 1953. 46 p.
I Call to You Across the Continent: Poems and Songs by Edith Segal for Morton Sobell in Alcatraz, and to the Memory of Ethel and Julius Rosenberg, Executed June 19, 1953. New York: People's Artists, Inc., 1953. 23 p.
Come with Me; Poems, Guessing Poems, Dance Poems for Young People. New York: Citadel Press, 1963. 63 p.
Take My Hand; Poems & Songs for Lovers & Rebels. New York: Dialog Publications, 1970. 127, [1] p.
Poems and Songs for Dreamers Who Dare. Westport, CT.: Lawrence Hill, 1975. 96 p.

SEGAL, JOSEPHINE
Driftings. Philadelphia: Press of Review Publishing & Printing Co., 1907. 108 p.
The Judge's Decision. Philadelphia: Press of Review Publishing & Printing Co., 1907. 37 p.
Wanderings of Christ. Philadelphia: Press of Review Publishing & Printing Co., 1908. 166 p.

SEIBERT, GERTRUDE ANTOINETTE (WOODCOCK)
Poems of Dawn. Brooklyn, N.Y.: Watch Tower Bible & Tract Society, 1912. 286 p.
The Sweet-Brier Rose and Other Poems. Miami, FL.: The Hefty Press, 1926. 97 p.

SEIFFERT, MARJORIE ALLEN [Full Name: Marjorie Stephens (Allen) Seiffert.]
Ballads of the Singing Bowl. New York: C. Scribner's Sons, 1927. xi, 126 p.
The King with Three Faces, and Other Poems. New York: C. Scribner's Sons, 1929. xiii, 120 p.
The Name of Life. New York: C. Scribner's Sons, 1938. xiii, 129 p.

SEIGFRED, SHIRLEY
Concerto for Two Voices; A Prose-Poem in Three Movements. New York: Exposition Press, 1957. 110 p.

SEIVER, ELIZABETH R.
Poems of the New Jerusalem; Battle Hymns of Armageddon, and Other Songs. New York, London: E. R. Seiver, 1918. 108 p.

SEIVWRIGHT, JEAN
...Errant Heart. New York: H. Vinal, Ltd., 1928. 5 p. ℓ., 54 p.

SELBER, LILLIAN (PERLSTEIN) (1894-)
Pastels. San Antonio, TX.: Naylor Co., 1954. xi, 50 p.
A Little Quiet Dreaming, a Little Time to Think. Houston, TX.: Pacesetter Press, 1973. 57 p.

SELBY, HAZEL BARRINGTON (1889-)
Stalks of Wind. Boston: B. Humphries, 1941. 78 p.

SELLARDS, OLLA JOSEPHINE (BEARD) (1871-)
'Twixt the Ox-Cart and the Auto. Pasadena, CA.: The Orant Press, 1924. 3 p. ℓ., 3-122 p.

SEMONOFF, SADIE
Impressions. Providence, R.I.: Oxford Press, 1958. 19 p.
Thoughts. 2d ed. Providence, R.I.: Oxford Press, 1958. 15 p.
Arts and Letters. Providence, R.I.: Oxford Press, 1965. 45 p.

SEMPLE, ANNE
Prairie-Born, A Book of Verse. Dallas, TX.: The Kaleidograph Press, 1940. xiii p., 1 ℓ., 17-77 p.

SERONDE, ADELE (HERTER)
Ask a Daffodil; A Completely Phonetic Poetry Book. Cambridge,

MA.: Wenkart Pub. Co., 1967. 2 p. ℓ., 40 p., 1 ℓ.
Ask a Cactus Rose. Cambridge, MA.: Wenkart Pub. Co., 1973. 40 p.

SESSIONS, LAURA HOOKER
Only a Wayside Flower. New York: Broadway Publishing Company, 1907. 2 p. ℓ., 143, [1] p.

SETON, GRACE (GALLATIN)
The Singing Traveller. Boston: The Christopher Publishing House, 1947. 96 p.

SETON, JULIA [SEARS, JULIA SEATON]
Shells from Life-Love-God. New York: Centre Publishing Co., 1909. 49 p.

SETTERSTROM, ZERA ELLEN (PARRISH)
Legacy of Love. Boston: Humphries, 1951. 64 p.

SEWALL, ALICE ARCHER see JAMES, ALICE ARCHER (SEWALL) (1870-)

SEWELL, ELIZABETH MARGARET (1919-)
Poems, 1947-1961. Chapel Hill, NC.: University of North Carolina Press, 1962. 76 p. (Contemporary poetry series)
Signs and Cities. Chapel Hill, NC.: University of North Carolina Press, 1968. 57 p.

SEXTON, ANNE (1928-1974)
To Bedlam and Part Way Back. Boston: Houghton Mifflin Co., 1960. 5 p. ℓ., 67 p.
All My Pretty Ones. Boston: Houghton Mifflin Co., 1961. 68 p.
Selected Poems. London: Oxford University Press, 1964. 95 p.
Live or Die. Boston: Houghton Mifflin Co., The Riverside Press, 1966. xiv p., 1 ℓ., 90 p.
Love Poems. Boston: Houghton Mifflin Co., 1967. 5 p. ℓ., 67 p.
Transformations. Boston: Houghton Mifflin Co., 1971. 111 p.
______. London: Oxford University Press, 1972. 95 p.
The Death Notebooks. Boston: Houghton Mifflin Co., 1974. 97 p.
The Awful Rowing Toward God. Boston: Houghton Mifflin Co., 1975. vii, 85 p.

SHACKLEFORD, RUBY P. (1913-)
Dreamer's Wine; Poems. New York: Exposition Press, 1957. 47 p.
Ascend the Hill, and Other Poems. Peterborough, N.H.: Windy Row Press, 1974. 64 p.

SHAFER, MINA (SPRUCK)
In Cupped Hands. Los Angeles: Wagon & Star Publishers, 1944. 3 p. ℓ., 25 p.

SHAFFER, ALICE HOEY (1886-)
Angel Timber. Boston: B. Humphries, 1948. 41 p.
Voices; Poems. New York: Exposition Press, 1958. 60 p.
Angel Timber, an Epic Poem of a Pioneer Woman. 2d rev. and enl. ed., New York: Exposition Press, 1962. 55 p.

SHALLENBERGER, CHRISTY ALICE
Fancy. Los Angeles, CA.: n.p., 1951. 3 p. ℓ., 20 p.

SHAMBURGER, PEARL ZORA
Pictures on My Heart. Dallas, TX.: Story Book Press, 1949. 55 p.

SHAMROY, AUDREY
The Leftover Smile. Los Angeles: George Yamada, 1950. 2 p. ℓ., [35] p., 1 ℓ.

SHANA BARRETT TUNSTALL, pseud. see TUNSTALL, VELMA BARRET (1914-)

SHANGE, NTOSAKE
For Colored Girls Who Have Considered Suicide/When the Rainbow Is Enuf. San Lorenzo, CA.: Shameless Hussy Press, 1975. [27] p.

SHANK, EDITH H.
Seed Time and Harvest. Philadelphia: Dorrance, 1956. 92 p.
The Key Ring. Philadelphia: Dorrance, 1958. 106 p.
Threads of Time. Philadelphia: Dorrance, 1961. 61 p.

SHANK, MARGERY RUEBUSH
...Years Between. Philadelphia: Dorrance & Company, 1945. 51 p.

SHANKS, EVA
Harvest; Poems. New York: Exposition Press, 1965. 64 p.

SHANNON, GERTRUDE (SPROUSE)
My Song. Nashville, TN.: Parthenon Press, 1951. 80 p.

SHANNON, JEANNE
The Colors of the World. Boulder Creek, CA.: Triton Press, 1974. 27 p.

SHAPLEIGH, KATHERINE CHASE (1875-)
Poems. Worcester? MA.: n.p., 1943. 53, [2] p.

SHARAUN, BLANCHE BRYANT
Goldfish, Geese and Kinka Joos. Boston: R. G. Badger, 1930. 64 p.

SHARP, GAZELLE STEVENS
Little Patch of Blue, and Other Poems. Boston: R. G. Badger, 1910. 144 p.

SHARP, SAUNDRA (1942-)
From the Windows of My Mind. New York: Togetherness Productions, 1970. 52 p.
In the Midst of Change. New York: Togetherness Productions, 1972. 40 p.

SHARPE, RUTH COLLIER
When Falcon from the Wrist, and Other Poems. New York: Greenberg, 1949. 76 p.

SHARPLESS, FRANCES M.
Poems. Priv. Print. J. B. Lippincott, 1911. 2 p. ℓ., 3-159 p.

SHARROW, BELLE
Poems. Philadelphia: Williams & Marcus, 1913. 2 p. ℓ., 9-67 p.

SHARTLE, ANNE
Verses. Coral Gables, FL.: Kells Press, 1945. 30 p.

SHARTLE, MILDRED
With My Love. Philadelphia: Dorrance, 1972. 74 p.

SHATFORD, SARAH TAYLOR
Birds of Passage. Boston: Sherman, French & Company, 1916. 10 p. ℓ., 510 p.
Zekiel's Homespun Philosophies. Boston: Sherman, French & Company, 1916. 3 p. ℓ., 81 p.

SHAW, ALICE JACQUELINE
The Children of Nazareth, and Other Poems. Boston: Four Seas Co., 1930. 59, [1] p.
The Morning Meal, and Other Poems. 3d ed. Boston: E. D. Abbott, Co., 1940. 5 p. ℓ., 13-194 p.

SHAW, AMANDA (1861-1941)
The Wondrous Hush. New York, Chicago: Fleming H. Revell Company, 1931. 48 p.

SHAW, BILLIE
The Heart Sings. Boston: B. Humphries, Inc., 1944. 31 p.

SHAW, CELIA VAN NESS
Poetic Moods and Memories. Jackson Heights, N.Y.: New Voices Pub. Co., 1949. 63 p.

SHAW, FRANCES WELLS (1872-1937)
Who Loves the Rain, and Other Poems. Chicago: R. R. Donnelley & Sons Co., 1940. xi, 63 p., 1 ℓ.

SHAW, LUCI
Listen to the Green. Wheaton, IL.: H. Shaw Publishers, 1971. 90 p.

SHAW, MARGARET (HORTON)
Birds of Memory. Philadelphia: Dorrance, 1955. 141 p.
The Bluebird's Tail; Poetry. New York: Exposition Press, 1955. 110 p.

SHAW, MAXINE
Beautiful Cages. Boston, MA.: Stone Soup Poetry, 1974. 47 p.

SHAW, PATRICIA
Lament for the Thunderbirds. New York: Vantage Press, 1957. 32 p.

SHAW, RUTH YOLANDE
The Things That Count. Quincy, IL.: n.p., 1923. 127 p.

SHAW, WINIFRED STOCKBRIDGE BARTLETT (1891-)
Love Rhapsodies of a Musician, and Other Poems. Boston: The Stratford Company, 1925. 4 p.ℓ., 42 p.

SHEAP, HARRIET
...Thinking in Verse. Philadelphia: Dorrance & Company, 1945. 53 p.

SHEARD, VIRGINIA (STANTON)
The Ballad of the Quest. New York: The James A. McCann Co., 1922. 6 p.ℓ., 52 p.

SHEEHAN, ELIZABETH
Poems. Staten Island, N.Y.: Stanley Vishnewski, 1955. [25] p.

SHEEHAN, ELIZABETH WINSTON (1882-)
Battle at the Bend. Montgomery?: n.p., 1959. [8] p.
Bright in Mosaic. Montgomery, AL.: Paragon Press, 1960? 43 p.
Poems. Montgomery, AL.: Shamrock Press, 1968. 64 p.

SHEEHAN, MARY EMELINE
Listening In. Philadelphia: Dorrance, 1950. 96 p.

SHEETS, BESS MAE
Thread Your Thoughts. Oklahoma City, OK.: Harlow Pub. Corp., 1955. 59 p.

SHEFFEY, MIRIAM
The Spirit-Mother, and Other Poems. New York: Broadway Publishing Company, 1905. 62 p.

SHEFFIELD, LEAH AUGUSTINE
I Can See from Here. Richmond, VA.: Whittet & Shepperson, 1940. 62 p.
Soulful Security. Richmond: n.p., 1952. 69 p.

SHEFFIELD, RENA CARY
On the Romany Road. Short Hills, N.J.: The Voxton Press, 1915. 3 p.ℓ., 11-104 p., 1 ℓ.

SHELBURNE, MARY WILLIS
Broken Pattern, Poems. Richmond, VA.: Dietz Press, 1951. xi, 65 p.

SHELL, WINNIE
Soul Poems. Appalachia, VA.: Designed and produced by Young Publications, 1968. ii, 60 p.

SHELLENBERGER, LAURA S.
Wings of Morning. New York: Exposition Press, 1948. 47 p.

SHELLEY, GLADYS
It's All Nonsense Anyhow. New York: The Poets Press, 1939. 3 p.ℓ., 9-50 p.

SHELLEY, HARRIET SPANGLER
Poems of Life and Loving. New York: Broadway Pub., 1902. unpaged.

SHELLEY, MARTHA
Crossing the DMZ. Oakland, CA.: Women's Press Collective, 1974. [3], 53 p.

SHELTON, ADA STEWART
...Garden Verses and Other Poems. Boston: The Stratford Company, 1927. 32 p. (The Stratford poets)

SHELTON, HELEN HIGGINS
Let Us Go Home. Philadelphia: Dorrance, 1951. 55 p.

SHELTON, JULIA BAGGETTE
The Blue Mirror. Prairie City, IL.: Decker Press, 1948. 60 p.

SHELTON, NATHALIE THURSTON
...Nature and Human Nature. Boston: The Stratford Company, 1930. 31 p. (The Stratford poets)

SHELY, PAT
The Thorns Cut Deeply. Emory University, Atlanta, GA.: Banner Press, 1963. 60 p.

SHEPARD, ELIZABETH (ALSOP)
White Fox. New York: Dodd, Mead, 1956. 111 p.

SHEPARD, KATHERINE
Farther Fairer Seas. Atlanta, GA.: E. Hartsock, The Bozart Press, 1928. 2 p.ℓ., [3]-56 p.
Manna Tree, Poems. New York: Exposition Press, 1954. 96 p.

SHEPARD, MARY NORSWORTHY
"Where It Listeth." Boston: Sherman, French & Company, 1912. 3 p. ℓ., 77 p.

SHEPHARD, ESTHER
Poems. Seattle, WA.: Printed by C. E. Shephard, 1938. 4 p. ℓ., 64, [1] p.
An Oriental Tale and A Romantic Poet. Santa Cruz, CA.: Pacific Rim Publishers, 1967. 47 p.
Selected Poems. Santa Cruz, CA.: Pacific Rim Publishers, 1968. 5 p. ℓ., 128, [4] p.

SHEPHERD, FLORENCE DOMBEY
Song of Life, and Other Poems. Boston: Stratford, 1920. 37 p.

SHEPPERSON, MARY FIDES, Sister [Secular Name: Isabel Shepperson.]
Cloister Chords. Pittsburgh, PA.: n.p., 1922. 142 p.

SHERLOCK, SOPHIE M.
Eve, and Other Poems. New York: Longmans, 1910. 60 p.

SHERMAN, CATHERINE (BARENGER)
A Gift Book of Poems. Baltimore, MD.: Stockton Press, 1925. 28 p.

SHERMAN, CORRINE
Time Stands Apart. New York: Vantage Press, 1953. 5 p. ℓ., 53 p.

SHERMAN, ELLEN BURNS (1867-)
Poems. London: The Mitre Press, 1936. 165 p.

SHERMAN, ELOISE LEE
Plantation Poems. New York: F. F. Sherman, 1910. 2 p. ℓ., 3-64 p.

SHERMAN, JORY
So Many Rooms. San Francisco: Galley Sail Publications, 1960. 30 p., 1 ℓ.
My Face in Wax. Chicago: Windfall Press, 1965. 56 p.
There Are Ways of Making Love to You. n.p.: Tecumseh Press, 1974.

SHERMAN, LEAH (1904-)
The Quickened Dream. Chicago: Dierkes Press, 1950. 48 p.

SHERMAN, MARTHA COLEMAN
Just a Dream of Childhood Days, and Other Verses. Chicago: Childhood Publishing House, 1914. 80 p.
Winter Dandelions and Other Poems. Boston: The Stratford Company, 1924. 2 p. ℓ., 91 p.

SHERMAN, SUSAN
The Perfect Creation. Berkeley, CA.: n.p., 1960. 2 ℓ.
Areas of Silence. New York: Hespiridian Press, 1963. 30 p.
Women Poems, Love Poems. Brooklyn, N.Y.: Two and Two Press, 1975. 24 p.

SHERMAN, SYLVIA
Pipes o' Pan: A Wood Dream. Boston: R. G. Badger, 1916. 81, [10] p.

SHERRILL, EVELYN NORCROSS
Peace Is the Pollen. Cincinnati, OH.: Talaria Publication, 1942. 70 p., 1 ℓ.

SHERRY, RUTH (FORBES)
...Hourglass in the Mojave. West Los Angeles, CA.: Wagon & Star, 1941. 48 p.
Lament and Prophecy. Gunnison, CO.: A. Swallow, 1942. 1 p. ℓ., [1], 10, [1] p.
Chart for Voyage. Los Angeles, San Francisco: H. Parker and Craftsmen, 1943. 70, [4] p.
Imperishable Gene. London: Outposts Publications; Alondra? CA.: Henny-Penny Press, 1958. 32 p.
Seize on Tragic Time. Boston: B. Humphries, 1963. 20 p.
Partisan. Lanham, MD.: Goosetree Press, 1964. [7] p.
Mojave. Homestead, FL.: Olivant-THVQ Books, 1966. 57, [1] p.
________. 1966. 76 p.
________. 3d. ed. 1967.

SHERWIN, ALBERTA McMAHON
Kansas City Beautiful. Kansas City, MO.: Burton Publishing Company, 1931. [32] p.
Tapers to the Sun. Mill Valley, CA., New York: The Wings Press, 1939. 64 p.

SHERWIN, JUDITH JOHNSON (1936-)
Uranium Poems. New Haven, CT.: Yale University Press, 1969. xii, 70 p. (Yale Series of Younger Poets)
Impossible Buildings. Garden City, N.Y.: Doubleday, 1973. 143 p.

SHERWOOD, ADA SIMPSON
Hungering for the Hills, and Other Poems. Philadelphia: Dorrance & Company, 1947. 4 p. ℓ., 11-72 p.

SHERWOOD, GEORGIA DAY
My Wealth. New York: H. Harrison, 1937. 63 p.

SHERWOOD, GRACE BUCHANAN (1884-)
Moon Shadows. Garden City, N.Y.: Grace B. Sherwood, 1935. xi, 73 p.

Winter Bird Song. Garden City, L.I.: Grace B. Sherwood, 1936. xi, 71 p.
Water Meadows. Dallas, TX.: The Kaleidograph Press, 1938. ix p., 1 ℓ., 13-97 p.
What If the Spring--. Dallas, TX.: The Kaleidograph Press, 1938. ix p., 1 ℓ., 13-97 p.
No Final Breath; A Book of Verse. Mill Valley, CA., New York: The Wings Press, 1940. 94 p.

SHERWOOD, GRACE MABEL (1886-)
Navigators. Providence: Priv. Print. C.R.B., 1923. 8 ℓ.
Gifts. Providence: The Oxford Press, 1935. 27 p.

SHERWOOD, MARGARET POLLOCK (1864-1955)
The Upper Slopes. Boston and New York: Houghton Mifflin Company, 1924. xi, 117 p.

SHIELDS, CLARA McGEORGE
Redwoods and Buttercups. Eureka, CA.: n.p., 1923. 4 p.ℓ., 11-65 p.

SHIELDS, ELIZABETH McEWEN (1879-)
In Tune with Nature's Voice. Richmond, VA.: John Knox Press, 1955. 48 p.

SHIELDS, ELLENIA BATES
Along the Golden Trail of Fancy. New York: Pegasus Publishing Co., 1936. 31 p.

SHIELDS, PAULINE RICE
Life's Windows. Cincinnati, OH.: n.p., 1925. 136 p.

SHIELDS, RUTH E. NEWTON
When God's Fire Comes. New York: Carlton Press, 1969. 63 p.

SHIELDS, SALLIE (WILSON) (1906-)
My Life in Poetry. Maryville? TN.: n.p., 1969. v, III, 148 p.

SHIFFERT, EDITH (MARCOMBE) (1916-)
In Open Woods. Denver, CO.: A. Swallow, 1961. 40 p.
For a Return to Kona; Island Poems. Denver, CO.: A. Swallow, 1964. 48 p.
The Kyoto Years. Kyoto, Japan: Kyoto Seika Junior College Press, 1971. 128 p.

SHILLITO, MARTHA LYMAN
Singing Flame. Dallas, TX.: The Kaleidograph Press, 1937. x p., 2 ℓ., 15-79 p.

SHIMER, FLORENCE HENRY (1879-)
Twelve Poems. Hingham, MA.: n.p., 1950. [23] p.

SHIPMAN, CLARE
Seven Stars, and Other Poems. San Francisco: J. J. Newbegin, 1918. x p., 1 ℓ., 76 p.

SHIPMAN, CLARE
Markers of Time. St. Paul, MN.: n.p., 1931. 1 p. ℓ., 32 p.
Poems and Verse. St. Paul, MN.: n.p., 1941? 242 numb. ℓ.

SHIPMAN, ELISABETH
Little Verse. Appalachia, VA.: Young Publications, 1969. 20 p.
Stories of the Gods in Verse. Appalachia, VA.: Young Publications, 1969. 22 p.
These Jewels. Appalachia, VA.: Young Publications, 1969. 20 p.

SHIPMAN, ELIZABETH GERWIG
Within a Tradition. London: Mitre Press, 1970. 64 p.

SHIPP, Mrs. ELLIS REYNOLDS
Life Lines. Salt Lake City, UT.: Sketon Publishing Company, 1910. 316 p.

SHIPPEY, MARY RANDALL
As Wild Birds Sing: Poems. New York: R. G. Cooke, 1904. 1 p. ℓ., viii, 118 p.
Soeur Marie: A. Poem. New York: R. G. Cooke, 1904. 3 p. ℓ., 96 p.

SHOEMAKER, DORA ADELE
Out o'Doors. Philadelphia: The Penn Publishing Company, 1932. ix p., 2 ℓ., 13-123 p.

SHOEMAKER, EDNA
The Speckled Butter Bean. Middletown, PA.: Barnet Print. Co., 1970. 44 p.

SHOEMAKER, LYNN
Coming Home. Ithaca, N.Y.: Ithaca House, 1973. 67 p.

SHOLL, BETSY
Changing Faces. Cambridge, MA.: Alice James Books, 1974. 72 p.

SHONYO, HATTIE CHRISTOPHEN (DIX) (1865-)
A Refuge in the Rockies. Salida, CO.: The Salida Mail Print, 1905. [26] p.

SHOWAKER, SARAH L.
God Is the Answer; A Devotional Poem. New York: Greenwich Book Publishers, 1958. 46 p.

SHRINER, LOUISA (ARNDT) (1876-1925)
Poems. Riverside, N.J.: The Press Printing Co., 1926. 240 p.

SHUEY, LILLIAN (HINMAN) (1853-)
Among the Redwoods. San Francisco: The Whitaker and Ray Co., 1901. 42 p.

SHUEY, MARY WILLIS (MILLER)
Some Kentuckians and Other People. Coconut Grove, FL.: Hurricane House, 1964. 71 p.

SHULL, EUNICE HAYNES
Bittersweet and Balsam. Dallas, TX.: The Kaleidograph Press, 1942. xiii p., 1 ℓ., 17-96 p.

SHULL, LENA MEARLE (1883-1960)
Rainbow Through the Web. Emory University, Atlanta, GA.: Banner Press, 1944. 73 p.
Night Is Always Kind. Dallas: Kaleidograph Press, 1948. 69 p.
Dark Salt. Dexter, MO.: Candor Press, 1954. 32 p.
Fire on the Mountain. Emory University, Atlanta, GA.: Banner Press, 1955. 86 p.
Red Leaf Carols. Dexter, MO.: Candor Press, 1961. x, 69 p.

SHULL, SALLIE JUANITA (1882-)
Flamingo Feather. West Los Angeles, CA.: Wagon & Star Press, 1950. 48 p.
Time of Dusk; Poems. Santa Monica, CA.: Vaughn Print. and Litho, 1959. 4 p. ℓ., 46 p.

SHULL, THELMA
The Button String. Chicago: Lightner Publishing Company, 1942. 71 p.

SHULTAS, LOUISE
The Sampler, and Other Poems. Boston: R. G. Badger, 1925. 79 p.

SHUMAKER, HARRIET HALL
A Garden with Gates. Boston: Marshall Jones Company, 1930. vii p., 1 ℓ., 11-104 p.

SHUMATE, FRANCES
From My Window; Poems. New York: Vantage Press, 1965. 78 p.

SHUMWAY, MARY L. (1926-)
Song of the Archer & Other Poems. Chicago: Regnery, 1964. 71 p.
Headlands. Port Clements, B. C.: Sono Nis Press, 1972. 63 p.
Time and Other Birds. Gulfport, FL.: Konglomerati Press, 1975. 20 p.

SIBLEY, IDA (WESTERVELT)
Wood Smoke, and Other Poems. Philadelphia: Dorrance, 1953. 73 p.

SIEGMEISTER, ALICE PAYFIEL
Poems. New York: n.p., 1932. x, 89 p.

SIEGRIST, MARY
You That Come After. New York: H. Vinal, 1927. xviii p., 1 ℓ., 144 p.
...Sentinel; Selected Poems. New York: H. Vinal, Ltd., 1928. 5 p. ℓ., 45 p.
Flames Rise on the Mountain. New York: The Exposition Press, 1942. 5 p. ℓ., 13-100 p.

SIGHTS, BETTIE NORMENT
Where Lilies Grow. Oklahoma City, OK.: Dunn Publishing Co., 1940. 85, [2] p.

SIGSBEE, A. ELIZABETH
Heart Poems. New York: Broadway Publishing Co., 1908. 3 p. ℓ., 46 p.

SILCOX, ETHEL AUDREY SMITH
Beginnings in Song. Newport, R.I.: The Milne Printery, 1918. [10] p.

SILKO, LESLIE MARMON
Laguna Women. Greenfield Center, N.Y.: Greenfield Review Press, 1974. 35 p.

SILL, LOUISE MORGAN (SMITH) (1889-)
In Sun or Shade. New York and London: Harper & Brothers, 1906. ix, [1] p., 2 ℓ., 226 p.

SILVER, ALICE MOOLTEN
There Must Be Beauty. New York: Philosophical Library, 1965. ix, 81 p.

SILVER, AUGUSTA HELEN
Over the Hills and Far Away. New York: Vantage Press, 1956. 39 p.

SILVER, DEBBIE H.
Scenario. New York: T. Seltzer, 1925. viii p., 1 ℓ., 11-95 p.

SILVERS, VICKI
Echoes on the Wind, A Collection of Haiku. Dexter, MO.: Candor Press, 1967. 1 p. ℓ., 52 p.
From the Heavens Above, and Other Poems. Dexter, MO.: Candor Press, 1967. 8 p.

SILVIA, MARY LAVINIA (1898-)
The Old Oaken Bucket. Dexter, MO.: Candor Press, 1958. 49 p.

SIMMERLEE, MAUDE M.
United States History in Rhyme. New York: H. Lechner, 1911. 2 p. ℓ., 3-239 p.

SIMMONS, JOY
This of Joy. Millbrae, CA.: Celestial Arts, 1975. 96 p.

SIMMONS, JUDY DOTHARD
Judith's Blues. Detroit: Broadside Press, 1973. 22 p.

SIMMONS, JULIA GARDEPHE
Rhymes from a Rural School; North Country Verse. New York: Exposition Press, 1962. 64 p.

SIMMONS, LAURA
Verses, Flights o' Fancy. Boston: The Atlantis Press, 1908. 63 p.
The Crannied Wall. Prairie City, IL.: J. A. Decker, 1941. 52 p.

SIMMONS, MADELEINE FOUCHAUX
Potpourri. Los Angeles: Printed by D. C. Welty, 1943. 61 p.
First Aid for Limping Verse. North Hollywood, CA.: Camas Press, 1953. 12 p.
_____. 2d ed. North Hollywood, CA.: Camas Press, 1954. 23, [1] p.

SIMON, ADELAIDE
Permit Me Voyage, Poems. Cleveland, OH.: Free Lance Press, 1964. 1 p. ℓ., [1]-22 p., 2 ℓ.

SIMON, DOROTHY (WILL)
A Mouse in the Corner. New York: Exposition Press, 1955. 63 p.

SIMON, HAZEL HARTWELL
The Heart Chalice, and Other Poems. Mountain View, CA.: Pacific Press Publishing Association, 1959. 32 p.

SIMON, KIA
Toddler. Berkeley, CA.: Aldebaran Review, 1975. 28 p.

SIMON, LORENA (COTTS) (1897-)
The Golden Keys. San Antonio, TX.: Naylor Co., 1958. viii, 59 p.
From My Heart. San Antonio, TX.: Naylor Co., 1960. viii, 80 p.

SIMON, MARY ANSPACH
The Hooky Well. Shelby? OH.: n. p., 1952. 95 p.

SIMONDS, MARY ETHEL (SANGER)
From the Rays of the Rainbow. New York, London: G. P. Putnam's Sons, 1926. viii, 55 p.

Bundles for Britain, Sonnets and Other Poems. Brattleboro, VT.: Printed by E. L. Hildreth & Company, 1944. 4 p. ℓ., 55 p.
The Sky, and Other Poems. New York: The Knickerbocker Press, 1947. v, 24 p.

SIMONS, KATHERINE DRAYTON MAYRANT (1892-)
The Patteran. Columbia, SC.: The State Company, 1925. ix, 129 p.
White Horse Leaping. Columbia, SC.: University of South Carolina Press, 1951. 71 p.

SIMONTON, ADELAIDE F.
Autumn Winds; Poems and Drawings. New York: Pageant Press, 1961. 6 p. ℓ., 77 p.

SIMPSON, CARRIE LEWIS
Picture Poems. New York: Vantage Press, 1956. 59 p.

SIMPSON, CONSTANCE DEIGHTON
Poems and Sonnets. Los Angeles, CA.: n. p., 1924. [36] p.

SIMPSON, DONITA
Tears and Stone. Flushing, N. Y.: New Voices Press, 1971.

SIMPSON, FANNIE LOUISE
Autumn Leaves. Nacogdoches, TX.: The Author, 1920. 100 p.

SIMPSON, MABEL
Poems. New York: H. Vinal, 1925. 5 p. ℓ., 81 p.

SIMPSON, MARGARET I.
Wind in the Hills. Boston: R. G. Badger, 1926. 38 p.

SIMPSON, MARIAN BERRY
Granite Soil, and Other Poems. Portland, ME.: Falmouth Publishing House, 1941. 1 p. ℓ., 3-94 p.

SIMPSON, MARY AURORA THOMPSON
Home Songs. New York: Fleming H. Revell, 1904. 228 p.

SIMPSON, MINERVA MALOON (1876-)
Songs from the Sky. New York: Exposition Press, 1947. 64 p.
Poems. Appalachia, VA.: Young Publications, 1968. 7 p. ℓ., 121 p.

SIMPSON, RUBY HUTCHINS
The Potter's Unfinished Vase. New York: Pageant Press, 1964. 4 p. ℓ., 40 p.

SIMPSON, RUTH M. RASEY (1902-)
Mountain Fortitude. Peterborough, N. H.: Windy Row Press, 1969. 70 p.

SIMRALL, MARGUERITE M.
...I Touched Her Hand and Other Poems. Philadelphia: Dorrance & Company, 1936. 80 p. (Contemporary poets of Dorrance, 146)

SIMS, LILLIAN
Collection of Poems. Chicago: The Author, 1971.

SINCLAIR, E. MARIE
Random Shots. Boston: R. G. Badger, 1910. 64 p.
Dream Dust. Boston: The Cornhill Company, 1919. 5 p. ℓ., 75 p.

SINCLAIR, GLADYS JULIETTE (MELLOR) (1908-)
Life, Love and Laughter. Hudson County, N. J.: La Pierrette Cie, 1948. 92 p.
Potpourri. Hudson County, N. J.: La Pierrette Cie, 1952. 59 p.

SINCLAIR, ISABEL (1845-)
From Gray to Gold. Boston: R. G. Badger, 1913. 47 p.

SINCLAIR, MARY CRAIG
Sonnets. Pasadena, CA.: U. Sinclair, 1924. 39 p.
Mississippi. Gulfport, MS.: The Dixie Guide, 1963. [4] p.

SINGER, ANNA LILLIAN
Garden of Treasures. Placentia? CA.: n. p., 1952? [64] p.

SINGER, SARAH
After the Beginning. Dublin, N. H.: William L. Bauhan, 1975. 74 p.

SIPFLE, LOUISE
Capture That Song; A Sampler of Poems... New and Old, Inspired and Contrived. Evanston, IL.: Schori Press, 1974. 52 p.

SIPLE, JESSIE (ALLEN)
Roses n' Everything. Los Angeles: Gem Publishing Company, 1925. 3 p. ℓ., [9]-60, [2] p.
Lavender and Old Gold. Boston: R. G. Badger, 1931. 6 p., 1 ℓ., 7-62 p.

SIROTKIN, JEANNE
An Unzipped Dress. San Francisco, CA.: Golden Mountain Press, 1975. 33 p.

SISSON, MARY JEANNE
Familiar Is the Wind. Dallas, TX.: Story Book Press, 1952. 48 p.

SITTIG, SIGRID
Remember My Love. Chicago: Folio Press, 1952. 63 p.

SIVLEY, MARY
May I Come In? 2d ed. Dallas, TX.: Kaleidograph Press, 1951. 64 p.
Horns and Halos; A Measure of Pleasure. Chicago: Windfall Press, 1967. 48 p.

SKIDMORE, HARRIET M(ARIE)
Roadside Flowers: A Book of Verse. San Francisco: A. M. Robertson, 1903. 99 p.

SKILLERN, HELEN REGAN
Flames from a Candle. Caldwell, ID.: The Caxton Printers, Ltd., 1938. 64 p.

SKINNER, CONSTANCE LINDSAY (d. 1939)
Song of the Coast Dwellers. New York: Coward-McCann, 1930. ix, [1], 85 p.

SKLAREW, MYRA
In the Basket of the Blind. Cherry Valley, N.Y.: Cherry Valley Editions, 1975. unpaged.

SKOGSBERGH, HELGA
Songs of Pilgrimage. Chicago: Covenant Press, 1962. ix, 117, [1] p.

SLAPPEY, MARY McGOWAN (1914-)
Crossroads of Eternity. Detroit: Harlo Press, 1964. 5 p.ℓ., 49 p., 2 ℓ.

SLATER, ELEANOR see MARY ELEANOR, Mother (1903-)

SLATER, MARY (WHITE) (1870-)
...The Child Book. Philadelphia: Dorrance and Company, 1940. 148 p. (Contemporary poets of Dorrance, 202)
Collected Poems. New York: Exposition Press, 1953. 160 p.

SLOAN, EMILY EVA (1878-)
Ballads of the Plains. Denver, CO.: Great Western Pub. Co., 1905. 35 p.

SLOAN, JANE
Prairie Vagabond. New York: H. Harrison, 1939. 63 p.
Moments Apart. Francestown, N.H.: Golden Quill Press, 1967. 79 p.

SLOAN, PAULINE BENNETT
Random Rhymes. Dallas, TX.: Johnston Printing & Advertising Co., 1931. 4 p.ℓ., 13-68 p.

SLOANE, MARY HUMPHREYS
Strong Cables Rising. New York: E. P. Dutton and Company, Inc., 1942. 5 p.ℓ., 9-89 p.

SLOCUM, GRACE L.
On the Face of the Waters, and Other Poems. Boston: R. G. Badger, 1911. 64 p.

SLONIM, RUTH
London, an American Appreciation. Boston: Bruce Humphries, 1954. 64 p.
San Francisco; "The City" in Verse. Pullman, WA.: Washington State University Press, 1965. 4 p. ℓ., 80 p.

SLOSS, EDITH TYNDALE
Echoes of the Old Plantation. Philadelphia: n. p., 1947. 152 p.

SLY, BLANCHE CAMPBELL
Seasons Through. Boston: The Four Seas Company, 1925. 32 p.

SLYE, MAUD (1879-)
Songs and Solaces. Boston: The Stratford Company, 1934. 3 p. ℓ., x, 416 p.
I in the Wind, Symphony No. 1, and Minor Songs. Boston: The Stratford Company, 1936. 2 p. ℓ., ix, 397 p.

SMALL, ELIZABETH FORESMAN
Ballads of Billy and Betty. Chicago: n. p., 1926. 1 p. ℓ., 5-38 p.

SMALLWOOD, VIVIAN
Window to the South. Mobile, AL.: n. p., 1972. xii, 87 p.

SMARIDGE, NORAH
What a Silly Thing to Do. Nashville, TN.: Abingdon Press, 1967. [40] p.
Teacher's Pest. New York: Hawthorn Books, 1968. [32] p.
Scary Things. Nashville, TN.: Abingdon Press, 1969. [40] p.
Your Five Gifts. Norwalk, CT.: C. R. Gibson Co., 1969. [25] p.
Raggedy Andy; The I Can Do It, You Can Do It Book. Racine, WI.: Golden Press, 1973. 20 p.
You Know Better Than That. Nashville, TN.: Abingdon Press, 1973. [32] p.

SMERDON, MARY E.
...Reveries. Philadelphia: Dorrance & Company, Inc., 1935. 50 p. (Contemporary poets of Dorrance, 133)

SMITH, AGNES M.
Down Memory Lane, Poems.... New York: William-Frederick Press, 1945. 16 p.
Words from My Heart. Milwaukee, WI.: Editions Unlimited, 1955. iv, 142 ℓ.

SMITH, AGNES (SMITH) (1862-)
Gethsemane, and Other Poems. San Diego, CA.: The Creller Press, 1915. 69 p.

SMITH, ALICE RAYMOND
Rhymes. Schenectady, N.Y.: n.p., 1947. 1 vol.

SMITH, ALICIA KAY (1913-)
Over the Moon's Edge. Medford, MA.: C. A. A. Parker, 1938. viii p., 2 ℓ., [3]-79 p. (Verse for children.)
Only in Whispers. Portland, ME.: Falmouth Pub. House, 1947. 4 p. ℓ., 45 p.

SMITH, ALLISON PARISH
The Friendly Kindly Man, and Other Poems. Newton, CT.: Press Bee Pub. Co., 1933. 18 p.

SMITH, ANITA SPEER
A Word in Its Own Tongue. Indianapolis, IN.: n.p., 1965. vi p., 1 ℓ., 45 p.

SMITH, ANNIE BURNETT (SWAN)
Songs of Memory and Hope. New York, Boston: H. M. Caldwell, 1911. 94 p.

SMITH, Mrs. ARTHUR PARKS
Questioned Hours. Springfield, MA.: n.p., 1911. 7-69 p.

SMITH, BERTHA WILCOX
A Bridge Is There. Pittsburgh? PA.: n.p., 1968. 80 p.

SMITH, BESS FOSTER
The Checkered Tablecloth. Caldwell, ID.: The Caxton Printers, Ltd., 1937. 111, [1] p.

SMITH, BETTY HUNTER
Flood-Gates, A Book of Verse. Boston: R. G. Badger, 1931. vi p., 2 ℓ., 3-145 p.
A Door to Happy Land. New York: Vantage Press, 1968. 48 p. (Verse for children.)

SMITH, BEULAH FENDERSON
Heartwood; Poems. Coral Gables, FL.: Wake-Brook House, 1964. 76 p.

SMITH, CAROLINE SPRAGUE
Tarry With Me, and Other Verses. New York: Printed for the author at the Cheltenham Press, 1909. x p., 2 ℓ., 3-185 p., [1] p.

SMITH, CAROLYN B.
A Little Book of American Verse. Englewood, N.J.: Englewood Press, 1920. 3 p. ℓ., 5-73 p.

SMITH, CLARA BELLE
Life's Musicale. Emory University, Atlanta, GA.: Banner Press, 1941. 40 p. (Verse craft series)

SMITH CORA ULTRA (COVIATT) (1901-)

If the Shoe Fits, Wear It. New York: Carlton Press, 1962. 143 p.

Through Hell in a Hand Basket. New York: Carlton Press, 1963. 144 p.

The Morning and the Evening. New York: Carlton Press, 1967. 176 p.

Ramrod. Charleston, IL.: Prairie Press Books, 1970. viii p., 1ℓ., 141 p.

Smitty's Shorts. Charleston, IL.: Prairie Press Books, 1972. ix, 141 p.

SMITH, DAISY F. DAVES

Half-Breed; Poems. New York: Exposition Press, 1956. 63 p.

A Fig and a Fither. New York: Carlton Press, 1967. 64 p.

SMITH, DAISY LYNNE (1864-)

"My Jim," and Other War Poems. Tacoma, WA.: Allen & Lamborn Printing Co., 1917. 14 p.

SMITH, DELPHIA

Along Life's Way, Poems. New York: Greenwich Book Publishers, 1961. 132 p.

So Swift the Night. Roma: Centro Studi e Scambi Internazionali, 1972. 16 p. (Quaderni di poesia)

To Catch a Dream Varied. Kanona, N.Y.: J & C Transcripts, 1973. 54 p.

Bright Remnants. Kanona, N.Y.: J & C Transcripts, 1974. 54 p.

Brocade and Denim. Kanona, N.Y.: J & C Transcripts, 1974. 54 p.

Out of the Mist. Kanona, N.Y.: J & C Transcripts, 1974. 54 p.

SMITH, DOLLILEE DAVIS

Today Is Mine! Dallas, TX.: The Kaleidograph Press, 1943. xiii p., 1 ℓ., 17-101 p.

SMITH, EDITH LIVINGSTON

A Garden of Yesterday. New York: E. P. Dutton & Company, 1921. 4 p.ℓ., 20 p.

SMITH, EDYTHE MAE

The Royal Visitor, and Other Poems. New York: Vantage Press, 1962. 48 p.

SMITH, ELEANOR SANDS

St. Martin's Summer. Manchester, ME.: Falmouth Pub. House, 1952. 70 p.

Everywhere Is Here and Lonesome. Manchester? ME.: n.p., 1959. 49 p.

SMITH, ELINOR HOWLAND
Harbor Lights. Dallas, TX.: Story Book Press, 1951. 48 p.

SMITH, ELOISE LANE
Historical Cocktales. New York: Vantage Press, 1963. 44 p.

SMITH, EMMA FRANCES LEE
The Fields of Peace, Poems and Ballads. Boston: R. G. Badger, 1919. 5 p., 1 ℓ., 7-124 p.

SMITH, ETHEL COLWELL
Courage Is Yours, and Other Poems. New York: The Hobson Book Press, 1947. 7 p. ℓ., 77, [1] p.

SMITH, ETHEL L. WORSLEY
Idle Hour Rhymes. Mendota, IL.: n. p., 1923. 4 p. ℓ., 13-62 p.

SMITH, EUGENIE MARIE (RAYE) (1871-)
The Battle of Brooklyn. Richmond Hill, N. Y.: E. M. Raye-Smith, 1913. 12 p.

SMITH, FRANCES LAURENCE
Wishful Thinking: Poems. Baltimore, MD.: Garland Press, 1953.

SMITH, GEORGINE (WETHERILL)
Poems and Paintings. New York: The Ram Press, 1953. 43 p.

SMITH, GOLDIE (CAPERS)
Sword of Laughter. Dallas, TX.: The Kaleidograph Press, 1932. 7 p. ℓ., 17-102 p.
Gardens Under Snow. Dallas, TX.: The Kaleidograph Press, 1942. xi p., 1 ℓ., 15-81 p.
Deep in This Furrow. Dallas, TX.: Kaleidograph Press, 1950. xi, 78 p.

SMITH, GRACE FRENCH
...Trumpet Call. New York: H. Harrison, 1935. 64 p.

SMITH, GRACE NOLL
...The Apple Is Eaten.... Philadelphia: Dorrance & Co., 1947. 61 p.

SMITH, GRACE TURNER
Clippings. New York: L. N. Green-Leach, 1930. 52 p.

SMITH, GWYNDOLYN
Blue Mist and Moonglow. Dallas, TX.: Story Book Press, 1953. 39 p.

SMITH, HARRIET G. (1894-)
Fire and Sleet and Candle-Lighte. San Antonio, TX.: Naylor Co., 1970. xii, 87 p.

SMITH, HAZEL E.
Across the Hills of Memories. New York: William-Frederick Press, 1947. 61 p.

SMITH, HAZEL LITTLEFIELD (1889-)
Mortal Harvest. Long Beach, CA.: Royal Press Printers, 1943. 57 p.
A Flame of Faith. Tujungs, CA.: C. L. Anderson, 1952. 74 p.

SMITH, HEATHER
Watch Out Brother, I'm Here! Berkeley, CA.: Shameless Hussy Press, 1971. 3 p. ℓ., 32 p.

SMITH, HELEN CATHARINE (1903-)
Stars in My Eyes. Dallas, TX.: Story Book Press, 1954. 35 p.

SMITH, HELEN ROGERS
The Call of God and Other Poems. n. p., 1965. 32 p.

SMITH, HILDA WORTHINGTON
Poems. Washington, D. C.: Merkle Press, 1964. xii, 106 p.

SMITH, J. PAULINE
"Exceeding Riches" and Other Verse. Detroit: n. p., 1922. xi p., 1 ℓ., 15-89 p.

SMITH, JEAN MOORE
Stormy Petrel. New York: Carlton Press, 1962. 8 p. ℓ., 47 p.

SMITH, JEANIE OLIVER (DAVIDSON)
Sonnets of Life. Boston: R. G. Badger, 1911. 71 p.

SMITH, JENNIE N.
Isles of Paisley. New York: H. Vinal, 1928. 7 p. ℓ., 102 p., 1 ℓ.

SMITH, JUANITA T.
A Bloom of Youth. Alvarado, TX.: Bulletin Print, 1900. 93 p.

SMITH, JULIET C.
Memorial Days and Other Poems. New York: Whittaker & Ray, 1901. 44 p.

SMITH, KATHARINE NEAL
"Poetry and Song." Columbus, OH.: F. J. Heer Pub. Co., 1946. 80 p.

SMITH, KATHARINE SCHOLL
October Garden; Poems. New York: Comet Press Books, 1959. 5 p. ℓ., 47 p.

SMITH, LATTA C.
Songs of a Young Heart; Poems. New York: Exposition Press, 1958. 47 p.

SMITH, LEAH WHITCANAK
From My Garden of Verse. Kansas City, MO.: Beacon Hill Press, 1956. 79 p.

SMITH, LOTTIE C.
Yuletide Musings. St. Mary's, WV.: Oracle Printing Office, 1920. 14 ℓ.

SMITH, LUCY COLEMAN
Linsey-Woolsey. Dallas, TX.: Story Book Press, 1948. 55 p.

SMITH, LUCY ELIOT
No Middle Ground; Poems. Philadelphia: Writer's Division, Phila. Council of the Arts, Sciences and Professions, 1952. 5 p. ℓ., 30 p.

SMITH, LUCY HAHN KING [Full Name: Lucy Maude Hahn King (Cunningham) Smith.]
Cadences. Cedar Rapids, IA.: The Torch Press, 1929. 175 p.

SMITH, LUCY (HYMPHREY) (1869-1939)
Memories and Poems. n. p.: Priv. Print., 1940. 2 p. ℓ., [3]-73 p.

SMITH, MARGARET HESS
The Cantos. Inglewood, CA.: n. p., 195-? 51 ℓ.

SMITH, MARGARET L.
Bittersweet Branches. Burlington, VT.: Printed by the Lane Press, 1946. 7 p. ℓ., 3-57 p.
Creative Poems. New York: Vantage Press, 1974. 47 p.

SMITH, MARIAN FLOSTER
The Other Self; Poems. Poland, OH.: Gold Seal Publications, 1952. 63 p.

SMITH, MARION COUTHOUY (1853-)
The Electric Spirit, and Other Poems. Boston: R. G. Badger, 1906. 94 p.
The Final Star, Poems. New York: J. T. White & Co., 1918. 110 p.
Sphinx of Flight. New York: H. Vinal, 1925. 3 p. ℓ., 43, [1] p.

SMITH, MARION ROBERTA MERRICK (1921-)
Prairie Child. Red Deer, Alta: Red Deer College Press, 1974. 38 p.

SMITH, MARJORIE BERTRAM
A Native's Notions; Poems. Chautauqua, N.Y.: n.p., 1953. 3 p. ℓ., 33 p.
No Ordinary Fire. Dallas, TX.: Triangle Pub. Co., 1962. 98 p.
The Road; A Collection of Poems. Kanona, N.Y.: J. & C. Transcripts, 1965. 3 p. ℓ., 50 p.
Letter from Chautauqua. Mayville, N.Y.: Chautauqua Press, 1967. 74 p.

SMITH, MARY CHAPIN
Earth Songs. Boston: R. G. Badger, 1910. 1 p. ℓ., 5-125 p.

SMITH, MARY ELIZABETH (1888-)
There Have Been Dreams. Boston: B. Humphries, 1935. 101 p.

SMITH, MARY FORBES
The Alabaster Box. Dallas, TX.: Story Book Press, 1950. 58 p.

SMITH, MAURINE
The Keen Edge. Evanston, IL.: M. Wheeler, 1921.

SMITH, MAY RILEY (1824?-)
The Lost Christmas and Other Poems. New York: E. P. Dutton & Co., 1901. 2 p. ℓ., [vii]-viii, [9]-129 p.

SMITH, MILDRED deWEIR see WATKINS, MILDRED deWEIR SMITH (1929-)

SMITH, NANA B.
Put My Tears in a Bottle. New York: Vantage Press, 1965. 64 p.

SMITH, NANCY
Contradictions. Burney, CA.: Hughes Printing, 1975.

SMITH, NANNETTE CARTER
Until the Night, Poems. Prairie City, IL.: Decker Press, 1948. 72 p.

SMITH, PATTI
Seventh Heaven. Yeadon, N.Y.: Telegraph Books, 1972. 47 p.
Witt. New York: Gotham Book Mart, 1973. 45 p.
Rimbaud. n.p.: Dot Books, 1974.

SMITH, SARAH HATHAWAY (BIXBY)
My Sagebrush Garden. Cedar Rapids, IA.: The Torch Press, 1924. 84 p.
Paesar; A Second Book of California Verse. Cedar Rapids, IA.: The Torch Press, 1926. 84 p.
The Bending Tree. Los Angeles: J. Murray, 1933. 87, [1] p.

SMITH, THEA HAGEN
Wind in the Trees. San Antonio, TX.: Carleton Printing Co., 1946. 48 p.
Golden Links. San Diego? CA.: Hecht Printing Co., 1955. 67 p.

SMITH, TINA B.
In Honor of My Mother. New York: Pyramid Press, 1940. 4 p. ℓ., 11-111 p.

SMITH, VERA KEEVERS
Poems of a Busy Mother. Hartford, CT.: Bond Press, 1959. vi, 46 p.

SMYTH, AMEY
Masks and Gypsy Music and Other Poems.... Philadelphia: Poetry Publishers, 1937. 36 p.
Shadows and Windy Places. A Collection of Verse. Philadelphia: Poetry Publishers, 1938. 36 p.
Songs of the Isles and Other Poems. New York: H. Harrison, 1940. 3-31 p.

SMYTH, FLORIDA (WATTS) (1873-)
Over the Hills and Far Away. Boston: The Poet Lore Company, 1913. 137 p.
Only on the West Wind. Middlebury, VT.: The Bread Loaf Printers, Middlebury College Press, 1940. ix, 21 p.
High Hill, Long River. Wilmington, DE.: Wilmington Poetry Society & Delaware Writers, Inc., 1951. 40 p.

SNEAD, HELEN (OLSEN)
My Kinsmen: All Danes. Lynchburg, VA.: J. P. Bell Co., 1961. 4 p. ℓ., 39, [1] p.
Standing Here. Kanona, N.Y.: J. & C. Transcripts, 1971. 29 p.

SNEDEKER, LUELLA G.
Thoughts Held Dear. New York: The Poets Press, 1942. 32 p.

SNELLING, FLORENCE D.
The Hidden Garden. Boston: The Ranger Company, 1916. 7 p. ℓ., 3-112 p.

SNOW, EDITH
Winter Tree. Auburn, CA.: Blue Oak Press, 1968. 78 p.
The Water Mill. Roseville, CA.: Blue Oak Press, 1971. 88 p.

SNOW, JANE ELLIOT
Bits of Verse. Cleveland, OH.: The Electric Printing Co., 1916. [16] p.

SNYDER, ELIZABETH JACQUES
Leaves. Seattle, WA.: Printed by Active Press, 1940. 77, [1] p.

SNYDER, ELOISE
Living Fire. Dallas, TX.: Story Book Press, 1953. 46 p.

SNYDER, EMILY EVELETH
Spin-Offs. Port Chester, N.Y.: Gothic Press, 1969. 27 ℓ. 7 pl. in folder.
Therefore; Poems. Rye? NY.: n.p., 1969? 21 ℓ. 6 pl. in folder.
The Hammond Swamp. Port Chester, N.Y.: Gothic Press, 1970. 48 p.
Patterns. Concord, N.H.: Evans Printing Co., 1971. 30 ℓ. 6 pl. in folder.

SNYDER, JUNE WINONA
Whispering Winds. Indianapolis?: n.p., 1928. 48 p.

SNYDER, MARIAN K.
Poetic Nuggets. New York: Carlton Press, 1965. 111 p.

SNYDER, MAUDE ALEXANDER
Near to Nature in the North Country. Watertown, N.Y.: n.p., 1928. 55, [1] p.

SNYDER, SARAH L.
Letters to My Friends. Brooklyn, N.Y.: Brooklyn Eagle Job Printing, 1915. 67 p.

SNYDER, ZILPHA KEATLEY
Today Is Saturday. New York: Atheneum, 1969. 56 p.

SOESTER, KATE
Woodnotes and Worship. Boston: B. Humphries, 1948. 77 p.

SOLEY, ISABELLA M.
Marian, a Prisoner's Soliloquy; A Temperance Poem. Pittsburgh, PA.: n.p., 1909. 47 p.

SOLOW, SOPHIE
A Reed for Pan. New York: Blue Faun Publications, 1924. 49 p.

SOLT, MARY ELLEN (1920-)
Flowers in Concrete. Bloomington, IN.: Designed and printed by John Dearstyne. Design Program, Fine Arts Dept., Indiana University, 1966. [29] p.
A Trilogy of Rain. n.p.: Priv. Print., 1970.
Eyewards. New York: White Rose Press, 1972.

SOLUM, SJANNA (1906-)
Lodestone. Chicago: Dierkes Press, 1950. 48 p.

SOMERS, SUZANNE
Touch Me. Los Angeles, CA.: Nash Pub., 1973. 64 p.

SOMERSET, JOYCE FLANAGAN
Leafy Heritage. Emory University, Atlanta, GA.: Banner Press, 1957. 77 p.

SONE, VIOLET WEST
Finger of Earth (Live Oak Peninsula) and Other Poems. Dallas, TX.: The Kaleidograph Press, 1942. x p., 1 ℓ., 13-68 p.

SORRELS, CLEO
Quest. Fayetteville, AR.: Rupert Publications, 1965. 32 p.

SORRELLS, HELEN
Seeds as They Fall; Poems. Nashville, TN.: Vanderbilt University Press, 1971. x, 85 p.

SOULE, BERTHA LOUISE (1863-)
The Joyous Traveler and Other Poems. New York: G. P. Putnam's Sons, 1934. iv p., 1 ℓ., 7-62 p.
Where No Fear Was. Portland, ME.: Printed by the Southworth-Anthoensen Press, 1941. ix, 66 p.

SOULE, FLOY DeVORE (PERFECT)
Told in a Patio. Boston: Christopher Pub. House, 1956. 180 p.

SOULE, HELOISE
Heartsease and Rue; Poems. Boston: R. G. Badger, 1904. 38 p.

SOUTHERLAND, MYRTELLA
Along the Gypsy Trail; A Book of Verse. Boston: The Stratford Company, 1971. 8 p. ℓ., 141 p.

SOUTHWICK, JESSIE ELDRIDGE (1865-)
Meditations in Verse. Boston: The Everett Press, 1913. 17 numb. ℓ.

SOUTHWORTH, GRACIA (1833-)
The Song of a Robin. Albion, MI.: n. p., 1900. 55 p.

SPANG, MARY LOUISE
Sounds and Silences; Poems. New York: Vantage Press, 1957. 48 p.

SPANGENBERG, FANNY (ILGENFRITZ) (1838-)
The Forest Land of Penn. Boston: R. G. Badger, 1909. 154 p.

SPARKS, CAROLYN
Conquests, 1918-1939; A Poem on the Search for Peace. New York: Exposition Press, 1952. 94 p.

SPARKS, MARY JANE
Wayside Fancies. Marion, IL.: The Author, 1900. 104 p.

SPARKS, VERNA
Come with Me to the Garden; Poems. New York: Exposition Press, 1963. 80 p.

SPARROW, LOUISE KIDDER
Narrative Poems, from Journal in Verse. Boston: Branden Press, 1970. 100 p.
Basket of Pansies. Kanona, N. Y.: J. & C. Transcripts, 1974. 15 p.

SPARROW, MARY O.
Songs by the Wayside. Harwich, MA.: Printed at Moody's Print Shop, 1930. [33] p.

SPATES, VIRGINIA
Wings Against the Wind. Atlanta, GA.: E. Hartsock, The Bozart Press, 1930. 68 p.
Dust from the Heels of Pegasus.... Dallas, TX.: The Kaleidograph Press, 1934. [20] p.
Enchanted Window. Dallas, TX.: The Kaleidograph Press, 1934. xi p., 1 ℓ., 15-112 p.

SPAULDING, FRANCESCA di MARIA PALMER
Voyager, and Other Poems. Piedmont-on-the-Hudson, N. Y.: n. p., 1912. 28 p.

SPAULDING, LOTTIE KINCHER
Hash; Poems. New York: Exposition Press, 1961. 61 p.

SPEAR, HELEN MAHLON (1886-)
The Private Life of a Public School Teacher. Philadelphia: Dorrance, 1975. xi, 163 p.

SPEARMAN, AURELIA L. (PRATT)
What Christ Means to Us; A Book of Religious Verse. New York: Carlton Press, 1964. 49 p.

SPEARMAN, DORIS WARREN
Angel in the House; A Book of Poems. Los Angeles, CA.: Spearman Pub. Co., 1966? [19] p.
Angels with Me. Los Angeles, CA.: Spearman Pub. Co., 1966? [12] ℓ.
Under Angel Wings. Los Angeles, CA.: Spearman Pub. Co., 1966. [15] p.
Verse for Little Angels. Los Angeles, CA.: Spearman Pub. Co., 1966? 12 ℓ.

SPEARS, MARGARET SKELLETT
Sunshine and Shadows. Philadelphia: Dorrance, 1971. 59 p.

SPECTOR, PEARL
The White Cloud, and Other Poem-Songs. New York: The Avondale Press, 1928. vii, 62 p.

SPEED, KATE MAUD (GREENER)
The Honeysuckle. Toledo, OH.: Alpha Publishing Co., 1914. 7 p. ℓ., 77 p.

SPEER, CLARA AIKEN
Sonnets for Eve, and Other Poems. New York: William-Frederick Press, 1952. 46 p.

SPENCE, ALMA (WOLDERT)
Southward Call. Dallas, TX.: Wilkinson Pub. Co., 1953. 130 p.

SPENCE, FLORENCE EVELYN
Glints. New York: n.p., 1922. 14 p.

SPENCE, IRENE
In Two Different Worlds We Live and Love. New York: Vantage Press, 1968. 87 p.

SPENCER, LILIAN (WHITE)
Arrowheads. New York: The Parade Pub. Co., 1929. 64 p.

SPENCER, MARGARET FRANCES
My Book of Catholic Poems. New York: Vantage Press, 1952. viii, 38 p.

SPENCER, MARTHA LINSLEY
Remembered Years, Collected Poems. Hartford? CT.: n.p., 1954. 7 p. ℓ., 175 p.

SPEYER, LEONORA (VON STOSCH) (1872-1956)
A Canopic Jar. New York: E. P. Dutton & Company, 1921. ix p., 1 ℓ., 92 p., 1 ℓ.
...Fiddler's Farewell. New York: A. A. Knopf, 1926. 113 p., 4 ℓ.
...Naked Heel.... New York, London: A. A. Knopf, 1931. xiv, 79 p., 1 ℓ.
Slow Wall, Poems New and Selected. New York: A. A. Knopf, 1939. ix, 140 p., 1 ℓ.
Slow Wall, Poems; Together with Nor Without Music. New York: A. A. Knopf, 1951. 235 p.

SPICER, ANNE HIGGINSON
Songs of the Skokie, and Other Verse. Chicago: R. F. Seymour, 1917. 169 p.
The Last Crusade. New York: J. T. White & Co., 1918. 128 p.
A Cookshire Lad. Chicago: S. Hinrichsen, 1922. 13-47 p.

SPICER, MYRA JANET LUNDERS
From My Heart; Poems. New York: Exposition Press, 1968. 46 p.

SPIEGELHALTER, MARIE A.
Star Dust. Boston: R. G. Badger, 1926. 43 p.

SPIEGNER, LUCILE MARSHALL
Fleeting Fancies. Boston: Meador Publishing Co., 1934. 80 p.

SPIERS, MARY BUCKNER
The Giant of the Blue Ridge, and Other Poems. Washington: The Neale Publishing Company, 1903. 96 p.

SPINGARN, AMY (EINSTEIN) (1883-)
New Houses; Twelve Poems. Amenia, N.Y.: Priv. Print. at the Troutbeck Press, 1925. 1 p. ℓ., 5-12 p. (Troutbeck leaflets, no. 7)
Humility and Pride. New York: Harcourt, Brace and Company, 1926. ix, 88 p.

SPIROU, EVELYN (1954-)
Nonstop to London. San Antonio, TX.: Naylor Co., 1975. 37 p.

SPIVACK, KATHLEEN
Flying Inland. Garden City, N.Y.: Doubleday, 1973. 93 p.
The Jane Poems. Garden City, N.Y.: Doubleday, 1974. xiii, 81 p.

SPIVAK, JENNIE CHARSKY
Lays. Denver, CO.: Big Mountain Press, 1961. 80 p.

SPIVEY, AMELLA JOSEPHINE
Memory Gold. Dallas, TX.: Story Book Press, 1949. 74 p.

SPOONER, ELLA BROWN (JACKSON) (1880-)
This Broad Land, Poems. New York: Exposition Press, 1949. 96 p.

SPOOR, ALETHA PHILLIPS
Other Ways and Other Days. Kalamazoo, MI.: Phil. Glover Publishing House, 1928. 112 p.

SPOOR, MARION ELLIOTT
Miniatures of Oaxaca; Poems of Mexico. New York: Exposition Press, 1955. 64 p.

SPRAGUE, HARRIET APPLETON
The Winds, and Other Poems. Milwaukee, WI.: Morehouse Pub. Co., 1923. vii, 61 p.

SPRAGUE, LILA (FROST)
A Bunch of Immortelles and Other Poems. Grand Rapids, MI.: Tradesman Company, 1900. [27] p.
Shadow People. Atlanta, GA.: By invitation only, J. B. Frost, 1913. 6 p. ℓ., 11-105 p.

SPRINGER, LOIS ELSIE
Chimes, a Collection of Bell Poems. Elgin, IL.: J. F. Cuneo Co., 1949. 110 p.

SPROTTE, LILLIAN ANN
Poetry for Lonely People. Philadelphia: Dorrance, 1967. 36 p. (Contemporary poets of Dorrance, 653)
Tragedy in Poetry. Philadelphia: Dorrance, 1968. 36 p. (Contemporary poets of Dorrance, 680)

SPROULE, DOROTHY (CORRIGAN)
The Gold of Dawn. New York: H. Harrison, 1938. 109 p.
A Garland of Orchids, Dedicated to Dorothy Sproule. New York: Banner Press, 1941? 2 p. ℓ., 3-19 p.

SPURLOCK, LIZZIE GIBBS
Poems. Oklahoma: n. p., 1931. 23 p.

SQUIRE, ANNETTE DAVISSON
...The Pass of Oaks. Philadelphia: Dorrance and Company, 1937. 74 p. (Contemporary poets of Dorrance, 158)

STAATS, MABEL MEADOWS
Bright Quarry; Poems. New York: Exposition Press, 1962. 63 p.

STACY, BELLE TOOLEY
Echoes of Life. Ogdensburg, N. Y.: The Ogdensburg Advance Co., 1933. 3 p. ℓ., 120 p.

STAFF, SUSAN
From the Fire. Pittsburgh, PA.: KNOW, Inc., 1972. 58 p. (Contemporary women poets series)

STAHL, MELITTA HEIDRICK
Moods. Dallas, TX.: Story Book Press, 1951. 58 p.

STAIRS, GORDON see AUSTIN, MARY (HUNTER)

STALEY, EMMA L.
Verses. Chicago: Priv. Print. R. R. Donnelley & Sons Co., 1938. 3 p. ℓ., 45, [1] p.
________. Chicago?: n. p., 1956. viii, 83, [1] p.

STAM, ELIZABETH ALDEN (SCOTT) (1906-1934)
The Faith of Betty Scott Stam in Poem and Verse. New York: Fleming H. Revell Co., 1938. 2 p. ℓ., iii-x, 129 p.
The Poems and Verse of Betty Scott Stam. Shanghai: Kelly & Walsh, Limited, 1938. 2 p. ℓ., iii-x, 129, [1] p.

STAMPER, GEORGIA MacSENTRE (1912-)
House of Hope. Emory University, Atlanta, GA.: Banner Press, 1938. 52 p. (Verse craft series)

Into the Room Beyond. Dallas, TX.: Story Book Press, 1949. 42 p.
Fulfillment. Emory University, Atlanta, GA.: Banner Press, 1950. 57 p.

STANFIELD, CLARIBEL LEONTINE see STANFIELD, LEONTINE (1866-)

STANFIELD, LEONTINE [STANFIELD, CLARIBEL LEONTINE]
Leontine Stanfield's Book of Verse. New York: J. S. Ogilvie Publishing Company, 1906. 9, [2], 6-61, 126, 45 p.

STANFORD, ANN (1916-)
In Narrow Bound. Gunnison, CO.: Swallow, 1943. 52 p.
The White Bird. Denver, CO.: Swallow, 1949. 58 p.
The Weathercock. San Jose, CA.: Talisman Press, 1956. 60 p.
Magellan; A Poem to Be Read by Several Voices. San Jose, CA.: Talisman Press, 1958. 86 p., 1 ℓ.
The White Bird. New York: Viking Press, 1966. 58 p.
The Weathercock. New York: Viking Press, 1966. x, 60 p.
The Descent. New York: Viking Press, 1970. xi, 83 p.

STANG, SARA KENNEDY
Tribute to Trifles, Poems. New York: Exposition Press, 1956. 72 p.

STANLEY, ADA M.
Morning Songs and Evening Vespers.... Cambridge: n.p., 1910. 4 ℓ., [3]-252 p.

STANLEY, MARGUERITE
Wind-Blown Petals. Emory University, Atlanta, GA.: Banner Press, 1947. 68 p.
Fifty Steps to the Moon. Emory University, Atlanta, GA.: Banner Press, 1952. 60 p.
The Highway Ahead. Atlanta, GA.: Banner Press, 1960. 66 p.

STANLEY, MAY [FINCH, MAY STANLEY]
A Minnesota Christmas, and Other Verses. Duluth, MN.: The U. F. Collier Press, 1915. 3 p. ℓ., 9-59 p., [1] p.

STANSBURY, MARY A.
The Path of Years. Appleton, WI.: n.p., 1907. 182 p.

STANTON, ADELE TOWNSEND
Poems and Sonnets of Adele Townsend Stanton. Cambridge: Printed at the Riverside Press, 1910. viii p., 1 ℓ., 64 numb. ℓ., 1 ℓ.

STANTON, MAURA (1948-)
Snow on Snow. New Haven, CT.: Yale University Press, 1975. xv, 62 p. (Yale Series of Younger Poets, v. 70)

STAPLER, HELEN L.
The Race, and Other Poems. New York: Pageant Press, 1954. 4 p. ℓ., 69 p.

STARBIRD, KAYE
Speaking of Cows, and Other Poems. Philadelphia: Lippincott, 1960. 70 p.
Don't Ever Cross a Crocodile, and Other Poems. Philadelphia: Lippincott, 1963. 62 p.
A Snail's Failure Socially, and Other Poems, Mostly About People. Philadelphia: Lippincott, 1966. 53 p.
The Pheasant on Route Seven. Philadelphia: Lippincott, 1968. 74 p.

STARBUCK, MARY ELIZA (1856-)
Nantucket, and Other Verses. New York: J. J. Little & Ives Company, 1911. 18 ℓ.
Nantucket, and Other Verses. Nantucket, MA.: n.p., 1924. 3 p. ℓ., 62 p.

STARKWEATHER, PAULINE (1885-)
When I Consider; Mid-Century Verse. New York: Pageant Press, 1959. 62 p.

STARR, ESTHER
Think to Myself Chapters. Boston: R. G. Badger, 1919. 46 p.

STARRING, ANNA MULLETT FARRAR
Thought Rays. Detroit: The Chas. F. May Co., 191-? 72 p.

STAVELY, MARGARET
Doors to a Narrow House. New York: The Hobson Book Press, 1946. vii p., 2 ℓ., 107 p.

STEARNS, FLORENCE (DICKINSON) (1883-)
Strange Dimension. New York: G. P. Putnam's Sons, 1938. x p., 1 ℓ., 13-94 p.

STECHER, GRACE NIXON
Wing-Beats. Portland, ME.: Falmouth Publishing House, 1940. 3 p. ℓ., 3-41 p.
Blossoms in the Wilderness. Mill Valley, CA.: Wings Press, 1953. 72 p.

STEELE, AGNES ELIZABETH
My Hour of Solitude; A Collection of Verses and Meditations. New York: Carlton Press, 1962. 4 p. ℓ., 63 p.

STEELE, FANNIE B.
The Pentateuch in Verse. Dansville, N.Y.: n.p., 1927. 47 p.
Life's Sunshine and Shadows. Boston: The Christopher Publishing House, 1929. 5 p. ℓ., [9]-92 p.

STEELE, MAUDE
Scenes and Dreams. New York: Pageant Press, 1957. 87 p.
Life's Golden Sunset. New York: Pageant Press, 1958. 133 p.

STEELE, ROSE YARBROUGH
Rainbow in the Sky. Dallas, TX.: The Story Book Press, 1947. 64 p.
The Wheel of Life. Dallas, TX.: The Story Book Press, 1947. 40 p.

STEEN, FRANCES COOK
Life Waves. Aledo, IL.: The Aledo Democrat Publishing Co., 1922. 125 p., [1] p.
Along the Way. Garden City, N.Y.: Doubleday, Doran & Co., 1931. 56, [2] p.

STEEVES, CATHERINE DUNLAP
From a Young Girl's Diary, Poems. New York: The William-Frederick Press, 1945. 15, [1] p.

STEGEMAN, THELMA I.
Seasonal Reflections. New York: Vantage Press, 1968. 106 p.

STEILER, IDA
Edelweiss and Alprose and Other Poems. Seattle, WA.: n.p., 1920.

STEIN, ANNA WOLTER
This I Ask. San Antonio, TX.: Naylor Co., 1966. vi, 50 p.

STEIN, EVALEEN (1863-1923)
Among the Trees Again. Indianapolis: The Bowen-Merrill Company, 1902. 5 p. ℓ., 90 p.

STEIN, GERTRUDE (1874-1946)
Tender Buttons: Objects, Food, Rooms. New York: Claire Marie, 1914. 1 ℓ., [1-8], 9-78, [79-80] p., 1 ℓ.
Have They Attacked Mary. He Giggled. (A Political Caricature). West Chester, PA.: Horace F. Temple, 1917. 1 ℓ., [1-4], 5-14 p.
Before the Flowers of Friendship Faded Friendship Faded. Paris: Plain Edition 27, Rue de Fleurus, 1931. 1 p. ℓ., 33, [1] p.
Prothalamium. Culver, IN.: Joyous Guard Press, 1939. 4 ℓ.
Kisses Can. Pawlett, VT?: The Banyan Press, 1947. 2 ℓ.
Two (Hitherto unpublished) Poems. New York: The Gotham Book Mart, 1948. 4 ℓ.
Bee Time Vine, and Other Pieces, 1913-1927. New Haven, CT.: Yale University Press, 1953. xii, 204 p. (Vol. 3, Yale ed. of the Unpublished Writings of Gertrude Stein)
Stanzas in Meditation and Other Poems, 1929-1933. New Haven, CT.: Yale University Press, 1956. xxiv, 298 p. (Vol. 6, Yale ed. of the Unpublished Writings of Gertrude Stein)

STEINBERGH, JUDITH
Marshmallow Worlds. New York: Grosset & Dunlap, 1972. 77 p.

STEINFELDT, ELEANOR LUETCKE
Petals. San Antonio, TX.: The Naylor Co., 1940. xi p., 2 ℓ., [3]-43 p.

STEINHAUER, LILLIAN
Poems. New York: Greenwich Book Publishers, 1961. 59 p.

STEINMETZ, MARGARET BIRD
Leaves of Life for Daily Inspiration. New York, Cincinnati: The Abingdon Press, 1914. 384 p.

STELLING, MARY ELLEN (TAYLOR) (1915-)
Peachtree Postscripts. Dallas, TX.: Story Book Press, 1948. 44 p.
Ridgewood Ramblings. Dallas, TX.: Story Book Press, 1949. 40 p.
Partial Payment. Francestown, N.H.: Golden Quill Press, 1958. 78 p.

STEMBRIDGE, JANE
Don't Ask Me to Sing if You Don't Want to Hear; Some Clues to What's Going on These Days. Selected Poems. New York: Seabury Press, 1968. 16 p.
I Play Flute, and Other Poems. New York: Seabury Press, 1968. 128 p.

STEPHAN, MARION (MORRIS)
Dragonfly Wings. Philadelphia: Dorrance, 1958. 63 p. (Contemporary poets of Dorrance, 501)

STEPHAN, RUTH WALGREEN (1910-)
Prelude to Poetry. Lima: Editorial Luman, 1946. 57 p., 1 ℓ.
Various Poems: Three Groups, Songs and Exercises, Daitokuji Poems [and] Love's Progress. New York: Gotham Book Mart, 1963. 77 p.

STEPHENS, KATE
Delphic Kansas. Woodstock, N.Y.: The Maverick Press, 1911. [20] p.

STEPHENS, LEILA
Enthralled. Emory University, Atlanta, GA.: Banner Press, 1956. 76 p. (Verse craft series)

STEPHENS, PAULINE ELEANOR (1903-) [STEPHENS, PAULINE FRANCIS, pseud.]
Doggerel, Early Poems. New York: The Alexander Press, 1934. 36 p.

Skinning the Snake and Other Poems. New York: The Alexander Press, 1936. 2 p. ℓ., 32 p.
Ebionite and Oracle of Dodona. New York: Priv. Print., The Alexander Press, 1937. [11] p.
Teller of Stars; A Sonnet Sequence. New York: Alexander Press, 1937. 1 p. ℓ., 10 p.
Columella; A Peace Offering. New York: Printed at the Sign of Hercules and the Hydra, 1939. 3 p. ℓ., 20 p.
De Profundis, and Other Poems. Horseheads, N. Y.: n. p., 1972. 14 p.
The Blow-Off. Horseheads, N. Y.: n. p., 1973. [4] p.
Grass Roots. New York: Peter Agostini, 1975. [2] p.

STEPHENS, PAULINE FRANCIS, pseud. see STEPHENS, PAULINE ELEANOR

STEPHENS, ROSEMARY
Eve's Navel. Fort Smith, AR.: South and West, 1975.

STERN, CAROLINE
At the Edge of the World. Boston: The Gorham Press, 1916. 6 p. ℓ., 9-131 p.

STERN, RITA
Jaundiced Eye Aglow; A Primer for Iconoclasts. New York: Anthem Press, 1964. xv, 167 p.

STERN, ROSE KAWA
Bits of Beauty, Poems. New York: Exposition Press, 1963. xiv p., 1 ℓ., 143 p.

STETSON, AUGUSTA EMMA SIMMONS (1842?-1928)
Poems Written on the Journey from the Sense to the Soul. New York: Holden & Motley, 1901. 3 p. ℓ., 11-151 p., 1 ℓ.
_______. 3d ed., 1910. 4 p. ℓ., 11-173 p., 1 ℓ.
_______. 4th ed., New York & London: G. P. Putnam's Sons, 1921. 132 p.

STETTHEIMER, FLORINE
Crystal Flowers. New York: n. p., 1949. vi, 82 p., 1 ℓ.

STEVENS, ADA BORDEN
Days Royal. A Triolet Sequence. Medford, MA.: n. p., 1930. 17 p.
The New England Coast. Medford, MA.: C. A. A. Parker, 1931. 16 p.
Colonial Tales in Verse. Cedar Rapids, IA.: The Torch Press, 1933. 25 p.
The Winged Season. Medford, MA.: C. A. A. Parker, 1933. [16] p.

STEVENS, BETH
Unicorn Country. n. p., 1972. 33 p.

STEVENS, CAROLYN
Delicate the Shell. Crescent City, FL.: New Athenaeum Press, 1964. 95 p., 1 ℓ.

STEVENS, ELSIE (STEVENS)
As They Came to Me. Philadelphia: Poetry Publishers, 1932. 46 p.

STEVENS, FLORA ELLICE
Lee; An Epic. Kansas City, MO.: Burton Publishing Company, 1917. 80 p.
Amphora of Castaly. Austin, TX.: n. p., 1967. 38 p.

STEVENS, HELEN FREEMAN
Breezes from Cape Cod. Chatham-on-Cape-Cod, MA.: n. p., 1925. 5 p. ℓ., 17, [1] p.

STEVENS, MARY PACE
...Through a Poet's Window. New York: H. Harrison, 1941. 3 p. ℓ., 9-64 p.

STEVENS, PEARLE MOORE
The Sighing Soul. Boston: The Stratford Company, 1929. 4 p. ℓ., 79 p.
Shadows of Dawn. Dallas, TX.: South-West Press, 1934. ix p., 1 ℓ., 88 p.
When Lights Burn Low. San Antonio, TX.: The Naylor Company, 1940. xi, 70 p.
Silver Wings Against the Sky. San Antonio, TX.: The Naylor Company, 1942. ix, 72 p.

STEVENSON, CANDACE THURBER
First the Blade. New York: Dutton, 1952. 61 p.

STEWART, ANNA BIRD
The Gentlest Giant (and Other Pleasant Persons); Poems from the Enchanting Realm of When We Were Little. New York: The Wayne Publishing Company, 1915. 142, [2] p.
_______. New York: R. M. McBride Company, 1929. 148, [2] p.
Builder of Bridges. New York: R. M. McBride & Co., 1929. ix, 70 p.
The Candy Box. New York: R. M. McBride & Company, 1929. x, 57 p. (Verse for Children.)
The Birds Began to Sing. New York: R. M. McBride & Company, 1930. 3 p. ℓ., ix-xi p., 3 ℓ., 3-131 p. (Verse for Children.)

STEWART, DOLORES
A Great Number Perished in the Catastrophe. Belmont, MA.:

Hellric Publications, 1971.

STEWART, ORA (PATE) (1910-)
Gleanings; Collected Poems. San Antonio, TX.: Naylor Co., 1948. xiii, 95 p.
I Talk About My Children. San Antonio, TX.: Naylor Co., 1948. 115 p.
Brown Leaves Turning. San Antonio, TX.: Naylor Co., 1953. 64 p.
Buttermilk & Bran. San Antonio, TX.: Naylor Co., 1964. xi, 181 p.
West Wind Song. Salt Lake City, UT.: Paragon Press, 1964. 94 p. (Verse for Children.)

STEWART, REBECCA TURNER
Love's Message. New York: n.p., 1915. 103 p.

STEWART, ROSALIE
The Doctor, Five Sonnets, and Other Verse. Evansville, IN.: n.p., 1902. 8 p.

STICKNEY, HELEN FRITH (1887-)
Verses. New York & London: G. P. Putnam's Sons, 1901. 6 p.ℓ., 125 p.
Prelude to Winter. Emory University, Atlanta, GA.: Banner Press, 1934. 71 p. (Verse craft series.)
Abigail's Sampler, and Other Poems. New York: The Fine Editions Press, 1943. 61, [1] p.

STICKNEY, JULIA (NOYES) (b. 1830)
In the Valley of the Merrimack. New York: The Grafton Press, 1901. 2 p.ℓ., 3-66 p.

STILLMAN, LISKA
A City Garden. Buffalo, N.Y.: n.p., 1908. 74 p.
A Knot, Poems. Buffalo, N.Y.: Otto Ulbrich Co., 1910? 142 p.

STILLMAN, MARGARET PRICE
The Gentle Magic of Remembered Dreams.... Atlanta, GA.: Martin-Johnson Printing Co., 1929. 7 p.ℓ., 17-55 p.

STILLMAN, MILDRED (WHITNEY)
Woodnotes. New York: Duffield & Co., 1922. 7 p.ℓ., 99 p.
Unknowing. New York: Duffield & Co., 1925. 7 p.ℓ., 3-70 p.
Queens and Crickets. New York: Duffield & Co., 1927. 5 p.ℓ., 3-77 p.
Apology to My Neighbors. New York: Frederick A. Stokes Company, 1934. xi, 112 p.
Sea-Gull in December. Cornwall-on-Hudson, N.Y.: Idlewild Press, 1943. 31 p.

STILSON, DOROTHY ELIZABETH
Christmas Every Day (Poems of Truth). San Gabriel, CA.: Willing Pub. Co., 1949. 64 p.

STIMSON, EDITH EVERETT BURGESS (1852-)
Glimpses, The Seen--The Unseen. Philadelphia: Dorrance & Co., 1928. 87 p. (Contemporary poets of Dorrance, 71)

STINE, ANNA DeVORA
Poems for Peace and Progress. New York: Pageant Press, 1961. 65 p.

STIRLING, SARAH VOWELL DAINGERFIELD
Thoughts. New York: The Poets Press, 1940. 4 p. ℓ., 11-50 p.

STIVER, MARY WEEDEN
Brief Argument. Sauk City, WI.: Printed and Published in England by Villiers Pub. for Hawk and Whippoorwill Press, 1964. 64 p.
Dreams Astonishments Realities. Manning, SC.: Clarendon Printing Co., 1972. 58 p.

STOCK, ETTA FLORENCE
Songs of Promise. Boston: The Four Seas Company, 1924. 16 p.

STOCKBRIDGE, DOROTHY
Paths of June. New York: E. P. Dutton & Co., 1920. ix p., 1 ℓ., 121 p.

STOCKDALE, ALICE BOYD
To Ireland with Love. Garden City, N.Y.: Doubleday, 1964. 89 p.

STOCKETT, MARIA LETITIA (1884-)
The Hoofs. Baltimore, MD.: The Norman, Remington Company, 1923. 56 p.

STOFFEL, BETTY W.
Moments of Eternity. Richmond, VA.: John Knox Press, 1954. 6 p. ℓ., 47 p.
Splendid Moments; Poems. Richmond, VA.: John Knox Press, 1965. 64 p.

STOKES, ELIZABETH STAPLETON
Small Wisdom; Poems. New York: H. Harrison, 1937. 63 p.

STOKES, MARY ROBERTINE
On a Green Slope; Poems. Boston: R. G. Badger, 1913. 55 p.

STOKES, ROSE PASTOR (WIESLANDER) (1879-)
The Woman Who Wouldn't. New York and London: G. P. Putnam's Sons, 1916. 2 p. ℓ., 183 p.

STOLOFF, CAROLYN

Triptych. Santa Barbara, CA.: Unicorn Press, 1970. folder.

Stepping Out. Santa Barbara, CA.: Unicorn Press, 1971. 79 p.

Dying to Survive. Garden City, N.Y.: Doubleday & Co., 1973. xi, 94 p.

In the Red Meadow; Poems. New York: New Rivers Press; dist. by Serendipity Books, Berkeley, CA., 1973. [31] p.

STOLZAR, BETSY H.

A Fair Share. San Antonio, TX.: Naylor Co., 1970. xi, 57 p.

STONE, ELLEN

Growing Down to Earth: Guatemala Poems, 1974. New Haven, CT.: Occum Press, 1975. 12 p.

STONE, FLORENCE (SYLVESTER) (1908-)

Rose That Opens. New York: Vantage Press, 1954. 4 p.ℓ., 80 p.

STONE, HELENA RIDGWAY

Burnt Offering; Poems. Los Angeles, CA.: Swordsman Publ. Co., 1964. 83 p.

STONE, JEWELL

Beautiful Thoughts in Verse. New York: Vantage Press, 1964. 80 p.

STONE, KATRINE FRANCES

...September Interlude. Philadelphia: Dorrance & Co., 1946. 82 p.

STONE, MARY D.

More Pebbles. Kanona, N.Y.: J. & C. Transcripts, 1974. 96 p.

STONE, NAOMI BORTON

To Be a Pilgrim. Winona, MN.: St. Mary's College Press, 1973. 88 p.

STONE, RUTH

In an Iridescent Time. New York: Harcourt Brace, 1959. [64] p.

Topography, and Other Poems. New York: Harcourt Brace Jovanovich, 1971. x, 116 p.

Cheap: New Poems and Ballads. New York: Harcourt Brace Jovanovich, 1975. 101 p.

STONE, VIDA REED

Winged Thoughts. San Gabriel, CA.: Willing Pub. Co., 1957. 58 p.

The Dawn of the Cosmic Age. Jayanthipura, Talangama, Ceylon: K. Ramachandria, 1962. 3 p.ℓ., 116 p.

STONER, MARIE LOUISE
Manana, for Those Who Believe in a Beautiful Tomorrow. Chambersburg, PA.: n.p., 1964. [15] p.
The Twelfth of Never. Chambersburg, PA.: n.p., 1965. [7] p.
The Singing and the Gold. n.p., 1966. [7] p.

STONER, MARY KIMBROUGH
The Cardinal Cat, and Other Verse. Lexington, KY.: Printed by Transylvania, 1941. 3 p. ℓ., 51 p.

STONER, MONA GRAY
Under Our Stars.... New York: The Exposition Press, 1944. 64 p.
Beyond the Stars.... New York: The Paebar Co., 1946. 2 p. ℓ., 75 p.

STOPPLE, LIBBY (1910-)
Never Touch a Lilac. San Antonio, TX.: Naylor Co., 1959. 3 p. ℓ., 10 p.
Peppermints; Poems of Childhood. Dallas: Dallas Records Pub. Co., 1970. [24] p.

STORCK, ADELE
Broken Chords. New York: Vantage Press, 1952. 39 p.

STOREY, VIOLET ALLEYN
Green of the Year. New York, London: D. Appleton and Company, 1927. x, 114, [1] p.
Tea in an Old House. New York: Print. by The Stratford Press, Inc., 1933. xii p., 1 ℓ., 173 p.
A Poet Prays. New York: Abingdon Press, 1959. 80 p.

STORM, HESTER G.
Wrongside-Up Rainbow. Denver, CO.: A. Swallow, 1964. 44 p. (Poets in Swallow paperbooks)
Fugue. New York: Pommel Press, 1966. [70] p.
Tears of Hecuba. Berkeley, CA.: Thorp Springs Press, 1974. 3 p.

STORM, MARIAN [Full Name: Marian Isabel Storm.]
Poems of Sun and Snow. Mexico, D. F.: For Sale at American Book Store, 1955. 91 p., 2 ℓ.

STOUT, MARY JANE
Gleanings from Life; A Collection of Poems. Kansas City, MO.: Burton Pub. Co., 1948. 139, [2] p.

STOUTENBURG, ADRIEN PEARL (1916-)
Heroes, Advise Us: Poems. New York: Scribner, 1964. 127 p.
The Things That Are. Chicago: Reilly & Lee Co., 1964. 55 p.

STOWE, EMILY
Desert Night. Washington, D. C.: Congressional Press, Inc., 1930. 4 p. ℓ., 40 p., 1 ℓ.

STRACHAN, PEARL [HURD, PEARL STRACHAN]
All in Black Flower, and Other Poems. Boston: n.p., 1946. 4 p.ℓ., 78 p.
Selected Poems. Boston: n.p., 1967. 3 p.ℓ., 86 p.

STRAHMAN, RUBY MacRAE
To the Mountain's Height, and Other Poems. New York: Exposition Press, 1956. 47 p.

STRAUGHN, HELEN A.
..."Ye Who Pass By." Philadelphia: Dorrance and Company, 1937. 74 p. (Contemporary poets of Dorrance, 161)

STRAYER, DOROTHA
The Singing Pen; Poems. New York: Greenwich Book Publishers, 1955. 3 p.ℓ., 57 p.

STREAMS, HAZEL LENA
My Verses. Seattle, WA.: Modern City Printing Co., 1973. 43 p.

STREET, MATTIE
Open Range and Open Doors. Denver, CO.: Big Mountain Press, 1964. 54 p.

STRICKER, VERA
Path to the Golden Years; Poems. New York: Exposition Press, 1966. 55 p.

STRODE, MURIEL
A Soul's Faring. New York: Boni and Liveright, 1921. 4 p.ℓ., 167 p.
At the Roots of Grasses. New York: Moffat, Yard and Company, 1923. 4 p.ℓ., 3-142 p.

STROH, DOROTHY ELIZABETH
Rain on the Rocks. Philadelphia: Dorrance & Co., 1932. 36 p. (Contemporary poets of Dorrance, 109)

STROMBERG, HELGA SOFIA (HENNING) (1886-)
Selected Poems. New York: Exposition Press, 1939. 4 p.ℓ., 11-94 p.
Through Windows of Love. New York: H. Harrison, 1940. 91, [5] p.
Worlds Within. New York: H. Harrison, 1941. 95 p.

STRONG, ANNA LOUISE (1885-)
Storm Songs and Fables. Chicago: The Langston Press, 1904. 45 p.
The Song of the City. Oak Park, IL.: Oak Leaves Press, 1906. 61 p.

STRONG, NELLE de LUCE
When the Sun Goes Low, and Other Verses. Los Angeles: Printed by A. K. Tate & Son, 1922. [27] p.

STRONGIN, LYNN (1939-)
The Dwarf Cycle. Berkeley, CA.: Thorp Springs Press, 1972. unpaged.
Shrift: A Winter Sequence. Berkeley, CA.: Thorp Springs Press, 1975. 36 p.

STROTHER, EMILY (VIELE) (1868-)
When We Are Old and Gay. New York: Comet Press Books, 1937. 5 p. ℓ., 68 p.

STROTHER, FLORENCE DAVIDSON
Hop Upon a Shadow. New York: Vantage Press, 1965. 47 p.

STROUSE, KATE CHIDSEY
Word Music. Norwich, CT.: n. p., 1930. 22 ℓ.
______. Boston: The Christopher Publishing House, 1932. 32 p.
Bouquet of Cheer. Norwich, CT.: Norwich Bulletin, 1941. 36 p.

STRUTHER, JAN, *pseud.* *see* TAYLOR, JOYCE (GRAHAM) (1901-)

STRYKER, LEONORA CLAWSON
Random Reflections. Washington: The Stylus Publishing Co., 1931. 2 p. ℓ., 7-94 p.
Indian Summer. Tujunga, CA.: C. L. Anderson, 1952. 105 p.
In Flower. Minneapolis, MN.: Lund Press, Inc., 1938. 4 p. ℓ., 11-95 p.

STUART, RUTH (McENERY) (1856-1917)
Plantation Songs and Other Verse. New York: D. Appleton and Co., 1916. vii, 135 p.

STUBBS, EDITH BLINE
Down to Earth Poems. New York: Vantage Press, 1966. 64 p.

STULL, DALENE WORKMAN
Spatter of Pearls. Francestown, N. H.: Golden Quill Press, 1966. 84 p.

STURDEVANT, EDITH MAY (1890-)
The King and His Glory, and Other Poems. Syracuse, N. Y.: Wesleyan Methodist Publishing Association, 1911. 97 p.

STURGEON, MYRTLE TITUS
Melodies of Love. New York: Greenwich Book Publishers, 1955. 64 p.

STURGES, EDITH MAIDA (LESSING)
Insurrection and Other Poems. San Diego, CA.: Silver Gate Press, 1905. [64] p.

STURGIS, EDITH BARNES
My Busy Days. New York: D. Appleton and Company, 1908. 50 p., 1 ℓ.
The Winged Messenger. New York: Coward-McCann, 1932. viii p., 1 ℓ., 40 p.

STUSSIE, LIDA PRINGLE
Horizon to Westward. Berkeley, CA.: Locksley Hall, 1949. vii, 117 p.

STUTEVILLE, MARY
Collected Poems. New York: Comet Press Books, 1954. 56 p.
Driftwood. New York: Comet Press Books, 1955. 4 p. ℓ., 75 p.

STUTZMAN, LUELLA WALDEN
A Tribute to Mother, and Other Poems. McPherson? KS.: n.p., 1910. 40 p.

STYRON, ROSE (BURGUNDER)
From Summer to Summer. New York: Viking Press, 1965. 64 p.
Thieves' Afternoon. New York: Viking Press, 1973. 87 p.

SUCCOP, MARGARET PHILLIPS (1914-)
Climb to the Stars. Philadelphia: Dorrance, 1952. 69 p.
Wakened Dreams. Philadelphia: Dorrance, 1953. 69 p.
Twenty-Four Sonnets and Other Poems. Peterborough, N.H.: Windy Row Press, 1971. 88 p.

SUKENICK, LYNN (1937-)
Houdini. Santa Barbara, CA.: Capra Press, 1973. [36] p. (Yes! Capra Chapbook no. 14)
Water Astonishing: Poems. Holly Springs, MS.: Ragnarok Press, 1974. [31] p.
Problems and Characteristics. n.p.: Avocet Press; Dist. by Serendipity Books, 1975. 32 p.

SULLIVAN, BETTY
Small Stones. New York: Carlton Press, 1969. 64 p.

SULLIVAN, KATHLEEN ANNE (1873-)
Thoughts of June. Milwaukee, WI.: Diederich-Schaefer Co., 1921. 3 p. ℓ., 11-103, [1] p.
God Is Near. New York: Vantage Press, 1953. 5 p. ℓ., 98 p.

SULLIVAN, MAY
Dust of Uncertain Journey. Detroit: Lotus Press, 1975. 72 p.

SULLIVAN, NANCY

The History of the World as Pictures: Poems. Columbia, MO.: University of Missouri Press, 1965. 8 p. ℓ., 79 p.

Body English. n. p.: Hellcoal Press, 1972.

Telling It. Boston: David R. Godine, 1975. 47 p.

SULLIVAN, SUZANNE

Coming Suddenly upon the Late Years. n. p.: Olympic Publishing, 1965. 65 p.

SUMMERROW, DOROTHY (EDWARDS)

Ten Angels Swearing; Sonnets. New York: Exposition Press, 1957. 64 p.

SUMMERS, LUCY (COOPER)

99 Patches. New York: Carlton Press, 1969. 64 p.

SUMMERS, MARY LYTTON

Echoes in the Wind. Philadelphia: Dorrance, 1964. 64 p. (Contemporary poets of Dorrance, 585)

SUMMERS, MILDRED PITT

Summer Verse; The Selected Poetry of Mildred Pitt Summers. New York: Pageant Press, 1961. 5 p. ℓ., 49 p.

SUMNER, CAROLINE LOUISE (1867-)

Thrills; A Group of Verse. Syracuse, N. Y.: Craftline Publishers, 1930. 22 p.

SURENSON, IRENE KIRBY

Singing Summer. Emory University, Atlanta, GA.: Banner Press, 1937. 54 p. (Verse craft series.)

On Wings Too Wide for Doubt, and Other Poems. Boston: The Christopher Publishing House, 1939. x, 13-64 p.

Beyond the Hills of Time, and Other Poems. New York: Harbinger House, 1945. 45 p.

The World Is a Contrast. Miami, FL.: Florida State Poetry Society, 1974. 108 p.

SUSLICK, EDITH

Interstices. Madison, WI.: Abraxas Press, 1970. [5] p.

SUTHERLAND, MAMIE ANGEL

Dream No More. Philadelphia: Dorrance, 1966. 28 p.

SUTHERLIN, IRENE

Song of Southern River, and Other Poems. Boston: R. G. Badger, 1930. 5 p. ℓ., 7-58 p.

SUTTERWAIT, ELIZABETH ALLEN

A Gentle Heart. Webster Groves, MO.: n. p., 1920.

SUTTON, KATHLEEN LIVINGSTON (STANLEY) (1898-)
Masquerade, a First Volume of Poems. New York: Paebar, 1932. 47 p.

SUTTON, LORRAINE
SAYcred LAYdy. Bronx, N. Y.: Sunbury Press, 1975. 32 p.

SUTTON, LOUISE WEIBERT
Through Lens of Poetry; Seasonal and Miscellaneous Poems. Kanona, N. Y.: J. & C. Transcripts, 1967. 4 p. ℓ., 43 p.
A Pen of Stars; Inspirational and Assorted Poetry. Kanona, N. Y.: J. & C. Transcripts, 1968. 44 p.
Songs from the April Hills; Nature Poetry Plus Animal and Inspirational Poems for All Seasons. Kanona, N. Y.: J. & C. Transcripts, 1968. 4 p. ℓ., 44 p.
The Voice of Verse; Varied Verses on Many Things. Kanona, N. Y.: J. & C. Transcripts, 1969. 36 p.

SUTTON, MARY DOROTHY (1902-)
Lyric Dawn. Philadelphia: Dorrance and Co., 1934. 62 p. (Contemporary poets of Dorrance, 118)

SUTTON, SIGRID
Dishpan Lyrics. Chicago: The Wildwood Press, 1932. 4 p. ℓ., 64 p.

SVENSON, LILLIAN MATHILDA
Spirit Free. Menasha, WI.: George Banta Publishing Company, 1933. 51 p., 1 ℓ.
Thoughtwaves. Philadelphia: Dorrance and Co., 1934. 3 p. ℓ., 5-16 p. (Contemporary poets of Dorrance, 123)
...A Thousand Years Ago. Philadelphia: Dorrance and Co., 1939. 39 p.
Sunshine Hill in Joyland. Philadelphia: Dorrance, 1950. 68 p.
Dancing Light Beams. Dallas, TX.: Story Book Press, 1954. 40 p.

SWAIM, ALICE MACKENZIE (1911-)
Up to the Stars. Denver, CO.: Big Mountain Press, 1954. 48 p.
Sunshine in a Thimble. Dillsburg, PA.: n. p., 1958. 58 p.
Crickets Are Crying Autumn. New York: Pageant Press, 1960. 69 p.
The Gentle Dragon. Francestown, N. H.: Golden Quill Press, 1962. 70 p.
October Caught Me Dreaming. Dillsburg, PA.: n. p., 1962. [12] p.
Here on the Threshold. Dillsburg, PA.: n. p., 1966. 24 p.
Pennsylvania Profile. Dillsburg, PA.: n. p., 1966. 24 p.
Scented Honeysuckle Days. Dillsburg, PA.: n. p., 1966. 24 p.
Beneath a Dancing Star. Rome: Quaderni di Poesia, 1967. 16 p.
Beyond My Catnip Garden. Francestown, N. H.: Golden Quill Press, 1970. 86 p.

SWAN, CAROLINE DAVENPORT
The Unfading Light. Boston: Sherman, French & Company, 1910. 5 p. ℓ., 171 p.

SWAN, EMMA (1914-)
The Lion & The Lady, and Other Poems. New York: New Directions, 1949. 76 p.
Poems. New York: New Directions, 1958. 70 p.
The Lion & The Lady, and Other Poems. London: Linden Press, 1961. 76 p.
Poems. London: Linden Press, 1961. 70, [2] p.

SWANN, MATTIE HOLLAND
Between Whiles; Poems. Cincinnati, OH.: The Editor Publishing Co., 1900. 2 p. ℓ., iii-v p., 1 ℓ., 89 p.

SWARTZ, ROBERTA TEALE (1903-)
Lilliput. New York: Harcourt, Brace & Co., 1926. vii, 57 p.
Lord Juggler & Other Poems. New York & London: Harper and Brothers, 1932. 2 ℓ., 3-78 p.

SWENSON, KAREN
An Attic of Ideals. Garden City, N.Y.: Doubleday, 1974. vi, 89 p.

SWENSON, MAY (1919-)
A Cage of Spines. New York: Rinehart, 1958. 96 p.
To Mix with Time, New and Selected Poems. New York: Scribner, 1963. viii, 183 p.
Poems to Solve. New York: Scribner, 1966. 72 p.
Half Sun, Half Sleep; New Poems. New York: Scribner, 1967. 128 p.
Iconographs; Poems. New York: Scribner, 1970. 88 p.
More Poems to Solve. New York: Scribner, 1971. 64 p.

SWENSON, MIRANDA POWERS
Pot-Pourri: Spice and Rose Leaves. Boston: The Gorham Press, 1904. 43 p.

SWIFT, CLARA POOR (WILDER)
Poems. New York: n.p., 1911. 39 p.

SWIFT, ELIZA MORGAN
...Summer Goodbye. New York: H. Vinal, 1926. 6 p. ℓ., 3-43 p.

SWIFT, JOAN
This Element. Denver: Alan Swallow, 1965. 47 p. (The New poetry series, 30)

SWIGART, MARGARET McGINNIS (1884-)
Colors of the Rainbow. Lawrence, KS.: Allen Press, 1950. 60 p.

SWIGGETT, GRACE RIESS
Welcome Dawn. Emory University, Atlanta, GA.: Banner Press, 1940. 5 p. ℓ., 9-48 p. (Verse craft series)

SYKES, EILEEN
The Gay Garland. New York: Pageant Press, 1954. 58 p.

SYLVESTER, GERTRUDE LYON
Country Airs. New York: Comet Press Books, 1957. 44 p.

SZERLIP, BARBARA
Teopantiahuac; Poetry. Santa Barbara, CA.: Water Table Press, 1971. 31 p. (Isla Vista street poets, no. 5)
Bear Dancing. n.p.: Doggerel Press, 1974.

TABER, GLADYS (BAGG) (1899-) [Full Name: Gladys Leona (Bagg) Taber.]
Lyonnesse. Atlanta, GA.: E. Hartsock, The Bozart Press, 1929. 3 p. ℓ., [5]-75 p.

TABER, MARGARET SYMONS
Echoes of a Singing Heart. New York: Comet Press Books, 1955. 3 p. ℓ., 37 p.

TABOR, EITHNE
The Cliff's Edge; Songs of a Psychotic. New York: Sheed & Ward, 1950. ix, 80 p.

TACY, ESTELLE
One Sovereign Song and Other Poems. Long Beach, CA.: Green's Inc., 1938. v, 48 p.

TAFT, GRACE ELLIS
Chimalman, and Other Poems. New York: Cameo Press, 1916. 96 p.

TAGGARD, GENEVIEVE (1894-1948)
For Eager Lovers. New York: T. Seltzer, 1922. 6 p. ℓ., 3-70 p.
...Hawaiian Hilltop. San Francisco: Wyckoff & Gelber, 1923. 3 p. ℓ., 15, [1] p.
...Words for the Chisel. New York: A. A. Knopf, 1926. 86, [2] p.
...Travelling Standing Still; Poems, 1918-1928. New York: A. A. Knopf, 1928. 5 p. ℓ., 3-56 p., 1 ℓ.
Monologue for Mothers (aside). New York: Random House, 1929. [4] p.
Remembering Vaughan in New England. n.p.: Arrow Editions Cooperative Association, 1933. [4] p.
Not Mine to Finish, Poems, 1928-1934. New York, London: Harper & Brothers, 1934. 6 p. ℓ., 93 p., 1 ℓ.
Calling Western Union. New York and London: Harper & Brothers, 1936. xxxii p., 1 ℓ., 74 p.

Collected Poems, 1918-1938. New York and London: Harper & Brothers, 1938. x, 164 p., 1 ℓ.
Falcon; Poems on Soviet Themes. New York: n.p., 1942. 18 p.
Long View. New York, London: Harper & Brothers, 1942. vii p., 1 ℓ., 3-113, [1] p.
A Part of Vermont. East Jamaica, VT.: River Press, 1945. 23 p.
Slow Music. New York and London: Harper & Brothers, 1946. x, 62 p.

TAINTER, LILA R. (MUNRO)
Caravel of Dreams: A Book of Verse. Boston: Sherman, French & Company, 1914. 7 p. ℓ., 127 p.

TALBOT, ANNE (RICHARDSON) (1857-)
Garden of Life, and Other Poems. Boston: Sherman, French & Company, 1913. 4 p. ℓ., 41 p.

TALBOT, FANNIE SPRAGUE
Poems. Boston: R. G. Badger, 1910. 48 p.
Nose Gay.... Cedar Rapids, IA.: The Torch Press, 1946. 31 p.

TALBOTT, DEANNA
Kewanee Boiler Poems. Sacramento, CA.: Grande Ronde Press, 1966. 32 p.

TALLY, STEPHANIE MARIE (1899-)
Pink Roses at Midnight. New York: Paebar Co., 1949. 50 p.

TANASSO, ELDA
The Dark Gaze. Boston: R. Humphries, Inc., 1944. 71 p.

TANDY, SARA ELLEN
Rhymes from Wildrose Terrace. St. Paul, MN.: n.p., 1925. 86 p.
...All Cupped in Beauty. Philadelphia: Dorrance & Co., 1941. 63 p. (Contemporary poets of Dorrance, 183)

TARDY, ANNE SOUTHERNE
Sun Through Window Shutters. Brattleboro, VT.: Stephen Daye Press, 1935. 100 p.

TARR, LAURA C. (FIELDS)
Singing in the Wilderness, A Book of Verse. New York: Greenwich Book Publishers, 1961. 57 p.

TATE, JANE BEVERLIN (1922-)
These Are For You. Portland, ME.: Falmouth Pub. House, 1949. 62 p.
Equinox, a Collection of Poems. New York: William-Frederick Press, 1952. 46 p. (The William-Frederick poets, 94)
One Long Summer. New York: Bookman Associates, 1957. 96 p.

TATHAM, SARAH THERESA (ROE) (1872-)
Airman. New York: The Poets Press, 1937. 61, [1] p.

TATUM, EDITH (1877-) [Full Name: Edith Brittain (Crenshaw) Tatum.]
Patteran. Emory University, Atlanta, GA.: Banner Press, 1931. 72 p. (Verse craft series)
The Awakening of Iseult. Oglethorpe University, GA.: Oglethorpe University Press, 1933. 6 p. ℓ., 9-44 numb. ℓ.
In a Chinese Garden, and Other Poems. Dallas, TX.: The Kaleidograph Press, 1939. xi p., 1 ℓ., 15-80 p.
Hills of the Spirit. Dallas, TX.: The Kaleidograph Press, 1945. xi p., 1 ℓ., 15-84 p.
Designs for Living. Dallas, TX.: The Kaleidograph Press, 1947. x p., 1 ℓ., 13-62 p.
Through a Window Toward the South. Dallas, TX.: Kaleidograph Press, 1950. 72 p.
Orchestra of Wind and Trees. Emory University, Atlanta, GA.: Banner Press, 1954. 91 p.

TAYLOR, ABIGAIL FLETCHER
Verse of Today and Yesterday. Boston: Small, Maynard & Company, 1920. 5 p. ℓ., 150 p.

TAYLOR, BELLE GRAY
War Verse. New York: The Knickerbocker Press, 1918. 16 p.

TAYLOR, CARRIE C. (1871-)
Silver Wings. Richmond, VA.: G. F. Gulley, 1951. 62 p.

TAYLOR, CHARLOTTE CARR
Out of the Night. Columbia, S.C.: The Letter Shop, 1941. 44 p.
Bond with Eternity, and Other Poems. Prairie City, IL.: Decker Press, 1949. 122 p.

TAYLOR, ELEANOR ROSS (1920-)
Wilderness of Ladies. New York: McDowell, Obolensky, 1960. 62 p.
Welcome Eumenides: Poems. New York: G. Braziller, 1972. xi, 55 p. (The Braziller series of poetry)

TAYLOR, ELETHA MAE
Love and Life and Other Poems. Anderson, IN.: The Herald Publishing Co., 1936. 5 p. ℓ., 13-163 p.

TAYLOR, FLORENCE MARIE (1897-)
Night of Stars. Greenfield, IN.: Mitchell-Fleming Printing, 1956. 96 p.

TAYLOR, GLORIA LEE (1916-)
Dreams for Sale. New York: Exposition Press, 1953. 64 p.

TAYLOR, JOYCE (GRAHAM) (1901-) [GRAHAM, JOYCE MAXTONE]
The Glass Blower. New York: Harcourt, Brace & Co., 1941. vii, 67 p.

TAYLOR, KATHERINE KELLEY
The Sea Gull's Daughter and Other Poems. Cleveland, OH.: William Feather Co., 1937. 104 p.

TAYLOR, LAUNORA
My First Poems. New York: Pageant Press, 1961. 60 p.

TAYLOR, LAURA TAITT
A String of Black Beads. n. p.: The Author, 1925.

TAYLOR, MARGARET
Caravan. n. p., 1973. 51 p.

TAYLOR, MARION ELIZABETH
Cocoons. Iowa City, IA.: Golden Scissors Press, 1971. 35 p.

TAYLOR, MARY ATWATER
Ropes and Threads. Portland, ME.: The Mosher Press, 1925. viii p., 2 ℓ., 3-69, [1] p.
October Orchard. Woodstock, N. Y.: The Maverick Press, 1934. 5 p. ℓ., 79 p.
... Turn of the Year. Prairie City, IL.: A. Decker, 1946. 5 p. ℓ., 9-78 p.

TAYLOR, MARY KEELY
In Many Keys. Cambridge, MA.: Priv. print. University Press, 1912. viii p., 1 ℓ., 100 p.

TAYLOR, MARY L. (PEARE)
Echoes from Girlhood, and Other Poems. Chicago: Bell Book Company, 1904. viii, [9]-140 p.
Reaping, and Other Poems. Chicago: Bell Book Company, 1915. 40 p.
Three Needs of Life, and Other Poems. Chicago: R. F. Seymour, 1929. 5 p. ℓ., 100 p.

TAYLOR, REBECCA NICHOLSON (1857-)
Songs of Hope: Poems. Boston: Sherman, French & Company, 1915. 3 p. ℓ., 28 p.

TAYLOR, ROBERTA NEWTON
Blue Heron. Dallas, TX.: Kaleidograph Press, 1952. 67 p.
The Place Called Morning. Richmond, VA.: Whittet & Shepperson, 1959. 72 p.

TAYLOR, SARAH WINGATE
Samphire, Herb of St. Peter: Poems. Duxbury, MA.: n. p., 1959. 64 p.
Yankee Island Ballads, and Other Poems. Duxbury, MA.: n. p.,

1962. 80 p.

Clark's in Plymouth Harbor; The Pilgrim Fathers' Island, 1620-1690. Peterborough, N. H.: Published for Cedarfield Clark's Island, Duxbury, MA. by R. R. Smith, 1965. 37 p.

TAYLOR, SUZANE

Youth's Enchantment. Boston: The Stratford Company, 1928. 4 p. ℓ., 42 p.

TAYLOR, WINIFRED SYLVIA GLADYS

Miscellaneous Verse. New York: McClunn & Co., 1921. 56 p.

TEASDALE, SARA (1884-1933)

Sonnets to Duse and Other Poems. Boston: The Poet Lore Co., 1907. 44 p.

Helen of Troy, and Other Poems. New York and London: G. P. Putnam's Sons, 1911. ix, 115 p.

Rivers to the Sea. New York: The Macmillan Company, 1915. xii p., 1 ℓ., 148 p.

Love Songs. New York: The Macmillan Company, 1917. xi, 91 p.

Flame and Shadow. New York: The Macmillan Company, 1920. 7 p. ℓ., 144 p.

Helen of Troy, and Other Poems. New and rev. ed. New York: Macmillan, 1922. xii p., 1 ℓ., 15-105 p.

Dark of the Moon. New York: The Macmillan Company, 1926. 92 p.

Stars To-Night; Verses New and Old for Boys and Girls. New York: The Macmillan Company, 1930. x, 49 p., 1 ℓ.

A Country House. New York: Alfred A. Knopf, 1932. [3] p. (The Borzoi chapbooks, no. 4)

Strange Victory. New York: The Macmillan Company, 1933. 37 p.

The Collected Poems of Sara Teasdale. New York: The Macmillan Company, 1937. xvi, 311 p.

The Collected Poems of Sara Teasdale. New York: Collier Books, 1966. xxxii, 224 p.

Those Who Love; Love Poems. Ed. by Arthur Wortman. Kansas City, MO.: Hallmark Editions, 1969. 61 p.

TEEPLE, SYLVIA CHASE

Favourite Poems. Beaver Springs, PA.: Printed by A. M. Aurand, 1912. 2 p. ℓ., 115 p.

TEJEDOR, CAROL

Scattered Leaves. Chicago: Dierkes Press, 1953. 40 p.

TEMPLE, ANNA

Kneeling Camel, and Other Poems. New York: Moffat, Yard & Company, 1920. 3 p. ℓ., ix-x p., 1 ℓ., 66 p.

TEMPLE, INEZ

Shelters & Pastures; Verse and Drawings. Boston: B. Humphries, 1951. 138 p.

TENNANT, DAISY ELMORE (1910-)
Shifting Sands. Odessa? TX.: n.p., 1954. 52 p.

TENNENT, SARAH MARGARET
Observations; Nature Verses and Others. New Philadelphia, OH.: The Acme Printing Co., 1925. 52 p.

TENNYSON, LAURA (MITCHELL)
Pilfered Moments, Poems. Chicago: Dierkes Press, 1952. 40 p.

TERSICH, MARILYN JEAN
Leaf and Feather. New York: Carlton Press, 1968. 63 p.

TETER, ELLEN KEENER
...Spring's Flower-Go-Round. Philadelphia: Dorrance and Company, 1940. 64 p. (Contemporary poets of Dorrance, 198)

TETER, MARIE (1890-)
The First Star, and Other Poems. New York: Exposition Press, 1962. 5 p. ℓ., 53 p.

TETTING, BELLE (1888-)
The Honor Roll, and Other Poems. New York: Carlton Press, 1969. 105 p.

TEUFEL, DOLORES E. (1921-)
Collected Poems. 2d ed. Hershey, PA.: Chapter 509. Order of the Eastern Star, 1963. 32 p.

THACHER, DELIA TUDOR
Separation, and Other Poems. New York: Duffield & Co., 1922. 4 p. ℓ., 3-56 p.

THACKER, LENA HAMMER
From the Heart of Carolina; Poems. New York: Exposition Press, 1963. 77 p.

THAYER, GEORGIANA
...Eve Passes. New York: H. Vinal, 1926. vi, 47 p.

THAYER, HARRIET MAXON
Anniversary and Other Poems. Chicago: R. F. Seymour, 1936. 2 p. ℓ., 7-78 p.

THAYER, MARY DIXON (1896-)
Songs of Youth. New York: A. A. Knopf, 1922. 6 p. ℓ., 3-149 p.
New York and Other Poems. Philadelphia: Dorrance & Co., 1925. 105, [1] p.
The Child on His Knees. New York: The Macmillan Co., 1926. 5 p. ℓ., 5-131 p.
...Songs Before the Blessed Sacrament. New York: The Mac-

millan Co., 1932. 56 p.
Sonnets. New York: The Macmillan Co., 1933. 4 p. ℓ., 39 p.

THAYNE, EMMA LOU
Spaces in the Sage; Poems. Salt Lake City, UT.: Parliament Publishers, 1971. 60 p.
Until Another Day for Butterflies. Salt Lake City, UT.: Parliament Publishers, 1973. 63 p.
With Love, Mother. Salt Lake City, UT.: Deseret Bk., 1975.

THÉRÈSE, Sister (1902-) [Secular Name: Florence Mae Lentfoehr.]
Now There Is Beauty, and Other Poems. New York: The Macmillan Company, 1940. viii, 82 p.
Give Joan a Sword. New York: The Macmillan Company, 1944. xii, 98 p.
Moment in Ostia. Garden City, N.Y.: Hanover House, 1959. 96 p.

THIERRY, ADELAIDE HAMLIN
Why and Whither? A Book of Poems. Boston: Chapman & Grimes, 1956. 64 p.
On Beauty Fed. Emory University, Atlanta, GA.: Banner Press, 1957. 97 p. (Verse craft series)
The Bitter and the Sweet. Emory University, Atlanta, GA.: Banner Press, 1958. 92 p. (Verse craft series)
Just About Folks. Boston: Chapman & Grimes, 1958. 102 p.
Fact and Fancy. Emory University, Atlanta, GA.: Banner Press, 1959. 69 p. (Verse craft series)

THOMAE, BETTY JANE KENNEDY (1920-)
Stand Still, Summer. Roma: Centro Studi e Scambi Internazionali, 1968.
Roses and Thorns. London: Mitre Press, 1970. 60 p.

THOMAS, ANNA ANDREWS
Star-Dust... Poems. Baltimore, MD.: H. G. Roebuck & Son, 1930. [36] p.

THOMAS, ANNE BUTLER
Golden Winged Days. Boston: R. G. Badger, 1907. 238 p.

THOMAS, CARA SCARBOROUGH
We Came Through, and Other Poems of Home. New York: Exposition Press, 1956. 64 p.

THOMAS, CARRIE S.
Little Lilting Lines. Boston: The Christopher Publishing House, 1925. 3 p. ℓ., 9-82 p.

THOMAS, CYNTHIA D. (HARVEY) (1841-)
Light in the Cloud. Jackson, MI.: Daily Citizen Printing House, 1905. 60 p.

THOMAS, EDITH ADDISON
There in the Woods, and Other Poems. Dallas, TX.: Triangle Pub. Co., 1958. 40 p.

THOMAS, EDITH MATILDA (1854-1925)
The Dancers and Other Legends and Lyrics. Boston: R. G. Badger, 1903. 93 p.
Cassia, and Other Verse. Boston: R. G. Badger, 1905. 89 p.
Children of Christmas, and Other Poems. Boston: R. G. Badger, 1907. 109 p.
The Flower from the Ashes and Other Verse. Portland, ME.: T. B. Mosher, 1915. 58 p.
The White Messenger, and Other War Poems. Boston: R. G. Badger, 1915. 5 p. ℓ., 9-91 p.
Selected Poems of Edith Matilda Thomas. Ed. by Jessie B. Rittenhouse. New York & London: Harper & Bros., 1926. xiii, 247 p.

THOMAS, ELIZABETH SIMONTON (1906-)
Mists of Daybreak. Boston: B. Humphries, Inc., 1944. 31, [1] p.

THOMAS, FLORA WATROUS
The Princess and the Fool. Pittsburgh, PA.: The Author, 1922. 52 p.

THOMAS, HATTIE (AVERILL)
At Break of Day. Dallas, TX.: Story Book Press, 1950. 64 p.

THOMAS, IDA WALDEN
... Twilight Fancies. Boston: The Stratford Company, 1928. 31 p. (The Stratford poets)

THOMAS, JESSIE GERTRUDE
Sugar and Spice. Dallas, TX.: The Kaleidograph Press, 1945. xiv p., 1 ℓ., 17-72 p.

THOMAS, JOYCE CAROL
Bittersweet. San Lorenzo, CA.: Shameless Hussy Press, 1973. 59 p.
Blessing. San Lorenzo, CA.: Shameless Hussy Press, 1975. 48 p.

THOMAS, KATHARINE GARFORD
Old Oak Tree. Oberlin, OH.: Oberlin Printing Co., 1946. viii, 56 p.

THOMAS, LETTA EULALIA
The Minor Chord and Other Poems. Grand Rapids, MI.: n. p., 1902. 10 p.

THOMAS, LILLIE JEWEL
The Passing Years.... Dallas, TX.: The Kaleidograph Press, 1930. 4 p. ℓ., 40 p.

THOMAS, LOUISA CARROLL (JACKSON)
Thyrsus, and Other Poems. Carmel-by-the-Sea, CA.: The Press in the Forest, 1925. 28 ℓ.
They Came Singing. Cedar Rapids, IA.: The Torch Press, 1939. 95 p.

THOMAS, MABEL CLARE
Sunlight and Shadows; Poems. San Antonio, TX.: Naylor Co., 1966. xii, 111 p.

THOMAS, MARGARET V.
Dreams of the Solitudes. Boston: R. G. Badger, 1925. 2 p. ℓ., 7-66 p.

THOMAS, MARY PETTUS (1857-)
Some Fancies in Verse. New York & Washington: The Neale Publishing Company, 1906. 104 p.

THOMAS, ROSEMARY (1901-1961)
Immediate Sun. New York: Twayne, 1951. 64 p. (Twayne library of modern poetry)
Selected Poems. New York: Twayne Publishers, 1968. 161 p.

THOMAS, RUTH
Flint and Fireflies. Boston: Manthorne & Burack, Inc., 1942. 64 p.

THOMPSON, ALYS H. R.
The Year's Rosary, by "Tipherith": A Cycle of Sonnets for Every Week in the Year. Chicago: The Library Shelf, 1910. 2 p. ℓ., 9-60 p., 1 ℓ.

THOMPSON, CLARA ANN
Songs from the Wayside. Rossmoyne, OH.: The Author, 1908.
A Garland of Poems. Boston: The Christopher Publishing House, 1926. 96 p.

THOMPSON, DOROTHENIA TINSLEY
Three Slices of Black. Chicago: Free Black Press, 1972.

THOMPSON, DOROTHY BROWN (1896-)
Subject to Change. Shawnee Mission, KS.: BkMk Press, 1973. 20 p.

THOMPSON, GENEVIEVE (1905-)
Tapestry, Poems. New York: Exposition Press, 1958. 45 p.

THOMPSON, HELEN WARD
O, Journey Again! and Other Poems. Atlanta, GA.: J. H. Thompson, 1925. 8-35 p.

THOMPSON, LUCILLE KEY (1892-)
Gracious Interlude. Emory University, Atlanta, GA.: Banner

Press, 1943. 62 p.
Blue Flags Waving. Emory University, Atlanta, GA.: Banner Press, 1951. 60 p. (Verse craft series)
Love Is a Certain Season. Emory University, Atlanta, GA.: Banner Press, 1958. 60 p. (Verse craft series)

THOMPSON, PHYLLIS (HOGE) (1926-)
Artichoke and Other Poems. Honolulu: University of Hawaii Press, 1969. 4 p. ℓ., 66 p.
The Creation Frame: Poems. Urbana, IL.: University of Illinois Press, 1973. vii, 83 p.

THOMPSON, PRISCILLA JANE
Ethiope Lays. Rossmoyne, OH.: The Author, 1900. 4 p. ℓ., 95 p.
Gleanings of Quiet Hours. Rossmoyne, OH.: The Author, 1907. 3 p. ℓ., 100 p.

THOMSON, CATHY
Special Echoes on a Difficult Day. Philadelphia: Dorrance, 1975. 54 p.

THORNBURY, KIZZIE (1865-)
Scattering Flowers. Cincinnati, OH.: Abingdon Press, 1919. 52 p.

THORNE, ELEANOR
The Missel Thrush.... New York: The Exposition Press, 1947. 91 p.

THORNE, ELINOR (INGERSOLL)
Facts and Fancies; in Verse. n.p., 1930. 2 p. ℓ., 9-61 p.

THORNE, EVELYN
The Winding Path. New York: The Avondale Press, Inc., 1927. 167 p.
Tapestries in Time. Branson, MO.: New Athenaeum Press, 195-? [14] p.
Fire in the Crystal. Branson, MO.: New Athenaeum Press, 1952. [20] p.
Design in a Web. Branson, MO.: New Athenaeum Press, 1955. 63 p.
From This Green Window. Crescent City, FL.: New Athenaeum Press, 1965. 57 p.
Answer in Bright Green. Crescent City, FL.: New Athenaeum Press, 1968. 56 p. Added t.p.: Specimen ed. published December 1, 1968 by Olivant Press, Homestead, FL.
Ways of Listening. Homestead, FL.: Olivant Press, 1969. 62 p.

THORNTON, BETTYE LOWE (1937-)
Invitations: Black and White. Montgomery, AL.: Paragon Press, 1973. 74 p.

THORPE, ROSE (HARTWICK) (1850-)
The Poetical Works of Rose Hartwick Thorpe. New York: The Neale Publishing Company, 1912. 137 p.

THRANE, JULIA (1890-1948)
The Willow Bridge. Fargo? N.D.: n.p., 1949. 64 p.

THURMAN, JUDITH (1946-)
Putting My Coat On. London: Covent Garden Press, 1971. 31 p. (Covent Garden Poetry, no. 6)

THURMAN, VIRGINIA (HILL)
Confettied Air. New York: Exposition Press, 1965. 61 p.

THURSTON, ELLA
Dreams of You: A Poem. Oneida, N.Y.: The Oneida Dispatch Press, 1914. 5 ℓ.

TIEMPO, EDITH L.
The Tracks of Babylon, and Other Poems. Denver, CO.: A. Swallow, 1966. 36 p.

TIETJENS, EUNICE (HAMMOND) (1884-1944)
Profiles from China, Sketches in Verse of People and Things Seen in the Interior. New York: A. A. Knopf, 1917. 75 p.
_______, Sketches in Free Verse.... 77, [1] p.
Body and Raiment. New York: A. A. Knopf, 1919. 5 p. ℓ., 13-84 p., 1 ℓ.
Profiles from Home; Sketches in Free Verse of People and Things Seen in the United States. New York: A. A. Knopf, 1925. 110 p.
Leaves in Windy Weather. New York: A. A. Knopf, 1929. 3 p. ℓ., ix-xi, 88 p., 1 ℓ.

TIFFT, ELLEN (1916-)
A Door in a Wall; Poems and Fables. Torrance, CA.: Hors Commerce Press, 1966. [37] p.
The Kissed Cold Kite; Poems and Fables. Torrance, CA.: Hors Commerce Press, 1968. [45] p.
Shaman, Tell. Belmont, WA.: Hellric Publications, 1971.
The Live-Long Day. Tacoma, WA.: Charas Press, 1973. 31 p.

TILDEN, ETHEL ARNOLD
Quest and Acceptance and Other Poems. New York: H. Vinal, 1925. 4 p. ℓ., 48 p.

TILDEN, NANCY LEE
A Winter Garden; Poems 1944-1974. San Francisco: Printed by L. & A. Kennedy, 1965. 42 p.

TILLERY, ANNE VYNE
Moods, Mystical and Otherwise. Boston: Sherman, Franch & Co., 1914. 5 p. ℓ., 68 p.

TIMMONS, ALICE HUNT
Portrait of a Lady. Francestown, N. H.: Golden Quill Press, 1958. 95 p.

TIMMONS, HAZEL BARBARA
My Book of Abstract Poems. New York: Vantage Press, 1963. 63 p.

TINGEY, ALICIA M.
Simple Philosophy; Verses. New York: Vantage Press, 1961. 64 p.

TINSLEY, MARGARET
Detours to Parnassus. Boston: R. G. Badger, 1930. 1 p. ℓ., 5-39 p.

TITMUS, THELMA PEARSON
Laughter's Dark Pools, Love Poems. New York: Exposition Press, 1953. 48 p.

TOBIAS, JEAN TERRY
Love, Life & Laughter. Peterborough, N. H.: Windy Row Press, 1973. 64 p.

TODD, GAIL
Family Way. San Lorenzo, CA.: Shameless Hussy Press, 1975. 32 p.

TOLDRIDGE, ELIZABETH
Mother's Love Songs. Boston: R. G. Badger, 1911. 52 p.

TOLMAN, EMILY
To a Summer Cloud, and Other Poems. Boston: Sherman, French & Co., 1914. 4 p. ℓ., 81 p.

TOLONEN, DOROTHY (DAILEY)
From Scarlet to Gold. Boston: Bruce Humphries, 1956. 43 p.

TOMKINS, MARGARET H.
These Are Ours. Chicago: Dierkes Press, 1952. 48 p.

TOMPA, LOIS
Above the Wall. New York: Vantage Press, 1967. 47 p.

TOMPKINS, DORA ELLA (1910-)
Rhymes. Kanona, N. Y.: J & C Transcripts, 1964. 3 p. ℓ., 30 p.
Nutmeg Rhymes. Danbury, CT.: T. N. P. C., 1966. 24, [1] p.
Patterned Poems. Danbury, CT.: T. N. P. C., 1966. 3 p. ℓ., 30 p.
Afterglow. Danbury, CT.: T. N. P. C., 1968. 22 p.

TOMPKINS, JANE HARRISON (1841-1912) [HARRISON, JENNIE, pseud.]
Poems of Life and Light: A Book of Devotional Verse. n. p.: Winston, 1906. 175 p.

TONEY, IEDA MAI
The Young Scholar and Other Poems. Boston: Meador Pub. Co., 1951. 32 p.

TONGUE, MARGARET
A Book of Kinds. Iowa City, IA.: Stone Wall Press, 1958. 39 p.

TOTTEN, MARY HOWE
Thorold, and Other Poems. New York & Washington: The Neale Publishing Company, 1904. ix, 11-110 p.

TOURTEL, MARY
A Horse Book. New York: F. A. Stokes Co., 1901. 2 p. ℓ., 94 p., 1 ℓ.

TOWER, BERYL (GOODWIN) (1898-)
Cabin in the Pines. Dallas, TX.: Kaleidograph Press, 1950. 95 p.

TOWER, FRANCES GATES
Come Spring. Nashville, TN.: Parthenon Press, 1955. 59 p.

TOWNE, MARY E.
Colorado Calls; Poems. Denver, CO.: Big Mountain Press, 1958. 56 p.
The Shining Path. Phoenix, AZ.: Stanley Publications, 1964? 98 p.

TRABAND, DORA WEAVER
Out of the Mist.... New York: The Exposition Press, 1940. 95 p.

TRACY, ALOISE
Memory Is a Poet. Chicago: Windfall Press, 1964. 48 p.
A Merry Heart. Charleston, IL.: Prairie Press, 1966. 36 p.

TRACY, ELIZABETH MOORE
To Each His Song; Selected Poems. Mill Valley, CA.: Wings Press, 1956. 84 p.

TRACY, VERA MARIE
Gold-Dusty. Milwaukee, WI.: The Bruce Publishing Co., 1937. x p., 1 ℓ., 83 p.

TRASK, ELIZABETH GUERRANT
The Gardener. Philadelphia: Dorrance & Co., Inc., 1933. 62 p. (Contemporary poets of Dorrance, 112)

TRASK, KATE NICHOLS (1853-1922)
Christalan. New York & London: G. P. Putnam's Sons, 1903. iii, 36 p.
Sonnets and Lyrics. 3d ed. Boston: R. G. Badger, 1903. 103 p.
Night and Morning. London: J. Lane; New York: John Lane Company, 1907. 3 p. ℓ., [3]-72 p.

TRAUTWINE, HANNAH DOAN
The Wings of Chance; A Collection of Poems. New York: n. p., 1927. viii, 104 p.
The Loom of Life, and Other Poems. New York: Printed by J. J. Little and Ives Co., 1929. 147 p.

TRAXLER, PATRICIA
Blood Calendar. New York: William Morrow, 1975. 96 p.

TREE, LETA BEATRICE (1884-)
North America, and Other Poems. Boston: Branden Press, 1968. 160 p.

TREMBLE, STELLA CRAFT (1897-)
Thorns and Thistledown; The Collected Poems of Stella Tremble. New York: Comet Press Books, 1954. 48 p.
Wind in the Reed; Poems. Boston: Bruce Humphries, 1957. 64 p.
The Crystal Prism. New York: The American Poets Free Press, 1959. 59 p.
Loom and Lyre. Dallas, TX.: Triangle Pub. Co., 1961. 85 p.
Telescope of Time. Chicago: Windfall Press, 1962. 4 p. ℓ., 27 p.
Songs of the Prairie. Chicago: Columbus Press, 1964. 79 p.
_______. 2d ed. Charleston, IL.: Prairie Press, 1965. 4 p. ℓ., 113 p.
In His Days. Charleston, IL.: Prairie Press, W. S. Tremble, 1966. 63 p.
Bells of Autumn. Charleston, IL.: Prairie Press Books, 1967. xiv, 118 p.
Hair, the Color of Clay and Sun. Charleston, IL.: Prairie Press Books, 1967. 78 p.
From Isles of Silence. Charleston, IL.: Prairie Press Books, 1968. 118 p.
Center and Circumference. Charleston, IL.: Prairie Press Books, 1971. xiii, 130 p., 1 ℓ.

TRENT, HATTIE (COVINGTON)
My Memory Gems. Salisbury, N. C.: Livingstone College, 1948. xiv, 87 p.

TRENT, LUCIA (1897-)
The Frigate of My Fancy. New York: Hudson Press, 1922. 21 p.
Dawn Stars. New York: H. Harrison, 1926. 95 p.

Children of Fire and Shadow. Chicago: R. Packard & Co., 1929. 95 p.

TREPTE, LOIS E.
...Pansies (Thoughts). Philadelphia: Dorrance & Co., Inc., 1934. 48 p. (Contemporary poets of Dorrance, 125)

TREVOR, DORIS E.
The Master's Violin: Poems. New York: Pageant Press, 1934. 38 p.

TRIEM, EVE (1902-)
...Parade of Doves. New York: E. P. Dutton & Co., 1946. 56 p.
Poems. Denver, CO.: Poetry and Prose Editions, 1965. 43 p.
Selected Poems. Homestead, FL.: Olivant Press, 1974.

TRIGG, EMMA GRAY (WHITE)
After Eden. New York: G. P. Putnam's Sons, 1937. 110 p.
Paulownia Tree. Francestown, N.H.: Golden Quill Press, 1969. 80 p.

TRIPP, LENA ELVINA
More Verses. Kanona, N.Y.: J. & C. Transcripts, 1970. 4 p. ℓ., 64 p.
Those Pets of Mine. Plymouth, CA.: n.p., 1971. 17 p.

TROTT, ROSEMARY CLIFFORD (1914-)
Sea Mist and Balsam, and Other Poems. Mill Valley, CA.: Wings Press, 1958. 50 p.

TROTTA, ANNA
Loving. Columbus, OH.: Edwin-Lee Publication, 1973.

TROUBETZKOY, AMÉLIE (RIVES) CHANLER (1863-1945)
Seléné. New York & London: Harper & Brothers, 1905. 3 p. ℓ., 88, [1] p.
Augustine the Man. London: John Lane; New York: John Lane Company, 1906. 5 p. ℓ., [3]-83 p.
As the Wind Blew. New York: Frederick A. Stokes Co., 1920. xii p., 4 ℓ., 3-229 p.

TROUBETZKOY, (DOROTHY) ULRICH (1914-)
Out of the Wilderness. Wilmington, DE.: Wilmington Poetry Society & Delaware Writers, 1957. 23 p.
Where Is Christmas? Richmond, VA.: Dietz Press, 1967. [16] p.
Bluebonnets and Blood. San Antonio, TX.: Naylor Co., 1968. xii, 80 p.
Sagamore Creek. Wilmington, DE.: Wilmington Poetry Society & Delaware Writers, 1969. 28 p.

TROUSDALE, ANNIE LAURIE
Winging Far. New York: G. P. Putnam's Sons, 1938. ix p., 1 ℓ., 13-125 p.
Beating Wings; Poems. New York: G. P. Putnam's Sons, 1940. x p., 1 ℓ., 13-89 p.

TRUEMAN, ANITA
Philo-Sophia; A Collection of Poems. New York: The Alliance Pub. Co., 1900. 100 p.

TRUESDELL, AMELIA WOODWARD (1839-1912)
Francisca Reina. Boston: R. G. Badger, 1908. 44 p., 1 ℓ.
The Soul's Rubaiyat. San Francisco: A. M. Robertson, 1911. 5-31 p.
Francisca Reina. San Francisco: A. M. Robertson, 1912. viii, 124 p.
All the Way; Being the Collected Poems of Amelia Woodward Truesdell. San Francisco: A. M. Robertson, 1913. ix, 228 p.

TRUESDELL, ELLA MARIA (1849-)
Over the Bridge, and Other Poems. Boston: R. G. Badger, 1905. 89 p.

TRUITT, BESS
Thistle Down and Prairie Rose. Kansas City, MO.: Burton Pub. Co., 1940. 6 p. ℓ., 15-96 p.

TRULLINGER, LILLIAN MAY (REED) (1882-)
An Isle and a Moon. Honolulu: n. p., 1925. 23 p.

TRUMBULL, ANNIE ELIOT (1857-1949)
Impressions. Hartford, CT.: E. V. Mitchell, 1927.

TRUSLOW, MARGUERITE (WALBRIDGE) (1877-)
Reprieve, and Other Poems. New York: William-Frederick Press, 1954. 61 p. (William-Frederick poets, 116)

TRUST, ESTELLE (1908-)
The Hazelwood Wand; Poems. Shreveport, LA.: Literary Calendar Press, 1958? 16 p. (Literary calendar press series, no. 2)

TRYON, MABEL B.
My Garden of Poems.... Huntington Park, CA.: Pub. by Glenn Printing Co., 1928. 2 p. ℓ., 40 p.

TUBBS, IDA PUTNAM
A Book of Poems. Waverly, N. Y.: National Protective Legion, 1913. 190 p.

TUCKER, AGNES (CARRUTH) (1910-)
...Dew on My Head.... Philadelphia: Dorrance & Co., Inc.,

1934. 52 p.
Songs from a Narrow Valley. New York: Paebar, 1934. 69 p.
Sonnets to the Sun. London: Linden Press, 1959. 96 p. (Poets of today)
The White Sparrow. London: Linden Press, dist. by Centaur Press, 1960. 71 p.
The Crystal Tree. Roma: Centro Studi e Scambi Internazionali, 1963. 16 p. (Quaderni di poesia)

TUCKER, BEVERLEY DANDRIDGE
Confederate Memorial Verses. Norfolk, VA.: Pub. by the Pickett-Buchanan Chapter, United Daughters of the Confederacy, 1904? 36 p.

TUCKER, BEVERLEY DANDRIDGE, bp. (1846-)
My Three Loves.... New York & Washington: The Neale Publishing Company, 1910. 106 p.

TUCKER, HELEN
Remembrance. Boston: B. Humphries, 1951. 48 p.

TUDOR, ELSA
Through a Broken Reed.... Boston: R. G. Badger, The Gorham Press, 1933. 32 p.
Love and Life. New York: Roerich Museum Press, 1935. viii p., 1 ℓ., 66 p.

TUDOR, MARIE see GARLAND, MARIE (TUDOR) (1870-)

TULL, MARY ESTHER
Stained Windows. Philadelphia: Dorrance & Co., 1927. 68 p.
Quest. London: The Mitre Press, 1932. 3 p.ℓ., 9-127, [1] p.

TUNNELL, SOPHIE
Blackberry Winter. Edwardsville, IL.: n.p., 1939. 106 p.

TUNSTALL, VELMA BARRET (1914-) [SHANA BARRETT TUNSTALL, pseud.]
Shadows on My Soul. Dallas, TX.: Royal Pub. Co., 1971. 43 p.

TUNSTALL, VIRGINIA HUNTER (LYNE)
A White Sail Set. New York: H. Vinal, Ltd., 1927. 5 p.ℓ., 67, [1] p.

TURNBULL, BELLE
Goldboat. Boston: Houghton, Mifflin Co., 1940. 3 p.ℓ., 76, [1] p.
The Tenmile Range. Iowa City, IA.: Prairie Press, 1957. 53 p.

TURNER, ALBERTA T. (1919-)
Need. Ashland, OH.: Ashland Poetry Press, 1971. 52 p.
Learning to Count. Pittsburgh, PA.: University of Pittsburgh Press, 1974. 45 p.

TURNER, JENNIE WILLING (McMULLIN) (1885-)
Sunburned Sands. Dallas, TX.: The Kaleidograph Press, 1942. xii p., 1 ℓ., 15-59 p.

TURNER, LIDA WILSON
Flagstones and Flowers. Oglethorpe University, GA.: Oglethorpe University Press, 1934. 3 p. ℓ., 9-60 p.
______. Emory University, Atlanta, GA.: Banner Press, 1943. 70 p. (Verse craft series)

TURNER, LILLIAN ELIZABETH
Shifting Sand. n.p., 1961. 85 p.

TURNER, LUCY MAE
'Bout Cullud Folkses. New York: H. Harrison, 1938. 64 p.

TURNER, MARTHA ANNE
...White Dawn Salutes Tomorrow. Philadelphia: Dorrance & Co., 1943. 85 p. (Contemporary poets of Dorrance, 260)

TURNER, NANCY BYRD (1880-)
Zodiac Town, The Rhymes of Amos and Ann. Boston: Atlantic Monthly Press, 1921. 5 p. ℓ., 131, [1] p.
Magpie Lane; Poems. New York: Harcourt, Brace & Co., 1927. x, 88 p.
A Riband on My Rein; Poems. Hartford, CT.: E. V. Mitchell, 1929. 3 p. ℓ., ix-xii p., 2 ℓ., 3-120 p.
______. New York: Dodd, Mead & Company, 1934. xii p., 1 ℓ., 122 p.
Star in a Well. New York: Dodd, Mead & Co., 1935. xii, 175 p.
Silver Saturday; Poems for the Home. New York: Dodd, Mead & Company, 1937. xii p., 1 ℓ., 125 p.
When It Rained Cats and Dogs. Philadelphia: J. B. Lippincott, 1946. [28] p.
Poems, Selected and New. Francestown, N.H.: Golden Quill Press, 1965. 122 p.

TURNER, VERNA STUART
Tear-Drop Bouquets and Other Lays. New York: Carlton Press, 1969. 64 p.

TUTTLE, EMMA ROOD (1839-)
Asphodel Blooms and Other Offerings. Chicago: J. R. Francis; London: H. A. Copley, 1901. 5 p. ℓ., [15]-285 p.

TUTTLE, STELLA WESTON (1907-)
Nor Bitter Nor Profane. Dallas, TX.: Kaleidograph Press, 1953. 72 p.

TWICHELL, ANNA SPENCER
With Star and Grass. Boston: The Cornhill Company, 1921. 11-59 p.

TWIGGS, SARAH LOWE
The Supreme Adventure. Bryn Athyn, PA.: n.p., 1919. 239 p.

TYLER, ELIZABETH PALMER (1881-1951)
The Quiver Full. Emory University, Atlanta, GA.: Banner Press, 1949. 67 p. (Verse craft series)

TYNES, MARY POLLARD
The Radiant Road.... Boston: B. Humphries, Inc., 1931. 64 p.
The Sunset Hill.... Dallas, TX.: The Kaleidograph Press, 1935. xi p., 1 ℓ., 15-82 p.
In Some Blue Dawn.... Dallas, TX.: The Kaleidograph Press, 1939. xi p., 1 ℓ., 15-75 p.

TYNG, HARRIET [Full Name: Harriet Morgan Tyng.]
...Open Letter, and Other Poems. Philadelphia: Dorrance & Co., 1938. 3 p.ℓ., 9-47. (Contemporary poets of Dorrance, 187)
Vermont Village. New York: Stephen Daye Press, 1947. 67 p.

TYRREL, EULALEE (1887-)
The Heart Will Sing Again. West Los Angeles, CA.: Wagon & Star Press, 1951. 58 p.

TYSON, ANNE ARRINGTON
Magdalene, and Other Poems. Montgomery, AL.: The Paragon Press, 1912. 37 p.
Magdalene; Poems and Lyrics. New York: Moffat, Yard & Company, 1923. 96 p.
Tomorrow, and Other Poems. N.Y.: H. Vinal, 1927. 3 p.ℓ., 57, [1] p.
Magdalen, and Other Poems. New York: The Knickerbocker Press, 1930. iv, 76 p.

ULLMANN, MARGARET
Tone-Poems. n.p.: Lakeside Press, 1908. 24 p.

ULRICH, BESSIE KENYON
The Winding Trail. Rochester, N.Y.: Verwey Printing Co., Inc., 1926. 31 p.

ULRICH, SHARON
I Am the Empress and No One Will Believe It. Milwaukee, WI.: Terrestrial Press, 1970. 28 p.

UNANGST, FLORENCE BECK (1911-)
Mainly Laughter. Chicago: Windfall Press, 1964. 32 p.
Mainly Quatrainly. Brooklyn, N.Y.: Serv-U-Press, 1965? 20 p.
The Searching Soul. Charleston, IL.: Prairie Press, W. S. Tremble, 1966. 39 p.
Love and Stuff. Danbury, CT.: Published by T.N.P.C., 1967. 32 p.

Past and Present. Danbury, CT.: T.N.P.C., 1967. 22, [1] p.

UNDERWOOD, EDNA (WORTHLEY) (1873-)
The Garden of Desire: Love Sonnets to a Spanish Monk. New York & London: Kennerley, 1913. 3 p. ℓ., 9-82 p.
Attic Twilights. Portland, ME.: The Mosher Press, 1928. 12, [1] p., 1 ℓ.
Egyptian Twilights. Portland, ME.: The Mosher Press, 1928. 10, [1] p., 1 ℓ.
Maine Summers; Sonnets to My Mother. Portland, ME.: The Mosher Press, 1940. vi, 25, [1] p.

UNGER, BARBARA
Basement: Poems, 1959-1961. San Francisco: Isthmus Press, 1975. 35 p. (Isthmus chapbook #4)

UNTERMEYER, JEAN (STARR) (1886-1970)
Growing Pains. New York: B. W. Huebsch, 1918. 64 p.
Dreams Out of Darkness. New York: B. W. Huebsch, Inc., 1921. 74 p.
Steep Ascent. New York: The Macmillan Company, 1927. 57 p.
...Winged Child. New York: The Viking Press, 1936. 77 p.
Love and Need; Collected Poems, 1918-1940. New York: The Viking Press, 1940. xvi, 239 p.
Later Poems. n.p.: Printed by E. and J. B. Roth, 1958. 24 p.
Job's Daughter. New York: W. W. Norton, 1967. 150 p.

UPTON, SUSAN CONDE OSGOOD
October Roses, and Other Verses. Los Angeles, CA.: The Neuner Company, 1915. 143 p.

URBANEK, MAE (BOBB) (1903-)
Songs of the Sage. Denver, CO.: Big Mountain Press, 1962. 242 p.

URDANG, CONSTANCE (HENRIETTE) (1922-)
Charades and Celebrations: Poems. New York: October House, 1965. 83 p.
The Picnic in the Cemetery. New York: G. Braziller, 1975. ix, 67 p. (The Braziller series of poetry)

URE, OLIVE E.
Gems from the Southland. Los Angeles, CA.: MasterMind Pub., 1919. 12 ℓ.

URIE, CAROLINE FOULKE
Vendemmia.... New York: Island Press, 1947. 63 p.

VAIL, RUTH (NEWBOLD)
River Acres. Dallas, TX.: The Kaleidograph Press, 1936. 103 p.
The Year's at the Spring. Emory University, Atlanta, GA.: Banner Press, 1954. 78 p. (Verse craft series)

VALENTINE, ELIZABETH UFFINGTON
The Ship of Silence, and Other Poems. n.p.: Bowen, 1901. 161 p.

VALENTINE, JEAN (1934-)
Dream Barker and Other Poems. New Haven, CT.: Yale University Press, 1965. 49 p. (Yale Series of Younger Poets, v. 61)
Pilgrims. New York: Farrar, Straus, and Giroux, 1969. 7 p. ℓ., 46 p.
Ordinary Things. New York: Farrar, Straus, and Giroux, 1974. 47 p.

VALENTINE, MARY A. (CLARK) (1853-)
Waiting for the Master, and Other Poems. Huntington, IN.: The U. B. Publishing Establishment, Printers, 1900. 26 p.

VALLÉ, ISABEL
Circle in the Sand. New York, London: G. P. Putnam's Sons, 1935. viii p., 1 ℓ., 11-108 p.

VAN BUREN, ALICIA (KEISKER) (1860-)
As Thought Is Led; Lyrics and Sonnets. Boston: R. G. Badger, 1904. 48 p.
Fireflies: Lyrics and Sonnets. Boston: R. G. Badger, 1913. 47 p.

VANCE, ELEANOR (GRAHAM) (1908-)
For These Moments. Brattleboro, VT.: Printed by Stephen Daye Press, 1939. 103 p.
Store in Your Heart. New York: Bookman Associates, 1950. 64 p.
It Happens Every Day. Francestown, N.H.: Golden Quill Press, 1962. 79 p.

VAN CLEEF, JEAN
The Golden Horse Cries. Briarcliff Manor, N.Y.: Printed by Easi-Bild Pub. Co., 1972. 55 p.

VAN CLEVE, ALICE DAVIS
Queen's Rosary, an Acrostic, Sixty Sonnets Celebrating an Event of Each of Sixty Years of the Most Glorious Reign of History. New York: R. H. Russell, 1902. [70] p.

VANDERBILT, GLORIA (1924-)
Love Poems. Cleveland, OH.: World Pub. Co., 1955. 63 p.

VAN DER VEER, KATHERINE
The Fire's By. Dallas, TX.: The Kaleidograph Press, 1934. 4 p. ℓ., xi-xiii p., 1 ℓ., 17-80, [1] p.

VANDIVER, JEWELL
Soundings. Emory University, Atlanta, GA.: Banner Press, 1954. 80 p. (Verse craft series)

VAN DUYN, MONA (1921-)
Valentines to the Wide World; Poems. Cummington, MA.: Cummington Press, 1958. 55 p.
A Time of Bees. Chapel Hill, N.C.: University of North Carolina Press, 1964. 57 p. (Contemporary poetry series)
To See, To Take: Poems. New York: Atheneum, 1970. viii, 94 p.
Bedtime Stories. Champaign, IL.: Ceres Press, 1972. [37] p.
Merciful Disguises: Poems Published and Unpublished. New York: Atheneum, 1973. x, 245 p.

VAN DYKE, CHERYL
Cheat Grass. Port Townsend, WA.: Copper Canyon Press, 1975. 28 p.

VAN EMDEN, FRIEDA W. (1891-)
Sure Enough, How Come? San Antonio, TX.: Naylor Company, 1933. 3 p.ℓ., ix-xvii, 70 p.
_______. rev. ed., 1938. xvi, 105 p.

VAN HORN, RUTH G.
Crooked Eclipses. Gunnison, CO.: A. Swallow, 1942. 23, [1] p.

VAN HOUTEN, ELINOR
Open Gates. New York: Vantage Press, 1956. 49 p.

VAN HOUTEN, LOIS
Behind the Door. Madison, N.J.: Stone Country Press, 197-. 40 p.
North Jersey Blues. New York: Cycle Press, 1972. 26 p.

VAN KIRK, ELIZABETH DAFFAN
Hawaiian Holiday. San Antonio, TX.: Naylor Co., 1959. viii, 42 p.

VANLANDINGHAM, LYNN
Alone I Wait. Flagstaff, AZ.: Northland Press, 1970. 67, [1] p.

VANLANINGHAM, EVELYN BOREN
Sorrows of a Changing Face: Poems. Champaign, IL.: Moneytree Press, 1973. [38] p.

VAN NAME, FRANCES A. R.
Let's Be Happy, Book of Verse.... Detroit: Radio Printing Co., 1939. 50 p.

VAN NESS, MAYE F.
Idle Hours. New York: The Exposition Press, 1948. 64 p.

VAN NORDEN, FAY JACKSON
Paths of Yesterday. San Francisco: Skyline Press, 1952. 57 p.

VAN ORDEN, AIDNA
In the Blue. New York: The Knickerbocker Press, 1913. vi p., 1 ℓ., 70 p.

VAN OVER, GRACE LEE (1930-1963)
A Bit of Clay. Philadelphia: Dorrance, 1966. 7 p. ℓ., 149 p. (Contemporary poets of Dorrance, 621)

VAN PELT, ALICE
The Pretty Letters. Toledo, OH.: The Hadley Printing & Paper Co., 1914. 4 p. ℓ., 7-77 p.

VAN RENSSELEAR, MARIANA GRISWOLD (1851-1934)
Poems. New York: The Macmillan Company, 1910. ix, 140 p.
Many Children. Boston: The Atlantic Monthly Press, 1921. xi, [1], 83, [1] p.

VAN SLINGERLAND, NELLIE BINGHAM
Passion and Picque Poesy. New York: Guarantee Pub. Co., 1905.
Patriotic Poesy. New York: Guarantee Pub. Co., 1905. 18 p.

VAN STEENWYK, MARION THOMPSON
Brittle, Bright. Chicago: The Black Archer Press, 1931. 5 p. ℓ., 13-68 p.

VAN STOCKUM, HILDA (1908-) [Full Name: Hilda Gerarda Van Stockum.]
...The Angels' Alphabet. New York: Viking Press, 1948. [64] p.

VAN TASSEL, ETTA MAY
Beyond Geography, A Few Poems. Stamford, CT.: The Overbrook Press, 1946. 2 p. ℓ., 45, [2] p.

VAN VLECK, NATALIE JOHNSON
Just One More; Verse and Pictures. Garden City, N.Y.: Doubleday, Page & Co., 1927. ix, [1], 84 p., 1 ℓ.

VAN VORST, MARIE (1867-1936)
Poems. New York: Dodd, Mead & Company, 1903. xi, 122 p.

VAN WICKLE, CARRIE ADELE
America's Lullaby, and Other Poems. Boston: The Christopher Publishing House, 1942. viii p., 1 ℓ., 13-142 p.

VAN WINKLE, ELEANOR
Verses of a Happy Lady. San Diego, CA.: T. G. Dawson, 1929. 5 p. ℓ., 13-112 p., 1 ℓ.
California and Other Verses. San Diego, CA.: The Torrey Pine Press, 1934. 62 p., 1 ℓ.

VAN ZANDT, GRACE GOODSPEED
Occasional Verses. San Diego, CA.: San Diego Printing Company, 1928. 40 p.

VAN ZANDT, KATHARINE
Singing Through the Year. Princeton, N.J.: Princeton University Press, 1940. 7 p. ℓ., 3-83 p.

VARDELL, PAT
Personally for You and Yours. Dallas, TX.: Book Craft, 1963. 3 p. ℓ., 170 p.
Personally. [Book two] Dallas, TX.: Book Craft, 1965. 60 p.
Candles in the Dark. Dallas, TX.: Book Craft, 1966. 90 p.
To Live Is to Love. Dallas, TX.: The Book Craft, 1968. 90 p.

VASSILION, AMELIA A. ANDRIELLO
Sing under the Breath. Syracuse, N.Y.: Vassilion, 1962. 63 p.

VAUGHAN, CARRIE BOURNE
Out of the Depths. Boston: R. G. Badger, 1908. 74 p.

VAUGHN, ADELIA (WITT) (1866-1935)
Selected Poems. Berkeley, CA.: n.p., 1935. [57] p.

VAUGHN, AGNES GORDON
So Many Worlds. Detroit? MI.: n.p., 1935. 4 p. ℓ., 32 numb. ℓ., 1 ℓ.
______. 2d ed., rev. and enl., 1936. 4 p. ℓ., 40 numb ℓ., 1 ℓ.

VAUGHN, DOROTHY
These Bits of Life; Poems. Dallas, TX.: Royal Pub. Co., 1965. 66 p.

VAUGHN, FRANCES LOIS
In Winged Sandals. Findlay, OH.: Ellisonia, 1951. 63 p.

VAUGHN, GERTRUDE THOMPSON
Across the Valley. New York: Avon House, 1942. 4 p. ℓ., 7-62 p.
With a Shield. New York: Exposition Press, 1948. 63 p.

VAUGHN, RUTH (1935-)
Celebrate with Words! Nashville, TN.: Broadman Press, 1972. 42 p.

VAUGHT, ESTELLA
Vengeance Is Mine. New York: Comet, 1959. 62 p.

VAUX-ROYER, ROSE M. de
Soul Shadows, Songs and Sonnets. New York: The Bookery, 1913. 99 p.
Rose of the Flame Immortal. New York: The Cameo Press and Publishing Company, 1920. xii, 88 p.

VEENENDAAL, CORNELIA
The Trans-Siberian Railway. Cambridge, MA.: Alice James Books, 1973. 62 p.

VEGA, JANINE see POMMY-VEGA, JANINE

VEGHTE, ADELINE HOLLISTER
Songs of the Spirit; Poems and Design. Pasadena, CA.: n.p., 1958. 116 p.

VEJTASA, FRANCES
...Prairie Phantasy. Philadelphia: Dorrance and Company, 1937. 48 p. (Contemporary poets of Dorrance, 170)

VENEN, BERTHA PIPER
Annals of Old Angeline. Seattle? WA.: Press of Denny-Coryell Co., 1903. [64] p.

VENEN, LAUREL PHILO
Kalethea; A Peep into the Realms of Poesy. Missoula, MT.: n.p., 1926. 117, [4] p.

VENTON, VIVA A.
The Gates of Paradise Ajar. Battle Creek, MI.: n.p., 1916. 67 p.

VERKENNES, GENEVA ALICE (Mc VAY)
Treasures of Truth. Flint, MI.: n.p., 1961? [18] p.

VERLAINE, DEE (1905-)
...Nets upon the Morning. Los Angeles, CA.: Gargoyle House, 1930. 42 p., 1 ℓ.

VERNER, ALICE CARRY
A Handful of Autumn Leaves. New York: H. Lechner, 1911. 87 p.

VERNON, ETHEL JOSLIN
A Voice from the Mountain Top. New York: The Exposition Press, 1944. 192 p.

VERNON, FREDA JESSIE
Revelation to Mankind: Gems of Spiritual Poetry. New York: Exposition Press, 1952. 128 p.

VERNON, LUCILE
Mephistopheles Puffeth the Sun Out, and Other Poems. Boston: The Stratford Co., 1920. 4 p. ℓ., 46 p.

VER SLUIS, EDITH
A Book of Verse. Grand Rapids? MI.: n.p., 1907. 29 ℓ.

VERTA MAE [GROSVENOR, VERTA MAE]
Plain Brown Rapper. Garden City, N.Y.: Doubleday, 1975.

VERVILLE, SONIA E.
...Bells Are Ringing, a Narrative Poem. Philadelphia: Dorrance & Company, 1946. 35 p. (Contemporary poets of Dorrance, 315)

VERY, ALICE (1894-)
The Human Abstract. Boston: B. Humphries, Inc., 1936. 62 p.
Write on the Water. Boston: Branden Press, 1972. 64 p.

VESTAL, GERTRUDE LA VINIA
Boundary Lines, a Book of Poems. New York: The Paebar Company, 1944. 3 p. ℓ., 3-60 p.
Salutation to Thought; Sonnets. Rome: Centro Studi e Scambi Internazionali, 1963. 16 p.
The Kingdom of the Mind. Philadelphia: Dorrance, 1969. 8 p. ℓ., 138 p.

VESTER, CLARA E.
Songs for Moments of Hope: Poems. Boston: R. G. Badger, 1904.
Singing Lines. Cedar Rapids, IA.: The Torch Press, 1928. 63 p.

VICTORIN, ANNETTE
Falling Feathers, Poems. Chicago: Dierkes Press, 1948. 48 p.

VIDAL, TERESA
The Gypsy's Curse; Love Poems. New York: Exposition Press, 1954. 89 p.

VIGER, MARY LOUISE
...Green-Wave. Philadelphia: Dorrance and Company, 1938. 5 p. ℓ., 9-85 p. (Contemporary poets of Dorrance, 184)

VIGGERS, LILLIAN
Out of the Dumps. Portland, OR.: Printed by the Metropolitan Printing Co., 1935. 7 p. ℓ., 65 p.
...Kiddie Shadows. Philadelphia: Dorrance and Company, 1941. 51 p. (Contemporary poets of Dorrance, 218)

VILAS, FAITH VAN VALKENBURGH
The Drummer of Fyvie, and Other Verse. New York: Reader Editors Inc., 1926. xvi, 95, [1] p.
Aromancy, and Other Poems. Philadelphia: Dorrance and Company, 1929. 71 p. (Contemporary poets of Dorrance, 75)
Roads of Earth. Philadelphia: Dorrance & Co., 1934. 125 p. (Contemporary poets of Dorrance, 119)
Certificate of Flight. New York: L. Raley, 1939. 79 p.
Sea Harvest, and Other Ballads. New Haven, CT?: Author, 1946? 1 p. ℓ., 46 p.

New Fields. New Haven, CT?: Author, 1951? [8] p.

VILLARD, MARIQUITA
Out of Night, Poems. Boston? n.p., 1952. 75 p.

VINES, EDA (HADRA)
Let Me Give Thanks for Life. Dallas, TX.: Kaleidograph Press, 1947. x p., 1 ℓ., 13-68 p.

VINOGRAD, JULIA (1943-)
Revolution & Other Poems. Berkeley, CA.: Oyez, 1970. 36 p.
The Berkeley Bead Game. Berkeley, CA.: Cody's Books, 1971. [39] p.
Uniform Opinions. Berkeley, CA.: Cody's Books, 1972. 31 p.
Street Spices: Poems. Berkeley, CA.: Thorp Springs Press, 1973. [28] p.
The Circus: Poems. Berkeley, CA.: Thorp Springs Press, 1974. 28 p.
Street Feet: Poems. Berkeley, CA.: Thorp Springs Press, 1974. 34 p.
Street Pieces: Poems. Berkeley, CA.: Thorp Springs Press, 1975. 32 p.

VINTON, ELEANOR (1899-)
Sounding Piquant Verses. Portland, ME.: Falmouth Publishing House, 1940. 5 p. ℓ., 3-52 p.
On the Contoocock, and Other Poems. Dublin, N.H.: W. L. Bauhan, 1974. 73 p.

VINYARD, MARY DICKSON
The Voice of Sooner-Land. New York: Vantage Press, 1956. 77 p.
The Voice of Sooner-Land, Number Two. New York: Pageant Press, 1961. 6 p. ℓ., 145 p.

VIORST, JUDITH
The Village Square. New York: Coward-McCann, 1966. 91, [2] p.
It's Hard to Be Hip Over Thirty, and Other Tragedies of Married Life. New York: World Pub. Co., 1968. 71 p.
______. New York: New American Library, 1970. 94 p. (A Signet book)
People & Other Aggravations. New York: World Pub. Co., 1971. 61 p.

VIOSCA, RENÉE
Tribute in Verse. New York: Carlton Press, 1970. 48 p.

VIRGIL, ANITA
A 2nd Flake. Paterson, N.J.: The Author. 72 p.

VISSER, AUDRAE
Rustic Roads, and Other Poems. New York: Exposition Press, 1961. 64 p.

VITORITTO, ELVIRA LANZA
Amaranth and Tumbleweed. Los Angeles, CA.: Swordsman Pub. Co., 1966. 48 p.
Dropping Pebbles in the Pond. Rome: Centro Studi e Scambi Internazionali, Academia Internazionale Leonardo da Vinci, 1969. 16 p.
Gentle on the Wind. Charleston, IL.: Prairie Press Books, 1969. 6 p. ℓ., 36 p.
Mediterranean Mood. Roma: Centro Studi e Scambi Internazionali, 1970. 16 p.
Substance and Dreams. Charleston, IL.: Prairie Press Books, 1972. xi p., 1 ℓ., 57, [1] p.

VOLGTS, MARIE
The Upward Look, Poems. Boston: J. W. Luce Co., 1949. 79 p.
"The Open Door"; Poems. Cicero, IL.: Quality Press, 1954. [40] p.

VOLLINTINE, MARIE
Crimson Feather. New York: H. Vinal, 1926. 5 p. ℓ., 3-93 p., 1 ℓ.

VOLLMAR, JOCELYN
Preludes. San Gabriel, CA.: Willing Pub. Co., 1959. 45 p.
Arabesques. San Gabriel, CA.: Willing Pub. Co., 1966. 31 p.

VON der LINDEN, MARGARET
These Small Songs. New York: House of Field, Inc., 1941. 23 p.

VON FINTEL, MITTIE ELIZA (SWANK) (1859-)
Sparklets. Delta, CO.: Stearns Bros. Co. Printers, 1913. 71 p.

VON SCHÖNBERG, ELIZABETH
Sonnets of San Francisco in Swingtime, and Other Poems. San Francisco: The Nookwood Press, 1937. 7 p. ℓ., 11-114 numb. ℓ.

VOSBURG, STELLA SHERWOOD
Desert Fables. Philadelphia, Chicago: The John C. Winston Company, 1934. 78 p.

VOSE, ELOISE FAUNTLEROY
Heart Echoes. Richmond, VA.: Guardian Pub. Co., 1945. 101 p.

VOSS, RITA, Sister (1901-) [Secular Name: Elizabeth Voss.]
The Soul's Voice. Boston: R. G. Badger, 1920. 4 p. ℓ., 5-40 p.
Shelter of Song. New York: H. Harrison, 1933. 63 p.

VOSWINKEL, LOIS ELEANOR
Silver Flutes. Minneapolis, MN.: The Lund Press, Inc., 1942. 64 p.

VOTAW, GRACE
Faggots of Faith. Dexter, MO.: Candor Press, 1949. 32 p.

VRBOVSKA, ANCA
Cyclone and Other Poems. New York: F. B. U. Fritts, 1934. 75 p.
The Gate Beyond the Sun; New and Selected Poems. New York: New Orlando Publications, 1970. v, 89 p.

VRBOVSKA, ANNA FRANCES
The Other Selves; Poems. New York? n.p., 1951. 32 p.

WACKMAN, MARY (BRABYN)
Lilacs by the Roadside. Dallas, TX.: The Kaleidograph Press, 1941. ix p., 1 ℓ., 13-79 p.
Primroses on the Hedges. Dallas, TX.: The Kaleidograph Press, 1943. ix p., 1 ℓ., 13-80 p.
Hollyhocks Are Sentinels. Dallas, TX.: The Kaleidograph Press, 1945. ix p., 1 ℓ., 13-79 p.

WADDELL, MAUDE
Brookgreen Ballads and Low Country Lyrics. Wendell, S.C.: The Gold Leaf Press, 193-. 3 p. ℓ., 16 p.
Saint Peters-by-the-Sea. Wendell, S.C.: Gold Leaf Press, 1940.
"Songs of the South." Charleston, S.C.: Southern Printing & Publishing Co., 1942. 7 p. ℓ., 17-205 p.

WADE, ALDA MADISON (1883-)
Belmont Park, and Other Poems. Boston: Christopher Publishing House, 1955. 209 p.

WADLEIGH, CHARLOTTE
The Miracle of Light, and Other Poems. New York: William-Frederick Press, 1954. 4 p. ℓ., 53 p.

WADSWORTH, LENORAH
To Meet Your Needs; Poems of Sunny Sanity. New York: The William-Frederick Press, 1946. 94 p.
Yours Sincerely. Norwood? OH.: n.p., 1952. vi p., 1 ℓ., 78 p.

WADSWORTH, MATTIE LEE
Mirage at Dawn. Dallas, TX.: Tardy Pub. Co., 1936. xii, 130 p.

WAECHTER, CARLA
Her Harvest. New York: W. Neale, 1923. 156 p.

WAER, LUCILE
Leaves in the Wind. New York: Vantage Press, 1954. 4 p. ℓ., 54 p.

WAGGONER, PEARL
Beyond the Shadow. Chicago: Rogers & Hall Company, 1913. 1 p. ℓ., 5-96 p.

WAGNER, LINDA WELSHIMER (1936-)
Intaglios. Fort Smith, AR.: South and West, 1967. 48 p.

WAGNER, MADGE (MORRIS)
The Lure of the Desert Land, and Other Poems. San Francisco: Harr Wagner Publishing Company, 1917. 7 p. ℓ., 122 p.

WAGNER, MARY BOYD
Roots. Mill Valley, CA.: Wings Press, 1954. 120 p.

WAGNER, MARY D.
So Grand as Ours! New York: Vantage Press, 1968. 27 p.

WAGNER, MARY SWAIN
Hungry Hands, and Other Poems. New York: The Paebar Company, Inc., 1937. 3 p. ℓ., 42 p.

WAGSTAFF, BLANCHE (SHOEMAKER) (1888-)
The Song of Youth. Boston: R. G. Badger, 1905. 95 p.
Woven of Dreams. New York: J. Lane Company, 1907. 138 p.
Narcissus, and Other Poems. New York: J. T. White & Co., 1918. 120 p.
Quiet Waters. New York: Moffat, Yard and Company, 1921. 122 p., 1 ℓ.
Mortality, and Other Poems. Boston: The Four Seas Company, 1930. 127, [1] p.
After the Flesh. Manchester, ME.: Falmouth Pub. House, 1953. 5 p. ℓ., 61 p.
Sonnets to Parsifal. Boston: Bruce Humphries, 1960. 46 p.

WAHL, JEAN
Voices in the Dark. Kirkwood, MO.: The Printery, 1974. 48 p.

WAID, EVA (CLARK) (1869-1929)
Poems. New York: Printing House of W. E. Rudge, Inc., 1932. 178 p., 1 ℓ.

WAIDE, ALICE (KIRKPATRICK)
Folklore Poems; Texas Style. San Antonio, TX.: Naylor Co., 1965. vi, 38 p.

WAINWRIGHT, VIRGINIA (1891-)
Youth, Love and Laughter. Brookline, MA.: V. Wainwright, 1931. 20 p.

WAITE, ALICE CROCKER

Bird Echoes; Songs of the Wildwood. Boston: R. G. Badger, 1907. 5 p. ℓ., 9-86 p.

WAITE, GERTRUDE HILDABRAND

Poems from My Heart. New York: Exposition Press, 1963. 72 p.

WAITE, SHIRLEY DILLON (1879-1958)

Hill Top Water. Atlanta, GA.: Banner Press, 1959. 62 p. (Verse craft series)

WAKOSKI, DIANE (1937-)

Justice Is Reason Enough. Berkeley, CA.: n.p., 1959. 2 ℓ. (California University. Emily Chamberlin Cook Prize in poetry)

Coins and Coffins. New York: Hawk's Well Press, 1962. 35 p.

Discrepancies and Apparitions; Poems. Garden City, N.Y.: Doubleday, 1966. 95 p.

The George Washington Poems. New York: Riverrun Press, 1967. 55 p.

The Diamond Merchant. Cambridge, MA.: Sans Souci Press, 1968. 34 p.

Greed, Parts One and Two. Los Angeles: Black Sparrow Press, 1968. 23 p.

Inside the Blood Factory. Garden City, N.Y.: Doubleday, 1968. 96 p.

Greed; Parts 3 and 4. Los Angeles: Black Sparrow Press, 1969. 29 p., 1 ℓ.

The Lament of the Lady Bank Dick. Cambridge, MA.: Sans Souci Press, 1969. [20] p.

The Moon Has a Complicated Geography. Palo Alto, CA.: Odda Tala, 1969. [17] p. (Odda Tala, no. 3)

Poems. Albany, CA.: Key Printing Co., 1969. [18] p.

Some Poems for Buddha's Birthday. Brooklyn, N.Y.: Pierrepont Press, 1969. 29 ℓ.

Thanking My Mother for Piano Lessons. Mt. Horeb, WI.: Perishable Press, 1969. [15] p.

Black Dream Ditty for Billy "the kid" M. Seen in Dr. Generosity's Bar Recruiting for Hell's Angels and Black Mafia. Los Angeles: Black Sparrow Press, 1970. [8] p.

The Magellanic Clouds. Los Angeles: Black Sparrow Press, 1970. 150 p., 2 ℓ.

Greed, Parts 5-7. Los Angeles: Black Sparrow Press, 1971. [1]-46 p., 3 ℓ.

The Motorcycle Betrayal Poems. New York: Simon & Schuster, 1971. 160 p.

On Barbara's Shore, A Poem. Los Angeles: Black Sparrow Press, 1971. [9] p.

The Pumpkin Pie: or, Reassurances Are Always False, Tho We Love Them. Only Physics Counts.... Los Angeles: Black Sparrow Press, 1972. [15] p.

Smudging. Los Angeles: Black Sparrow Press, 1972. 153 p.

Dancing on the Grave of a Son of a Bitch. Los Angeles: Black Sparrow Press, 1973. 137 p.
Greed, Parts 8, 9, 11. Los Angeles: Black Sparrow Press, 1973. [1]-50 p., 3 ℓ.
Stillife: Michael, Silver Flute and Violets. Storrs, CT?: n.p., 1973. folder [4] p.
Abalone. Los Angeles: Black Sparrow Press, 1974. [9] p.
The Wandering Tatler. Driftless, WI.: The Perishable Press Limited, 1974.
Virtuoso Literature for Two and Four Hands. Garden City, N.Y.: Doubleday, 1975. x, 85 p.

WALDMAN, ANNE (1945-)
On the Wing. New York: Boke Press, 1967. [18] p.
Giant Night. New York: Angel Hair Books, 1968. [4] ℓ.
O My Life! New York: Angel Hair Books, 1969. [35] ℓ.
Baby Breakdown. New York: Bobbs-Merrill, 1970. 6 p. ℓ., 115 p.
Giant Night; Poems. New York: Corinth Books, 1970. 94 p.
Up Thru the Years. New York: Angel Hair, 1970. [2] ℓ.
Goodies from Anne Waldman. London: Strange Faeces Press, 1971.
Holy City. n.p.: Priv. Print., 1971.
Light and Shadow. New York?: Priv. Print., 1972. folder, [4] p.
Spin Off. Bolinas, CA.: Big Sky Books, 1972. [20] p.
West Indies Poems. New York: Boke Press, 1972. [16] ℓ.
Life Notes: Selected Poems. Indianapolis: Bobbs-Merrill, 1973. 117 p.
Fast Speaking Woman. Detroit: Red Hanrahan Press, 1974. [9], 17, [1] p.
Fast Speaking Woman & Other Chants. San Francisco: City Lights Books, 1975. 76 p.
Sun the Blond Out. Berkeley, CA.: Arif Press, 1975. [13] p.
Poems. London: Opal & Ellen Nations, 197-? [41] p. (Strange Faeces, no. 5)

WALDROP, ROSEMARIE
A Dark Octave. Providence, R.I.: Burning Deck, 1967.
The Relaxed Abalone; or, What-You-May-Find. Providence, R.I.: Burning Deck, 1970. [16] ℓ.
Spring Is a Season and Nothing Else. Mount Horeb, WI.: Perishable Press, 1970. [17] p.
The Aggressive Ways of the Casual Stranger. New York: Random House, 1972. 91 p.
Eating. Providence, R.I.: Diana's Bimonthly, 1974. 10 p.
Kind Regards. Providence, R.I.: Diana's Bimonthly, 1975. 12 p.

WALDSMITH, RUTH
...The Ancient Life Within Me. Philadelphia: Dorrance and Company, 1939. 38 p. (Contemporary poets of Dorrance, 185)

WALKER, ALICE (1944-)
Once; Poems. New York: Harcourt, Brace & World, 1968. 5 p. ℓ., 81 p.
Revolutionary Petunias & Other Poems. New York: Harcourt, Brace Jovanovich, 1973. 70 p.

WALKER, BERTHA ELLINWOOD
Feathers from the Starry Swan. Hollywood: H. Parker, 1940. 7 p. ℓ., 17-81 p.

WALKER, BETH
Dream Ships, a Book of Poems. New York: P. G. Boyle, 1923. 62 p.
Psalms for Lovers. Boston: R. G. Badger, 1925. 4 p. ℓ., 7-46 p.

WALKER, CAROLINE A.
High Notes and Other Poems. Dedham, MA.: The Transcript Press, Inc., 1928. 2 p. ℓ., 54 p.
A Song Wreath. Islington, MA.: n. p., 1930. 3 p. ℓ., 55 p.

WALKER, CARRIE D.
Treasured Memories. Encinitas, CA.: Print. by the Coast Dispatch, 1930. 3 p. ℓ., 104, [1] p.

WALKER, CATHERINE POYAS RAVENEL
Poems. Limited ed. Charlottesville, VA.: Priv. Print. The Michie Company, 1934. 3 p. ℓ., 47 p.

WALKER, DEE LAWRENCE
Salt Spray and Honey. Dallas, TX.: Wilkinson Pub. Co., 1951. 94 p.
Sky Trails. Dallas, TX.: Story Book Press, 1952. 79 p.

WALKER, EDITH E.
Bright Pathways. New York: The Exposition Press, 1945? 4 p. ℓ., 11-62 p.
You Shall Remember. New York: The Exposition Press, 1946. 63 p.

WALKER, ELMA GLENN
... Poems of Wyalusing. Philadelphia: Dorrance & Company, Inc., 1935. 44 p. (Contemporary poets of Dorrance, 122)

WALKER, EMELINE TATE
Poems of the Red, White, and Blue. Chicago: Chicago Chap. D. A. R., 1903. 19 p.

WALKER, EVELYN H.
Altar-Side Messages. Chicago: Unity Publishing Company, 1912. 47 p.

WALKER, GERTRUDE BOND
Thoughts Along the Way. New York: Exposition Press, 1958. 63 p.

WALKER, JEAN (RICHET) (1884-) [Full Name: Eugenie Frankie (Richet) Walker.]
Weldings. New York: The Spinner Press, Inc., 1936. [56] p.

WALKER, LAURA MARGARET (MARQUAND)
Songs of Then and Now. Lakewood: Press of Lakewood Times and Journal Publishing Company, 1905. 3 p. ℓ., 40 p., 1 ℓ.
Twenty-Four Quatrains. Newark, N. J.: Borden Press, 1914. 2 p. ℓ., 24 numb. ℓ., 1 ℓ.

WALKER, LUCYE
A Choice of Sound. New York: Exposition Press, 1954. 52 p.

WALKER, MARGARET (1915-)
For My People. New Haven, CT.: Yale University Press, 1943. 58 p. (Yale Series of Younger Poets, 41)
Ballad of the Free. Detroit: Broadside Press, 1966.
Prophets for a New Day. Detroit: Broadside Press, 1970. 32 p.
October Journey. Detroit: Broadside Press, 1973. 38 p.

WALKER, Mrs. MAT M.
When Universes Fade. Rogers, AR.: Avalon Press, 1946. 3-45 p.

WALLACE, EDNA KINGSLEY
Feelings and Things, Verses of Childhood. New York: E. P. Dutton & Company, 1916. viii p., 1 ℓ., 102 p.
Wonderings and Other Things. New York: E. P. Dutton & Company, 1919. xi p., 1 ℓ., 86 p.
The Stars in the Pool; A Prose Poem for Lovers. New York: E. P. Dutton & Company, 1920. 3 p. ℓ., 111, [1] p.

WALLACE, FRANCES REVETT
The Chinaware of Dreams, and Other Poems. Berkeley, CA.: Printed by W. and F. Bentley, 1939. 4 p. ℓ., 39, [1] p.

WALLACE, MARY IMELDA, Sister (1884-) [Secular Name: Lorabel Marie Wallace.]
The Harp of Dawn, and Other Poems. Springfield, KY.: Dominican Sisters, St. Catherine's Academy, 1924. 62 p.

WALLACE, ZELLA
On Such a Night. New York: H. Harrison, 1940. 63 p.
Laced with Laughter, Poems. New York: Exposition Press, 1949. 64 p.

WALLBAUM, SARAH ROBERTS
The Palace of the Night, and Other Poems. Chicago: Printed by Hack and Anderson, 1912. [25] p.

WALLER, EFFIE
Rhymes from the Cumberland. New York: Broadway Publishing Company, 1909. 3 p. ℓ., 53 p.
Songs of the Months. New York: Broadway, 1909.

WALLIS, ELEANOR (GLENN)
Child on a Mill-Farm. Dallas, TX.: The Kaleidograph Press, 1937. ix p., 2 ℓ., 15-94 p.
Natural World. Prairie City, IL.: J. A. Decker, 1940. viii, [9]-41 p., 1 ℓ.
Tidewater Country. Prairie City, IL.: Press of J. A. Decker, 1944. 52 p.
Design for an Arras. Baltimore: Contemporary Poetry, 1949. 43 p.

WALLIS, KATHERINE E.
Chips from the Block; Poems. New York: Exposition Press, 1955. 56 p.

WALLS, NORAH SPENCER
Looking Back; Recollections in Verse. New York: Exposition Press, 1959. 127 p.

WALSH, VIRGINIA JANE
With Love to the Passionate Shepherd. New York: Vantage Press, 1959. 65 p.

WALTER, CARRIE (STEVENS)
Rose-Ashes, and Other Poems. San Jose: A. C. Eaton & Co., 1907. vii, [5], 14-149 p.

WALTER, DONNA JOAN
Illusions of a Mid-Western Frontier. Bloomington, IN.: Woodhix Press, 1972. [22] p.

WALTER, NINA WILLIS (1900-)
Brush Strokes. Los Angeles, CA.: n.p., 1948. ix p., 2 ℓ., 47 p., 1 ℓ.
People-Watching. Pico Rivers, CA.: n.p., 1966. 23 p.

WALTHALL, ANNABEL JORDAN
In the Fire Light. Dallas, TX.: The Story Book Press, 1953. 70 p.

WALTHALL, FRANCES GEORGE
Red Roses Growing. Dallas, TX.: Dealey and Lowe, 1937. 4 p. ℓ., 74 p.

WALTON, BEULAH EARLE
Thoughts, Trivial and Solid. Morrisville? N.C.: n.p., 1964. 71 p.

WALTON, EDA LOU (1896-)
Dawn Boy: Blackfoot and Navajo Songs. New York: E. P. Dutton and Company, 1926. xxiii p., 2 ℓ., 3-82 p.
Jane Matthew, and Other Poems. New York: Brewer, Warren and Putnam, 1931. 147 p.
So Many Daughters. New York: Bookman Associates, 1952. 62 p.

WALTON, MARY ALICE
Poems. Baltimore? n.p., 1910. [34] p.

WALTON, MARY ETHEL
Words Have Breath. Philadelphia: Dorrance, 1951. 127 p. (Contemporary poets of Dorrance, 419)

WALTON, MILDRED EMMA
Rhymes Here and There. Washington, D.C.: Columbian Printing Company, 1920. 54 p.

WALTON, MILLY
Some Small Delight. Chicago: Dierkes Press, 1949. 55 p.
The Magic Shell. Eureka Springs, AR.: Dierkes Press, 1955. 55 p.

WANGSGAARD, EVA (WILLES) (1893-) [WANGSGARD, EVA (WILLES)]
Singing Hearts. Caldwell, ID.: The Caxton Printers, Ltd., 1935. 120 p.
...Down This Road. Mill Valley, CA., New York: Wings Press, 1940. xiii, [1] p., 1 ℓ., 75 p.
After the Blossoming. Mill Valley, CA., New York: The Wings Press, 1946. 74 p., 1 ℓ.
Shape of Earth. Mill Valley, CA.: Wings Press, 1959. 88 p.

WANGSGARD, EVA (WILLES) see WANGSGAARD, EVA (WILLES)

WANN, BONNIE HARRELL
Grandma Said. New York: Vantage Press, 1964. 78 p.

WARBURG, PHYLLIS BALDWIN
New Deal Noodles. Garden City, N.Y.: Doubleday, Doran & Co., Inc., 1936. 4 p.ℓ., 51 p.

WARD, ANNA MARIA WEBSTER (b. 1828)
Verses. Lowell, MA.: Press of Butterfield Printing Company, 1906. 71 p.

WARD, ELLA J. MAYO
Purple Wings: A Book of Verse. Charlottesville, VA.: The Michie Company Printers, 1941. vii, 87 p.
Bougainvillea and Desert Sand. Charlottesville, VA.: The Michie

Company Printers, 1942. vii, 72 p.

WARD, LILLIAN HOPWOOD
Violet Verses. Buffalo, N.Y.: Press of the White-Evans-Penfold Co., 1903. 25 ℓ.
_______. Boston: R. G. Badger, 1911. 63 p.

WARD, LYDIA (AVERY) COONLEY (1845-1924)
The Melody of Childhood. New York: J. T. White, 1921. 7 p. ℓ., 166 p.
The Melody of Life. New York: J. T. White & Co., 1921. 7 p. ℓ., 145 p.
The Melody of Love. New York: J. T. White & Co., 1921. 7 p. ℓ., 178 p.

WARD, MAY (WILLIAMS)
Seesaw. Atlanta, GA.: E. Hartsock, The Bozart Press, 1929. 60 p.
From Christmas-Time to April. Dallas, TX.: The Kaleidograph Press, 1938. xi p., 1 ℓ., 15-78 p.
Wheatlands; Poems. Wellington, KS.: n.p., 1954. 64 p.
No Two Years Alike. Dallas, TX.: Triangle, 1960. 72 p.
In That Day; Poems. Lawrence, KS.: University Press of Kansas, 1969. xii, [4], 80 p.

WARD, SIBYL
Over the Footlights; Verses. Boston: Popular Poetry Publishers, 1940. 20 p.

WARE, AMY (ROBBINS)
Echoes of France, Verses from My Journal & Letters. Minneapolis, MN.: The Farham Company, 1920. 3 p. ℓ., [iii]-xix, 139 p.

WARFIELD, WENDY
These Are Mine, a Book of Poems. Prairie City, IL.: The Decker Press, 1948. 82 p.

WARING, MALVINA SARAH (BLACK) (1842-)
Between Whiles. Columbia? SC.: n.p., 192-? 36 p.

WARNE, DOROTHY BAYS
Melody of Thoughts. New York: Vantage Press, 1956. 74 p.

WARNER, ELEANOR S.
Men of Earth. New York: Vantage Press, 1953. 3 p. ℓ., 69 p.
Lilacs in the Rain. New York: Exposition Press, 1956. 71 p.

WARNER, NELLY
A Military Alphabet and Other Rhymes. Kansas City: The Standard Press, 1920. 31 p.

WARREN, GRETCHEN (OSGOOD)
Trackless Regions, Poems. Oxford: B. H. Blackwell; New York: Longmans, Green & Co., 1917. 118 p.
The Sword. Oxford: B. H. Blackwell; New York: Longmans, Green & Co., 1919. 4 p. ℓ., 151, [1] p.
Humanity; Twenty-Six Poems. Oxford: R. H. Blackwell, 1953. 40 p.
________. 1954. 43 p.

WARREN, KATHARINE
Early and Late. New York: Duffield & Company, 1921. viii p., 1 ℓ., 89 p.

WARREN, MARY ELIZABETH
Candle Lights. San Francisco: Portal Press, 1943. [54] p.

WARREN, MARY FLORENCE (1884-)
A Few Verses. Philadelphia: Printed by A. Anderman, 1916. 33 p.
Twilight and Other Poems. Boston: R. G. Badger, 1916. 16 p.

WARSAW, IRENE (1908-)
A Word in Edgewise; A Book of Light Verse. Francestown, N.H.: Golden Quill Press, 1964. 80 p.

WASHBURN, GWENDOLYN JANE (1942-)
Poems of Inspiration. New York: Vantage Press, 1969. 64 p.

WASHINGTON, EDNA (DANIEL)
I Dip My Pen. Emory University, Atlanta, GA.: Banner Press, 1940. 6 p. ℓ., [11]-80 p.
Swing Oh Pendulum. Dallas, TX.: American Guild Press, 1956. 70 p.

WASSALL, IRMA
Loonshadow. Golden, CO.: Sage Books, 1949. 48 p.
________. 2d ed. Denver, CO.: Experiment Press, 1958. 48 p.

WASSON, PEARL (RANDALL) (1878-)
Sonnets & Lyrics. Burlington, VT.: n.p., 1926. [20] p.

WATERS, MARY S.
Sense and Nonsense, from the Pen of Mary S. Waters, a Miscellany. New Haven, CT.: Printed by Quinnipiack Press, Inc., 1957. 46 p.

WATERS, SHIRLEY A.
Psalms of a Black Woman. Los Angeles: Hopkins-Thomas, 1969.

WATKINS, ANNE S.
A Basketful of All Sorts of Eggs. New York: Press of Vechten Waring Company, 1911. 28 p.

WATKINS, MARTHA HEROLD
Pleasing Poems for Young and Old. New York: Greenwich Book Publishers, 1958. 108 p.

WATKINS, MILDRED deWEIR SMITH (1929-) [SMITH, MILDRED deWEIR]
Vignettes. New Orleans, LA.: Pelican Pub. Co., 1952. 64 p.

WATKINS, VIOLETTE PEACHES
My Dream World of Poetry; Poems of Imagination, Reality, and Dreams. New York: Exposition Press, 1955. 128 p.

WATSON, AMELIA B.
Sonnets. Columbus, OH.: F. J. Heer Printing Company, 1934. 57 p.

WATSON, ANNAH WALKER (ROBINSON) (1848-)
Passion Flowers; Poems. Richmond, VA.: Whittet & Shepperson, 1901. 90 p.
The Victory. Memphis, TN.: Foster Printing and Publishing Company, 1909. 5 p. ℓ., 8-69 p.
Pre-Ordained. Memphis, TN.: Press of Early-Freeburg Co., 1928. [28] p.

WATSON, CHRISTINE HAMILTON
Crumpled Leaves. New York: J. T. White & Co., 1921. 102 p.
Poems. New York: H. Harrison, 1937. 94 p.
Periphery of Time, Sonnets. New York: The Fine Editions Press, 1941. 62 p., 1 ℓ.

WATSON, ELIZABETH LOWE (1843-)
Song and Sermon. Cupertino, CA.: E. L. Watson, 1906. 187 p.

WATSON, EVELYN MABEL PALMER (1886-)
Divine Fire and Other Poems. Philadelphia: Dorrance, 1922. 60 p.
Kingdom Beautiful. Philadelphia: Dorrance, 1923. 5 p. ℓ., 9-70 p.
Flames of Stars. Philadelphia: Dorrance, 1924. 67 p. (Contemporary poets of Dorrance, 11)
Lighted Tapers. London: E. MacDonald, Ltd., 1925. 120 p.
Niagara. Buffalo: Aries Book Club, 1925? 2 p. ℓ., 6 ℓ.
Flame Wings; A Book of Bird Poems. Boston: The Christopher Publishing House, 1927. 7-124 p. (Syndicate series)
Lifted Torches: Lyrics, Ballads, and Odes. London: E. MacDonald, Ltd., 1927. 3 p. ℓ., 9-153 p.
Candle Gold; Lyrics of Love & Death. Boston: The Christopher Publishing House, 1928. 144 p.
Happy Heart Songs for Tots and Teens and Inbetweens. Boston: The Christopher Publishing House, 1928. 6 p. ℓ., [15]-139 p.
A Book of Rainbows. Boston: The Christopher Publishing House, 1929. 14-120 p.
Poems of the Niagara Frontier. New York: Dean & Company,

1929. 2 p. ℓ., 7-128 p.
Clustering Stars. Ed. by Alan Frederick Pater. New York: Literary Publications, 1931. 74 p.
Symbols of Immortality. Boston: Christopher Pub. House, 1931. 3 p. ℓ., 5-162 p.
...Jewel Dust. New York: The Paebar Company, 1932. 6 p. ℓ., 68 p.
A Network of Stars; A Compilation of Quatrains. Boston: The Christopher Publishing House, 1932. 3 p. ℓ., 5-183 p.
End o' My Gardens, Songs of a Renewed Faith. New York: The Paebar Company, 1933. 155 p.
As from a Minaret; A Book of Sonnets. Boston: Humphries, 1936. ix, 13-326 p.
Anthem of the Ages. Ed. by Jethra Hart. Buffalo, N.Y.: Niagara Bookcraft, 1938. 4 p. ℓ., 5-200 p.

WATSON, FRIEDA K.
Feelin's. Los Angeles: A. Kirzna Publication, 1971.

WATSON, GENNEVA DICKEY
On Other Hills. Tacoma, WA.: n.p., 1947. 96 p.

WATSON, HELEN FIELD
Field Notes. Mill Valley, CA.: Wings Press, 1949. 88 p.

WATSON, JEANIE DOWNS
The Middle Course. New York: H. Harrison, 1940. 63 p.

WATSON, KATHLEEN
Litanies of Life. New York: A. Wessels & Co., 1901. 168 p.

WATSON, MARY
Pedestrian Sketches. Kansas City: The Lowell Press, 1930. 3 p. ℓ., ix-x p., 1 ℓ., 13-75 p.
The Shepherd and the Stars.... Kansas City: Lowell Press, 1936. [29] p.

WATSON, MARY FRANCINE
Sunshine and Shadow. Alpine, CA.: Visions Press, 1938. [72] p.

WATSON, MARY HAYES
Verses. Flint, MI.: Smith, Bristol, and Phillips, 1913. 1 p. ℓ., [5]-27 p.

WATSON, MARY LAURA
September's Child. West Los Angeles, CA.: Wagon & Star Press, 1951. unpaged.

WATSON, MARYLAND
Destiny and Desire; Poems Passionate and Perverse. New York: Casino Publishing Company, 1908. 63 p.

WATSON, NANA
Reap the Harvest. New York: William-Frederick Press, 1952. 31 p.

WATSON, NETTIE WALTON
One Small Key. 2d ed. Corpus Christi, TX.: Jones Pub. Co., 1943. 31 p.

WATSON, SARAH ANN (MOONEY) (1841-1904)
Poems. St. Albans, VT.: Messenger Co. Print., 1905. 171, [4] p.

WATSON, SUSAN TABITHA (YARBROUGH)
By-Ways and Hedges. Calhoun, MA.: Printed by Amateur Notes & Quotes, 1956. 4 p. ℓ., 53 p.

WATT, MARION FRANCES
Cypress and Rose. Seattle, WA.: The Ivy Press, 1902. 183 p., 1 ℓ.

WATT, NELL HODGSON
Ball of Southern Yarns. Greenville, SC.: Hiott Press, 1953. 4 p. ℓ., 54 p.

WATTS, MARJORIE SEYMOUR
Do You Remember? Boston: The Four Seas Company, 1927. 29 p.

WAYT, JENNIE R. JELLISON
Diamonds in the Rough. Denver, CO.: The Smith-Brooks Press, 1912. 92 p.
________. Los Angeles: n. p., 1931. 96 p.

WEAGE, MARY (DUDLEY) (1831-)
Songs of the Unseen. Seattle, WA.: The Socialist Publishing Ass'n., 1915. 47 p.

WEATHERMAN, ROSA
Driftwood, Facts and Fancies, Picked up from the Stream of Time Along the Pathway of Life. Boston: The Christopher Publishing House, 1932. 111 p.

WEAVER, ADA MARY (PALMER)
Morning in the Heart; Selected Poems. Denver, CO.: Big Mountain Press, 1958. 93 p.

WEAVER, GERTRUDE
Patterned Thought. Grand Rapids, MI.: Bardic Echoes, 1968. 24 p.

WEAVER, IDA
Clouds and Sunshine: Poems. Washington, D. C.: Hayworth Publishing House, 1904. 62 p.

Love Lyrics, and a Home in the Hills. Boston: Chapman & Grimes, 1956. 64 p.

WEAVER, MABEL DUNNIGAN
Simple Thoughts in Rhyme. New York: Carlton Press, 1968. 64 p.

WEAVER, MAY MARSHALL
Thoughts and Memories Ring a Bell. San Antonio, TX.: Naylor Co., 1960. vi, 69 p.

WEBB, ELISABETH HOLDEN
Shining Grass. New York: Gramercy Park Press, 1926. [30] p.

WEBB, JOYCE W.
Dark Earth. Madison, WI.: Wells Printing Co., 1965. 40 p.

WEBB, JULIA CLAY BARRON
Tall White Candle, Lighted. Emory University, Atlanta, GA.: Banner Press, 1957. 61 p. (Verse craft series)

WEBB, ROZANA (1908-)
The Thirteenth Man; Poems. New York: 7 Poets Press, 1962. 17, [1] p. (7 poets press series one, no. 6)
The Monsoon Breeds. Fort Smith, AR.: Border Press, 1965. 38 p.
Eternal the Flow. Fort Smith, AR.: South and West, 1966. 34 p.
The Coffee Break. Fort Smith, AR.: South and West, 1967. [7] p.
The Way. Fort Smith, AR.: South and West, 1969. 45 p.

WEBB, TESSA (SWEAZY)
Life's Tilted Cup. Atlanta, GA.: Ernest Hartsock, The Bozart Press, 1927. 69 p.
Window by the Sea. Columbus, OH.: The Hilltop Record, Inc., 1942. 79 p.

WEBB, VADA HART
Claudia and Other Poems. Mansfield, OH.: n.p., 1946. 94, [2] p.

WEBBER, GEORGIANNA TOMLYN
Song at Even. Boston: Bruce Humphries, 1954. 96 p.

WEBER, MARY BOND
Dreams. Oakland, MD.: The Sincell Printing Company, 1933. [39] p.

WEBSTER, LILLIAN
Memories of Mine. Austin, TX.: n.p., 1952. 54 p.

WEBSTER, MARJORIE FRASER (1896-)
A Corner of My Heart. Baltimore? MD.: n.p., 1953. 104 p.

WEDDENDORF, LUCILE BENDER
Conquest, and Other Poems. Los Angeles, CA.: Wetzel Publishing Co., 1930. 3 p. ℓ., 13-107 p.

WEEDEN, Miss HOWARD (1847-1905)
Songs of the Old South; Verses and Drawings. New York: Doubleday, Page & Company, 1900. xii, 94 p., 1 ℓ.
Old Voices.... New York: Doubleday, Page & Company, 1904. xii, [96] p.

WEEG, SARAH CATLIN
Twilight Reveries. Chicago: The Gallop Publishing Company, 1934. 5 p. ℓ., 15-80 p.

WEEKS, ANNA ROSS
Cobwebs, and Other Poems. New York: The Grafton Press, 1929. 53 p.

WEEKS, IDA AHLBORN
Poems of Ida Ahlborn Weeks. Sabula, IA.: Pub. by her friends, 1910. xi, [1], 136 p.

WEEKS, LEONIE BELLE
Scribblings. San Francisco, CA.: n.p., 1928. [20] p.
Leaves in the Sun. San Francisco, CA.: J. H. Nash, 1935. 1 p. ℓ., 53 p., 1 ℓ.

WEEKS, RAMONA (1934-)
About Armadillos and Others. Phoenix, AZ.: The Baleen Press, 1972. [12] p.
Lincoln County Poems, and Poems from Other Places. Winters, CA.: Konocti Books, 1973. 43 p.

WEGNER, LAURA BRAECKLY
The Service of a Smile. Brooklyn, N.Y.: Press of Braunworth and Company, Incorporated, 1928. x, 181 p.
Roses of Hope, and Other Homespun Verse. South Bend, IN.: Mirror Press, 1940. 1 p. ℓ., v-xi, 148 p.

WEHMILLER, DOROTHY HELEN (1909-)
Cancers in the Earth. Boston: R. G. Badger, 1930. 25 p.

WEHR, OLIVE C.
God's Forgotten Garden and Vintage Poems. New York: n.p., 1917. 46 p.

WEIGAND, ANN
Poems and Meditations. New York: Vantage Press, 1961. 49 p.

WEIK, MARY
Adventure; A Book of Verse. Boston: The Poet Lore Co., 1919. 32 p.

WEINBAUM, ELEANOR (1900-)
From Croup to Nuts. Dallas, TX.: The Kaleidograph Press, 1941. v, 7-92 p.
The World Laughs with You. San Antonio, TX.: Naylor Co., 1950. 42 p.
Jest for You. San Antonio, TX.: Naylor Co., 1954. 64 p.

WEINER, DIANE (1953-)
Masques of Fall. Philadelphia: Dorrance, 1973. 30 p.

WEINIG, MARY ANTHONY, Mother (1920-)
Rain in the Chimney. Fort Smith, AR.: South and West, 1972. 41 p.

WEIR, CLARA TREADWAY
Kinnikinic, a Book of Western Verse. New York: I. Somerville & Co., 1907. 118 p.

WEIS, LYDIA MARGUERITE
The Handless Clock. San Francisco: J. T. Campbell Pub. Co., 1964. 32 p.

WEISS, RUTH
Steps. San Francisco: Mel and Ruth Weitsman, 1958. 11, 41 p.
Gallery of Women. San Francisco: Adler Press, 1959. [52] p.
South Pacific. San Francisco: Adler Press, 1959. [32] p.
Blue in Green. San Francisco: Adler Press, 1960. 12 p., 1 ℓ.

WEITZEL, LOUISE ADELINE
A Quiver of Arrows. Lititz, PA.: The Express Printing Co., 1908. 244 p.
Shpectakel. Lititz, PA.: n.p., 1931. [33] p.

WEIXELBAUM, ALMA LOUISE
More Verses. Springfield, OH.: Alma L. Weixelbaum, 195-? 64 p.

WELCH, AGNES SHEFFIELD
Afterglow, a Book of Poems. Boston: B. Humphries, 1931. 5 p. ℓ., 3-55 p.
Panorama, Poems. Boston: B. Humphries, Inc., 1933. 95, [1] p.
Of Life and Love. Boston: B. Humphries, Inc., 1938. 62 p.

WELCH, EMILY M.
Woman, Wife, Mother. Philadelphia: Dorrance, 1975. 26 p.

WELCH, LEONA NICHOLAS
Black Gibraltar. San Francisco: Leswing Press, 1971. 75 p.

WELCH, MARIE de L.
...Poems. New York: The Macmillan Company, 1933. ix, 86 p.
This Is Our Own. New York: The Macmillan Company, 1940. xi, 75 p.

WELCH, MARY ARTIE (BARRINGTON)
Wayside Windows. Dallas, TX.: The Kaleidograph Press, 1945. x p., 1 ℓ., 13-70 p.

WELCH, MARY ROSE
Prouder Than Wine. Dallas, TX.: Royal Pub. Co., 1965. 40 p.

WELCH, MYRA BROOKS
The Touch of the Master's Hand, Ninety Other Poems. Elgin, IL.: Elgin Press, 1941. 110 p.
Chariots on the Mountains. Elgin, IL.: Brethren Publishing House, 1945. 111 p.
The Touch of the Master's Hand, and Ninety-three Other Poems. Elgin, IL.: Brethren Publishing House, 1957. 96 p.

WELLES, BETTIE PAYNE
Harbor Hunger, and Other Poems. Los Angeles, CA.: New Age Publishing Co., 1949. 70 p.

WELLES, WINIFRED (1893-1939)
The Hesitant Heart. New York: B. W. Huebsch, 1919. 56 p.
This Delicate Love. New York: The Viking Press, 1929. 5 p. ℓ., 3-77 p.
Skipping Along Alone. New York: Macmillan, 1931. viii p., 1 ℓ., 52 p. (Verses for Children)
Blossoming Antlers. New York: The Viking Press, 1933. 4 p. ℓ., 3-58 p.
A Spectacle for Scholars. New York: The Viking Press, 1935. 4 p. ℓ., 3-59 p.
The Park That Spring Forgot. New York: E. P. Dutton and Company, 1940. 4 p. ℓ., 15-90 p.
...The Shape of Memory. New York: H. Holt and Company, 1944. xvii, 62 p.

WELLINGTON, KAY
...White Christmas. New York: Harbinger House, 1943. 58 p.
Comfort Me with Apples. Philadelphia: Dorrance, 1954. 65 p.

WELLINGTON, MAUD KILBOURN
Rhymes. Boston: G. H. Ellis Co., Printers, 1903. 2 p. ℓ., 58 p.

WELLMAN, ESTHER TURNER (1893-)
Democracy, and Other Verse. Gardena, CA.: Spanish American Institute Press, 1925. 39 p.
A Rosary of Madrigals. Gardena, CA.: Spanish American Institute Press, 1925. 37 p., 1 ℓ.

WELLS, FLORENCE HORTON
Poems. Oneida, N. Y.: Printed by the McHenry Press, Inc., 1931. 31 p.

WELLS, GRACE SHERMAN (d. 1900)
Verses. Chicago: Priv. Print. R. R. Donnelley and Sons Company, 1909. 126 p., 1 ℓ.

WELLS, MILDRED TATE
When Goldenrod Blooms, and Other Poems. Memphis, TN.: Press of S. C. Toof & Company, 1914. 32 p.

WELSH, MARY ELIZABETH (1840-)
Kapiolani: A Tale of Hawaii. N. Y., London: The Abbey Press, 1902. 1 p. ℓ., 46 p.

WELSHIMER, HELEN
Singing Drums. New York: E. P. Dutton & Co., 1937. 159 p.
Shining Rain. New York: E. P. Dutton & Co., 1943. 157 p.

WENDT, VIOLA SOPHIA (1907-)
You Keep Waiting for Geese. Waukesha, WI.: Carroll College Press, 1975. 101 p.

WENNER, BLANCHE HOWARD
Hawaiian Memories. New York: Cochrane Publishing Company, 1910. 30 p.

WENTWORTH, ALICE LOVERING
Commending the Troops, and Other Poems. New York: Exposition Press, 1967. 46 p.

WENTWORTH, MARION JEAN (CRAIG) (1872-)
Iridescent Days. Santa Barbara, CA.: J. F. Rowny Press, 1939. 109 p.

WERNER, MABEL TYSON
Glad Wilderness. Lawrence, L. I.: Golden Galleon Press, 1933. 5 p. ℓ., [13]-67 p.

WERNER, MARY KATHLEEN (1948-)
A Child's Thoughts in Poetry. New York: Greenwich Book Publishers, 1959. 31 p.

WESCOTT, KATHERINE SARAH (ROBERTS)
Salt and Sand. Ononcock, VA.: Eastern Shore News, 1963. 65 p.

WESCOTT, MABEL INGALLS
Let Me Linger, and Other Poems. Boston: Meador Publishing Company, 1937. 143 p.
Into the Dawn. Boston: Meador Publishing Company, 1945. 62 p.

WEST, ANNE DRUMMOND
Pipes of Indian Summer.... New York: Exposition Press, 1944. 62 p.

WEST, IRENE
A Soul's Appeal, and Other Poems. Huntington, IN.: Our Sunday Visitor Press, 1917. 102 p., 3 ℓ.
The Twain Shall Meet (A Volume of Race Poems by an All White Author). Los Angeles, CA.: n.p., 1943. 52 p.

WEST, LULAMEADE
The Isle of Me. Emory University, Atlanta, GA.: Banner Press, 1952. 61 p.

WESTCOTT, JOAN C.
Fragments of Stained Glass. Philadelphia: Dorrance, 1965. [64] p. (Contemporary poets of Dorrance, 613)
More Fragments of Stained Glass. Philadelphia: Dorrance, 1966. [62] p. (Contemporary poets of Dorrance, 626)
Bits of Chaff. Philadelphia: Dorrance, 1967. 42 p.

WESTCOTT, MARGERY DUNBAR
The Country of My Dreaming. New York: The Knickerbocker Press, 1926. vi, 52 p.

WESTON, MILDRED
The Singing Hill. New York: H. Vinal, 1926. 63 p.

WETHERALD, ETHELWYN (1857-) [Full Name: Agnes Ethelwyn Wetherald.]
Tangled in Stars: Poems. Boston: R. G. Badger, 1902. 45 p.
The Radiant Road. Boston: R. G. Badger, 1904. 43 p.
Tree-top Mornings. Boston: The Cornhill Publishing Company, 1921. ix p., 1 ℓ., 65 p.

WETHERILL, CATHARINE HALL
For You and For Me; A Book of Verse. Philadelphia: Campion and Company, 1909. 105 p.

WETHERILL, HILDA (FAUNCE)
Navajo Indian Poems; Translations from the Navajo, and Other Poems. New York: Vantage Press, 1952. 5 p. ℓ., 53 p.

WETZLER, JOSEPHINE BOWMAN
Strange Companions. Eureka Springs, AR.: Dierkes Press, 1962. 55 p.

WEYBREW, GERTRUDE M.
Stepping-Stones. Emory University, Atlanta, GA.: Banner Press, 1941. 64 p.

WEYGANT, NOEMI, Sister
It's Autumn! Philadelphia: Westminster Press, 1968. 63 p.

It's Spring! Philadelphia: Westminster Press, 1969. 63 p.
It's Winter! Philadelphia: Westminster Press, 1969. 63 p.
It's Summer! Philadelphia: Westminster Press, 1970. 63 p.

WHARTON, CARRIE M.
Waiting Women. Kansas City, MO.: Burton Publishing Company, 1943. 5 p. ℓ., 13-61 p.

WHARTON, EDITH NEWBOLD (JONES) (1862-1937)
Artemis to Actaeon, and Other Verse. New York: C. Scribner's Sons, 1909. v, [1], 90 p.
Twelve Poems. London: Medici Society, 1926. 5 p. ℓ., 3-51, [1] p., 2 ℓ.

WHEELAN, ALBERTINE RANDALL
To Love and to Cherish: A Collection of Sonnets. New York: Dodge Pub. Co., 1903.

WHEELER, ANNIE BALCOMB
Footpaths and Pavements. Philadelphia: Dorrance & Company, 1929. 87 p. (Contemporary poets of Dorrance, 81)
Along the North Shore. Boston: Humphries, 1949. 90 p.

WHEELER, CATHERINE
Bright Little Poems for Bright Little People. San Francisco: The Whitaker and Ray Company, 1902. 120 p.

WHEELER, DELLA J.
Wings of Verse. Carmel, CA.: Carmel Press, 1941. [23] p.

WHEELER, ELIZABETH HOWLAND
Poems of the Dawn-Light. n.p.: Wheeler, 1913.

WHEELER, KATHARINE (WELLES)
Filled Flagons. Mill Valley, CA., New York: The Wings Press, 1944. 63 p.

WHEELER, MARGARET ALEXANDER (1903-)
...The Abundance of Life. Philadelphia: Dorrance and Company, 1937. 56 p. (Contemporary poets of Dorrance, 163)
These My Brethren. Philadelphia: Dorrance, 1948. 78 p. (Contemporary poets of Dorrance, 377)

WHEELER, MARY BLACKBURN
Roses Among Thorns, and Other Poems. Dallas, TX.: Story Book Press, 1954. 62 p.

WHEELER, RUTH GUNTHER (WINANT) (1885-)
Seeing Through. Boston: R. G. Badger, 1920. 12 p., 1 ℓ., 13-138 p.
Bright Star Above the Hill. New York: The Poets Press, 1942. 40 p.
With God for Company. New York: Pageant Press, 1956.

7 p. ℓ., 118 p.
Road Song. New York: Vantage Press, 1965. 96 p.

WHEELER, SYLVIA
City Limits. Shawnee Mission, KS.: BkMk Press, 1973. 20 p.

WHELESS, JENNIE NOONAN
Poems. Yazoo City, MS.: Mississippi Stationery Co., 1900. 70 p.
A Book of Verse.... Yazoo City, MS.: Yazoo Sentinel, 1919. 40 p.

WHELPLEY, JULIA GOODCHILD
...Small Domain. New York: The Fine Editions Press, 1944. 43 p.

WHITAKER, CHRISTINE D.
The Singing Teakettle: Poems for Children. New York: Exposition Press, 1956. 40 p.

WHITAKER, CICELY MAUD
Poems. Philadelphia: H. W. Fisher & Co., 1903. 1 p. ℓ., 59 p.

WHITCOMB, CHARLOTTE
Verses. Boston: R. G. Badger, 1907.

WHITE, ANNA GRIMSTAD
Homespun Writings in Rhyme; My Contribution. Fresno, CA.: Williams, 1951. 182 p.

WHITE, BARBARA
Poems. Johnstown, PA.: Benshoff Ptg. Co., 1919. 48 p.

WHITE, EDITH PARENT
Family Fare, Poems. New York: Exposition Press, 1956. 71 p.

WHITE, ELLA MAY
Weed Blossoms. Chicago: W. H. Wilton Co., 1920. [33] p.

WHITE, ETHEL FAIRFIELD
Laughing Giraffe, and Other Verses. Spokane, WA.: C. W. Hill Printing Company, 1942. 69, [1] p.
Jester at Heart. Mill Valley, CA., New York: The Wings Press, 1943. 54 p.
Rocky Hill. Mill Valley, CA.: Wings Press, 1957. 64 p.

WHITE, ETHYLE
Arabella of Trinity Bay. Anahuse? TX.: n. p., 1954. 63, [1] p.

WHITE, FRANCES LAING

Tides. New York: H. Vinal, 1925. 5 p. ℓ., 24 p.

Weaving. Shreveport, LA.: Journal Publishing Company, 1928. 3 p. ℓ., 32 p.

Tapestry. Shreveport, LA.: Journal Pub. Co., 1935. 3 p. ℓ., 27 p.

WHITE, GEORGIA

The Jingle Book; A Collection of Verses Written Now and Then. Concord, N.H.: Rumford Printing Co., 1909. 64 p.

WHITE, GRACE HOFFMAN

Christus; A Story of Love. New York: Priv. Print., 1909. 3 p. ℓ., 64 p., 1 ℓ.

WHITE, GRACE MILLER

Wings to Dare. Portland, ME.: The Mosher Press, 1925. ix, [1] p., 45, [1] p.

WHITE, GRACE (SHILLING)

The Legend of Dessardee, and Other Poems. Knox, IN.: Democrat Office, 1941. 44 p.

Unhoarded Gold; A Book of Poems. New York: Exposition Press, 1953. 96 p.

WHITE, JEANNIE COPES

Poems. Boston: Sherman, French & Company, 1916. 4 p. ℓ., 153 p.

WHITE, LAURA WATSON

Rhymeland. Philadelphia: Press of J. B. Lippincott Company, 1927. 255 p.

WHITE, LOURINE

Echo from a Sheltered Valley. Fort Smith, AR.: South and West, 1965. 42, [11] p.

Promenade; A Book of Poems. Homestead, FL.: Olivant Press, 1969. 82 p.

WHITE, LUCY ANNE (BARDON) (1892-)

Lingering Memories. Easton, PA.: The John S. Correll Co., Inc., 1941. 48 p.

WHITE, MARGARET McFADDEN

For We Know Not What We Do, and Other Poems. New York: Exposition Press, 1963. 48 p.

If, and Other Poems. New York: Vantage Press, 1970. 64 p.

WHITE, MARION STRONG

The Living Stone. New York: Coward-McCann, Inc., 1946. viii p., 1 ℓ., 85 p.

WHITE, MARTHA SPERBECK
Old Fashioned Poems. Boston: The Christopher Publishing House, 1933. 108 p.

WHITE, MARY
Orchids and Onions. New York: H. Harrison, 1948. 63 p.

WHITE, MARY LOUISE
...Jacpot. Philadelphia: Dorrance and Company, 1937. 58 p. (Contemporary poets of Dorrance, 173)

WHITE, MAY (SMITH)
Forty Acres. Cincinnati, OH.: n.p., 1949. 75 p.
Always Another Spring. New Orleans, LA.: Pelican, 1967. 63 p.

WHITE, PAULETTE C.
Love Poem to a Black Junkie. Detroit: Lotus Press, 1975. 40 p.

WHITE, VIOLA CHITTENDEN (1890-)
Horizons. New Haven, CT.: Yale University Press, 1921. 80 p., 1 ℓ. (Yale Series of Younger Poets, 9)
Blue Forest, and Other Poems. Boston: The Four Seas Company, 1929. 62 p.

WHITEFIELD, FANNIE SPRAGUE
Five Seasons. Boston: The Christopher Publishing House, 1943. ix p., 1 ℓ., 13-94 p.

WHITEHEAD, DAISY CRUMP
Heart Lines. Raleigh, N.C.: Pittman Printing Company, 1937. 56 p.

WHITEHEAD, LORITA
First Poems. Madison, WI.: Abbot Press, 1962. 4 p. ℓ., 33 p., 1 ℓ.

WHITEHURST, MOLLIE JEANETTA DUPUY
Temptations of Eden. Norfolk, VA.: n.p., 1923. 23 p.

WHITEKER, MYRTLE (NICHOLSON)
We Sing in Texas. Dallas, TX.: Mathis, Van Nort, 1947. 70 p.

WHITELEY, MARY N. S.
Sea Born, Poems.... Prairie City, IL.: The Press of J. A. Decker, 1947. 61 p.

WHITING, ROBERTA HARRISS
Rose Petals. New York: Broadway Publishing Company, 1914. 1 p. ℓ., 5-51 p.

WHITLEY, OPAL STANLEY
The Flower of Stars. Washington, D.C.: n.p., 1923. 286 p.

WHITLOCK, GENEVIEVE HALE (1875-1903)
Poems. New Haven, CT.: C. E. H. Whitlock, 1906. xi, 126 p.

WHITMAN, ALICE
Fragments from Flowerland. Palatka, FL.: M. M. Vickers, 1901. 57 p.

WHITMAN, RUTH (1922-)
Blood & Milk Poems. New York: Clarke & Way, 1963. 54 p.
The Marriage Wig, and Other Poems. New York: Harcourt, Brace & World, 1968. ix, 67 p.
The Passion of Lizzie Borden; New and Selected Poems. New York: October House, 1973. 116 p.

WHITMAN, TANIA CROCKER
Poems. San Francisco: J. H. Nash, 1934. 18 p.

WHITMORE, LAURA ANN (1855-)
Aurora, & Other Poems. Boston: The Heintzemann Press, 1903. 5 p.ℓ., 7-112 p.
Aurora, and Other Poems. Boston: Sherman, French & Company, 1913. 5 p.ℓ., 171 p.

WHITNEY, ADELINE DUTTON TRAIN (1824-1906)
Pansies: "...for thoughts." Boston & New York: Houghton, Mifflin and Company, 1900. vi, 111 p.

WHITNEY, ANNE (1821-1915)
Poems. Boston: Priv. Print. The Merrymount Press, 1906. x p., 2 ℓ., 170 p., 2 ℓ.

WHITNEY, BARBARA (SCHMITT)
Descent of the White Bird. New York: Fine Editions Press, 1955. 57 p., 1 ℓ.

WHITNEY, GERTRUDE CAPEN (1861-)
Roses from My Garden. Boston: Sherman, French & Company, 1912. 4 p.ℓ., 92 p.

WHITNEY, GERTRUDE CLARA LOUISE (1899-)
Sled Against the Door. Boston: B. Humphries, 1935. 51 p.

WHITNEY, GERTRUDE (SCHUYLER)
The Poems of Gertrude Schuyler Whitney. Cambridge, MA.: Crimson Printing Co., 1967. vi, 57 p.

WHITNEY, HELEN (HAY)
The Rose of Dawn; A Tale of the South Sea. New York: R. H. Russell, 1901. 2 p.ℓ., 57 p.

Sonnets and Songs. New York & London: Harper & Bros., 1905. ix, [1], 81 p.
Verses for Jock and Joan. New York: Fox, Duffield and Company, 1905. 32 p.
The Bed-Time Book. New York: Duffield and Company, 1907. 31, [1] p. (Verses for Children.)
Gypsy Verses. New York: Duffield & Company, 1907. ix, 76 p.
Herbs and Apples. New York: John Lane Co., 1910. xi p., 1 ℓ., 65, [1] p.

WHITNEY, MINNIE LOOMIS
Songs of Life. Boston: H. Vinal, Ltd., 1932. 60 p.

WHITSELL, BETTY L.
California Nuggets. Dallas, TX.: The Kaleidograph Press, 1939. x p., 1 ℓ., 13-71 p.
From Four Windows. Dallas, TX.: The Kaleidograph Press, 1941. xi p., 1 ℓ., 15-75 p.

WHITSITT, CADDIE MAY
Meditations of a Wanderer. Fort Worth, TX.: Vestal Ptg. Co., 1917. 32 p.
Meditations of a Wanderer, and Other Poems. Charleston, SC.: Son. Prt'g. & Pub. Company, 1919. 47 p.

WHITSON, EMMA J. (TURNEY) (d. 1905)
The Bluebell, and Other Verse. San Jose, CA.: Melvin, Hillis & Black Printers, 1906. 56 p.

WHITTELSEY, DELIA MARIA (TAYLOR) (1861-)
Thoughts by the Way. Seattle, WA.: Print. by F. McCaffrey, 1933. 85 p.

WHITTEMORE, GRACE CONNER
August Night Orchestra, and Other Poems. New York: Exposition Press, 1953. 88 p.

WHITTIER, SOPHIA (1897-)
Hearts and Flowers. n.p., 1971. x, 32 p.

WICKENDEN, HELEN SLACK
A Quebec Bouquet. Boston: The Stratford Company, 1930. 5 p. ℓ., 35 p.

WICKHAM, ANNA
The Contemplative Quarry. London: The Poetry Bookshop, 1915. 40 p.
The Contemplative Quarry, and the Man with a Hammer. New York: Harcourt, Brace and Company, 1921. xv p., 1 ℓ., 136 p.

WICKLIFFE, ELIZABETH LOCKHART
Flights and Fancies. Wickliffe? KY.: n.p., 1909. 4 p. ℓ., 11-143 p.

WICKLUND, MILLIE MAE
The Marisol Poems. New York: New Rivers Press, dist. by Serendipity Books, 1975. 39 p.

WIDDEMER, MABEL (CLELAND)
Souvenir. Francestown, N.H.: Golden Quill Press, 1957. 88 p.

WIDDEMER, MARGARET (1897-)
The Factories, with Other Lyrics. Philadelphia: The John C. Winston Company, 1915. 7 p.ℓ., 13-160 p.
Factories, Poems. New York: H. Holt and Company, 1917. 154 p.
The Old Road to Paradise. New York: H. Holt and Company, 1918. x, 124 p.
Cross-Currents. New York: Harcourt, Brace and Company, 1921. 6 p.ℓ., 3-112 p.
A Tree with a Bird in It: A Symposium of Contemporary American Poets on Being Shown a Pear-Tree on Which Sat a Grackle. New York: Harcourt, Brace & Co., 1922. 3 p.ℓ., v-ix, 102 p.
Little Girl and Boy Land; Poems for Children. New York: Harcourt, Brace & Company, 1924. viii, 97 p.
Ballads and Lyrics. New York: Harcourt, Brace & Company, 1925. ix, 107 p.
Collected Poems of Margaret Widdemer. New York: Harcourt, Brace and Company, 1928. xii, 279 p.
The Road to Downderry & Other Poems. New York: Farrar and Rinehart, Inc., 1932. xii, 112 p.
Hill Garden; New Poems. New York: Farrar & Rinehart, Inc., 1936. viii, 72 p.
The Dark Cavalier; The Collected Poems of Margaret Widdemer. Garden City, N.Y.: Doubleday, 1958. 279 p.

WIDEN, RUTH
In Praise of Pain. New York: Parnassus, 1928.

WIEAND, HELEN EMMA
Spring Moods and Fancies; A Book of Verse. Boston: Sherman, French & Company, 1914. 69 p.

WIEGNER, KATHLEEN (KNOPP) (1938-)
Encounters. Milwaukee, WI.: Membrane Press, 1972. [38] p.
Country Western Breakdown. Trumansburg, N.Y.: Crossing Press, 1974. 64 p. (Crossing Press series of poets)

WIEWEL, PHILOMENA
Silent Symphonies. New York: The Exposition Press, 1944. 62 p.

WIGGINS, BERNICE LOVE (1897-)
Tuneful Tales. El Paso, TX.: n.p., 1925. 174 p.

WIGHT, CAROL VAN BUREN
Sir Thomas More, and Other Verse. Baltimore, MD.: The Johns Hopkins Press, 1925. 116 p.
Star-Dust; A Sonnet Sequence. Baltimore, MD.: n.p., 1926. v p., 24 numb. ℓ.
From a Scallop Shanty. Hyannis, MA.: Printed by F. B. and F. P. Goss, 1934-1941. 2 vol. vol. 2 printed in Harwich, MA.
The Crimson Rambler, and Other Selected Poems. Boston and Los Angeles: Walter H. Baker Company, 1938. 71 p.

WIGHTMAN, WILLA M.
My Heart Sings. New York: Vantage Press, 1957. 63 p.

WIGREN, BESSIE C.
Summer Wind. Boston: The Poet Lore Company, 1919. 45 p.

WILCOX, ELLA WHEELER (1855-1919)
Poems of Pleasure. Chicago: W. B. Conkey Company, 1902. 158 p.
Poems of Power. Chicago: W. B. Conkey Company, 1903. 157 p.
Poems of Love. Chicago: M. A. Donohue & Co., 1905. 1 p. ℓ., 5-144 p.
Poems of Reflection. Chicago: M. A. Donohue & Co., 1905. 160 p.
New Thought Pastels. Holyoke, MA.: E. Towne, 1906. 1 p. ℓ., 7-45 p.
Poems of Sentiment, Containing An Erring Woman's Love, Love's Supremacy, and Worthwhile, etc., etc. Chicago: W. B. Conkey Co., 1906. 1 p. ℓ., 7-163 p.
Poems of Progress, and New Thought Pastels. Chicago: A. Whitman & Co., 1909. 4 p. ℓ., 7-177 p.
Picked Poems. Chicago: W. B. Conkey Company, 1912. 3 p. ℓ., 176 p.
Poems of Problems. Chicago: W. B. Conkey Company, 1914. 176 p.
Sonnets of Sorrow and Triumph. New York: George H. Doran Company, 1918. viii p., 1 ℓ., 11-69 p.
Poems. London: Gay and Hancock, Limited, 1919? xvi, 413 p.
Collected Poems of Ella Wheeler Wilcox. London: L. B. Hill, 1924. xxp., 1 ℓ., 517 p.

WILDE, EDNA MAY (JUDSON) (1872-)
Traveller's Joy. Boston: B. Humphries, 1947. 117 p.

WILDE, IRENE
Driftwood Fires. San Francisco: Harr Wagner Publishing Co., 1928. viii p., 1 ℓ., 40 p.
Fire Against the Sky. New York: Liveright Pub. Co., 1938. xiv p., 1 ℓ., 144 p.

WILDER, CHARLOTTE (1898-)
Mortal Sequence. New York: Coward-McCann, Inc., 1936. xi,

65 p.
Phases of the Moon. New York: Coward-McCann, Inc., 1936. 7 p. ℓ., 3-90 p.

WILDER, CORDELIA BEARDSLEY
Kitchen Visits with the Muses. Coventry, N.Y., Binghamton, N.Y.: Press of the Chronicle Publishing Co., 1902. 83 p., [2] p., 1 ℓ.

WILDES, ADELINE WILKINS (d. 1914)
The Rainbow Bridge and Other Poems. Boston?: n.p., 1900. 1 p. ℓ., 5-14 p.

WILDMAN, ANNETTE (1897-)
Mosaic of Living; A Collection of Poems, 1915-1950. Kansas City, MO.: Burton Pub. Co., 1951. 144 p.
Sonnettones. Kansas City, MO.: Burton Pub. Co., 1951. 210 p.
Moments of Mood. Kansas City, MO.: Burton Pub. Co., 1952. 223 p.
Of Heart and Home. Kansas City, MO.: Burton Pub. Co., 1956. 201 p.

WILDS, MYRA VIOLA
Thoughts of Idle Hours. Nashville, TN.: The National Baptist Publishing Board, 1915. 81 p.

WILDWOOD, FLORA, pseud. see HINES, MARCELLA MELVILLE (1828-)

WILEY, SARA KING (1871-1909)
Alcestis, and Other Poems. New York, London: The Macmillan Company, 1905. 4 p. ℓ., 60 p.

WILKIE, ISABELLA
Sonnets of the Sierra. San Francisco: Johnck & Seeger, Printers, 1922. 9 ℓ.

WILKINS, ALICE GARRETT
...Arcana. New York: H. Vinal, Ltd., 1927. 5 p. ℓ., 3-31, [1] p.

WILKINS, ELSIE (1905-)
Hideaway. Boonville, N.Y.: Willard Press, 1954. 83 p.

WILKINSON, ELIZABETH HAYS
The Lane to Sleepy Town, and Other Verses. Pittsburgh, PA.: Reed and Whitting, 1910. vii, 66 p.

WILKINSON, FLORENCE see EVANS, FLORENCE (WILKINSON)

WILKINSON, MARGUERITE OGDEN (BIGELOW) (1883-1928)
In Vivid Gardens; Songs of the Woman Spirit. Boston: Sherman, French & Co., 1911. 5 p. ℓ., 72 p.

By a Western Wayside. Santa Barbara, CA.: Craft Camarata, 1912. [14] p.
Bluestone, Lyrics. New York: The Macmillan Company, 1920. xxxiii p., 1 ℓ., 129 p.
The Great Dream. New York: The Macmillan Company, 1923. 5 p. ℓ., 42 p.
The Way of the Makers. New York: The Macmillan Company, 1925. xxii, 316 p.
Citadels. New York: The Macmillan Company, 1926. 6 p. ℓ., 11-86 p.

WILKINSON, ROSEMARY CHALLONER (1924-)
A Girl's Will. Charleston, IL.: Prairie Poet Books, 1973. 24 p.

WILLARD, JULIA COLTON
The Garden Path, and Other Verses. Boonville, N.Y.: G. A. Willard, 1920. 49 p.

WILLARD, LUVIA MARGARET (1882-)
Bric-A-Brac. New York: n.p., 1932. 92 p.

WILLARD, NANCY
In His Country. Ann Arbor, MI.: Generation Press, 1966. 56 p.
Skin of Grace. Columbia, MO.: University of Missouri Press, 1967. 45 p.
A New Herball. Baltimore, MD.: Ferdinand Roten Galleries, 1968. 32 p.
19 Masks for the Naked Poet. Santa Cruz, CA.: Kayak Books, 1971. 45 p.
The Carpenter of the Sun: Poems. New York: Liveright, dist. by Norton, 1974. 55 p.

WILLIAMS, BERTHA
Luminous Token. New York: H. Harrison, 1935. 63 p.
God Gave Me a Poem. San Antonio, TX.: Naylor Co., 1965. 26 p.

WILLIAMS, BERTYE (YOUNG)
Rhymes in the Rough. Boston: The Stratford Company, 1926. 3 p. ℓ., 55 p.
House of Happiness. New York: G. Sully & Co., 1928. xiii, 140 p.
Apples of Gold. New York: G. Sully & Co., Inc., 1932. 140 p.
... Far Is the Hill. Cincinnati, OH.: Talaria Publications, 1939. 94 p., 1 ℓ.

WILLIAMS, BLANCHE ROBINSON (1895-)
Fragile Hands. Richmond, VA.: The Dietz Press, 1940. 5 p. ℓ., 65 p.
Ultimate Plea. Richmond, VA.: The Dietz Press, 1942. 65 p.

White Barrier. Richmond, VA.: Dietz Press, 1947. 68 p.
In the Hushed Leaf. Richmond, VA.: Dietz Press, 1951. 80 p.
Poems Selected Old and New. Richmond, VA.: Dietz Press, 1963. 115 p.

WILLIAMS, EDITH JEANETTE
The Star-Dust Trail. Los Angeles: Westwood Hills Press, 1930. 1 p. ℓ., 19 p., 1 ℓ.

WILLIAMS, ELLA O.
Designs for Liberation; Symbolic Truisms. Tacoma, WA.: n. p., 1973. 52 p.

WILLIAMS, ELSETTA R.
The Silver Flute. Philadelphia: Dorrance, 1961. 27 p. (Contemporary poets of Dorrance)

WILLIAMS, ELVA
Night in a Rented Room. New York: Elektra Press, 1939. 3 p. ℓ., 3-59 p.

WILLIAMS, ETHEL SCOTT
A Little Patch of Blue, and Other Poems. Chicago: Printed for the Author by the Methodist Book Concern, 1925. 90 p.

WILLIAMS, FLORENCE
The Guiding Light. Nashville, TN.: National Baptist Training School Board, 1963.

WILLIAMS, HELEN EVELYN (1906-)
Driftwood of Dreams. San Leandro, CA.: The Greater West Publishing Co., 1939. 61 p.

WILLIAMS, HELEN SHERMAN
... Ground-Swell. Philadelphia: Dorrance & Co., 1937. 40 p. (Contemporary poets of Dorrance, 172)

WILLIAMS, HELEN WOODBRIDGE (1888-)
Discoveries. Philadelphia: Dorrance, 1948. 74 p.

WILLIAMS, JEANETTE MARIE
Soul of a Sapphire. Chicago: Free Black Press, 1969? [24] p.

WILLIAMS, MANUELLA
Pebbles. Ames, IA.: Printed by the Milepost, 1932. 5 p. ℓ., 3-39 p.

WILLIAMS, MARGARET PITCHER
For This Gift. San Antonio, TX.: Naylor Co., 1964. 60 p.

WILLIAMS, MARGARET WINSLOW
Thoughts. New York: The Knickerbocker Press, 1925. v, 43 p.

WILLIAMS, MARY A.
Pitter, Patter, Roundabout. New York: Vantage Press, 1959. 66 p.

WILLIAMS, MARY BRADBURY
Life the Huckster and Other Poems. Boston: R. G. Badger, 1931. 141 p.

WILLIAMS, MONA (GOODWYN) (1906-)
Voices in the Dark. Garden City, N.Y.: Doubleday, 1968. 116 p.

WILLIAMS, NELLIE LOWMAN
Songs in the Night. Emory University, Atlanta, GA.: Banner Press, 1951. 65 p.
Sincerely Yours. Emory University, Atlanta, GA.: Banner Press, 1953. 55 p.

WILLIAMS, SARAH A.
Goldenglow, a Book of Poems. Evanston, IL.: n.p., 1923. 35 p.

WILLIAMS, SHIRLEY ANNE
The Peacock Poems. Middletown, CT.: Wesleyan University Press, 1975. 87 p. (The Wesleyan poetry program)

WILLIAMSON, ALICE (BOORMAN)
Cinderella's Slippers. Richmond, VA.: Dietz Press, 1950. 96 p.

WILLIAMSON, CLARA MARION (YOUNG) (1860-)
Easter Lilies. New Orleans, LA.: Palfrey-Rodd-Pursell Co., 1907. 38 p.

WILLIER, ELIZABETH CHAPMAN
Dreamer's Gold. New York: Pageant Press, 1959. 60 p.

WILLS, ROBERTA JUNE
Sea Shells. Dallas, TX.: American Poetry Association, Inc., 1938. 2 p. ℓ., vii-x, 100 p.

WILSON, ABBA (GOULD)
With Garlands Green. Cambridge, MA.: n.p., 1915. 195 p.

WILSON, ALICE (1869-)
Actaeon's Defense, and Other Poems. Boston: R. G. Badger, 1906. 2 p. ℓ., [6]-90 p.
The Lutanist. Boston: R. G. Badger, 1914. 46 p.

WILSON, ALICE MARIE
Forget-Me-Not. New York: Paebar Co., 1949. 32 p.

WILSON, ANNE WASHINGTON
Scrimshaw. Baltimore, MD.: The Norman, Remington Co., 1925. 38 p.

WILSON, ANNE WILSON
Pansies.... San Francisco: The Church Book Shop, 1929. 2 p. ℓ., 3-85, [2] p., 1 ℓ.

WILSON, ANNIE SHIPMAN
Gold Gleams of Poetry. St. Joseph, MO.: Combe Printing Co., 1914. 160 p.

WILSON, BEULAH HASTINGS
The Heart That Understands, Poems. New York: Exposition Press, 1963. 72 p.

WILSON, CAROLYN CROSBY
Fir Trees & Fireflies. New York & London: G. P. Putnam's Sons, 1920. ix p., 1 ℓ., 69 p.

WILSON, CATHERINE NUNLEY
Falling Leaves. Granbury, TX.: Granbury News, 1924. 40 p.
Light on the Hills. Dallas, TX.: Kaleidograph Press, 1949. 85 p.

WILSON, CLOVER
Poems of Love, Faith and Friendship. New York: Pageant Press, 1958. 112 p.

WILSON, ELIZABETH DIXON
In Retrospect; Poems. New York: Vantage Press, 1968. 71 p.

WILSON, EMILY H.
Down Zion's Alley. n.p.: Drummer Press, 1972.
Balancing on Stones. Winston-Salem, NC.: Jackpine Press, 1975. 63 p.

WILSON, FLORA McCULLOUGH (1927-)
Not by Bread Alone. New York: Carlton, 1970. 64 p. (A Lyceum book)

WILSON, GRACE BARKER
Miles to Go. Mill Valley, CA.: Wings Press, 1960. 78 p.
Wide Horizons. Clarendon, TX.: Clarendon Press, 1968. 82 p.

WILSON, IBBIE McCOLM (1834-1908)
Miscellaneous Poems. Des Moines, IA.: Lewis-Wallace Printing Company, 1909. vii, 182 p.

WILSON, IONE
Belle-Fleur; A Book of Verses. San Leandro, CA.: The Greater West Publishing Co., 1937. 63 p.

WILSON, IVA BAKER
My Swinging Lantern; Poems and Illustrations. Portland? OR.: n.p., 1946. [92] p.

WILSON, LORETTA POWER
The Gypsy Heart. Baltimore, MD.: The Norman, Remington Company, 1927. 72 p.
Leaves of Love and Petals from Life; New Poems. New York: Galleon Press, 1934. 63 p.

WILSON, LOUISE B.
Horns in Velvet. New York: The Harbor Press, 1930. 4 p. ℓ., 59, [1] p.

WILSON, MABEL REED
My Garden of Dreams. Boston: The Christopher Publishing House, 1928. 6 p. ℓ., [9]-35 p.
Rosemary for Remembrance. New York: Avon House, 1937. 64 p.
Wings of the Morning. New York: Avon House, 1939. 64 p.
A Gleam of Sunset Gold. New York: Avon House, 1941. 64 p.
Grey Dawn. New York: Exposition Press, 1941. 5 p. ℓ., 13-94 p.

WILSON, MARTHA (1900-)
Testament. London: Richards, 1938. 68 p.
Penitent Earth. Hartland, VT.: Solitarian Press, 1940. 62 p.

WILSON, MIRIAM
Etchings for Someone You Love; Poems. New York: Exposition Press, 1963. 63 p.
The Journey. New York: Exposition Press, 1964. 71 p.

WILSON, RACHEL MACK
The Sacred Acre; Poems. New York: H. Vinal, Ltd., 1928. 6 p. ℓ., 46 p., 1 ℓ.
Last Days of Sappho. Chicago: Excaliber Press, 1936. 3 p. ℓ., 33 p.

WILSON, RUTH MARIAN
My Garden of Time, and Other Poems. Boston: Bruce Humphries, 1954. 64 p.

WILTON, MABEL A.
Down Childhood Lane. Los Angeles, CA.: Paul Moran Print Shop, 1936. 56 p.

WILTON, MABEL ALBERTHA (1894-)
These Jewels I Share. Los Angeles: Willing Pub. Co., 1949. 143 p.

WINANT, FRAN (1943-)
Looking at Women: Poems. New York: Violet Press, 1971. 34 p.

WINANT, RUTH GUNTHER (1885-)
Seeing Through. Boston: R. G. Badger, 1920. 138 p.

WINCHESTER, MARIE MOON
Other Worlds Are Empty. New York: H. Harrison, 1941. 63 p.

WINES, VIETTA B.
Wines and Roses. Big Fork, MN.: Northwoods Press, 1974. 48 p.

WING, FLORENCE ANNETTE
Moon of the Desert. New York: H. Vinal, 1927. x p., 1 ℓ., 41 p.

WINGATE, MAUDE (LAMB)
Poems. New York: G. P. Putnam's Sons, 1938. 90 p.

WINKLEBLACK, GLADYS C.
Wind Songs. Charleston, IL.: Prairie Press, 1965. 59 p.

WINSHIP, MARY GRAY
Autumn Leaves and Other Poems. Flatbush, N.Y.: n.p., 1909. 20 ℓ.

WINSLOW, ANNE GOODWIN
The Long Gallery. New York: Harcourt, Brace and Company, 1925. vii, 128 p.

WINSLOW, GRACE SEWELL
Wayside Inn, and Other Poems. Framingham, MA.: Peerless Press, 1940. 64 p.

WINSTEAD, HULDAH LUCILE
In the Land of Dakota; A Little Book of North Dakota Verse. Boston: R. G. Badger, 1920. 45 p.
America Makes Men, and Other Poems; A Second Book of North Dakota Verse. Boston: R. G. Badger, 1924. 67 p.

WINSTON, BESSIE BRENT
Alabaster Boxes. Washington, D.C.: Review & Herald Publishing Assoc., 1947. 160 p.
Life's Red Sea, and Other Poems. Washington, D.C.: Review and Herald Pub. Assoc., 1950.

WINSTON, LULA GAINES
The Mosaic of Calvary. n.p.: Winston, 1923.

WINTERS, BERNICE (1921-)
The Tropic of Mother; Poems, 1966. 2d ed. Homestead, FL.: Olivant Press, 1967. [20] p.
Bitchpoems. Homestead, FL.: Olivant Press, 1970. [87] p.

WINTERS, JANET LEWIS <u>see</u> LEWIS, JANET (1899-)

WIREN, MYRA PAGE
<u>The Poems of the Pioneers, and Other Verses.</u> Garden City, N.Y.: The Country Life Press, 1923. 5 p. ℓ., ix-xi, 73 p.

WISE, HILDA JOHNSON
<u>The Optimist, and Other Verses.</u> New York: C. Scribner, 1900. 72 p.

WISEMAN, ADA POTTER
<u>The Call of the Woods, and Other Poems.</u> Los Angeles, CA.: Wetzel Publishing Co., 1927. 71, [1] p.

WISTER, MARINA
<u>Helen and Others.</u> New York: The Macmillan Company, 1924. xiii, 112 p.
<u>Night in the Valley.</u> New York: The Macmillan Company, 1930. viii, 64 p.
<u>Fantasy and Fugue.</u> New York: The Macmillan Company, 1937. ix, 108 p.

WITHERS, Mrs. B. T.
<u>Lean Lines & Love-ly.</u> San Angelo, TX.: Press of Holcombe-Blanton, 1951. 48 p.

WITHERSPOON, PATTIE FRENCH
<u>Elizabeth of Boonesborough, and Other Poems.</u> Boston: The Poet Lore Company, 1909. 122 p.

WITHROW, LILLIE McFADDEN
<u>Meadow Flowers.</u> Philadelphia: Dorrance, 1956. 105 p. (Contemporary poets of Dorrance, 484)

WIXON, PEARL E.
<u>The Master.</u> Parma, MI.: W. E. Beebe, Printer, 1923. 61 p.

WOELLWARTH, MARY ELISE
<u>Mother, Read Us a Poem.</u> St. Louis, MO.: The Queen's Work, 1938. 46, [1] p.

WOLCOTT, EDNA (THOMPSON)
<u>Weavings from My Loom.</u> Philadelphia: Dorrance, 1951. 95 p.

WOLCOTT, KATHARYN
<u>Wind Across the Threshold....</u> Prairie City, IL.: The Decker Press, 1948. 66 p.

WOLF, EDITH (AINSFIELD) (1889-)
<u>Cinquainian, a Bookful of Cinquains.</u> Flint, MI.: Verse-Land Press, 1935. 68 p., 1 ℓ.
<u>Balance; A Bookful of Little Thought.</u> Cleveland, OH.: The Erie Press, 1942. 5 p. ℓ., 50 p.

Wordmobile; Collected from the Writer's Poems Appearing Through the Years in Blue River Publications. Shelbyville, IN.: Blue River Press, 1956. [16] p.

WOLF, EILEEN
Tidemark. Boston: Printed by the Nimrod Press, 1971. unpaged.

WOLF, GERALDINE (ARBUCKLE)
The Crowded Eye. Philadelphia: H. Wolf, 1951. 155 p.

WOLFE, MARIANNE
The Berrypicker; Poems. Port Townsend, WA.: Copper Canyon Press, 1973. 42 p.

WOLFE, MARJORIE LOUISE
Many Moods. Boston: The Stratford Company, 1927. 3 p. ℓ., 37 p.

WOLFERT, ADRIENNE
7 Day World. Fort Smith, AR.: South & West, 1966. 31 p.

WOLFERT, HELEN X. (HERSCHDORFER) (1904-)
Nothing Is a Wonderful Thing. New York: Simon & Schuster, 1946. 4 p. ℓ., 118 p., 1 ℓ.
The Music. New York: Norton, 1965. 85 p.

WOLFF, MARY EVALINE see MADELEVA, Sister (1887-)

WOLPERT, PAULINE
A Book of Joy, Poems. New York: Exposition Press, 1948. 6 p. ℓ., 131 p.

WOLSTON-HALLETT, MARY
Morning Glories & Love; Poems. New York: New Orlando Publications, 1964. 28 p.

WOMACK, BESS FOSTER
Next to My Heart. Dallas, TX.: Mathis, Van Nort & Company, 1939. vii, [1], 56 p.

WONG, MAY (1944-)
A Bad Girl's Book of Animals. New York: Harcourt, Brace & World, 1969. 83 p.
Reports: Poems. New York: Harcourt, Brace, Jovanovich, 1972. 140 p.

WONSON, AGNES CHOATE
Candles of Memory. Gloucester, MA.: Press of L. A. Chisholm, 1925. [84] p., 1 ℓ.

WOOD, ALICE IRENE
Battle Hymn, and Other Poems. Newark, N.J.: Franklin Press, 1917. 1 p. ℓ., 45 p.

WOOD, ANNA HAMILTON
The Flame. Baltimore, MD.: The Stockton Press, 1924. 4 p. ℓ., 45 p., 1 ℓ.

WOOD, CHARLOTTE E.
"Woodside" Reveries & Rambling Rhymes. Concord, CA.: Poets Press, 1927. 5 p. ℓ., 9-75 p.

WOOD, DIAMIA FRANKLIN
Unto the Hills. San Antonio, TX.: Naylor Co., 1966. vii, 32 p.

WOOD, ELEANOR DUNCAN
Largesse. Louisville, KY.: J. P. Morton & Company, 1926. 4 p. ℓ., 74 p.

WOOD, ELIZA T.
In His Hands. Baton Rouge, LA.: Claitor's Book Store, 1965. 57 p.

WOOD, ELIZABETH (LAMBERT)
Face of the West. Portland, OR.: Binfords & Mort, 1952. 98 p.

WOOD, ESTHER
The Wind-Carved Tree. Manchester, ME.: Falmouth Pub. House, 1953. 6 p. ℓ., 105 p.

WOOD, FLORIAN E.
Now Sleeps the Rose. New York: Carlton Press, 1968. 40 p.

WOOD, LAURA HOPE
Meditations. Kansas City, MO.: Frank Glenn Pub. Co., 1959. 5 p. ℓ., 67 p.

WOOD, ODELLA PHELPS
Recaptured Echoes. New York: The Exposition Press, 1944. 64 p.

WOODALL, ELIZABETH GREY
Beauty; God's Gift. New York: Pageant Press, 1956. 5 p. ℓ., 118 p.
My Yoke Is Easy & There Is Life Everlasting. New York: Pageant Press, 1956. 6 p. ℓ., 43 p., 4 ℓ., 63 p.

WOODLEY, KATHERINE KELLY
Echoes Through the Years; Poems for Sharing & Enjoyment. New York: Exposition Press, 1959. 47 p.

WOODMAN, HANNAH REA (1870-)
The Heart & the Crown. New York & Washington: The Neale Publishing Company, 1905. 64 p.

Tumbleweed. Poughkeepsie, N. Y.: A. V. Haight Co., 1909. 3 p. ℓ., xi-xiii, 128 p.
The Open Road; A Book of Outcast Verse. Poughkeepsie, N. Y.: Priv. Print. by the Author, 1910. 4 p. ℓ., xiii-xv, 138 p.

WOODRUFF, CAROLINE SALOME (1866-)
My Trust, and Other Verse. Rutland, VT.: The Tuttle Company, 1928. 3 p. ℓ., 5-126 p.

WOODRUFF, HILDA ELIZABETH
False Dawn. Boston: R. G. Badger, 1931. 76 p.

WOODS, BERTHA GERNEAUX (DAVIS) (1873-)
Verses. Washington, D. C.: The Neale Publishing Company, 1903. 120 p.
The Guest, and Other Verse. College Park, MD.: The University Press, 1926. 3 p. ℓ., 51 p.
Patient Scientists, and Other Verse. College Park, MD.: University Press, 1928. 9-55 p.
"The Little Gate" Opening into Nature, Humanity, Life. North Montpelier, VT.: W. J. Coates, The Driftwind Press, 1935. 4 p. ℓ., [7]-85, [1] p.

WOODS, HELEN GEE (1897-)
This Love I Sing. Idaho Falls, ID.: Guild Quarterly Press, 1968. 5 p. ℓ., 48 p.

WOODS, JANE AMIDON
Today Is a Poem. New York: Vantage Press, 1963. 64 p.

WOODS, WINIFRED
Snow in April. Lincoln Park, MI.: n. p., 1935. 40 p.

WOODWARD, HELEN DE LONG
A Song of Exultation; A Sheaf of Recollections. New York: Comet Press Books, 1957. 6 p. ℓ., 39 p.

WOODWARD, JOAN
The Glow Worm & Other Poems. Mill Valley, CA., New York: The Wings Press, 1943. 40 p.

WOODWARD, MARY ALETHEA
Songs of the Soul. Boston: The Stratford Company, 1924. 5 p. ℓ., 102 p.
_______. 2d ed. rev. and amplified. Portland, OR.: Binfords & Mort, 1939. 8 p. ℓ., 3-210 p.

WOODWARD, MARY C. (SLOAN) (1833-)
Darkness and Dawn. Dayton, OH.: Press of United Brethren Publishing House, 1903. xviii p., 1 ℓ., [21]-157 p.

WOOLDRIDGE, IRIS
A Touch, a Smile, a Memory. New York: Vantage Press, 1975. 53 p.

WOOLEVER, MARY STAUFFER
We Two Are Kin, Oh Tree; A Sonnet Sequence & Miscellaneous Poems. North Montpelier, VT.: The Driftwind Press, 1944. 65 p.

WOOLLEY, FRANCES
State Flower Poems. Boston: Meador Pub. Co., 1941. 46 p.

WOOLSEY, SARAH CHAUNCEY (1835-1905)
Last Verses. Boston: Little, Brown and Company, 1906. xix, 167 p.

WOOSTER, NITA KIBLER
Of a Number of Things. Grand Rapids, MI.: Dickinson Bros., 1941. 5 p. ℓ., 68 p.

WORCESTER, BLANCHE RULLSON (1871-)
From a Walled Garden. Boston: R. G. Badger, 1929. 179 p.

WORKMAN, RONA MORRIS
Just Loggin'. Portland, OR.: Metropolitan Press, 1936. 46 p.

WORLEY, INDIA B.
Poems for Daily Living. Radford, VA.: Commonwealth Press, 1958. 2 v.

WORREL, RUTH
Heart's Journey. New York: William-Frederick Press, 1949. 3 p. ℓ., 119 p.

WORTH, KATHRYN
...Sign of Capricornus. New York: A. A. Knopf, 1937. 6 p. ℓ., 3-65, [1] p.

WORTHINGTON, ANNE (1943-)
Circling Clouds of Imagination; Poems, 1960-1969. Bowie, MD.: Golden Triangle Pub. Co., 1973. 97 p.

WRAY, FLORENCE RUBERT
Spring Tide; A First Collection of Poems. Fort Smith, AR.: South & West Publications, 1963. 40 p.

WRAY, MARGARET TOWNE
For Betty Coed & Joe College. Chicago: Inland Press, 1941. 79 p.

WRAY, RUBY MARION
So Flows the Spring. Philadelphia: Dorrance, 1949. 76 p.

WRIGHT, BEATRICE
Color Scheme; Selected Poems. New York: Pageant Press, 1957. 59 p.

WRIGHT, BERNICE LONG
Catalina Mists. Boston: R. G. Badger, 1924. ix, 11-92 p.

WRIGHT, CATHARINE MORRIS (1899-)
Seaweed Their Pasture. Wyncote, PA.: Endsmeet Farm, 1946. 3 p. ℓ., 112 p.

WRIGHT, CELESTE TURNER (1906-)
Inscription Rock and Other Poems. Davis, CA.: University of California, 1963. 97 ℓ.
Etruscan Princess, & Other Poems. Denver, CO.: A. Swallow Press, 1964. 48 p.
A Sense of Place. Francestown, N. H.: Golden Quill Press, 1973. 96 p.

WRIGHT, DAISY McLEOD
Little John Bull, and Other Poems. Boston: The Gorham Press, 1915. 60 p.

WRIGHT, ETHEL WILLIAMS
Of Men & Trees; Poems. New York: Exposition Press, 1954. 64 p.

WRIGHT, IDA FLORENDA (SAMPSON) (1858-)
A Message Dedicated to Those I Love & Those I Know Are True. Portland, OR.: The Columbian Press, Inc., 1924. 2 p. ℓ., 7-115, [1] p.

WRIGHT, JEAN
A Fool on a Roof, et in Arcadia Ego, and Other Poems. Boston: R. G. Badger, 1911. 56 p.
An Urban Faun, and Other Poems. Boston: R. G. Badger, 1912. 3 p. ℓ., 5-74 p.

WRIGHT, MARGARET WHITE
White Heather. Philadelphia: Dorrance, 1960. 31 p.

WRIGHT, MARTHA ELIZABETH (BURT) (1846-)
Oakham, a Retrospect in Rhyme. New Haven, CT.: Tuttle, Morehouse & Taylor Co., 1928. 102 p.

WRIGHT, MARY M. (1894-)
Beyond Bewilderment. Emory University, Atlanta, GA.: Banner Press, 1942. 53 p.
Not for Oblivion. Alpine? TX.: n. p., 1956. 42 p.
Light from Other Stars. New York: Poets of America Pub. Co., 1963. 99 p.

WRIGHT, MARY PAULINE
Poems. . . . Lowell, MA.: Alentour House, 1929. 3 p. ℓ., 11-66 p.

WRIGHT, MAUDE (FABLE)
The Gossip of a Stream. Marshall, IN.: Press-Craft, 1940. [76] p.

WRIGHT, NATHALIA
The Inner Room. Windham, CT.: Hawthorn House, 1938. 3 p. ℓ., 9-37, [1] p. (Modern American poets, v. 3)

WRIGHT, ROXANNE SEABURY
In April, & Other Songs. Carmel-by-the-Sea, CA.: n. p., 1925. 2 p. ℓ., 9-41 p., 1 ℓ.

WRIGHT, SARAH E.
Give Me a Child. n. p.: Kraft, 1955.

WRIGHT, SARAH MARTYN
A Book of Verse. Boston: The Jordan & More Press, 1921. 7 p. ℓ., [3]-67 p.

WRINN, MARY J. J.
Cock on the Ridge. New York & London: Harper & Brothers, 1940. xi p., 1 ℓ., 139, [1] p.

WUESTHOFF, MABEL GREGORY
The Seal of Faith. Boston: B. Humphries, 1946. 80 p.

WUPPERMANN, VIRGINIA F. (1914-1932)
The True Seeker. New York: J. D. Brooks & Co., 1933. 5 p. ℓ., xii-xvi, 134 p.

WURDEMANN, AUDREY (1911-)
The House of Silk. New York: H. Vinal, 1927. 6 p. ℓ., 9-85 p., 1 ℓ.
Bright Ambush. New York: The John Day Co., 1934. 7 p. ℓ., 76 p., 1 ℓ.
______. New and enl. ed. New York: Reynal and Hitchcock, 1935. 7 p. ℓ., 78 p.
The Seven Sins. New York & London: Harper & Brothers, 1935. vii p., 1 ℓ., 59, [1] p.
Splendour in the Grass. New York & London: Harper & Brothers, 1936. xi p., 1 ℓ., 95, [1] p.
Testament of Love; A Sonnet Sequence. New York & London: Harper & Brothers, 1938. vii p., 2 ℓ., 49 p., 1 ℓ.

WURL, EMILY SPRAGUE
To Those Who Dream. New York: Avon House, 1941. 62 p.

WYATT, ANDREA
Three Rooms; Poems. Berkeley, CA.: Oyez, 1970. [37] p.

Poems of the Morning and Poems of the Storm. Berkeley, CA.: Oyez, 1973. 57 p.

WYATT, CAROLINE (COX)
My Heart Sings. Chattanooga, TN.: Andrews Printing Co., 1944. 5 p. ℓ., 13-61 p.

WYATT, EDITH FRANKLIN (1873-1958)
The Wind in the Corn, and Other Poems. New York, London: D. Appleton & Co., 1917. xii p., 1 ℓ., 124 p.

WYATT, FARICITA (HALL)
The River Must Flow. Berkeley, CA.: n.p., 1965. 25 p.

WYATT, MARGARET
Treasured Thoughts; A Volume of Miscellaneous Verse Dealing with Common Everyday Experiences of Life. Cedar Rapids, IA.: The Torch Press, 1925. 73 p.

WYLIE, ELINOR (HOYT) (1885-1928)
Incidental Numbers. London: Printed by Wm. Clowes & Sons, 1912.
Nets to Catch the Wind. New York: Harcourt, Brace & Company, 1921. 47 p.
Black Armour; A Book of Poems. New York: George H. Doran, 1923. viii, 1 ℓ., 11-77 p.
Elinor Wylie. Ed. by Laurence Jourdan. New York: Simon & Schuster, 1926. 31 p. (The Pamphlet poets)
Black Armour; A Book of Poems. London: M. Secker, 1927. 77 p.
Nets to Catch the Wind. London: A. A. Knopf, 1928. v, 41 p.
Trivial Breath. London, New York: A. A. Knopf, 1928. vii, 80 p.
...Angels and Earthly Creatures. New York, London: A. A. Knopf, 1929. xi, 63, [2] p.
Birthday Sonnet. New York: Random House, 1929. [4] p. (The poetry quartos)
Nets to Catch the Wind. New York: A. A. Knopf, 1929. 47 p.
Rondeau; A Windy Day. n.p., 193-? 4 ℓ.
Collected Poems of Elinor Wylie. New York: A. A. Knopf, 1932. xviii, 2 ℓ., 3-311 p., [1] p.
Last Poems of Elinor Wylie; Poems transcribed by Jane E. Wise with other poems hitherto unpublished in book form. New York: A. A. Knopf, 1943. xix p., 1 ℓ., 105, [1] p.
Collected Poems. New York: Alfred A. Knopf, 1963. 318 p.

WYLIE, LOLLIE BELLE
Arcades. Atlanta, GA.: A. B. Caldwell, 1916.

WYLY, RACHEL LUMPKIN
Fifty Little Lyrics. Asheville, NC.: Daniels Business Services, Inc., 195-? 29 p.
Sifted Memories. Boston: Branden Press, 1968. 70 p.

WYMAN, LILLIE BUFFUM (CHACE)
Interludes & Other Verses. Boston: W. B. Clarke Company, 1913. xv, 183 p.

WYMORE, MARY ISABEL
Adrienne and Other Poems. Boston: R. G. Badger, 1907. 43 p.

WYNNE, ANNETTE
For Days and Days; A Year-Round Treasury of Child Verse. New York: Frederick A. Stokes Company, 1919. xxvi, 276 p.
All Through the Year; Three Hundred and Sixty-five New Poems for the Holidays and Every Day. New York: Frederick A. Stokes, 1932. xxv, 364 p.
Treasure Things. New York, Chicago: P. F. Yolland Co., 1932. [39] p.

WYNNE, MADELINE (YALE) (1847-1918)
Si Briggs Talks. Boston & New York: Houghton Mifflin Co., 1917. v, [1] p., 1 ℓ., 71, [1] p., 1 ℓ.

WYNNE, MAMIE FOLSOM (1885-)
Remember Me. Dallas? TX.: n.p., 1957. 3 p. ℓ., 89 p.

WYSE, LOIS
Love Poems for the Very Married. Cleveland, OH.: World Pub. Co., 1967. 55 p.
Are You Sure You Love Me? New York: World Pub. Co., 1969. 63 p.
I Love You Better Now. New York: Garret Press, dist. by World Pub. Co., 1970. 55 p.
Come Live with Me. Cleveland, OH.: American Greetings Corp., 1971.
How Come Holding Hands Feels So Good? Cleveland, OH.: American Greetings Corp., 1971. 28 p.
I Am So Glad You Married Me. Cleveland, OH.: American Greetings Corp., 1971.
I Will Wait for You. Cleveland, OH.: American Greetings Corp., 1971. 28 p.
Love Poems for a Wedding Day. New York: Bantam Books, 1971. 64 p.
Love Will Come Again. Cleveland, OH.: American Greetings Corp., 1971.
More Love Poems for the Very Married. Cleveland, OH.: American Greetings Corp., 1971. 28 p.
One and One Make Love. Cleveland, OH.: American Greetings Corp., 1971.
So What Are You Waiting for, Darling? Cleveland, OH.: American Greetings Corp., 1971. 28 p.
The Start of Love. Cleveland, OH.: American Greetings Corp., 1971.
Who But Me? Cleveland, OH.: American Greetings Corp., 1971.

You Are the Love I Want.... Cleveland, OH.: American Greetings Corp., 1971.
A Father Is Love & Other Nice Things. Garden City, N.Y.: Dist. by Doubleday, 1972. 23 p.
A Grand-(Kind-of-a-)Father. Garden City, N.Y.: Dist. by Doubleday, 1972. 23 p.
I'm Glad You Are My Son. New York: Garret Press; dist. by Doubleday, Garden City, N.Y., 1972. 23 p.
My Mother and Me. New York: Garret Press; dist. by Doubleday, Garden City, N.Y., 1972. 23 p.
Oh, Grandmother, What a Big Heart You Have. New York: Garret Press; dist. by Doubleday, 1972. 23 p.
Small Poems for the Daughter I Love. New York: Garret Press; dist. by Doubleday, Garden City, N.Y., 1972. 23 p.
A Weeping Eye Can Never See. Garden City, N.Y.: Doubleday, 1972.
Lovetalk; How to Say What You Mean to Someone You Love. Garden City, N.Y.: Doubleday, 1973. 96 p.

YAFFE, LEONA (1913?-)
Bits o' Life. Chicago: W. Ransom, 1923. 5 p. ℓ., 9-89 p.

YALE, MARGARET E.
Long After You. Pasadena, CA.: Ampersand Press, 1948. 4 p. ℓ., 68 p.

YANCEY, BESSIE (WOODSON) (1882-)
Echoes from the Hills; A Book of Poems. Washington, D.C.: The Associated Publishers, Inc., 1939. vi, 62 p.

YANES, ROSEANNE
The Hurdy-Gurdy Man. Campbell, CA.: Poet & Printer Moses Yanes, 1973.

YARNALL, ANNA
Golden Memories. Philadelphia: Innes & Sons, 1919. 5 p. ℓ., 3-113 p.

YARRELL, Mrs. THOMAS, Sr.
Poems. New York: The Cosmopolitan Press, 1913. 85 p.

YATES, ELIZABETH CRAWFORD (1885-)
Wind Carvings. Portland, OR.: Binfords & Mort, 1953. 7 p. ℓ., 78 p.

YATES, MAGDALENA EUGENIE
Poems. New York: Exposition Press, 1965. 55 p.

YATES, MARGARET PEARL
The Charm of the Castle. San Francisco: W. Kibbee & Son, 1944. 3 p. ℓ., [11]-62 p.

YAUGER, FAY McCORMICK
Planter's Charm. Dallas, TX.: The Kaleidograph Press, 1935. xi p., 1 ℓ., 15-78 p.

YEATMAN, JENNETTE
Four Men West & Other Poems. Chicago: Dierkes Press, 1952. 48 p.

YEISER, IDABELLE
Moods; A Book of Verse. Philadelphia: The Colony Press, 1937. xiii p., 2 ℓ., 19-83 p., 1 ℓ.
Lyric and Legend. Boston: Christopher Publishing House, 1947. 77 p.

YEO, WILMA
Mrs. Neverbody's Recipes. Philadelphia: Lippincott, 1968. 34 p.

YERBURY, GRACE HELEN (DAVIES) (1899-)
Reed Song. San Antonio, TX.: Naylor Co., 1965. xii, 71 p.
Vistas Unvisited. Charleston, IL.: Prairie Press Books, 1973. vii, [1], 19 p.

YOCHIM, RACHEL
Meandering Thoughts. New York: Simplicity Press, 1966. 11 p.

YOFFIE, LEAH RACHEL
Dark Altar Stairs. Saint Louis: The Modern View Publishing Company, 1926. 5 p. ℓ., [13]-61 p., 1 ℓ.

YORK, ESTHER BALDWIN
Scarf of Stars. Orange? CA.: n. p., 1953. 137 p.

YORK, MABEL LUCE
Wild Quail at Play. Denver, CO.: Big Mountain Press, 1955. 80 p.

YORKE, ELENOR
Anthills of Joy. Ed. & pub. by Lew Lauria. Hollywood, CA.: n. p., 1941. 4 p. ℓ., 59 p.
Direct Current. Chicago: Oceanic Pub. Co., 1953. 88 p.

YOST, FRANCES CARTER (1914-)
Brim with Joy. Dexter, MO.: Candor Press, 1950. 48 p.
While Orchids Bloom. Bancroft? ID.: n. p., 1954. 64 p.

YOUNG, ANNA E.
My Mystic Realm. Dallas, TX.: Story Book Press, 1950.

YOUNG, ANNETTE M. (1892-)
M'Dawg & I, and Other Verses. Philadelphia: Dorrance, 1949. 59 p. (Contemporary poets of Dorrance, 382)

YOUNG, ANNIE WIER
Poems: Echoes from Life. Beacon, N.Y.: C. E. Spaight, Printer, 1 p. ℓ., [5]-62 p.

YOUNG, ARETTA (1864-1923)
After Sunset; Poems. Provo, UT.: Brigham Young University, 1925. 6 p. ℓ., 45, [1] p.

YOUNG, BARBARA
The Keys of Heaven; A Book of Poems. New York: Fleming H. Revell Company, 1927. 4 p. ℓ., 7-159 p.
I Go A-Walking & Other Poems. New York: The Paebar Company, 1933. 4 p. ℓ., 11-62 p.
No Beauty in Battle; A Book of Poems. New York: The Paebar Company, 1937. 6 p. ℓ., 113 p.

YOUNG, CARRIBEL (SCHMIDT) (1901-)
Some Links from a Chain. South Bend, IN.: Mirror Press, Inc., 1947. 3 p. ℓ., 25 p.

YOUNG, CELIA
Poems for Madeline Swansen. Milwaukee, WI.: Monday Morning Press, 1972. 4 p.

YOUNG, CHARLOTTE
The Heart Has Reasons. Emory University, Atlanta, GA.: Banner Press, 1953. 60 p. (Verse craft series)
...Speak to Us of Love. Emory University, Atlanta, GA.: Banner Press, 1959. 60 p. (Verse craft series)

YOUNG, ELEANOR G. R.
Days That Are Tapestries, & Other Poems. Wilmington, DE.: The Progressive Press, 1932. 4 p. ℓ., 87 p.

YOUNG, ELLA (1867-1956)
Marzilian & Other Poems. Oceano, CA.: Harbison & Harbison, 1938. 6 p. ℓ., 2-90, [1] p., 1 ℓ.
Seed of the Pomegranate, and Other Poems. New York: Graphic Arts Press, 1949. 42 p.
Smoke of Myrrh, and Other Poems. n.p.: Pacific Coast Pub. House, 1950. 135 p.

YOUNG, EMILY MAY
Out of the Dark; Poems. New York: Exposition Press, 1955. 64 p.
Into the Light, Poems. New York: Exposition Press, 1962. 64 p.

YOUNG, FLORNIE BAXTER
Songs from [illegible]awartha. New York: Vantage Press, 1959. 221 p.

YOUNG, J [illegible]
Black Ev[illegible]. A Tale of "The 45" in Verse. New York: F. T.

Neely, 1901.
Glynne's Wife: A Novelette in Verse. New York: F. T. Neely, 1901.
The Story of Saville: A Poem. New York: F. T. Neely, 1901.

YOUNG, JULIA EVELYN (DITTO)
Barham Beach: A Poem of Regeneration. Buffalo, N.Y.: Floyd-Genthner Press, 1908. 6 p. ℓ., [19]-142 p.

YOUNG, KATHLEEN T. (d. 1933)
Ten Poems. New York: Priv. Print. Parnassus Press, 1930. [21] p.
The Dark Land. Ithaca, N.Y.: Dragon Press, 1932. 44 p. (The Dragon series)

YOUNG, LIVIA IONE
At Evening Time. New York: The Grafton Press, 1907. 32 p.

YOUNG, MARGUERITE (1909-)
...Prismatic Ground. New York: Macmillan, 1937. viii, 63 p.
...Moderate Fable. New York: Reynal & Hitchcock, 1944. 3 p. ℓ., 50 p.

YOUNG, MARTHA (1868-)
Minute Dramas, the Kodak at the Quarter. Montgomery, AL.: The Paragon Press, 1921. 74 p.

YOUNG, MARY OLIPHANT
Record of a Few Published Poems. Latonia, KY.: V. Carter Service, 1947. 21 p.

YOUNG, OLIVE EMILY
Theme for a Threnody. New York: Vantage Press, 1958. 63 p.

YOUNG, OLIVIA (RUDOLPH) (1894-)
Take the Dirt Road: California in Photographs and Poems. Sanbornville, N.H.: Wake-Brooke House, 1960. 55 p.

YOUNG, SUSIE CARR
Dents: A Souvenir of Lewiston, Maine. Lewiston, ME.: The Journal Printshop, 1916. 32 p.

YOUNG, VIRGINIA BRADY
Circle of Thaw. New York: Barlenmir House, 1972. [64] p.

YOUNGS, FLORENCE EVELYN (PRATT) (1868-)
Songs of Many Days. Boston: R. G. Badger, 1907. 80 p.

YOUSE, ALICE MAY
The Power of Prayer, a Musical Poem Narrating a True Incident of the Civil War. Wilmington, DE.: The J. M. Rogers Press, 1901. 41 p.

ZAGOREN, RUBY
Meandering Meditations. Dallas, TX.: The Kaleidograph Press, 1938. x p., 1 ℓ., 13-78 p.

ZATURENSKA, MARYA (1902-)
Threshold and Hearth. New York: Macmillan, 1934. x, 58 p.
Cold Morning Sky. New York: Macmillan, 1938. viii, 1 ℓ., 62 p.
The Listening Landscape. New York: Macmillan, 1941. x, 87 p.
The Golden Mirror. New York: Macmillan, 1944. viii, 73 p.
Selected Poems. New York: Grove Press, 1954. 130 p.
Terraces of Light. New York: Grove Press, 1960. 77 p.
Collected Poems. New York: Viking Press, 1965. xi, 210 p.
The Hidden Waterfall: Poems. New York: Vanguard Press, 1974. 69 p.

ZEALEAR, IDA
Yosemite & Other Poems. Oceanside, CA.: The Langford Press, 1941. [24] p.

ZELIMA
Soy. Oakland, CA.: Women's Press Collective, 1974. 80 p.

ZELL, RUTH O. CARLSON
Prairie Wildflowers; Poems from the Big Sky Country. New York: Exposition Press, 1967. 96 p.

ZERBEY, DOROTHEA (1884-)
Ends. Wilkes-Barre, PA.: n.p., 1935. [23] p.

ZIMMER, MARY HONORA
Saint Francis Would Know Answers. Sanbornville, N.H.: Wake-Brook House, 1961. 63, [1] p.
White Dove in the Oak. Sanbornville, N.H.: Wake-Brook House, 1963. 94 p.

ZIMMERMAN, EDNA M.
Alleluia Gems. New York: Carlton Press, 1968. 48 p.

ZIMMERMAN, HAZEL LOUISE
Green Grows the Laurel. New York, London: G. P. Putnam's Sons, 1936. 94 p.
The Wind Returns. (Sonnets in the Petrarchan Form). New York: G. P. Putnam's Sons, 1939. 64 p.

ZIMMERMAN, MARY H.
A Gallery of Women's Portraits, Poems. Chicago: Dierkes Press, 1950. 48 p.
Written on the Lamb's Skin. Eureka Springs, AR.: Dierkes Press, 1959. 48 p.

ZINNES, HARRIET
Waiting and Other Poems. Lanham, MD.: Goosetree Press, 1964.
An Eye for an I; Poems. New York: Folder Editions, 1966. 57 p.
Entropisms. New York: New Directions, 1973.

ZIPP, ETHEL
A Bit of Everything. Philadelphia: Dorrance & Co., Inc., 1931. 77 p. (Contemporary poets of Dorrance, 99)

ZOLOTOW, CHARLOTTE (SHAPIRO) (1915-)
All That Sunlight. New York: Harper & Row, 1967. [31] p.

ZUBENA, Sister (Cynthia Conley)
Calling All Sisters. Chicago: Free Black Press, 1970.
Om Black. Chicago: The Author, 1971.

ZUKIN, REBECCA H.
The Pixie Pool; Poems. New York: Exposition Press, 1964. 47 p.

TITLE INDEX